SOCIOLOGY IN FOCUS
for OCR A2 Level

Edited by
Michael Haralambos and Peter Langley

Written by
**Michael Haralambos, Peter Langley,
Andrew Pilkington, John Richardson**

Dedication

To Kate, Jane, James, Sally and Sam

Acknowledgements

Cover and page design	Caroline Waring Collins (Waring Collins Ltd)
Graphic origination	John A Collins (Waring Collins Ltd)
Graphics	Tim Button, Kevin O'Brien (Waring Collins Ltd)
Author index and typing	Ingrid Hamer
Reader	Mike Kidson
Special thanks	Steve Chapman

Picture credits

Advertising Archives 8; Art Directors & TRIP Photo Library 129; Associated Press 6(tr), 12 (br), 36, 52(br), 57(tl), 108, 147, 176(t), 188, 291(m); BBC Photograph Library 229(bl,br); BMW 239(tr); Brian Smith 204, 205(l); David Hoffman 201(t,m), 209(m); David Hoffman/Janine Wiedel 228; Granada TV 168; Guardian Newspapers 57(mr); Guy Birkin Ltd 239(ml); John Collins 195(br), 223; Mary Evans 214, 216(r); Michael Haralambos 78; National Museums of Canada 226; Peter Newarks American Pictures 85(r); PhotoDisc 208; Photofusion 5(br), 9(ml,mr,bl), 39(tl,br) 89, 93, 106, 122(t,m), 123, 128, 130, 152, 153, 166(bl), 167(tl), 172(br), 230(b), 250, 263(l,r), 293; Popperfoto.com 101, 206(l); Press Association 97; Refuge 185; Rex Features 6(mr), 7, 28(tr), 39(tr,mr,bl), 41, 52(mr), 65(tl, tr), 85(l), 86, 139, 151, 161, 166(br), 167(tr), 170, 173, 179(t,b), 195(ml, mr), 206(r), 238, 255(l,r), 300, 311; Robert Yager 31(tl,tr); Sally and Richard Greenhill 117, 227(r); TopFoto 5(bl), 6(tl,ml), 9(br), 24(tl), 28(tl), 35, 49(tr,bl), 49(ml,mr), 61, 65(mr), 82, 95, 110(tr), 137(tr), 149, 155, 158, 159, 160, 165, 166(bm), 174, 179, 194, 246, 258(l,r), 275, 279, 288, 291(b), 294, 295, 316; Womens Aid 12(tr).

Cartoons

The cartoons in this book have been specially drawn by BRICK www.brickbats.co.uk

Cover picture

Hundertwasser
THE RAIN FALLS FAR FROM US FALLS THE RAIN, 1970
© J. Harel, Vienna

Every effort has been made to locate the copyright owners of material used in this book. Any omissions brought to the attention of the publisher are regretted and will be credited in subsequent printings.

British Library Cataloguing in Publication Data
A catalogue record for this book is available from the British Library.

ISBN 978-1-902796-96-5

Pearson Education
Edinburgh Gate, Harlow, Essex CM20 2JE

© Michael Haralambos, Peter Langley, Andrew Pilkington, John Richardson

First impression 2005
Reprinted 2007
Printed and bound in China WC/03

Contents

1 Crime and deviance

Introduction

We are fascinated by crime and deviance. This is evident from the mass media – from crime series on TV and crime reports in newspapers, from detective novels which are concerned with finding the criminal and explaining the crime, and from movies which often portray the more colourful, lurid and violent aspects of crime.

Why this fascination? Criminal behaviour appears unusual and different. It involves risks which endanger those who commit crimes and their victims. For many people, out-of-the-ordinary behaviour seems much more interesting than their own humdrum activities. And to those of us looking on, the risks and dangers involved are often experienced as exciting and entertaining – from a safe distance!

Crime and deviance break social norms – they deviate or diverge from conventional behaviour. This can be disturbing. We often fear crime and feel worried and anxious when taken-for-granted norms are broken. Why? Because such activities disrupt our sense of social order and threaten our view of the way things should be.

And this adds to our fascination with crime. It should therefore come as no surprise that crime and deviance is one of the most popular topics in sociology.

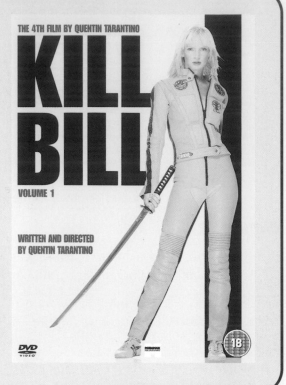

chaptersummary

▶ **Unit 1** looks at the meanings of deviance, crime and social control.

▶ **Unit 2** investigates evidence on the extent of crime, trends in the crime rate, and the identity of offenders.

▶ **Unit 3** examines media representations of crime and deviance.

▶ **Units 4, 5 and 6** outline and evaluate various sociological theories of crime and deviance, including functionalist, interactionist and Marxist approaches.

▶ **Units 7 and 8** examine two opposing theories of crime and social control – right realism and left realism.

▶ **Units 9, 10 and 11** look at the relationship between ethnicity and crime, gender and crime, and age and crime.

▶ **Unit 12** examines the spatial distribution of crime.

▶ **Unit 13** looks at social control, crime reduction and social policy.

Unit 1 The nature of crime, deviance and social control

keyissues

1 What are crime, deviance and social control?
2 What is distinctive about the sociological approach to crime, deviance and social control?

1.1 Defining crime and deviance

Human social life is governed by norms and values – by norms which define appropriate and acceptable behaviour, and by values which define behaviour as right or wrong.

Sociologists have long been concerned with how society's norms and values are maintained.

However, there is another side to the story – how and why are norms broken and values rejected? In other words, how and why does *deviance* occur?

Deviance

Deviance is usually defined as behaviour which goes against conventional norms and generally accepted values. In terms of this definition, deviance is behaviour which most people would regard as inappropriate, or more strongly, as unacceptable and wrong. As a result, deviance is usually subject to a variety of social controls ranging from mild disapproval to severe punishment.

This view of deviance is reflected in the following definition by Downes and Rock (2003). 'Deviance may be considered as banned or controlled behaviour which is likely to attract punishment or disapproval.' This definition covers acts such as murder and rape which are explicitly banned in most cultures and subject to severe punishment. It also covers relatively trivial acts such as burping and farting in public which usually attract little more than a disapproving glance or a negative comment.

Crime

At first sight, *crime* is a much more specific category than the wide and varied range of activities covered by deviance. Often, crime is simply defined as an infraction of the criminal law – as lawbreaking. Crimes are usually seen as particularly serious and negative forms of deviance – hence laws which ban them and agents of social control such as the police and judges who deal with them. This view of crime is reflected in the following definition. 'Crimes are those actions deemed so disturbing to citizens or disruptive to society as to justify state intervention' (Pease, 2002).

This type of definition has its limitations. We cannot assume that crimes are always more disturbing to citizens or more disruptive to society than non-criminal behaviour. Think of all the non-criminal behaviour that contributes to global warming, global pollution and the destruction of the world's wildlife. In Muncie's (2001) words, 'Any number of damaging events are far more serious than those that make up the "crime problem" '.

What is more, breaking the criminal law covers a vast array of actions from the trivial to the serious. Crime, like deviance, covers a highly varied range of behaviour. This leads some sociologists to talk about crimes in the plural rather than crime in the singular. In other words, there's 'crime and crime'.

There are many different definitions of deviance and crime. None are without their problems as Activity 1 illustrates. It looks at vandalism which the *Concise Oxford Dictionary* defines as the wilful or malicious destruction or damage of property. This destruction or damage may or may not be seen as deviant. It may or may not be defined as criminal damage.

key terms

Deviance Actions which deviate from the norms and values of society.
Crime A form of deviance which breaks the law.

activity1 vandalism

Item A

Item B

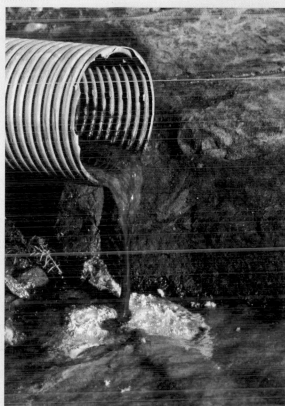

Item C

Item D

Item E

Item F

questions

1 Look at the pictures. Which (if any) would you see as examples of vandalism? Give reasons for your answer.

2 Using examples from this activity, briefly discuss the problems of defining crime and deviance.

1.2 The contexts and diversity of deviance

Deviance takes varied forms in society. For example, we can distinguish between secret and private deviance as against open and public deviance, and between individual deviance as against collective deviance.

Secret and private deviance This form of deviance is often concealed – not least due to the heavy personal costs of exposure to the public gaze. It is often undercover and may be hidden in normal settings such as the home or the workplace. Secret deviance may be legal – for example, a group with unusual sexual practices who meet in each other's homes. Or it may be illegal, as in the case of the Gloucester serial killer, Frederick West.

West appeared to be a fairly average family man with a normal occupation as a self-employed builder. Yet, in the privacy of his home, he murdered two members of his family and a number of vulnerable young women. Furthermore, he was able to use his 'normal' skills as a builder to hide the dead bodies in his house and garden.

Open and public deviance This form of deviance often involves conforming to the norms and values of a clearly defined outsider group – norms and values which differ from those of the wider society. Take the example of the so-called New Age Travellers in Britain today. Their lifestyle is very different from that of the mainstream population. They tend to be seen as a deviant group and are viewed with distaste and hostility by some members of society. They are an example of public and collective deviance.

1.3 The relativity of crime and deviance

Crime and deviance are relative to time, place and culture. In other words, what counts as crime and deviance varies from time to time, place to place and culture to culture.

Societal and situational deviance Ken Plummer (1979) captures this point in his distinction between societal and situational deviance. Societal deviance refers to behaviour which breaks the law or which is seen as deviant by most members of society. It is judged to be deviant on the basis of their shared values and beliefs and what 'common sense' tells them. There is general agreement about the identification of societal deviance – for example, most people regard armed robbery as wrong, as deviant and as criminal.

Situational deviance refers to the effect of the context or situation on the classification of deviance. In one situation an act may be seen as deviant, in another situation it may not. People interpret what counts as deviance in their personal worlds of friends, colleagues and acquaintances. Plummer accepts that the beliefs and values of the wider society affect views of situational deviance. However, he argues that in certain contexts people either neutralise or reject the societal version of deviance.

Plummer uses the example of homosexuality to illustrate this point. Homosexuality is societally deviant but not always situationally deviant. In certain contexts, such as gay bars and clubs, homosexuality is no longer deviant – it becomes the norm.

Culture and deviance Crime and deviance are relative to culture. Different cultures have different norms and values. As a result, what is considered normal and deviant will vary from one culture to another. For example, in many non-Western societies marriage is polygynous – a man may have two or more wives. In the West, this is not only deviant, but criminal.

As cultures change, so do definitions of deviance and crime. At certain times in Western societies it was considered deviant for women to use make-up and consume alcoholic drinks in public. Today, this is no longer the case. In the same way, definitions of crime change over time. Sexual relations between men were once a criminal offence in Britain. Since 1969, homosexual acts between consenting adults in private have no longer been illegal.

activity2 deviance is relative

Item A Smoking banned

On Saturday, 29 March 2003, Robert de Niro and Danny de Vito joined 280 guests in the ballroom of the Regent Wall Street Hotel in New York for a $95-a-head Last Smoke dinner. The prime rib steak smoked in tobacco leaves went down well. De Niro and De Vito lit up their Cuban Montecristo cigars.

When the clock struck midnight, the Last Smoke was over. Smoking was banned in 13,000 New York bars and restaurants which were not covered by an earlier smoking ban.

The city hired an army of inspectors to tour bars and restaurants, confiscating ashtrays and issuing warnings in a 30-day grace period before fines of up to $3000 start being slapped on owners.

Adapted from *The Observer*, 30.3.2003

After the ban

Item B *Endorsing Camels*

The late American film star John Wayne advertising Camel cigarettes.

questions

1 Use information from Items A and B to illustrate the point that deviance is relative to time and place.

2 Look at Item B. Why would it be unlikely for a film star today to endorse cigarettes?

1.4 Social control

Every society has methods of making its members toe the line, of making sure that they stick to the straight and narrow. These methods are known as mechanisms or methods of *social control*. They ensure that most of the people, most of the time, conform to society's norms and values. For social order to exist, shared norms and values are necessary and conformity to them must be enforced. Enforcing conformity means discouraging deviant and criminal behaviour – behaviour which breaks social norms and goes against shared values.

Social control takes many forms. Some researchers have distinguished between *formal* and *informal* methods of social control.

Formal methods of social control Formal methods refer to institutions specifically set up to enforce social control. In modern industrial societies, this mainly involves institutions which create and enforce the law – for example, parliament which enacts the law and the police, judiciary and prison service which enforce the law.

The ultimate and most obvious form of social control is physical force. Under certain circumstances, some have the right to use physical force against others in an attempt to control their behaviour. In modern industrial societies, the police are an obvious example. Other formal methods of social control include judicial punishments such as fines and imprisonment.

Informal methods of social control Informal methods of social control involve institutions and social groups which are not directly concerned with enforcing social control and upholding the law. These groups and institutions include the family, schools, religious organisations and significant others.

The family and the school socialise young people, teaching them the norms and values of the wider society. Conformity to these norms and values is usually rewarded, deviance from them is usually punished.

Religious teachings often reinforce the values of society. For example, the Christian Commandments you shall not kill and you shall not steal reinforce the values placed on human life and private property. And, in turn, they back up secular laws protecting life and property. Religions offer rewards to those who follow their teachings and punishments to those who deviate from them. In this way, religion acts as a mechanism of social control.

Significant others are people who matter to an individual. They usually include his or her immediate family, friends, neighbours and workmates. People are concerned about what significant others think about them. Their approval makes them feel good, their disapproval upsets them. Because the opinion of significant others is held so highly, they can play an important part in controlling the behaviour of an individual. People often conform to social norms in order to gain the approval and acceptance of significant others and to avoid their disapproval and rejection.

Many sociologists see informal social controls as more important and effective than the more obvious formal controls.

key terms

Social control Methods of controlling people's behaviour – encouraging them to conform to society's norms and values and discouraging deviant and criminal behaviour.
Formal methods of social control Institutions specifically set up to enforce social control – in particular, institutions which create and enforce the law.
Informal methods of social control Institutions and groups which are not directly concerned with enforcing social control yet still play an important part in controlling the behaviour of others.

summary

1. The term deviance covers a wide range of behaviour which deviates from the norms and values of society.

2. The term crime also covers a variety of activities – from the trivial to the serious.

3. Crime and deviance may be secret and private or open and public; individual, involving one person, or collective, involving a group of people.

4. Crime and deviance are relative to time, place and culture. What counts as crime and deviance varies from time to time, place to place and culture to culture.

5. Every society has mechanisms of social control which discourage crime and deviance.

6. Formal mechanisms of social control include institutions which create and enforce the law – for example, parliament, the police and the judiciary.

7. Informal mechanisms of social control include the family, schools, religious organisations and significant others. Although not directly concerned with social control, sociologists see them as powerful control mechanisms.

activity3 social control

Item A Police

Item B Family

Item C Friends

Item D Prison

Unit 2 Crime statistics

keyissues

1 How are the volume and trends in crime measured?

2 How are offenders identified?

3 How valid and reliable are data on crime and offenders?

2.1 Measuring crime

The two main measures There are two main measures of crime in Britain. The first, *police recorded crime*, is based on police records – on records kept by the police of crimes which they have recorded. The second, the British Crime Survey (BCS), is based on interviews with a representative sample of adults. It asks whether they have been victims of particular crimes during the previous year.

Sections 2.2 and 2.3 look at the 'official' picture of crime presented by police recorded crime. Section 2.4 looks at the picture presented by the British Crime Survey.

The official picture Each year statistics produced from police records provide an official account of the volume of crime and trends in crime. In addition, statistics compiled from court records and police cautioning records give an official picture of those responsible for criminal offences – that is the 'criminals'. Together, these statistics present a picture of the 'crime problem' – a picture interpreted for us by politicians and transmitted to us by the mass media.

But are official statistics a valid measure of crime? Do they provide an accurate measure of the extent of crime and of trends in crime? Do they present a true picture of those who commit crimes? The short answer to all these questions is probably not.

2.2 The volume of crime

According to official statistics based on police records, there were 6,468,000 cases of recorded crime in the United Kingdom in 2002/03 (*Social Trends*, 2004). Four-fifths of these were offences against property – theft, handling stolen goods, criminal damage, burglary, fraud and forgery.

These statistics do not represent the total volume of crime. There is a so-called 'dark figure' or 'hidden figure' of unrecorded crime. There are various reasons why the official picture is incomplete. And there are reasons why this picture may be systematically biased – for example, it may repeatedly underestimate certain kinds of crime.

Recorded versus known offences Official statistics do not even give a complete record of criminal offences known to the authorities. For example, until 1998 they didn't cover *summary offences* – those tried in Magistrates Courts as opposed to Crown Courts. Such offences include driving after consuming alcohol over the legal limit. Nor do statistics on recorded crime cover offences dealt with *administratively* by organisations such as the Inland Revenue. Generally speaking, the Inland Revenue negotiate a monetary settlement with people who commit a tax offence – for example, with a business which does not record all its takings and so pays less tax than it should.

There may be some justification for omitting the above offences if they were trivial. But consider this. Two-fifths of crime statistics are made up of criminal damage and theft from a vehicle or from shops. Often such crimes involve small amounts of damage or loss. It is questionable whether they can be seen as more serious than summary offences or offences dealt with administratively.

Police recording practices A further example of known offences not appearing in official statistics is provided by police recording practices. Over 30% of offences reported to the police in 2002/03 were not recorded (Simmons & Dodd, 2003). While the police have a statutory obligation to record crimes, they also have some discretion over whether a crime is serious enough to warrant their attention.

This discretion can be used in different ways by different police forces. For example, in 1981, Nottinghamshire appeared to be the most criminal area in the country. This was largely due to many more crimes involving £10 or less being recorded in Nottinghamshire than in comparable counties such as Leicestershire and Staffordshire (Holdaway, 1988).

The Home Office provides police forces with 'counting rules' to calculate the extent of crime. The basic rule is that the statistics should indicate the number of victims rather than the number of criminal acts. For example, if a single victim has been assaulted by the same person on several occasions, only the most serious offence is counted (Maguire, 2002). This can make some crimes appear less serious than they are. For example, it can understate the extent of domestic violence which often involves numerous assaults over a prolonged period.

Police priorities The number and type of offences discovered by the police in the course of their operations will vary according to their priorities. And this, in turn, will affect crime statistics.

Police priorities are influenced by the concerns of local and national government, pressure groups, public opinion and the media. For example, in recent years, the police have directed more resources to combat paedophilia, due, in part, to increased media concern with this offence.

An ongoing police priority is to improve their clear-up rate – solve more crimes and catch more offenders. With this in mind, resources tend to be targeted at certain crimes. In the words of a retired police officer, 'If you don't catch a burglar, he will go out and he will commit a lot of crime which will then be reported and it will damage your detection rate' (Davies, 1994).

Reporting and non-reporting Over 80% of all recorded crime results from reports by the public (Bottomley & Coleman, 1981). Some types of crime are more likely to be reported than others. For example, 97% of thefts of vehicles were reported to the police in 2002/03, as an official record of the incident is needed for insurance purposes. This compares with estimates which suggest that only around a third of incidents of vandalism and theft from the person are reported (*Social Trends,* 2004).

There are many reasons why crimes are not reported to the police.

- There may be a lack of awareness that a crime has taken place – eg, fraud.
- The victim may be relatively powerless and frightened of the consequences of reporting – eg, child abuse and domestic violence.
- The offence may seem too trivial – eg, vandalism.
- There is no apparent victim – eg, prostitution.
- A view that the police can't do anything about the incident.
- The matter was dealt with privately.

Crime statistics rely heavily on the public reporting incidents to the police. Since some types of crime are more likely to be reported than others, official statistics will not reflect the overall pattern of crime.

The significance of crime statistics Numbers aren't everything. For example, violence against the person, sexual offences and fraud may form a relatively small proportion of recorded crime, but there are other ways of measuring their significance.

Violent and sexual offences often have a traumatic effect upon victims and their seriousness is evident from the number and length of prison sentences they bring – around a third of prisoners are serving sentences for violent or sexual offences.

Fraud may only account for 6% of recorded crime but its monetary value is far greater than this suggests. In Mike Maguire's (2002) words, 'If one measures the importance of property offences in terms of the value stolen, rather than the quantity of incidents, fraud comes out as of enormously greater significance than other categories'. If we take any one of the major cases of alleged fraud investigated by the Serious Fraud Office in the early 1990s – Barlow Clowes, Guinness, Maxwell, BCCI, Polly Peck – we find that, by itself, it exceeded the total amount stolen in thefts and burglaries recorded by the police (Levi, 1993).

Conclusion Official statistics on recorded crime are drawn from police records – they are based on data collected by the police. The evidence presented in this section indicates that these statistics fail to provide a reliable and valid measurement of crime. And they may be systematically biased in underestimating the extent of certain crimes.

Official statistics on recorded crime are *not* simple, straightforward facts. Instead, they are a *social construction* – they are constructed during the process of social interaction, they are based on a series of interpretations, definitions and decisions which are influenced by a variety of factors, and vary from situation to situation. In the words of Simon Holdaway (1988), 'Official statistics of crime are not so much the facts about crime, as the end product of a complex series of decisions. An incident occurs and someone decides that it is a crime. A decision is made to telephone a police officer and the police officer receiving the call decides to regard the incident as a crime. Another officer attends the scene and, hearing the various accounts of the incident, makes a further decision about its being a crime, and so on. The official statistics are socially constructed; they are the end product of a range of decisions.'

key terms

Police recorded crime Crimes recorded by the police from which official statistics on crime are drawn.
Summary offences Crimes dealt with by Magistrates Courts as opposed to Crown Courts. They were not included in official statistics until 1998.
Crime dealt with administratively Crimes which are not prosecuted – not taken to court. They are dealt with by organisations such as the Inland Revenue and do not appear in police recorded crime.
Social construction Definitions and meanings constructed in the course of social interaction.

The 2002/03 BCS

The 2002/03 British Crime Survey provides the following picture of crime in England and Wales.

The volume of crime On the basis of interviews conducted in 2002/03, the BCS estimates that 12.3 million crimes were committed against adults living in private households. Police recorded crime for England and Wales for the same period was just under 5.9 million. The BCS estimate is, therefore, more than double police recorded crime.

Unreported and unrecorded crime Not all BCS crimes can be directly compared with police figures – for example, thefts involving household and personal property are placed by the police in the same category as thefts of business property and shoplifting, crimes which are not included in the BCS. However, just over 9.5 million BCS crimes are comparable with those in police statistics. Of these, 43% were reported to the police, and of those reported, 68% were recorded by the police. This means that only 29% of all BCS crimes were actually recorded by the police and entered the official statistics of police recorded crime (Simmons & Dodd, 2003).

Since the BCS includes both unreported and unrecorded crime, it gives a more complete estimate of many crimes than police records.

Trends in crime From 1981 to 1995, British Crime Survey estimates show a steady rise in crime. Since then, there has been a steady fall – by 2002/03, the estimates were only slightly above the 1983 level – see Activity 5, Item C.

In general, the BCS trends in the volume of crime are reflected in the trends in police recorded crime. However, they diverged when a new counting rule for recorded crime was introduced in 1998 and the National Crime Recording Standard came into operation in 2002. These

key term

Victim study/survey A study of the victims of crime. Such studies usually ask people to report the crimes that have been committed against them, or any other member of the household, during the previous year.

activity5 the British Crime Survey

Item A The BCS and police recorded crime

	% BCS crimes reported to the police	% of reported BCS crimes recorded by the police	% of all BCS crimes recorded by the police
Vandalism	31	70	22
PROPERTY CRIME	50	75	38
Burglary	65	71	46
Burglary attempts and no loss	49	42	21
Burglary with loss	87	94	81
All vehicle thefts	50	84	42
Thefts from vehicles	47	75	35
Thefts of vehicles	97	84	81
Attempted vehicle theft	36	100	38
Bicycle theft	50	56	28
Thefts from the person	33	59	19
VIOLENCE	41	52	21
Common assault	34	46	16
Wounding	46	57	26
Robbery	53	54	28
ALL COMPARABLE CRIME	43	68	29

Adapted from Simmons & Dodd, 2003

Item B *Police recorded crime trends*

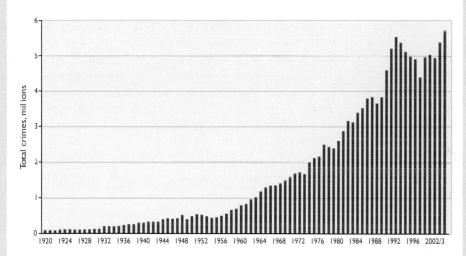

Crimes recorded by the police, England and Wales, 1920–2002/03

Note: From 1997, the figures are based on the financial year (ie, April to March).
Adapted from Home Office, 2001 and *Annual Abstract of Statistics*, 2004

Item C *BCS trends*

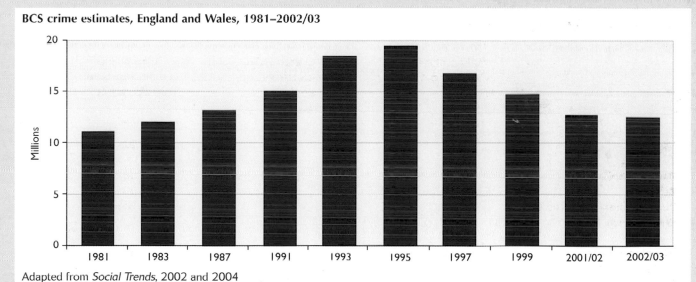

BCS crime estimates, England and Wales, 1981–2002/03

Adapted from *Social Trends*, 2002 and 2004

questions

1 a) Briefly summarise the differences between the police and BCS figures in Item A.

   b) Why are some crimes more likely to be reported to the police than others?

   c) Why are some crimes reported to the police more likely to be recorded than others?

2 a) Briefly summarise the trends shown in Items B and C.

   b) Suggest reasons for the differences in recent trends (2001/02 and 2002/03) between police recorded crime and BCS estimates.

new measures increased the volume of police recorded crime. For example, the National Crime Recording Standard raised the volume of police recorded crime by 10% in 2002/03. This 10% 'increase' was simply due to a change in recording practice, it does not reflect a real increase in crime.

Without these changes in recording practices, the trends in police recorded crime would be similar to the BCS trends – they would show a steady decline in the volume of crime from the mid-1990s (Simmons & Dodd, 2003).

Evaluation of the BCS

Advantages For the crimes it covers, the British Crime Survey provides a more accurate picture of the extent of crime and of trends in crime than police recorded crime. There are two main reasons for this.

- First, BCS estimates include unreported and unrecorded crime.
- Second, the trends identified by the BCS are not affected by changes in recording practices, unlike the trends identified from police records.

Disadvantages There are a number of disadvantages of the BCS. They include the following.

- Only three-quarters of BCS crimes can be directly compared to police recorded crime.

- Because it is a household survey, the BCS does not cover a range of crimes which appear in police statistics. These include crimes against corporate and commercial organisations – such as fraud and shoplifting – motoring offences and so-called victimless crimes – such as possession or dealing in drugs (Maguire, 2002).
- Locally-based surveys of women indicate that the BCS underestimates assaults committed by people known to the victims – for example, partners.
- The BCS is a national survey. However, crime is not spread evenly across the country. In certain inner-city areas, the risks of serious crime are high. A local victim survey in Islington revealed that one-third of all households reported being a victim of burglary, robbery or sexual assault within the previous year (Jones et al., 1986). This is considerably higher than the national figure.

2.5 The social characteristics of offenders

Sociologists often explain behaviour in terms of people's social characteristics – for example, their social class, ethnicity, gender and age. Sociologists are therefore interested in the social characteristics of offenders. For instance, if offenders are primarily young, male and working class, then these factors may help to explain their criminal behaviour.

There are two main sources for identifying the social characteristics of offenders – official sources and self-report studies.

The official picture

Known offenders Statistics compiled from court records and police cautioning records provide an official picture of offenders. It is important to note that the number of 'known offenders' is small compared to the number of recorded offences. For example, in 2000, some 325,000 people were sentenced in court in England and Wales and 151,000 were cautioned by the police. This compares with over 5 million recorded crimes. The proportion of known offenders becomes even smaller when a comparison is made with BCS data. According to one estimate, only 3 in 100 BCS crimes resulted in an offender being convicted or cautioned (Barclay & Tavares, 1999).

We cannot assume that all offenders are similar to this small proportion of known offenders. In other words, we cannot generalise from such a small, and probably unrepresentative, sample.

Social characteristics Of the 476,000 offenders convicted or cautioned in 2000, 80% were male and 41% under the age of 21. Often gender and age are the only characteristics of offenders available from court and police cautioning records.

A fuller picture is provided by the National Prison Survey which was conducted in England and Wales in 1991 (Walmsley et al., 1992). The main findings were as follows.

- 62% of inmates were under 30 compared with 25% in the population as a whole.
- A disproportionate number were from the lower levels of the class system – 41% of males formerly had unskilled or partly-skilled manual jobs compared with 18% of the population as a whole.
- Given their numbers in the general population, a disproportionate number of prisoners came from ethnic minorities – particularly African Caribbean.

Overall, the findings of the National Prison Survey reveal a very different pattern than that found in the wider population.

Mike Maguire (2002) describes the picture presented by official sources of the social characteristics of offenders. 'There are many more males, young people, Black people, poor people, poorly-educated people, and people with disturbed childhoods than one would find in a random sample.'

Self-report studies

Only some 3% of crimes result in a conviction or caution. What about the other 97%? Do those who committed these offences share the same characteristics as the 3%? *Self-report studies* may help to provide an answer to this question.

Self-report studies of crime ask people whether they have committed a series of offences. They are usually based on a self-completed questionnaire or an interview. Respondents are presented with a list of offences and asked which they have committed over a period of time – for example, during the past 12 months or during their lifetime.

Crime is normal Self-report studies suggest that most of us have committed at least one crime at some stage in our lives. This questions the view that a clear distinction can be made between law-abiding people and offenders. Gabor (1994) argues that many of us have done one or more of the following: 'taken home linens, silverware, art and other "souvenirs" from hotels in which we have stayed; made inflated insurance claims following a fire or theft; illegally copied computer software or videos; used prohibited drugs or abused prescription drugs; exhibited disorderly conduct in public; physically struck another person intentionally'.

It is possible to argue that crime is 'normal'. If this is the case, then there is nothing particularly distinctive about the social characteristics of those who break the law. However, there are problems with this view. What kinds of crime are we talking about? Many of the crimes committed by most people can be seen as fairly trivial. And how many crimes do most people commit? Self-report studies indicate that committing one or two criminal acts is a 'normal' part of growing up for most boys. However, frequent lawbreaking is relatively rare (Hood & Sparks, 1970).

Gender Self-report studies indicate that far more males than females commit crimes. This reflects the picture given by official statistics. In a self-report study conducted by the

Home Office, over 30% of 22-25 year-old males admitted a criminal offence within the previous year, compared with only 4% of females in the same age group (Graham & Bowling, 1995).

Social class Most self-report studies suggest a link between social class and criminal behaviour. They indicate that the lower a person's position in the class system, the more likely they are to commit a crime. Again, this reflects the picture given by official statistics (Coleman & Moynihan, 1996).

This link appears strongest in terms of 'street crime' – burglary, robbery, theft of or from a vehicle – and the so-called *underclass* – those at the base of the class system, the long-term unemployed and those dependent on welfare benefits (Farnworth et al., 1994).

However, there are problems with this apparent link between class and crime. Street crimes are the typical crimes of the poor. They are a police priority and are the types of crime which the police are most likely to deal with. And they are the types of crime which tend to be listed by researchers in self-report questionnaires and structured interviews. Other types of crime, such as fraud, domestic violence and child abuse, are less visible and less likely to appear on a list in self-report studies. In view of this, it is not surprising that the poor appear to commit more crimes than their better-off counterparts (Maguire, 2002).

Age Self-report studies, like official statistics, suggest that crime is a 'young person's game'. However, it is important to note that young people tend to offend in groups and in public – they are more visible and more likely to be apprehended. Also the crimes young people commit are more likely to be listed in self-report studies (Coleman & Moynihan, 1996). And they are more likely to be reported to the police – for example, vehicle theft.

Ethnicity There is little difference between Blacks and Whites in self-reported crime. This is at odds with the picture presented by official statistics which shows a relatively high proportion of Black offenders.

Evaluation and conclusion

Official statistics reveal the social characteristics of those who have been processed by the criminal justice system – that is, those who have been cautioned, those found guilty by the courts, and those imprisoned. They reflect the priority given by the police to certain kinds of crime and certain types of lawbreakers. As such, they are useful.

However, official statistics are unlikely to present a picture of the social characteristics of lawbreakers in general. They indicate that young, working-class males are a major crime problem. But this may simply reflect the fact that 'most police resources are devoted to uniformed patrol of public space' where most young working-class males are likely to spend their social lives (Reiner, 1994). And police priorities and perceptions might well be the main reason for the apparent class/crime link. According to William Chambliss (1969) 'The lower class person is (i) more likely to be scrutinised and therefore to be observed in any violation of the law, (ii) more likely to be arrested if discovered under suspicious circumstances, (iii) more likely to spend the time between arrest and trial in jail, (iv) more likely to come to trial, (v) more likely to be found guilty, and (vi) if found guilty, more likely to receive harsh punishment than his middle or upper-class counterpart.'

Self-report studies The results of self-report studies must be approached with caution. Traditionally, they have focused on male juvenile delinquency – the criminal behaviour of young men. And the lists of crimes presented in self-report studies tend to reflect those typically committed by young working-class males – in particular 'street crime'. They tend to omit 'hidden crimes' and adult crimes, such as domestic violence and child abuse, crimes which are likely to be spread more evenly across age and class groups. And they are unlikely to include fraud, often committed by middle-class, middle-aged men. As a result, self-report studies provide only a partial view of crime. And this leads to a one-sided picture of the social characteristics of offenders.

key terms

Self-report study A survey in which respondents report on aspects of their behaviour - in the case of crime, the offences they have committed over a period of time.
Underclass Some sociologists claim that an underclass, a class below the working class, has developed in modern societies. Characteristics of the underclass include dependency on welfare benefits and long-term unemployment.

summary

1. There are two main measure of crime in Britain – police recorded crime based on police records, and the British Crime Survey (BCS), a victim study based on a representative sample of adults.

2. Police recorded crime statistics do not represent the total volume of crime. There is a 'dark figure' or 'hidden figure' of unrecorded crime.

3. Certain offences, for example many tax offences, do not enter police records because they are dealt with administratively by organisations such as the Inland Revenue.

4. Many of the offences reported to the police are not recorded – over 30% in 2002/03. Often this is because the offences are seen as too trivial to record.

5. Police priorities affect the crimes they target, the number and

type of offences they discover, and the crime statistics they produce.

6. Some crimes are more likely to be reported to the police than others. For example, vehicle theft is much more likely to be reported than domestic violence.

7. Police recorded crime provides statistics. It has nothing to say about the significance of crime. For example, in monetary terms fraud is much more significant than other property offences.

8. Police recorded crime fails to provide a reliable and valid measure of crime. It may be significantly biased in underestimating certain types of crime – for example, fraud and domestic violence.

9. Police crime statistics are a social construction. They are constructed during the process of social interaction and based on a series of interpretations, definitions and decisions.

10. Police recorded crime provides the following picture of trends in crime. There is little change in the annual crime figures from 1876 until the 1930s. Then, there is a gradual rise to the 1950s, followed by a sharp increase until the early 1990s. Since then, the figures have gone up and down, but remained high compared to earlier years.

11. The following reasons have been given for the increase in police recorded crime.
    - The proportion of crime reported to the police rose significantly between the early 1980s and mid-1990s.
    - New crimes and new opportunities for crime have developed – for example, credit card fraud.
    - Changes in police recording practices have increased the total of recorded crime.

12. The rise in police recorded crime does not necessarily mean that more crimes are being committed. However, evidence from the British Crime Survey indicates an actual rise in crime from the early 1980s until 1995.

13. The British Crime Survey (BCS) is a victim study based on a representative sample of adults in England and Wales.

14. It estimates that the total volume of crime is more than double the total given by police recorded crime.

15. The BCS indicates a steady rise in crime from 1981 to 1995, followed by a steady fall to 2002/03.

16. Differences between BCS and police recorded crime trends since 1995 are probably due to changes in police recording practices. These changes increased the level of recorded crime.

17 Compared to police recorded crime, the BCS has the advantage of including both unreported and unrecorded crime. Also, it is not affected by changes in recording practices.

18. The BCS has a number of disadvantages. They include:
    - The BCS does not cover certain crimes which appear in police statistics – for example, fraud.
    - It underestimates certain crimes – for example, domestic violence.

19. There are two main sources for identifying the social characteristics of offenders - official sources and self-report studies.

20. Statistics from court records and police cautioning records provide an official picture of offenders. However, the number of 'known offenders' is small compared with the number of recorded offences.

21. This number becomes even smaller when BCS crimes are taken into account. Only around 3 in 100 BCS crimes result in an offender being convicted or cautioned. We cannot generalise from such a small and probably unrepresentative sample.

22. According to official sources, the typical offender is young, male and working class.

23. Self-report studies indicate that most people have committed at least one crime. In this respect, there is nothing distinctive about people who break the law.

24. Self-report studies give the following picture of the social characteristics of offenders. It reflects the picture provided by official statistics.
    - Significantly more males than females commit crimes.
    - The lower a person's position in the class system, the more likely they are to commit crimes.
    - Younger people are more likely to commit crimes than older people.

25. The social characteristics of offenders provided by official statistics reflect the priorities given by the police to certain kinds of crime and certain types of lawbreakers.

26. Self-report studies tend to focus on the types of crime committed by young working-class males. They tend to omit adult crimes, such as domestic violence and fraud, which are likely to be spread more evenly across age and social class groups.

27. Both official sources and self-report studies give only a partial view of crime. This leads to a one-sided picture of the social characteristics of offenders.

activity6 your self report

Incident	Offence	Maximum Penalty
1. Have you ever bought goods knowing or believing they may have been stolen?	Handling stolen property	£5,000 and/or 6 months imprisonment
2. Have you taken stationery or anything else from your office/work?	Theft	£5,000 and/or 6 months imprisonment
3. Have you ever used the firm's telephone for personal calls?	Dishonestly abstracting electricity	£5,000 and/or 6 months imprisonment
4. Have you ever kept money if you received too much change?	Theft	£5,000 and/or 6 months imprisonment
5. Have you kept money found in the street?	Theft	£5,000 and/or 6 months imprisonment
6. Have you taken 'souvenirs' from a pub/hotel?	Theft	£5,000 and/or 6 months imprisonment
7. Have you tried to evade customs duty on a small item bought on holiday?	Intending to defraud	Three times value of goods or £5,000 fine, whichever is greater and/or 3 years imprisonment
8. Have you used a TV without buying a licence?	Using a TV without a licence	£400 fine
9. Have you ever fiddled your expenses?	Theft	£5,000 and/or 6 months imprisonment
10. Have you ever driven a car knowing you are 'over the limit'?	Driving with excess alcohol	£5,000 and/or 6 months imprisonment

questions

1 a) How many of these offences have you committed?

   b) Add up the maximum penalties which you could have received.

   c) Compare your answers to a) and b) with those of other students.

2 What do your answers to Question 1 suggest about a) the accuracy of official statistics and b) the picture of the 'typical criminal' drawn from official statistics?

Unit 3 Media representations of crime

keyissues

1 What pictures of crime do the media present?

2 What factors influence media representations of crime?

3 To what extent do the media shape popular perceptions of crime?

3.1 Media images of crime

The previous unit looked at the pictures of crime and the criminal presented by official statistics, victim studies and self-report studies. This unit looks at the pictures presented by the mass media.

Judging by the output of the media, the public have an enormous appetite for crime. A significant proportion of newspaper articles, broadcast news (TV and radio), films, novels, comics, drama, documentaries and reality TV focuses on crime. And the pictures of crime and the criminal presented by the media are often different from those provided by official statistics, victim studies and self-report studies.

Methodology

Most of the studies of media representations of crime are based on content analysis.

Formal content analysis This method aims to classify and quantify media content in an objective manner. For example, it is used to measure the amount of space devoted to crime and the types of crime covered in newspapers. Researchers usually have a checklist of crimes

Item B *Prostitution*

A prostitute in New York City

Item C *Riots*

Bradford, 2001

question

Suggest how the activities in Items A, B and C can be seen as functional for society.

4.3 Strain theory

In the 1930s, the American sociologist Robert K. Merton wrote an article entitled *Social Structure and Anomie*. It became one of the most influential explanations of crime and deviance. Merton's theory was sociological – he offered a social rather than a psychological or biological explanation. In particular, it was a *structuralist theory* as it saw the structure of society shaping people's behaviour.

Culture and norms According to Merton, American culture attaches great importance to success – and success is measured in terms of money and material possessions. There are norms which define legitimate means for achieving success. These legitimate means include gaining skills and qualifications and career advancement. The American Dream states that anybody can make it to the top if they try hard enough.

Anomie So much emphasis is placed on material success that many people experience pressure to deviate from accepted norms and values. Deviance occurs when they reject the goal of success and/or the legitimate means of reaching that goal. For example, some people are tempted to use any available means of getting to the top – even if this involves criminal behaviour.

Merton refers to this pressure to deviate as a 'strain to anomie'. *Anomie* means normlessness – it refers to a situation where norms no longer guide behaviour, where 'anything goes'.

Social structure Despite what the American Dream says, not everybody has an equal chance of success. The social structure prevents equal opportunity. In particular, the strain to anomie is most strongly felt by those at the bottom of the

class structure. They are less likely to acquire the skills and qualifications needed to reach the top. As a result, they are more likely to seek alternative routes to success.

Adaptations Merton identifies five possible adaptations or responses to the strain to anomie in American society – see Table 1. The first is conformity – aiming for success and sticking to the rules. The other four are deviant adaptations – they reject the goal of success and/or the norms for achieving it.

Table 1 *Goals and means*

	Cultural goal	Normative means
Conformity	acceptance	acceptance
Deviant adaptations		
Innovation	acceptance	rejection
Ritualism	rejection	acceptance
Retreatism	rejection	rejection
Rebellion	replacement	replacement

Conformity According to Merton, most people conform despite the strain to anomie. Even if they don't make it, they continue to strive for success and follow the normative means of getting there.

Innovation People who adopt this deviant adaptation accept the goal of success but, in Merton's words, they have 'little access to conventional and legitimate means for becoming successful'. As a result, some innovate – they turn to illegitimate means, to crime. The pressure to select this adaptation is greatest for those in the lower levels of the class system.

Ritualism People who follow this deviant route abandon the goal of success, but stick rigidly to the rules – for example, people in dead-end, white-collar occupations who follow their job descriptions to the letter.

Retreatism This deviant adaptation involves a rejection of both the goal of success and the normative means of achieving it. It applies to people who 'drop out' – tramps, drug addicts and habitual drunkards.

Rebellion This involves a rejection of conventional goals and means and their replacement with alternatives. The revolutionary who seeks to change society illustrates this type of deviant adaptation.

Evaluation of strain theory

Advantages Merton's strain theory was an early attempt to explain crime and deviance in terms of the culture and structure of society. It provided a sociological alternative to biological and psychological theories. In particular, it offered an explanation for working-class crime. Whatever its weaknesses, Merton's work provided a spur for the development of further sociological theories of crime and deviance.

Disadvantages Merton's theory raises a number of unanswered questions.

- First, why do some people but not others adopt deviant adaptations? For example, why do some people in the lower levels of the class system turn to crime but others do not?
- Second, Merton's theory focuses on individuals rather than groups. Crime and deviance are often collective activities. How can this be explained in terms of strain theory?
- Third, crime and deviance are not always motivated by a desire for monetary gain. How can activities such as vandalism and fighting between rival gangs be explained in terms of Merton's theory?

In search for answers to these questions, subcultural theory was born.

4.4 Subcultural theory

Albert Cohen – status frustration

Albert Cohen (1955) was the first sociologist to develop a subcultural theory of working-class crime and deviance. He examined delinquent gangs in low-income, inner-city areas. Delinquency refers to the criminal and anti-social acts of young people.

Cohen agreed with Merton that the mainstream value of success creates problems for young working-class males. Many do badly at school and fail to acquire the skills and qualifications needed for success.

Status frustration Defined as failures by the wider society, many working-class adolescents experience *status frustration*. They are frustrated with their low status as 'losers' and are given little or no respect.

A subcultural solution Faced by a common 'problem of adjustment' – a problem they share – some working-class adolescents develop a deviant solution. They create their own *subculture* – their own norms and values which differ from those of mainstream society. In Cohen's words, 'the delinquent subculture takes its norms from the larger culture but turns them upside down'.

Anti-social and criminal behaviour, which are condemned by the wider society, are valued by the delinquent subculture. And, most importantly, they provide a means by which 'failed' working-class young people can solve the problem of status frustration. By succeeding in terms of the values of the delinquent subculture, they gain respect and admiration from their peers – those in a similar situation.

This is where *collective* deviant activities come in. Gang members require an audience to gain respect. The 'successful' delinquent gains status in the eyes of his peers.

Non-utilitarian crime If status frustration is the main problem, then criminal activities to achieve monetary success – Merton's 'solution' – may not be necessary. Vandalism, joy-riding, fighting, anti-social behaviour such as giving cheek to teachers and disrupting the classroom, can bring respect. These are examples of *non-utilitarian* crime and deviance – not 'useful', not directed to monetary gain.

Acting in terms of the deviant subculture, young men not only gain status in each other's eyes, they also hit back at a society which has denied them the opportunity to succeed and branded them as failures.

Evaluation Cohen's subcultural theory offered explanations for non-utilitarian crime and collective deviance – explanations which Merton's strain theory failed to provide. However, there are other explanations for working-class delinquency, as the following sections illustrate.

Cloward and Ohlin – opportunity structures

The American sociologists Richard Cloward and Lloyd Ohlin (1961) provide an explanation for different types of working-class delinquency. They argue that both Merton and Cohen fail to explain why delinquent subcultures take different forms. Why, for example, are some gangs mainly concerned with theft while others focus on violence?

Cloward and Ohlin agree with Merton that delinquency results from legitimate opportunity structures being largely closed to many young, working-class males. However, their response to this situation varies depending on the social environment in which they grow up. Different social environments provide different opportunities for crime and deviance which, in turn, encourage the development of different delinquent subcultures. Cloward and Ohlin identify three types of delinquent subculture.

The criminal subculture This type of subculture tends to develop in areas where there is a well-established pattern of adult crime. This provides an illegitimate opportunity structure. Young men are presented with role models from whom they can learn the tricks of the trade. They are given the opportunity to climb the professional criminal hierarchy and to become 'successful' by participating in crime which brings monetary gain.

The conflict subculture This type of subculture tends to develop in areas where an *illegitimate opportunity structure* is absent. These areas usually have a high turnover of population and a low level of social cohesion – this prevents established patterns of adult crime from developing.

With little opportunity to succeed by either legitimate or illegitimate means, young men become frustrated and angry. They often respond to this situation with gang violence which gives them the opportunity to gain status and respect from their fellow gang members.

The retreatist subculture This type of subculture tends to emerge among those who have failed to succeed either by legitimate means or as members of either criminal or conflict subcultures. These 'double failures' sometimes form retreatist subcultures based on illegal drug use.

Evaluation Cloward and Ohlin develop both Merton's strain theory and Cohen's subcultural theory. They show that working-class delinquency is not simply concerned with material gain. And they identify, and provide explanations for, a number of delinquent subcultures.

However, Cloward and Ohlin tend to box off the subcultures they identify and ignore the overlaps between them. For example, gangs involved in the conflict subculture often deal in drugs and make large sums of money in the process. The same applies to members of the retreatist subculture – some addicts also 'successfully' deal in drugs (Winlow, 2001).

key terms

Structuralist theory A theory which sees the structure of society shaping people's behaviour.
Anomie A state of normlessness – where norms no longer direct behaviour.
Delinquency The criminal behaviour of young people.
Status frustration Dissatisfaction and frustration with the status and respect given by others.
Subculture Distinctive norms and values shared by a group within society. These norms and values differ from those of the mainstream culture.
Non-utilitarian crime Crime which is not directed to monetary gain – for example, vandalism.
Illegitimate opportunity structure A structure which provides illegal opportunities for monetary gain.

Lower-class subculture

The theories we've looked at so far present a similar picture of society. They assume that there is a consensus or agreement about values. Members of society are socialised into a common value system and become committed, at least in the USA, to the ideal of success in monetary terms. Criminal and deviant subcultures are seen as reactions by young working-class males to their inability to obtain this goal by legitimate means.

The American sociologist Walter B. Miller (1958) takes a different view. He sees society as consisting of different social classes, each with a distinct set of values. Miller argues that there is a distinctive lower-class subculture which is passed on from generation to generation. It arose partly from the experience of low-skilled labour which involved boring, repetitive, dead-end jobs, interspersed with periods of unemployment. Lower-class subculture provides ways of living with this situation and of finding satisfaction outside of work.

*activity*11 *hispanic gangs*

Item A **Hispanic gangs in LA**

East Los Angeles is a mainly Hispanic area. Hispanics or Latinos have their origins in Spanish speaking countries in Central and South America. Hispanics in the USA are twice as likely to live in poverty as White Americans.

East LA has at least 800 Hispanic gangs with more than 100,000 members. The level of gang violence is extremely high. LA is known as the murder capital of the USA. Most of these murders are gang-related.

The Hispanic gangs are split into two groups. The *chicanos* are Mexican-Americans born in the USA who often don't speak any Spanish. Their rivals are gangs whose members are recent immigrants from Mexico and other Spanish speaking countries who have evolved a language of their own called *calo*. Older members *(veteranos)* are held in great respect by their 'home boys', having defended the honour of their neighbourhood with fierce urban warfare.

Each gang has its own initiation ceremony. For example, to become a Playboy, a new member has to get 'jumped in' – beaten up – by a minimum of three gang members. While the beating takes place, others look on and count up to 13 slowly. Once initiated, members take on nicknames and adopt the dress codes of their comrades.

Many gang members deal in drugs. At the age of 15, former gang member Luis Rivera was earning 1000 dollars a day selling crack cocaine. 'I had my first car at the age of 16. I had no shortage of money.'

Adapted from the *Observer*, 6.2.94, 7.7.2002 and Winant, 1994

Item B Hand signals and tattoos

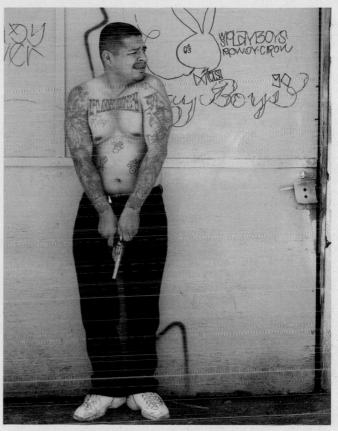

Hand signals representing the Playboys

Hand signals and tattoos are important signifiers of gang loyalties. Tattoos are usually done by *carnals* (fellow gang members) often using home-made instruments. They are a symbol of identity and defiance.

Young men who want to escape from gang life sometimes get their tattoos removed with a laser gun. Jose, a former gang member, states, 'The quicker I get 'em off, the quicker I get out of the gang. If I get them removed, then I'll no longer be a gang member.'

Adapted from the *Observer*, 6.2.1994, 7.7.2002

A member of the Playboys

question

Read Items A and B and look at the pictures.

Explain the behaviour of Hispanic gangs in terms of a) Merton's strain theory, b) Cohen's subcultural theory, and c) Cloward and Ohlin's opportunity structure theory.

Focal concerns According to Miller, lower-class subculture has a number of *focal concerns* – major interests and involvements. They include a desire for excitement and thrills, an emphasis on toughness – on a macho form of masculinity – and a concern with 'smartness' – with conning and outwitting others. These concerns are exaggerated by lower-class young men because of their desire for status in the eyes of their peer group.

Lower class delinquency results from young men acting out the concerns of lower-class subculture. In doing this, they often break the law. The concern with toughness can lead to fights, the concern with excitement can result in a range of criminal activities from joy-riding to robbery, and the concern with smartness can be seen in the repertoires of the hustler and the con man.

Evaluation Miller pictures lower-class subculture as a 'distinctive tradition, many centuries old'. Lower-class young men are seen to act out this subculture with little reference to mainstream society. They appear to live in a world of their own. While accepting that a lower-class subculture may well exist, it is unlikely that lower-class young men are as insulated from the wider society and its values as Miller suggests (Bordua, 1962).

4.5 Delinquency and drift – David Matza

The theories examined so far tend to see criminal and deviant behaviour resulting from forces beyond the individual's control. For example, in terms of Merton's strain theory, those at the bottom of the class structure are under considerable pressure to turn to crime. And Cohen's subcultural theory suggests that the deviant behaviour of many young working-class males is directed by a delinquent subculture. To an extent, these theories picture people as prisoners of the social structure, acting out predetermined roles with little or no say in the matter.

David Matza (1964) sees three main problems with this approach.

- First, it tends to make deviants more distinctive than

they really are. For example, the idea of deviant subcultures suggests that those involved are very different from members of mainstream society.

- Second, it 'over-predicts' delinquency – it accounts for more delinquency than there actually is. Why doesn't everybody in a particular position in society become a delinquent?
- Third, it suggests that the deviant has little or no freedom of choice – that their behaviour is determined by social forces beyond their control.

How different are delinquents?

Matza rejects Cohen's view that delinquents are different, that they have a distinctive subculture in opposition to mainstream society.

Subterranean values Matza argues that delinquent behaviour is often directed by *subterranean values* which are found throughout society. These 'underground values' are only expressed in particular situations. They include an emphasis on excitement and toughness. In mainstream society they are expressed in competitive sports – for example, on the football field. If, as Matza claims, they often direct delinquent behaviour, then in this respect, delinquents are little different from other young people (Matza & Sykes, 1961).

Techniques of neutralisation How do young people view their delinquent behaviour? According to Matza, many express guilt and shame for their delinquent acts. This suggests at least some commitment to mainstream norms and values. If this is so, why does delinquent behaviour occur? Part of the answer is *techniques of neutralisation* which open the door to delinquency and provide a justification for it. Matza identifies five techniques which neutralise the blame for delinquent acts and make them acceptable (Sykes & Matza, 1962).

- **Denial of responsibility** This technique states the delinquent was not responsible for his own actions. He got in with a bad crowd and came from a poor neighbourhood. As a result, 'It wasn't my fault'.
- **Denial of injury** Nobody was really hurt. For example, stealing from those who could afford it, 'borrowing' a car for joyriding.
- **Denial of the victim** They had it coming to them – the person concerned was not a victim but someone who deserved to be punished.
- **Condemning the condemners** Those who condemn the delinquent are themselves wrongdoers – for example, the police are corrupt and brutal.
- **Appeal to higher loyalties** Criminal behaviour is justified in terms of mainstream values such as duties and obligations to families and friends – stealing to provide food for their family, fighting to defend their friend.

According to Matza, techniques of neutralisation suggest that delinquents largely accept the values of the wider society. They justify their criminal acts in terms of mainstream values. And there is little evidence for a distinctive delinquent subculture. Delinquents are therefore similar to young people in general.

Drifting into delinquency Subcultural theory suggests that many young males are committed to a distinctive subculture and a deviant lifestyle. In *Delinquency and Drift*, David Matza (1964) rejects this view. He argues that many young men drift in and out of delinquency. Their delinquent acts are casual and intermittent rather than a way of life. This fits with evidence indicating that most young people have little difficulty giving up delinquent activities as they grow older.

Again, the delinquent is pictured as little different from young people in general.

Evaluation of Matza

Advantages Matza provided a view of delinquency which answers the criticisms of strain theory and subcultural theory. Delinquents are no longer seen as prisoners of the social system directed by their position in the social structure and/or their distinctive subcultures.

According to Downes and Rock (2003), Matza's view describes the criminal behaviour of many young men in Britain. The most frequent reason they give for their delinquency is boredom. And delinquency offers plenty of opportunity for risk, daring and excitement to relieve boredom.

Disadvantages

- In seeking to remedy theories which over-predict delinquency, Matza may have gone too far in the opposite direction – and under-predicted. For example, one in three British men born in a single month in 1953 had a criminal record by the time they reached 30 (Carrabine et al., 2002).
- Matza's picture of young men drifting in and out of delinquency with little commitment to a deviant lifestyle does not fit the highly organised gangs in the USA. The life of the young men in the Hispanic gangs described in Activity 11 shows a real commitment to a deviant subculture. If there are over 100,000 Hispanic gang members in Los Angeles, this is hardly casual and intermittent behaviour.
- According to Stanley Cohen (2003), techniques of neutralisation don't necessarily indicate a commitment to conventional norms and values. They may simply be a public justification and excuse for criminal behaviour. For example, at the Nuremburg trials after World War II, neutralisation techniques were used by Nazis in their defence for the murder of millions of Jews.

key terms

Subterranean values Values which are only expressed in particular situations.
Techniques of neutralisation Techniques which neutralise the blame for actions which are defined as unacceptable or wrong by society's norms and values.

4.6 White-collar crime

The starting point for the theories of crime and deviance examined so far is the social pattern reflected in official statistics – that most offences are committed by young working-class males. As a result, these theories have little to say about *white-collar crime*

Defining white-collar crime

The American criminologist Edwin Sutherland (1949) defined white-collar crime as 'a crime committed by a person of respectability and high social status in the course of his occupation'. He challenged the view that crime was mainly a 'working-class problem', claiming that the financial cost of white-collar crime was probably several times greater than the cost of working-class crime.

Today, many researchers identify two types of white-collar crime – *occupational crime* and *corporate crime*. Occupational crime refers to crimes committed at the expense of the organisation, for example employees stealing money or goods from their employer. Corporate crime refers to crimes committed on behalf of the organisation, such as non-payment of VAT.

Some researchers identify a third type of white collar crime – *state crime*. This involves crimes committed by the state or agencies of the state such as the police or the military. Such crimes are committed on behalf of the state. For example, many people regard the treatment of suspected terrorists held by the US government at Guantanamo Bay in Cuba as a criminal offence.

Corporate crime

There are many types of corporate crime. They include the following.

Crimes against consumers These include manufacturing or selling food which is unfit for human consumption, manufacturing or selling dangerous goods, and falsely describing the contents of goods – for example, of food.

These crimes can have disastrous consequences. In the 1970s, mechanical defects in the Ford Pinto may have led to between 500 and 900 deaths in the USA. The company was fully aware of these defects (Box, 1983). Again from the 1970s, the deliberate fabrication of test data on the fertility drug thalidomide resulted in the births of thousands of deformed babies.

Many instances of companies harming consumers are not dealt with as a criminal offence. Accidents and 'disasters' for which companies are held to be responsible provide an example. In 1987, the capsizing of the cross-Channel ferry *Herald of Free Enterprise* led to the deaths of 154 passengers and 38 crew members. An official inquiry blamed the owners, P&O Ferries, for failing to provide a safe operating system. However, attempts to prosecute the company for 'corporate manslaughter' failed (Croall, 2001).

Crimes against employees These include failing to meet health and safety regulations which can lead to the injury or death of employees. Between 1965 and the mid-1990s in the UK, around 25,000 people were killed at work. According to the Health and Safety Executive, 70% of these deaths were due to the failure of management to meet safety regulations (Hughes & Langan, 2001).

Environmental offences These include polluting the environment with toxic waste. For example, ICI was fined £300,000 by the Environment Agency in 1999 for polluting groundwater in Runcorn. However, most fines are much lower, averaging £4300 in 1998 (Croall, 2001).

Financial frauds These include false accounting, insurance frauds and the making of false claims by sellers about the benefits of pension schemes and savings plans. Fraud can involve vast sums – over $4 billion in the case of WorldCom's false accounting (see Activity 4, Item B). And the consequences can be extremely serious – in WorldCom's case, 17,000 workers were made redundant and many investors lost their life-savings.

Views of white-collar crime

Compared to more visible and obvious types of crime such as burglary and murder, white-collar crime is often seen and treated differently by the public, police, courts and regulatory bodies. According to Gordon Hughes and Mary Langan (2001), this is due to four main factors.

Low visibility Street crimes and their consequences are highly visible. White-collar crimes are largely hidden from the public gaze. And when they are detected, it is often difficult to pinpoint blame – for example, which individuals were responsible for neglecting health and safety regulations?

Complexity Large-scale frauds are highly complex operations. They are difficult to unravel and it is hard to allocate blame. They involve different companies, various bank accounts, a multitude of transactions, and a variety of individuals who are more, or less, aware of what's going on. Teams of expert investigators spend years attempting to get to the bottom of large-scale frauds.

Diffusion of responsibility Responsibility for corporate crime is often diffused – widely spread. It is difficult to allocate blame to particular individuals. In the case of the *Herald of Free Enterprise* disaster, a variety of people and organisations were blamed – crew members, their commanding officers, the company and the regulatory authorities.

Diffusion of victimisation Many white-collar crimes are described as 'crimes without victims'. In many cases, there is no obvious victim as in cases of murder or robbery. However, there are victims but they are spread out or diffused. For example, environmental pollution can affect thousands of people. And we all have to pay for white-collar crime – in higher prices, insurance premiums and taxes (Hughes & Langan, 2001).

Regulating corporate crime

Compared to many other forms of crime, corporate crime

has a lower rate of detection and prosecution, and more lenient punishments (Croall, 2001).

Regulatory offences Many corporate offences are dealt with by regulatory bodies rather than the criminal justice system. Bodies such as the Health and Safety Executive, the Environment Agency and the Trading Standards Agency deal with violations of health and safety, environmental health and trading standards regulations. They are more likely to issue 'official warnings' to put matters right rather than pursue prosecutions.

In the case of professionals, such as doctors and lawyers, 'misconduct' is usually dealt with by professional associations such as the British Medical Association. Only the most serious cases result in prosecution.

Many private companies operate a system of self-regulation. For example, the London Stock Exchange and Lloyds attempt to regulate their own affairs, even if this means a certain amount of loss through fraud.

Risk of prosecution Regulatory bodies are primarily concerned with securing compliance with regulations rather than identifying offenders. They advise and warn rather than punish.

Organisations such as the Inland Revenue and Customs and Excise tend to deal with offences administratively rather than prosecute. Their main aim is to recover the money lost from tax evasion and VAT fraud rather than charge the offender with a criminal offence.

Lenient punishment When white-collar offenders are prosecuted and found guilty of a criminal offence, their punishment tends to be lenient. Compared to 'ordinary criminals' such as burglars, they are more likely to be 'punished' with community service, a fine, or a short sentence in an open prison.

Explaining white-collar crime

White-collar crime covers a vast array of offences from petty occupational crime, such as fiddling expenses and stealing small items from employers, to corporate crime such as large-scale frauds. It is difficult to find an explanation for this variety of offences.

Strain theory revisited Merton's strain theory has been developed in an attempt to explain white-collar crime. A typical explanation goes as follows. All members of society face the same success goals – there is pressure on all social classes to succeed. When people in white-collar occupations find the routes to pay increases and promotion

summary

1. Sociologists look to society for an explanation of crime and deviance rather than the biological or psychological makeup of the individual.

2. According to Durkheim, a certain amount of crime is not only 'normal' but also an 'integral part of all healthy societies'. Society's values and norms must not be too strong - this would prevent the innovation and change necessary for a healthy society. Crime can be seen as a byproduct of this necessity.

3. Some crimes can be functional for society - for example, they may indicate that something is wrong with the way society is organised.

4. Merton's strain theory argues there is a 'strain to anomie' when the normative means for attaining cultural goals are blocked. This strain is most strongly felt by those at the bottom of the class structure. Some 'innovate' and turn to crime to attain monetary success.

5. Cohen's subcultural theory argues that many young working-class males experience status frustration. Some respond by developing a delinquent subculture in terms of which they can gain status and respect.

6. Cloward and Ohlin provide an explanation for different types of working-class delinquency. They argue that different social environments provide different opportunities for crime and deviance. This encourages the development of different delinquent subcultures.

7. David Matza argues that many sociological theories picture delinquents as more distinctive than they really are. He sees delinquents responding to subterranean values which are found throughout society. They use techniques of neutralisation which indicates that they largely share the values of the wider society. And they drift in and out of delinquency rather than being committed to a delinquent subculture.

8. Many sociological theories of crime and deviance tend to ignore white-collar crime.

9. There are two main types of white-collar crime - occupational crime and corporate crime.

10. Corporate crime includes crimes against consumers, crimes against employees, environmental offences and fraud.

11. Corporate crime is seen and treated differently from crimes such as burglary and murder. Reasons for this include:
    - Its low visibility
    - Complexity
    - The diffusion of responsibility
    - The diffusion of victimisation.

12. Compared to many other forms of crime, corporate crime has a lower rate of detection and prosecution, and more lenient punishments.

13. Merton's strain theory has been adapted to explain white-collar crime. This version states that some middle-class people experience relative deprivation when they make comparisons with those better off than themselves. In the absence of legal means to reach this level of success, some turn to crime.

14. Subcultural theory has been developed to explain middle-class crime. Many corporations have a subculture which emphasises the pursuit of wealth and profit. For some, the pressure to succeed in terms of this subculture leads to criminal acts.

blocked, they sometimes 'innovate', just like members of the working class. In other words, they turn to illegal means to become successful and attain monetary goals. They experience the same strain to anomie, to normlessness. This weakens the mechanisms of social control – the norms which would otherwise restrain criminal behaviour.

But why should middle-class people experience a strain to anomie when they are better off than those at the bottom of the class structure? One suggestion is that deprivation is relative. Middle-class people may feel deprived relative to, that is in comparison to, others who are considerably better off than themselves. And, given the pressure to succeed, they experience a strain to anomie. As a result, they innovate, just like their working-class counterparts.

In much the same way, corporations may find that legal ways of maintaining or increasing their profits are ineffective. As a result, there is a strain to anomie and pressure to turn to illegal means. The desired result may be obtained by fraud or by ignoring health and safety and environmental regulations (Box, 1983).

Subcultural theory revisited The hero of the film *Wall*

key terms

White-collar crime The crimes of people in white-collar occupations. It includes occupational crime and corporate crime.
Occupational crime Crimes committed by employees at the expense of the organisation.
Corporate crime Crimes committed on behalf of and for the benefit of the organisation.
State crime Crimes committed by the state or by agencies of the state on behalf of the state.

Street – the street where the big New York stockbroking firms are located – stated that 'greed is good'. Some sociologists have argued that many corporations, especially financial institutions, have a subculture which emphasises the pursuit of wealth and profit. This so-called enterprise culture places a high value on risk-taking and monetary success. For some, it is a short step to 'success at all costs', even if this means fraud, bribery and corruption.

Further explanations of white-collar crime are examined in Unit 6 which looks at Marxist theories of crime.

activity 12 corporate crime

Item A Enron

Under its president Kenneth Lay, the US company Enron became the world's largest energy trading company. It specialised in contracts to deliver natural gas and electricity to customers at a future date. In December 2001, Enron filed for bankruptcy, billions of dollars in debt.

Investors lost a fortune with Enron shares practically worthless. Enron's 19,000 employees lost both their jobs and their savings because they belonged to a retirement plan based on Enron shares. 20,000 creditors were owed an estimated $67 billion. Most received less than 20 cents for every dollar they were owed.

Investigations revealed fraud on a vast scale. Top executives lined their pockets while concealing massive debts. False accounting practices boosted reported income and lowered reported debt. As a result, share prices remained high, bearing no relationship to the true value of the company.

Shortly before bankruptcy was declared, the company president Kenneth Lay borrowed $74 million and repaid it with company shares. And a number of senior executives were given payments totalling $55 million.

Adapted from various issues of the *Guardian*, 2001, 2002, 2003

An effigy of Enron president Kenneth Lay (right) at an anti-capitalist demonstration in New York

Item B *The Piper Alpha disaster*

On July 6, 1988, there was an explosion on the oil rig Piper Alpha, 100 miles off the east coast of Scotland. It was caused by an escape of flammable gas and resulted in the deaths of 167 workers. The rig was owned by the Occidental Group.

A public enquiry led by Lord Cullen looked into the causes of the disaster. They included:

- An inadequate assessment by the company of the risks involved
- A failure to put right known deficiencies in the system
- Management neglect of safety standards and regulations.

Adapted from SafetyLine Institute, 1998, www.safetyline.wa.gov.au

Piper Alpha two days after the explosion

Dear G E Rald,

We should like to take this opportunity to inform you that on 12th of March this year you were seen entering empty handed into the private premises of Ms P C Edwards of Convent St, Folkestone, and leaving shortly afterwards with your hands full.

In our opinion, this constitutes a violation of the Theft Act 1968 subsection 32(c) and we would be grateful if you would consider the following advice: please stop going down Convent St and entering houses without the owners' permission.

We should warn you that next March 12th another police constable will be on foot duty in Convent St, and should he notice a repetition of your behaviour, we shall have to consider the possibility of taking even more stringent action than we have on this occasion.

Item C *A warning*

Many regulatory bodies inspect companies to check that regulations, for example on health and safety, have been followed. Warnings are issued if any regulations have not been met and companies are revisited to check that matters have been put right. On the left is a spoof letter, using similar procedures, written to a young burglar.

From Box, 1983

questions

1 The consequences of corporate crime can be extremely serious. Discuss with reference to Item A.

2 Would you describe the Piper Alpha disaster (Item B) as a crime? Give reasons for your answer.

3 How does Item C illustrate the difference between the way many corporate offences and 'ordinary crimes' are seen?

Unit 5 *Interactionism and labelling theory*

keyissues

1 What is distinctive about the interactionist approach to crime and deviance?

2 What are the strengths and weaknesses of labelling theory?

5.1 The interactionist approach

To move from functionalism to interactionism is to move to a very different theoretical perspective. Gone are the social systems and social structures which direct behaviour. In their place are small-scale interaction situations in which people act in terms of meanings and definitions of the situation. The interactionist approach to crime and deviance became popular in the 1960s.

The interactionist perspective According to Herbert Blumer (1969) interactionism, or more specifically symbolic interactionism, is based on three central views.

- First, 'human beings act towards things on the basis of the meanings that things have for them'. Human behaviour is not determined by social forces. Rather, people are self-conscious beings who choose what to do on the basis of their subjective perceptions – how they see things.

- Second, 'the meaning of things is derived from, or arises out of, the social interaction that one has with one's fellows'. Meanings are not fixed but are continually modified as people negotiate with each other.

- Third, 'group action takes the form of a fitting together of individual lines of action'. Society is not so much a determinant of human action as a product of human activity. People make society, rather than society making people.

The challenge to functionalism In terms of its approach to crime and deviance, functionalism was challenged on three grounds.

- First, the assumption that there is agreement about what forms of behaviour constitute crime and deviance. What intrigued interactionists was why the same behaviour is defined as criminal or deviant in some contexts but not others.

- Second, the claim that deviants are somehow distinctive, comprising a specific group of the population. We are asked instead to look at the process of interaction and question why certain individuals or groups are more likely to be defined as deviant.

- Third, the search for the causes of deviance is seen to be fruitless. We all commit acts which break rules. What is more interesting is the way that agencies of social control respond to different individuals and the effects of that response on their future actions.

5.2 Labelling theory

From an interactionist perspective, deviance is an act which is labelled as such. There is nothing essentially or intrinsically deviant about any act. It only becomes deviant when it is seen as such and labelled as such.

The classic statement of this view is given by Howard Becker (1963). In his words, 'social groups create deviance by making the rules whose infraction constitutes deviance and by applying those rules to particular people and labelling them as outsiders. From this point of view, deviance is not a quality of the act the person commits but rather a consequence of the application by others of rules and sanctions to an "offender". The deviant is one to whom that label has successfully been applied; deviant behaviour is behaviour that people so label.'

Becker's words are frequently quoted because they represent a new approach within the sociology of crime and deviance. The focus moves away from a concern with the deviant and the causes of deviance to a concern with the agencies of social control – with the process by which they label certain acts as deviant and the consequences of this labelling. How, then, is deviance created?

Defining deviance Society creates the rules. Deviant behaviour is not a distinctive form of behaviour but behaviour which is seen to contravene these rules. Becker (1963) illustrates this point well. 'The act of injecting heroin into a vein is not inherently deviant. If a nurse gives a patient drugs under a doctor's orders, it is perfectly proper. It is when it is done in a way that is not publicly defined as proper that it becomes deviant.' What applies to the use of drugs also applies to other forms of behaviour. Even the act of taking someone else's life is, in some contexts, considered appropriate. Indeed, in a war it is the refusal to kill which is often seen to be deviant.

Labelling Acts labelled as deviant tend to be committed by certain types of people. For example, the police tend to target specific groups. Studies of policing indicate that 'those who are stopped and searched or questioned in the street, arrested, detailed in the police station, charged, and prosecuted are disproportionately young men who are unemployed or casually employed, and from generally discriminated against ethnic minorities' (Reiner, 1994). For labelling theorists, this is due to the perceptions held by the police of the 'typical criminal'. They are more likely to see the activities of young men from the lower levels of the class structure and from certain ethnic minority groups as suspicious.

Aaron Cicourel's (1976) study of police and juvenile (probation) officers in California illustrates this point. Both groups held a similar picture of the 'typical delinquent' – as 'coming from broken homes, exhibiting "bad attitudes" towards authority, poor school performance, ethnic group membership, low-income families and the like'. As a result, young people who fitted this picture were more likely to be arrested and handed over to the juvenile officers. And, in turn, those who came closest to the picture of the 'typical delinquent' were more likely to be charged with a criminal offence by the juvenile officers. The middle-class minority who were arrested were usually 'counselled, cautioned and released' by the juvenile officers.

In the process, the police and probation officers not only created typical delinquents, they also created the social characteristics of the typical criminal shown in official statistics – young, working class and male.

Primary and secondary deviance

Edwin Lemert (1972) makes a distinction between *primary* and *secondary deviance*. Primary deviance refers to deviant acts which have not been publicly labelled. Most of us have engaged in such acts at one time or another, and for all sorts of reasons. Usually, this has little effect on our identity and status in society, or on our future lives.

Secondary deviance refers to acts which have been publicly labelled as deviant and to the deviance which is generated by this labelling.

Societal reaction The reaction of society – the way others react to someone labelled as deviant – may have a dramatic effect on that person's status and identity and may lead to further deviant acts.

Labelling people as deviant will tend to mark them out. The label may become a *master status* which overrides all other statuses. As a result, the individual is no longer seen as a parent, a friend or a worker but only as a criminal. Rejected by conventional society, they may embark on a deviant career – engage in further deviant acts and ultimately join an organised deviant group. Public labelling may result in a *self-fulfilling prophecy* whereby the person labelled deviant not only commits further deviant acts but also accepts the label.

Jock Young's (1971) study of hippie marihuana users in Notting Hill during the 1960s illustrates this process. The police targeting of a group, whose lifestyle included smoking marihuana, served to widen the differences between the hippies and conventional society. In the process, drug taking, which had been 'essentially a peripheral activity' became 'of greater value to the group as a symbol of their difference and of their defiance against perceived injustices' (Young, 1971). In this context, a deviant subculture developed. Individuals labelled outsiders began to see themselves as different from non-drug takers, all of which made it difficult for them to re-enter the wider society.

Evaluation of labelling theory

Advantages Labelling theory has a number of advantages.

- First, it has drawn attention to the importance of labelling and societal reaction. These processes can, in themselves, generate deviant and criminal behaviour.
- Second, it has shown that certain types of people are singled out for labelling.
- Third, it has shown that this results from the definitions and perceptions of the agents of social control – for example, their perceptions of the 'typical delinquent'.

Disadvantages Critics have pointed to the following weaknesses of labelling theory.

- **Origins of deviance** Labelling theorists see the search for the origin of deviant acts as largely fruitless. But deviance is not simply created by the label. People do not become burglars simply because they are labelled as such. They know that their actions are deviant, they are aware that they are breaking the law. Why do they become burglars? This example suggests that looking for the origins of deviance is an important sociological question.
- **Selection of deviants** Labelling theory fails to explain why certain types of people are selected as likely deviants rather than others. It is not sufficient to say that they fit definitions of likely deviants held by the agents of social control. Where do these definitions come from? They don't appear to be simply created in interaction situations. The picture of the 'typical

delinquent' is common to criminal justice systems in the UK, USA and elsewhere.

- **Who makes the rules?** According to Howard Becker (1963), 'social groups create deviance by making rules whose infraction constitutes deviance'. But who are these people who make the rules? And why do they make these particular rules? For example, are rules made by the powerful for their own benefit? This possibility is examined in the next unit which looks at Marxist approaches to crime and deviance.

key terms

Primary deviance Deviant acts which have not been publicly labelled.

Secondary deviance Acts which have been publicly labelled as deviant and the deviance which is generated by the label.

Societal reaction The reaction of others to an individual. In this case, the reaction of others to someone labelled as deviant.

Master status A status which overrides all other statuses. The status in terms of which a person is seen by others.

Self-fulfilling prophecy A prophecy which comes to pass simply because it has been made. The prophecy therefore fulfils itself.

5.3 Deviancy amplification

A number of sociologists who do not share the same theoretical perspective as the interactionists have also focused on societal reaction. The following study looks at societal reaction to mods and rockers in the mid-1960s.

Mods and rockers Mods and rockers are youth groups who differed from each other in terms of dress, musical tastes and modes of transport – mods rode scooters, rockers rode motor bikes. Stanley Cohen's (1987) study looked at societal reaction to disturbances involving mods and rockers which took place in Clacton over the Easter bank holiday in 1964.

The mass media represented these disturbances as a confrontation between rival gangs 'hell bent on destruction'. On inspection, however, Cohen discovered that the amount of serious violence and vandalism was not great and that most young people who'd gone to the seaside that weekend did not identify with either the mods or the rockers. The mass media had produced a distorted picture of what went on.

Deviancy amplification spiral Media coverage led to considerable public concern with mods and rockers. And this set in motion a *deviancy amplification spiral*. Sensitised to the 'problem', the police made more arrests, the media reported more deviance, and young people were more likely to identify with either mods or rockers. Further disturbances followed on subsequent bank holidays, attracting more police attention, more arrests, increased media interest and more young people reacting to what they saw as heavy-handed and unjustified treatment from the police.

activity 13 labelling theory

Item A *Defining deviance*

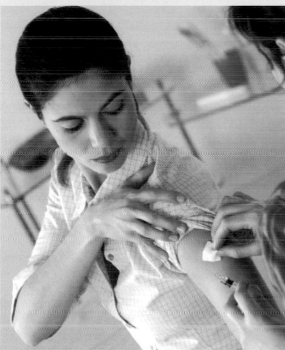

Item B *Labelling deviance*

Item C *Secondary deviance*

Stop and search

questions

1 Which act or acts in Item A might be defined as deviant? Give reasons for your answer.

2 If there was trouble at a soccer match, which of the people in Item B would the police be more likely to question and arrest? Give reasons for your answer.

3 How might the police activity in Item C lead to secondary deviance?

The reaction to the initial disturbances over the Easter bank holiday not only exaggerated the amount of deviance, it also generated more deviance.

Moral panics

Stanley Cohen claimed that the reaction of the media to events in Clacton generated a *moral panic*. A moral panic occurs when 'a condition, episode, person or group of persons emerges to become defined as a threat to societal values and interests' (Cohen, 1987). In the above case, mods and rockers were singled out as 'folk devils' whose behaviour constituted a threat to the social order. The 1960s were a decade of widespread social change, in which cherished norms were challenged. The mods and rockers served as symbols of what was wrong with society. In subsequent decades, young people continued to be the focus of moral panics. The 1970s saw the moral panic of mugging, and the 1980s the moral panic of football hooliganism (see Activity 14).

More recently, moral panics have focused on threats to children with concerns over child abuse, paedophilia and the influence of violent films on young viewers (Critcher, 2003).

The media's reaction to deviance may lead to a deviancy amplification spiral, a moral panic and more authoritarian forms of control. This process is illustrated in Figure 1.

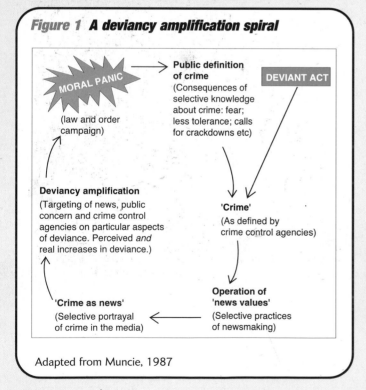

Figure 1 A deviancy amplification spiral

Adapted from Muncie, 1987

Evaluation

There is evidence that societal reaction can amplify deviance. And there is evidence that this reaction can reach the level of a moral panic. When it reaches this level, it is out of proportion to the situation – it is 'over the top'.

But who's to say that a so-called moral panic is unreasonable? Jock Young (1986) criticises the concept of a moral panic because it implies that crime is, in large part, constructed by the media. Young accepts that the media may exaggerate the 'crime problem', but it does not create it. He argues that the reality of crime, and the human suffering it produces, must be taken seriously and not reduced to a media construction.

key terms

Deviancy amplification spiral A process in which deviance is increased by societal reaction.
Moral panic According to Cohen (1987), a moral panic occurs when 'a condition, episode, person or group of persons emerges to become defined as a threat to societal values and interests'.

summary

1. From an interactionist perspective, people act in terms of meanings and definitions which arise in social interaction. The interactionist approach to crime and deviance became popular in the 1960s.

2. Interactionists challenge the view that deviants are essentially different from non-deviants.

3. In terms of labelling theory, deviance is behaviour which is labelled as such, a deviant is someone to whom a label has successfully been applied.

4. Labelling theory focuses on the agents of social control, on the way they define certain acts and certain kinds of people as deviant, and the consequences of this.

5. Societal reaction to someone labelled as deviant can lead to a self-fulfilling prophecy. Individuals so labelled may be encouraged to commit further deviant acts and may see themselves in terms of the label.

6. Although it has a number of advantages – for example, showing the importance of societal reaction – labelling theory has been criticised for failing to explain:
   - The origins of deviance
   - Why certain types of people are seen as likely deviants
   - Who makes the rules.

7. Societal reaction can lead to a deviancy amplification spiral in which the response to the initial deviance generates further deviance.

8. Societal reaction can take the form of a moral panic.

9. The idea of a moral panic has been criticised because it implies that crime is largely constructed by the media. According to Jock Young, it tends to ignore the reality of crime.

activity14 football hooliganism

Item A *Moral panics and social control*

> **IDENTIFICATION OF A PROBLEM**
> (eg football hooliganism)
>
> ↓
>
> **Identification of a subversive minority**
> (eg the 'few who spoil the enjoyment of millions': identification by styles - skinheads, etc)
>
> ↓
>
> **Simplification of cause**
> (eg decline in moral standards, lack of discipline etc)
>
> ↓
>
> **Stigmatisation of those involved**
> (Media use of emotive and disparaging significations eg 'morons'; 'animals'; 'savages' etc)
>
> ↓
>
> **Stirring of public indignation**
> (eg media campaigns calling for 'action': criticism of 'soft' sentences; evocation of the 'national image', etc)
>
> ↓
>
> **Stamping down hard**
> (eg government responds to 'public demand' as presented by the media. Stiffer sentences; more 'anti-hooligan' legislation; bans on spectators etc)
>
> **MORE AUTHORITARIAN FORMS OF CONTROL**

Adapted from Muncie, 1987

Item E *The police response*

In the last twenty years increasing attempts by police to control football hooliganism have included separating rival groups at matches in pens surrounded by spiked fences; closed circuit television crowd surveillance techniques; the use of identity card schemes; soccer hooligan group infiltration through police undercover operations and the formation of a National Football Intelligence Unit with computerised data banks on known soccer hooligans.

Adapted from Kerr, 1994

Item F *A hooligan's view*

We just don't have the time we used to have. The moment a fight starts we're immediately surrounded by dogs and horses. That's why everyone has started using knives. I suppose it might sound stupid but, because the policing has got so good, we've got to the point where we have to inflict the greatest possible damage in the least amount of time, and the knife is the most efficient instrument for a quick injury. In fact the knifings – because there is so little time – have been quite symbolic. When someone gets knifed, it amounts to an important victory to the side that has done the knifing. If the policing was not so good, I'm sure the knifings would stop.

Quoted in Kerr, 1994

Item B *Newspaper headlines, 1988*

Before the European Championship
Sun Euro hoolies league
Daily Mirror Plague of the Euro yob: Dutch go top of the Thug's Table

During the European Championship
Sun World War III
Star Yobs Plot War

Item C *Reaction in Parliament*

'We must really eradicate this blot on our reputation We want those guilty of it caught and convicted, and given a severe sentence as an example to others.'

Margaret Thatcher, 1988, after rowdiness by some English fans at the European championships.

Item D *Pictured in the media*

Liverpool vs Juventus, European Cup Final, Brussels, 1985

questions

1 To what extent does the societal reaction in Items B to E fit the process outlined in Item A?

2 How might societal reaction generate further and more serious deviance? Refer to Item F in your answer.

Unit 6 Marxism and radical criminology

keyissues

1 What is distinctive about the Marxist approach to crime, deviance and social control?
2 What are the strengths and weaknesses of this approach?

6.1 Traditional Marxist approaches

This unit examines two Marxist approaches to crime and deviance which emerged in the 1970s. The first is a fairly traditional development of Marxist ideas. The second – radical criminology – incorporates certain aspects of the interactionist approach.

From a Marxist perspective, crime and deviance in Western society can only be understood in terms of capitalism and the class struggle. Coercion and conflict are seen as the key features of capitalist society in contrast to functionalism's emphasis on consensus and integration. However, like functionalism, Marxism sees the structures and institutions of society as largely determining how people behave.

Causes of crime From a Marxist viewpoint, crime is systematically generated by the structure of capitalist society. Capitalism is an economic system based on the private ownership of the means of production and the maximisation of profit. As such, it emphasises individual gain rather than collective wellbeing. Capitalism is a competitive system which encourages aggression and emphasises the importance of winning. It is also an exploitative system in which some gain at the expense of others.

Given these priorities it is a short step to seeing the end as justifying the means – to be so obsessed with personal gain and coming out on top that breaking the law seems a minor barrier to success. Pressures to break the law will affect people across the social spectrum from wealthy business people to the poverty-stricken unemployed. In this respect, fiddling business expenses and fiddling the dole have similar causes.

From a Marxist perspective, capitalism encourages greed and self-interest, it generates frustration and aggression. Breaking the law can be seen as a rational step in order to satisfy these desires and express these feelings. Crimes motivated by financial gain can be seen as a logical outcome of the priorities of profit. Crimes with no apparent financial motive can be seen as an expression of the frustration, aggression and hostility which the system produces.

The law Laws in capitalist society are seen to reflect the interests of the dominant capitalist class. Thus the many laws protecting private property, which have appeared on the statute books over the past 200 years, reflect the growth of industry and the expansion of trade and commerce. In this respect, private property, the essence of capitalism, is protected.

Laws which appear to protect the interests of workers can be seen as concessions to the working class to maintain, if not its loyalty, then its acceptance of the system. For example, health and safety laws protecting workers can be seen in this light – and they have the additional benefit to capitalism of helping to provide a fit and healthy workforce.

Law enforcement 'There is one law for the rich and another for the poor.' This piece of folk wisdom summarises how many Marxists characterise law enforcement in capitalist society. The law is enforced selectively – there is a systematic bias in favour of those at the top. The crimes of the powerful such as corporate crime – for example, failing to pay business taxes and breaking trading laws – if discovered are rarely prosecuted. By comparison, those at the bottom of the class system who are caught breaking the law are regularly prosecuted. Yet in monetary terms their crimes are a drop in the ocean compared to the vast sums involved in the criminal activities of those at the top. Some of the evidence for this claim can be seen in Activity 15.

Evaluation Marxist approaches have the advantage of combining explanations of crime which cover members of all social classes, a wide variety of offences, the nature of law in capitalist society and the selective enforcement of the law. However, these explanations are very general and depend for their force on an acceptance of a Marxist view of capitalism. Many sociologists reject the view that there is a fundamental conflict of interest between the ruling and subject classes in capitalist society and the exploitation of one by the other.

6.2 Radical criminology

Radical criminology is the most influential attempt to apply a Marxist perspective to the study of crime and deviance. It emerged in Britain in the 1970s out of dissatisfaction with existing theories – including the more traditional Marxist approaches.

Radical criminology focuses on the process by which the state defines certain activities as criminal and thereby criminalises certain groups, particularly the oppressed and disadvantaged. This stress on the process of criminalisation is reminiscent of labelling theory. While accepting that interaction between lower-level agents of social control, such as the police, and deviants is important, radical

activity15 scrounging

Item A *Two views of capitalist society*

'I got the loot, Charlie, but after bank costs, services and handling charges, we owe them £6.25p.'

Item B *'The real scroungers'*

| Cost of dole fraud | £500 million | Cost of tax fraud | £5,000 million |
| Number of prosecutions | 14,000 | Number of prosecutions | 20 |

In the eyes of the law, all people may be equal but the government's treatment of tax and social security offenders suggests there is one law for the rich and another for the poor. For every individual who is pursued through the courts for tax fraud, about 700 are prosecuted for welfare offences. This disparity cannot be accounted for by arguing that benefit fiddling is a more serious social menace than tax fraud. Official estimates indicate that losses from benefit abuses are dwarfed by losses from tax evasion. The Inland Revenue sees prosecution as a last resort and seeks to secure 'a reasonable settlement by agreement'. As one tax accountant put it, 'You have to be very unlucky, very stupid and very crooked to be done by the Revenue'.

Adapted from the *Observer*, 23.10.1988

questions

1 Using a Marxist perspective, briefly comment on the cartoons in Item A.

2 Read Item B. Suggest reasons for the different treatment of tax fraud and welfare fraud.

---

criminology demands a wider focus. It looks at the process of criminalisation in relation to the state as it seeks to manage the capitalist system.

A 'fully social theory of deviance'

The ambition of radical criminology is evident in the final chapter of *The New Criminology* by Ian Taylor, Paul Walton and Jock Young (1973). There the authors outline a model which they term a 'fully social theory of deviance'. The model has seven dimensions:

1 'The wider origins of the deviant act'

   The radical criminologist needs to locate the deviant act within the wider social system – capitalism and its class divisions.

2 'The immediate origins of the deviant act'
   They then need to look at the immediate social context within which an individual chooses to commit an act of deviance.

3 'The actual act'
   Attention needs to be given to what the deviant act means to the individual concerned.

4 'The immediate origins of social reaction'
   They need to look at the immediate response of other people, such as members of the deviant's family and the police, to the discovery of deviance.

5 'Wider origins of deviant reaction'

   The immediate reaction needs to be located within the wider social system, with particular attention given to the question of who has the power to define certain activities as deviant.

6 'The outcomes of social reaction on the deviant's further action'

While most deviants recognise that there will be a reaction against them, it is important to examine the effects of the labelling process on the deviant.

7 'The nature of the deviant process as a whole'

Finally the six aspects of the deviant process need to be connected together for there to be a 'fully social theory of deviance'.

The closest approximation to a 'fully social theory of deviance' is *Policing the Crisis* by Stuart Hall et al. (1978). It is a study of the moral panic which took place in the early 1970s over 'mugging'. In the following summary, particular attention is given to the way this study illustrates a 'fully social theory of deviance'.

Policing the crisis

The wider origins of mugging Mugging is a term imported from America. It refers to the street crime of robbery or theft involving the threat or actual use of violence. During the early 1970s in Britain, a moral panic developed about the dangers of street crime and, in particular, the threat of the young Black mugger. Stuart Hall et al. (1978) argue that this societal reaction to mugging must be seen in the wider context of capitalism and the class system.

Street crime has traditionally been one 'survival strategy' for those at the bottom of the class system, particularly during an economic crisis.

Partly as a result of racism, the first generation of African-Caribbean migrants were the most disadvantaged members of the working class. The majority found low-paid employment and made the best of their situation.

The immediate origins of mugging Acutely aware of the racism of British society, Black youth were less willing than their parents to accept the situation. This sometimes caused conflict between the generations, resulting in some young people leaving home, taking to the streets and drifting into petty crime. In this context, a small minority of Black youngsters adopted the 'mugging solution' as a survival strategy.

The immediate origins of the social reaction to mugging The media were central in 'orchestrating public opinion' against the Black mugger. Between August 1972 and August 1973, the national daily newspapers reported 60 incidents as 'muggings'. They pictured Black youth creating mindless havoc in the inner cities. Yet mugging was neither a new problem, nor was it growing at an alarming rate – in fact, the rate of growth was less than half the rate in the 1960s. Hall et al. see the societal reaction to mugging as a moral panic.

The wider origins of the social reaction to mugging Hall et al. argue that this moral panic must be seen in the context of the problems that British capitalism was experiencing in the early 1970s.

Since 1945, full employment, rising living standards and the growth of welfare services resulted in the working class accepting the authority of the state. However, an economic crisis in the early 1970s brought rising unemployment, a slowing down of the rise in people's living standards and a halt to the expansion of welfare services. As a result, the authority of the state came under challenge from various groups, especially trade unions. For example, in 1972, there were more workdays lost by strikes than in any year since 1919. (See Chapter 4, Activity 7, pages 178-179.)

The state reacted by presenting this challenge to its authority as a 'law and order' issue. The stability of society was threatened by lawlessness and the state must respond. The focus on the Black mugger served to symbolise this threat to social order. The result was to divide the working class on 'racial' grounds, so weakening any challenge to the state. And, the apparent need to stamp out mugging as quickly as possible justified the state increasing its powers.

The outcome of social reaction Responding to the perceived threat of mugging, the police targeted this crime and Black youth in particular. Increasing numbers of young Black men were randomly stopped, searched and questioned in the street. Many saw this as unjustified and some responded with verbal abuse or violence. This often led to their arrest and appeared to confirm that they were indeed prone to crimes of violence. The result was a process of deviancy amplification. The labelling of Black youth as deviant led to more arrests which, in turn, justified even stronger police measures against so-called Black muggers, all of which provided further headlines for the newspapers.

A fully social theory *Policing the Crisis* looks at the moral panic of mugging from a variety of viewpoints. It analyses the crisis faced by British capitalism in the early 1970s and the resulting threat to the authority of the state. It argues that the state responded to this crisis by mounting a law and order campaign which led to a moral panic over mugging. As a result, Black youth became increasingly criminalised and the state was able to justify its growing powers. This analysis looks at the 'problem of mugging' on various levels – from society as a whole right down to street level.

Evaluation of radical criminology

Advantages Radical criminology combines a number of different perspectives in an attempt to provide a fully social theory of deviance. Within a Marxist framework, *Policing the Crisis* includes labelling theory along with concepts such as societal reaction, moral panics and deviancy amplification. In doing so, it offers a more comprehensive picture than previous perspectives.

Disadvantages In adopting a Marxist framework, radical criminology ultimately explains crime and deviance in terms of the nature of capitalist society, the conflict of interest between social classes and the role of the state in representing the capitalist class. Can all crime and deviance be explained in terms of this framework? Critics argue that many laws and much police activity cannot simply be seen as an expression of the interests of the capitalist class - for example, traffic laws and their enforcement (Rock, 1979).

According to Lea and Young (1993), radical criminology tends to trivialise and underplay the reality of crime. While moral panics do occur and societal reaction can amplify deviance, crime has risen. And the consequences are serious. Both the victims and the perpetrators of street crime are usually working class and, in many inner-city areas, this is a major problem. Radical criminology has little to say about the victims of crime.

According to Downes and Rock (2003), *Policing the Crisis* was a brave but unsuccessful attempt to provide a fully social theory of deviance. In particular, the authors failed to demonstrate that the societal reaction to mugging was caused by a crisis of capitalism. At the very least, they needed to show a link between economic crises and moral panics at other times and places. And this was not done.

summary

1. Marxist theories of crime and deviance became popular in the 1970s.
2. Traditional Marxist approaches argued that:
   - Crime is systematically generated by the structure of capitalist society.
   - Laws reflect the interests of the dominant capitalist class.
   - Laws are enforced selectively - there is a systematic bias in favour of those at the top.
3. Radical criminology adopts a Marxist framework but includes other perspectives - for example, interactionism.
4. It focuses on the process by which the state defines certain activities as criminal and thereby criminalises certain groups, particularly the disadvantaged. It looks at the process of criminalisation in relation to the state's management of the capitalist system.
5. Radical criminology aims to provide a 'fully social theory of deviance' - to explain every aspect of deviance from the activity of the state to crime on the streets.
6. Policing the crisis argued that the state manufactures a crime problem in order to justify strengthening its control over the population.
7. Radical criminology has been criticised for:
   - Seeing the actions of the state and the agents of social control as solely serving the interests of the capitalist class.
   - Downplaying the significance of crime and largely ignoring the victims of crime.

Unit 7 *Right realism and social control*

keyissues

1. What is distinctive about right realist approaches to crime?

2. What are the strengths and weaknesses of these approaches?

7.1 Recent developments in the sociology of crime

New approaches to crime and deviance are partly a reaction to the shortcomings of previous approaches, partly a reflection of changing academic and political priorities, partly a response to changing fashions.

In the 1980s and 90s there was increased concern about law and order in Britain and the USA. This was accompanied by a growing awareness of high levels of unreported victimisation, especially amongst the most vulnerable sections of the population. These concerns were reflected in two new approaches to the study of crime –

right realism and *left realism*. Both see crime as a major problem in society, especially for its victims, and both claim to take crime seriously and to put forward practical proposals to combat it. 'Realist' approaches can be seen as a reaction to both labelling theory and radical criminology. Neither of these perspectives appeared to show much concern for the victims of crime. Indeed, labelling theory implied that in many cases the 'victim' was the person who had been labelled as 'criminal'.

7.2 The right realist approach

Conservative theorists were the first to adopt a realist approach. James Q. Wilson (1975), an American New Right theorist and policy adviser to President Reagan, was one of the earliest authors to question the predominant liberal and left analyses of law and order which prevailed in sociology. What then are the central features of the right realist analysis of crime?

Poverty, unemployment and crime

First and foremost, right realists question the view that

economic factors such as poverty or unemployment are responsible for the rising crime rate. In the following passage, Wilson makes a telling critique of this view by arguing that affluence and prosperity may go hand in hand with rising crime.

'If in 1960 one had been asked what steps society might take to prevent a sharp increase in the crime rate, one might well have answered that crime could best be curtailed by reducing poverty, increasing educational attainment, eliminating dilapidated housing, encouraging community organisation, and providing troubled or delinquent youth with counselling services.

Early in the decade of the 1960s, this country (the USA) began the longest sustained period of prosperity since World War II. A great array of programmes aimed at the young, the poor and the deprived were mounted. Crime soared. It did not just increase a little; it rose at a faster rate and to higher levels than at any time since the 1930s, and, in some categories, to higher levels than any experienced in this century' (Wilson, 1975).

Explaining rising crime

According to James Q. Wilson and Richard Hernstein (1985), 'crime is an activity disproportionately committed by young men living in large cities'. They explain this in terms of both biological and social factors. In their words,

'It is likely that the effect of maleness and youthfulness on the tendency to commit crime has both constitutional [biological] and social origins: that is, it has something to do with the biological status of being a young male and with how that young man has been treated by family, friends and society.'

Wilson and Hernstein picture young men as 'temperamentally aggressive'. This aggression is partly biologically based and makes them prone to crime.

An increase in the proportion of young men in the population is therefore likely to increase the crime rate. In the USA and Britain in the 1970s, the proportion of young men in the population and the crime rate both increased. Since the early 1980s, the proportion of young men has decreased but the crime rate has continued to increase. Wilson and Hernstein offer a social explanation for this increase.

Culture and socialisation Wilson and Hernstein argue that the way young men are socialised in the family, school and wider community has an important effect on their behaviour. Consistent discipline inside and outside the home encourages individuals to learn and follow society's norms and values and develop self control.

Wilson and Hernstein see the growth of a culture which emphasises *immediate gratification* – the immediate satisfaction of wants and desires – *low impulse control* – less control over desires and emotions, fewer restraints and checks on behaviour – and *self-expression* – the outward expression of feelings. These aspects of culture have produced a less effective learning environment for many young men and reduced the restraints on their behaviour. As a result, they are less likely to conform to society's norms and values and more likely to commit crime.

Costs and benefits Wilson and Hernstein argue that the crime rate will change with changes in the costs and benefits of crime, particularly property crime. The more the benefits rise – for example, the more successful criminals are – and the more the costs fall – for example, the less likely they are to be caught – the more the crime rate will rise.

7.3 Social control

Control theory

Many right realists argue that individuals are more likely to commit crime when the social constraints on their behaviour are weakened. Control theory is mainly concerned with identifying the factors which prevent individuals from committing crimes.

According to the American sociologist Travis Hirschi (1969), none of us is immune from the temptations of crime. What stops most of us from committing crime are strong social bonds which link us together. Social bonds consist of four main elements: attachment, commitment, involvement and belief. The stronger our attachments to key social institutions such as the family and school, the more we develop commitments to those involved – parents and teachers. Such commitments in turn foster involvement in family life and learning, and encourage a belief in conforming to the rules. Effective social bonds mean that we have too much to lose by committing crime. To do so would risk losing the good opinion of significant others – those who matter to us.

In support of his theory, Hirschi reports the findings of a large-scale self-report study of over 4000 young people aged 12-17 in California. Variations in their reported bonds with parents and teachers were much more significant than economic factors in accounting for variations in reported delinquency. Drawing on a range of studies, Hirschi has put forward a general theory of crime. He argues that the primary distinguishing feature of offenders is a lack of self-control. This, in turn, stems from poor socialisation in families and schools (Gottfredson & Hirschi, 1990).

Social control and the underclass

The American New Right theorist Charles Murray (1990, 1996) claims that an underclass is emerging in modern Western societies. For Murray, an underclass does not simply consist of those with the lowest income at the base of the class system. Instead, it consists of those with low income who behave in a certain way. In Murray's words, 'When I use the term *underclass*, I am indeed focusing on a certain type of poor person defined *not* by his condition, eg long-term unemployed, but by his deplorable behaviour in response to that condition, eg unwilling to take the jobs that are available to him'.

Murray sees births outside marriage 'as the leading indicator of an underclass'. Such births often lead to lone-parent families, the majority of which are headed by women. When lone-parent families become widespread, they form the basis of and the 'breeding ground' for an underclass. And 'proof that an underclass has arrived is that large numbers of young, healthy, low-income males choose not to take jobs'.

Inadequate socialisation Many of these young men have grown up in a family without a father and male wage earner. As a result, they lack the male role models of mainstream society. Within a female-headed family dependent on welfare benefits, the disciplines and responsibilities of mainstream society tend to break down. Murray believes that work must become the 'centre of life' for young men. They must learn the disciplines of work and respect for work. And they must learn to become 'real fathers', accepting the responsibilities of parenthood. However, 'Little boys don't naturally grow up to be responsible fathers and husbands. They don't naturally grow up knowing how to get up every morning at the same time and go to work. They don't naturally grow up thinking that work is not just a way to make money, but a way to hold one's head high in the world.' Murray believes that the socialisation and role models required to develop these attitudes are often lacking in female-headed low-income families.

Crime and the underclass According to Murray (1990), crime is a characteristic of the underclass. He argues that 'men who do not support families find other ways to prove that they are men, which tend to take various destructive forms'. Many turn to crime – particularly violent street crime – and to drug abuse. The high crime rate and high levels of victimisation result in fragmented communities which reinforce already inadequate socialisation.

Welfare benefits and family Although Murray appears to blame members of the underclass for their situation, he places most of the blame on government policy. It is the availability of overgenerous welfare benefits which has allowed the underclass to develop. Members of the underclass have become dependent on the state which has funded their unproductive lifestyles. Murray's solution is a sharp reduction or withdrawal of welfare benefits in order to force people to take responsibility for their own lives. In addition, Murray (1996) recommends penalising births outside marriage and reaffirming 'the value of marriage and the nuclear family'.

Without these changes, Murray believes that the underclass will reproduce itself from generation to generation.

7.4 Social order and crime prevention

Right realists are concerned with practical measures to reduce crime and maintain social order. Some of those measures are based on *rational choice theory*.

Rational choice theory As noted earlier, Wilson and Hernstein (1985) argue that there is an important element of choice when deciding whether or not to commit a crime. They picture the individual weighing up the costs and benefits of criminal activity and coming to a rational decision. In terms of this view, crime reduction means increasing the costs of crime and raising the benefits of conformity.

Two measures which increase the costs of crime are *target hardening* and *surveillance*. Target hardening reduces the physical opportunities for offending. Examples include installing tougher coin boxes in phone kiosks, making it more difficult to break into buildings, and gated communities with security guards. Surveillance refers to systems like CCTV (closed circuit television) which can film criminal activities. These measures increase the costs of crime – the cost of failure and the cost of getting caught.

Informal social controls In James Q. Wilson's view, it is not practical to deal with the fundamental causes of crime – the biological and social factors outlined in Section 7.2. The central concern of the criminal justice system should be the maintenance of social order. Since informal controls are fundamental in preventing crime, the police should seek to prevent further deterioration of communities before it is too late.

In a highly influential article, Wilson and Kelling (2003) argue that crime and social disorder are closely connected. Leaving broken windows unmended and ignoring anti-social behaviour can result in a vicious cycle whereby graffiti proliferates, noise levels increase, vandalism grows and more windows get broken. The consequence of inaction is to tip a neighbourhood into decline – property values spiral downwards, respectable members of the community are afraid to go out, they eventually leave the neighbourhood, and crime and disorder become widespread.

The role of the police is to prevent an area from deteriorating by clamping down on the first signs of petty crime and disorderly behaviour. By working with local residents to deal with undesirable behaviour, the police can help to prevent the deterioration of neighbourhoods and reinvigorate informal social controls. Since the police have limited resources, prioritising areas where there is still a possibility of regenerating communities means that there is little point in wasting valuable resources on the worst inner-city areas. The most that can be done there is to contain the crime problem by adopting more punitive measures – for example, longer prison sentences – to deal with 'wicked people' (Wilson, 1975). The prison population in the US has tripled since the late 1970s (from 500,000 to 1.8 million in 1998) and is now the highest per capita in the world (Carrabine et al., 2002).

7.5 Evaluation of right realism

What's 'real' about right realism? Right realists see the rising crime rate as a real indicator of a *real* social problem

– a problem which must be tackled with practical methods. However, as discussed in Unit 2, at least part of the rise in crime indicated by official statistics may result from changes in recording and reporting crime (Walklate, 2003).

Economic change and crime Right realists make an important point when they argue that economic growth and rising living standards have gone hand in hand with rising crime since the 1960s. However, this does *not* mean that social inequality ceases to be an important factor in generating crime. Despite rising living standards, the gap between top and bottom has widened over the past 25 years. This can result in a sense of relative deprivation which may lead to an increase in crime.

Disorder and community deterioration Do signs of disorder – 'broken windows' and anti-social behaviour – lead to a vicious cycle of community deterioration and rising crime? A study of 196 neighbourhoods in Chicago questions this view. It found that economic disadvantage underpinned *both* growing disorder and crime (Sampson & Raudenbush, 1999). Again, this points to the importance of relative deprivation in generating crime.

Young males Right realists focus on young males and street crime. They are the real problem, and the type of crimes they commit are the real threat to social order. This view is questionable. Other types of crime may be equally, if not more harmful – for example, corporate crime and domestic crime.

Right realists assume that young males in inner-city areas are responsible for most crimes. Again, this is questionable. It assumes that official statistics provide a valid picture of the typical offender.

Crime prevention According to Wilson (1975), 'wicked people exist' and the only thing that works is to 'set them apart from innocent people'. More imprisonment and longer sentences keep wicked people out of circulation and reduce the crime rate. Not only is this a very expensive measure, there is no sound evidence that it works (Walklate, 2003).

Civil liberties The major concern of right realists is to maintain order in society. For some, their prescription for producing order is based on a 'culture of control' – social control, situational control and self-control. This has alarmed some sociologists who see it as a threat to civil liberties – for example, the widespread use of surveillance techniques intruding on people's privacy (Hughes, 2000).

summary

1. Right realists accept the view that the crime rate rose dramatically in the second half of the 20th century.

2. They reject the view that economic factors and social inequality explain this rise.

3. Wilson and Hernstein argue that the rise in crime results from the growth of a culture which emphasises immediate gratification, low impulse control and self-expression. This results in a less effective learning environment for many young men. As a result, they are less likely to conform to society's norms and values.

4. Control theory states that strong social bonds result in high levels of social control. These are the main factors which prevent criminal behaviour.

5. Charles Murray argues that the underclass is a 'breeding ground' for crime. The 'deplorable behaviour' of young males results from inadequate socialisation in female-headed families and a lack of mainstream role models. Murray argues that overgenerous welfare benefits have allowed the underclass to develop.

6. Rational choice theory states that individuals weigh up the costs and benefits of criminal activity. Crime reduction therefore means increasing the costs of crime and the benefits of conformity.

7. Target hardening, surveillance, more imprisonment and longer sentences increase the costs of crime.

8. The primary role of the criminal justice system is to maintain public order. According to Wilson, strong informal social controls are the most effective method for maintaining order.

9. Disorder indicates a weakening of informal controls. The police should clamp down on the first signs of disorder to prevent community deterioration and rising crime.

10. Right realism has been criticised for:
    - Accepting the picture of crime presented by official statistics
    - Rejecting the view that economic factors and social inequality can generate crime
    - Focusing on young males and street crime and largely ignoring other types of offenders and crime.
    - Placing too much emphasis on control which some see as a threat to civil liberties.

activity16 controlling crime and anti-social behaviour

Item A Maintaining order

How to sweep these beggars from our streets

by David Marsland

In all of our major cities and larger towns beggars have multiplied over recent years like fungus spreading in a damp cellar. Their aggressive hassling of men, women, and children is an intolerable blot on the complex but orderly copy-book of a modern civilised society.

Their arrogant contempt for the values of most decent, ordinary people - honesty, hard work, and civility foremost among them - is intolerable. Their possessive occupation - like locusts swarming on the harvest - of the most celebrated and attractive streets and squares they can find, is contemptible.

Analysis of historical and international evidence serves to disprove most fashionable explanations of begging. Neither 'capitalism' nor poverty is the cause. Begging on any scale is unheard of in some of the richest countries in the world - such as Switzerland - and some of the poorest - such as Malaysia.

Nor is it unemployment which causes begging. The current scale of begging was unheard of in the Britain of the 1930s, when unemployment was at much higher levels and much crueller in its impact.

Victorian experience provides the clue to the real explanation. Faced with a problem very like today's, politicians, businessmen and community leaders carefully analysed cause and effect, and rapidly set up a practical system which solved the problem in short order.

The Poor Laws and the work-houses were modernised and toughened up.

Help without a return of effort was outlawed. The values of hard work, self reliance and respectability were reinforced and unapologetically defended by a powerful consensus of public opinion in the schools, the churches, the media and Parliament. Begging was shamed out of existence.

What is causing the escalation in modern begging is:

- The hand-out culture of the decaying welfare state.
- The cultivation of tolerance for 'doing nothing' and 'doing your own thing' by teachers, intellectuals and political leaders.
- The impact on established British values of the sloppy, alien thinking of the Sixties.

Adapted from *Daily Mail*, 1994

Item B Controlling crime

Closed circuit television

Gated community

Metropolitan Police Chief Sir Paul Condon (centre) promoting the Neighbourhood Watch Scheme

questions

1 In what ways does Item A reflect the right realist approach?

2 How do the pictures in Item B illustrate right realist views on crime control?

Unit 8 Left realism

keyissues

1 What is distinctive about the left realist approach?

2 What are its strengths and weaknesses?

8.1 The left realist approach

The emergence of left realism Left realism developed in the early 1980s. It was a reaction to both right realism and radical criminology. It was led by the British sociologist Jock Young.

Left realism accused the right of over-dramatising the crime problem with its picture of crime rates out of control. It rejected right realism's view of moral decay and sick societies. And it accused the right of failing to understand the real causes of crime.

Marxism and radical criminology were criticised for focusing on the crimes of the powerful and for failing to understand working-class crime. In particular, left realism argued that street crime could not simply be dismissed as a moral panic fuelled by a crisis of capitalism. Left realism accused radical criminology of failing to take working-class crime seriously.

Taking crime seriously Left realism, as its name suggests, claims to focus on the reality of crime. Its rallying cry to sociologists is to 'take crime seriously'. And this means starting from 'problems as people experience them' (Young, 1986). Although left realists do not discount the importance of white-collar and corporate crime, they see street crime as 'the most transparent of all injustices' (Lea & Young, 1993). Its effects can be traumatic, it can leave people living in fear, it can impoverish victims. Left realists see crime committed by working-class people against working-class people as a problem of the first order.

Explaining crime Left realists argue that earlier explanations of crime failed to see the whole picture. For example, they looked at offenders and ignored victims, or focused almost exclusively on the criminal justice system. Left realists argue that an understanding of the reality of crime requires an examination of four basic elements and how they interact (Young, 1997).

- The victims – how they see and experience crime
- The offenders – why they commit crime
- The reaction of the formal agencies of the state – for example, the police and the courts
- The response of the public and the nature of informal methods of social control.

8.2 The victims

Left realists see crime as a real problem and the public's fear of crime as largely rational and justified. And they see the social survey as the main research method for studying the victims of crime.

Victim studies According to Jock Young (1992), victim surveys 'allow us to give voice to the experience of people' and to take their needs seriously. They reveal the extent of victimisation, the concerns and priorities of the victims of crime, and they provide information on which to base policies of crime prevention.

Left realists accept that estimates from national surveys, such as the British Crime Survey, show that the average chance of being a victim of crime is small. However, national surveys underestimate the risks faced by low-income groups in inner-city areas. For example, the Islington Crime Survey found that 36% of local residents saw crime as a major problem, 56% were anxious about being burgled, 46% had been a victim of a street robbery and a third of women avoided going out after dark for fear of sexual harassment (Jones et al., 1986).

In contrast to some earlier approaches, such as labelling theory and radical criminology, left realists highlight the plight of victims. It is disadvantaged groups living in the inner cities who are most at risk from being harmed by street crime. And since these groups are on low incomes, they often suffer more – petty theft is a lot more serious when people are living in poverty.

8.3 The offenders

Left realists largely accept the picture presented by official statistics – that there has been a significant growth in crime, especially working-class crime. They see the increase in working-class crime as a particularly disturbing development – most of the victims are not the rich but the most vulnerable members of society. And most of the offenders come from the same social groups as their victims.

Why do people commit crime? The key concept used by left realists to answer this question is *relative deprivation*.

Relative deprivation Jock Young notes that the rise in crime between 1960 and 1975 occurred at a time of full employment and rising living standards. And since then 'as the West became wealthier, the crime rate rose' (Young, 1999). Deprivation, as such, clearly does not cause a rise in crime. What does, according to left realists, is how people see or perceive deprivation. In other words, what matters is relative deprivation.

People see themselves as deprived in comparison to, or relative to, other people. This comparison may be relative to people in the same social category as themselves – for example, in the same social class or ethnic group – or to people in other social categories – for example, in different social classes or ethnic groups to themselves.

In late modern society – from the 1970s onwards – there has been an increase in relative deprivation. And this increase has been particularly acute for those at the base of the class structure and for those in certain ethnic groups. Reasons for this will be examined shortly.

Relative deprivation does not necessarily lead to crime. It breeds discontent which can be expressed in many different ways – crime is only one of them. It is the combination of relative deprivation and *individualism* that provides a recipe for crime. In Jock Young's (1999) words, 'The lethal combination is relative deprivation and individualism'.

Individualism A number of sociologists see the rise of individualism as one of the main characteristics of late modern society. Individualism refers to a focus on and concern with the self, to a demand for individual freedom and autonomy. It is partly responsible for, and partly a result of, the breakdown of close-knit communities and the break-up of families. It undermines the relationships and values necessary for social order and weakens the informal mechanisms of social control in the community. And it often results in the pursuit of selfish interests.

According to Jock Young (1999), the combination of relative deprivation and individualism is the main cause of crime in late modern society. As a result of this combination, 'the working-class area implodes upon itself', anti-social behaviour is widespread, 'neighbours burglarise neighbours' and 'aggression is widespread'.

Late modern society and rising crime

What are the changes in late modern society that have led to the disintegration of community, the increase in relative deprivation and rising crime rates? Left realists provide the following picture with particular reference to the lower working class.

Changes in the economy There has been a rapid decline in manufacturing and manual jobs, particularly unskilled and semi-skilled occupations. Lower working-class males have been particularly hard hit, as have African Caribbeans in Britain and African Americans and Hispanics in the USA. And within these groups, the young are most likely to experience unemployment – many have never had full-time work. This has led to acute feelings of relative deprivation because of a lack of fit between their situation and what they see as reasonable expectations in terms of jobs and material rewards.

Changes in the economy have led to the disintegration of many lower working-class families and communities, and the informal social controls they provided.

Government policy has not helped. Most Western governments have adopted free-market policies which discourage state intervention in the economy to provide jobs. Alongside this, many governments have reduced welfare benefits.

Exclusion Those at the base of the class structure are increasingly excluded from mainstream society.

- They are largely excluded from the labour market.
- They face increasing social exclusion as the middle classes flee from the inner city to areas where the poor cannot afford to live and, in some cases, cannot enter as the rich increasingly live in gated communities with security guards at the entrance.
- And they are excluded from society, as prison populations increase dramatically. For example, in the USA, 1 in 9 Black males in their 20s are in prison compared to 1 in 135 of the total population (Mauer, 1997).

The mass media and inclusion There is one area where those at the base of the class structure are included – the mass media, especially television. Living in a world which excludes them, they remain 'glued to the television sets which alluringly portray the glittering prizes of a wealthy society' (Young, 1999). And, sharing the materialistic values of the mainstream culture, they are faced every day with comparisons which fuel relative deprivation.

Jock Young (2002) argues that the lower working class live in a *bulimic society* – a society constantly exposed to the material goods taken for granted by most of the population, but unable to consume them. In this sense, they are starving. In Young's words, 'The process is not that of a society of simple exclusion. Rather it is one where both inclusion and exclusion occur simultaneously – a *bulimic society* where massive cultural inclusion is accompanied by systematic structural exclusion.'

8.4 Dealing with crime

The public and informal control

Left realists agree with the right realists that the police and other criminal justice agencies can only play a limited role in preventing crime. Far more important are the forces of informal control. 'It is not the "Thin Blue Line" but the social bricks and mortar of civil society which are the major bulwarks against crime. Good jobs with a discernible future, housing estates that tenants can be proud of, community facilities which enhance a sense of cohesion and belonging, a reduction in unfair inequalities, all create a society that is more cohesive and less criminogenic' (Young, 1992).

On the local level, what's needed is a concerted effort by all the agencies which may have an impact on crime. Left realists refer to this as *multi-agency intervention*. Local authorities must coordinate their various departments – for example, housing, education, social services and planning – in order to rebuild disintegrating communities. On the national level, the state must reduce economic inequalities and create a more just society.

The police and formal control

Left realism accepts that good policing can play an important part in reducing crime. But, low clear-up rates and a decline in public confidence have made members of some communities reluctant to help the police. Where the

activity 17 Life at the bottom

Item A Watching TV

A study of a low-income Black ghetto in Philadelphia found that African Americans watch TV half as much again as whites – in the average Black household TV is on for 11 hours a day. By the age of five and six, children are familiar with adult luxury – from Gucci, Evan Piccone and Pierre Cardin, to Mercedes and BMW. By the age of ten they are thoroughly engrossed in Nike's and Reebok's cult of the sneaker.

Adapted from Nightingale, 1993

Item B Dealing in drugs

A study of Puerto Rican immigrants in East Harlem drew the following conclusion.

I want to place drug dealers and street level criminals into their rightful position within the mainstream of US society. They are not 'exotic others' operating in an irrational netherworld. On the contrary they are 'made in America'. Like most other people in the United States, drug dealers and street criminals are scrambling to obtain their piece of the pie as fast as possible. They are aggressively pursuing careers as private entrepreneurs: they take risks, work hard, and pray for good luck. They are the ultimate rugged individualists, braving an unpredictable frontier where fortune, fame, and destruction are all just around the corner, and where the enemy is ruthlessly hunted down and shot.

Adapted from Bourgois, 1995

Item C Riots

Two youths stole a police BMW motorbike in Hartcliffe, Bristol. In the police chase which followed, they crashed and were killed. Trouble ensued – crowds of young people, White and Black, set fire to the local library and community centre, and looted shops. The following night, there were more riots. It is a familiar pattern, repeating what has occurred in depressed estates from Teeside to Salford.

The affluent societies of the West have fostered new expectations. Advertising and the rules of an economy based on mass consumption teach us that if we are truly to belong to our society, we must possess its glittering prizes. Hunger no longer propels riots – in its place are the DVD player, the mobile phone and the BMW.

Adapted from Young, 1992

Looting during a riot in Miami, Florida 1990

Item D Exclusion

US population in prison, on parole or on probation, 1995		
	In prison	In prison, on parole or on probation
Total population	1 in 135	1 in 37
Black males	1 in 24	1 in 13
Black males in 20s	1 in 9	1 in 3

Adapted from Mauer, 1997

Inmates from a maximum security prison, Miami

questions

1 In what way does Item A illustrate Young's view of the bulimic society?

2 How does Item B indicate that those at the bottom share the values of mainstream society?

3 Use the concept of relative deprivation to explain the behaviour outlined in Items B and C.

4 How can Item D be seen as the ultimate form of exclusion?

flow of information from the public – which is crucial to the solution of many crimes – has ground to a halt, the police have responded with more direct methods such as stopping and searching large numbers of people.

This can lead to 'a drift towards military policing' which can make it well nigh impossible to police with the consent of the community (Lea & Young, 1982). In some Black low-income inner-city areas, the police are regarded by some as an army of occupation. And in Brixton in 1981, a police operation, which swamped an area with officers on a stop and search mission, triggered riots.

In line with its concern about what is to be done about law and order, left realism calls for greater democratic control of the police. A genuinely accountable police force will be more efficient since it will restore the flow of information from the public. And it will reflect the concerns and priorities of the community.

In addition, left realism urges the state to decriminalise minor offences such as the possession of cannabis, find more alternatives to imprisonment, and develop multi-agency and community-based forms of crime prevention.

8.5 Evaluation of left realism

Left realism is a genuine attempt to take crime seriously. And it is a comprehensive approach which looks at both victims and offenders, and informal and formal methods of social control. Despite these advantages, it has been criticised in various ways.

Focus on street crime While left realists accept that crime takes place across the class structure, their primary focus is on street crime and lower working-class offenders and victims. In their defence, such crimes loom large in victim surveys and are particularly harmful to victims. However, some sociologists criticise left realists for neglecting white-collar and corporate crime – which may be even more harmful (Walklate, 2003)

Over-predicting crime The view that relative deprivation plus individualism and economic inequality generate crime 'over-predicts the level of crime' (Jones, 1998). Since this explanation appears to fit most people, why isn't there more crime?

A trend towards inclusion Some sociologists question whether the trends identified by left realists are as serious and permanent as they suggest. According to the British Crime Survey, crime rates have been falling since the mid-1990s. And so have unemployment rates.

It is possible to detect trends towards inclusion as well as exclusion in late modern societies (Downes & Rock, 2003). For example, the Labour government in Britain has introduced the minimum wage, raised child benefits, set up the New Deal to help the unemployed return to work, and created the Social Exclusion Unit with the aim of bringing the excluded into mainstream society.

Victim surveys Left realists rely heavily on victim surveys to measure the type, extent and fear of crime in low-income inner-city areas. As outlined earlier, victim studies have their limitations (see pages 212-123). Certain types of crime are under-reported or not reported – for example, domestic violence and child abuse. And victim studies do not capture how people define and experience criminal victimisation – for example, do women define domestic

summary

1. Left realism aims to 'take crime seriously'. It sees street crime as particularly damaging to victims.

2. Understanding crime requires an examination of four basic elements and how they interact – victims, offenders, the police and the criminal justice system, and the public and informal control.

3. Local victim studies reveal the type and extent of crime in low-income, inner-city areas. They present a disturbing picture.

4. Relative deprivation is the key concept used by left realists to explain crime. Relative deprivation is felt most acutely by those at the base of the class structure.

5. In late modern society, the combination of relative deprivation and individualism is the main driving-force generating crime.

6. Changes in late modern society have led to the disintegration of community and informal social controls, an increase in relative deprivation, and rising crime rates. These changes include:
   - Economic change and the loss of many unskilled and semi-skilled jobs
   - The growing exclusion of those at the base of the class structure from mainstream society.

7. One area where those at the bottom are included is the mass media. They are presented daily with expensive goods and lifestyles but are unable to consume them. In Jock Young's words, they live in a 'bulimic society'. The media fuels relative deprivation.

8. Left realists argue that the criminal justice system has only a limited role in preventing crime. Informal mechanisms of social control are far more important.

9. Left realists argue that multi-agency intervention on the local level can help to reduce crime rates.

10. The police have an important part to play but they need the support of the public. This requires an accountable police force under local democratic control.

11. Left realism has been criticised for:
    - Paying too much attention to street crime and largely ignoring white-collar and corporation crime
    - 'Over-predicting' the level of crime
    - Ignoring trends towards inclusion in late modern society
    - Relying too heavily on victim studies as a source for information.

violence by their partner as a crime and, if so, what level of violence? In-depth interviews rather than survey questionnaires are more likely to answer this and similar questions.

Unit 9 Ethnicity and crime

key issues

1 Are some ethnic groups more likely to commit crimes than others?

2 Are some ethnic groups more likely to be victims than other groups?

3 Is the criminal justice system biased?

9.1 The ethnicity and crime debate

Questions of ethnicity and gender were barely looked at by sociologists of crime and deviance until the 1970s. The primary focus was on class. Since the 1970s, sociologists have recognised the need to examine ethnicity and gender. This unit focuses on the ethnicity and crime debate. Issues relating to gender and crime are examined in the following unit.

In the early phase of post-war migration, there was a widespread assumption that members of ethnic minority groups were no more likely to be offenders or victims than the majority White group. It was also assumed that the criminal justice system treated all ethnic groups fairly. Indeed, according to a major investigation into police-immigrant relations in 1972, 'Black people were more law abiding than the general population' and there was little evidence of racist attacks against Black and Asian immigrants (Layton-Henry, 1992). During the following ten years, however, relations between the police and the Black community deteriorated and evidence mounted of increasing racist attacks.

Two reports published in November 1981 signalled the onset of official concerns. The Scarman Report (1981) into the Brixton disorders emphasised how the riots were essentially an outburst of anger and resentment by young African Caribbeans against perceived harassment by the police. And a Home Office report into racial attacks revealed that South Asians were 50 times, and African-Caribbeans 36 times, more likely to be the victims of racially motivated attacks than Whites. There was growing evidence that Black and Asian people were increasingly involved with the criminal justice system.

Two issues in particular have given rise to concern – the racist violence and harassment experienced by ethnic minority groups and the criminalisation of Black people.

Criminalisation The issue which initially attracted most attention concerned the criminalisation of Black people. At the end of the criminal justice process, 'Black people are about six times as likely to be in prison as White people or South Asians' (Smith, 1997). Two broad explanations have been put forward for this. The first sees Black people as disproportionately criminal. This explanation tended to be adopted by the police and other criminal justice agencies and reproduced in the media (Hall et al., 1978). The second sees the criminal justice system as inherently racist and discriminating against Black people. This explanation has received some support from radical sociologists (Gilroy, 1983). Until the 1990s, the ethnicity and crime debate was primarily concerned with this issue.

Victimisation More recently, attention has turned to another question. The murder of Stephen Lawrence, a Black teenager, and the failure of the criminal justice system to convict those responsible, led to an official inquiry, the Macpherson Report in 1999. The report found serious failings with the police investigation into this racially motivated murder. It not only challenged the dominant picture of the criminal justice system as unbiased, but also raised the profile of another question. Are ethnic minority groups more likely to be victimised than the White majority ethnic group?

9.2 Ethnicity and offending

To discover whether there are differences between ethnic groups in rates of offending, we can turn to three sources – official statistics, victim surveys, and self-report studies.

Official statistics

Table 2 presents the official statistics detailing the ethnic groups at different stages of the criminal justice system.

The table indicates that in 2000/01, Black ethnic groups were particularly over-represented at different stages of the criminal justice system. While they comprised only 1.8% of the population, they made up 7.7% of arrests, 6.2% of cautions and 12.1% of the prison population. Asian groups,

Table 2 Representation of ethnic groups at different stages of the criminal justice process, 2000/01

	Ethnicity					
	White	Black	Asian	Other	Not known	Total
Population (aged 10 and over)	94.5%	1.8%	2.7%	1.1%	0.0%	100.0%
Stops and searches	82.7%	10.1%	4.9%	1.0%	1.2%	100.0%
Arrests	86.3%	7.7%	4.4%	0.9%	0.6%	100.0%
Cautions	85.7%	6.2%	4.6%	1.0%	2.0%	100.0%
Youth offenders	77.9%	5.8%	2.7%	1.9%	11.6%	100.0%
Prison receptions	85.6%	8.9%	2.4%	3.1%	0.0%	100.0%
Prison population	81.9%	12.1%	2.8%	3.1%	0.1%	100.0%

Adapted from Home Office, 2002

by comparison, were slightly over-represented. Comprising 2.7% of the population, they made up 4.4% of arrests, 4.6% of cautions and 2.8% of the prison population. In contrast to these ethnic minority groups, White ethnic groups were under-represented – they were less likely to be arrested, cautioned or sent to prison.

While the official statistics point to ethnic differences at different stages of the criminal justice system, they do not demonstrate that there are ethnic differences in rates of offending. The higher arrest rate of Black ethnic groups could reflect the fact that these groups are more likely to be targeted by the police. Similarly, the higher rate of imprisonment could reflect the fact that these groups are more severely sentenced by the courts.

Victim surveys

At first sight victim studies, such as the British Crime Survey, provide a more effective way of discovering whether there are ethnic differences in rates of offending, since they include questions asking victims about the ethnic identity of offenders. Unfortunately, victims are usually only aware of offenders when it comes to personal crimes, which account for only 20% of all crimes. These surveys show that, in many cases, both offenders and victims come from the same ethnic group. An analysis of the 1988 and 1992 British Crime Surveys (Mayhew et al., 1993) revealed that 88% of White victims of violence identified the offenders as White. In the majority of violent offences against ethnic minority groups, the offenders were also identified as White (51% in the case of Black victims and 62% in the case of Asian victims). This is to be expected since the general population is overwhelmingly White. Once account has been taken of White offenders, a majority of Black victims of violence identified Black offenders (42%) and the majority of Asian victims identified Asian offenders (19%).

Mugging The offence that has given rise to most controversy has been 'mugging'. Although this term is a criminal label that has no formal legal standing, it has been taken up widely since its arrival from the USA in 1972. It has been used by the police and the BCS to refer to robbery and some thefts from the person. Victim surveys suggest that Black ethnic groups are significantly more likely to commit this offence than other ethnic groups. Mayhew et al. (1993) point to 42% of muggings being committed by Black offenders in the early 1990s, while Clancy et al. (2001) point to a slightly lower figure of 31% in the late 1990s. BCS figures are similar to police data on the ethnicity of those arrested for robbery and therefore suggest that the Black over-representation amongst muggers indicates a higher Black offending rate (Clancy et al., 2001).

A word of caution is in order, however. 'The effects of stereotyping and prejudice may lead White victims sometimes to say that offences committed against them have been committed by Black people, even when they are not sure who was involved' (Bowling & Phillips, 2002). What is more, mugging constitutes only a small proportion of crime – only 2.8% of offences recorded by the BCS. While Black ethnic groups may have a higher offending rate for this crime, victim surveys do not point to significant over-representation of Black or other ethnic minority groups among offenders for other crimes.

Self-report studies

In contrast to both the official statistics, which measure the outcomes of the actions of criminal justice agencies, and victim surveys, which are only able to reveal the ethnic identity of offenders for a small proportion of crime, self-report studies address the question of offending directly. Self-report studies ask people whether they have been engaged in criminal and disorderly behaviour.

The major study conducted in Britain which expressly pays attention to the question of ethnicity is the Home Office study, *Young People and Crime* (Graham & Bowling, 1995). Based on a large sample of young people, 'this study found that White and Black respondents had very similar rates of offending (44% and 43% respectively), while Asian respondents – Indians (30%), Pakistanis (28%) and Bangladeshis (13%) – had significantly lower rates' (Phillips & Bowling, 2002).

This study challenges the widespread view that the rate of offending of Black ethnic groups is higher than that of White ethnic groups. And it supports the suggestion that the rate of offending of Asian groups is somewhat lower. However, we cannot infer that this study reveals the true rate of offending. Self-report studies rely on the honesty of respondents and exclude from their sample people in institutions who may be more involved in offending. They also underplay the more serious offences.

Evaluation

The evidence from the three sources on the extent and nature of offending by different ethnic groups is inconclusive. The sources of data are all flawed in some way, with self-report studies pointing in one direction and arrest data in the other (Bowling & Phillips, 2002).

However, there are two exceptions to this. Homicide statistics, which are more reliable than other official statistics, do 'indicate that a disproportionate number of homicides involve people from ethnic minorities [especially African Caribbeans] as both victims and suspects' (Bowling & Phillips, 2002). And victim reports do point to the greater involvement of African Caribbeans in robbery. While homicide and robbery represent only a small proportion of recorded crime, the data for these offences suggests somewhat higher rates of offending by African Caribbeans (Phillips & Bowling, 2002).

9.3 Racism and the criminal justice system

Some researchers argue that the greater likelihood for ethnic minority groups, particularly Black ethnic groups, to be criminalised (arrested and imprisoned, for example) reflects their greater involvement in crime. Other researchers argue that ethnic differences in criminalisation stem from institutional racism within the criminal justice system. This view received support from the Macpherson Report.

The Macpherson Report

Institutional racism The 1999 Macpherson Report on the police investigation into the murder of Stephen Lawrence concluded that 'institutional racism' in the police force was widespread. The Macpherson Report agreed with the earlier Report of Lord Scarman into the 1981 Brixton disorders that the police do not 'knowingly as a matter of policy, discriminate against Black people' (Scarman, 1981). However, it did not accept Scarman's view that 'institutional racism does not exist in Britain' (Scarman, 1981).

For Macpherson, the concept of institutional racism does not imply that the policies of organisations are racist. The term instead is defined as: 'the collective failure of an organisation to provide an appropriate and professional service to people because of their colour, culture or ethnic origin. It can be seen or detected in processes, attitudes

and behaviour which amount to discrimination through unwitting prejudice, ignorance, thoughtlessness and racist stereotyping' (Macpherson, 1999, para 6.34).

The Macpherson Report gives official recognition to the fact that the police in particular, and the criminal justice system in general, are biased against ethnic minority groups.

Policing For Macpherson, the failure of the police investigation into the murder of Stephen Lawrence was not due to acts of discrimination by individual officers acting out their personal prejudices. Instead, it stemmed from the occupational culture of the police. In an occupation that may entail danger, great emphasis is placed on teamwork, with jokes and banter being used to cement solidarity. A number of studies have discovered that derogatory stereotypes about ethnic minority groups are prevalent among police officers, the vast majority of whom are White (Smith & Gray, 1995, Holdaway, 1996, Graef, 1990). Jokes and banter often take a racist form and reinforce a negative perception of Black and Asian people.

While we cannot assume that such racism leads to discriminatory policing, it can do so. A case in point is Dwayne Brooks, Stephen Lawrence's companion on the night of his murder. As a Black young man at the scene of a knifing, he was regarded by the police as a suspect rather than a witness. In seeking to protect society from crime and disorder, the police identify certain groups as more likely to mean 'trouble'. Black young men and, more recently, Muslim young men are often viewed in this way. As a result, their actions are more likely to be regarded with suspicion (Kalra, 2003).

Stop and search The Macpherson Report identified the use of stop and search powers by the police as a key factor in contributing to poor relations between the police and ethnic minority groups. In 1998/99, Black people were six times and Asians twice as likely to be stopped and searched as Whites. The police have considerable discretion in the use of these powers, which can be used on the basis of 'reasonable suspicion'. At the time of the inquiry, the BCS revealed that ethnic differences in the likelihood of being stopped and searched could not be accounted for by other factors such as age or social class. This suggests that discrimination may be responsible.

The Macpherson Report's judgement on the use of stop and search powers by the police states: 'we are clear that the perception and experience of the minority communities that discrimination is a major element in the stop and search problem is correct' (Macpherson, 1999). In the immediate aftermath of the report, the use of stop and search powers fell and, at the same time, the ethnic differences declined. In addition, the 2000 BCS indicates that the ethnic differences in foot stops, as opposed to car stops, could now be accounted for by factors other than ethnicity – for example, by social class (Clancy et al., 2001). While this suggests that ethnic discrimination may have fallen, the official statistics in Activity 18 indicate that the fall may have been short-lived.

activity 18 stop and search

Item A *Stop and search statistics*

Stop and search in Brixton, South London

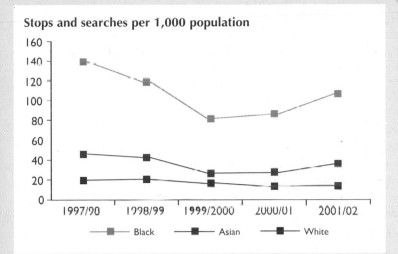

Stops and searches per 1,000 population

Years: 1997/98, 1998/99, 1999/2000, 2000/01, 2001/02

Legend: Black — Asian — White

Adapted from Home Office, 2002

Item B *'It makes you feel stigmatised.'*

Wesley Walters-Stephenson is a race relations trainer for the police. He is an African Caribbean.

'How many times have I been stopped and searched? It happens so often. I become defensive when I am stopped because I am weary of being pulled up and it makes you feel stigmatised, it makes you feel like a criminal. It can happen any time and I try to stay off the streets as much as possible.

My worst experience was when I got my shoulder busted and went unconscious for a short while after I was stopped and searched. I was 26. It is no wonder they have problems with youth culture when the police have criminalised two generations of Black people.'

Adapted from *The Guardian*, 8.11.2002

Wesley Walters-Stephenson

questions

1 Summarise the trends in Item A.

2 Read Item B. What are the likely effects of being regularly stopped and searched?

Arrests Figure 2 shows ethnic differences in arrest rates. Black people are approximately six times and Asians approximately twice as likely to be arrested as Whites. Most arrests result from the police responding to reports from the public. However, a significant minority are due to the police targeting particular ethnic minority groups through their use of stop and search powers (Phillips & Bowling, 2002).

Once arrested, and in contrast to other ethnic groups, Blacks are less likely to admit the offence. As a result, they are less likely to escape with a caution and more likely to face formal action (Home Office, 2002). Black juveniles are less likely than other groups to have their cases referred to multi-agency panels and thus more likely to go to court. This holds true even when 'admission of the offence' has been taken into account (Phillips & Bowling, 2002).

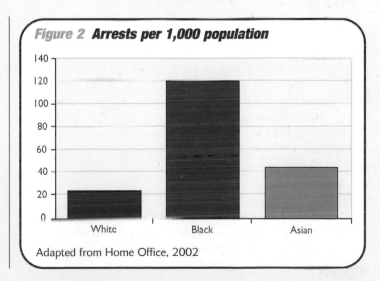

Figure 2 Arrests per 1,000 population

White, Black, Asian

Adapted from Home Office, 2002

Prosecution Before a case goes to court, the Crown Prosecution Service (CPS) decides whether to proceed with a prosecution. It does so when it believes that there is a 'realistic prospect of conviction' and that it is in the public interest to do so. The CPS is more likely to terminate cases that involve ethnic minority groups. This suggests that the police may, as a result of holding negative stereotypes, put forward cases against ethnic minorities where the evidence is weak (Phillips & Bowling, 2002).

Once the decision to prosecute has been made, the next step is to decide whether to remand a defendant in custody or grant bail. Ethnic minorities are more likely to be remanded before and during a trial 'partly because they have an increased risk of being "of no fixed abode", a key criterion on which courts refuse bail' (Phillips & Bowling, 2002). Those remanded in custody are more likely to be given a custodial sentence if found guilty.

There is a greater likelihood of defendants from ethnic minority groups pleading not guilty and electing for trial in a Crown Court rather than a Magistrate's Court. If found guilty, they are likely to face a more serious sentence than they would if they had entered a guilty plea or opted for trial in a Magistrate's Court.

Ethnic minority defendants are more likely to be acquitted than White defendants (Home Office, 2002). This finding reinforces the suggestion above that cases involving ethnic minorities are more likely to be brought forward by the police where the evidence is weak. It also suggests that the CPS still allows 'a disproportionate number of weak cases against ethnic minorities to go to trial' (Denman, 2001).

Sentencing and imprisonment

Sentencing The most significant study on ethnic differences in sentencing was conducted in five Crown Courts in the West Midlands in 1989. All male ethnic minority defendants found guilty were compared to an equivalent sample of male White defendants. After taking the seriousness of the offence and previous convictions into account, the study revealed that Black men were 5% more likely to be given a custodial sentence. What is more, for defendants who pleaded not guilty and were sent to prison, Asian men were given sentences 9 months longer and Black men 3 months longer than Whites (Hood, 1992). Sentencing is a clear example of discrimination against ethnic minority groups.

Imprisonment In comparison with other ethnic groups, Black people have significantly higher rates of imprisonment. This is illustrated in Figure 3. Some of the reasons for this difference have already been mentioned. Further reasons are given in the following section.

Evaluation

The evidence clearly points to racial discrimination in the criminal justice system. However, an important question still remains. Does discrimination wholly account for the greater criminalisation of ethnic minority groups? The two

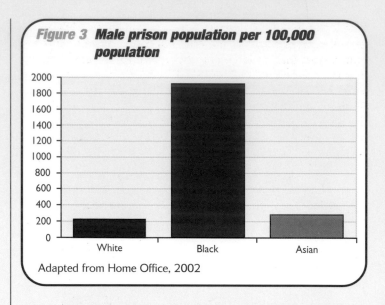

Figure 3 Male prison population per 100,000 population

Adapted from Home Office, 2002

most recent overviews that have looked at this question reach somewhat different conclusions.

Evidence of bias The first review acknowledges 'evidence of bias' against Black people at various stages of the criminal justice system – in the use of stop and search powers, in the decision to prosecute juvenile offenders, and in sentencing by the Crown Courts (Smith, 1997). Such bias does not demonstrate, however, that the criminal justice system is institutionally racist. For bias is not evident at all stages in the criminal justice system. What is more, if the criminal justice system were institutionally racist, it is difficult to understand why Black people are much more likely to be criminalised than Asians. The extent of the disproportionate imprisonment of Black people is, in this view, too great to be explained by racial discrimination in the criminal justice system.

Discrimination A more recent review is more sympathetic to the view that discrimination in the criminal justice system has a cumulative effect on Black people and helps to explain their over-representation in the prison population. 'It is not necessary for there to be discrimination at each and every stage in the process in order for the over-representation of Black people in prison to be the result of cumulative discrimination' (Bowling & Phillips, 2002).

The criminal justice system can still be racist even though Black people are treated more harshly than Asians. This may reflect the fact that Black people are more likely to be viewed with suspicion, itself a result of contrasting stereotypes held of Black (violent and dangerous) and Asian people (passive and traditional).

Despite the fact that the two most recent overviews reach somewhat different conclusions, they agree that the available evidence is not able to demonstrate whether the over-representation of Black people in prison is better explained in terms of their higher rate of offending or discrimination by the criminal justice system. There is now widespread agreement among sociologists that we need to move beyond the 'either/or of racist criminal justice vs

Black criminality' (Reiner, 1993). While acknowledging bias at various stages of the criminal justice system, Smith emphasises that 'in large part the difference in rate of arrest and imprisonment between Black and White people arises from a difference in the rate of offending' (Smith, 1997). Similarly, Phillips and Bowling (2002) – after highlighting the discriminatory nature of the criminal justice system – acknowledge 'somewhat "elevated" rates of offending by African Caribbeans'

Discrimination and criminalisation In short, both discrimination in the criminal justice system and the greater involvement of young Black men in street crime contribute to the criminalisation of Black people (Hudson, 1993). The two are linked – 'discrimination on the one hand, and Black crime on the other, reinforce and feed off one another in a vicious cycle of amplification' (Reiner, 1993).

Lea and Young (1982) illustrate how this vicious circle develops. For there to be policing by consent, a community must act as a source of information to the police so that they can 'catch and/or deter individual lawbreakers'. As unemployment generates an increasing crime rate in inner cities, however, the police begin to adopt a more aggressive policing policy and turn to operations which involve the random stopping of 'suspicious' youth. This inevitably results in large numbers of innocent people being stopped and searched. Once this happens, the community 'begins to become alienated from the police'. It 'comes to see any attempt at an arrest by officers as a symbolic attack on the community' and ceases to provide the police with any information which can help them identify individual offenders. Faced with this situation, the police adopt an even more aggressive policing policy and so the vicious circle continues. In this context, 'whatever racist sentiments exist within the police force are reinforced' (Lea & Young, 1982; Pilkington, 2003).

9.4 Ethnicity and victimisation

Racist incidents

Although racist violence and harassment is by no means new, mounting evidence indicates the scale of the problem in Britain. The police recorded 23,049 racist incidents in 1998/9, a massive increase since 1988 (4,383 incidents) when records of such incidents were first collected. The police statistics – though they cover the majority of the most serious cases – represent the tip of an iceberg if we include all racially motivated crimes. The 2000 British Crime Survey discovered, for example, 280,000 racially motivated offences in 1999. If we also include 'forms of racially insulting and threatening behaviour which are not seen as criminal events in themselves', the extent of racist victimisation becomes even more evident (Modood et al., 1997). The Policy Studies Institute Survey provides an estimate of such low-level racist harassment in 1994. It concludes 'that over a quarter of a million people were subjected to some form of racial harassment in a 12-month period' (Modood et al., 1997).

While all ethnic groups face the risk of being the victim of racist harassment, the risk is significantly greater for members of ethnic minority groups. In 1999, for example, 'the annual risk of being the victim of a racially motivated offence was 0.3% for White respondents, 2.2% for Black groups, 3.6% for Indians and 4.2% for Bangladeshis and Pakistanis' (Clancy et al., 2001). The consequences of such racist harassment are extremely damaging. A range of studies confirms how they can create a climate of continual insecurity for victims and their families (Chahal & Julienne, 1999). Such everyday harassment provides the backdrop to racist violence. The murder of Black teenager Stephen Lawrence at a bus stop by five White youths in 1993 is the most notorious example.

The Macpherson Report considered the reluctance of the police to acknowledge the existence of racially motivated offences and to protect ethnic minority groups from victimisation to be a serious failing. Its conclusion outlined a series of recommendations related to the handling of racist incidents. A plethora of activity has followed. A code of practice on the reporting and recording of racist incidents has been produced by the Home Office (2000); the Association of Chief Police Officers (ACPO, 2000) has produced a guide to identifying and combating hate crime; and Her Majesty's Inspectorate of Constabulary has produced a succession of reports on community and race relations (HMIC, 2001). Whether significant progress has been made in the handling of racist incidents remains to be seen.

Victimisation and fear of crime

Ethnic minority groups also face a higher risk of a range of 'household crimes' such as burglary and theft (Clancy et al., 2001). The same applies to violent crime, although in this case, ethnic minority groups are much more likely to see these incidents as racially motivated.

The 2000 British Crime Survey points out that a significant proportion of the increased risk of victimisation faced by ethnic minority groups is due to factors such as area of residence and age. However, even with regard to these factors, racial discrimination may still play a part in increasing the risk of victimisation – it can influence the area in which people choose to live. And finally, the increased victimisation faced by ethnic minorities is reflected in their increased fear of crime.

summary

1. The ethnicity and crime debate has addressed two key questions:
   - Why are some ethnic groups, especially Black groups, more likely to be criminalised?
   - Are some ethnic groups more likely to be victimised than others?
2. We cannot reach a definite conclusion as to whether there are ethnic differences in the rate of offending. For specific offences, such as mugging, there is some evidence of a higher rate of offending by Black ethnic groups.
3. There is clear evidence of racial discrimination at various stages of the criminal justice system.
4. It is likely that ethnic differences in rates of offending and a discriminatory criminal justice system combine to produce ethnic differences in criminalisation.
5. Ethnic minority groups face a higher risk of victimisation and suffer disproportionately from racially motivated offences. As a result, they are more likely to express fear of crime than other groups.

Unit 10 Gender and crime

keyissues

1. Why are there gender differences in crime?
2. Is there a gender bias in the criminal justice system?

10.1 The gender and crime debate

Official statistics indicate that men are much more likely to commit crime than women. For example, in 2002, over 80% of known offenders were men (Home Office, 2003). This ratio is found in other Western countries and has remained remarkably similar over time.

In the past, sociologists paid little attention to these marked gender differences. They tended to take them for granted. Instead, they focused on why some men rather than other men were more likely to commit crime or become labelled as criminals.

Things began to change in the 1970s. Feminists, such as Carol Smart (1977), as challenged what they saw as the male dominance of the subject. They opened up new lines of inquiry into women and crime and asked a new set of questions.

- Why do women commit fewer crimes than men?
- Why are women more likely to conform to social norms than men?
- Is there anything distinctive about women's experience as offenders and as victims of crime?
- Are women treated differently than men by the criminal justice system?

Today, there is widespread agreement that the sociology of crime and deviance must take account of gender. This means examining both women and crime *and* men and crime. And this also means asking a new set of questions about men – for example, what is the relationship between crime and masculinity?

10.2 Gender and offending

In 2002, over 481,000 people in England and Wales were cautioned for, or found guilty of, criminal offences. Just over four-fifths were men (Social Trends, 2004). These figures are drawn from official statistics based on police and court records. As outlined in Unit 2, there are a number of problems with the reliability and validity of official statistics (see pages 207-214).

Self-report studies provide an alternative source of information for gender differences in offending. For example, the 1998/9 Youth Lifestyles Survey, based on 4,849 12 to 30-year-olds, found that males were two-and-a-half times more likely to have offended in the last year than females (Home Office, 2003). However, there are also problems with self-report studies (see pages 213-214).

Despite these problems, all sources of data point in the same direction. As a result, there is now general agreement that:

- Significantly more men than women commit crime.
- Men are more likely to commit serious offences.
- Men are more likely to re-offend (Heidensohn, 2002).

Sex role theory

Sex role theory argues that boys and girls are socialised differently and, as a result, boys are more likely to become delinquent. There are a number of versions of this theory.

Edwin Sutherland According to Sutherland (1949), there are two main gender differences in the socialisation process. First, girls are more closely supervised and more strictly controlled. Second, boys are more likely to be encouraged to take risks and to be tough and aggressive. As a result, boys have more opportunity and more inclination to commit crime.

Talcott Parsons According to Parsons (1955), there are clearly defined gender roles in the modern nuclear family. The father performs the instrumental role of leader and provider, the mother performs the expressive role of giving

activity19 gender and offending

Offenders found guilty or cautioned, 2002

England & Wales					Rates per 10,000 population
	10-15	16-24	25-34	35 and over	All aged 10 and over (thousands)
Males					
Theft and handling stolen goods	86	183	104	17	131.5
Drug offences	18	159	62	9	84.1
Violence against the person	31	77	32	9	51.8
Burglary	29	49	21	2	30.4
Criminal damage	13	18	7	2	12.5
Robbery	6	14	4	0	7.2
Sexual offences	3	4	3	2	5.0
Other offences	11	102	59	12	69.0
All offences	196	606	292	53	391.5
Females					
Theft and handling stolen goods	51	67	32	6	50.1
Drug offences	2	15	9	1	9.8
Violence against the person	11	12	5	1	9.5
Burglary	3	3	1	0	2.1
Criminal damage	2	2	1	0	1.6
Robbery	1	1	0	0	0.9
Sexual offences	0	0	0	0	0.1
Other offences	3	20	13	2	14.4
All offences	74	119	61	12	88.6

Adapted from *Social Trends*, 2004

Shoplifting – according to official statistics, a typical female offence

questions

1 Summarise the data in the table.

2 Briefly outline the problems with official crime statistics.

---

emotional support and socialising children. These gender roles are rooted in biology since women give birth to and nurse children.

While girls usually have a readily available female role model at home – their mother – boys have less access to a male role model. Largely socialised by their mother, they tend to reject any behaviour seen as feminine and to compulsively pursue masculinity. There is an emphasis on toughness and aggression which can encourage anti-social behaviour and delinquency.

Albert Cohen According to Cohen (1955), socialisation can be a difficult process for boys. Without a readily available male role model, they can experience anxiety about their identity as young *men*. One solution to this is the all-male peer group or street gang. In these social contexts, aspects of masculinity can be expressed and rewarded. Being tough, taking risks and breaking rules can help to confirm a masculine identity. But, they can also encourage delinquent behaviour.

Evaluation Sex role theory is an early sociological theory which attempted to explain gender differences in crime. It

has the advantage of explaining these differences in terms of learned behaviour rather than earlier theories which looked for explanations in biological differences between males and females. However, something of this earlier approach remains in the work of Talcott Parsons. He sees women as biologically adapted to a nurturing and caring role. As a result, they are mainly responsible for socialising children.

Feminist writers criticise sex role theory for failing to consider gender differences in power – In particular, the power that men have over women. This view is considered in the following section.

10.3 Feminist perspectives

Feminist perspectives start from the view that society is patriarchal. It follows that the behaviour of women can only be understood in the context of male dominance. In terms of women and crime, this viewpoint leads to new questions and new answers. The research examined in this section combines feminist insights with control theory.

Female crime as rational

Pat Carlen (1990) argues that women's crimes are largely 'the crimes of the powerless'. Many women who commit crimes are powerless in various ways. They often live in poverty with little power to change their situation. As children, many have been harshly supervised, and sometimes abused by their fathers. And as adults, they have often lived under the dominance of male partners who, in some cases, used violence in an attempt to assert control.

Carlen (1988) conducted in-depth interviews with 39 working-class women aged 15-46 convicted of a range of offences. She draws on control theory, arguing that people turn to crime if the advantages outweigh the disadvantages. For the women Carlen interviewed, crime appeared as a rational choice. Their experience of low-paid work and unemployment had not led to the standard of living and lifestyle they had hoped for. And their experience of family life, both as children and adults, had been unhappy and unfulfilling.

Unrewarded in the family and in the workplace and with little power to change their situation by legitimate means, they saw crime as a rational alternative. And the crimes they typically committed were seen as a rational choice. In Carlen's words, 'Property crime was *chosen* because certain types (eg, shoplifting and cheque fraud) were seen to be "easy" '.

Evaluation Carlen's sample of 39 women is too small to generalise from. However, her research suggests that conformity to social norms tends to break down when the rewards for doing so are largely absent. But, as the next section indicates, it may be much more difficult for women than men to deviate from society's norms.

Conformity and control

According to Frances Heidensohn (1996, 2002), the most striking thing about women's behaviour is their conformity to social norms. Drawing on control theory, she argues that women have more to lose than men if they deviate from norms. And drawing on feminism, she argues that in a male-dominated society, the control of women by men discourages deviance from norms.

Home and family Women still have the primary responsibility for raising children and domestic work. Their commitment to raising children and to family life also involves a commitment to conformity – to the traditional mother-housewife role and to socialising children in terms of society's norms and values. From the point of view of control theory, women have more to lose than men by deviating from social norms.

Women have been socialised to conform. Girls are more strictly supervised than boys, given less freedom and expected to perform more household duties. And these controls, duties and expectations continue into adult life. As adults, women are not only controlled by their childhood socialisation but also by their male partners. Women who challenge their traditional roles are often brought into line by men's financial and physical power. According to Heidensohn, wife-battering is an 'assertion of patriarchal authority'.

Women's socialisation and domestic responsibilities plus the controls imposed on them by men discourage deviance from social norms. Their lives are centred on the private sphere of the home and they have less freedom to go out. As a result, they have less inclination, less time and fewer opportunities to commit crime.

Beyond the home Outside the home, women's freedom to come and go as they please and to deviate from social norms is limited in various ways. For example, women are often reluctant to go out after dark, particularly in inner-city areas, for fear of attack or rape by men. And they are less likely to deviate from norms of respectability for fear of being labelled a slag or a bitch.

At work, men are more likely than women to be in control – in managerial and supervisory roles. And surveys indicate that sexual harassment is common in the workplace. This is a further indication of male power and control as it is often experienced as intimidating by women.

Both inside and outside the home, there is pressure for women to conform – pressure which is reinforced by male power.

Evaluation Heidensohn's combination of a feminist perspective with control theory provides an explanation for women's conformity to social norms and for their low crime rate. However, critics have made the following points. First, it presents women as passive, as simply accepting their situation (Naffine, 1987). The feminist movement from the 1960s onwards suggests a rather different picture. Second, Heidensohn makes sweeping generalisations about women and men. In doing so, she fails to recognise the differences between women, and the differences between men (Walklate, 2003).

10.4 Crime and masculinities

Research into gender and crime over the last 25 years has been mainly concerned with women and crime. Feminists focused on women, and men enter the picture in terms of their control over women.

Researchers now recognise that there is another side to the gender issue – men and masculinity. Why are men more likely to commit crime than women? Is there a relationship between male crime and masculinity?

Men, masculinities and crime

James Messerschmidt (1993) has presented the most influential and comprehensive view of the relationship between masculinity and crime.

Accomplishing masculinity Messerschmidt starts from the position that gender identity is a vital part of the individual's sense of self. It is something that people accomplish – they are continuously constructing, expressing and presenting themselves as masculine or feminine. And, in the case of males, crime can be a resource for accomplishing masculinity. It can be used in the construction of masculinity so that men can express their masculinity both to themselves and to others.

Masculinities Messerschmidt identifies a number of different masculinities which are shaped by social class, ethnicity, age and sexual orientation. Men's position in society provides differential access to power and resources which leads to different constructions and expressions of masculinity. And this, in turn, leads to different types of crime.

Messerschmidt refers to the dominant form of masculinity as *hegemonic masculinity*. It is the 'idealised' form which is 'defined through work in the paid-labour market, the subordination of women, heterosexism and the driven and uncontrollable sexuality of men'. This is the form of masculinity that most men seek to accomplish. However, for various reasons, some men are unable to, or do not wish to, accomplish this dominant form.

Messerchmidt calls the alternatives to hegemonic masculinity *subordinated masculinities*. They include masculinities which develop in some ethnic minority and lower-class groups, and homosexual masculinity.

Crime, masculinities and youth Young middle-class White males are usually able to demonstrate some of the characteristics of hegemonic masculinity through success at school and college. However, this comes at a price – subordination to teachers. Some assert their masculinity outside school through vandalism, petty theft and heavy drinking.

White working-class young men are less likely to be successful in education. They sometimes resist school and construct their masculinity around physical aggression, anti-social behaviour, delinquency and, in some cases, violence towards gays and members of ethnic minority groups.

Lower working-class young men from ethnic minority groups with little expectation of educational success or secure employment sometimes assert their masculinity in street gangs. With little chance of accomplishing hegemonic masculinity by legitimate means, they are more likely to turn to robbery and serious property crime.

Social class and masculinities Even middle-class males who have the resources to accomplish hegemonic masculinity use crime to express masculinity. Messerschmidt argues that white-collar and corporate crime are not simply a means for profiting the individual or the organisation. They are also a means of accomplishing hegemonic masculinity – as a successful breadwinner and as an aggressive, risk-taking male.

Working-class crime in the workplace can also be seen as a means of accomplishing masculinity. Workers sometimes resist the authority of management by theft and industrial sabotage.

Ethnicity and masculinities Messerschmidt uses the example of African Americans to illustrate a subordinated masculinity. Lower-class African-American males often lack the resources to accomplish hegemonic masculinity. The pimp and the hustler – long-established roles in African-American subculture – offer an alternative subordinate masculinity.

The pimp dominates a string of prostitutes and lives off their earnings. With his 'pimp walk', soft-top Cadillac, diamond rings, gold chains, and prowess with and power over women, the pimp demonstrates a highly visible alternative masculinity to himself and others.

Evaluation Messerschmidt has provided a sophisticated analysis of the relationship between masculinities, age, class, ethnicity and crime. His focus on accomplishing masculinity is an original explanation of the high level of male crime. However, there are a number of criticisms of his research.

- First, it over-predicts crime (Jones, 1998). For example, pimps are the exception rather than the rule in low-income African-American areas. And why do only a minority of men from all social classes and ethnic groups feel the need to assert their masculinity through crime?
- Second, the claim that hegemonic masculinity is the ideal which all men aspire to is questionable. It can be seen as little more than a popular stereotype. Masculinities may be considerably more complex and diverse than Messerschmidt claims.
- Third, Messerschmidt uses the idea of masculinity to explain practically every crime that men commit – theft, burglary, rape, domestic violence, joy-riding, white-collar and corporate crime. According to Richard Collier (1998), this stretches the explanatory power of the concept of masculinity much too far.
- Fourth, there is an element of tautology in Messerschmidt's argument – in other words, his argument tends to be circular. Masculinity explains male crimes. How do we know? Because males have committed those crimes.

key terms

Hegemonic masculinity The dominant and ideal form of masculinity which most men seek to accomplish.
Subordinated masculinities Less desirable forms of masculinity which some men seek to accomplish because they lack the resources required for hegemonic masculinity.

Masculinity and crime in late modern society

A crisis of masculinity Late modern societies have seen an economic transformation. There has been a rapid decline in manufacturing industry and a rise in service industries. This has resulted in a fall in unskilled and semi-skilled manual jobs and a rise in working-class male unemployment.

These changes have been particularly unsettling for men who, in the past, were able to express their masculinity through physical labour. In addition, unemployment and intermittent employment mean they can no longer accomplish their masculinity through full-time work and support for their families. This can lead to a *crisis of masculinity* (Campbell, 1993).

According to Jock Young (1999), this crisis is particularly acute for young men who have never had a job and have little prospect of getting one. They are 'cast adrift' and are not even suitable marriage material.

Some respond by creating subcultures of machismo which glorify an exaggerated form of masculinity – toughness, aggression, sexual prowess, and respect for manhood backed up by physical strength and, in some cases, by guns. This can be seen in gangsta rap where women are portrayed as whores, bitches and sex objects to be exploited, where pimping, hustling and gun law are expressions of masculinity, and men earn respect by defending their reputation with violence.

The night-time economy In recent years there has been a massive expansion in the night-time leisure economies of many towns and cities in Britain. Local authorities, anxious to regenerate their communities through attracting private investment to the inner cities, have adopted increasingly liberal attitudes towards alcohol and entertainment licensing. Night clubs have mushroomed, with large numbers of young people flocking to them.

A two year research project studied this development (Hobbs et al., 2003). The researchers used both participant observation and interviews with bouncers, police, council staff, night-club managers, licensees and other key players in order to understand how the night-club economy worked. To facilitate access, three of the project team trained as bouncers and one of the research assistants worked underground as a bouncer.

According to Dick Hobbs, 'The night time economy is currently an unplanned largely unregulated zone where alcohol-related violence and disorder is rife'. Any control that does exist is mainly in the hands of bouncers who fill the void left by the police. The activities of these men (only 7% are women) are not effectively regulated and order is maintained by frequent threat or use of violence. While being a hard man has always been a source of status in many working-class communities, in the night-time economy it becomes a means of earning a living as a bouncer. What is more, being a bouncer provides opportunities for engaging in lucrative criminal activities. These include protection rackets, drug dealing, and importing duty-free cigarettes and alcohol and selling them at cut-price to clubs and pubs. With the loss of many working-class jobs, these men assert their masculinity through being hard, working as bouncers and, in many cases, getting involved in criminal activities.

Joy-riding A study of crime and riots in the early 1990s on two deprived council estates in Newcastle-upon-Tyne and Oxford points to the pleasures gained by working-class young men asserting their masculinity through joy-riding (Campbell, 1993). High unemployment on these estates meant that many young men could not look forward to a secure job that would enable them to support a family. They asserted their masculinity by manufacturing excitement through joy-riding and ram raiding. Brought up in a consumer society where high performance cars are associated with power and status, they drove stolen cars at speed around local estates and in some cases smashed them into shops to gain entry. This often led to a car chase with the police which added to the excitement.

Evaluation The case studies examined above relate to specific contexts. As a result, we cannot generalise from these studies. However, they do suggest that some working-class men turn to crime to accomplish masculinity. While research on masculinities and crime indicates there is a link between the two, it has yet to demonstrate that most, let alone all, male crime can be explained in these terms.

10.5 Gender and the criminal justice system

Is there a gender bias in the criminal justice system? Are women and men treated differently by the police and the courts? There are two schools of thought on this issue.

The chivalry thesis Chivalry means treating others, especially women, with courtesy, sympathy and respect. The *chivalry thesis* states that women are treated more leniently than men by the criminal justice system. Male chivalry means that the police are less likely to charge women and the courts will tend to give women lighter sentences, even when they have committed the same offences as men.

Double deviance This argument states that women are treated more harshly by the criminal justice system. This is because they are doubly deviant – they have deviated from social norms by breaking the law and deviated from gender norms which state how women should behave.

Many women feel they have been treated harshly by the criminal justice system. They see it as a male-dominated institution and feel their treatment has been unsympathetic and unjust (Heidensohn, 2002).

The evidence

Official statistics reveal the following.

- After arrest, women are more likely than men to be cautioned rather than charged.
- They are less likely than men to be remanded in custody or committed for trial.
- Women offenders are more likely than men to be discharged or given a community sentence and less likely to be fined or sentenced to prison.
- Women sent to prison receive shorter sentences than men (Home Office, 2003).

At first sight, these figures suggest that the criminal justice system treats women more leniently. They appear to

activity20 *subordinated masculinities*

Item A **Gangsta rap**

Gang members in Los Angeles

Tupac Shakur

The rapper Tupac Shakur died from gunshot wounds at the age of 25. He now sells more CDs dead than alive. He often used to pose with guns and had THUG LIFE tattooed on his stomach.

Gangsta rap reflects the violence of low-income ghetto areas. Rappers boast about using guns to defend their reputation, to settle scores and to avenge murdered 'homies' (friends from the neighbourhood). In one rap, Ice Cube refers to himself as a 'natural born killer' and states:

'When I grab my sawnoff (shotgun)

Niggas get hauled off.'

Women are often referred to as 'hoes' (whores) and bitches. Rappers boast about their sexual exploits and their prowess with women.

When work is mentioned, it is usually pimping, hustling, dealing in dope and the rewards they bring.

Adapted in part from Light, 1998

Item B **Bouncers**

Bouncers need to present themselves as hyper-masculine. This form of masculinity has the following characteristics: toughness, autonomy, vitality, power, dominance, respect, honour, pride, and of course violence. Body size and shape are accentuated, and stance, clothing, facial expression and general demeanour are often tailored to display the mental and physical toughness required.

A licensee of a pub gives the following description of a bouncer. 'I already knew Jimmy for a few years. I knew he did the doors at some of the pubs in town so I just asked him to call in. I just picked a time when I knew some of the local lads would be in. We talked for about five minutes and you can hear them go quiet then start talking about him. After a few minutes, he just walked over and said 'all right' to them, and that he was working here now. They didn't say a fucking word. They knew who he was obviously, everyone knows Jimmy don't they? It's not like you can miss him. And that's it. I gave him twenty quid that first time, and fifteen quid a week after that. He gave me his mobile number to "phone if there's any bother" and he comes in every now and then. With someone like Jimmy doing that, I don't need a bouncer on at all really. I'm still here all the time and I keep a pickaxe handle behind the bar.'

Adapted from Hobbs et al., 2003

Bouncer outside the Chunnel club in London

questions

1 How do Items A and B illustrate subordinate masculinities?

2 Suggest reasons why these masculinities are developed by men from particular social groups.

provide support for the chivalry thesis. Matters are not that simple, however. To compare like with like, we need to take into account the seriousness of the offence and differences in offending history. The higher cautioning rate for women and the lower likelihood of being remanded in custody or sent for trial mainly reflect differences in the type of offence and past offences (Home Office, 2003). Women's offences tend to be less serious and women are less likely to have a criminal record. This suggests that there is no systematic bias for or against women.

Sentencing The evidence on sentencing is conflicting. Farrington and Morris (1983) examined sentencing in Cambridge City Magistrates Court over a one year period. They found that men and women received similar sentences, once relevant factors such as the seriousness of the offence and the offender's previous record were taken into account. By contrast, Hood's (1992) study of sentencing in Crown Courts in the West Midlands found that women were treated much more leniently, even when relevant factors were taken into account. A review of a range of studies on sentencing found that, on the whole, women and men received similar treatment. However, there is some evidence of women being treated more leniently, including avoiding imprisonment where men would not (Cavadino & Dignan, 2002).

There is evidence that courts treat some women differently than other women. This appears to be based on the view that the primary role of women is as a mother. On the basis of interviews with Scottish sheriffs (judges), Carlen (1983) concludes that women who are considered good mothers are unlikely to be imprisoned. Such leniency towards some women was accompanied by harshness towards others. Women who were not considered good mothers and whose children were in care received harsher sentences, including imprisonment.

Evaluation It is not possible to reach a definite conclusion about gender bias in the criminal justice system. There are clearly differences in the likelihood of men and women being sent for trial and placed in custody. However, many but not all of these differences disappear when the severity of the offence and the offender's record are taken into account. In addition, there is evidence that some women are treated more harshly than others on the basis of how well they are judged to have performed their role as mothers.

10.6 Gender and victimisation

Victim surveys consistently show that men are more likely to be the victim of violent crime than women. The British Crime Survey 2002/03 reveals that 5.3% of adult males and 2.9% of adult females had been the victim of at least one violent crime in the preceding twelve months (Home Office, 2003). The type of violent crime men and women experience tends to differ. Men are more likely to be the victims of violent attacks by strangers and other men in

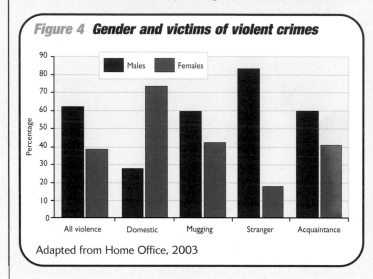

Figure 4 **Gender and victims of violent crimes**

Adapted from Home Office, 2003

summary

1. Available sources of data indicate that:
   - Significantly more men than women commit crime.
   - Men are more likely to commit serious offences.
   - Men are more likely to re-offend.

2. Sex role theory argues that boys and girls are socialised differently and, as a result, boys are more likely to become delinquent.

3. Feminists argue that the behaviour of women can only be understood in the context of male dominance.

4. Pat Carlen argues that women's crimes are largely 'crimes of the powerless'. She draws on control theory, arguing that working-class women turn to crime when the advantages appear to outweigh the disadvantages.

5. According to Frances Heidensohn, the most striking thing about women's behaviour is their conformity to social norms. She explains this in terms of their socialisation and control over their behaviour by men. As a result, women have less inclination, time and opportunity for crime.

6. James Messerschmidt argues that male crime can be seen as an expression and assertion of masculinity.

7. He distinguishes between hegemonic masculinity – the ideal which most men strive for – and subordinate masculinities – constructed by men who lack the resources to accomplish the dominant form.

8. Masculinities are shaped by class, ethnicity, age and sexual orientation. Different masculinities lead to different forms of crime.

9. A number of researchers argue that there is a 'crisis of masculinity' in late modern society. This is due to the decline in manufacturing and the resulting loss of many unskilled and semi-skilled jobs. As a result, some men have turned to crime in order to assert their masculinity.

10. At first sight, it appears that men and women are treated differently by the criminal justice system. However, when the seriousness of offences and the history of offending are taken into account, most of these differences disappear.

11. There is evidence that some women are treated more leniently than others on the basis of how well they are judged to have performed their role as mothers.

12. Men are more likely to be the victims of violent crime. Women are more likely to be the victims of domestic violence and sexual violence.

13. Woman tend to express more fear of violent crime than men. This places constraints on their behaviour.

public spaces. Women, on the other hand, are more likely to know their attacker and to be victimised at home. The British Crime Survey 2002/03 reveals that 73% of domestic violence incidents were against women. In the case of homicide, 46% of female victims were killed by current or former partners compared to only 5% of males. Women are also more likely to be the victims of sexual violence. According to the British Crime Survey 2000, around one woman in 20 has been raped since the age of 16, with strangers accounting for only 8% of those rapes (Home Office, 2003).

Feminism and women's victimisation Feminists have highlighted the extent and seriousness of crimes such as rape and domestic violence. These crimes, which usually involve women as victims, are seen to reflect male power in a patriarchal society. They differ from most other crimes since they often continue over long periods of time. Male violence against women is not limited to the home – it also occurs at work and in public places.

Women tend to express more fear of violent crime than men, despite the fact that they are less likely to be victims. This can place constraints on women's lives. They may avoid going out after dark for fear of being attacked. And they may take measures to dress and behave in ways that prevent them being seen as provocative by men (Stanko, 1994).

Unit 11 *Age and crime*

keyissues

1　What is the relationship between age and offending?

2　What explanations have been given for this relationship?

11.1 Sources of data

Data from official statistics and self-report studies indicates that most offences are committed by young people – by teenagers and by adults in their early 20s. This section looks at the evidence.

Official statistics In 2002, over 481,000 people in England and Wales were sentenced in court or cautioned by the police for an offence. Compared to other age groups, young people offended most – the highest rate for males was at age 19, for females at age 15. Theft was the most common crime committed by young people, followed by drug offences, violence against the person and burglary (*Social Trends*, 2004).

Official statistics from various Western societies show a similar age-crime curve. Offending rises steeply from ages 10 to 18, declines sharply to around age 24, followed by a long, slow decline through the remaining age groups. This generalisation applies to different historical periods and different social groups – for example, males, females and ethnic minorities (Smith, 2002). Table 3 shows the age-crime curve for England and Wales in 2002.

Self-report studies Self-report studies of crime ask people whether they have committed a series of offences. They are usually based on a self-completed questionnaire or an interview. Respondents are presented with a list of offences and asked which they have committed over a period of time – for example, during the past 12 months or during their lifetime.

Self-report studies present a similar picture to official statistics of the relationship between age and offending. They mirror the age-crime curve shown by convictions and cautions.

Evaluation – official statistics As outlined in Unit 2, official statistics provide information on only a small proportion of offenders. For example, there were nearly 5.9 million recorded crimes in England and Wales in 2002/03. This compares with only 481,000 people convicted or cautioned. The proportion of known offenders becomes even smaller when a comparison is made with British Crime Survey data. According to one estimate, only 3% of BCS crimes resulted in an offender being convicted or cautioned (Barclay & Tavares, 1999).

We cannot assume that all offenders are similar to this small proportion of known offenders. In other words, we cannot generalise from such a small, and probably unrepresentative, sample.

The information provided by official statistics may exaggerate the proportion of young offenders. Young people are more likely to offend in groups and in public – they are more visible and more likely to be apprehended. And the crimes they tend to commit – for example, vehicle theft – are more likely to be reported to the police. By comparison, white-collar crimes, which a higher proportion of older people may well commit, are less visible and less likely to be reported.

Table 3 *Offenders found guilty or cautioned*

England and Wales				Rates per 10,000 population
Age group	10-15	16-24	25-35	35 and over	All aged 10 and over (thousands)
Males	196	606	292	53	391.5
Females	74	119	61	12	88.6

Adapted from *Social Trends*, 2004

Evaluation – self-report studies Research indicates that most people are prepared to admit to offences – even serious ones – when asked to take part in a confidential self-report study. And, in direct comparisons with individuals' official records, self-report studies reveal far more offences (Smith, 2002).

However, the results of self-report studies must be approached with caution. Traditionally, they have focused on male juvenile delinquency – the criminal behaviour of young men. And the lists of crimes presented in self-report studies tend to reflect those typically committed by young males – in particular, 'street crime'. They tend to omit 'hidden crimes' and adult crimes, such as domestic violence and child abuse, crimes which are likely to be spread more evenly across age groups. And they are unlikely to include fraud, often committed by middle-aged men. As a result, self-report studies provide only a partial view of crime. And this may lead to a distorted picture of the age-crime curve.

key term

Age-crime curve A curve showing the relationship between age and offending.

11.2 Explaining the age-crime curve

Control theory

Control theory – sometimes known as social control theory – has been used to explain the age-crime curve. It was outlined on page 46-47. To recap, control theory argues that what stops people from committing crime are the strong social bonds which join us together – for example, the bonds with family, friends and work colleagues. Effective social bonds mean that we have too much to lose by committing crime. To do so would risk losing the good opinion of significant others – those who matter to us (Hirschi, 1969).

Control theory provides the following explanation for the age-crime curve. Most children have strong bonds with their parents. Most adults have strong bonds with their partners, children, friends and work colleagues. However, many adolescents and young adults loosen the bonds with their parents and have yet to form relatively permanent adult relationships and commitments. As a result, their behaviour is less likely to be constrained by social bonds and they are more likely to deviate from conventional norms and values and become involved in crime (Sampson & Laub, 1990).

Evaluation There is evidence to support this view. Regular offenders who formed a stable relationship with a partner in young adulthood were more likely to stop offending than those who did not (Quinton et al., 1993). Similarly, offenders who found a steady job were more likely to stop offending (Sampson & Laub, 1990). In both cases, the former offenders were making commitments and establishing bonds.

Judging from both police recorded crime figures and from victim studies, the crime rate rose significantly for most of the second half of the 20th century. During this time, the gap between childhood and adulthood widened. The period of compulsory education lengthened and growing numbers of young people continued their education beyond the minimum school leaving age. Full-time employment was postponed and people married at a later age. As a result, the traditional bonds created by marriage and work were not established until later in life. This may help to explain the rising crime rate from the 1950s to the mid-1990s (Rutter & Smith, 1995). However, it fails to explain the apparent decline in the crime rate indicated by the British Crime Survey from the mid-1990s onwards.

According to control theory, adolescence and young adulthood provide a window of opportunity for many young people to turn to crime. During this period, they are largely free from the constraints of both childhood and adulthood. But, why should they express this freedom in crime rather than other activities? Control theory fails to provide a satisfactory answer.

Independence and status

Adolescence is a period of transition from childhood to adulthood. It is a time when young people seek independence from their parents and look for status and respect as developing adults. Often, both independence and respect are in short supply – in many ways, young people remain dependent on their parents and they are not yet able to claim the status of fully-fledged adults.

A solution to the dependency problem is to seek out or create situations in which to express independence, freedom and autonomy. A solution to the status problem is to seek respect in the eyes of the peer group – those in a similar situation to themselves.

But, how does this argument help to explain the age-crime curve? Independence can be seen as freedom from constraints. In this respect, deviant and criminal activities – which reject the constraints of conventional society – can be seen as an expression and indication of independence. And, in the context of the peer group, these activities can bring the status and respect which the adult world largely denies young people (Caspi & Moffit, 1995).

Albert Cohen's (1955) subcultural theory of working-class delinquency provides an extreme example of this process (see page 29). Many of these young men do badly at school and fail to acquire the skills and qualifications needed for success. Defined as failures by the wider society, they experience status frustration – they are frustrated with their low status as 'losers'. Add this to the problems of young people in general, and their sense of status frustration is particularly acute.

According to Cohen, their creation of a delinquent

subculture can be seen as a solution to the problems they share. The 'successful' delinquent gains respect and admiration from his peers. And it allows him to hit back at a society which has denied him the opportunity to succeed and branded him as a failure.

summary

1. Data from official statistics and self-report studies indicates that most offences are committed by young people. There are problems with both sources of data.

2. Official statistics provide information on only a small proportion of offenders. And the crimes young people typically commit are more likely to be reported to the police.

3. Self-report studies reveal far more offences when compared to an individual's police record. However, they tend to list offences typically committed by young people and omit those which are likely to be spread more evenly across the age group.

4. Control theory argues that young people are more likely to offend because they have loosened the bonds with their parents and have yet to form relatively permanent adult relationships and commitments. Without strong bonds to constrain their behaviour, they are more likely to deviate from conventional norms and values.

5. Some researchers have seen young people's high rate of offending as a response to their desire for independence and status.

As the age-crime curve shows, most young offenders stop their criminal activity as they grow older. When they really become independent and adopt adult status, they no longer need the 'gestures of independence' of their youth (Smith, 2002).

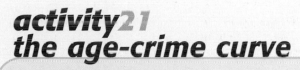

activity 21
the age-crime curve

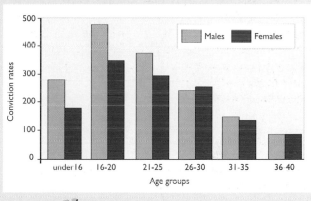

Conviction rates for different age groups

questions

1 What does the bar chart show?

2 Why is this pattern called the age-crime curve?

Unit 12 Location

key issues

1 What is the spatial distribution of offenders?

2 What is the spatial distribution of offences?

3 What explanations have been given for these distributions?

Offenders tend to be concentrated in particular areas. They are likely to live in particular places in towns and cities. In other words, the spatial distribution of offenders is not random.

The same applies to offences. Crimes tend to occur in particular areas. Again, the spatial distribution of offences is not random.

This unit looks at environmental criminology. It is concerned with mapping the spatial distribution of offenders and offences, and with explanations for these distributions.

12.1 The Chicago School

During the 1920s, a group of sociologists based in Chicago, who later became known as the Chicago School, argued that the growth of cities produced distinctive neighbourhoods, each with its own characteristic lifestyle. Clifford Shaw and Henry McKay (1942) applied this perspective to the study of delinquency.

They divided the city of Chicago into five zones, drawn at two mile intervals, radiating outwards in concentric circles from the central business district (CBD). They then mapped the residences of male delinquents. Figure 5 shows the delinquency rates for boys aged 10 to 16 living in each zone from 1927 to 1933. For example, 9.8% of boys in zone 1 were charged with criminal offences during this period. The rates steadily declined from zone 1 to zone 5. Shaw and McKay found similar patterns in Chicago from 1900 to 1906 and from 1917 to 1923.

Zone 1 has the highest rate of delinquents. It is characterised by a high population turnover and *cultural heterogeneity* – a mixture of different cultures. Newcomers

Figure 5 Spatial distribution of delinquents in Chicago

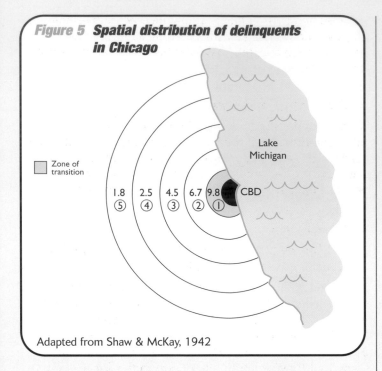

Zone of transition

Lake Michigan

1.8 ⑤ 2.5 ④ 4.5 ③ 6.7 ② 9.8 ① CBD

Adapted from Shaw & McKay, 1942

to the city usually begin their urban life in zone 1 – they often have little money and zone 1 provides the cheapest accommodation. And they come from a variety of cultural backgrounds – in the case of Chicago, Black and White rural migrants from the southern states and immigrants from various European countries such as Ireland, Italy, Greece and Poland. Zone 1 is a *zone of transition* – many migrants move out to higher income areas once they have become established, so making room for new arrivals. As a result, zone 1 has a shifting population.

Social disorganisation A high rate of population turnover plus cultural heterogeneity result in *social disorganisation*. There is a lack of social cohesion, little sense of community and weak social controls. Controls such as gossip, public disapproval and public surveillance are not strong enough to prevent the development of deviant norms and criminal behaviour.

Evaluation Shaw and McKay's methods were applied to a number of American cities and produced largely similar results. Where results were different, they tended to confirm Shaw and McKay's conclusions. For example, Bernard Lander's (1962) study of Baltimore found a high proportion of offenders in areas of shifting population in zone 1. However, there were also areas of stable population within zone 1 where the proportion of offenders was relatively low. Since both types of area were low income, this suggests that the level of population stability was a major factor accounting for the level of offenders.

Shaw and McKay note that the rate of delinquents corresponds closely to economic factors. Income rises steadily from zone 1 to zone 5. Rates of delinquents decline steadily from the inner-city slums to the tree-lined suburbs. A part of their explanation echoes Merton's views.

Shaw and McKay argue that crime in low-income areas 'may be regarded as one of the means employed by people to acquire, or attempt to acquire, the economic and social values generally idealised in our culture, which persons in other circumstances acquire by conventional means'.

key terms

Zone of transition An area with a shifting population – people moving in and out.
Cultural heterogeneity An area with people from a number of different cultural backgrounds.
Social disorganisation A low level of social cohesion and weak social controls.

12.2 Area offender rates in Britain

Croydon Research on area offender rates in Britain has not supported the neat and tidy zonal pattern found in many American cities. For example, a study of Croydon by Terence Morris (1957) suggested that area offender rates reflected local authority housing policies. Concentrations of delinquents were found on estates where the local council had housed high numbers of so-called 'problem families', some of whom already had members with a history of delinquent behaviour.

Sheffield Research in Sheffield also failed to reflect American findings. A study by Bottoms, Mawby and Xanthos (1989) looked at two council estates – Stonewall and Gardenia – separated by a main road. Recorded offender rates for Gardenia were 300% higher than those for Stonewall. Both estates were built in the 1920s. Each had a stable population of 2500 to 3000, with 60% of adults in both areas having lived in the same residence for 10 years or more. And there was little or no difference between the estates in terms of social factors such as class, ethnicity, age, gender, income and employment levels.

The researchers offered the following explanation for the differences in offender rates between Stonewall and Gardenia. Sometime in the 1940s, Gardenia 'tipped' – started a downward spiral towards a high crime area. This appears to have influenced the council's housing policy. Those with severe housing needs and various other social problems were allocated to Gardenia – the very people most at risk of crime. Gardenia developed a negative reputation which resulted in some residents leaving and others refusing to move on to the estate.

Evaluation The Sheffield study is important for three main reasons (Bottoms & Wiles, 2002).

- Since the two estates are almost identical in terms of social class, it challenges those who argue that offender rates on the local level simply reflect the link between class and offending on the national level.

- Shaw and McKay's explanation based on high population turnover and cultural heterogeneity does not apply to the Sheffield estates.

- The operation of the local housing market is a key factor in explaining area offender rates in Sheffield.

12.3 Area offence rates

So far this unit has focused on area offender rates – the rate of *offenders* living in a particular area. This section looks at area offence rates – the rate of *offences* in a particular area.

In traditional cities, offences tend to be clustered in and around the city centre. For example, in Sheffield in 1966, 24% of offences occurred within a half mile radius of the city centre – which made up only 3% of the city's total land area. Typical city-centre offences include theft of and from cars, theft from the person and violence and vandalism in public places. This pattern can change with the development of shopping malls and entertainment complexes away from the city centre. For example, the building of the Meadowhall shopping mall on the outskirts of Sheffield was a factor in reducing city-centre offences from 24% in 1966 to 10% in 1995 (Wiles & Costello, 2000).

In residential districts, offence rates tend to be highest in low-income, inner-city areas and in high-income neighbourhoods in cities which are close to areas with high offending rates. According to the 2002/03 British Crime Survey, the highest levels of burglary, vehicle-related crime and violent crime occur in low-income council estates with a high proportion of elderly, lone parent and unemployed residents; in multi-ethnic, low-income areas; and in town and city areas which house well-off professional singles and couples.

The following explanations have been suggested for the spatial distribution of offences.

Opportunity theory

Opportunity theory, as its name suggests, is concerned with the opportunities for crime. It focuses on *target attractiveness* and *accessibility* (Clarke, 1995).

Target attractiveness In terms of property, a target is attractive if its monetary value is high and if it can be easily transported and sold. Obviously, a laptop in the back seat of a car is a more attractive target than a bag of groceries.

Accessibility A target is accessible if it can be seen, if physical access is easy and the chances of being observed are low.

On its own, opportunity theory cannot account for the spatial distribution of offences. For example, the highest level of vehicle-related crime is in low-income multi-ethnic neighbourhoods where 21% of vehicle-owning households are victims of this crime. The rate for professionals living in towns and cities is 16%, while the rate for wealthy home-owning areas is only 8% (British Crime Survey, 2002/03). In terms of target attractiveness, vehicles and their contents in low-income multi-ethnic areas would be less attractive than those in the other areas. Despite this, they have the highest level of vehicle-related crime.

Routine activities theory

Because of the shortcomings of opportunity theory, it is often combined with routine activities theory to explain the spatial distribution of offences. Routine activities theory states that crimes are likely to occur in particular places because three things tend to come together in those places:

- Likely offenders
- Attractive targets
- An absence of 'capable guardians' – for example, the property owners (Cohen & Felson, 1979).

Routine activities theory, as its name suggests, is concerned with the routine, everyday activities of those who may be involved with crimes – the possible offenders, the possible victims and the possible observers. For example, studies of convicted burglars show that they weigh up the opportunities for a successful crime. But, they also base their decisions on their routine activities and the knowledge they gain from those activities.

For example, their everyday movements are centred on their residential area, place of work, the shopping and entertainment centres they frequent and the routes they travel to and from these places. These are the places offenders are familiar with *and* the places where they tend to commit offences (Wright & Decker, 1994). This brings together explanations of the spatial distribution of offences and offenders.

> ### key terms
>
> **Target attractiveness** The attractiveness of a possible target for crime – for example, its monetary value.
> **Target accessibility** A target is accessible if it can be seen, access to it is easy and the chances of being observed are low.
> **Routine activities** A person's normal, everyday activities.

12.4 Explaining the spatial distribution of offenders and offences

So far, the spatial distributions of offenders and offences have been examined separately. This section looks at the relationship between them.

Most offences occur within a short distance from the offender's home. For example, a study in Sheffield found that, on average, offenders travelled only 1.93 miles from their home to commit a crime (Wiles & Costello, 2000). A number of studies suggest that this is related to offenders' routine activities and their normal use of space.

Cognitive maps

Patricia and Paul Brantingham (1984) argue that we have *cognitive maps* inside our heads which outline our perception of the geography of our local area. These maps contain the places we are familiar with – for example, home, work or school, shops and places of entertainment. They also include our routes to and from these places.

The Brantinghams suggest that most offenders will commit crimes in areas they are familiar with – that is, in areas which are clearly shown on their cognitive maps. Figure 6 illustrates this idea. It shows the suggested relationship between offenders' awareness of space, opportunities for crime, and areas where offences occur.

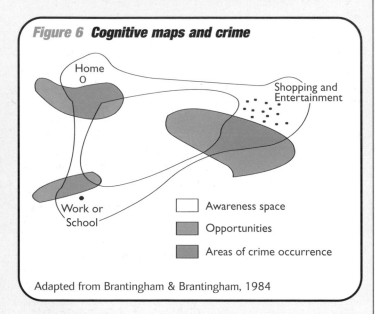

Figure 6 Cognitive maps and crime

Home

Shopping and Entertainment

Work or School

☐ Awareness space

▨ Opportunities

▨ Areas of crime occurrence

Adapted from Brantingham & Brantingham, 1984

Evidence There is some evidence to support the connection between familiarity, cognitive maps and offence location. A study of convicted burglars in Pennsylvania showed that most of their offences were committed near their regular routes to work and recreation (Rengert & Wasilchick, 2000). Research in Oklahoma City, which is divided into Black and White areas, showed that most offenders committed their crimes within their own ethnic group area – that is, in places they were familiar with (Carter & Hill, 1979).

A study in Sheffield by Wiles and Costello (2000) categorised neighbourhoods in terms of high, medium or low offence rates and offender rates. High offender and high offence rates were found in the same area – there were no cases of high offender rates and low offence rates in the same neighbourhood. This can be explained in terms of the routine activities of the offenders and their familiarity with their own neighbourhoods.

There were a few cases of low offender rates and high offence rates. This usually occurred in high-income neighbourhoods close to areas regularly used by offenders – for example, adjacent to their own neighbourhood, shopping or entertainment area.

12.5 Further explanations

Why do some areas have high offender and offence rates? Part of the explanation has been given in the previous section. Offenders tend to commit crimes in areas with which they are familiar. But why are offenders often clustered in the same area? Many of these areas are low-income, inner-city neighbourhoods. The common-sense answer is poverty breeds crime. But, as the Sheffield study of Stonewall and Gardenia indicates, this is not necessarily so. Both were low-income council estates, but the recorded offender rates for Gardenia were 300% higher than those of Stonewall. The reason given earlier was the council's policy of housing so-called 'problem families' in Gardenia. But how does a neighbourhood 'tip' into an area with high levels of offenders and offences?

Social disorganisation One explanation has already been examined – Shaw and McKay's theory of social disorganisation. To briefly recap – high population turnover and cultural heterogeneity lead to social disorganisation which results in weak social controls. These controls are not strong enough to prevent the development of criminal behaviour. This explanation may fit the development of certain American cities but does not fit British examples. As noted earlier, it does not explain the difference in offender rates between Stonewall and Gardenia in Sheffield. Both estates had both stable populations and culturally homogeneous populations.

'Broken windows' As noted in an earlier unit (see page 47), Wilson and Kelling (2003) provide the following explanation for *tipping* – the downward spiral of certain neighbourhoods. Informal social controls are essential for crime prevention. They are likely to break down when buildings are left in a state of disrepair – for example, with broken windows – and when disorderly and anti-social behaviour is left unchallenged. In this situation, graffiti spreads, noise levels increase, vandalism grows and more windows get broken. Failure to do anything about these developments tips a neighbourhood into decline – property values plummet, law-abiding members of the community are afraid to go out, many leave the neighbourhood, informal social controls break down and crime and disorder become widespread. (For further discussion of Wilson and Kelling, see pages 47-48).

Spiral decay Wesley Skogan's (1990) analysis of the 'spiral decay of American neighbourhoods' echoes many of the points made by Wilson and Kelling. Skogan identifies two types of disorder – physical disorder, such as dilapidated buildings, broken streetlights and litter, and social disorder such as drinking on the street and prostitution. These two types of disorder tend to occur together. They have the following effects.

- Undermining neighbourliness – residents were less willing to help each other and take part in activities which reduce crime, such as keeping a watch on each other's houses when they were on holiday.

- Increasing concerns about safety – people were fearful

of going out, especially at night. This weakens social controls such as public surveillance.

- The area becomes stigmatised as a 'bad neighbourhood', property values decline, and those who can afford to do so move out.

- As a result of the 'spiral of decay' produced by disorder, the informal social controls which tend to prevent crime are weakened.

Evaluation The processes described by the 'broken windows' and 'spiral decay' arguments may well be an important part of tipping a neighbourhood into a high-crime area. But how do they begin in the first place? For example, how does the disorder which generates the spiral of decay start? The following study provides possible answers.

A three-stage process A study of juvenile offender rates in different areas of Los Angeles from 1950-1970 examined the changes that occurred in low-rate offender areas which later became high-rate offender areas (Schuerman & Kobrin, 1986). This study is important because it looks at changes over time – this may help to establish what causes what.

The researchers identified a three-stage process which, they argue, led to the development of high-rate offender areas.

- First, there were changes in land-use – for example, an increase in apartment buildings and in renting as opposed to owner occupation.

- Second, there were changes in the size and make-up of the population – for example, a decline in population size and an increase in the proportion of unrelated individuals – more single people and fewer families.

- Third, there were changes in the economic status of the population – for example, an increase in the proportion of unskilled and unemployed workers.

Conclusion

Local, national and global Location studies of offender and offence rates are based on local areas. As such, they take little account of wider social and economic changes. Although they add to our understanding of crime, they are limited. Clearly, national and global changes will impact on local areas. A fuller understanding of local areas therefore requires an analysis which incorporates these wider changes. For example, the decline in manufacturing in Western societies has led to a reduction in the demand for manual labour and to high unemployment rates in certain urban areas (Bottoms & Wiles, 2002).

Methodology Studies of the distribution of offender and offence rates are based on data from police recorded crime and victim studies conducted in local areas. The validity of both types of data is questionable. As outlined earlier, police recording practices and priorities for investigation vary from area to area (see pages 10-12). For example, burglary may be a priority in one area, drug dealing in another. Similarly, the willingness of the public to report crimes to the police or to participate in victim surveys may also vary from one area to another.

key term

Tipping The process by which an area moves from a low to a high offender and offence rate.

summary

1. Environmental criminology looks at the spatial distribution of offences and offenders.

2. Shaw and McKay claimed that delinquents were concentrated in zones of transition in American cities. They argued that this was due to high population turnover and cultural heterogeneity which led to social disorganisation. This, in turn, weakened informal social controls.

3. Area offender rates in British cities do not reflect the American pattern. Research indicates that the housing of so-called 'problem families' on particular estates by local councils can result in a concentration of offenders.

4. In traditional cities, offences tend to be clustered in and around the city centre. 'Out-of-town' shopping malls and entertainment centres can change this pattern.

5. In residential districts, offences tend to be highest in low-income, inner-city areas, and in high-income neighbourhoods close to areas with high offending rates.

6. Opportunity theory states that targets with high attractiveness and high accessibility are likely to be selected by offenders.

7. Routine activity theory states that the spatial distribution of offences is linked to the routine activities of offenders.

Offenders tend to commit crimes in areas they are familiar with.

8. The Brantinghams argue that we have cognitive maps of the areas we are familiar with. To some extent, these maps guide offenders' selection of places to commit offences.

9. Wilson and Kelling argue that a neighbourhood 'tips' when buildings are left in disrepair and anti-social behaviour is unchallenged. Informal social controls break down and crime becomes widespread.

10. Skogan argues that physical and social disorder undermine neighbourliness, increase concerns about safety and stigmatise the neighbourhood. This weakens informal social controls.

11. A longitudinal study in Los Angeles suggests a three-stage process leading to tipping.
    - A change in land-use
    - A change in the size and make-up of the population
    - A change in the economic status of the population.

12. Critics argue that location studies of offender and offence rates should incorporate wider social and economic factors.

13. The validity of the data on which location studies are based is questionable.

activity22 neighbourhoods and crime

Item A Neighbourhoods and offence rates

The bar chart looks at the percentage of household victims of burglary, vehicle-related crime and violent crime in different types of residential neighbourhoods in England and Wales. The data is drawn from the 2002/03 British Crime Survey. The types of neighbourhood are defined in the box on the right.

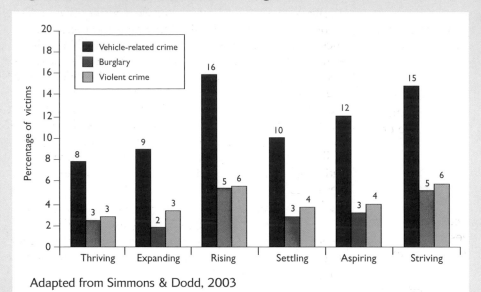

Adapted from Simmons & Dodd, 2003

Item B Type of neighbourhood

Thriving – wealthy, affluent home-owning areas. Commuters and prosperous older people.

Expanding – affluent working couples and families with mortgages, plus homeowners.

Rising – well-off professional singles and couples, living in town and city areas.

Settling – established home-owning areas, skilled workers.

Aspiring – mature communities, new homeowners and multi-ethnic areas.

Striving – council estates with elderly, lone parent or unemployed residents. Multi-ethnic, low-income areas.

questions

1 Briefly summarise the data in the bar chart.

2 Suggest reasons why different types of neighbourhood have different offence rates.

Unit 13 Social control, crime reduction and social policy

keyissues

1 What are the main approaches to crime reduction?

2 What are the crime policies of British governments since 1945?

The idea of social control was introduced on page 8. Various aspects of social control have been examined throughout this chapter in the context of theories of crime and deviance – for example, in terms of right realism (see pages 45-49). This unit looks at methods of social control with specific reference to crime reduction.

The terms crime reduction and crime prevention are often used interchangeably. However, the term crime reduction is now more popular and will be used in this unit.

13.1 Approaches to crime reduction

There are three main approaches to crime reduction – 1) structural or societal 2) individual 3) situational (Pease, 2002).

Structural/societal approaches These approaches see the basic causes of crime in society. For example, crime is generated by inequalities in income and wealth, or by inequalities of opportunity. Crime reduction therefore involves changes in society.

Individual approaches These approaches see particular individuals as prone to crime. Crime reduction therefore involves changing the behaviour of those at risk of starting a criminal career, or ending the criminal career of those with a history of lawbreaking.

Situational approaches These approaches seek to reduce the opportunities for crime by changing the settings in which crime occurs. Examples include surveillance – for

Crime and deviance 75

instance, CCTV – and target hardening – for instance, steering locks on cars.

Evaluation No one approach provides a solution to the 'crime problem'. Crime is extremely varied – it ranges from vandalism to fraud, from domestic violence to street robbery. It is unlikely that one approach will provide an across-the-board reduction in this variety of crime (Pease, 2002).

A number of researchers recognise this point. For example, Jock Young (1992) argues for both a reduction in social inequality on a national level, and intervention on the local level by various agencies in order to reduce crime.

Finally, classifications of approaches to crime reduction provide only a rough framework. Some approaches don't fit neatly into a particular category, others overlap two or three categories.

13.2 Structural/societal approaches

Many of the sociological theories of crime examined in this chapter suggest that crime reduction involves major changes in society. The following examples illustrate this approach.

Strain theory Robert K. Merton's strain theory argues that the social structure prevents equal opportunity (see pages 28-29). It states that those at the bottom of the class structure are less likely to acquire the skills and qualifications needed to reach the top. As a result, some turn to crime in order to obtain the material rewards which are highly valued in Western society. The solution suggested by strain theory is the removal of barriers which prevent equal opportunity.

Subcultural theory Albert Cohen's subcultural theory starts from a similar position (see page 29). As a result of their position in society, many young working-class males do badly at school and fail to acquire the skills and qualifications needed for success. As a result of this failure, they experience status frustration. One way out of this situation is to develop a delinquent subculture in terms of which they can gain status and respect. As with Merton, the solution suggested by subcultural theory is the removal of barriers which prevent equal opportunity.

Marxist approaches From a traditional Marxist perspective, crime is systematically generated by the structure of capitalist society. The solution to crime is a classless society – communism – free from exploitation, oppression, conflicts of interest and inequalities of income and wealth. In terms of Marxist theory, people would then work for the common good, and crime as we know it would largely disappear.

Evaluation Apart from general statements about reducing social inequality and increasing equality of opportunity, strain theory and subcultural theory offer few if any practical proposals for achieving these aims. And, apart from predicting the eventual overthrow of capitalism,

traditional Marxism offers little in the way of practical solutions to the reduction of crime.

Left realism Unlike the theories outlined so far, left realism argues for both change on the societal level and for practical steps to reduce crime. In this respect, it claims to 'take crime seriously' (Young, 1986).

Jock Young (1999) sees relative deprivation as the major cause of crime in late modern society (see pages 50-51). Relative deprivation is generated by a society which is seen as blatantly unfair and unjust, in which inequalities of income and wealth are becoming greater, and in which equality of opportunity is blocked by barriers of class, race, gender and age. Young calls for a society in which rewards are based on talent and merit, and in which citizens become increasingly involved in the democratic process on both national and local levels. He hopes that this will lead to a society which will be seen as just and fair. If so, this will result in a reduction in relative deprivation, and to a reduction in the crime which relative deprivation generates.

Evaluation Jock Young provides a general outline of the way forward for late modern society, but gives little indication of how to get there. However, left realism does suggest practical solutions for crime reduction for the here and now (see pages 51-53).

13.3 Individual approaches

A variety of different approaches are examined under this broad heading. Their aim is to change the behaviour of individuals who are seen to be particularly at risk of crime. Although these have been termed individual approaches, they also refer to the groups to which at-risk individuals belong – for example, low-income groups in inner-city areas.

Early intervention

Early intervention programmes intervene in the lives of children, particularly children from disadvantaged groups. Their aim is to improve children's chances of success. The programmes assume that if children are caught young enough, then their chances of success at school and in later life can be improved. And their risks of turning to crime can be reduced.

There is some evidence that early intervention programmes can help to reduce the crime rate. The following programmes appear to have been particularly successful.

Pregnant mothers were seen in their homes by health visitors during their pregnancy and for two years after the birth of their child. Fifteen years later, their children had less than half the number of arrests compared with the children of a comparable sample of mothers who received no visits (Olds et al., 1997).

The Perry pre-school enrichment programme aimed to

give children from low-income families a head start when they began school. Parents were encouraged to 'enrich' their children's lives with books, toys and educational activities. By the age of 27, the children who participated in the programme had been arrested only half as often as a sample of similar age and background (Schweinhart et al., 1993).

Evaluation There is evidence that some early intervention programmes appear to reduce crime. However, there is evidence that others appear to have little or no effect. In the USA in the 1960s, there was a massive programme of early intervention in low-income, inner-city areas. Known as Operation Head Start, it was designed to provide pre-school children with the skills, aptitudes and motivation to succeed in the school system.

Head Start assumed that enrichment in the early years would open doors and provide greater opportunities in the later years. Although crime reduction was not the major aim, it was assumed that young people who went through the programme would have less reason to turn to crime.

In terms of improving educational performance, Operation Head Start appeared to have, at best, short-term and limited success. Children in the programme sometimes made short-term gains when they began school but soon fell back to the level of their peers (Jensen, 1973). In terms of crime reduction, it is difficult to estimate the programme's effect. However, James Q. Wilson (1975) believes it had little or no effect. He notes that in the USA during the early 1960s:

> A great array of programmes aimed at the young, the poor and the deprived were mounted. Crime soared. It did not just increase a little; it rose at a faster rate and to higher levels than at any time since the 1930s, and, in some categories, to higher levels than any experienced in this century (Wilson, 1975).

Wilson also applies his comments to later intervention – programmes designed for older people. For example, Operation Head Start was accompanied by programmes for unemployed young people which attempted to provide 'work experience' and instil 'work habits' and 'work incentives'. In general, the evidence suggests that the later in life the intervention, the less likely it is to produce the desired effects (Pease, 2002).

Imprisonment

The responses of the criminal justice system to people who have broken the law can be seen as an attempt to change individual behaviour. Prison and the various alternatives to prison are obvious examples. Prison provides *incapacitation* – it prevents those inside from committing crimes on the outside. So, as long as habitual criminals remain behind bars, the crimes they would probably commit on the outside will be halted.

Apart from incapacitation, do prisons deter those who have already embarked on a career of crime? In other words, does the threat of future imprisonment make them change their behaviour and stop committing crimes? Or, do prisons *reform* those inside? One of the stated aims of the Prison Service is to rehabilitate offenders – to change them into law-abiding citizens who are ready to take up a normal life on release. Many prisons have programmes which seek to improve educational and work skills and promote law-abiding behaviour after release (Prison Service, 2001).

Available evidence suggests that imprisonment neither deters nor rehabilitates many of those who have broken the law. In Britain during the early 1980s, prison expenditure rose by 85% and courts were encouraged to hand out longer sentences. By the late 1980s, Britain's rate of imprisonment was the highest in Europe. Yet the rate of recorded crime continued to grow rapidly. And nearly half of adult prisoners and around two-thirds of young prisoners were re-convicted within two years of release (McLaughlin & Muncie, 2001).

Prisons do not appear to be effective in terms of either deterrence or rehabilitation. Programmes designed to rehabilitate prisoners seem to have little or no effect. Those who participate in these programmes usually re-offend as often as those who do not participate (von Hirsch, 1976).

In view of this, some researchers argue that the main contribution of prison to crime reduction is incapacitation. For example, James Q. Wilson (1983) argues that the most active criminals should be removed from circulation and given long sentences. In his view, this will have a major impact on crime reduction.

The evidence suggests that incapacitation is not particularly effective. From 1987 to 1995, the USA increased its prison population by 124% and during that time there was a 2% increase in crime. Over the same period, Denmark increased its prison population by 7% and had a 3% increase in crime. As frequently noted in this chapter, any measurement of crime must be treated with extreme caution. However, available evidence suggests that the use of imprisonment to reduce the crime rate has not been very successful (Young, 1999).

key terms

Incapacitation Making someone incapable of doing something. In this case, using imprisonment to prevent offenders from committing crimes during their length of stay.
Deterrence Discouraging or preventing a person from doing something for fear of the consequences. In this case, using prison as a deterrent for lawbreaking.
Rehabilitation Restoring someone to a normal life. In this case, restoring offenders to law-abiding citizens.

Community sentences

In recent years there have been growing demands for alternatives to prison. This has been accompanied by a rise in *community sentencing* which involves the punishment, rehabilitation, treatment or supervision of offenders in the community (Hughes, 2001). Community sentences include:

- Community rehabilitation orders – the offender is supervised by a probation officer and may be required to take part in various programmes.
- Community punishment order – the offender is required to perform unpaid work for the benefit of the community under the supervision of a probation officer.
- Curfew orders – the offender is required to remain at a particular location during fixed times for up to six months (Raynor, 2002).

By the end of the 1990s, around 50% of all youth sentences in England and Wales were community-based. In 2002, 33% of all offenders were given community sentences and 25% were given prison sentences (*Social Trends*, 2004).

How effective are community sentences in reducing crime? In particular, how do they compare with prisons in terms of re-offending? A review of the evidence indicates that they are at least as effective as imprisonment (Brownlee, 1998). Although this isn't particularly impressive, some researchers argue that, given the dehumanising effects of prison, community sentencing is much more preferable.

It would be wrong to dismiss community sentencing on the basis of the overall re-offending rate. Research indicates that certain types of community-based programmes can reduce re-offending by up to 20%. The more effective programmes are 'highly structured, they make clear and explicit demands' on the offender, they are well resourced and supervised by trained staff (Raynor, 2002).

13.4 Situational approaches

Situational approaches to crime reduction are concerned with changing aspects of the environment to:

- increase the chances of detection when committing a crime
- increase the chances of failure when committing a crime.

Together, these measures increase the risks and reduce the rewards of crime. In theory, this should deter people from breaking the law.

Many offences are 'crimes of opportunity'. For example, if a car is left unlocked, it presents a far better opportunity for theft than a locked car with a steering column lock. Situational approaches to crime reduction seek to reduce the opportunities for crime.

Examples of situational approaches

Target hardening This refers to reducing the physical opportunities for crime. Examples include more secure doors and windows, toughened-glass screens in banks and building societies separating staff and customers, steering column locks on vehicles, entryphones to buildings, and gated communities which provide barriers to outsiders.

Surveillance This refers to various means of observing people's behaviour. It ranges from closed circuit television (CCTV) whereby cameras keep watch on city streets, malls and shops, to improvements in street lighting which increase the chance of people being seen in the dark.

The effectiveness of situational approaches

There have been many evaluations of situational approaches. Most techniques appear to result in crime reduction. The following examples indicate the effect of surveillance (Clarke, 2003).

- Vandalism is considerably reduced on buses with conductors.
- Public telephones in pubs and launderettes suffer almost no vandalism compared to those in kiosks.
- Car parks with attendants have lower rates of auto-crime.
- Apartment blocks with CCTV or doormen have fewer burglaries.

Informal social control At first sight, it seems obvious why situational approaches often work. However, a closer look suggests that the reasons are not so obvious. For example, gated communities appear to reduce crime because they present barriers to entry. But they also make residents feel safer and encourage a sense of community. Because of this, people tend to spend more time on the street, and are more likely to get to know each other. As a result, they are more likely to identify strangers and question their presence on the estate. Informal social controls such as gossip, public opinion, parental control and public surveillance tend to develop. And these controls can lead to a reduction in crime.

Similarly, street lighting appears to work because it increases surveillance in the dark. *But* it also reduces the amount of crime in daylight. Again, this suggests an increase in community solidarity and informal social control (Painter & Farrington, 1999).

Evaluation Situational approaches to crime reduction may not be as successful as they appear. In particular, they may result in *displacement* in the place, type, method and time of the offence. For example, target hardening and surveillance may simply move crime from one area to another, or from a protected to an unprotected building. Offenders may select alternative types of crime, use different methods and/or choose different times.

Research indicates that if displacement does occur, it is fairly limited. And some studies suggest the opposite of displacement – that crime reduction sometimes extends beyond the area where situational measures have been introduced (Pease, 2002).

key terms

Displacement Removing something from one place to another. In this case, changing the place, type, method and/or type of crime without changing the extent of crime.

activity23 situational approaches

Item A Gated communities

This picture shows the entrance to a gated community in Memphis, Tennessee. The houses and apartments are rented. Residents use a swipe card to enter the estate. The owners have an office at the entrance which arranges access for visitors. The office provides a number of facilities for residents – computers, faxes and a library of DVDs and videos, all at no charge. Alongside the office are tennis courts, an outdoor swimming pool and a gym – all available free to residents and their friends.

CAUTION!
AUTOMATIC GATES

Gate timed for ONE vehicle.
NO PLAYING OR CLIMBING
on or around gate.
Owner and management not
liable for any injury, damage
or loss caused by problems
or malfunction of gates.

Item B Decoy vehicles

Vehicles can be adapted in various ways to detect anyone entering them illegally. Methods include tracking or camera systems, or physical restraints which prevent intruders from leaving the vehicle.

Specially adapted decoy vehicles were used in Stockton-on-Tees in an attempt to reduce vehicle theft. The result was a small reduction. The vehicles were then withdrawn. However, it was widely publicised that the initiative was still in operation. This time the reduction in vehicle theft was much greater.

Adapted from Sallybanks, 2000

questions

1 In what ways might gated communities reduce crime?

2 Use the idea of informal social control to explain the results of the decoy vehicle initiative in Item B.

Broken windows and informal social control

In a famous article entitled 'Broken windows: The police and neighbourhood safety' first published in 1982, James Q. Wilson and George L. Kelling (2003) argue that informal social control is the key to crime reduction. They claim that disorder and anti-social behaviour – 'incivility' – are closely linked to crime. For example, if a window is broken and left unrepaired, the remaining windows in the building will soon be broken. If nothing is done, it appears that nobody cares, and 'untended property becomes fair game for fun and plunder'. Similarly, 'untended behaviour' – that is behaviour which is not checked, challenged and controlled – can become increasingly anti-social. Incivilities such as rudeness, excessive noise and vandalism become common. This leads to a breakdown in community controls and produces a situation in which crime can flourish.

According to Wilson and Kelling, the main job of the police is to halt this downward spiral of disorder and maintain informal social controls in communities. In other words, their main job is to maintain order. This involves enforcing rules of orderly behaviour and doing this in partnership with people in the neighbourhood. For example, noisy teenagers should be told to keep quiet, begging should be forbidden, and drunks and addicts should be prevented from sleeping or lying down on the street.

James Q. Wilson (1983) argues that most police work occurs after crime has been committed and reported. Reducing crime therefore involves preventing crime in the first place. And this means maintaining 'orderly neighbourhoods'. Some neighbourhoods are beyond repair – the best the police can do is attempt to deal with crimes which have been committed by responding to calls and trying to catch offenders. They are not very good at this – most crimes remain unsolved. Other neighbourhoods are 'stable and serene' – they do not even need foot patrols. Where the police can make a difference is in neighbourhoods at the 'tipping point' – where public order is deteriorating but can be restored (see also pages 47-49).

Evaluation Wilson and Kelling's argument is based on evidence which indicates that policing has only limited effects on the crime rate. Rather than concentrate on crimes which have already occurred, the police should focus on strengthening the informal social controls which prevent disorder.

But do disorder and incivility lead to rising crime? As noted earlier (see page 48), a study of 196 neighbourhoods in Chicago suggests that as neighbourhoods became poorer there was an increase in both disorder and crime. In other words, it was economic disadvantage rather than disorder as such which led to a rise in crime (Sampson & Raudenbush, 1999).

Zero-tolerance policing

Wilson and Kelling's views suggest that the police should clamp down on a wide range of behaviour which is not necessarily criminal and take so-called 'petty offences' seriously. In other words, there should be zero-tolerance of all anti-social behaviour.

In 1994, William J. Bratton was appointed police commissioner for New York City. He introduced a policy of zero-tolerance policing. This meant that the police clamped down on all types of crime, however petty and insignificant. No longer did they turn a blind eye to people riding bikes on the sidewalk, urinating in public, small-time drug dealers, graffiti, beggars and street prostitution. In Bratton's words, 'If you don't stop the small offenders, it emboldens the really bad guys. It creates an atmosphere of lawlessness.' Within two years of the introduction of zero-tolerance, homicides in New York City were halved and robberies dropped by a third (Chaudhary & Walker, 1996).

So-called zero-tolerance policing in New York was not a get-tough policy imposed by the police on unsuspecting neighbourhoods. According to Commissioner Bratton, it involved a partnership with local communities and took account of their concerns and priorities (Young, 1999).

Evaluation Does zero-tolerance policing work? Certainly the results from New York City are impressive. But were they due to zero-tolerance policing or to other factors?

From 1993 to 1996 the crime rate declined in 17 out of the 25 largest cities in the USA. In some of these cities there had been no change in policing policy and in some cases there had been a reduction in the number of police officers. Some cities specifically adopted a less aggressive policing policy – for example, Los Angeles after the riots – and they too saw a reduction in crime. In addition, the crime rate in New York had started to decline before the appointment of Commissioner Bratton and zero-tolerance policing (Young, 1999).

At a minimum, this suggests that differing police methods do not necessarily have a marked effect on the crime rate. If this is the case, how else can the overall reduction in crime during this period be explained?

From 1990 to 1993, there was a crime wave in the USA. This coincided with an economic recession and high unemployment. From 1994 to 1996, 10.5 million new jobs were created in the USA. In addition, there was a marked decline in the crack-cocaine epidemic. Factors such as these, rather than zero-tolerance policing, may provide a better explanation for the decline in crime in New York City (Chaudhary & Walker, 1996).

Conclusion

It is difficult to evaluate the various approaches and strategies to crime reduction. First, the reliability and validity of crime statistics are questionable. As a result, any measurement of the effectiveness of crime reduction strategies must also be questionable. Second, many of the approaches to crime reduction are directed towards particular crimes – for example, street crime – and particular groups, for example, the working class. In view of the variety of both crime and of groups in society, it is unlikely that any single approach can provide a solution to the 'problem of crime'. Third, there are many factors which affect the crime rate. It is extremely difficult to isolate a particular factor and say with any degree of certainty that it is responsible for a reduction in crime.

13.5 Social policy and crime

Social policy refers to government policy on a range of social issues – for example, education, the family and health. This section looks at the crime policies of British governments from 1945 onwards. It also considers their relationship to sociological theories of crime.

1945-1979

Elected in 1945, the Labour Party set the early post-war agenda for dealing with crime. Crime reduction meant the reduction of social inequality. In this respect, Labour policy reflected sociological theories which see the roots of crime within the structure of society – the structural/societal approaches outlined in Section 12.2. In practice, this meant dealing with poverty, unemployment and educational failure, and reducing inequalities in income, wealth and opportunity. In terms of offenders, the focus was on treatment and rehabilitation rather than imprisonment and punishment (McLaughlin & Muncie, 2001).

From 1945-1959, crime was not a major political issue. It was hardly mentioned in the manifestos or election campaigns of the main political parties (Downes & Morgan, 2002).

Things started to change in the 1960s. The recorded crime rate rose rapidly during these years, particularly the rate for young offenders. Crime was becoming a political issue. So much so that by 1979, the Conservatives were talking about a 'law and order crisis'.

Conservative policy, 1979-1997

The Conservative Party won the 1979 election and remained in power for the next 18 years. Crime was a major issue in the election campaign. Labour maintained its traditional policy of dealing with 'the social deprivation which allows crime to flourish'. The Conservatives rejected this approach. They promised to restore the 'rule of law' with a 'war on crime'. Criminals rather than society were to blame for the rocketing crime rate. And they had been allowed to get away with it because of the 'soft' policies of Labour governments.

The emphasis now was on apprehending and punishing criminals. Muggers, burglars and hooligans were to blame for rising crime. They, not society, were responsible for their criminal behaviour. As a result, they deserved to be punished. Money was pumped into the criminal justice system. During the first half of the 1980s, expenditure on the police force rose by 40%. Courts were encouraged to give tougher sentences in an effort to deter offenders. Expenditure on prisons rose by 85% in the first half of the 1980s. And by 1988, the rate of imprisonment in Britain was the highest in Europe. Despite the Conservative policy of getting tough on crime, the rate of recorded crime continued to grow rapidly (McLaughlin & Muncie, 2001).

In line with their rejection of structural/societal approaches to crime reduction, the Conservatives looked to situational approaches such as target hardening and surveillance. Crime control was not just the responsibility of government – it was also the duty of every citizen and local community. Individuals must make their homes more secure and take action to protect their neighbourhoods with schemes like Neighbourhood Watch.

New Labour policy, 1997-2004

In the 1980s, the Conservative's catch-phrase was 'Labour's soft on crime'. In the 1990s, the soundbite of Tony Blair's New Labour was 'Tough on crime and tough on the causes of crime'.

Tough on crime New Labour, like the Conservatives before them, argued that offenders should be held responsible for their criminal acts and be given their just deserts – that is be punished in relation to the seriousness of their crimes. The criminal justice system should 'come down hard' on persistent offenders. One of the results of this policy has been a further increase in the prison population. In England and Wales in 2003, there were nearly 73,000 people in prison, an increase of over 25,000 since 1990 (*Social Trends*, 2004).

In 2001, Tony Blair set out Labour's crime policy for his second term in office. 'We will take further action to focus on the 100,000 most persistent offenders. They are responsible for half of all crime.' As part of this response, New Labour has favoured a zero-tolerance policy – clamping down on petty criminals, drunkenness, vandalism and a range of anti-social behaviour in order to prevent the development of environments in which more serious crime can flourish. This can be seen from the introduction of ASBOs – Anti-social Behaviour Orders – which can result in curfews for young people and banning them from certain areas. Failure to comply with an ASBO is a criminal offence.

To a large extent, New Labour has seen crime reduction as 'a local problem requiring local solutions' (Cook, 2001). A *multi-agency approach* has been encouraged. This involves various local authority agencies – for example, social services, health, housing and criminal justice agencies – working together to combat crime. Wherever possible, local people should participate in this process (Cook, 2001).

Tough on the causes of crime When New Labour came to power in 1997, they offered a 'Third Way' in politics – neither the traditional left-wing policies of 'old' Labour, nor the right-wing policies of the Conservatives. The Third Way sought new directions and new solutions to old and new problems.

Much of this was influenced by one of Britain's leading sociologists, Anthony Giddens, who has been described as Tony Blair's favourite guru. Giddens' *The Third Way: The Renewal of Social Democracy* was published in 1998.

Giddens saw *social exclusion* as the main threat to social order and social solidarity. Society would tend to fracture and disintegrate if groups became excluded from the mainstream. For example, if the poor or ethnic minorities were detached from the wider society, they would not feel part of the national community.

Social Exclusion Unit Giddens' Third Way is reflected in New Labour's social policy. In their first year of government, Labour set up the Social Exclusion Unit to find solutions to the problem of exclusion. The Unit is directly responsible to the Cabinet and it attempts to ensure that all policies – health, education, poverty, crime, urban renewal – are part of a coordinated strategy to deal with social exclusion (MacGregor, 2001).

Poverty Living in poverty means exclusion from many of the activities that most people take for granted. The largest group in poverty are low-paid workers and their dependent children. Labour's policy to reduce poverty has focused on this group. It has introduced the following:

- A minimum wage
- The Working Families Tax Credit to top up the wages of low-paid workers
- A significant increase in Child Benefit allowances
- The National Childcare Strategy which provides money for the development of childcare centres
- The Sure Start programme which provides health and support services for low-income families with children under four (Donnison, 2001; Page, 2002).

Unemployment Labour's New Deal, introduced in 1998, was part of their programme for social inclusion. The New Deal offered education and training for young people between the ages of 18 and 24 who had been out of work for more than six months. It was later extended to older people.

The New Deal provided personal advisors who offered direction and support to the unemployed, guiding them through the various options – academic courses, vocational training, self-employment, or voluntary work.

The New Deal emphasised the duties of citizenship. It was the duty of unemployed people to take up work and training opportunities. If they didn't, their benefits might be withheld until they did.

Education Shortly after their election in 1997, Labour promised to 'overcome economic and social disadvantage and make equality of opportunity a reality' (DfEE, 1997).

The focus was reaching out to the excluded and providing them with opportunities to enter mainstream society. This involved finding new ways of motivating young people in deprived inner-city areas and of improving 'underachieving schools'. For example, Education Action Zones were set up in urban areas which had low levels of educational attainment.

Crime and social exclusion In terms of New Labour's policy, crime is generated by social exclusion. Crime reduction in the long term can only result from policies of social inclusion. This means opening doors and providing opportunities, particularly for those at the bottom of the class system. In practice, this means reducing poverty, reducing unemployment and reducing educational failure. The aim is to give the excluded opportunities to enter mainstream society and to encourage them to do so.

Evaluation In terms of crime reduction, has Labour's policy worked? According to the British Crime Survey, crime in England and Wales has been steadily falling since 1995. Whether this has anything to do with Labour's policies of crime reduction and social inclusion is difficult to say.

Traditional Labour policy for tackling the causes of crime was based on a structural/societal approach. It was concerned with reducing social inequalities by redistributing income and wealth from the top to the bottom. New Labour is primarily concerned with reducing inequality of opportunity rather than redistribution. Many sociologists argue that inequality of opportunity cannot be significantly reduced unless economic inequalities are reduced. And this is particularly true when the gap in wealth and income between top and bottom is widening as it has under New Labour (Paxton & Dixon, 2004).

Labour's emphasis on social inclusion and increasing opportunity as a means for dealing with the causes of crime has been strongly criticised. For many sociologists, the target should be economic inequalities. In David Marquand's (1998) words, 'No project for social inclusion will work unless it captures some of the winners' gains and redirects them to the losers'.

Can social exclusion be seen as *the* cause of crime? What about the white-collar crimes of the socially included? In Dee Cook's (2001) words, 'It is unclear how tackling social exclusion would reduce racially motivated crime, domestic violence or white-collar crimes such as embezzlement, fraud, pollution and tax evasion'.

summary

1. There are three main approaches to crime reduction – a) structural/societal, b) individual, c) situational.
2. Structural/societal approaches see the basic causes of crime in society – for example, crime is generated by social inequality. Crime reduction therefore involves changes in society.
3. Individual approaches aim to change the behaviour of those seen to be at risk of crime.
4. There is some evidence that early intervention can reduce the risk of crime in later life. However, there is also evidence that it has little or no effect.
5. Evidence indicates that prison as a means of rehabilitation or deterrence has little effect. Some argue that the main value of prison is incapacitation. However, this appears to have little effect on the crime rate.
6. In terms of re-offending, community sentences are little different from imprisonment. However, certain types of community-based programmes can reduce re-offending by up to 20%.
7. Situational approaches seek to reduce the opportunities for crime by changing the settings in which crime occurs. Examples include target hardening and surveillance.
8. There is evidence that most situational approaches have some success, particularly if they lead to the strengthening of informal social control.
9. Wilson and Kelling see informal social control as the key to crime reduction. Disorder and anti-social behaviour lead to a breakdown in informal controls which allows crime to flourish. The main job of the police is to maintain order.
10. Zero-tolerance policing may be a successful method of crime reduction. However, the evidence is not clear-cut. Many other factors may account for a reduction in crime.
11. After 1945, crime reduction for the Labour Party meant a reduction in social inequality.
12. Conservative policy from 1979 to 1997 tended to blame the offender rather than society. Offenders must be given the punishment they deserve. Despite a rapidly growing prison population, the crime rate grew rapidly.
13. Like the Conservatives, New Labour claimed to be 'tough on crime'. They favoured a zero-tolerance policy and argued that offenders should be punished in relation to the seriousness of their crime.
14. New Labour saw social exclusion as the main cause of crime. Their policies were designed to reduce exclusion, provide equality of opportunity, and so reduce crime.
15. This view has been criticised. For example, some sociologists argue that inequality of opportunity cannot be significantly reduced until economic inequalities are reduced.

activity24 New Labour and crime

Item A Tony Blair

Tony Blair in the House of Commons

'If you are tolerant of small crimes, and I mean vandalism and the graffiti at the end of the street, you create an environment in which pretty soon the drug dealers move in, and then after that the violent people with their knives and their guns and all the rest of it, and the community is wrecked.'

Item B A critical view

In 2001, Tony Blair outlined New Labour's crime policy for his second term in office.

'We will take further action to focus on the 100,000 most persistent offenders. They are responsible for half of all crime. They are the core of the crime problem in this country. Half are under 21, nearly two-thirds are hard drug users, three quarters are out of work and more than a third were in care as children. Half have no qualifications at all and 45% are excluded from school.'

Jock Young makes the following comments on this statement.
'Let us note that these figures are as hypothetical as they are politically convenient. They ignore the fact that a large proportion of young people commit crime, that only a few are caught, and that generalisation about their background from these few is grossly unreliable. Further, that the number of crimes committed is based on police interviews with apprehended young offenders, who are encouraged to exaggerate in order to boost the clear-up figures; and that even given this, only one-quarter of offences are cleared up, so that for four million uncleared offences we do not have the faintest idea of the identity of the offenders. Furthermore, that for youth offences such as burglary and robbery the clear-up rate is even lower, 18% and 13% respectively, and the culprits even more unknown and indescribable.'

Adapted from Young, 2002

questions

1 Critically assess Tony Blair's claim in Item A.

2 One of the main problems with developing policies to fight crime is that governments know very little about the majority of lawbreakers. Discuss with reference to Item B.

Education

Introduction

Why do we spend the best years of our life in school? Until recently, most people managed quite well without a formal education. They learned what they needed from family, friends, and neighbours.

This type of informal education continues to be an important part of the socialisation process. What's new is a state system of formal education. It consists of specialised institutions – schools, colleges and universities – and selected knowledge and skills transmitted by professionals – teachers and lecturers.

Education is important. It takes up a significant proportion of people's lives – at least eleven years. And it affects them for the rest of their lives. It's very expensive – in 2001 government expenditure on education in the UK was £47 billion, 11.8% of all public expenditure. And the cost rises year by year (*Social Trends*, 2003).

Starting out

chaptersummary

▶ **Unit 1** looks at the relationship between education, socialisation and identity.

▶ **Unit 2** examines social relationships within educational institutions.

▶ **Units 3, 4 and 5** outline sociological explanations for the differences in educational attainment between social classes, gender and ethnic groups.

▶ **Unit 6** examines the relationship between education and the economy.

▶ **Unit 7** looks at social policy and education.

Unit 1 Education, socialisation and identity

keyissues

1 What are the main views of the relationship between education and socialisation?

2 What are their strengths and weaknesses?

This unit looks at the role or function of education in society. In simple terms, this means what does education do? Some theories argue that it is beneficial to society whilst others argue that it benefits only a minority at the expense of the majority.

1.1 Functionalist theories of education

The key influences on functionalist thinking in the past century were Emile Durkheim and Talcott Parsons. Both were concerned with explaining the social order that characterises modern industrial societies. Both saw this order as underpinned by:

- Value consensus – an agreement about the central values of society.
- An integrated division of labour – a complex structure of specialised occupations into which people were allocated according to their skills and ability.

Society and social order Both Durkheim and Parsons stressed the central role of the educational system as an agency of *secondary socialisation* functioning to ensure that both the value system and the division of labour are reproduced from generation to generation. This process of social reproduction ensures that society continues above and beyond the individual. In other words, people are born into society, they live their lives and they eventually die but society does not stop or break down into chaos or confusion. Rather society continues with very little disruption because new generations continue to subscribe to similar shared beliefs, values and traditions, and willingly replace those who drop out of the division of labour. Each generation conforms and social order is assured. This is not to say that society does not change and progress. Social change occurs but it is gradual and evolutionary rather than radical and revolutionary.

Society as a social system Functionalists see society as an integrated and interdependent *social system* made up of key social institutions or sub-systems such as the family, education, the mass media, religion, the legal system (ie the law and agents of social control such as the police and judiciary), the political system (central and local government, parliament and the civil service) and the economic system (ie employers and employed).

These social institutions work together for the benefit of society as a whole. They are concerned with the maintenance of social order. Some institutions achieve this by focusing on the reproduction of the culture of society through the process of socialisation. Some are mainly concerned with making sure that members of society are allocated to suitable positions in the division of labour. Social institutions usually work together to achieve these goals. For example, the educational and economic systems are often seen as working hand in hand as schools, colleges and universities develop the skills required for the world of work.

Emile Durkheim

Social solidarity Writing over 100 years ago, the French sociologist Emile Durkheim argued that *social solidarity* – social unity – is essential for the survival of society. Social solidarity is based on 'essential similarities' between members of society. According to Durkheim, one of the main functions of education is to develop these similarities and so bind members of society together.

Durkheim believed that for society to operate effectively individuals must develop an identity based on a sense of belonging to something wider than their immediate situation. They must become *social beings* with a loyalty and commitment to society as a whole. Durkheim saw education as playing an important part in this process.

History, religion and social solidarity Durkheim suggested that subjects such as history, language and religious studies link the individual to society and affirm a sense of belonging to society. He argued that children should be encouraged to take pride in the historical achievements of their nation and to understand that they were part of a greater whole – that is, a community united by shared history and sentiment. For example, the National Curriculum, with its emphasis on British history, can be seen as a means of developing this link by showing young people that they are part of something larger than their immediate family or neighbourhood.

We can illustrate Durkheim's ideas with reference to the Welsh education system. In Wales, the Welsh language is compulsory in schools up to year 11, despite the fact that it is the first language for only a minority of the population. All subjects in secondary schools are expected to have a 'Welsh dimension'. History, for example, partly focuses on Welsh resistance to English occupation, on freedom fighters such as Owen Glendower, and the influence of the Welsh on the Tudor kings. Pupils are also expected to study Welsh poets and novelists. Schools are encouraged to organise their own Eisteddfod, a cultural celebration involving Welsh songs, poetry and literature. All these aspects of a specifically Welsh (as opposed to British) educational experience are aimed at making young people feel part of a wider group – that is, Wales.

The USA provides a vivid illustration of Durkheim's views. Its population is drawn from all over the world. A common educational system has helped to weld this diverse mass of human beings into a nation. It has provided common norms and values, a shared sense of history and a feeling of belonging to a wider society.

American pupils often start their day with an oath of allegiance to their flag and country. History lessons focus on American heroes such as George Washington, Abraham Lincoln and Davy Crockett. There is an emphasis in their biographies on the American Dream – the idea that it doesn't matter what your background is, if you work hard enough you can be a success.

With a shared history, people feel part of a wider social group – it is their country, made up of people like themselves. In this way, education contributes to the development of social solidarity and a national identity.

In summary, Durkheim saw the function of education as socialising the individual to fit into a society 'which already has an identity of its own' by 'passing on the collective consciousness, or culture, of that pre-existing society' (McKenzie, 2001). This process of cultural reproduction ensures the commitment of each new generation to the maintenance of social order.

Modern schools and social solidarity More recently, functionalists have applied Durkheim's ideas to contemporary education. For example, it is argued that assemblies, school uniforms, sports teams, sports days and house competitions can all play a role in constructing a sense of social solidarity.

David Hargreaves (1982) agrees with Durkheim's views. However, he criticises the emphasis in today's schools on competition and examination performance. Hargreaves argues that this emphasis serves to divide pupils into successes and failures rather than uniting them into an integrated group.

Hargreaves believes that schools often alienate pupils, particularly the less able and those from low-income backgrounds. He argues that many of these young people take their sense of rejection and failure into their dealings with the wider society. And this can lead to disorder – for example, delinquency – rather than the order which a smooth-running and integrated society requires.

activity1 education and socialisation

Item A Durkheim on education

Education consists of a systematic socialisation of the younger generation. In each of us, it may be said, there exists two beings which, whilst inseparable, remain distinct. One is made up of all the mental states which apply only to ourselves and to the events of our personal lives. This is what might be called the individual being. The other is the system of ideas, sentiments and practices which express in us, not our personality, but the group or different groups of which we are a part. These are religious beliefs, moral beliefs and practices, national or occupational traditions, collective opinions of every kind. Their totality forms the social being. To constitute this being in each of us is the end (the purpose) of education.

Adapted from Durkheim, 1961

Item B Oath of allegiance

American schoolchildren pledging loyalty to their flag and country

Item C Teaching history

Davy Crockett's story has been retold on countless occasions in schools across the USA. Davy Crockett pulled himself up by his own bootstraps. He became a skilled hunter and marksman in the backwoods of Tennessee, before joining the US army as a scout. He was elected three times as a Congressman. Hearing of the Texans' fight for freedom against Mexico, he gathered a dozen volunteers to help them. He died fighting the Mexican army in 1836.

Adapted from Newark, 1980

Davy Crockett at the Alamo

questions

1 Using Durkheim's ideas in Item A, suggest how the British education system transmits a British identity.

2 How can Items B and C be used to illustrate the view that education helps to unite members of society?

Talcott Parsons

The American sociologist Talcott Parsons (1961) developed Durkheim's ideas. He too argued that in modern industrial societies education performs important integrating and socialising functions. Like Durkheim, he noted that education helps individuals feel part of a wider social system. Parsons saw the school classroom as a 'microcosm of society'. This miniature society provides the training ground in which children can experience society beyond the family and so eases the transition from childhood to adulthood. By transmitting the culture of society to new generations, education helps to ensure the continuity of norms and values. As McKenzie (2001) notes, this process 'teaches us not only how to conform, but also how to think'.

Ascribed vs achieved status Parsons argued that education acts as a social bridge between the family unit and wider society. In the family, the child's status is *ascribed* – fixed at birth. This means that our parents will usually love us

regardless of our talents or lack of them. However, in the wider society, status is *achieved* through education, qualifications and the jobs we do. We are judged on the basis of achieved status. It is a big jump from the ascribed status of the family to the achieved status of society as a whole. Schools help to bridge this gap because they free children from dependence on the family and judge them in terms of their educational achievements (McKenzie, 2001).

Parsons noted that education is our first experience of being judged for what we achieve rather than for who we are. We learn that status is no longer guaranteed but must be earned. We learn that in the wider society people are judged in terms of universal, society-wide standards. We learn that status is achieved on the basis of merit – that is, through effort, ability and hard work. And, in this way, we learn that education and society are meritocratic.

Central values Parsons argued that schools socialise young people into the key values of society in order to prepare them for their adult roles. In Western societies, the central values transmitted by schools are achievement, individualism, competition and equality of opportunity. In schools, young people are encouraged to achieve, they are assessed as individuals rather than as members of a group, they compete against each other and everyone is given an equal chance to succeed.

Social order Parsons saw such values as having both a social and economic function. In social terms, the value of equality of opportunity ensures social order since both high and low achievers see the system as offering everybody an equal chance to succeed and, therefore, as fair and just. Outcomes in terms of success and failure are consequently rarely questioned. As a result, the risk of conflict between the successful and unsuccessful is minimised and social order maintained.

Role allocation In economic terms, Parsons argued that capitalism requires a highly motivated achievement-orientated workforce. The existence of a hierarchy of academic examinations and qualifications justifies different rewards for different levels of ability. Competition and individualism ensure that those with greater talents and skills are motivated to achieve those higher academic and economic rewards. Schools therefore help to select young people and allocate them to their adult roles. Pupils are assessed and sorted in terms of their talents and abilities and this helps allocate them to appropriate occupations. This ensures that the division of labour operates efficiently because people are allocated to jobs that best suit their ability. Parsons, therefore, saw the transmission and internalisation of these values as essential for effectively managing the movement of young people into the world of work. Parsons' view of the selection and allocation function of schools is similar to the functionalist theory of stratification (see page 131).

In summary, functionalists see education as a crucial part of the socialisation process.

- It transmits and reinforces society's norms and values in order to maintain value consensus and social solidarity.
- It prepares young people for their adult roles as motivated and achievement-orientated workers, prepared to take their place in a specialised division of labour.
- It selects young people in terms of their abilities for occupational roles, thus maintaining the efficiency of the economic system.

Functionalism and education – evaluation

Questioning value consensus Functionalists have emphasised the importance of education as a means of transmitting society's values. However, they assume that there is a single set of values to transmit. It can be argued that society today is no longer characterised by value consensus – an agreement about shared values – but by cultural fragmentation and diversity. For example, the UK is often described as a multicultural society consisting of various groups with different and even conflicting sets of values.

Marxists have argued that education does not transmit common values – rather it transmits ruling class values. Other sociologists have pointed out that the dominant value systems are often patriarchal, middle class and White – that is they reflect the values of White, middle-class males. For example, feminists often argue that women are

activity2 examinations

questions

In terms of Parsons' theory, how can the type of formal examination pictured here:

a) Help to transmit the central values of society - that is, the values of achievement, individualism, competition and equality of opportunity?

b) Form part of the process of role allocation?

largely invisible in history books. And many ethnic minority groups are demanding that history teaching reflect their historical experience and their viewpoint. For example, in the USA, African-American history is now a major part of the history curriculum.

Social conflict rather than social order Other critics have suggested that education can generate social conflict rather than social order. Hargreaves (1982) argues that community solidarity and cohesion are declining in modern societies. He believes that schools can reverse this decline by encouraging allegiance to group life. However, for many pupils, especially those from low-income and ethnic minority backgrounds, the experience of school leads to alienation and anti-social behaviour as they react to their perception that the institution does not value them.

Determinism The functionalist view of schools turning out conformist citizens has been criticised as deterministic. Pupils are not passively shaped into educational products that uncritically take their place in society as good citizens and workers. Rather, studies of schools and classrooms suggest that education is often a site of conflict, confrontation and pupil resistance.

Questioning meritocracy Functionalists often assume that Western education systems are meritocratic – that all pupils have an equal chance and are rewarded primarily on the basis of objective criteria such as achievement, ability, intelligence and effort. However, as later units show, there are significant inequalities in society – such as those based on social class and ethnicity – which prevent equality of opportunity. For example, many working class and ethnic minority pupils underachieve in school. As a result, the extent to which the educational system is able to develop and assess pupils' 'real' ability is questionable. The inequalities of opportunity which exist both inside and outside schools suggest that education is not a meritocratic process.

Confirming status It can be argued that the educational system confirms people in their social positions rather than provides opportunities for advancement. Middle-class pupils tend to get middle-class jobs. In general, they get higher qualifications than their working-class counterparts. These qualifications can be seen as a 'rubber stamp' confirming their right to middle-class occupations. Their 'success' in school may result from the advantages of their class position rather than their ability. If this is the case, then the functionalist claim that schools efficiently select and allocate pupils in terms of ability is questionable.

Education and the economy Critics argue that the relationship between education and the economy is not as simple and straightforward as Parsons suggests. As noted above, his claim that schools allocate individuals to appropriate positions in the occupational system is challenged by evidence that there are barriers preventing many students from achieving their potential.

The relationship between education and the economy is far from clear. It is discussed in detail in Unit 6.

Conclusion Functionalism has often been criticised as a conservative theory – as a theory which is largely uncritical of modern society, which focuses on the positive contributions of social institutions, and which implies things should be maintained the way they are. While there is some truth in this view, it should not be used to dismiss functionalism out of hand. Durkheim's insights into the relationship between education and social integration are still relevant today. For example, our sense of local and national identity is partly shaped by our experience of the education system. And Hargreaves' view of the potential for schools to contribute to the re-establishment of community is an important contribution to the debate about education.

key terms

Social solidarity Social integration, social unity.
Social system The idea that society forms a system of interdependent parts which work together for the benefit of the whole.
Specialised division of labour A labour force with a large number of specialised occupations.
Secondary socialisation The process of socialisation which builds on the primary socialisation usually conducted by the family.
Value consensus An agreement about the major values of society.
Social status A position in society, eg father, nurse, teacher.
Ascribed status A status that is largely fixed and unchangeable.
Achieved status A status that involves some degree of choice and results partly from individual achievement.
Individual achievement Achieving success as an individual rather than as a member of a group.
Equality of opportunity A system in which every person has an equal chance of success.
Role allocation The system of allocating people to roles which suit their aptitudes and capabilities.

1.2 Marxist theories of education

The infrastructure The Marxist theory of education cannot be separated from the Marxist theory of class stratification. Karl Marx (1818-1883) saw capitalist societies such as the UK and USA as largely shaped by their economic systems or *infrastructure*. He argued that a minority class, the bourgeoisie or capitalist class, owned and controlled the means of production – that is, the wealth (capital), land, factories and raw materials needed to produce manufactured goods. However, the capitalist class need the labour power of the majority class, the proletariat or working class, in order to transform the means of production into manufactured goods.

The relationship between the bourgeoisie and the proletariat (which Marx referred to as the *social relations of production*) is that of a ruling class and a subject class. And this relationship is an exploitative one because the wage

Item B Two views of role allocation

questions

1 How does the ideologically sound young woman in Item A illustrate Bowles and Gintis's theory of the role of education in society?

2 Using Item B, briefly compare functionalist and Marxist views of role allocation.

that the lads were shaped by the educational system. Instead, the lads rejected school and created their own *counter-school culture*. But, it was this very rejection of school which prepared them for the low-skill, low-status jobs they were to end up in.

The lads rejected educational success as defined by the school. They saw the conformist behaviour of hardworking pupils – the ear 'oles – as a matter for amusement and mockery. School was good for a laugh and not much else. Boredom was relieved by mucking around and breaking rules. The lads actively created a counter-school culture based on opposition to authority. In some respects this behaviour made sense. They were destined for low-skill jobs so why bother to work hard.

So, like Bowles and Gintis, Willis argues for a correspondence between school and work. But this is not produced by the school – the lads are not the docile, obedient pupils of Bowles and Gintis's study. The lads themselves have produced the correspondence by their

rejection of the school. And in doing so they have prepared themselves for their place in the workforce. They have learned to have a laugh, to put up with boredom and monotony, and to accept the drudgery of low-skill jobs.

Ideology But the lads' culture is not entirely adapted to the requirements of the capitalist workforce. It contains an important, albeit largely hidden, criticism of the dominant ideology of individualism and equality of opportunity. There is an implicit recognition that individual effort does not necessarily bring success, that the meritocratic society does not exist and that collective action is needed to improve the position of the working class. However, this is a long way from recognising the true nature of capitalist exploitation and oppression.

Twenty years on Willis's study was conducted in a secondary school in Birmingham in the 1970s. Twenty years later, a similar study was conducted in the West Midlands by Máirtín Mac an Ghaill (1994). Some of the working-class young men – the 'macho lads' – were similar to Willis's lads. They rejected the authority of the teachers and the values of the school. However, this was a time of high unemployment when many traditional low-skill working-class jobs were disappearing. Because of this, the macho lads' behaviour was 'outdated' – the jobs it prepared them for were fast becoming a thing of the past.

Evaluation Willis is sometimes criticised for using a small and unrepresentative sample – 12 boys. However, his research was intended as a case study of a particular group of lads in a particular school rather than a social survey based on a representative sample from which generalisations could be made. Willis's study was based on participant observation and informal interviews. It is unlikely that the insights and rich data which resulted from his research would have been produced by a survey based on questionnaires.

Willis's research is important for its attempt to link structure and action, to link the wider society with the day-to-day activities of a small number of people.

activity4 learning to labour

Item A From school to work

Item B Opposing authority

The most basic, obvious and explicit dimension of counter-school culture is entrenched, general and personalised opposition to 'authority'.

(In a group discussion on teachers)

Joey: they're able to punish us. They're bigger than us, they stand for a bigger establishment than we do, like, we're just little and they stand for bigger things, and you try to get your own back. It's, uh, resenting authority I suppose.

Eddie: The teachers think they're high and mighty 'cos they're teachers, but they're nobody really, they're just ordinary people ain't they?

Bill: Teachers think they're everybody. They are more, they're higher than us, but they think they're a lot higher and they're not.

This opposition involves an apparent inversion of the usual values held up by authority. It is lived out in countless small ways which are special to the school institution, instantly recognised by the teachers, and an almost ritualistic part of the daily fabric of life for the kids.

Adapted from Willis, 1977

Item C Discrediting qualifications

The lads reject the idea of qualifications. Since knowledge is opposed, so must qualifications be resisted and discredited. As in other things, the principal means of discrediting formal standards is to 'see behind' them to 'how things really work'. At a certain level, the lads really feel they know better. It is possible to get on without qualifications and school work because what really matters is 'knowing a bit about the world', 'having your head screwed on', and, 'pulling your finger out' when necessary.

Qualifications, to them, seem to be a deflection or displacement of direct activity. They feel that they can always demonstrate any necessary ability 'on the job', and that the doing of a thing is always easier than the account of it, or its representation in an exam, or its formal description seem to imply.

Adapted from Willis, 1977

High achievement is rewarded with praise, high status, good grades and valuable qualifications. In this way, young people are encouraged to value individual achievement. And this prepares them to achieve as individuals in the wider society.

Marxist views As outlined earlier, Marxists argue that the main job of schools is social reproduction – producing the next generation of workers *schooled* to accept their roles in capitalist society.

For Bowles and Gintis (1976), this is done primarily through the hidden curriculum. They claim that schools produce subordinate, well-disciplined workers who will submit to control from above and take orders rather than question them. Schools do this by rewarding conformity, obedience, hard work and punctuality, and by penalising creativity, originality and independence.

Conclusion

The idea of a hidden curriculum is useful. Clearly, there's a lot more being taught and learned in schools than the formal curriculum of English, maths, science, and so on. And clearly much of this is 'hidden' – teachers and learners are often unaware of what's going on.

The content of the hidden curriculum is open to interpretation. Have the functionalists got it right? Have the Marxists got it right? This partly depends on how you see capitalist society.

Further aspects of the hidden curriculum will be examined throughout this chapter.

summary

1. From a functionalist perspective education:
   - Is the major agency of secondary socialisation which transmits the central values of society from one generation to the next
   - Provides the skills and knowledge required for a specialised division of labour
   - Makes an important contribution to social solidarity and social order
   - Develops and assesses the talents and abilities of young people and allocates them to appropriate roles in the wider society.

2. The following criticisms have been made of functionalist views.
   - The values transmitted by education may be those of a powerful minority rather than those of society as a whole.
   - Schools may generate social conflict rather than social order.
   - Functionalist views tend to be deterministic.
   - The assumption that schools and society operate as meritocracies is questionable.
   - Education may simply confirm status rather than provide opportunities for advancement.
   - Role allocation may not be as effective as functionalists argue.

3. From a Marxist perspective education:
   - As part of the superstructure reflects ruling class interests

   - As an ideological state apparatus transmits ruling class ideology
   - Legitimises inequality and disguises exploitation
   - Rewards conformity and obedience
   - Reproduces new generations of workers, schooled to accept their place in capitalist society.

4. The following criticisms have been made of Marxist views.
   - They are based on a value judgement - that capitalism is an evil and exploitative system.
   - They are often deterministic.
   - They fail to recognise pupil resistance (though this does not apply to Willis).
   - They fail to appreciate the *lack* of correspondence between aspects of schooling and the requirements of capitalism.
   - They over-estimate the power of the infrastructure to shape the superstructure.

5. The hidden curriculum transmits messages which pupils and teachers are largely unaware of. It consists of ideas, beliefs, norms and values which are embedded in the normal routines and procedures of school life.

6. From a functionalist view, the transmission of society's core values can be seen as part of the hidden curriculum.

7. From a Marxist view, social reproduction is part of the hidden curriculum.

activity6 *views of the hidden curriculum*

Item A Prize day

Awards for academic excellence in an American school

Item B *Learning to submit*

In a study of 237 students in their final year at a New York high school, the researchers claimed that high grades were linked with perseverance, obedience, consistency, dependability and punctuality. Students with high grades were often below average when measured in terms of creativity, originality and independence of judgement.

Adapted from Bowles & Gintis, 1976

questions

1 How can Item A be used to support a functionalist view of the hidden curriculum?

2 How can Item B be used to support a Marxist view of the hidden curriculum?

Unit 2 *Institutional processes*

keyissues

1 What insights have interpretivist approaches provided?

2 What effect do streaming, setting and labelling have on educational attainment?

3 What is the significance of 'classroom knowledge'?

This unit looks at processes which take place within educational institutions. For example, it examines the way teachers define students and the effect this might have on students' progress.

2.1 Systems theories

The theories outlined in Unit 1 – functionalism and Marxism – are known as systems or structuralist theories They picture society as a social system or a social structure and examine the relationship between the parts of society and society as a whole. They are concerned with the contribution of the various parts to the maintenance of the whole.

In line with this focus on society, functionalists ask how the education system functions to maintain social order. And one answer to this question is establishing value consensus by socialising young people in terms of the core values of society. Similarly, Marxists ask how the education system meets the needs of capitalism and maintains ruling class dominance. And the main answer to this question is

the transmission of ruling class ideology.

As a result of this focus on society as a whole, systems theories tend to neglect small-scale interaction situations – in particular, what actually happens in the classroom. There are exceptions, such as Willis's study of the 'lads' which looked at 12 young men in a particular school.

This unit narrows the focus. In doing so, it uses different theoretical perspectives – interpretivist and interactionist approaches.

2.2 Interpretivist approaches

Willis's study looked at small-scale interaction situations. It attempted to discover the meanings which the lads gave to their actions and to those of others. It tried to show how they constructed their own social reality. In these respects Willis used an interpretivist approach.

Interpretivist approaches usually focus on small-scale interaction. They assume that people interpret the world in terms of meanings which are constructed in interaction situations. They are often critical of structural approaches such as Marxism and functionalism which tend to see behaviour as shaped by the social system.

In terms of education, interpretivist approaches often focus on classroom interaction, on the meanings which direct that interaction, and the relationships which develop from it.

Defining others

Symbolic interactionism, one of the main interpretivist approaches, emphasises the importance of a socially constructed identity. This identity is shaped in part by people's perception of how others see them. It may become a *self-fulfilling prophecy* if people act in terms of the image of themselves which others project.

Social identities are often constructed rapidly and on the basis of very little evidence. John Beynon (1985) examined how boys classified and evaluated each other during their first three months of secondary school. Their classifications included *good kids* (who stood up to teachers), *TPs* (teachers' pets), *bullies*, *dippoes* or *weirds* and *snobs* or *toffees*. On the basis of these and other categories, the boys formed friendship groups. Social classifications are important as they define what a person is and what others think about and expect from them.

Labelling A label is the major identifying characteristic of a person. For example, if a pupil is labelled a *troublemaker,* then it is likely that all their actions will be interpreted in terms of this label. Thus, even if they are seen to be behaving well, this will be judged as unusual, as out of character.

One of the first studies which tried to uncover the meanings which teachers use to classify pupils was made by the American sociologist Howard Becker (1971). He interviewed 60 Chicago teachers and found they tended to share a picture of the *ideal pupil*. This was used as a benchmark to judge the pupils they taught. The ideal pupil was highly motivated, intelligent and well-behaved. Pupils judged to be closest to this ideal were likely to come from middle-class backgrounds, those furthest from it from lower working-class backgrounds. As a result, the latter were often labelled as discipline problems, as unmotivated and as unlikely to succeed. These labels may well have a significant effect on their educational careers. This point is examined in more detail in Unit 3.

Negotiation From an interactionist perspective, meanings and roles are not fixed and given, they are negotiated in interaction situations. David Hargreaves (1975) examined how teachers and pupils negotiate a 'working consensus' in the classroom. Each attempts to define and control classroom interaction. Teachers use a range of tactics to 'get their own way'. They might, for instance, make excessive demands and then compromise – perhaps setting a lengthy homework assignment and agreeing to reduce it in response to their pupils' groans. They offer rewards and punishments – 'if you'll work hard now, then I won't set any homework later'. They use cautionary tales of what happened to previous students as warnings to their current pupils. Teachers are in a more powerful position than pupils – they have formal authority which is backed up by sanctions. Nonetheless, pupils have ways of influencing the actions of teachers. For example, they can appeal to justice – 'you let 3B off homework' – and try to set one teacher against another – 'Mr … lets us do this'. Hargreaves argues that the order in classrooms is a negotiated order based on

a consensus worked out between teachers and pupils.

Evaluation Interpretivist approaches have provided valuable insights by focusing directly on interaction situations. However, it is this very focus which has been criticised. It has been seen as too narrow, looking at classroom interaction in isolation from the rest of society. What about, for example, the distribution of power in society as a whole? Won't this affect interaction situations and influence the construction of meanings and the outcome of negotiations?

Many sociologists argue that good sociology should combine a study of both interaction situations and the wider society. In this way, it is possible to study both social action and social structure and to examine the relationship between the two.

key terms

Systems theories Theories which see society as a system made up of interconnected parts.
Interpretivist approaches Approaches which seek to discover the meanings which direct action.
Symbolic interactionism An interpretivist approach which focuses on small-scale interaction situations and the negotiation of meaning.
Labelling theory A theory which states that when someone is labelled as a certain kind of person, they will tend to see themselves in terms of the label and act accordingly.
Self-fulfilling prophecy A prophecy or prediction which tends to fulfil itself simply because it has been made and people believe it to be true.

2.3 Teacher expectations

This section looks at an early study of the way teachers classify and evaluate pupils, their resulting expectation of pupils, and how this might affect pupils' behaviour. Further studies of the possible effects of teacher expectations are examined in Units 3, 4 and 5.

A famous study conducted in 1964 by Robert Rosenthal and Leonora Jacobson looked at the effects of teachers' expectations on pupils' behaviour. The researchers told teachers in a primary school in California that they had identified a number of pupils – the 'spurters' – as likely to make rapid progress. Unknown to the teachers, these pupils were selected at random. Yet, judging from the results of intelligence tests, the spurters made greater progress than their classmates over the next year.

Rosenthal and Jacobson concluded that their progress was due to the way they were defined. Their teachers expected more from them, conveyed this expectation to them, and the pupils acted accordingly. Yet, in Rosenthal and Jacobson's (1968) words, the only difference between the 'spurters' and their classmates was 'entirely in the minds of teachers'.

Rosenthal and Jacobson used the idea of a *self-fulfilling*

activity7 be realistic!

The following extract is taken from *The Autobiography of Malcolm X*. Malcolm, a Black American, went to school in Lansing, Michigan in the 1940s. In the 1960s he became leader of the Black Muslims and a spokesperson for many Black Americans. He was assassinated in 1965.

One day something happened which was to become the first major turning point of my life.

Somehow, I happened to be alone in the classroom with Mr Ostrowski, my English teacher. He was a tall, rather reddish White man and he had a thick mustache. I had gotten some of my best marks under him, and he had always made me feel that he liked me.

I know that he probably meant well in what he happened to advise me that day. I doubt that he meant any harm. It was just in his nature as an American White man. I was one of his top students, one of the school's top students - but all he could see for me was the kind of future ' in your place' that almost all White people see for Black people.

He told me, 'Malcolm, you ought to be thinking about a career. Have you been giving it thought?'

The truth is, I hadn't. I never have figured out why I told him, 'Well, yes, sir, I've been thinking I'd like to be a lawyer.' Lansing certainly had no Black lawyers - or doctors either - in those days. to hold up an image I might have aspired to. All I really knew for certain was that a lawyer didn't wash dishes, as I was doing.

Mr Ostrowski looked surprised, I remember, and leaned back in his chair and clasped his hands behind his head. He kind of half smiled and said, 'Malcolm, one of life's first needs is for us to be realistic. Don't misunderstand me, now. We all of us here like you, you know that. But you've got to be realistic about being a nigger. You need to think about something you can be. You're good with your hands - making things. Everybody admires your carpentry shop work. Why don't you plan on carpentry? People like you as a person - you'd get all kinds of work.'

The more I thought afterwards about what he said, the more uneasy it made me. It just kept treading around in my mind.

What made it really begin to disturb me was Mr Ostrowski's advice to others in my class - all of them White. They all reported that Mr Ostrowski had encouraged what they had wanted. Yet nearly none of them had earned marks equal to mine.

It was then that I began to change - inside.

I drew away from White people. I came to class, and I answered when called upon. It became a physical strain simply to sit in Mr Ostrowski's class.

Adapted from Malcolm X, 1966

Malcolm X

questions

1 What effects might Mr Ostrowski's advice have had on Malcolm's educational career?

2 How might a knowledge of the structure of American society add to our understanding of the interaction between Malcolm and Mr Ostrowski?

---

prophecy to explain their results. If people are defined in a certain way, this definition includes a prediction or prophecy of their future behaviour. If others act as if the prophecy is true, then there is a tendency for it to come to pass – to fulfil itself.

The definition acts as a *label*. According to *labelling theory*, if someone is labelled as a certain kind of person, others will respond to them in terms of the label. And there is a tendency for the person to adopt that identity and act in terms of it.

Evaluation Rosenthal and Jacobson's research has been extremely influential. However, attempts to replicate (repeat) their study have produced mixed results with some suggesting that labelling was of little or no significance. However, many researchers argue that labelling is important, that the self-fulfilling prophecy is real, and that it can help to explain differences in educational attainment.

activity8 an ideal pupil

questions

1 How does this cartoon illustrate the ideas of labelling and the self-fulfilling prophecy?

2 Suggest why interactionists sometimes use the term 'looking-glass self' to explain the source of a person's identity?

2.4 Pupil subcultures

If a group of pupils are defined in a similar way by their teachers, they will tend to see themselves as part of a group with similar characteristics. They will tend to interact with members of this group and develop a group identity and shared behaviour patterns. In other words, they will develop a *pupil subculture*. Pupil subcultures are the distinctive norms and values developed by groups of young people and acted out in schools.

This section asks three questions.

- First, do subcultures develop in response to pupils' experience within schools – for example, the way they are defined and evaluated by teachers?

- Second, are subcultures a reflection of life outside the school – do pupils bring their subculture from the neighbourhood into the school?

- Third, do pupil subcultures develop from young people's experiences both inside and outside the school?

Subcultures developed inside schools

One of the earliest studies of pupil subcultures was conducted in the late 1950s/early 60s by Colin Lacey (1970). The pupils were mainly middle class and attended Hightown Grammar School (not its real name). Many had been high achievers at their local primary school – they were the 'top scholars, team leaders, head boys and teachers' favourites'.

In their first year, all new boys showed high levels of commitment to the school, proudly wearing their school caps and jackets, and enthusiastically attending school functions and clubs. In class, they were eager, straining to answer questions, cooperating with their teachers and competing among themselves. Six months into the second year, one class was seen by their teachers as difficult to teach. In the words of one teacher, 'They're unacademic, they can't cope with the work'. What had happened to transform a group of high-achieving, academically-able first year pupils into 'unacademic' second year pupils? To help explain this, Lacey introduced two concepts – *differentiation* and *polarisation*.

Differentiation This is the process by which teachers judge and rank pupils in terms of their academic ability (as perceived by the teachers) and their behaviour. On this basis, they are differentiated into streams. As time goes on, pupils get a sense of how both teachers and fellow pupils rate and rank them.

Polarisation Gradually, a gap opened up – and kept growing – between the pupils who were defined as successful and those defined as unsuccessful. The two groups became polarised.

The subculture of success Pupils in the top stream accepted the value system of the school – they worked hard and were well-behaved. The system rewarded them with prestige – they were praised and respected by teachers. And the boys reinforced each other's behaviour – they were members of a successful peer group sharing the same values.

The subculture of failure Pupils in the bottom stream developed an anti-school subculture which became more extreme as the years went by. The school's values were turned upside down – boys gained prestige for giving cheek to a teacher, truanting, refusing to do homework, and for smoking and drinking.

This was a group thing – boys gained respect from other members of the group for anti-school behaviour. In this way, they reinforced each other's behaviour. And in the process, their school work steadily deteriorated.

Conclusion Lacey's study suggests that pupil subcultures develop within the school. They are a response to the way pupils are perceived by teachers, by other pupils, and by themselves. And they are a reaction to the way school classes are organised – in this case, streamed – and all that this 'says' about pupils in different streams.

Subcultures developed outside schools

As outlined earlier, Paul Willis studied a small group of working-class boys – the 'lads' – during their last year and a half at school (see pages 89, 91-92). In many ways the anti-school subculture developed by the lads was similar to the behaviour of the boys in the bottom stream in Lacey's study of Hightown Grammar. However, Willis's explanation of the subculture's development is very different.

According to Willis, the lads' behaviour reflected a) their expectations of future employment and b) the working-class subculture they brought to school with them. The lads were keen to leave school as soon as possible and looked forward to 'real' work – adult, male, manual jobs. School was a waste of time.

- The lads didn't need academic qualifications for the jobs they wanted.
- They despised those who conformed to the school's values – who they called the 'ear 'oles' – seeing them as cissies.
- They wanted a context – manual work – where they could be real men.

The lads' anti-school subculture reflected the working-class culture they'd learned from their fathers, elder brothers and other men in the neighbourhood. Having a 'laff', a lack of respect for authority and messing around are aspects of manual working-class male subculture. The lads are attracted to this kind of behaviour and reproduce it in the classroom.

For Willis, the lads' anti-school subculture is shaped mainly by their expectations about the jobs they hope to get and by the working-class subculture they bring with them to school.

Conclusion

Although the explanations of the origins of pupil subcultures given by Lacey and Willis are very different, there is probably some truth in both. Studies have shown that the pupils placed in lower streams tend to be from working-class backgrounds. Although all the pupils in Lacy's study started their secondary school career with enthusiasm, those relegated to the bottom stream would probably have reacted negatively to teacher expectations and drawn from their working-class background to express their dissatisfaction.

While the pupils in Willis's study may well have brought their subculture into school, the expectations of teachers probably reinforced this subculture. In view of their behaviour, teachers were likely to have low expectations of their progress and place them in the bottom stream. As a result, their anti-school subculture may well have been magnified.

> **key terms**
>
> **Pupil subcultures** The distinctive norms and values developed by groups of young people in schools.
> **Differentiation** Separating pupils into groups on the basis of their perceived ability and behaviour.
> **Polarisation** The widening gap in terms of measured ability and behaviour between top and bottom streams.

2.5 The organisation of teaching and learning

This section looks at how pupils are allocated to teaching groups, and how this shapes what they are taught and the examinations they take.

There are two main types of teaching groups – *ability groups* and *mixed-ability groups*.

Ability groups These are groups of pupils who are seen to have similar abilities. *Setting* and *streaming* are two ways of dividing students into ability groups. Setting allocates pupils to subject groups – a pupil could be in set 1 for English and set 3 for maths. Streaming places pupils in the same ability group for all subjects – for example, a pupil is placed in class 3 and taught at that level for all subjects.

Mixed-ability groups In these groups, pupils are randomly or intentionally mixed in terms of their perceived ability.

Setting is the most common form of ability grouping in schools in England and Wales. It becomes increasingly common as pupils approach GCSE. Streaming was typical of primary schools in the 1940s and 50s. It began to die out with the decline of the 11-plus exam. Mixed-ability teaching throughout pupils' school careers is found in only a small number of schools.

Ability groups

Supporters of ability groups make the following points.

Different abilities – different teaching Young people have different abilities. This means they need to be taught:

- At different speeds
- In different ways
- At different levels.

The most efficient way of doing this is to create teaching groups of pupils with similar abilities.

Different abilities – different tasks There's no point in giving the same tasks to pupils of different ability. For example, only some can cope with higher level maths.

Different abilities – different exams Because pupils have different abilities, they need different exams at different levels – for example, GCSE maths at higher, intermediate and foundation levels.

Mixed-ability groups

Supporters of mixed-ability groups make the following points.

Social benefits Mixed-ability groups encourage cooperation and friendly relationships between students. For the wider society, they reduce class differences and class conflict.

Ability is not fixed Most pupils remain in the same set or stream. This assumes that their ability is fixed – that it won't change. However, there is a lot of evidence which suggests that ability – as measured by tests – is not fixed.

Setting affects attainment The set or stream in which a pupil is placed can affect their attainment. For example, it can raise attainment in the top set and lower attainment in the bottom set. This is unfair – all pupils should have an equal chance.

Setting discriminates Those allocated to lower sets or streams tend to be from working-class or ethnic minority backgrounds. This can prevent them from obtaining the knowledge required for a high grade in examinations – for example, at GCSE level. In contrast, a disproportionate number of White, middle-class pupils are placed in the upper sets/streams. Ability groups discriminate in favour of the White middle classes and against those from working class and ethnic minority backgrounds.

Behaviour rather than ability This can be used as a basis for allocating pupils to ability groups. For example, there is evidence that African-Caribbean pupils have been placed in examination sets which were below their measured ability because their behaviour was seen as unsuitable for higher sets (see pages 126-128).

What are the effects of ability grouping?

A large number of studies have been carried out on the effects of ability grouping on pupils' attainment. Here are the conclusions of two surveys of these studies.

- 'In general, the research findings indicate that streaming and setting compared with mixed-ability teaching have no effect, either positive or negative, on average pupil achievement (across the ability range) at either primary or secondary level' (Sukhnandan & Lee, 1998).
- 'The weight of evidence from research on ability groupings within schools indicates that they have rather little impact on overall attainment' (Ireson & Hallam, 2001).

So, what's all the fuss about? It appears that allocating pupils to ability groups makes little or no difference. There is *some* research, however, which indicates that it does make a difference. This research suggests that although the *overall* attainment level may remain the same, this is because those in the top sets do better and those in the bottom sets do worse. Possible reasons for this have already been outlined – labelling, the self-fulfilling prophecy, teacher expectations, and pupil subcultures.

Where does this leave us? The short answer is we don't really know. Research evidence on the effects of ability grouping is inconclusive – it is not clearcut.

Setting and tiered exams

League tables and setting From 1992 onwards, the test and examination results of every secondary school in the country were published. Results from primary schools were published from 1997. This led to local and national 'league tables' as schools were ranked in terms of their results. In the words of one Head of Year in a London comprehensive, 'A school now lives or dies on its results' (quoted in Gillborn & Youdell, 2001).

The pressure to improve results led to an increase in setting in the belief that this would lead to improved examination performance. This belief was reinforced by government policy. The Labour Party's election manifesto of 1997 stated that:

> 'Children are not all of the same ability, nor do they learn at the same speed. That means "setting" children in classes to maximise progress, for the benefit of high fliers and slower learners alike.'

Tiered exams and setting GCSE exams are tiered. Pupils are allocated to sets for examination entry. For example, they may be allocated to the higher, intermediate or foundation set for mathematics. And this is where ability grouping in terms of sets has a major effect. It actually prevents those in lower sets from having *any* chance of attaining higher grades.

Most GCSEs have two levels – higher and foundation. The highest grade that pupils entered for foundation level can attain is grade C. There is no way they can get an A*, A or B.

> ### key terms
>
> **Ability groups** Groups of pupils who are seen to have similar abilities.
> **Setting** Allocating pupils to ability groups in terms of subjects – for example, set 1, 2 or 3 for English.
> **Streaming** Placing pupils in the same ability group for all subjects – for example, class 1, 2 or 3.
> **Mixed-ability groups** Groups in which pupils are randomly or intentionally mixed in terms of their ability.
> **Tiered exams** Exams with two or three levels. The maximum possible grade varies with each tier.

2.6 Classroom knowledge and 'ability'

The previous section looked at the relationship between setting and GCSE examination entry. Pupils defined as 'less able' were placed in lower sets and entered for lower tiers at GCSE. As a result, they were denied access to the knowledge required for success in higher tier exams and denied entry to those exams. This process will now be examined in more detail.

Classroom knowledge

In a study of a London comprehensive, Nell Keddie (1973) explored the meanings behind 'what counts as knowledge

activity9 setting

Item A Tony Blair

Tony Blair visits the Ridings School in Halifax

Different children move at different speeds and have differing abilities. The modernisation of the comprehensive principle requires that all pupils are encouraged to progress as far and as fast as they are able. Grouping children according to ability is an important way of making that happen.

Tony Blair quoted in Chitty, 2002

Item B Tiered exams

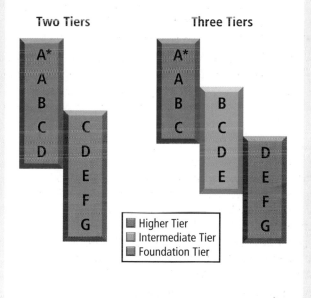

Adapted from Gillborn & Youdell, 2001

Item C Teachers' comments

Teacher A: You don't find any behaviour problems with the top set – they've got the intelligence.

Teacher B: When you get your next year's timetable and you see that it is a top or bottom set then you get certain images. If you get a top set you tend to think that their behaviour will be better. You tend to think with a bottom set you will get more discipline problems. I look forward to teaching my top-set third year but dread my bottom-set third year. With the bottom group I go in with a stony face but I know that with the top set if I say fun's over they will stop. But if I give a bottom set rope they'll take advantage of you.

Adapted from Abraham, 1995

questions

1 Write a letter of no more than 100 words to Tony Blair about his views in Item A.

2 Using the information in Item B, state why setting for examinations can make a real difference to pupils' attainment.

3 How might the teachers' views in Item C affect pupils' attainment?

---

to be made available and evaluated in the classroom'. She found that teachers graded knowledge. Knowledge was regarded as significant and important if it was appropriate for a particular course. And, the higher the level of course, the higher the grade of knowledge seen to be required.

In practice, teachers tended to see abstract knowledge as superior to specific pieces of concrete information. And teachers regarded the knowledge they presented as superior to the pupils' own knowledge drawn from their experience.

The level of classroom knowledge made available to pupils depended on the teachers' perception of the pupils' ability. High-grade knowledge was presented to supposedly high-ability pupils who were placed in top sets. Even when pupils were supposed to be taught the same material, teachers still filtered the information they presented in terms of their views of pupils' ability. The result was that high-grade knowledge was often withheld from supposedly low-ability pupils.

The social construction of ability

In a study of two London secondary schools, David Gillborn and Deborah Youdell (2001) explored the meanings given to the idea of 'ability'. They argue that ability is socially constructed. Teachers operate in terms of a taken-for-granted view of ability which is socially constructed during routine interactions in schools. In terms of this view, ability has the following characteristics.

- It is relatively fixed. Ability doesn't change or develop to any great extent.
- It is assumed that ability can be measured. For example, in some secondary schools, pupils are given a 'cognitive ability' test in year 7. This cognitive or 'thinking' test is seen as an effective measure of ability.
- Ability is seen as an indicator of academic potential. For example, a year 7 cognitive ability test is seen as a good predictor of year 11 GCSE results.

On the basis of this view of ability, teachers place students into sets, provide them with different levels of classroom knowledge, and enter them for different tiers in GCSE exams.

The problem of 'ability' Gillborn and Youdell argue that ability is a 'highly dangerous concept' that 'draws on common-sense prejudices and misconceptions'. They make the following points.

- Ability is *not* fixed.
- Ability is learned. Those who obtain high ability scores have learned the skills to do well in tests.
- Ability scores are not necessarily an indicator of future academic performance. To say a pupil is 'more' or 'less' able refers to their past performance.

In terms of this view, the concept of ability used by teachers closes down opportunities for many students. It leads teachers to separate the 'more' from the 'less' able, and provide each with the 'appropriate' classroom knowledge.

To make matters worse, some teachers see ability as unevenly distributed between social groups. Certain class groups and certain ethnic groups are seen as less able than others – in particular, the working class and African Caribbeans. In Gillborn and Youdell's words, the concept of ability 'acts to legitimate the systematic failing of Black and working-class young people'.

summary

1. Systems theories tend to focus on society as a whole. By comparison, interpretivist and interactionist theories tend to focus on small-scale interaction situations.

2. Concepts such as labelling, negotiation and the self-fulfilling prophecy have provided valuable insights into classroom interaction.

3. The way teachers define, classify and evaluate pupils can affect pupils' behaviour and teacher-pupil relationships.

4. Pupil subcultures can reflect:
   - Neighbourhood subcultures
   - Ability groupings within the school
   - A combination of both.

5. There are two main types of teaching groups - ability groups and mixed-ability groups.

6. Research indicates that in general ability groups, eg sets or streams, compared with mixed-ability groups have no significant effect on overall attainment.

7. However, there is some evidence that higher ability groups increase attainment levels and lower ability groups decrease attainment levels.

8. The pressure in schools to improve exam results has led to an increase in setting.

9. Setting for exams can have a real effect on attainment - for example, placing students in sets for GCSE foundation tiers denies them any opportunity of achieving the higher grades.

10. Classroom knowledge is socially constructed and evaluated by teachers. High-grade knowledge is presented to supposedly high-ability pupils and often withheld from those seen as less able.

11. The idea of ability is socially constructed by teachers. It is seen as:
    - Fixed
    - Something that can be measured
    - A good predictor of academic progress.

12. Gillborn and Youdell see this view of ability as a 'highly dangerous concept'. It can close off opportunities for those defined as 'less able'.

Unit 3 Social class and educational attainment

keyissues

1 What are the differences in educational attainment between social class groups?

2 What explanations are given for these differences?

3.1 Class and attainment – the evidence

In Western industrial societies there is general agreement that education should be based on equality of opportunity. Everybody should have an equal chance to develop their talents and abilities to the full, regardless of their class, ethnicity, gender and other social characteristics. However, the evidence shows clearly that in terms of educational qualifications people with certain social characteristics are likely to do better than others.

Class, ethnicity and gender make a significant difference to educational attainment.

- **Class** is most important. Its effect on educational attainment is nearly three times greater than ethnicity.

- **Ethnicity** comes next. It has about twice the effect of gender.

- **Gender** Despite capturing public attention in recent years, gender is least important. Class has over five times the effect on educational attainment (Gillborn & Mirza, 2000).

This unit looks at class differences in educational attainment. The next two units look at ethnic and gender differences.

In general, the higher a person's social class of origin – the class they were born into – the higher their educational qualifications. This has been shown time and time again over the past 50 years by sociological research and government statistics. Activity 10 looks at some of this evidence.

activity10 educational attainment and social class

Item A GCSE and social class, 2002

Pupils achieving five or more GCSE grades A* to C

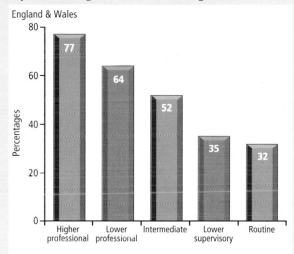

Adapted from *Youth Cohort Study*, 2002 (National Statistics Online, 20.02.03)

Item B GCSE and social class, 1989 and 2000

Pupils achieving five or more GCSE grades A* to C

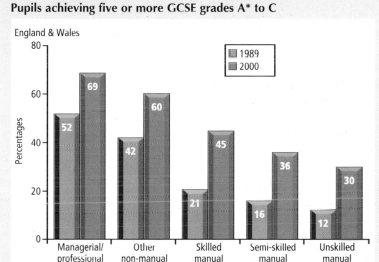

Adapted from *Social Trends*, 2001

Item C Higher education and social class

Great Britain	Participation rates in higher education										Percentages
Social class	1991	1992	1993	1994	1995	1996	1997	1998	1999	2000	Gain 1991-2000
Professional	55	71	73	78	79	82	79	82	73	76	+21
Intermediate	36	39	42	45	45	47	48	45	45	48	+12
Skilled non-manual	22	27	29	31	31	32	31	29	30	33	+11
Skilled manual	11	15	17	18	18	18	19	18	18	19	+8
Partly skilled	12	14	16	17	17	17	18	17	17	19	+7
Unskilled	6	9	11	11	12	13	14	13	13	14	+8
All social classes	23	28	30	32	32	33	33	31	32	33	+10

Adapted from *Age Participation Index*, Department of Education and Skills, 2003

The table shows the percentage of people under 21 from each social class who enter undergraduate courses in higher education. The figures on the right show the increase in percentage points for each class from 1991 to 2000.

questions

1 What does Item A suggest about the relationship between social class and educational attainment?

2 No matter what definition of social class is used, there are significant class differences in educational attainment. Comment on this statement using Items A and B which use different definitions of class.

3 What changes does Item B indicate between 1989 and 2000?

4 Summarise the trends shown in Item C.

Primary and secondary education The evidence clearly supports the view that children from working-class backgrounds underachieve compared with their middle-class peers. Jefferis et al. (2002) studied 11,000 children born in 1958 and found that those who experienced childhood poverty had significantly fallen behind children from middle-class backgrounds in terms of mathematics and reading by the age of 7. The research also found that the gap in educational attainment between children of higher and lower social classes widened as time went on.

The National Children's Bureau (2003) reported that students from families living on state benefits were two-thirds less likely to get at least five A*-C GCSE grades than those from well-off backgrounds. The 2003 GCSE results revealed that only 18% of White boys and 25% of White girls from low-income backgrounds achieved five or more A*-C grades compared with national averages of 50% and 61% respectively.

Further and higher education Research shows that the higher a student's class background, the more likely they are to stay on into further education, and the more likely they are to take A levels. For example, in 2000, 82% of the children of professionals and managers were in further education compared with 60% of the children of semi-skilled and unskilled manual workers (Payne, 2001).

Young people from manual working-class backgrounds are under-represented in higher education in Britain. Although their participation rate increased from 11% in 1991/92 to 19% in 2001/02, it remains well below that of the non-manual middle classes whose participation rate increased from 35% to 50% over the same period (*Social Trends*, 2004). The gap between the classes has widened from 24 percentage points in 1991/92 to 31 percentage points in 2001/02. And the more prestigious the university, the greater the proportion of students from higher social class backgrounds. For example, in 1998, 79% of students attending Oxford and Cambridge universities were from professional and managerial backgrounds compared with 70% at the London School of Economics and 70% at Durham and Nottingham universities. In contrast, only 35% of students at the new universities of Wolverhampton and Central Lancashire (both formerly polytechnics) were from professional and managerial backgrounds (Connor & Dewson, 2001).

This section has looked at some of the evidence for class differences in educational attainment. The following sections examine explanations for these differences.

3.2 Intelligence and educational attainment

Those who do well in education tend to do well in intelligence tests – they have a high IQ (intelligence quotient). This has led many people to argue that intelligence is a major factor in determining educational attainment.

Heredity There is a general agreement that intelligence results from the interaction of genetic and environmental factors. A person's intelligence is due in part to the genes they inherit from their parents, in part to their social environment. Some researchers, such as the psychologist Hans Eysenck (1971), argue that the genetic component (heredity) is the most important. In Eysenck's words, 'What children take out of schools is proportional to what they bring into the schools in terms of IQ'. From this viewpoint it has been argued that class differences in educational attainment largely result from class differences in genetically based IQ.

Few if any sociologists would go this far. However, the British sociologist Peter Saunders (1996) gives more credit to heredity than most. He argues that, to a large extent, Britain is a meritocratic society with equal opportunity for all. Saunders accepts that environmental factors such as parental encouragement at school do make a difference. But, at the end of the day, 'what matters most is whether you are bright and whether you work hard'. And whether you are bright depends in large part on your genetic inheritance. Saunders supports his argument with an analysis of children's IQ data, their educational performance and their job status as adults. He concludes the IQ has far more effect on a person's educational and occupational success than their class background.

Environment While not denying the importance of heredity, most sociologists have emphasised environmental factors in explaining IQ differences. A person's score on an IQ test is seen to result mainly from their motivation, knowledge and skills, all of which are learned rather than genetically determined. Motivation, knowledge and skills may vary between social classes. If this is the case then class differences in educational attainment may be due to differences in class backgrounds rather than class genes.

If there are cultural differences between social classes then this might explain why those in higher social classes tend to score more highly in IQ tests. The tests may be biased in their favour. For example, the language used in IQ tests may be closer to middle rather than working-class speech.

Many researchers have argued that this is indeed the case. Given this argument, comparisons of social groups in terms of IQ are invalid. And it is not therefore possible to explain class differences in educational attainment in terms of 'intelligence'.

Cause or consequence? How can the link between IQ and educational attainment be explained? One explanation states that both IQ tests and education are biased in favour of the middle and upper classes, hence members of those classes will tend to do well in both. Intelligence, as such, is not the cause of educational success.

Another argument states that both qualifications and IQ are directly related to length of stay in the educational system. The longer people stay, the more qualifications they get and the more their IQ develops. And middle-class students are more likely to stay longer in education than working-class students.

Conclusion Most researchers would argue the following. IQ is a result of the interaction of heredity and environment. It is not possible to measure the contribution of each to a person's IQ. It is not possible to produce a 'fair', culture-free IQ test so we cannot compare the IQs of people from different social groups. If it were possible we would probably find that individuals would differ in intelligence but large social groups such as classes, ethnic and gender groups would not. The same range of intelligence would be present in each group. Given this, differences in educational attainment between social groups must be due to factors other than intelligence.

activity11 intelligence tests

- Underline the odd one out:

  House   Igloo   Bungalow   Office   Hut

- Underline which of these is not a famous composer:

  ZOTRAM   SATSURS   REVID   MALESO

- Insert the word missing from the brackets:

  Fee (Tip) End
  Dance (....) Sphere

- Underline the odd one out:

- Draw the next one in the sequence:

  1   3   6   10

questions

1 Answer the test questions.
2 Why might some or all of these questions be biased in favour of middle-class children?

3.3 Material factors

Children raised in poverty have the lowest levels of educational attainment. This is evident even before they start primary school, judging from the results of tests of educational development (Flaherty et al., 2004). And the attainment gap between the poor and the rest of the population widens steadily throughout the years of compulsory education. Fewer young people raised in poverty go on to further education and even fewer to higher education.

Material deprivation During the 1960s, sociologists claimed that the low attainment of many low-income, working-class pupils resulted from a lack of something. They were *deprived*. This deprivation was *material* – a lack of money and the things that money could buy – and *cultural* – an absence of the attitudes and skills that were needed for educational success. This section looks at the impact of material or economic factors on educational attainment.

In general, the higher a child's class of origin, the higher their family income. High income can provide many educational advantages – a comfortable well-heated home, spacious rooms with a desk to work at, a home computer with internet access, reference and revision books, private tuition and the option of private education.

At the other end of the scale, children in poverty often live in cramped, cold and draughty conditions. Shortage of money means they are more likely to have part-time jobs in the evenings and at weekends, and to leave school at the minimum leaving age. Poverty often leads to ill health. And this can result in absence from school, tiredness and irritability.

The costs of education Traditionally, many working-class students left school at the minimum leaving age because their parents could no longer afford to support them. However, since the introduction of the GCSE examination in 1988, a far higher proportion of 16-19 year olds have continued into further education.

More recently, the introduction of tuition fees and the abolition of student grants has meant that many young people with working-class backgrounds feel they cannot afford to go on to higher education. As Item C in Activity 10 shows, it is those at the top of the class system who have benefited most from the expansion of university places. Even though grants are available for students from low-income families, many are still put off by the costs of higher education (Machin, 2003). They are fearful of getting into serious debt and of putting financial pressure on their parents (Connor & Dewson, 2001).

Buying success Money can buy educational advantage. A study of 3000 students aged 11, 16 and 18 conducted at London University found that 27% had a private tutor. Estimates by agencies who supply tutors suggest that around 65% of students have had a private tutor at some time during their school career (Harris, 2004). Affording private tuition is beyond the means of many working-class families.

It is not unusual for middle-class parents to move house in order to get their children into the school of their choice. A study of two areas in Coventry found that house prices within the catchment areas of two popular comprehensives were between 15% and 19% higher than similar homes just outside these areas. Parents were prepared to pay this premium for schools with a good reputation and successful exam results. And the rise in house prices meant that many working-class parents could not afford houses in these areas.

3.4 Cultural factors

Class differences in educational attainment have often been seen as a result of differences in class cultures. For example, a number of studies have argued that the values, attitudes and aspirations of parents have an important effect on their young people's education. If these values and attitudes vary between social classes then this may account, at least in part, for class differences in educational attainment.

Parental interest

Many sociologists in the 1960s saw differences in primary socialisation as the main reason for class differences in attainment. In a large-scale study of British children entitled *The Home and the School*, J.W.B. Douglas (1964) claimed that middle-class children received more attention and encouragement from their parents during their early years. This provided a foundation for high attainment in their later years.

Douglas found that the degree of parents' interest in their children's education was the single most important factor affecting educational progress. His research suggested that in general middle-class parents showed more interest than working-class parents. They were more likely to visit the school and to encourage their children to continue education beyond the minimum school leaving age.

Evaluation Douglas measured parental interest in terms of how often parents visited the school and how teachers viewed the parents. There are problems with this. Teachers will probably assess parental interest in terms of number of visits. For example, Douglas found the most striking difference was between fathers. Working-class fathers seldom visited school to discuss their children's progress. However, this may have more to do with working practices than interest. Manual workers are more likely to work longer hours, shifts, and to have more difficulty taking time off work. Also they are less likely to feel at ease in a middle-class institution such as a school. Factors such as these, rather than lack of interest, may explain infrequent school visits.

Recent research More recent research provides some support for Douglas's claim that parental interest is the key factor explaining class differences in educational attainment. Leon Feinstein (2003) examined data from two large-scale longitudinal studies – the National Child Development Study and the British Cohort Study. He

activity12 material deprivation

Item A Growing up poor

question

How might growing up in poverty disadvantage children at school?

Item B Homelessness

A report on the effects of homelessness on schoolchildren by Her Majesty's Inspectorate for Schools makes the following points.

Their chances of doing well are slim. 'Sustainable achievement is often beyond their reach.' Cramped sleeping conditions leave the children tired, listless and unable to concentrate. In one London school, a four-year-old boy spent a whole day sleeping outside the headteacher's office.

The inspectors found evidence of ill health caused by poor diet, and stress from permanent insecurity. For some, the crises which led to homelessness produce social and emotional difficulties.

Weak reading, writing and verbal skills among primary school children are combined with a poor self-image. 'I can't read,' a seven-year-old girl told her teacher. 'Don't you know I'm simple?'

The report notes that many hostel rooms lack such basics as chairs and table. As a result, children often find it hard to do homework. A fourth year GCSE pupil had to work on her bed and could only start when the sisters she shared the room with were asleep.

Adapted from *The Times Educational Supplement.* 10.8.90

claimed that the main factor accounting for class differences in attainment was the degree of parental interest in their children's education. However, as in Douglas's study, the degree of parental interest was assessed by teachers. And the same criticisms of this form of assessment apply – working-class parents may feel ill at ease in a middle-class institution such as a school and the demands of their jobs (long hours and shift work) may make school visits difficult.

Class subcultures

Differences in *social class subcultures* – the norms, attitudes and values typical of each class – were often seen as part of the explanation for class differences in attainment.

The British sociologist Barry Sugarman (1970) described working-class subculture as:

- *Fatalistic* – accepting the situation rather than working to improve it
- *Present-time orientated* – living for the moment rather than planning for the future
- Concerned with *immediate gratification* – taking pleasures now rather than making sacrifices for the future.

By comparison, middle-class subculture was seen as non-fatalistic, future-time orientated and concerned with deferred gratification.

These differences in class subcultures were seen to place pupils from working-class backgrounds at a disadvantage. For example, fatalism will not encourage pupils to improve their grades. And present-time orientation and immediate gratification will discourage sustained effort for examination success.

Evaluation The idea of distinctive class subcultures has been questioned. Critics point to a number of studies which suggest that if there are differences, they are slight. Sugarman's research was based on questionnaires given to 540 boys in a London secondary school. Responses to questionnaires may not reflect behaviour in everyday life.

A number of researchers argue that the main difference between the middle and working classes is not their culture but their situation. They share the same norms and values but respond to different situations. As Smithers (2003) notes, 'if you come from a low-income background, part of the script is to get out of the education system as quickly as possible to earn money'. And this response can be seen as realistic rather than fatalistic, as a necessity rather than immediate gratification.

Speech patterns and class

A number of researchers have claimed that there are class differences in speech patterns and these may partly account for class differences in educational attainment.

Restricted and elaborated codes The British sociologist Basil Bernstein identified two forms of speech pattern, the *restricted code* and the *elaborated code*. The restricted

code is a kind of shorthand speech, usually found in conversations between people who have a lot in common, eg friends and family members. It is often tied to a context, eg it cannot be fully understood outside the family circle, and its meanings tend to be particularistic, that is, specific to the speaker and listener. Sentences are often short, simple and unfinished, detail is omitted, explanations not given and information taken for granted. This is because a considerable amount of shared knowledge between speaker and listener is assumed.

By comparison, the elaborated code spells out what the restricted code takes for granted. Meanings are made explicit, explanations provided, details spelt out. As such, the elaborated code tends to be context-free (not tied to a context such as a particular friendship group) and its meanings are universalistic (they can be understood by everybody).

Class and speech codes According to Bernstein, most middle-class children have been socialised in both the restricted and elaborated codes and are fluent in each, whereas many working-class children are limited to the restricted code. Since teachers use the elaborated code, working-class pupils are placed at a distinct disadvantage. They are less likely to understand what teachers say and are more likely to be misunderstood and criticised for what they themselves say.

Bernstein insists that working-class speech patterns are not substandard or inadequate. However, they do place working-class pupils at a disadvantage since the elaborated code is the language of education.

Evaluation Bernstein's research shows how schools can contribute to class differences in educational attainment. Because schools demand the use of the elaborated code, middle-class pupils have a built-in advantage.

Some researchers have questioned Bernstein's view that members of the working-class are limited to the restricted code. He provides little hard evidence to support his view. And much of this evidence comes from interviews given by middle-class adults to five-year-old working-class boys. Such interviews may reveal little about the linguistic ability of young people – see Activity 13, Item B.

William Labov Some researchers have seen the speech patterns of those at the bottom of the class structure as inferior. For example, the American psychologist Carl Bereiter argued that the speech patterns of many low-income children are inadequate to meet the demands of the education system. As a result, they directly contribute to educational failure.

This view has been rejected by the American linguist William Labov (1973). He examined the speech patterns of low-income African-American children from Harlem in New York. Labov claimed that their speech patterns were not inferior to standard English, they were just different. Those who saw them as inferior simply failed to understand low-income Black dialect. Some of the evidence Labov used to support his views is given in Activity 13, Item B.

Questioning Bourdieu's theory So far, Sullivan's findings support Bourdieu's theory. But, her survey found that although social capital had an important effect on GCSE results, it 'leaves most of the social class differential in attainment unexplained'. This means that factors other than cultural capital cause most of the class differences in educational attainment. Sullivan suggests that these factors include 'material resources and educational aspirations'.

Class, mothers and cultural capital

In an important study entitled *Class Work: Mothers' involvement in their children's primary schooling*, Diane Reay (1998) states that, 'It is mothers who are making cultural capital work for their children'. Her research is based on interviews with the mothers of 33 children at two London primary schools.

All the mothers are actively involved in their children's education. The working-class mothers worked just as hard as the middle-class mothers. But it was not hard work that counted. Instead, it was the amount of cultural capital available. And the middle-class mothers had most.

Middle-class mothers had more educational qualifications and more information about how the educational system operated. They used this cultural capital to good effect – helping children with their homework, bolstering their confidence and sorting out problems with their teachers. Where the middle-class mothers had the confidence and self-assurance to make demands on teachers, the working-class mothers talked in terms of 'plucking up courage' and 'making myself go and see the teacher'. Where middle-class mothers knew what the school expected from their children and how to help them, working-class mothers felt they lacked the knowledge and ability to help their children.

Middle-class mothers not only have more cultural capital, they also have more material capital. Over half the middle-class mothers had cleaners, au pairs or both. This gave them more time to support their children. Working-class mothers could not afford help with domestic work. Nor could they afford private tuition which many middle-class mothers provided for their children.

According to Diane Reay, it is mothers who have the main influence on their children's education. Their effectiveness depends on the amount of cultural capital at their disposal. And this depends on their social class.

Social capital, class and choice

In recent years, government education policy has encouraged schools to compete, and offered parents and students choices between schools. Choosing the 'right' primary and secondary school is important. It can make a difference to students' examination results and their chances of climbing the educational ladder.

In *Class Strategies and the Education Market: The middle classes and social advantage*, Stephen J. Ball (2003) argues that government policies of choice and competition place

the middle class at an advantage. They have the knowledge and skills to make the most of the opportunities on offer. Compared to the working class, they have more material capital, more cultural capital and more *social capital* – access to social networks and contacts which can provide information and support. In Ball's words, middle-class parents have 'enough capitals in the right currency to ensure a high probability of success for their children'.

Strategies The aim of parents is to give their children maximum advantage in the education system. The choice of school is vital. And this is where middle-class parents come into their own. Compared to working-class parents, they are more comfortable, more at home in dealing with public institutions like schools. They are more used to extracting and assessing information. For example, they use their social networks to talk to parents whose children are attending the schools on offer. They collect and analyse information – for example, the GCSE results of the various schools. And they are more used to dealing with and negotiating with teachers and administrators. As a result, when entry into a popular school is limited, they are more likely to gain a place for their child.

The school/parent alliance Middle-class parents want middle-class schools. In general, schools with mainly middle-class pupils have the best results and the highest status. And these schools want middle-class pupils. They are seen as easy to teach and likely to perform well. They will maintain or increase the school's position in the exam league table and its status in the education market.

Conclusion Many middle-class parents work extremely hard to get their children into the most successful schools. But what they gain for their children can be at the expense of working-class children.

> ## key term
>
> **Social capital** The support and information provided by contacts and social networks which can be converted into material rewards.

3.7 Social class in schools

This section examines a number of studies which explain class differences in educational attainment in terms of the meanings and relationships which are socially constructed in classroom interaction. Many of these studies are based on interpretivist and interactionist approaches. These approaches were outlined in Unit 2.

Teachers' perceptions and social class

Pupils are constantly being assessed. On the basis of this assessment, they are defined as able or less able, placed in particular sets or streams, entered for particular examinations and given or denied access to certain parts of the school curriculum.

activity14 cultural and social capital

Item A Supporting your child

Liz, a middle-class mother, spells out how she supports her son at primary school.

'One is the support I give him at home, hearing him read, making him read every night, doing homework with him, trying to get the books he needs for his project. I see that as a support role. The other side, in the particular case of Martin, is where he has had difficulties and finds reading very, very difficult. So a lot of my time has been spent fighting for extra support for him and I mean fighting.'

Later in the interview, she discusses the tuition Martin receives.

'Well he just wasn't making enough progress in school so we decided we'd have to get him a tutor.'

Josie, a working-class mother talks about her son's reading difficulties.

'I have tried, I really have. I knew I should be playing a role in getting Leigh to read but I wasn't qualified. Therefore it put extra pressure on me because I was no good at reading myself, it was too important for me to handle and I'd get very upset and angry at Leigh.'

'I always found if I went to the class teacher, she'd take it very personal and think I was attacking her. I wasn't. I was just bringing it to her attention in case she didn't know, you know, that in my opinion he's not progressing.'

Adapted from Reay, 1998

Item B Choosing a school

Here are some comments from middle-class mothers about choosing schools for their children.

'You talk to other people who've got children there who come from Riverway, how are they coping. You spend a lot of time talking outside the school gates to people you know in the same situation, that's how you discover things really.'

(Mrs Grafton)

'We spoke to teachers in the schools, spoke to other parents, and spoke to my friends who are scattered across the borough and where their children went and what they thought about it.'

(Mrs Gosling)

'There was definitely a feeling that this step into secondary education would have a very, very big influence on what they do in the rest of their life. So you had to put a lot of your attention into each school and approach each school as if your child was definitely going to go there, and size it up, assess your own reactions to it and all the rest of it.'

(Mrs Cornwell)

Adapted from Ball, 2003

Item C The school/parent alliance

questions

1 Using Item A, suggest how cultural capital might give middle-class children an advantage.

2 Using Item B, suggest how social capital might give middle-class children an advantage.

3 How does the cartoon in Item C illustrate the school/parent alliance?

How do teachers assess pupils' ability? Assessments are based on exam results, on judgements of pupils' progress and potential, and perceptions of their conduct. In addition, there is evidence that assessments can be affected by pupils' social class.

Class and the 'ideal pupil' An early study looking at the influence of pupils' class on teachers' perceptions was conducted in the early 1950s by the American sociologist Howard Becker. He interviewed 60 teachers from Chicago high schools and found they tended to share an image of the 'ideal pupil'.

Teachers perceived middle-class pupils as closest to this

ideal, and pupils from the lower working class as furthest from it. Those in the lowest class grouping were seen as less able, lacking motivation and difficult to control. As a result, teachers felt the best they could do was 'just try to get some basic things over to them' (Becker, 1971).

Teachers were unaware that the social class background of pupils influenced their assessments. Nor did they realise that perceptions of class also influenced the level of work they felt appropriate for pupils.

Class in a nursery school An American study of children starting nursery school shows how early and how quickly the link between class and ability can be made. By the eighth day, children had been allocated to one of three tables depending on the teacher's perception of their ability. And this perception, unknown to the teacher, was based on the child's class background, with working-class children being placed on the 'lower-ability' table (Rist, 1970).

Class and 'ability' Research in Britain presents a similar picture. David Gillborn and Deborah Youdell (2001) conducted research in two London secondary schools from 1995 to 1997. They discovered that teachers had a 'common sense understanding of ability'. Using this as a yardstick, they allocated pupils to different examination sets.

Working-class pupils were more likely to be seen as disruptive, as lacking in motivation and lacking in parental support. As a result, they 'face a particular problem in convincing teachers that they have "ability" '. And because of this, they are more likely to be placed in lower level sets and entered for foundation tier examinations.

As a result of making a link between so-called 'ability' and social class, teachers systematically discriminated against working-class pupils (Gillborn & Youdell, 2001).

Class and teacher-pupil relationships Teachers' perceptions of students can have an important effect on day-to-day relationships. Generally, teachers prefer to teach pupils they see as able and highly motivated. They place these students in higher sets and respond more favourably towards them. As a result, teacher-pupil relationships tend to be positive.

Conversely, teachers' views of students who have been defined as less able and placed in lower sets tend to be less favourable. These students may respond with resentment and hostility. And this can result in discipline problems and negative relationships between teachers and pupils.

Labelling and the self-fulfilling prophecy

These ideas were introduced in Sections 2.2 and 2.3 (see pages 95-97). A label is a major identifying characteristic. If middle rather than working-class pupils are labelled 'able' and 'well behaved', this may well disadvantage working-class pupils. If a person is defined as 'less able' or 'badly behaved', others tend to respond to them and interpret their actions in terms of these labels.

There is a tendency for a self-fulfilling prophecy to develop. Pupils may see themselves in terms of the label

and act accordingly – so fulfilling the prophecy others have made about them.

The picture is more complicated than this outline suggests. David Hargreaves (1975) argues that whether or not a label 'sticks' – is accepted by the pupil – depends on a number of factors. These include: 1) how often the pupil is labelled 2) whether the pupil sees the teacher as someone whose opinion counts 3) the extent to which others support the label and 4) the context in which the labelling takes place, eg in public or private.

Research has also indicated that some types of label are more readily accepted than others. Bird (1980) found that pupils were more likely to accept 'academic labels' (referring to academic ability) than 'behavioural labels' (referring to conduct). She notes that consistent behavioural labelling is less likely in large secondary schools. In such schools a teacher may see up to three hundred pupils in one week and a pupil may be taught by up to fifteen teachers. The time for teachers to establish labels is limited as is the likelihood of them all applying the same labels. Different teachers have different interpretations of acceptable and unacceptable behaviour. Thus, a pupil who behaves consistently may be told off for misbehaving by one teacher but not another.

Evaluation It is difficult to assess the importance of labelling and the self-fulfilling prophecy. As noted in Section 2.3 (pages 96-97), attempts to replicate (repeat) Rosenthal and Jacobson's famous experiment on the self-fulfilling prophecy have produced mixed results. Some suggest that labelling is of little or no significance. Other researchers reject this view, arguing that labelling and the self-fulfilling prophecy help to explain class differences in educational attainment.

Setting and streaming and social class

Most secondary schools have some system for placing pupils in teaching groups in terms of their perceived ability. These groups include sets in which pupils are placed in subject groups (they may be in set 1 for maths, set 3 for art) or streams in which they are placed into class groups (class 1, 2, 3) and taught at that level for all subjects.

A number of studies (eg Hargreaves 1967, Lacey 1970) have looked at the effects of ability grouping in secondary schools. In general, they have found the following. There is a tendency for middle-class pupils to be placed in the higher groups and for working-class pupils to be placed in the lower groups. The 'ability gap' between these groups is likely to widen from year 7 to year 11. Most teachers prefer to teach higher ability groups. The conduct of pupils in higher groups is likely to be better than that of those in lower groups. Those in lower groups will tend to develop an *anti-school subculture* in which breaking school rules is highly regarded by some pupils. Teachers spend more time controlling behaviour in these groups at the expense of teaching. They expect less from these pupils, deny them access to higher level knowledge and skills and enter them for lower level examination tiers.

Evaluation To what extent does setting and streaming advantage the largely middle-class higher groups and disadvantage the largely working-class lower groups? The evidence is inconclusive – it is not possible to reach a firm conclusion. In general, research indicates that setting and streaming have little or no effect on pupils' overall achievement. However, there is some evidence that ability grouping may raise attainment in the top groups and lower it in the bottom groups (Ireson & Hallam, 2001).

Where ability groups do have a major effect is in setting for examination entry. As noted earlier, lower sets are denied entry into higher tier GCSEs. And the reason pupils are placed in lower sets may have as much, if not more, to do with their social class and perceived conduct as their actual ability (Gillborn & Youdell, 2001).

Pupil subcultures

A number of researchers argue that pupil subcultures often develop from grouping pupils into sets and streams (see pages 98-99). Defined in a similar way by teachers, they will tend to interact with members of their own group, and develop a group identity along with distinctive norms and values.

As noted earlier, Colin Lacey (1970) identified two distinctive subcultures (see pages 98-99).

- **The subculture of success** which developed in the largely middle-class top stream. The pupils worked hard, they were well behaved, and they were respected and praised by teachers
- **The subculture of failure** In the largely working-class lower stream, the pupils developed an anti-school subculture. Denied respect from teachers and defined as failures, these pupils turned the school values upside down. They gained prestige from their peer group by misbehaving – giving cheek to teachers, refusing to do homework and truanting. As a result, their school work steadily deteriorated.

Working-class subcultures

Máirtín Mac an Ghaill (1994) studied Year 11 students in the early 1990s, in Parnell School (not its real name), a comprehensive in the West Midlands. He identified three working-class male peer groups, each with a distinctive subculture.

Mac an Ghaill argues that to some extent these subcultures are shaped by:

- the way students are organised into sets
- the type of curriculum they follow
- the teacher-student social relations which result from the above.

Macho Lads The Macho Lads were relegated to the bottom two sets for all their subjects. They were academic failures and treated as such by their teachers. They rejected the school's values and the teachers' authority. Their concerns were acting tough, having a laugh, looking after their mates

and looking smart. The teachers viewed them with suspicion and policed their behaviour, banning certain clothes and hairstyles, and making constant demands – 'Sit up straight', 'Look at me when I'm talking to you' and 'Walk properly down the corridor'.

Academic Achievers Apart from the Macho Lads, Mac an Ghaill identified two other working-class pupil subcultures. The Academic Achievers saw hard work and educational qualifications as the route to success. They were in the top sets, and received preferential treatment in terms of timetabling, books and experienced teachers. The Academic Achievers tended to come from the upper levels of the working class.

New Enterprisers The New Enterprisers saw a different route to success. They focused on vocational subjects such as business studies and technology and looked forward to a future in high-skilled areas of the labour market.

Evaluation of pupil subcultures

The evidence presented so far suggests that the way teachers define pupils and allocate them to ability groups generates different pupil subcultures. In the case of the largely middle-class higher sets, the 'subculture of success' benefits their progress, as pupils reinforce each other's behaviour. In the case of the largely working-class lower sets, the anti-school subculture has a negative effect on educational progress. This argument provides a further explanation for class differences in educational attainment.

The summary in the previous paragraph contains broad generalisations. A study by Meyenn (1980) of girls' friendship groups warns against this. There were groups of girls who were quiet, well behaved, caused no trouble, said they were happy at school yet showed absolutely no interest in academic work and accepted their position in the lowest ability groups. On the other hand, some groups of girls who were much more successful academically were strongly opposed to certain school rules and enjoyed 'messing about' and 'causing trouble'. It appears that not all pupils follow the pattern described in the previous paragraph.

As discussed earlier, Paul Willis's study of the 'lads' questions whether pupil subcultures are generated within schools. For Willis, the lads' anti-school subculture is shaped mainly by their expectations about the jobs they hope to get and by the working-class subculture they bring with them to school (see pages 89-91 and 99).

Conclusion

This section has looked at class differences in educational attainment in terms of what happens within the school. Much of the research is based on interpretivist and interactionist approaches. It argues that class differences in attainment result from teachers' perceptions and expectations, their assessment of pupils, the allocation of pupils to ability groups and the pupil subcultures generated by this process. Class differences in attainment are seen to be socially constructed during classroom interaction.

Critics of this view argue that it largely ignores what happens outside the school. They claim that class differences in attainment are primarily due to the social inequalities generated by the class system. From this point of view, schools do little more than reflect and rubber stamp existing inequalities.

Other researchers see class differences in attainment resulting from a combination of what happens inside and outside the school. From this viewpoint, the inequalities of the class system are reinforced by interaction in the classroom.

summary

1. There are significant class differences in educational attainment. Despite an overall rise in attainment in recent years, class differences remain, and in some cases have increased.

2. The following explanations have been given to explain why pupils with working-class backgrounds are less successful.
   - Class differences in intelligence. Most sociologists reject this view.
   - Material deprivation - a lack of money and the things that money can buy.
   - A lack of encouragement, stimulation and interest from parents.
   - Working-class subculture with its emphasis on fatalism, present-time orientation and immediate gratification.
   - Cultural deprivation - an absence of the norms, values and skills needed for high attainment. This view has been strongly criticised.
   - The use of the elaborated code in schools which disadvantages many working-class pupils.

3. In the 1960s and 70s, programmes of compensatory education were developed to compensate for the supposed deficiencies of 'culturally deprived children'. Evaluations suggest that, in most cases, the benefits were at best short term.

4. More recent attempts at compensatory education, such as Education Action Zones, have so far produced disappointing results.

5. Many sociologists argue that reducing inequality of educational opportunity requires a reduction in social inequality. Recent Labour governments have focused on reducing poverty rather than redistributing income and wealth from the better to the worse off.

6. Pierre Bourdieu argues that the main function of the education system is social reproduction. Education discriminates against the working class because they lack the cultural capital to succeed.

7. Ann Sullivan tested Bourdieu's theory. Her results indicated that cultural capital explained a part of class differences in attainment, but left most of those differences unexplained.

8. According to Diane Reay, it is mothers who have the main influence on education. Their effectiveness depends on the amount of cultural capital at their disposal. Middle-class mothers have most.

9. Stephen Ball's research argues that social capital is vital when choosing schools. Middle-class mothers, with their wide social networks, have most.

10. Interpretivist and interactionist approaches argue that class differences in attainment result from teachers' perceptions, expectations and assessment of pupils. Middle-class pupils are seen as more likely to succeed.

11. Working-class pupils are more likely to be seen as less able and more disruptive. This may lead to a self-fulfilling prophecy.

12. Middle-class pupils are more likely to be placed in higher sets, working-class pupils in lower sets. In general, research indicates that ability groupings have little or no effect on pupils' overall achievement. However, they may raise attainment in the top groups and lower it in the bottom groups.

13. What does have an effect is the tendency to enter more working-class pupils for lower level exams, so denying them the opportunity to obtain the top grades.

14. Allocating pupils to ability groups may lead to the development of pupil subcultures. Those in the largely working-class lower sets may develop an anti-school culture. This may contribute to class differences in attainment.

15. Critics argue that focusing on classroom interaction largely ignores what happens outside the school. They claim that class differences in attainment are mainly due to the social inequalities generated by the class system.

activity 15 teachers and pupils

Item A The 'ideal' pupil

Teachers tend to use class differences in classifying their pupils and such differences lead to variations from the image of the 'ideal' pupil held by teachers. Children of the lowest group, from slum areas, are characterised as the most difficult to teach successfully, lacking interest in school, learning ability and outside training. They are seen as not having the right kind of study habits or being able to apply themselves as well as other pupils.

In definite contrast are the terms used to describe children of the upper groups: 'In a neighbourhood like this there's something about the children, you just feel you're accomplishing so much more. The children know what you're talking about and they think about it.'

In the lower-class school a major part of the teacher's time must be devoted to discipline. This emphasis on discipline detracts from the school's primary function of teaching, thus discriminating, in terms of available educational opportunity, against the children of these schools.

Adapted from Becker, 1971

Item B Class and ability

Teacher A: Some of the class have written to Oldham Town Council for material for the New Town project.

Teacher B: They're really bright, are they?

Teacher A: Mostly from middle-class families, well motivated.

Adapted from Keddie, 1973

A Head of Faculty in a secondary school explains the school's poor showing in the 'league tables'. 'We are weighted down the lower end, unfortunately, because we are a working-class school.'

Adapted from Gillborn & Youdell, 2001

Item C The Macho Lads

Darren: It's the teachers that make the rules. It's them that decide that it's either them or us. So you are often put into a situation with teachers where you have to defend yourself. Sometimes it's direct in the classroom. But it's mainly the headcases that would hit a teacher. Most of the time it's all the little things.

Interviewer: Like what?

Gilroy: Acting tough by truanting, coming late to lessons, not doing homework, acting cool by not answering teachers, pretending you didn't hear them; that gets them mad. Lots of different things.

Noel: Teachers are always suspicious of us (the Macho Lads). Just like the cops, trying to set you up.

Adapted from Mac an Ghaill, 1994

Messing around

questions

1   How might Item A help to explain class differences in educational attainment?

2   What does Item B suggest about teachers' perceptions of middle and working-class pupils?

3   a)   Suggest explanations for the attitudes and behaviour of the Macho Lads in Item C.

b)   How might their attitudes and behaviour affect their educational attainment?

Unit 4 Gender and educational attainment

keyissues

1 What are the gender differences in educational attainment?

2 What explanations are given for these differences?

In the 1960s and 70s, sociologists were concerned about the apparent underachievement of girls. Why weren't they more ambitious? Why did fewer girls than boys take high status subjects such as maths, physics and chemistry? Why were girls less likely to go to university?

By the 1990s, the concern had shifted to underachieving boys. The so-called *gender gap* in education now meant failing boys and successful girls. For Professor of Education, Ted Wragg, 'the underachievement of boys has become one of the biggest challenges facing society today'. For the former Chief Inspector of Schools, Chris Woodhead, underachieving boys are 'one of the most disturbing problems facing the education system'.

The impression sometimes given by the media is of boys failing in droves and of girls racing ahead. But is there really a gender crisis in education? Work carefully through Activity 16. It contains the kind of statistics on which claims of a gender crisis are often based. Then we'll look at various ways of interpreting this evidence.

Statistical evidence provides the following picture of gender differences in educational attainment. In England, from Key Stage 1 (5-7 years old) through to Key Stage 4 (14-16 years old), girls consistently score higher than boys, though the difference is much less marked in maths and science than in English. As girls and boys move through primary and secondary school, the attainment gap widens. And, over the past 10 years, the attainment gap between girls and boys at all Key Stages and at GCSE has widened.

The picture at A-level reflects these trends with women outperforming men and the attainment gap widening over recent years. The same applies to vocational qualifications.

The number of women in higher education has now overtaken men. In 2002, women and men were almost as likely to achieve a first class honours degree (9% of women compared to 10% of men). However, a greater proportion

activity16 gender and educational attainment

Item A GCSEs

Attainment of 5 or more GCSEs A*- C in Year 11

England and Wales   Percentages

Year	1989	1992	1994	1996	1998	2000	2002
Males	28	33	37	40	42	44	46
Females	31	40	46	49	51	54	56

Adapted from *Youth Cohort Study*, 2002

Item B A levels

Attainment at GCE A level or equivalent qualification

England and Wales   Percentages

	Males		Females	
	2 or more A levels	1 A level	2 or more A levels	1 A level
1995/96	27	7	33	9
1996/97	27	7	33	8
1997/98	30	6	37	7
1998/99	30	6	37	7
1999/2000	31	6	39	7
2000/01	33	4	42	5

Adapted from *Social Trends*, 2003

Item C Higher education

Students in higher education

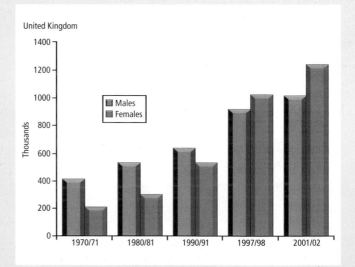

Adapted from various issues of *Social Trends*

question

Briefly summarise the trends shown in Items A, B and C.

of women achieved an upper second (49% compared to 40% of men). (National Statistics Online – Education, 8.1.2004).

4.1 Interpreting the statistics

The picture of failing boys and achieving girls is based on the kind of statistics presented in Activity 16. What's wrong with this picture?

Both girls and boys are doing better Over the past 50 years, the educational performance of boys and young men has steadily improved. The performance of girls has risen at a faster rate at some levels and in some subjects. However, this hardly justifies blanketing all boys as underachievers. Many boys are doing extremely well (Coffey, 2001).

Only some boys are failing Only certain groups of boys are underachieving. There is a close link between male underachievement and social class – compared to other groups, a high proportion of working-class boys are failing (Epstein et al., 1998).

What's new? In some respects, there's nothing new about girls outperforming boys. When the 11-plus exam was introduced in the 1940s, more girls passed than boys. The results were fiddled so that roughly equal numbers of boys and girls went to grammar schools. If the results hadn't been 'adjusted', then two-thirds of grammar school places would have gone to girls (Chitty, 2002).

Hiding girls' failure The preoccupation with so-called 'failing boys' diverts attention from underachieving girls. A high proportion of working-class girls are failing in the school system (Plummer, 2000).

What has changed? In general, the educational performance of girls has improved significantly since the 1980s. And, in general, their improvement has been greater than that of boys. But this does not mean that boys as a group are failing. As noted earlier, the educational performance of most boys is improving.

4.2 Explaining girls' improvement

Why are girls doing so well? Here are some of the explanations suggested by researchers.

Changing attitudes

Judging from a number of studies, girls and young women's attitudes towards education, work and marriage have changed in recent years. Sue Sharpe compared the attitudes of working-class girls in London schools in the early 1970s and 1990s (Sharpe, 1976 & 1994). She found that the 1990s girls were:

- more confident
- more assertive
- more ambitious
- more committed to gender equality.

The main priorities of the 70s girls were 'love, marriage, husbands and children'. By the 1990s, this had changed to 'job, career and being able to support themselves'. And education was seen as the main route to a good job and financial independence.

Changes in the adult world

Changes in the world of work, in the home and in adult relationships may have changed attitudes.

- There has been a steady rise in the numbers of women in the labour force. By 2002, the number of men and women in paid employment was virtually the same (*Social Trends,* 2003). Working mothers provided role models for their daughters. As a result, girls were more likely to see their future in the workplace and to value education as a means to a good job.
- According to Sue Sharpe (1994), girls were increasingly wary of marriage. They had seen adult relationships breaking up all around them. And they had seen women coping alone in what was once a 'man's world'. Girls were now concerned with standing on their own two feet rather than being dependent on a man. As a result, they were more likely to see education as a means to financial independence.

Changes in schools

The abolition of the 11-plus exam and the introduction of comprehensive schools by most local education authorities has removed some of the barriers to girls' achievement. No longer are girls artificially 'failed' in order to get equal numbers of boys and girls into grammar schools.

There has been a growing awareness of gender bias in schools and attempts to remove it. For example, there was a recognition that girls were put off by what were traditionally seen as 'boys' subjects' such as maths, technology, physics and chemistry. This led to the introduction of equal opportunity initiatives such as Girls into Science and Technology.

In 1988, the National Curriculum provided a compulsory core curriculum for all students up to the age of 16 – no matter what their gender. Although the compulsory core has now been slimmed down, all students still have to take English, maths and science.

4.3 Why are some boys failing?

As noted earlier, most boys and young men are improving their performance in primary, secondary, further and higher education. However, their levels of attainment are rising more slowly than those of girls. And some boys are doing badly – in particular some working-class boys.

Working-class boys have always had problems with the educational system for the reasons outlined in Unit 3. Some researchers believe that these problems have grown in recent years for the following reasons.

Changes in the job market

Manual jobs With the decline in manufacturing and the

activity 17 changing girls

Item A *Girl power*

Item B *Changing times*

Celebrating straight As at A level at Colchester County High School for Girls.

Twenty years ago you watched bright girls leave before A levels, planning only a stop-gap job between marriage and motherhood. Between the extremes of university and supermarket checkout stretched an endless wasteland of dreary typing jobs with criminal rates of pay. If you were one of the tiny minority hoping for university, you worked hard; if not, why bother?

Item C *Changing drinks*

Early 1970s

Early 1990s

But now that middle ground has been filled with a shimmering improvement of choices – service industries, media jobs and information technology, providing a sexless workplace paradise with no barriers and no preference for men. Whether they get the message from the Spice Girls, Madonna, or their savvy mothers, girls now know that independence means power, and both start with a decent job. This translates into an ambition to get on, and never be financially dependent on a man if you can help it. About time too.

Adapted from White, 1998

question

How might Items A, B and C help to explain girls' rising educational attainment?

increasing automation of production, there has been a rapid reduction in semi-skilled and unskilled jobs. The shrinking of this section of the job market has hit working-class males hard. In 2002, the highest unemployment rate – at 10% – was for men in semi-skilled and unskilled occupations which do not usually require formal qualifications (*Social Trends*, 2003).

Manual 'macho' jobs fitted traditional working-class masculine identities. The collapse of this sector of the job market has left these identities uncertain, threatened and confused (Jackson, 1998).

Service sector jobs The new jobs in the service sector tend to be desk jobs in offices and call centres, or jobs involving care for others which require sensitivity and interpersonal skills. These jobs do not sit happily with traditional working-class masculine identities. And even the more 'macho' jobs in the public services – eg, police, fire service and paramedics – now require higher levels of sensitivity and social skills (Mahony, 1998).

Changes in male roles

Traditionally the working man was a father, husband and breadwinner. With increasing numbers of lone-parent families, over 90% of which are headed by women, these roles are closed to many men. And boys growing up in these families lack the role models of father, husband and breadwinner.

Lone-parent, mother-headed families are concentrated in the lower working class. Growing up in such families can threaten traditional working-class masculine identities (Jackson, 1998).

A crisis in identity In recent years, working-class boys have become increasingly vulnerable and insecure. They have seen jobless men in the neighbourhood, dependent on welfare with little hope for the future. They have seen traditional working-class jobs drying up. They have seen more and more men fail as breadwinners and fathers.

According to some sociologists, the result is a 'crisis' in working-class masculinity. How do boys deal with this crisis at school?

School and male underachievement

According to Mac an Ghaill (1994), some working-class boys attempt to deal with the 'crisis in masculinity' by adopting an aggressive, macho 'laddishness'. There is nothing new about this – it reflects behaviour described by Willis (1977) over 15 years earlier. However, it many have become more common in recent years. The Macho Lads in Mac an Ghaill's study defined schoolwork as 'sissy' work. As one boy put it, 'The work you do here is girls' work. It's not real work'. In other words, it's not the kind of work that 'real' men do. Those who work hard are put down as 'swots' and 'keenos'.

In the late 1990s, Frosh, Phoenix and Pattman (2002) conducted group interviews with 11-14 year-old boys in 12 London schools on the subject of 'growing up as a man'.

They found that few boys managed to be both popular and academically successful. Boys who identified with the academic values of the school were sometimes subjected to homophobic abuse. They were labelled as 'gay' because conscientiousness and commitment to schoolwork were interpreted by male peer group culture as 'feminine'.

This 'macho' maleness can result in the anti-school subculture described in previous units (see pages 98-99 and 115). Rejecting the values of the school, some boys look for acceptance, recognition and respect by acting out the norms and values of the anti-school subculture. Reinforced by their peers, they make a considerable contribution to their own educational failure.

Why do many boys see academic work as 'feminine'? One suggestion is that educational development in the early years is largely the responsibility of mothers. And it's mothers who usually help with homework. A survey of 17,000 children born in 1958 suggests that educational performance improves when fathers are involved in the child's early development and help with homework (Buchanan, 2001). However, according to the British Market Research Bureau (2002), only 12% of fathers provide this kind of educational support.

Key Stage tests and GCSE results indicate that the gender gap in attainment widens throughout secondary education – from years 7 to 11. These are the years when boys are particularly concerned about establishing a male identity. And this can involve a rejection of behaviour and attitudes seen as 'feminine'.

summary

1. The educational performance of females has improved significantly since the 1980s. They have overtaken males at every level from primary to higher education.

2. Overall, the performance of males has also improved, but at a slower rate.

3. The following reasons have been suggested for the improvement in female performance:
   - Changing attitudes, eg more ambitious
   - Changes in the adult world, eg growing numbers of women in the labour force
   - Changes in schools, eg reduction in gender bias.

4. In recent years, the attainment levels of some working-class boys have been particularly low. Suggested reasons for this include:
   - Changes in the job market, eg rapid reduction in semi-skilled and unskilled jobs
   - Changes in male roles, eg growing number of female-headed, lone-parent families
   - An adoption of aggressive masculinity along with an increasing rejection of the school and its values and a definition of academic work as 'feminine'.

Conclusion

Gender differences in educational attainment must be put into perspective.

- First, as noted earlier, class has over five times the effect on educational attainment compared to gender, and ethnicity has about twice the effect (Gillborn & Mirza, 2000). In terms of those comparisons, the effect of gender is relatively small.

- Second, male underachievement has often been exaggerated. As Activity 16 shows, male educational performance has improved – at GCSE, A level and in higher education. The difference is that female educational performance has improved more rapidly. However, there is evidence that significant numbers of working-class pupils, particularly males, are not part of this overall improvement.

activity 18 a changing world

Item A The decline of manufacturing

Derelict engineering works, Willenhall, West Midlands

Item B Aggressive masculinity

For many working-class boys, the traditional route to status, pride and security is closed. What some boys are left with is a bitter sense that trying to get work is pointless, and an aggressive culture of masculinity to fill in the despairing gaps.

Adapted from Jackson, 1998

Item C New opportunities

Working in a call centre

If the sort of work available to young working-class people is largely in the service industries, they will need qualities such as warmth, empathy, sensitivity to unspoken needs, and high levels of interpersonal skills to build an effective relationship with customers.

Adapted from Mahony, 1998

question

Use Items A to C to provide an explanation for the educational failure of some working-class boys.

Unit 5 *Ethnicity and educational attainment*

key issues

1 How does ethnicity affect educational attainment?

2 What explanations have been given for ethnic differences in attainment?

In 2000, the Office for Standards in Education (OFSTED) published a report entitled *Educational Inequality*. Based in part on information from 118 local education authorities, the report showed that:

- All groups – Whites and ethnic minorities – have improved their educational attainment.

- There are significant differences in the attainment of

ethnic groups (Gillborn & Mirza, 2000).

The following section looks at some of the evidence on which these statements are based.

5.1 Ethnicity and attainment – evidence

Activity 19 looks at ethnicity and educational attainment at GCSE level.

activity 19 ethnicity and attainment

Attainment of 5 or more GCSEs A*- C in Year 11
England and Wales (percentages)

Ethnic group	1988	1995	1997	2000	2002	Improvement (1988-2002)
White	26	42	44	50	52	+26
Black	17	21	28	39	36	+19
Indian	23	44	49	60	60	+37
Pakistani	20	22	28	29	40	+20
Bangladeshi	13	23	32	29	41	+28

Note: Black includes people of African-Caribbean and Black African origin.

Adapted from various *Youth Cohort Studies*

question

Summarise the relationship between ethnicity and educational attainment indicated by the table.

Change over time Activity 19 presents a snapshot of educational attainment at Year 11. It tells us nothing about educational attainment before or after Year 11. It is important to recognise this. For example, the attainment of Pakistani and Bangladeshi pupils is low in the early years of schooling but shows significant improvement once their English improves in secondary school. By comparison, African-Caribbean students make a good start in primary school but their performance shows a marked decline as they move through secondary school (Gillborn & Mirza, 2000).

Gains and losses The table in Activity 19 indicates that, in general, all groups have improved their performance since the introduction of GCSEs. Some have made greater gains than others – for example, the Indian group with an increase of 37 percentage points. However, the Black group have caused concern with a decline in their performance between 2000 and 2002.

Ethnicity, gender and class Just how much are the differences in attainment at GCSE due to ethnicity? We already know that social class and gender affect attainment. Before going further, it is important to look at their effects in order to assess the effect of ethnicity.

Work through Activity 20 now in order to assess the effect of gender.

activity 20 ethnicity, gender and attainment at GCSE

Attainment of 5 or more GCSEs A*- C in Year 11, 2001

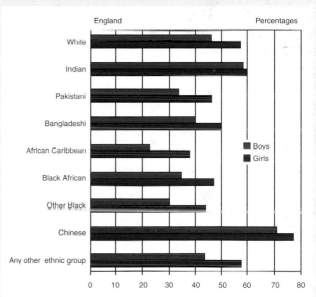

Adapted from National Statistics Online - Education, 8.1.2004

question

What relationships between ethnicity, gender and educational attainment are indicated by the bar chart?

The bar chart in Activity 20 shows that in each of the ethnic groups, girls do better than boys. Clearly, there is a gender gap in attainment. But, even taking this into account, there are still important ethnic differences. For example, Chinese girls do better than Chinese boys, but they also do better than girls from other ethnic groups.

Now work through Activity 21 in order to assess the effect of class.

School effectiveness

Some schools are better than others when it comes to exam results. In *The School Effect*, David Smith and Sally Tomlinson (1989) followed the progress of over 2400 pupils from the age of 11 to 16 in 18 multi-ethnic comprehensives. They found that different schools achieved very different results with children of similar background and ability. According to the authors, 'what school a child goes to makes far more difference than which ethnic group he or she belongs to'.

Evaluation Reviewing *The School Effect*, David Gillborn and David Drew (1992) state that, 'Crucially the work reminds us that individual schools possess the power to influence the educational experiences, achievements and future life chances of their pupils'.

But they see two major problems. The first concerns methodology – in particular, the size and nature of the sample. For example, there were only 146 African-Caribbean pupils at age 16, too small a number on which to base conclusions. A second concern is Smith and Tomlinson's view that racism was not a significant factor in the education of ethnic minorities. The results of their questionnaire given to parents and teachers suggested that racism was not a problem in school. But there is a growing body of research which suggests that racism is widespread in many schools. And it may well have a significant effect on educational attainment.

Racism in schools

Racism refers to *prejudice* and *discrimination* against groups seen as racially different. Prejudice means members of those groups are prejudged in terms of negative stereotypes – sweeping generalisations are made about all members of the group – for example, they are aggressive, lazy and so on. Discrimination means acting against people simply because they are seen to be members of a particular group – for example, not giving them a job because of their group membership.

People may be completely unaware that they are discriminating against others. And they are often shocked when this is revealed to them.

Discrimination and setting Jayleigh – not its real name – is a comprehensive school. In 1988, 41% of its pupils were of Asian origin.

At Jayleigh a greater proportion of White pupils (77%) were entered for GCSEs than Asian pupils (70%). In addition, White pupils were entered for more GCSEs (an average of 6.2) than Asian pupils (5.8). Whether or not pupils could take GCSEs depended largely on teachers' assessment of their attainment and potential.

Pupils at Jayleigh were set in terms of ability. Asian pupils were more likely to be placed in lower sets even when they had the same assessment from the same primary school as White pupils. And to get in the top sets, Asians generally needed higher marks than Whites. Pupils tended to remain in the same sets throughout secondary school.

And set placement largely determined GCSE entry. As a result, fewer Asians were entered for GCSEs, and those that were entered took fewer GCSEs.

This study by the Commission for Racial Equality (1992) concluded that, 'Here was a school which, however unintentionally, was using a setting system that appears to have set up barriers to a significant number of Asian pupils, and, in some instances, might have discriminated against them unlawfully'.

It is impossible to estimate the extent of the 'Jayleigh situation'. However, similar examples of systematic discrimination on ethnic grounds have been found in other schools. This can be seen from Activity 22 which looks at setting in a Midlands comprehensive school. It refers to CSEs and O levels which have been replaced by GCSEs. CSE is a lower level examination. A CSE grade 1 is equivalent to an O level grade C.

Classroom interaction

Primary schools The evidence examined so far suggests that ethnic minority students experience discrimination during their school careers. Studies of classroom interaction support this. Cecile Wright's research, conducted in 1988/89, was based on classroom observation in four inner-city primary schools (Wright, 1992). It found that teachers perceived and treated ethnic minority children differently from White children.

Asian children, especially the younger ones, were often seen as a problem, but as a problem that could be largely ignored. They received least attention, were often excluded from classroom discussions and rarely asked to answer questions. Teachers tended to assume that their command of English was insufficient for full classroom participation. Yet they also saw Asian pupils as well disciplined and highly motivated.

African-Caribbean children – especially boys – were expected to behave badly. They received considerable attention – nearly all of it negative. Their behaviour was usually seen as aggressive, disobedient and disruptive. They were often singled out for criticism, even for actions which were ignored in other pupils. As a result, they often felt picked on and treated unfairly.

Secondary schools Research by David Gillborn (1990) largely reflects Wright's findings. He spent two years studying an inner-city comprehensive school gathering data from classroom observation and interviews with teachers and students. He found that the vast majority of teachers tried to treat all students fairly. However, they perceived students differently and on this basis treated them differently. In particular, they often saw the actions of African-Caribbean students as a threat where no threat was intended. And they reacted accordingly by disciplining them.

African-Caribbean students were more likely to be criticised and punished, even when members of other ethnic groups committed the same offence. As a result,

activity22 ethnicity and setting

Item A Allocation to exam sets

		Third year exam results (marks out of 100)				Set placement (O – GCE O level)			
Ethnicity	Pupil	English	Maths	French	Physics	English	Maths	French	Physics
African-Caribbean	A	73	44	58	---	CSE	CSE	CSE	---
	B	62	63	60	59	CSE	CSE	CSE	CSE
	C	64	45	56	72	CSE	CSE	---	CSE
	D	68	37	82	---	CSE	CSE	CSE	---
Asian	E	51	77	---	55	O	O	---	O
	F	60	56	58	---	O	O	O	---
	G	61	62	55.5	---	O	O	O	---
	H	54	55	---	40	O	O	---	O
White	I	61	62	---	62	O	O	---	O
	J	52	57	55	---	O	O	O	---
	K	75	82	77.5	72	O	O	O	O
	L	54	75	64	72	O	O	O	O

A CSE grade 1 is equivalent to an O level grade C. Adapted from Wright, 1986

Item B Setting and perceived behaviour

The deputy head admitted that setting was not based solely on exam results – 'It is the case that the school tends to put the dutiful children in O level groups'. Some teachers saw African-Caribbean students as 'less cooperative'. One English teacher described all her African-Caribbean students as 'a disruptive influence'. It appeared that at least some students were placed in lower sets on the basis of teachers' views of their behaviour rather than ability.

Adapted from Wright, 1986

question

In view of Items A and B, do you think that racial discrimination played a part in the setting of students? Explain your answer.

---

there was considerable tension and conflict between White teachers and African-Caribbean students.

Máirtín Mac an Ghaill (1988) studied a boys' comprehensive in the early 1980s. The school was streamed with boys being demoted to lower streams for what was seen as bad behaviour. In the words of one teacher 'There are boys of relatively higher ability in the lower sets, especially among the West Indians. I've told you before Johnson and Brian were marvellous at Maths, especially problem-solving. But it's their, it's the West Indians' attitude and that must decide it in the end. You can't promote a boy who is known to be a troublemaker, who's a dodger. It will look like a reward for bad behaviour.'

Many African-Caribbean pupils responded with resistance. They formed an anti-school peer group, the Rasta Heads, which rejected many of the school's norms and values.

Exclusion Exclusion is one of the methods of social control which schools can use to deal with pupils they regard as troublesome. Exclusion can be permanent – the pupil is not allowed to return to that school – or temporary – the pupil is excluded from school for a fixed term.

In 2001/02, African-Caribbean pupils had the highest permanent exclusion rate in English schools at 42 per 10,000. This was three times the rate for White pupils. Chinese (2 per 10,000) and Indian pupils (3 per 10,000) had the lowest permanent exclusion rates (National Statistics Online – Education, 8.1.2004).

Why are so many African-Caribbean students permanently excluded? According to Jenny Bourne, there is a tendency for even well meaning White teachers to see 'Black youth as undermining their authority and even threatening to them personally' (Bourne et al., 1994). A second explanation argues that African-Caribbeans are more likely to experience the frustrations of racism and to express these frustrations in their behaviour in the classroom.

Racism in schools – evaluation

Methodology Wright, Gillborn and Mac an Ghaill's studies use a research method known as *ethnography*. This involves direct observation of relatively small groups, often over fairly long periods of time. Because the samples are small, it is not possible to make generalisations – ie, to say that the findings apply to all multi-ethnic schools.

However, the insights ethnography provides are unlikely to come from research methods such as questionnaires. For example, in *The School Effect*, Smith and Tomlinson's questionnaire to parents revealed little evidence of racism in schools. Ethnographic methods often give a very different picture. But not always.

An alternative view Peter Foster (1990) conducted an ethnographic study of a multi-ethnic comprehensive between 1985 and 1987. He found no evidence of racism. Students from ethnic minorities were not treated differently from White students. In fact, minority students, especially African-Caribbean girls, achieved better results than White pupils.

Foster admitted that the school he studied was distinctive. It was situated in a community with a long history of ethnic cooperation. And, at the time of his study, the staff were involved in an anti-racist programme. Whatever the differences between this school and others, Foster's study warns against the dangers of generalising from a few examples.

Despite this warning, there is evidence of racism in schools. Ethnic minority pupils tend to be over-represented in the lower sets and in the lower tiers for GCSE exam

activity23 different treatment

The following is taken from observation of a nursery class of four-year-olds.

Teacher:	Let's do one song before home time.
Peter:	(*White boy*) Humpty Dumpty
Teacher:	No, I'm choosing today. Let's do something we have not done for a while. I know, we'll do the Autumn song. What about the Autumn song we sing. Don't shout out, put your hand up nicely.
Mandy:	(*shouting out*) Two little leaves on a tree.
Teacher:	She's nearly right.
Marcus:	(*African-Caribbean boy with his hand up*) I know.
Teacher:	(*talking to the group*) Is she right when she says 'two little leaves on a tree'?
Whole group:	No.
Teacher:	What is it Peter?
Peter:	Four.
Teacher:	Nearly right.
Marcus:	(*waving his hand for attention*) Five.
Teacher:	Don't shout out Marcus, do you know Susan?
Susan:	(*White girl*) Five.
Teacher:	(*holding up one hand*) Good, because we have got how many fingers on this hand?
Whole group:	Five.
Teacher:	OK, let's only have one hand because we've only got five leaves. How many would we have if we had too many. Don't shout out, hands up.
Mandy:	(*shouting out*) One, two, three, four, five, six, seven, eight, nine, ten.

Teacher:	Good, OK how many fingers have we got?
Marcus:	Five.
Teacher:	Don't shout out Marcus, put your hand up. Deane, how many?
Deane:	Five.
Teacher:	That's right, we're going to use five today, what makes them dance about, these leaves?
Peter:	(*shouting out*) The wind.
Teacher:	That's right.

Adapted from Wright, 1992

question

Make out a case that the teacher's treatment of Marcus is
a) racist   b) non-racist.

entry. And African-Caribbean boys in particular tend to be regarded as badly behaved and troublesome by many teachers, even when their behaviour is similar to that of White boys. This can only disadvantage ethnic minority pupils (Pilkington, 2003).

African-Caribbean male subcultures

Anti-school subcultures As noted earlier, a number of studies have identified African-Caribbean anti-school subcultures. These subcultures are seen to develop from factors both inside and outside the school (Gaine & George, 1999).

Within schools, teachers tend to see African-Caribbean males as aggressive, challenging and disruptive. Often this is a misreading of African-Caribbean youth subculture – ways of walking, talking and dressing are sometimes interpreted by teachers as a challenge to their authority when none is intended. As a result of these misconceptions, African-Caribbean students tend to be singled out for punishment when White and Asian students are just as guilty. This leads some pupils to suspect teachers of racism. And this can lead to anti-school subcultures (Connolly, 1998).

As a result of both their class and ethnicity, a disproportionate number of African-Caribbean students are labelled as less able and placed in lower sets. Again, this can lead to anti-school subcultures.

As noted earlier, African-Caribbean students sometimes bring Black street culture into the classroom. And this can be seen by some teachers as disruptive with its emphasis on aggressive masculinity.

A variety of subcultures Sociologists tend to focus on anti-school subcultures. In some ways, they are more interesting and colourful than conformist subcultures. Particularly in the case of African-Caribbeans, this tends to overlook the variety of responses to schooling.

In a study of African-Caribbean students in a boys-only, 11-16 comprehensive school, Tony Sewell (1997) identifies four main responses.

- **Conformists** These pupils (41%) accepted the value of

education and the means to achieve educational success – behaving well and working hard. Conformists felt they couldn't succeed educationally *and* embrace the values and norms of their own Black peer group. This is a gamble, because if they don't succeed, they may lose the security which comes from being seen as a part of the Black community.

- **Innovators** These students (35%) accepted the value of education and wanted academic success but rejected the schooling process. Although anti-school, they tried to keep out of trouble. They attempted to distance themselves from the conformists and from teachers.

- **Retreatists** A small group (6%) of loners who made themselves as inconspicuous as possible. Many had special educational needs.

- **Rebels** These students (18%) rejected the school and projected an image of aggressive masculinity. Some modelled themselves on the Jamaican Yard Man, noted for his supposed physical and sexual prowess. They treated the Conformists with contempt, they were challenging and confrontational, and sometimes violent. Many saw academic qualifications as worthless – White racism would prevent them from achieving high status occupations.

Conclusion The above study is important because it shows the variety of African-Caribbean pupil subcultures rather than simply focusing on anti-school subcultures.

This study also shows how pupil subcultures are influenced by what goes on inside and outside the school. For example, the Rebels drew on Black street culture, arriving at school with patterns in their hair. This was banned, despite White boys being allowed to wear ponytails. This was seen as a lack of respect and pupils responded aggressively. Teachers punished them and so an anti-school subculture developed, shaped by factors from both inside and outside the school (Sewell, 1997).

African-Caribbean female subcultures

A number of studies of African-Caribbean female pupil subcultures have produced the following picture (Mac an Ghaill, 1988, 1992; Gillborn, 1990; Mirza, 1992). These findings apply to many, though by no means all, students.

Generally, African-Caribbean girls are pro-education – they are ambitious, determined to succeed, and are aiming for high-status, well-paid occupations. However, they tend not to identify with their teachers and school. This is partly in response to the open racism of a small number of teachers and the clumsy, well-meaning but often unhelpful 'help' offered by many teachers in response to the girls' ethnicity (Mirza, 1992).

African-Caribbean girls usually keep a low profile, keep their distance and avoid confrontation. In this way, they maintain their self-respect and don't have to compromise.

Conclusion

Ethnic differences in educational attainment are not static – they change over time. For example, the performance of Indian students at GCSE has improved remarkably from 1988 to 2002, and since the mid-1990s they have out-performed the White majority.

Statistics on ethnic differences in attainment are usually two to three years out of date when published. It is important to bear this in mind. As past statistics indicate, a lot can change in two or three years (see Activity 19).

Explanations of ethnic differences in attainment are often multi-dimensional – it is unlikely that any one factor or any one approach can explain these differences.

summary

1. There are significant differences in the educational attainment of ethnic groups.
2. The following factors outside the school have been seen to affect ethnic differences in attainment.
   - Social class - ethnic groups with the lowest attainment have the highest proportion of people in the working class.
   - Material factors - low attainment is linked to low income. The lower a person's social class, the lower their income.
   - Cultural factors - for example, language differences.
3. The following factors within the schools have been seen to affect ethnic differences in attainment.
   - Racism - particularly directed against African Caribbeans
   - Discrimination in setting and exam entry
   - Discrimination in everyday classroom interaction
   - Discrimination in discipline - for example, in exclusion
   - Pupil subcultures.
4. Many researchers argue for a multi-dimensional approach in order to explain ethnic differences in attainment.

activity24 African-Caribbean students

Item A Working for himself

Calvin has set up in business as a 'mobile barber'. Although still at school, he says he can make up to £300 a week.

Interviewer: How important is it for you to own your own business?

Calvin: It is important for Black people to make money because White people don't take us seriously because we're poor.

Interviewer: Is education important to you?

Calvin: Not really. I know what I need to know from the street. I'll give it three years and I bet no-one will bother with school. There ain't no jobs for no-one and they don't want to give jobs to Black people.

Adapted from Sewell, 1997

Item C Celebrating

Celebrating successful GCSE results

Item B Setting a good example

Interviewer: Do you belong to a gang?

Kelvin: No, because my mum says I shouldn't hang around students who get into trouble. I must take my opportunity while I can.

Interviewer: What students in this school do you avoid?

Kelvin: They are fourth years, you can easily spot the way they walk around in groups, they are mostly Black with one or two Whites. They're wearing baseball hats and bopping (*Black stylised walk*).

Interviewer: Don't you ever bop?

Kelvin: Sometimes for a laugh, but it's really a kind of walk for bad people. I wouldn't walk like this in school in front of the teachers. It sets a bad example.

Adapted from Sewell, 1997

questions

1 It is important not to see the anti-school subculture as the typical response of African-Caribbean young men. Discuss with some reference to Items A and B.

2 Suggest why African-Caribbean girls often do well at school and college.

Unit 6 Education and the economy

keyissues

1 What are the main theories of the relationship between education and the economy?

2 What are their strengths and weaknesses?

6.1 Functionalism, education and the economy

Emile Durkheim – the specialised division of labour

Writing in the late 19th and early 20th century, the French sociologist Emile Durkheim contrasted the skills needed by the workforce in pre-industrial and industrial societies. In pre-industrial societies, the division of labour was relatively unspecialised. By comparison with industrial societies, there were few specialised occupations. The skills needed by the workforce could usually be passed on from parents to children without the need for formal education.

As industrial society developed, the division of labour became more and more specialised. The number of different occupations increased rapidly in order to meet the variety of skills required by the economy. For instance, the design, manufacture and sale of motor cars involves the combination of a large number of specialist occupations – for example, designers, engineers, assemblers, salespeople and advertisers.

Social solidarity in industrial society is largely based on this interdependence of specialised skills. Members of society are united by the necessity of combining their particular occupational skills to produce goods and services.

Durkheim argued that a formal system of education was needed to teach the skills required by a specialised division of labour.

Talcott Parsons - role allocation

As outlined in Unit 1, the American sociologist Talcott Parsons (1961) sees role allocation as one of the main functions of education. This involves directing young people to the occupational roles which are best suited to their talents. In Parsons' words, schools 'allocate these human resources within the role structure of adult society'.

Parsons claims that schools operate on meritocratic principles. All pupils have an equal opportunity to succeed and their progress is based on merit – on talent and motivation. They are objectively assessed by examinations and high achievement is rewarded by high qualifications. Within schools, their status is achieved rather than ascribed (fixed at birth). The same principles operate in the wider society – individuals achieve their occupational status. Schools therefore prepare students for their adult life.

According to Parsons, modern industrial society requires a highly motivated, achievement orientated workforce. By offering high rewards for high achievement, schools help to produce this type of workforce. In the wider society, people achieve their occupational status and are rewarded accordingly – for example, those in top jobs receive high salaries.

Davis and Moore – education and stratification

The American sociologists Kingsley Davis and Wilbert E. Moore (1945) see the main function of social stratification as ensuring that the most able people are allocated to the most important positions in society. This is accomplished by attaching high rewards to those positions. These rewards will motivate people to compete for them and, in theory, the most able will win through. And this will benefit both the economy and society as a whole.

Davis and Moore see education as an important part of this process. High academic qualifications provide entry into the most functionally important positions. According to Kingsley Davis, education is the 'proving ground for ability and hence the selective agency for placing people in different statuses according to their capacities'.

Functionalism and the economy – an evaluation

There have been numerous criticisms of the functionalist perspective. They include the following.

- First, there is evidence that schools do not operate on meritocratic principles. As previous units have indicated, class and ethnic differences influence the assessment of pupils within schools. This suggests that judgements of ability are not necessarily based on objective principles.

- Second, rather than social stratification operating as Davis and Moore argue, it might actually work against their claim that schools are a 'proving ground for ability'. As Unit 3 on social class and educational attainment has shown, social inequalities can prevent equal opportunity in schools – they can prevent pupils from realising their potential.

- Third, just how much education does the workforce in modern industrial society actually require? Randall Collins (1972) argues that only 15% of the increase in education of the US workforce can be attributed to a rise in the proportion of jobs with high skill requirements. Alternatively, it could be argued that the skill demands of existing jobs have risen – for example, managers today need more knowledge and higher level skills than in the past. Even taking this into account, Collins estimates that educational qualifications have outpaced this requirement. He concludes that the contribution of education to the economy has been exaggerated.

6.2 Marxism, education and the economy

Where functionalists see the economic functions of education benefiting society as a whole, Marxists argue that they benefit only a small minority – the ruling capitalist class. Marxist views on the relationship between education and the economy were discussed in Unit 1, pages 87-89. They will be briefly summarised here.

- As part of the superstructure, the education system is largely shaped by the infrastructure – the economic base of society.

- The education system serves the interests of the capitalist class – those who own and control the means of production.

- According to Louis Althusser (1972), the main role of education is the reproduction of labour power which involves two processes. First, the reproduction of the skills necessary for an efficient labour force. Second, the reproduction of ruling class ideology and the socialisation of workers in terms of it.

- Bowles and Gintis (1976) argue that the main role of education is the reproduction of new generations of workers appropriately schooled to take their place in capitalist society. This involves the following processes – learning to accept and obey a hierarchy of authority, to find satisfaction in external rewards rather than work itself and to believe that social inequality is just and legitimate. Schools reward hard work, obedience, conformity and punctuality. These are the qualities required for a subordinate, disciplined and obedient workforce.

- An evaluation of Marxist views is given on page 92.

6.3 Social democratic perspectives

Social democratic perspectives on education developed in the 1960s. They have had an important influence on government educational policy.

Social democratic theorists start from the view that everybody should have an equal chance to succeed in the educational system. This is not only fair and just, it also brings practical benefits. A well-educated workforce will lead to economic growth.

Equal opportunity

The British sociologist A.H. Halsey is one of the leading social democratic theorists. He criticised functionalist views which claimed that the education system in Western industrial societies provided equality of opportunity. Halsey's work from the 1960s onwards showed clearly that social class has a significant effect on educational attainment. In general, the higher a person's social class of origin – the class into which they were born – the higher their educational qualifications. This suggests that schools are not providing equality of opportunity for all young people (Halsey et al., 1961; 1980).

According to social democratic theorists, this is both wrong and inefficient. It is wrong because in a democracy, everybody has a right to equal opportunity. It is inefficient because it wastes talent. If people don't have the opportunity to develop their aptitudes and abilities, then their contribution to the economy and society as a whole will be reduced. Inequality of educational opportunity means that everybody suffers.

Education and the economy

According to social democratic theorists, there is a close link between education and economic growth. Modern economies require an increasingly specialised and highly-trained workforce. The educational system reflects this requirement (Halsey et al., 1961).

Over the past 50 years there has been more education, and more specialised education. The school leaving age has steadily risen and growing numbers of young people are continuing into further and higher education. There has also been a rapid growth in *vocational education* – education which aims to provide specific workplace skills.

According to Halsey and Floud (1961), the economies of advanced industrial societies are 'dependent to an unprecedented extent on the results of scientific research, on the supply of skilled and responsible manpower, and consequently on the efficiency of the educational system'.

Social democratic perspectives – evaluation

It is difficult to unravel the relationships between education and the economy. Some researchers argue that the growth in education greatly exceeds the needs of the economy. For example, Randall Collins (1972) points to studies which suggest that once mass literacy has been achieved, education makes little difference to economic growth. He claims that when companies do require specific skills, they usually provide their own training courses. (See page 131 for further aspects of Collins' argument.)

Alison Woolf (2002) has also questioned the view that more education leads to economic growth. She gives the example of Switzerland, one of the richest countries in the world, where expenditure on education has been relatively low. And Egypt, which invested heavily in its education system in the late 20th century, saw no apparent change in its economic position compared to similar countries.

Other researchers claim that the growth in vocational education with its focus on workplace skills is vital for economic development. And still others argue that the increased pace of technological and economic change calls for a flexible workforce with a good general education rather than specific vocational training (Brown et al., 1997).

key term

Vocational education Education which aims to provide specific workplace skills.

activity25 a social democratic view

question

How does this cartoon illustrate the social democratic view of education?

6.4 New Right perspectives

New Right ideas developed in the early 1980s. They took a very different view of the route to educational and economic success.

The problem

According to New Right thinkers, advanced industrial economies such as the USA and Britain were declining. Much of this decline was due to social democratic policies. These policies resulted in:

- Too much state control – the 'nanny state' got too involved in people's lives.

- This crushed people's initiative and stifled their enterprise. They relied on the state rather than taking responsibility for their own lives.

- This can be seen in welfare dependency – the poor had come to depend on state 'handouts' rather than pulling themselves up by their own bootstraps.

- State control and welfare benefits cost a lot of money which meant high taxation.

- Because of this there was less money to invest in private industry – the really productive sector of the economy.

The solution

The New Right offered the following solution to the decline of advanced industrial societies.

- Restore enterprise and initiative.

- Roll back the state and make people responsible for their own destiny rather than relying on state institutions, state guidance and state handouts.

- Increase competition not only in the private sector but also the public sector – schools and hospitals should compete in much the same way as companies in the private sector.

- This will increase productivity and efficiency, and result in economic growth.

Education

Where does education fit into all this? The job of schools is to raise educational standards and instil enterprise, drive and competitive spirit.

The New Right's programme for raising educational standards runs as follows.

- Competition between schools and colleges – the best will attract more students, the worst won't get any and go out of business. This means that teachers and administrators will have real incentives to improve standards. And parents and their children will have real choice.

- Allowing schools and colleges to become self-managing. This means giving teachers and administrators control over finance, staffing and school policy. This encourages grassroot initiative and enterprise rather than reliance on direction from above. And this will motivate teachers to improve standards.

- The above measures will lead to better school management and higher quality teaching. This is what's needed to raise educational standards for all (Chubb & Moe, 1997).

- Higher standards will mean higher qualifications, particularly for those at the bottom. And this will give them a better chance of escaping from welfare dependency.

New Right perspectives – evaluation

New Right views leave a number of unanswered questions (Halsey et al., 1997).

First, does competition between schools raise standards? Measured in terms of GCSE and A level results, standards are improving. However, this may have little or nothing to do with competition between schools.

Second, is a choice of schools and colleges available? In some areas, there is no alternative to the local comprehensive. In other areas, where choice exists, middle-class parents are in a better position to get their children into the best schools. For example, where there are limited places, they tend to be more successful at negotiating with teachers.

Third, can schools make up for inequalities in the wider society? For example, with good management and high quality teaching, can schools provide equality of opportunity for students from low-income backgrounds? Available evidence suggests that the answer is 'no' (Halsey et al., 1997).

key term

Welfare dependency Depending on state benefits for support and accepting this as a way of life.

summary

1. From a functionalist perspective, education performs the following economic functions:
    - Providing the skills and knowledge required for a specialised division of labour
    - Assessing young people in terms of their talents and abilities and allocating them to appropriate roles in the wider society.

2. From a Marxist perspective, education:
    - Transmits ruling class ideology
    - Prepares pupils for their role in the workplace
    - Legitimises inequality and disguises exploitation
    - Rewards conformity and obedience
    - Reproduces new generations of workers, schooled to accept their place in capitalist society.

3. From a social democratic perspective, education:
    - Should provide every young person with an equal chance to develop their talents and abilities
    - This will benefit society as a whole by producing economic growth.

4. According to the New Right, the role of education is to instil drive, initiative and enterprise. This will come from:
    - Competition between schools and colleges
    - Motivating teachers to improve standards
    - Providing parents and students with a choice of schools and colleges.

activity26 *the educational market-place*

question

How does this cartoon illustrate New Right views of education?

Unit 7 Social policy and education

keyissues

1 What have been the main policies on education from 1870 onwards?

2 To what extent have they been shaped by economic concerns?

7.1 The 1870 Education Act

Before 1870, public schools educated the children of upper classes, and grammar schools taught the children of the middle classes. Both types of school were fee-paying. Working-class children were limited to elementary schools run by churches and charities. Standards were often appallingly low and around one third of children received no schooling at all (Royle, 1997).

The 1870 Education Act aimed to 'fill the gaps' left by church and charity schools. It provided state-run elementary schools for five to eleven-year-olds. They charged a maximum fee of nine pence a week.

In 1880, elementary education was made compulsory up to the age of 10. It aimed to teach basic literacy and numeracy, 'morality' and Biblical knowledge. In 1891, elementary education was made free. The school leaving age was raised to 12 in 1889 and to 14 in 1918.

Elementary education and the economy One of the main aims of the 1870 Act was economic. In a speech introducing his Education Bill into the House of Commons, W.E. Forster stated: 'Upon the speedy provision of elementary education depends our industrial prosperity. It is of no use trying to give technical teaching to our artisans without elementary education. Uneducated labourers are, for the most part, unskilled labourers, and if we leave our workfolk any longer unskilled, they will become overmatched in the competition of the world'.

The provision of mass elementary education in Britain in 1870 can be seen as a response to the needs of industry for a literate and numerate workforce at a time when industrial processes were becoming more complex, the demand for technical skills was steadily growing, and competition from other industrial nations was becoming more intense.

The 1902 Education Act This Act made local authorities responsible for secondary education. It encouraged the building of fee-paying grammar schools, many of which offered free places to children from low-income backgrounds who passed a scholarship exam. Again one of the main aims was economic. Britain's economic growth was falling behind other industrial countries, particularly Germany and the USA. The government saw secondary education as a means of catching up.

In broad terms, up to the Second World War (1939-1945), there were three types of school for children from different class backgrounds:

- elementary schools for the working classes
- grammar schools for the middle classes
- public schools for the upper classes.

7.2 The 1944 Education Act

During and after the Second World War, there was widespread debate over the kind of society that should follow the war. Education was a central issue in this debate. It was felt that the nation was not making full use of the talents of its people, particularly those in the lower classes. Changes in the education system were seen as a way to remedy this.

The 1944 Education Act aimed to give every pupil an equal chance to develop their abilities to the full within a free system of state education. The Act reorganised the structure of education in England and Wales into three stages.

- Primary for 5 to 11-year-olds
- Secondary for 11 to 15-year-olds
- Further/higher education.

The tripartite system

The major changes were in the secondary sector. The question was, what sort of secondary education would provide equality of educational opportunity for all children from the age of 11?

Types of pupil The response owed much to the theories of psychologists and educationalists of the 1920s and 1930s. These theories were based on the idea that there were different types of pupils, with differing aptitudes and abilities, and that a child's type could be identified by intelligence testing. On the basis of this, the 1944 Act introduced a national test for 11-year-olds – the 11-plus test – as a means of allocating children to one of three types of secondary school.

Types of school The three types of secondary school were grammar schools, technical schools and secondary modern schools. This became known as the *tripartite system* of secondary education.

Grammar schools were intended for pupils defined as bright and academic – those whose abilities lay in reasoning and solving logical problems. They were to study classics, mathematics, science and other 'difficult' subjects in preparation for GCE O and A-level exams. Around 20% of the school population went to grammar schools. Technical schools were intended for children with an aptitude for technical subjects. These schools emphasised vocational training and technical skills and were attended by around 5% of the school population. Most children

results of working-class pupils would improve compared to those of middle-class pupils. Although the educational qualifications of *all* school leavers improved, class differences remained largely unchanged. In other words, examination results in general got better but the gap between top and bottom stayed more or less the same (Ferri et al., 2003).

Breaking down class barriers Many of those who supported the comprehensive system looked forward to schools attended by pupils from across the entire social class spectrum. They hoped that this social mix would help to break down class barriers. However, most comprehensives recruit from a local catchment area. Often, these areas are largely middle class or working class. As a result, many comprehensives are primarily 'single class', so tending to reinforce rather than break down existing class divisions.

Streaming and setting Many comprehensives divide pupils into ability groups. A disproportionate number of middle-class pupils are placed in the top streams and sets and a disproportionate number of working-class pupils in the bottom streams and sets. Some see this as another form of selection, not unlike the tripartite system.

7.4 Conservative educational policy, 1979-1997

In May 1979, the Conservative Party, led by former Education Minister Margaret Thatcher, were elected. Their aims were to:

- Develop an educational system which met the needs of industry
- Raise standards throughout Britain's schools and colleges.

The new vocationalism

Until the 1970s, vocational training – training for work – was seen as the responsibility of employers. They would teach new recruits the skills needed in the workplace. This view began to change with the rise in youth unemployment in the 1970s. Schools, it was argued, were producing young people who lacked the skills required by industry. And industry in turn was suffering from a skills shortage. This line of argument led to the *new vocationalism* – direct government involvement in youth training.

Training schemes Conservative governments introduced a number of training schemes for young people. For example, the Youth Training Scheme (YTS), started in 1983,

activity28 class in the comprehensive

question

What problems of comprehensive schools are illustrated by this cartoon?

was a one-year, work-based training scheme for school leavers. It was replaced by Youth Training (YT) in 1990. In addition to workplace training, YT offered young people the chance to take vocational qualifications.

Vocational qualifications The development of training schemes was accompanied by new vocational qualifications. The National Council for Vocational Qualifications, set up in 1986, established National Vocational Qualifications (NVQs) for a range of specific occupations.

More general vocational qualifications were also introduced. General National Vocational Qualifications (GNVQs) allowed young people to keep their options open rather than specialise in a particular occupation. GNVQs assessed skills, knowledge and understanding in broad occupational areas such as Art and Design, Business, Health and Social Care, Manufacturing, and Leisure and Tourism. They have now been replaced by Applied GCSEs and Applied A levels.

The new vocationalism – evaluation

Jobs not training are needed A number of critics argued that youth unemployment was due to a lack of jobs, not to a lack of skills. In other words, the problem was with the economy, not with young people and their education (Finn, 1987).

Quality and relevance of training According to Phil Cohen (1984), many trainees spent most of their time 'running errands' and 'being useful'. Few received any real occupational training, most were a source of cheap labour.

Not all youth training fitted this description. The better schemes and employers offered effective training in skills that were in demand in the labour market.

A second-best option Middle-class students usually avoided Youth Training, seeing it as a second-best option to staying on at school or college. In practice, YT students tended to be young people from working-class backgrounds who couldn't get a job. It has been argued that YT was training for the less able which channelled them into low status, low paid occupations (Lee et al., 1990).

Status of vocational qualifications Traditionally, vocational qualifications have been seen as inferior to GCSEs and A levels. The introduction of NVQs and GNVQs may have

activity29 youth training

Item A Training at the bank

Each year about 20 young people, many with no qualifications, are recruited from the inner-city area to train under the Bank of England's clerical youth training scheme.

18-year-old Elton Thomas is in his second year, and came in without any qualifications. However, he's working towards achieving an NVQ this summer.

'I use computers a lot at the moment. I spend a lot of time on the phone chasing statements and invoices. I've worked in four different offices and gained a variety of experience. It's great working here. I really like wearing a suit to work and looking sharp. I'm in the bank's football team. We play other banks and companies and win a few and lose a few!'

Adapted from Employment Department Group and BBC Radio One, 1991

Item B Cheap labour

Well, the thing is, my son's education was all right until he left school and he'd got no job to go to. So he went to these job creation schemes, which is the biggest con there ever was. All it was was cheap labour. I mean, I saw all this because the firm I worked for actually got kids in and they were working as hard, if not harder, than the men that earned the money, but they never got paid for it. He was a damn good worker, keen to learn, but as soon as the training period was over, they got rid of him and started a new one, because it was cheap labour.

Adapted from McKenzie, 2001

Trainees at the Bank of England

question

The quality of youth training depends on who's providing the training. Briefly discuss with reference to Items A and B.

improved their status. Applied GCSEs and Applied A levels may continue this improvement.

Raising standards

The first major aim of Margaret Thatcher's Conservative government was to make education more responsive to the needs of industry. The second major aim was to raise standards throughout Britain's schools and colleges.

Where Labour had been influenced by social democratic ideas, Conservative governments were influenced by the New Right (see pages 133-134). In line with New Right ideas, the aim was to create an education market-place in which the providers – schools and colleges – competed, and the consumers – parents and students – made choices. This would drive up standards since the consumers would choose successful schools and colleges, leaving unsuccessful institutions to go out of business.

To put these ideas into practice, the Conservatives gave schools more freedom and self-government in some areas and increased government control in other areas. This can be seen clearly from the Education Reform Act.

The Education Reform Act

The 1988 Education Reform Act is the most important and far reaching educational legislation since the 1944 Education Act. It established a national curriculum for all state schools in England and Wales and a national system of testing and assessment. It reduced the role of local education authorities by giving greater control to individual schools and their governing bodies. It established city technology colleges and grant-maintained schools, both independent of local authority control.

Competition and choice Part of the thinking behind the Education Reform Act can be seen from a government circular entitled *Our Children's Education: The Updated Parent's Charter* (Department of Education, 1994). It tells parents that, 'Your choice of school directly affects that school's budget; every extra pupil means extra money for the school'. And 'the right to choose will encourage schools to aim for the highest possible standards'. From this point of view, parental choice means that schools will compete in order to attract pupils (and money) and in the process standards of education will rise.

Diversity and choice Will parents have a real choice? Aren't all comprehensives much of a muchness? In an attempt to offer real choice, the Education Reform Act encouraged diversity. It introduced two new types of school.

- **Grant-maintained schools** are created when sufficient parents vote to withdraw the school from local authority control. They are financed directly by central government. They are self-governing with governors and headteachers taking decisions about the employment of staff, the curriculum, the provision of goods and services and the way pupils are selected for entry. The idea was to free schools to specialise – for

example, in particular subjects or particular types of pupils such as the 'more academically able'. In this way, the choice for parents was seen to be widened.

- **City technology colleges** for 11 to 18-year-olds are financed by central government and private sector sponsorship. Located mainly in inner-city areas, they teach the National Curriculum while concentrating on maths, science and technology.

In the 1990s, the Conservatives introduced two further types of schools – schools specialising in either languages or technology. They were called colleges to indicate their prestige and importance.

By 1996, there were 1,100 grant maintained schools, including 660 secondary schools, accounting for one in five of all secondary students. There were 15 city technology colleges, 30 language colleges and 151 new technology colleges (Chitty, 2002).

The National Curriculum The Education Reform Act introduced the National Curriculum. For the first time in the history of state education, the government told teachers in England and Wales exactly what to teach. From the age of 5 to 16, all pupils in state schools must study three *core subjects* – English, maths and science – and seven *foundation subjects*. Pupils were tested in the core subjects by Standard Assessment Tasks (SATs – now renamed National Tests) at the ages of 7, 11 and 14. SATs results provided parents with information on which to judge the performance of schools.

League tables In 1992, all state secondary schools were required to publish the results of their SATs, GCSEs and A levels. In 1997, primary schools had to publish their SATs results. Local and national 'league tables' of schools were based on these results. They provided parents with information on which to base their choice of school. They were also intended to encourage competition between schools by spurring headteachers and staff to improve their position in the league.

Evaluation of Conservative policy

Choice Do parents have a real choice of schools? Popular schools are likely to be full, or to have only limited places. Where places are available, it is the articulate middle-class parents with their social and cultural capital who tend to obtain them. And in this situation, schools have more choice than parents – they are likely to choose middle-class pupils to maintain their position in the league tables. As a result, what choice exists is not equal – it operates on class lines and favours the middle class (Ball, 2003; Smith & Noble, 1995).

League tables Parents often look closely at examination results when assessing and choosing schools. But a simple league table which ranks schools in terms of results can be very misleading. There is evidence that some of the best schools in Britain do poorly in this kind of league table. These schools, often in run-down inner-city areas, are achieving extremely good results given the social background of their pupils. They may be doing a far better job than schools well above them in the league table (see Activity 31).

There is some evidence that secondary schools have concentrated on pupils likely to get A* to C grades at GCSE in order to improve their position in the league tables. This may have a detrimental effect on the progress of less able pupils (Garner, 2004).

Selection There is some evidence of selection on academic and/or social grounds in popular schools. They may be reluctant to accept pupils with special needs, low academic ability or so-called behaviour problems, seeing them as a threat to their standing in the league tables. In the early 1990s, around one-third of grant-maintained schools selected pupils on the basis of interviews with parents and/or pupils and reports from previous schools (Bush et al., 1993).

Critics have seen this as a means of 'back door selection'. They see a return of the grammar school in the guise of the grant-maintained secondary school. And there will be no need for a selection process like the 11-plus. The government will have provided the evidence with SATs at age 11.

Marketing schools Increased competition has led to schools using a variety of marketing strategies to present themselves in an attractive and positive light. These include glossy brochures, mission statements, open evenings and adverts in the local press. The resources devoted to marketing mean that less money is available to spend on things which directly benefit pupils – for example, teachers and textbooks (Gewirtz et al., 1995).

However, this emphasis on marketing has its benefits. Schools now give more attention to academic standards, to pastoral care, to discipline, and the state of their buildings. In the words of one researcher, schools have had to 'address their academic weaknesses and capitalise on their strengths' (Coffey, 2001).

7.5 Labour educational policy, 1997-2005

During the election campaign of 1997, Tony Blair proclaimed that Labour's top three priorities were 'education, education, education'. New Labour was elected in May 1997 with surprisingly little in the way of new policies for education.

Diversity and choice

In many ways the Labour government continued the Conservatives' policies of diversity and choice.

activity30 the educational market-place

question

How does this cartoon illustrate the aims of the Education Reform Act?

Modernisation and comprehensives Tony Blair rejected what he called the 'one-size-fits-all' idea of comprehensive education. He saw the existing comprehensive system as providing the same type of school for everyone. Past Labour governments had seen this uniformity and standardisation as a way of providing equal opportunities for all. New Labour rejected this view, arguing that schools should reflect the diversity of young people – their particular aptitudes and talents, and their varying abilities.

Comprehensives should be 'modernised'. And part of this process involved more specialist schools.

Specialist schools In May 1997, Labour inherited 196 specialist schools from the Conservatives. By late 2002, they had almost 1000 in place. The plan is to have at least 2000 by 2006 and eventually to transform all comprehensives into specialist schools. By 2003, sports, arts, business and enterprise, engineering, maths and computing, music, and humanities colleges had been added to the Conservatives' specialist schools.

The idea of specialist schools is to provide centres of excellence and expertise in particular subject areas. They are intended to raise local standards of teaching and learning in these subjects and to open their doors to pupils from other schools and to community groups. They can select up to 10% of their pupils, choosing those who have an aptitude for their specialist subject.

Diversity within schools The diversity of aptitude and ability must also be reflected *within* schools. Tony Blair rejected mixed-ability groups, arguing that ability grouping is the best way of making sure that *all* pupils progress as far and fast as they can. In his view, this was essential for the modernisation of comprehensive schools.

Evaluation Many of the criticisms of Conservative policy also apply to Labour's policy of diversity and choice – see pages 140-141. Choice usually means limited places and selection at the more popular schools. In this situation, the middle class with their cultural and social capital have the advantage.

Measuring success The government now has three ways of measuring the success of schools on the basis of exam results.

- **Examination results** Until recently, official league tables were based simply on examination results. In terms of this measure, selective secondary schools had the best GCSE results in 2004. And specialist schools had improved their GCSE results at a faster rate than standard comprehensives (Garner, 2004; Taylor, 2005).

- **Value added** This measure looks at pupils' attainment when they enter secondary school and when they leave. It attempts to measure how much schools have improved attainment over the five years of secondary education – that is, how much value, if any, has been added by the school (see Activity 31). In 2004, comprehensive schools dominated the top 20 in the value-added league table.

- **Most improved** This measure looks at the improvement of GCSE results in particular schools. For example, The North School in Kent improved it's A* to C pass rate at GCSE by 51% from 2001 to 2004, coming first in the most improved league table. As with the value-added measure, comprehensive schools dominated the top 20 in the most improved league table in 2004 (Taylor, 2005).

Underachievement in disadvantaged areas

Within three months of their election, the new Labour

activity31 a value-added league table

This league table refers to the top 20 local education authorities in England. The figures in brackets are taken from the league table based on exam results from secondary schools. The placings from 1 to 20 are based on 'value-added scores'. These scores look at pupils' attainment levels when they first arrive at secondary school then see how much schools improve on these levels – that is, how much value is added.

The results show that schools can – and do – make an enormous difference. There are local authorities with a high proportion of very poor children who do badly in both tables. But the most significant finding is the number of inner-city authorities, languishing in the lower regions of the exam results table, who do exceedingly well in the value-added table.

Adapted from *The Observer*, 20.3.1994

1	Wirral	(31)	11	Bolton	(42)
2	Camden	(57)	12	Hackney	(102)
3	Barnet	(3)	13	W. Sussex	(2)
4	Kingston	(1)	14	E. Sussex	(17)
5	Sutton	(9)	15	Dorset	(12)
6	Bromley	(4)	16	Wigan	(30)
7	Liverpool	(98)	17	Harrow	(7)
8	Tower Hamlets	(105)	18	Cheshire	(18)
9	Lambeth	(100)	19	Redbridge	(23)
10	Bucks	(5)	20	Herts	(10)

question

Why is a league table based on value-added scores important?

government published a policy document entitled *Excellence in Schools* (DfEE, 1997). It stated that they intended 'to overcome economic and social disadvantage and to make equality of opportunity a reality'. This involved finding new ways of motivating young people in deprived inner-city areas and doing something about 'underachieving schools'. New types of schools and new programmes were developed for this purpose.

Beacon schools These schools were 'centres of excellence'. Their job was to share their expertise with other schools, particularly those in inner-city areas.

City academies These were formerly failing inner city schools which were taken over by central government in

activity32 *diversity and choice*

Item A *Specialist schools*

Specialist schools and colleges will have a key contribution to make in raising standards and delivering excellence in schools. They will help thousands of young people to learn new skills and progress into employment, further training and higher education, according to their individual abilities, aptitudes and ambitions.

Former Education Minister Estelle Morris, quoted in Chitty, 2002

Item B *Diversity and inequality*

In a class-divided and competitive society, specialisms are not equal: they rapidly become ranked in a hierarchy of status.

A divided secondary system, with its hierarchy of schools firmly established, will continue to work to the advantage of the powerful, the influential and the articulate; while large numbers of children find themselves in less favoured institutions which attract the sort of criticisms once levelled at the secondary modern schools.

Adapted from Chitty, 1997

questions

1 How does the cartoon illustrate Labour's policy of diversity and choice?

2 With some reference to Item B, discuss how diversity can lead to inequality of educational opportunity.

partnership with businesses, churches, or voluntary organisations. They could offer special bonuses to teachers to attract and keep the best. Up to 200 city academies are planned by 2010.

Judging by exam results, city academies have had only limited success. Of the 11 city academies in 2004, six have improved their results at GCSE but five have shown no improvement. However, since some of the academies had been open for little more than a year in 2004, it may be too early to make a judgement (Taylor, 2005).

Education Action Zones (EAZs) These zones were located in disadvantaged urban areas with low levels of educational attainment. By April 2003, there were 72 EAZs, each run by an Action Forum made up of parents, representatives from local schools and businesses and from local and national government. Each zone was given £1 million to spend. Teachers and schools were encouraged to be flexible and innovative – for example, running Saturday classes and a variety of work-related courses.

As noted earlier, the results are disappointing with some schools in the EAZs performing less well than those in similar areas outside the zones. EAZs are now being phased out and replaced by the Excellence in Cities initiative which provides extra money for schools in disadvantaged areas and targets specific programmes such as educating gifted children (Garner, 2004).

Evaluation Education Action Zones ploughed money and energy into disadvantaged areas, they encouraged innovation, and brought together expertise from local and national government. However, like similar experiments in the 1960s, such as Educational Priority Areas, they may fail to make up for the economic and social disadvantages of pupils from low-income, inner-city areas (Kirton, 1998). Similar criticisms have been made about city academies.

Excellence in Cities (EiC) Education Action Zones have now been replaced by Excellence in Cities (EiC), a larger programme which aims to improve the standards of schools in disadvantaged areas. It covers more schools and provides more money. EiC targets its funding for particular purposes – for example, employing learning mentors, educating gifted children, providing learning support units and City Learning Centres. After the first two years, schools in the EiC programme have shown modest improvements, particularly for pupils with lower levels of attainment (McKnight et al., 2005).

Vocational education and training

Aims Labour's policies for vocational education have focused on two main areas.

- First, to provide the training needed for a high wage/high skill economy, so that the UK can compete successfully in world markets.
- Second, to reduce unemployment, particularly for young people (Strathdee, 2003).

New qualifications GNVQs were replaced by Applied GCSEs and Applied A levels. Part of the reason for this change was to raise the status of vocational qualifications to the level of academic qualifications.

National Vocational Qualifications (NVQs) were extended. They now ranged from an Initial Award – gained after a 26 week introductory training period – to a Level 5 award which is equivalent to a degree.

summary

1. The 1870 Education Act provided the first state-run schools. The main aim of the Act was economic – to meet the needs of industry for a numerate and literate workforce.

2. The 1944 Education Act set up the tripartite system of secondary education – grammar, technical and secondary modern schools.

3. The tripartite system provided schools of unequal status and unequal quality. Middle-class pupils tended to go to high-status grammar schools, working-class pupils to low-status secondary modern schools.

4. The comprehensive system was designed to provide equality of opportunity by replacing the tripartite system with a single type of school for all young people.

5. Class differences in attainment remained, partly because pupils were placed in streams or sets with a disproportionate number of middle-class pupils in higher ability groups and working-class pupils in lower ability groups.

6. Conservative governments from 1979 to 1997 introduced work-related training schemes and vocational qualifications.

7. The Education Reform Act of 1988 aimed to provide competition between schools, a variety of schools, and choice for parents. In theory, standards would rise as parents chose successful schools, while failing schools would go out of business.

8. Choice usually meant limited places and selection at the more popular schools. In this situation, the middle class with their cultural and social capital have the advantage.

9. The National Curriculum, introduced in 1988, was assessed by SATs in its core subjects. The results of these tests provided parents with information by which to judge the performance of schools.

10. Labour continued the Conservatives' policy of diversity and choice. The idea of a single type of secondary school for all was rejected in favour of a range of specialist schools.

11. Labour introduced new types of schools and new programmes which aimed to raise standards in deprived inner-city areas.

12. The New Deal offered education and training for young people who had been out of work for over six months.

13. Labour aims to increase the number of students participating in higher education and to increase the proportion of working-class students. The impact of student loans on this policy is not clear.

Evaluation NVQs have yet to prove themselves. Surveys suggest that about two-thirds of employers see little value in these qualifications. The government may have overestimated the demand for highly-skilled workers. In the 1990s, the fastest growing job was care assistant in hospitals and nursing homes (Strathdee, 2003).

The New Deal Labour introduced the New Deal in 1998. It offered education and training for young people between the ages of 18 and 24 who had been out of work for more than six months. It was later extended to older people.

The New Deal provided personal advisors who offered direction and support to the unemployed, guiding them through the various options – academic courses, vocational training, self-employment, or voluntary work.

Evaluation Two years into the New Deal, Tony Blair claimed that it had helped more than 250,000 young people to find jobs. However, this estimate is probably exaggerated. Youth unemployment was falling rapidly before the New Deal was introduced due to an upturn in the economy. Estimates by academic researchers suggest that the New Deal raises youth employment by around 17,000 a year (McKnight, 2005).

Higher education In 2000, around 30% of the 18-30 age group participated in higher education. Labour aims to increase this figure to 50% by 2010. This aim will not be met unless more young people from disadvantaged areas go on to university.

Over the past 20 years, the numbers and proportion of all social classes participating in higher education have increased. Despite this, the gap between top and bottom has widened. In other words, the growth in university

places has benefited the middle class to a greater extent than the working class (see pages 103-104).

Labour aims to widen participation in higher education – to increase the level of working-class participation (DfES, 2003). The Office of Fair Access was set up for this purpose. It has the power to issue fines of up to £500,000 for a 'serious and wilful' breach of a university's commitment to expand access for working-class students.

In 1998, Labour replaced student maintenance grants by low-cost loans and required students to pay tuition fees. Some researchers argue that these measures have widened the class gap in access to higher education. There is evidence that worries about debt are deterring some students, particularly those from low-income backgrounds, from going to university (Universities UK Online, 2003). Other researchers argue that student loans have had little or no effect on participation in higher education. They see the widening class gap as part of a longer-term trend (Galindo-Rueda et al., 2004).

activity33 grants not fees

National Union of Students demonstrate against tuition fees and the student loans scheme.

question

Would you support this demonstration? Give reasons for your answer.

3 Applied sociological research methods

Introduction

Want to put up some shelves? You're going to need to do some preparation first. You need to decide where exactly the shelves are going, measure up and buy some shelving. You're going to need some tools – for example, a screwdriver and a drill. And you're going to need some screws and some wall plugs. A well-stocked toolkit means that you will be able to choose the right tools and the right equipment for each part of the job.

The job of the sociologist is to find out about the social world. Just like the DIY enthusiast, the sociologist needs to prepare before they start the job of actually collecting data. The exact aims of the research need to be decided, background reading completed and ethical issues taken into account.

They need a toolkit too. The sociological research toolkit contains methods of data collection – questionnaires, interviews, observation and so on. The sociologist will try to select the most suitable method for their particular study. Participant observation might be the best tool to understand the motivations of illegal drug users but it may not work as well if the research aims to find out patterns of participation in religious organisations.

This chapter examines these practical aspects of doing sociological research – from designing a plan for the study, to collecting data, to interpreting and finally reporting the results. It builds on the knowledge and skills developed during the Research Skills part of your AS Sociology course. It encourages you to apply what you learned to a range of practical research problems, as well as introducing some new concepts and debates. The material here will enable you to prepare for the written exam or, if you are taking the coursework option, to build up the skills required for a successful Personal Study.

chaptersummary

▶ **Unit 1** considers various aspects of research design.

▶ **Unit 2** focuses on the ways sociologists prepare for research including background reading, gaining access to research participants and meeting ethical guidelines.

▶ **Unit 3** is concerned with the different methods of sampling – the selection of people to act as participants in the research.

▶ **Unit 4** covers quantitative data collection including operationalising concepts and the design and piloting of questionnaires and structured interviews.

▶ **Unit 5** focuses on the process of qualitative data collection including different types of open-ended interviews and observation.

▶ **Unit 6** considers the advantages of mixing quantitative and qualitative methods.

▶ **Unit 7** examines the ways in which secondary data has been used in sociological research.

▶ **Unit 8** looks at the interpretation, evaluation and reporting of research findings.

Unit 1 Research design

keyissues

1 What are the purposes of research?
2 What is research design?
3 How do sociologists break down a research topic?

1.1 Purposes of research

What is the point of sociological research? Schutt (1996) divides research into four broad types according to its purpose. He uses homelessness as an example of each of these.

1 Descriptive research This sets out to develop a clear understanding of a topic and to describe its key features.

Defining homelessness is not simple. Do you include those in temporary shelters? Or those housed in emergency accommodation? Do you have to be actually sleeping on the street to be homeless? What sort of people are homeless? What are their backgrounds? What about their age, gender and ethnic group? How many homeless people are there?

2 Exploratory research This kind of investigation explores the views and feelings of the participants in the research. Exploratory research is often qualitative, using methods such as unstructured interviews and participant observation.

In the case of homelessness, how do the homeless feel about their situation? What are their hopes, worries and expectations of the future? How do they get along with other homeless people, the public, welfare workers and the police?

3 Explanatory research This attempts to identify causes and effects. Why do people become homeless? What effects does homelessness have on the homeless and on society?

4 Evaluation research Local and central governments along with a variety of other organisations are responsible for taking action to improve aspects of society. Evaluation research aims to assess the effectiveness of their policies.

What has been done to help the homeless? What have been the results? What should happen in the future?

activity1 types of research

These examples of research into homelessness were all carried out in the USA.

Homeless in Cincinnati, Ohio

Item C

Dee Roth's (1990) study of homelessness - like many others - faced the problem of identifying a sample. She asked workers in shelters, homeless support and mental health organisations to identify homeless people who had used their facilities. As a result, she was able to interview 979 homeless people.

She found that 80% of her sample were male, two thirds White, 50% were high school graduates and 10% were married. Health problems were common. Almost a third had been in a psychiatric hospital, a third reported physical health problems and 20% reported problem drinking.

Item D

For one year David A. Snow and Leon Anderson (1987) followed homeless people through their daily routines and asked them about their lives. Six were studied more intensively with taped in-depth interviews. The researchers were trying to find out how the homeless come to terms with their homelessness.

Examples adapted from Schutt, 1996

Item A

Peter H. Rossi (1989) surveyed a sample of homeless people in Chicago. He found that extreme poverty meant that people became homeless due to the high cost of housing. Those most likely to become homeless were individuals with problems of substance abuse or mental illness.

Item B

A team of sociologists led by Goldfinger (1990) recruited 118 homeless people to take part in an experiment to test the effectiveness of different types of housing for the homeless. They placed half of the sample in small flats where individuals lived completely independently. The rest went to live in group houses. The group homes were designed to assist residents to take control of their own affairs. Residents were encouraged to set rules for the household and eventually become fully independent.

80% of the residents of the group homes were still in the houses one year after the study. A higher proportion of those in independent flats had left their housing and returned to the streets or shelters.

questions

1 Match the research described in each of the items to one of the types of research identified by Schutt on this and the previous page. Explain your choices.

2 Give suggestions for descriptive, exploratory, explanatory and evaluative research on the educational underachievement of African-Caribbean boys.

1.2 Research design

Whatever its purpose, all research needs to be planned out carefully. Decisions need to be made about key issues and concepts, sampling, methods and so on. This planning is sometimes referred to as *research design*.

The process of research design can be broken down into four parts (Punch, 1998).

1 Strategy This refers to the overall approach to research. If research is quantitative, what *correlations* need to be made? Is it appropriate to study a group of people over a long period – a *longitudinal survey*?

In the case of quantitative research about the effects of divorce, the researcher may start with the *hypothesis* that the effects of divorce on children will depend on the age of the child at the time of the divorce. If so, then it may be necessary to find a way of comparing the effects of divorce on samples of children who experienced divorce at different ages. Alternatively, a longitudinal strategy may be possible where one group of children are monitored over a long period. This may indicate that different problems emerge as the child grows older.

Qualitative researchers also have to make decisions. They may wish to take a *case study* approach and use a range of methods to find out about one particular group, place or organisation. Alternatively, an *ethnographic* approach may be taken where participant observation or unstructured interviews are used to explore the way of life of a group of people – their culture, experiences and the ways they make sense of the world around them.

Take the example of gender and subject choice. One school might be studied in detail using school records and policies, marked work, observation and interviews – a case study approach. Alternatively, the researcher might feel that unstructured ethnographic interviews with pupils and teachers might be more appropriate to explore the meanings boys and girls give to the subjects they choose.

2 Concepts What are likely to be the most important concepts in the research? How will they be *operationalised* – defined in such a way that they can then be measured?

key terms

Correlation A measurement of the strength of the relationship between two or more variables.
Longitudinal study A study of the same group of people at various times over a period of years.
Hypothesis A statement that can be tested about the relationship between two or more variables.
Case study A study of one particular case or instance of something.
Ethnography The study of the way of life of a group of people. It often involves an attempt to see the world from their point of view.
Operationalise Translating concepts into a form which can be measured.
Research design The process of planning research.

In the example of research into the effects of divorce discussed earlier, how will the concept of 'the effects of divorce' actually be measured? By the level of emotional stability of the child? By their school performance? By their use of alcohol and drugs? Or by some combination of a range of indicators?

A researcher will not get far without clear definitions of concepts. The process of operationalising concepts is explored in more depth on pages 165-167.

3 Sample The issue of sampling is discussed in Unit 3.

4 Data collection, analysis and interpretation Data collection is covered in Units 4, 5, 6 and 7. Data analysis and interpretation can be found in Unit 8.

1.3 Quantitative and qualitative research design

At the centre of research design is the identification of a set of steps the researcher will take in order to reach conclusions. This process is different for quantitative and qualitative research.

Quantitative research This type of research tends to follow a linear approach – one step follows another – starting with a theory or hypothesis that requires testing, then reviewing existing literature on the subject, identifying key concepts, sampling, collecting and interpreting data before validating, rejecting or adapting the initial theory (see the diagram in Activity 2).

Something of this approach can be seen in the example of research into the effects of divorce on children described above. After the initial hypothesis has been developed – that the effects of divorce on children will depend on the age of the child at the time of the divorce – researchers are likely to start by reading a range of psychological and sociological background material about relevant issues such as child development. Then key concepts such as 'effects' will have to be operationalised (see above) and a suitable sample identified. One approach might be to take three samples – one group of children who had experienced divorce at an early age, one at a later point in their lives and a control group who had not experienced divorce at all. A possible method of data collection could be structured interviews, the results of which could then be analysed to see if there were statistically significant differences between the samples. At this point, the researchers may be able to draw some preliminary conclusions about their original hypothesis. Is it holding up to the investigation or does it need adapting or even rejecting?

Qualitative research This type of research takes a more circular route in which 'there is mutual interdependence of the single parts of the research process' (Flick, 1998). The researcher often starts the research as soon as possible and key questions, concepts and background reading emerge as the research progresses. Theories can also develop as a result of research in a process known as *grounded theory* – the theory is 'grounded' in the data (Glaser & Strauss, 1967).

activity2 quantitative and qualitative research design

Item A *Research models*

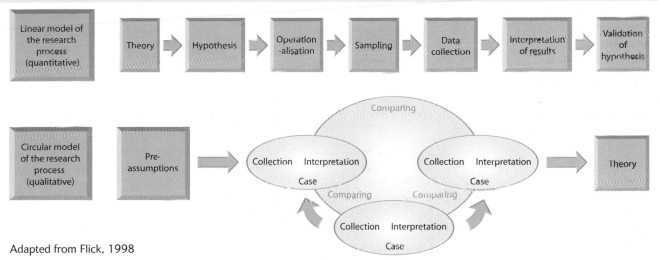

Adapted from Flick, 1998

Item B *Lesbian parents*

questions

You are undertaking research into the effects on children of being brought up by lesbian parents. Using the procedures described above and in Item A:

1 Produce a quantitative research design for this research, using a hypothesis.

2 Produce a qualitative research design for this research, showin how the theory is grounded in the data.

Qualitative research into the effects of divorce may begin with unstructured interviews with children and parents who have experienced relationship breakdown. After comparing the results, an initial grounded theory may be developed – perhaps that a key factor is the parents' handling of the break up – the more amicably the divorce is managed, the less stressful it is for children. A key concept appears: divorce management. The researchers may now be drawn to some background reading on the way relationships end while they plan some more interviews to further investigate and develop their grounded theory.

1.4 Developing research questions

All sociological research starts with the identification of a problem of some sort – something that needs explaining. The problem might be the decline of mainstream churches, the impact of CCTV cameras in city areas, or the increase in single-person households.

But the problem identified is usually too general to enable research to start immediately. The next stage is to ask a series of research questions which will help clarify the focus of the research. For example, using the example of the decline in church attendance above, what are the patterns of attendance in different churches? What sorts of people attend church? How regularly do they attend church? Why do they attend church? Why do some people stop going to church?

activity3 research questions

Social research involves detective work. You begin with a problem and then ask a number of questions about it, such as 'What?' 'Who?' 'Where?' 'When?' 'How?' and 'Why?' In some research, the most important question may be 'What are the consequences?' Consider research on discrimination.

- **What** is discrimination? Is it possible to begin with a clear definition? A starting point would be to look at existing literature on the subject and to work out how the concept of discrimination can be operationalised.
- **Who** experiences discrimination? People with disabilities? Ethnic minority groups? Gays and lesbians? Particular age groups? Residents of certain areas?
- **Where** does the discrimination take place? In the workplace? Schools? On the streets?
- **When** does the discrimination occur? How often? For what length of time? Is it a large part of people's everyday lives?
- **How** does it occur? You might want to measure levels of abuse or more indirect discrimination in organisations. You might concentrate on the effects of unfair treatment on people's lives, or how organisations deal with unfair practice.
- **Why** does discrimination occur? The purpose of the study may be to find an explanation.

Adapted from Gilbert, 2001

questions

Break down the following issues into research questions using the same approach as Gilbert.

1 Marital and relationship breakdown.
2 Deviant behaviour in classrooms.

key terms

Grounded theory An approach to qualitative research in which theories are developed as the data is collected. Theories are 'grounded' in the data.
Research questions Key questions identified by researchers to help break down and narrow the focus of a general topic of research.

summary

1. Research can be divided into different types according to its purpose. It may be descriptive, exploratory, explanatory or evaluative.
2. Research design involves the development of a strategy, the identification of key concepts, the selection of a sample and the collection, analysis and interpretation of data.
3. Quantitative research design usually takes a linear form, beginning with a theory or hypothesis and then collecting data in order to test it.
4. Each part of qualitative research is interdependent, with theories developing as the research progresses.
5. Sociologists develop research questions to help clarify and narrow the focus of research.

Unit 2 Preparing for research

keyissues

1 How is background reading used in research?
2 How do sociologists gain access to people and organisations?
3 How do ethical issues affect sociological research?

2.1 Literature reviews

It seems obvious that the first thing anyone should do when starting a piece of research is to read up on the topic. And for many researchers this is exactly what happens. The traditional approach is to conduct a *literature review* at a very early stage as part of the process of research design.

Francis (2000) identifies four purposes of the traditional literature review.

1 It can indicate what kind of research has already been conducted on a topic and where there are particular gaps in knowledge.
2 It can help make sure that the research avoids the mistakes of previous studies.
3 It can identify good ideas from previous research.
4 It can help identify key concepts and theories for the research.

However, some qualitative researchers adopt a different

approach. They do not want their interpretation of data to be influenced by the categories and concepts used previously. Instead, they want their own to emerge from data collection in the process known as grounded theory (see pages 148-149). This means that background reading may be delayed until their data provides a clear direction (Punch, 1998).

activity4 the literature review

Item A Unemployment and mental health

If your research question is 'What is the effect of unemployment on mental health?' you might first consider searching literature on unemployment and mental health. You could then search for studies on specific effects that unemployment may have on mental health, such as depression, suicide, demoralisation and aggressiveness. Other issues might include gender differences in the effects of unemployment and the relationship between social support and the impact of long-term unemployment.

Adapted from Schutt, 1996

Item B Racial harassment

A national literature review covering all aspects of the issue was undertaken. The review focused on current sources of statistical evidence, the recognition of racial harassment as a social problem, locality surveys, racial harassment and housing, and finally the effects of racial harassment on ordinary lives.

Adapted from Chahal & Julienne, 1999

questions

Using similar approaches to the literature reviews described in Items A and B, suggest three different topics that would be suitable as background reading for each of the following pieces of research.

1 An investigation of the relationship between church attendance and social class.

2 An investigation into the meaning of politics to young people.

3 An investigation into asylum seekers' adaptation to life in Britain.

2.2 Gaining access

The first stage of carrying out any primary data collection is to find a way of getting into the group or organisation you are studying. This is known as *gaining access*. Gaining access usually involves explaining to the group or key individuals exactly what the research involves. Hopefully, they will then give their permission – their informed consent – for the research to take place.

Gatekeepers

This is the term used to describe the key individuals who can provide access. They are 'those individuals in an organisation or another social situation who have the power to grant or withhold access to people or situations for the purposes of research' (Hughes, 2000).

Gaining access usually involves negotiation with a range of people. Gatekeepers may be those formally in charge of organisations. In the case of research in a school, the most obvious person to approach would be the Headteacher. However, if a sociologist wanted to observe in classrooms then further access would have to be negotiated with

individual departments and teachers. And if interviews with pupils were also part of the research, then the pupils would also have to be consulted.

The research bargain

In official organisations, access can be a very formal affair with the researcher left quite powerless. They may have to enter into a *research bargain* where access is granted only with various strings attached. Large organisations may demand to check all research findings in return for their cooperation. Or they may provide a 'chaperone' to monitor the researcher at all times. Organisations may even try to control the methods of the researcher. Often they will prefer quantitative approaches which they see as generating 'hard facts'. These can be controlled far more than the uncertain and spontaneous nature of qualitative methods such as participant observation.

For example, a piece of research about a crime prevention unit in Northamptonshire involved very difficult negotiations. The researchers wanted to use a mixture of unstructured interviews and observation to uncover the workings of the organisation. However, the management were keen to get 'hard' quantitative data which would demonstrate clearly the success of the unit (Hughes, 2000).

Research into informal groups can also involve research bargains. Val Hey studied friendships between girls. Her research was based on observation in two schools. She would sometimes give the girls small gifts and excuses to miss lessons in exchange for cooperating in her research (Hey, 1997).

Although research bargains are necessary if research is to take place, there are dangers. Serious ethical issues are raised by tactics such as Hey's. And objectivity will suffer if methods and findings are influenced by the groups and organisations being researched.

Access and power

In general, groups with the least power are much more accessible to research than powerful groups. Hughes (2000) contrasts researching criminality among London's homeless youth with an investigation of unreported crime among city financiers. As he puts it, ' "Studying down"

(that is, studying vulnerable minority groups) is much easier and commonplace than is "studying up" of powerful elites'.

The study of shoplifting, vagrancy and begging among homeless youth is relatively simple, especially if it involves known offenders. The young homeless are a vulnerable group who lack any protection from academic scrutiny. Studying city financiers, on the other hand, the researcher may well experience closed doors, many gatekeepers, threats of legal action and a privileged culture of privacy.

key terms

Gatekeepers Individuals who can provide the researcher with access to a group, place or situation.
Research bargain Formal or informal agreement reached between the researcher and gatekeeper where access is agreed only if certain conditions are met.

activity5 gaining access

Item A Research in prisons

Experienced prison researchers who have already worked with the Prison Service are likely to be given a high level of cooperation by management. A study commissioned by the Home Office or Prison Service and employing Home Office researchers would probably gain the highest level of cooperation, enabling carrying of keys and access to all parts of the prison and prison records. If problems are encountered, such as officers refusing to unlock subjects for interview or denying access to records, help can be enlisted from the governor. However, this approach would not promote a happy atmosphere between researcher and officer and would probably be counterproductive. A high level of management cooperation does not prevent hostility from staff and prisoners. If the research is oriented towards prisoner welfare, staff may be resentful and reluctant to allow access to prisoners. If the research requires lengthy interviews with staff, then prisoners may decide the researchers are 'on the staff's side' and thus not to be trusted.

Adapted from Martin, 2000

Prison wing at Portland Young Offenders Institution, Portland, Dorset

Item B Research with the police

Robert Reiner has conducted extensive research into the workings of the police. Here he writes about the 'research bargains' he has experienced.

The researcher is likely to give undertakings such as protecting the confidentiality of individuals. What is more of a problem is the question of editorial control of the final report. It is common to show a draft for comment to the organisations that allow access. However, allowing the organisation to censor parts of a study undermines any value the research might have. However, it would be legitimate to edit out errors of fact pointed out by the organisation or any information that might be harmful if published - for example, because it could endanger or discourage witnesses or make detection methods widely known. Restrictions may also be put on methods such as not allowing tape recording or restricting areas of questioning. For example, I was prohibited from asking questions about political opinions when interviewing police officers.

Adapted from Reiner, 2000

Item C Extract from a research diary

Karen Sharpe researched prostitutes in an English city. At first she faced serious problems of access but after one year had interviewed an estimated 95% of women working regularly as prostitutes in that area. This extract from her research diary was written at an early stage of the research.

'The women are practically ignoring me as if I do not exist. Some of them look straight through me, some of them look me up and down, some of them leave me in no doubt that if looks could kill ... I have the feeling that any other intelligent person doing this kind of research would know exactly what to do and would say all the right things and everything would be fine, but I seem to be having to make this up as I go along and adapt to whatever situation I find myself in. I have been sworn at, spat at, laughed at, ridiculed and threatened. This is much harder in reality than I ever imagined it would be.'

Teenage prostitute, Walsall, West Midlands

Adapted from Sharpe, 2000

questions

1   Read Item A. How does this passage show that gaining access is a complex process involving negotiation with a wide range of people?

2   Using Item B, explain the problems in creating a 'research bargain'.

3   Suggest how Sharpe (Item C) might have been more successful in gaining access to her sample of prostitutes.

4   Suggest how access might be gained to the following groups.
    a) Marijuana smokers
    b) Pregnant women
    c) Gay men and women

2.3 Ethical issues

Ethical issues – matters of moral principle – can affect all aspects of the research process from beginning to end. At the start of research the choice of topic is a matter of moral judgement – for example, should I study the crimes of the poor or the crimes of the powerful? And at the end of the research there is the question of whether research participants should be able to check the final report.

Martin Bulmer (2001) provides an overall view of ethics. He argues that sometimes the researcher will have to compromise to protect both themselves and the participants in the research. Sacrifices may have to be made in order to respect the rights of individuals and groups.

'Ethics is a matter of principled sensitivity to the rights of others. Being ethical limits the choices we can make in the pursuit of truth. Ethics say that while truth is good, respect for human dignity is even better' (Bulmer, 2001).

Ethical decisions are rarely straightforward in the real world and often confront researchers with really difficult problems. Subject associations such as the British Sociological Association have drawn up guidelines to assist ethical decision making (see Activity 6, Item B).

activity6 ethical guidelines, ethical problems

Item A Some principles of ethical research

1   **Informed consent** - participants in research should be free to choose whether to take part or not on the basis of full information about the nature of the research.

2   **Respect for privacy** - researchers should respect the privacy of the participants.

3   **Safeguarding the confidentiality of data** - steps should be taken to ensure that individuals cannot be identified from any stored data.

4   **Protection from harm** - research should not harm the researcher or the participants.

5   **Avoiding deception** - deceit and lying should be avoided.

6   **Awareness of the consequences of publication** - sociologists should ensure they can publish their results without undue influence from sponsors. And they should also be aware of the effects of publication on the research participants.

Adapted from Bulmer, 2001

Item B Extracts from the British Sociological Association's Statement of Ethical Practice

- Sociologists have a responsibility to ensure that the physical, social and psychological well-being of research participants is not adversely affected by the research. They should strive to protect the rights of those they study, their interests, sensitivities and privacy, while recognising the difficulty of balancing potentially conflicting interests.

- In some cases, where the public interest dictates otherwise and particularly where power is being abused, obligations of trust and protection may weigh less heavily. Nevertheless, these obligations should not be discarded lightly.

- As far as possible, participation in sociological research should be based on the freely given informed consent of those studied. This implies a responsibility on the sociologist to explain in appropriate detail, and in terms meaningful to participants, what the research is about, who is undertaking and financing it, why it is being undertaken, and how it is to be disseminated and used.

- Research participants should be made aware of their right to refuse participation whenever and for whatever reason they wish.

- Research participants should understand how far they will be afforded anonymity and confidentiality and should be able to reject the use of data-gathering devices such as tape recorders and video cameras.

- In some situations access to a research setting is gained via a 'gatekeeper'. In these situations members should adhere to the principle of obtaining informed consent directly from the research participants to whom access is required, while at the same time taking account of the gatekeeper's interest.

- Researchers should be aware of the possible consequences of their work. Wherever possible they should attempt to anticipate, and to guard against, consequences for research participants which can be predicted to be harmful. Members are not absolved from this responsibility by the consent given by research participants.

- Special care should be taken where research participants are particularly vulnerable by virtue of factors such as age, disability, their physical or mental health.

Adapted from the British Sociological Association's Statement of Ethical Practice

questions

For each of the following research situations:

a) Use the BSA guidelines and Bulmer's principles to identify the main ethical problems involved.

b) Suggest the most appropriate ethical course of action for the researcher, carefully explaining each decision.

1 You are researching delinquency and want to interview some residents of a young offenders' institution. You approach the manager for permission and she agrees as long as she can read all the interview notes and make any alterations she wants in the final report.

2 You are researching the work of local councillors. In the course of your research you find out that one councillor has been falsifying their expenses for the past four years. What do you do?

3 The research concerns the effect of divorce on 10-11 year old children. You ask a local school for a list of children who have experienced the divorce of their parents in the last two years and plan to give each child a questionnaire.

4 Research into the lives of pupils at a local private school finds that marijuana smoking is seen as a 'normal' social activity. The local newspaper gets hold of a draft of the research report and a journalist rings you for more information. They are planning to expose the use of drugs at the school.

Ethical issues in quantitative research

When questionnaires are being designed and interviewers trained, a number of ethical issues need to be taken into account. Before data collection begins respondents need to be informed about the nature and purposes of the study, how the data will be used, how their anonymity will be respected and how the confidentiality of their answers will be safeguarded.

Asking questions An interviewer may be able to check on any possible harm or upset to the respondent by building up a friendly relationship or rapport with them. In this way the respondent should feel confident to refuse to answer certain questions, or the interviewer can simply avoid asking them.

However, some interviewers are trained to ask every respondent every question in the same way. In this case showing individual sensitivity would compromise the reliability of the data.

It is not always possible to anticipate the issues that will cause upset or harm. A question about frequency of contact with the extended family may appear harmless but if the respondent has just experienced the death of a grandparent the question could be upsetting.

Uses of data Large-scale quantitative research generates huge amounts of survey data which are usually stored electronically. The data must be kept securely and in line with the Data Protection Act. In the case of the official census, although the main results are freely available, individual data never leave the Census office.

Most survey data leaves out names and addresses to ensure confidentiality. Sometimes computer-assisted self-interviewing (CASI) is used (see page 163). Here the respondent types their answers to questions into an interviewer's laptop. This ensures answers are private and the data confidential.

Ethical issues in qualitative research

Qualitative research, consisting of methods such as unstructured interviews and participant observation, raises many ethical issues. This is because it is more open and unpredictable than quantitative research and relies heavily on the individual judgements and skills of the researcher.

It is often difficult to get informed consent from every person encountered by a participant observer. In his research about a school in the Midlands, Bob Burgess observed some job interviews for teachers. He 'reached an agreement with the head whereby he would either introduce me to all candidates or he would give me an opening to do this for myself' (Burgess, 1989). However, Burgess does not consider that this constituted informed consent because the candidates were not really in a position to object to his presence in the middle of their job interview.

Sometimes participant observers find it hard to avoid illegal actions. Dick Hobbs (1988) conducted research about petty criminals and police in the East End of London.

He had to participate in some criminal activities in order to be accepted fully into the culture and to get a complete picture of what was going on. He had to show: 'A willingness to abide by the ethics of the researched culture and not the normal ethical constraints of sociological research' (Hobbs, 1988).

But Hobbs did draw the line at racism. He comments that he sacrificed important information because people were not open with him once he had objected to their racism.

Covert research A key area of debate about the ethics of qualitative research is the question of *covert* or hidden research. Is it ever justifiable to deceive participants by failing to reveal that research is taking place?

Failing to reveal the true purpose of your presence contradicts three standard ethical guidelines. There is no attempt to gain informed consent, the participants are deceived and their privacy is invaded. So can it ever be justified?

activity7 ethics and covert research

Item A *Stealing and fiddling*

Jason Ditton studied stealing and 'fiddling' at work by employees at a bakery. He worked at the bakery without revealing his research to anyone. He writes:

I decided to return to Wellbread's where I had worked the previous summer. I worked in the plant while also being an undercover observer. By now I knew most of the men and so had none of the usual problems of getting permission, and getting accepted. In fact, I had far greater problems getting out. Every attempt to leave was brushed aside and I was plied with furious pleas to stay and help out for the summer.

Adapted from Ditton, 1977

Item B *Desiree's world*

Julia O'Connell Davidson conducted research into sex work based around a prostitute called 'Desiree'.

Although I have full and informed consent from Desiree, her receptionist and her 'hangers on', my research involves covert observation of her clients and this raises some ethical issues.

When I answer the phone and offer to provide details of services offered and prices charged, the men making enquiries take me to be a prostitute or a receptionist. No clients have consented to Desiree providing me with information about their sexual preferences, physical and psychological defects and so on. When I take coffee to a waiting punter, he is not aware that I am making notes about him.

It could be argued that I am invading these men's privacy and that, since I am firmly convinced that few would give their informed consent, this is unethical. Yet I find myself untroubled by my uninvited intrusion into these men's worlds. This is mainly because the clients remain completely anonymous to me. Moreover, Desiree has willingly offered to provide me with the details of their interaction and since this knowledge belongs to her it seems to me that she is entitled to do what she likes with it.

Adapted from O'Connell Davidson & Layder, 1994

questions

1 How could it be argued that Jason Ditton's easy access into the bakery created ethical problems (Item A)?
2 In your own words, justify the covert observation described in Item B.

Those who tolerate covert research argue that no harm can come to participants if their identities are not revealed in the published research. What is more, covert research is the only possible method of gaining access to certain groups – particularly deviant groups. In these cases, the benefits to society of knowing more about the lifestyle and motivations of group members may outweigh the ethical problems associated with covert research.

key terms

Informed consent Agreement to participate in research based on a full knowledge and understanding of its methods, aims and the uses to which the data will be put.
Covert research Hidden research where the sociologist does not reveal that they are conducting research.

summary

1. Research usually starts with a literature review. Some qualitative researchers prefer to start research with an open mind and read up on issues as they arise.

2. All researchers need to gain access to a group, place or organisation. Gatekeepers often provide the key to access.

3. Sometimes researchers have to enter into research bargains with gatekeepers where access is only granted if certain conditions are met.

4. Gaining access to less powerful groups is usually easier than to more powerful groups who can protect themselves from research.

5. Ethical issues such as gaining informed consent, respect for

privacy and protection of participants from harm, affect all aspects of the research process.

6. The British Sociological Association produces a Statement of Ethical Practice to guide researchers.

7. Particular care must be taken to preserve the anonymity of participants and the confidentiality of data.

8. Qualitative research - particularly participant observation - is unpredictable. This makes it difficult to gain the informed consent of everyone who participates in the research.

9. Covert research involves particular ethical problems as informed consent cannot be obtained.

Unit 3 Quantitative data collection – sampling

keyissues

1 How do sociologists select samples?

2 What are the advantages and disadvantages of different sampling methods?

Quantitative data is numerical. It is often presented in the form of tables, graphs and charts and is normally collected by asking all respondents the same questions in the same order.

Social surveys are based on quantitative data. They aim to make general statements about a particular population – for example sixth-form students, teenage mothers, or people who play the National Lottery. One of the largest social surveys in Britain is the government's General Household Survey. This takes place almost every year and is based on interviews with every adult in over 13,000 households. The survey collects information on topics such as education, marriage and cohabitation, smoking and drinking, and ownership of various consumer goods.

Sampling With the exception of the national census, all social surveys are based on a sample. The need for sampling is neatly summarised by Miles and Huberman (1994): 'You cannot study everyone, everywhere doing everything'.

In virtually every piece of research a sample needs to be selected. Even in qualitative studies, choices have to made

about where the study will take place and exactly which groups and individuals will be the focus of attention.

Researchers refer to the whole group being studied as the *sample population*. This may be as small as students studying Sociology A level in a particular school or college, or as large as all of the households in Britain. On most occasions, researchers do their best to ensure that the sample selected is an accurate cross section of the whole group being studied. That is, they aim to make their sample *representative* of the sample population.

Once the sample is selected, it should be possible to apply the findings to the sample population as a whole. In other words, it should be possible to generalise the results from the sample to the whole group.

Figure 1 provides a simple illustration of the process of sampling.

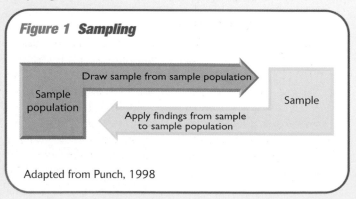

Figure 1 Sampling

Draw sample from sample population

Sample population

Sample

Apply findings from sample to sample population

Adapted from Punch, 1998

key terms

Quantitative data Data in a numerical form.
Social survey A study of a particular population in which members of the sample are usually asked the same questions in the same order.
Sample population The group or population being studied.
Sample A selection from the sample population which provides the focus for research.
Representative sample A sample which represents or reflects the sample population as a whole.
Generalise In this case, applying findings from the sample to the sample population as a whole.

3.1 Probability samples

There are several types of sampling, each of which can be divided into one of two categories: *probability* and *non-probability* samples.

The essence of a probability sample is that each person in the sample population has an equal chance of being selected as part of the sample. This means that there is no possibility of the researcher applying bias by choosing people for a particular reason – for example, because they appear cooperative or attractive.

Sampling frames

In order to select a probability sample, the researcher needs a complete list of everybody in the sample population. This list is known as a *sampling frame*. Two commonly-used sampling frames are the Electoral Register and the Postcode Address File.

The Electoral Register covers everyone over the age of 18 who is registered to vote. It is widely available in public libraries and can actually be purchased from local authorities. However, it excludes those who are ineligible to vote, such as prisoners, as well as those who have not registered to vote. This means that groups such as young adults, members of ethnic minority groups and unemployed people are under-represented (Butcher & Dodd, 1983).

A more common choice of sampling frame is the Postcode Address File. This is a list of addresses in Britain, updated regularly by the Post Office. It has the advantages of being more up to date and more easily accessible than the Electoral Register. However it lists only addresses, not the individuals who live at those addresses (Arber, 2001).

In many cases, sociologists are not interested in the whole population but in smaller groups such as school pupils in a particular town or pregnant women under the age of 18. In these cases, researchers have to be creative in identifying and then gaining access to relevant lists. Sometimes several lists have to be used and it can take months to gain access to these (see Item A in Activity 8).

Evaluating sampling frames Sara Arber (2001) identifies two key criteria for assessing sampling frames:

- How complete is the information on the sample population?
- Are there any omissions or duplicate entries in the sampling frame?

Arber goes on to give an example. Say the research is a questionnaire study of employees of a large corporation. It may be possible to obtain names and addresses of employees from the company. However, by the time the questionnaires are sent out, some employees may have left and new employees joined. Those who have left would simply be excluded from the sample. This is not a problem as they are no longer part of the sample population. However, the omission of new employees is more serious because the resulting sample may under-represent recent recruits. Another potential problem is that employees may have moved factory or office as a result of promotion. If the lists were updated at different times, the same individual might appear on more than one list. The problem here is that the sample may then over-represent those who are successful and ambitious.

key terms

Probability sample A sample in which each member of the sample population has an equal chance - the same probability - of being selected.
Non-probability sample A sample in which each member of the sample population does *not* have an equal chance of being selected.
Sampling frame A list of everybody in the sample population.

activity8 sampling frames

Item A Family fragments

Carol Smart and Bren Neale's book *Family Fragments* is based on interviews with 60 recently divorced or separated parents. They planned to recruit the sample through local solicitors so that the parents would be as close to the conclusion of legal proceedings as possible. The legal firms they chose dealt with very different types of client. The researchers told the solicitors that they wanted a range of parents - not just those who were bitter or who had experienced difficult separations.

Some solicitors did provide respondents but many did not. The researchers felt unable to put pressure on them - after all, they were only helping as a favour. Smart and Neale turned to support groups for divorced parents and also advertised through employers' newsletters. Of the final sample of 60, 29 were contacted through solicitors, 19 through support groups, 7 through advertising and the remaining 5 were recruited through existing members of the sample.

Adapted from Smart & Neale, 1999

Item B   Marriages

Mansfield and Collard (1988) wanted to study how marriages develop. They needed a sampling frame of all recent marriages. However, they were unable to gain access to a list of civil marriages that had taken place in Registry Offices so had to use a sampling frame consisting only of church marriages. This may have affected the research because couples with civil marriages are more likely to have cohabited before marriage, and they may differ in age and class from those who married in church.

Adapted from Arber, 2001

Leaving church after the wedding ceremony

questions

1   Identify the sampling frames used by Smart and Neale (Item A) and Mansfield and Collard (Item B).

2   Evaluate the likely representativeness and generalisability of each of the samples.

3   Suggest possible sampling frames for the following research topics.

   a)   Sexually active teenagers under the age of 16 in a particular town.

   b)   Those who participate in badminton.

   c)   Users of illegal drugs in a local area.

4   For each of the examples above, evaluate the extent to which your choice of sampling frame is likely to provide a complete list of the sample population.

Simple random sampling

The most basic type of probability sampling involves choosing randomly from a sampling frame. Random in this case does not refer to a haphazard selection of names or addresses, but means ensuring that each name or address has a mathematically equal chance of selection by using a computer or a table of random numbers to make selections.

But *simple random sampling* may not produce a representative sample. Imagine a simple random sample taken from a sampling frame of a secondary school roll. There is nothing to prevent the sample from including a disproportionate number of girls or of year 9 pupils, for example.

Stratified sampling

Stratified sampling is designed to produce more representative samples than simple random sampling. Sampling frames can be sub-divided into smaller lists and then random samples taken from each list. This process is known as stratifying a sample.

In the example above, the school roll could be sub-divided into a list of all the boys and a list of all the girls in the school. These two lists could then be divided into lists of the boys and the girls in each different year group. Then random samples could be taken from each of these lists. In this way, a sample could be selected which was representative of both the gender and age of the school pupils.

Typical criteria for stratifying a sample are gender, social class, age group and ethnicity but these criteria will vary according to the purpose of the research.

Systematic sampling

Imagine a sampling frame consisting of 1000 names. It is decided that the sample size is to be 100. The sample is selected by simply choosing every tenth name on the sampling frame. This is known as *systematic sampling*.

The problem with this method is illustrated by the following example provided by Tim May (2001).

'Some years ago a certain London borough conducted a survey of residents of several blocks of high-rise flats asking them about their attitudes to their housing. The results showed that a frequent complaint was noisy lifts, but the problem had its origin in the sample selection of every fourth flat, which, as a result of a common building design, happened to be the one closest to the lift!'

So systematic sampling does not always provide a representative sample.

Multi-stage cluster sampling

Sometimes it is impractical to randomly sample from huge national sampling frames such as the Postcode Address File. One thousand people may be chosen randomly from all over the country, making interviewing a lengthy and impractical task – and not necessarily covering every area. In this case, a sample of areas may be chosen (the first stage) and then a random sample taken from each of these selected 'clusters' (second stage). If stratifying takes place, then the sampling can go through even more stages.

---

key terms

Simple random sample A sample in which members are selected randomly from the sampling frame.

Stratified sample A sample which attempts to reflect particular characteristics of the research population. The population is divided into strata in terms of age, gender etc, and the sample is randomly drawn from each stratum.

Systematic sample A systematic selection of people from the sampling frame, eg every 10th member.

Multi-stage cluster sampling A method of reducing the size of large sampling frames, and then selecting a random sample from these reduced units or 'clusters'.

3.2 Non-probability samples

Sometimes sampling frames are not available for particular groups. Sometimes researchers only have sufficient resources to study a small group of people. And sometimes researchers may feel that the representativeness of a sample is less important than other factors such as the need for in-depth and detailed information that a survey is unlikely to produce. In these cases non-probability samples are used.

Opportunity sampling

Sometimes known as convenience or availability sampling, *opportunity sampling* involves selecting participants simply because it is convenient to do so. School or college students might be approached at break time, or a magazine might ask readers to respond to a survey.

Sociologists rarely use opportunity sampling. Findings based on this method are not generalisable to the wider sample population, making analysis beyond simply describing the sample virtually impossible (David & Sutton, 2004).

Quota sampling

This is a more commonly used sampling method, particularly in market research interviewing. *Quota sampling* involves dividing the population according to characteristics such as age, gender and ethnicity. These categories are known as 'quotas' and each interviewer is given a quota of, say, 10 males and 10 females. They then select males and females on an opportunity basis until their quotas are met.

Quota sampling does allow comparisons to be made, for example between different age groups or genders, but its representativeness is limited by the fact that subjective factors such as 'looking friendly' may affect the interviewer's choice of respondents.

---

activity9 quota sampling

Interviewers stand on a busy high street on a Tuesday afternoon. Each interviewer has a quota of 5 men and 5 women in three age categories: 18-30, 35-47 and 51-65. The interviewers have to conduct brief interviews with 30 people altogether.

A member of a quota sample being interviewed by a market researcher

question

To what extent is the eventual sample likely to be representative of adults in the local town? Explain your answer.

The following two types of sampling are usually associated with qualitative research, which is the subject of Unit 5.

Purposive or theoretical sampling

On some occasions a researcher will want to select research participants because of their usefulness to the development of the research. In these cases, the representativeness of the sample is seen as less important than the need to move the research forward.

For example, in his research on youth subcultures, David Muggleton (2000) selected his sample by approaching young people whose appearance seemed to deliberately reflect the norms of different subcultures. His sample may not have been representative of young people as a whole, but it was useful in providing access to those who showed strong commitment to a particular subculture.

Snowball sampling

A snowball rolls down a hill, becoming larger as it picks up snow along the way. This is the principle of *snowball sampling.* One person introduces the researcher to another who in turn introduces them to one or two more and so on.

Snowball sampling is used when a sample population is 'hidden' and cannot be contacted by more conventional methods. Jessica Jacobson (1998) used this approach in her qualitative study of the importance of religion for the identities of young British Pakistanis. No sampling frame was available and she needed an initial contact to 'smooth the ground' for her as her interviews were time consuming – between one and two and a half hours.

Snowball sampling is often used in the study of deviant groups, such as illegal drug users, since members of these groups are unlikely to respond positively to conventional approaches from researchers.

However, this method of sampling can only work where there are informal social networks of people who share the characteristic that is the focus of the research. This has the disadvantage that the sample tends to reflect the values, tastes and interests of the person who originated the 'snowball'.

What is more, it is virtually impossible for the researcher to assess the extent to which a snowball sample is representative of the sample population.

Mixing probability and purposive sampling

In practice, sociologists use the sampling method or methods that best suit the aims of their research. Often this involves mixing sampling methods, as the example below illustrates.

'In a study of the occupational aspirations of secondary school children the researcher may only have sufficient resources to study a small number of schools. These should be selected using purposive sampling to represent the range of types of school that are expected to influence their pupils' aspirations. However, within each school, the sample of students to be surveyed should be selected using probability sampling.' (Arber, 2001)

Volunteer sampling

Volunteer sampling provides an alternative to snowballing. Advertisements, leaflets, posters, radio or TV broadcasts, newspaper or magazine articles announce the research and request volunteers for the sample. Annette Lawson (1989) wrote a newspaper article about her study of adultery. She used the article to obtain a volunteer sample by asking readers who had experienced adultery to complete a questionnaire. Five hundred and seventy-nine readers responded to her request.

Volunteer sampling has much the same advantages and disadvantages as snowballing. In addition, volunteer samples are *self-selected* which may systematically bias the sample in a particular direction. For example, those who volunteer may have a particular reason for doing so.

Sample size

What proportion of the sample population does a sample need to be for it to provide an accurate representation? This is a complex mathematical question but there are two key points (May, 2001).

1. A large, poorly-chosen sample will probably be less accurate than a small carefully-chosen one.

2. The smaller the sample population, the bigger the ratio of sample to population needed.

Non-response

There is little point in making a careful selection of 1000 people using probability sampling if a significant

activity10 evaluating samples

Smoking marijuana

Item A Marijuana users

I conducted 50 interviews with marijuana users. I had been a professional dance musician for some years when I conducted the study and my first interviews were with people I had met in the music business. I asked them to put me in contact with other users who would be willing to discuss their experiences with me. Although in the end half of the 50 interviews were conducted with musicians, the other half covered a wide range of people, including labourers, machinists, and people in the professions.

Adapted from Becker, 1963

Item B TV news

Cottle's study of television news coverage of environmental risks is based on a content analysis of a sample of 40 news programmes drawn from a two-week period. The programmes were taken from eight television news outlets between 25th January and 5th June 1995. Such a sampling strategy attempts to ensure that variation in media content over different days of the week, and seasonal differences, is taken into account.

Adapted from David & Sutton, 2004

Item C Shopping

Daniel Miller led a team of sociologists in a study of shopping. Part of their research involved a survey of shoppers at Brent Cross Shopping Centre in North London.

The survey was completed over a 12 week period as shoppers left the centre, concentrating on the main exits but also including some interviews at less busy exits. We did not attempt to secure a quota or random sample but asked every person who passed by, and who did not obviously look in the other direction or change their path, to complete a questionnaire. In order to confirm the representativeness of our survey, various checks were used. Survey results were compared with census data for the local areas and with other surveys of local shopping centres.

Adapted from Miller et al., 1998

questions

1 Identify the types of sampling outlined in Items A, B and C.

2 Evaluate the likely representativeness and generalisability of each of the samples.

3 Suggest possible methods of sampling for the following pieces of research.

a) The ways in which applications for asylum are processed by the Home Office.

b) Young people who 'joyride' (steal cars and drive them for pleasure).

c) The religious beliefs of members of a particular church.

---

proportion of those people end up not responding to your questions. High levels of non-response can really damage a sample, especially if those non-responses are not spread evenly through the sample population.

For example, in the 1994 General Household Survey the response rate was 83.5% in rural areas and 75.6% in Greater London. Low response rates in London and other inner-city areas are common in surveys and can result in the under-representation of poorer people and ethnic minorities.

key terms

Non-probability sampling Methods of sampling in which members of the sample do not have an equal chance of being selected.

Opportunity sample Members of the sample are chosen because of their availability or convenience.

Quota sample A stratified sample in which selection from the strata is not random.

Purposive or theoretical sample Members of the sample are specifically chosen because they fit the priorities and concerns of the researcher.

Snowball sample Members of the sample select each other.

Volunteer sample Members of the sample are self-selected – they offer to participate in the research.

Response rate The percentage of the sample that participates in the research.

Non-response Members of the sample who, for whatever reason, do not participate in the research.

summary

1. Social surveys are designed to provide quantitative data from particular populations.

2. They are usually based on probability samples which aim to represent the sample population as a whole.

3. Whatever type of probability sample is used, there is no guarantee that it will be representative.

4. However, some types of probability sample - eg stratified samples - are more likely than others - eg simple random samples - to be representative.

5. Non-probability samples are used when:
    * sampling frames are not available
    * researchers only have sufficient resources to study a small group
    * other factors are seen as more important than representativeness.

6. A high level of non-response can result in an unrepresentative sample.

activity11 the National Survey of Sexual Attitudes and Lifestyles

This survey used the Postcode Address File as a sampling frame and aimed to interview one person between 16 and 59 in each of 50,010 selected private addresses. The interviewer would call four times at an address before classifying it as 'non-contact'.

Sources of non-response in the National Survey of Sexual Attitudes and Lifestyles

	Number	%
Total addresses	50,010	100
Non-private addresses, eg shops	5,980	12
No eligible resident	14,228	28
Potentially eligible addresses	29,802	60
Of which		
Completed interviews	18,876	63
Refusals	9,278	31
Non-contacts	1,027	2
Not interviewable, eg doesn't speak English	621	2
Total eligible sample	29,802	100

Adapted from Devine & Heath, 1999

questions

1 What was the response rate in this survey?

2 Explain the following reasons for non-response in the survey and give your own example of each:
  a) Non-private addresses
  b) No eligible resident
  c) Refusal
  d) Non-contact
  e) Not interviewable.

Unit 4 Quantitative data collection – asking questions

keyissues

1 What are the main ways of asking questions in quantitative research?

2 What are their strengths and weaknesses?

There are two methods of asking questions in quantitative sociological research.

1. The questions are put by an interviewer using a fixed interview schedule. This is known as a *structured interview*. The interview may take place in person or over the telephone.

2. The respondent is sent or given a questionnaire and they fill in answers themselves. This is known as a *self-completion questionnaire*.

Whatever approach is used, the aim is to achieve reliability by collecting data in a standardised and consistent manner.

4.1 Structured interviewing

Structured interviews involve interaction between the interviewer and respondent. This has both advantages and disadvantages.

The interviewer is able to establish a *rapport* with the respondent, to note down non-verbal aspects of the interview and to prompt and probe for more detail. However, the interviewer may affect responses in a process known as *interviewer effect*. Perhaps some respondents will answer according to the level of social desirability attached to different answers. People may not want to admit to drinking excessive amounts of alcohol for example.

The skill of the interviewer is crucial in maintaining a balance between flexibility and consistency in the interview. Fowler (1988) identifies the following key roles for the interviewer.

• To locate and secure the cooperation of the respondent

• To motivate and guide the respondent through the questions

• To ask questions in a clear, standardised and concise way

• To record the answers carefully in accordance with instructions

• To maintain a rapport with the respondent.

Recent developments in technology have enhanced the process of interviewing.

Computer-assisted interviewing

The use of *computer-assisted personal interviewing* (CAPI) is growing rapidly. The interviewer asks questions displayed on a computer screen and then inputs answers directly into the computer. This approach is now used in many major social surveys such as the government's Labour Force Survey and Family Resources Survey.

CAPI has several advantages over the usual paper and pen approach to interviewing (Sainsbury, Ditch & Hutton, 1993).

- Questions can be customised. For example, information given earlier in the interview can be remembered so later questions can be personalised and irrelevant questions not asked.

- Inconsistent or contradictory responses can be identified.

- The process of data analysis is speeded up as mathematical calculations can be made immediately.

- Answers can be kept confidential by allowing the respondent to type directly into the computer – a method known as *computer-assisted self-interviewing*.

Feminist criticisms

Many feminists criticise the use of structured interviews. They argue that this formal approach to questioning exploits the respondent: 'the researcher extracts information from the research subject and gives nothing in return' (Bryman, 2004).

Interviewers are trained to ask every question in the same way and to avoid becoming too familiar with the respondent. This creates consistency and thus improves the reliability of the data gathered. However, feminists believe that structured interviewing creates a hierarchical relationship where the interviewer is powerful and the respondent powerless.

key terms

Structured interview An interview in which each respondent is asked a fixed set of questions. The interviewer records the responses.
Rapport In this case, a friendly and understanding relationship between interviewer and respondent.
Interviewer effect The unintended effects of the interviewer on the interviewee's responses.
Computer-assisted personal interviewing (CAPI) The interviewer asks questions displayed on the computer and inputs the respondent's answers.
Computer-assisted self-interviewing (CASI) The respondent inputs their answers.

Feminists such as Oakley (1981) believe that the barriers between the interviewer and respondent need to be broken down. They advocate the use of less structured interviews which they believe are more equal. Semi-structured and unstructured interviews are covered in Unit 5.

Order of questions

Can the order in which questions are asked in an interview affect responses? The answer is almost certainly 'yes'. An example of the effect of question order is provided by the annual British Crime Survey (BCS). The BCS always uses the question:

Taking everything into account, would you say the police in this area do a good job or a poor job?

Because of an error, this question appeared twice in the 1988 survey, once early in the interview schedule and once near the end. The duplication of the question raised an interesting point about question order. 66% of respondents gave the same answer to both questions, but 22% gave a more favourable rating to the police the

activity12 computer-assisted self-interviewing

The British Crime Survey

The British Crime Survey provides an annual estimate of the number of incidents of domestic violence. However, it has been acknowledged that this is likely to be an under-estimate. This is mainly because of face-to-face interviewing. The switch to computer-assisted interviewing for the main British Crime Survey provided the opportunity to introduce computer-assisted self-interviewing (CASI).

The interviewer passes the laptop computer over to the respondent who reads the questions on the screen and inputs responses directly into the computer. The method was first used in the 1994 survey to measure illegal drug use and sexual victimisation. The 1996 BCS included a new CASI component designed to give a measure of domestic violence committed by partners and ex-partners against men and women aged 16-59.

Adapted from Mirrlees-Black & Byron, 2000

questions

1 How might the introduction of computer-assisted self-interviewing in the British Crime Survey improve the quality of data about domestic violence?

2 Identify three other topics where interview data may be improved by the use of CASI. Explain your answers.

second time and 13% a less favourable rating. This may have been due to respondents becoming more sensitive to the difficulties facing the police as the interview developed (Mayhew, 2000).

activity13 From Here to Maternity

Ann Oakley (1981) provides a well-known example of the feminist criticism of structured interviews based on her own research with pregnant women. She points out that many research methods textbooks state that interviewers should avoid directly answering respondents' questions.

They advise that such questions as 'Which hole does the baby come out of?' 'Does an epidural ever paralyse women?' and 'Why is it dangerous to leave a small baby in the house?' should be met with such responses as 'I guess I haven't thought about it enough to give you an answer right now', or a head-shaking gesture which suggests 'that's a hard one'.

Adapted from Oakley, 1981

questions

1 According to many research methods textbooks, how should interviewers react to respondents' questions?

2 Why do you think Oakley disagreed with this approach?

4.2 Self-completion questionnaires

Self-completion questionnaires require respondents to read and answer questions themselves. These may be sent out by post to be completed in respondents' own homes. Sometimes they are completed in exam-type conditions to ensure confidentiality and anonymity. This is particularly common in surveys aimed at discovering the extent of deviant behaviour among young people (see Activity 15).

A particular problem associated with postal questionnaires is a low response rate. This is particularly important when using a probability sample. Bryman (2004) identifies a variety of ways of improving response rates in postal questionnaires.

- A good covering letter accompanying the questionnaire
- Use of stamped addressed envelopes
- Following up individuals who fail to respond
- Keeping the questionnaire as short as possible
- Making instructions and layout simple and clear
- Beginning with interesting questions
- Personalising letters and signing them
- Providing an incentive for respondents such as a small payment.

key term

Self-completion questionnaire A questionnaire completed by respondents.

activity14 question order

A controversy about question order surrounds the research on social class by Gordon Marshall et al., (1988). The authors concluded that social class was still important as a source of identity. However, Peter Saunders (1989) attacked these conclusions, arguing that the socialist values of the authors, which led them to see class as the major division in society, influenced their research. In particular, the order and quantity of questions about social class encouraged respondents to accept that social class was still important.

Item A Socialist bias?

A glance at the questionnaire reveals that respondents were bombarded with questions about class right from the start of the interview. Following no fewer than 28 detailed questions about the class system, respondents were then asked if they thought they belonged to any social class. Not surprisingly, most agreed that they did belong to one class or another. Armed with their 'findings', the authors conclude that class identity is still more important than other identities.

Adapted from Saunders, 1989

Item B The case for the defence

The question about class was preceded by 30 questions. Six of these have no obvious relation to the issue of identities. No less than 17 were specifically designed to make interviewees see the world in terms other than those of social class. They invited people to see themselves as consumers, as voters, as members of ethnic or gender groupings, as employees; in short, as everything but members of an identifiable social class.

Adapted from Marshall & Rose, 1989

questions

1 How does Saunders argue that question order reflected the researchers' values?

2 How do Marshall and Rose defend their research?

activity 15 the self-completion questionnaire

Smith and McVie (2003) conducted a longitudinal study of youth and crime in Edinburgh. They describe the conditions under which the questionnaires were completed:

'Desks were spaced out as much as possible, and in most cases questionnaires were completed in exam-like conditions, with talking strongly discouraged, and little or no over-looking of others' questionnaires.'

Adapted from Smith & McVie, 2003

questions

1 Identify the advantages and disadvantages of this approach to completing questionnaires.

2 Suggest two other research topics that might be suitable for this approach. Explain your answer.

Internet-based surveys

The growth of the Internet has created new possibilities for social surveys. Questionnaires can be administered through email, or respondents can be directed to a website where they can fill in the questionnaire on-line.

Internet surveys allow very large numbers of people nationally and internationally to be surveyed quickly at a very low cost. However, there are disadvantages, such as low response rates.

Sampling is a particular problem. Internet users are by no means a representative sample of the population. They tend to be better educated, younger, wealthier and to be members of the White majority (Couper, 2000).

4.3 Constructing questions

Reliability and validity

Whether self-completion questionnaires or structured interviews are used, sociologists try to make sure that their questions generate data that is both reliable and valid.

Reliability Data is said to be reliable when different researchers using the same methods get the same results. Simmons (2001) provides the following guidelines for researchers in order to ensure that their study is reliable.

1. Questions should be worded clearly so that all respondents understand them in the same way.

2. Instructions for the interviewer or, in the case of a self-completion questionnaire, for the respondent, should be the same in every case.

3. The sample selected should be well defined and there should be an explanation of how the sample was selected.

4. Explicit details of the methods used will allow other researchers to follow them exactly in order to replicate (repeat) the study.

Validity Data is said to be valid if it 'actually measures what it sets out to measure' (Simmons, 2001). For example, official statistics of crime are valid if they provide an accurate measurement of the extent of crime.

key terms

Reliability Data is seen to be reliable when different researchers using the same methods get the same results.
Validity Data is seen to be valid when it provides an accurate measurement - when it actually measures what it is intended to measure.

Operationalising concepts

A crucial process in achieving reliability and validity is the operationalisation of concepts. *Operationalising* involves putting a concept into a form which can be measured. This involves identifying *indicators* of the concept – specific examples of the concept which can be directly measured. For example, indicators of the concept 'religious belief' might include a belief in a supernatural being and regular prayer. Questions can then be constructed to discover whether such beliefs and actions exist. Respondents' answers can be quantified and, in this way, the concept of religious belief can be measured.

Many researchers argue that operationalisation is essential for reliability – without a standard method of measurement, how can different researchers get the same results? They also argue that operationalisation is essential for validity – how can concepts be accurately measured unless they are translated into indicators which can be quantified?

However, things are not as simple as this.

• First, sociologists often disagree about how to operationalise a concept. Look at concepts like class, poverty and religion. They have been operationalised in many different ways.

activity16 reliable and valid?

Wine on Monday

Beer on Friday

questions

1 Is the data gathered by the researchers reliable? Explain your answer.

2 Is the data gathered by the researchers valid? Explain your answer.

• Second, how do we know that operationalisation produces valid data? For example, does regular attendance at a religious institution provide a valid measure of religious belief? Maybe. But people can attend for social rather than religious reasons, and some non-attenders may be deeply religious.

Operationalisation – an example Zeller (1997) illustrates the stages of the process of operationalising through the example of research by Rosenberg (1979) measuring young people's self esteem.

1 Defining the concept Rosenberg defined self esteem as a positive or negative orientation towards oneself. A person with low self esteem for example, 'lacks respect for himself, considers himself unworthy, inadequate or

otherwise seriously deficient as a person'.

2 Identifying indicators Rosenberg used a series of statements as indicators. Respondents expressed strong agreement, agreement, disagreement, or strong disagreement with each of these statements. Some of these statements were positive and some negative. Examples included:

'On the whole I am satisfied with myself.'
'I feel that I'm a person of worth, at least on an equal plane with others.'
'I feel I do not have much to be proud of.'
'I wish I could have more respect for myself.'

In all, Rosenberg used five positive and five negative indicators.

activity17 indicators of homelessness

Sleeping rough in Harrow, Middlesex

All that's left of their home after the tsunami struck Indonesia in 2005

Hippy travellers in the Malvern Hills

Mother and baby placed by the council in bed and breakfast

Centre for the homeless, London

questions

1 How do the pictures illustrate problems in operationalising the concept of 'homelessness'?

2 Define the following concepts and then identify at least three indicators for each. What problems do you face?

a) Attitude to marriage

b) Poverty

c) Educational achievement.

3 Collecting data for these indicators A sample of young people was then asked to respond to these statements. The more an individual agreed with the positive indicators of self esteem, the higher their self esteem was judged to be.

key terms

Operationalise Putting a concept into a form which can be measured.

Indicators Specific examples of a concept which can be directly measured.

Constructing questions

After a concept has been operationalised and indicators have been identified, the next step is to translate the indicators into questions.

There are two main types of questions used in self-completion questionnaires – *closed* and *open*. In closed questions, the range of responses is fixed by the researcher. The respondent usually has to select one answer from a series of alternatives. Questions with two alternatives are known as *dichotomous questions*, whereas *multiple-choice questions* provide the respondent with three or more options to select from. Open questions, on the other hand, allow the respondent to answer in their own words.

Closed questions are often used to collect information about the social and personal characteristics of individuals – for example, their gender and marital status. These tend to be simple, straightforward matters. For example, in

nearly every case gender is easily dealt with by a dichotomous question which asks respondents to circle either male or female.

Open questions are more likely to be used to discover attitudes and beliefs. For example, political or religious beliefs are fairly complex matters that cannot easily be reduced to multiple-choice questions.

Coding answers

Constructing questions is the first stage of translating indicators into quantified data. The next stage is *coding* the answers to those questions. Coding refers to the process of classifying respondents' answers into categories so they can be quantified.

Closed questions are much easier to code than open questions. The respondent has a number of choices available to them and each possible choice is given a code. In the example below, the respondent is asked to choose one of six options, each with a separate code.

Which do you most prefer in a job?

A Work that pays well

B Work that gives a feeling of accomplishment

C Work where there is not too much supervision and you make most decisions yourself

D Work that is pleasant and people are nice to work with

E Work that is steady with little chance of being laid off

F Other/don't know

This question is precoded. As a result, it is very easy to quantify the responses – for example, 21% A, 19% B, and so on.

activity18 types of questions

1 Write the following types of question to find out the age or age group of a respondent.
   a) An open question
   b) A question based on a dichotomy
   c) A multiple-choice question.
2 What are the advantages and disadvantages of these three types of question in finding out:
   a) A person's age   b) Their marital status
   c) Their attitudes to illegal drugs?

3 The following points are advantages of either open or closed questions. Identify which is which.
   • Answers can be easily compared
   • Unusual and unexpected responses can be given
   • Answers are not suggested to respondents
   • Answers can be easily quantified
   • Respondents can answer in their own terms.

The question could also be asked as an open question – for example, 'What do you most prefer in a job?' In this case, the researcher would code respondents' answers in terms of a number of categories. Possible categories include:

feeling of accomplishment, control of work, pleasant work, security, opportunity for promotion, short hours/lots of free time, working conditions, benefits, satisfaction, other responses.

Sometimes open questions are used in preliminary studies in order to help the researcher develop categories for what will eventually become closed questions. In fact, this was the case with the question above (Schuman & Presser, 1981).

activity19 coding open questions

Suggest categories for coding the following open questions.
1 Why are you studying A level Sociology?
2 What do you think are the main causes of crime?
3 What influences your choice of clothes?

key terms

Closed questions Questions in which the range of responses is fixed by the researcher.
Open questions Questions in which the respondent is free to answer in their own words.
Dichotomous questions Closed questions with two alternative responses.
Multiple-choice questions Closed questions which provide three or more options to choose from.
Coding Classifying respondents' answers into categories so they can be quantified.

Writing closed questions

There are three main principles that guide the writing of closed questions (de Vaus, 2001).

1 Exhaustiveness The categories provided should account for every possible response. Piloting the questionnaire (see Section 4.4) is usually necessary to check that this is the

case. Final options such as 'other' or 'none of the above' are often used to take account of unanticipated responses.

2 Exclusiveness Respondents should be able to select only one response from those available. This is a particular consideration when there is a long list of options.

3 Balancing Where respondents have to place their own attitudes on a scale, there should be equal amounts of positive and negative categories. Having too many categories at either end of a scale will distort answers. It is also useful to have an option in the middle such as 'neutral' as many people do not have strong feelings for either side of an issue.

activity20 constructing closed questions

Coronation Street

1 Comment on the following two questions in terms of their exhaustiveness and exclusiveness.
   How did you travel to college this morning?
   a) Bus b) Train c) Walked d) Taxi
   Which of the following statements best reflects your own view of TV soap operas?
   a) TV soap operas help people deal with their own problems.
   b) TV soap operas are a useful reflection of society today.
   c) TV soap operas are very good entertainment.
   d) TV soap operas are dangerous because some people believe they are real.
2 Write a closed question to discover which newspapers people read. Try to make it meet the criteria of exhaustiveness, exclusiveness and balance.

Measuring attitudes

Do you think that cannabis should be legalised?

Yes

No

The question above is aiming to discover respondents' attitudes to the legalisation of cannabis. But you may already have noticed some problems. What if the respondent has never considered the issue? What if they have considered at great length, discussing it with their friends and researching it on the Internet? What if they agree it should be legalised only in some circumstances, for example for medical purposes?

The sort of dichotomous yes/no approach in the question above is rarely an effective method of finding out about people's attitudes and beliefs.

Rating scales

Sociologists have developed *rating scales* to provide a better way of measuring attitudes and beliefs. These have the advantages of being closed questions – they can be quantified and tested for reliability – but they can also provide a measure of the actual strength of opinions, thus improving validity. Two examples of rating scales are *semantic differential scales* and *Likert scales*.

Semantic differential scales place two extremes at either end of a series of numbers. Respondents are given a statement and then circle the number that most closely reflects the strength of their opinion about that statement. For example:

How important is living in a nuclear family for the wellbeing of children?

Absolutely essential 1 2 3 4 5 Totally unimportant

Likert scales are sometimes used in situations where a number of indicators are being used to measure a particular concept. For example a respondent's 'religious beliefs' may be measured by their belief in an ultimate being, the power of prayer, heaven and hell, superstition and so on. A list of statements is provided, each with a scale of 1 to 5, with 'strongly agree' at one end of the scale, and 'strongly disagree' at the other. The respondent's answers can then be added up and they can be given a 'score' for the strength of their religious beliefs.

	Strongly agree				Strongly disagree
	1	2	3	4	5
1. I believe in the power of prayer.					
2. I believe in the existence of an ultimate force in the universe.					
3. I am a superstitious person.					
4. Heaven and hell exist.					

In this case, the lower the respondent's score the stronger their 'religious beliefs'.

In actual research, the emphasis of statements is often mixed up so the respondent does not get into the habit of always opting for the same number. Likert scales work well when people have strong views in one consistent direction. They are more difficult to interpret where scores are in the middle areas, or where people have strong views in different directions. In these cases, both types of respondent may end up with the same score.

activity21 attitude scales

1 Design a question using a semantic differential scale to find out respondents' fear of crime.
2 Construct a Likert scale to measure young people's interest in politics.

4.4 Piloting questions

As you can see from the previous discussions, writing questions for sociological research is a difficult and complex process. This is why most questionnaires and interview schedules are tested out before the main study gets underway. This process is known as *piloting*. Piloting questions serves several purposes.

1 If closed questions are to be used in the main study, open questions can be used in the pilot to help form the fixed choice options.
2 Interviewers can gain confidence by practising the interview schedule.
3 Questions that make respondents feel uncomfortable can be identified.
4 Questions that are not understood clearly can be identified and clarified.
5 The order of questions can be tested to see how well they flow from each other.
6 Instructions to respondents or interviewers can be checked.

(Adapted from Bryman, 2004)

summary

1. There are two main methods of asking questions in quantitative sociological research - structured interviews and self-completion questionnaires.

2. Structured interviewing has the advantage of having an interviewer on hand to clarify questions. However, it has the disadvantage of possible interviewer effects.

3. Feminists have criticised structured interviewing, seeing it as a one-way process in which the interviewer exploits the respondent.

4. The order in which questions are asked in a structured interview can affect the responses.

5. Self-completion questionnaires require respondents to read and answer the questions themselves.

6. Often the response rate is low, particularly in the case of postal questionnaires.

7. In order to produce quantified data, concepts must be operationalised. This involves:
   - Identifying indicators of the concept
   - Translating those indicators into questions
   - Coding the responses to the questions.

8. Ideally, operationalisation will produce reliable and valid data.

9. Questions on a self-completion questionnaire may be closed or open. Closed questions are easier to code. Open questions give respondents more freedom to express themselves.

10. Various rating scales have been developed to measure the strength of opinions and attitudes.

11. Ideally, questions should be piloted to iron out any problems with them.

activity22 pilot studies

Item A Plans for FE

The following questions are taken from a questionnaire designed for year 11 students about their plans for further education.

1 List the subjects you plan to take at AS level.

2 Which of these will you continue to A2 level?

3 What are the advantages and disadvantages of vocational (applied) A levels?

4 How are your subject choices related to your future career?

Item B Suspects' rights

Carole Adams researched suspects about their rights when detained in police custody.

The questionnaire was checked in the usual way for ease of completion, problems with question wording, and problems relating to layout and format. However, an informal chat with a respondent who had completed the pilot questionnaire caused me to seriously doubt the usefulness of my research device.

We were talking about his views on the tape recording of formal interviews at the police station. He mentioned several reasons why he thought this procedure was useful, and then sighed and exclaimed that it made no real difference in his case as his interview had not been tape recorded. I was surprised by this statement and reminded him that on his questionnaire he had ticked to say he had been formally interviewed at the police station. He told me that was correct, he had been given a formal interview but there had been no tape recorder available at the time to tape his interview. 'They don't put them in the back of the van and the cells you know.'

Respondents believed they had been formally interviewed by the police when they had been asked questions about the offence for which they had been arrested and detained. They were not aware that to be 'formal' police interviews had to be tape recorded.

Adapted from Adams, 2000

A tape-recorded formal interview in a police station

questions

1 You conduct a pilot study using the questions in Item A. What problems might you encounter with the questions? Suggest ways of solving them.

2 Why was Carole Adams' pilot study (Item B) useful?

Unit 5 *Qualitative data collection*

key issues

1 What is qualitative data?
2 How do sociologists conduct observation?
3 How do sociologists conduct qualitative interviews?
4 What are the strengths and weaknesses of qualitative research?

Qualitative data emphasises words rather than numbers. It may take the form of quotations from interviews, notes made from observation, written sources such as diaries and autobiographies, even films and recorded music.

Qualitative data can often provide a richer and more in-depth picture of social life than the numbers provided by quantitative data. However, many sociologists combine quantitative and qualitative data in their research (see Unit 6).

5.1 The features of qualitative research

Bryman (2004) identifies four key features of qualitative research.

Seeing through the eyes of the people being studied

People are different from the chemicals, rocks and other objects that make up the natural world and which are the focus of the natural sciences. People are different because they are able to reflect on their experiences and to plan their actions on the basis of how they understand things. In other words they give meaning to the social world.

Many qualitative researchers try to understand these meanings by using approaches which allow them to see through the eyes of the people being studied. They try to empathise with the research participants. Max Weber called this empathic understanding *verstehen*.

The approach described above is sometimes known as

interpretivist methodology and more detail can be found in Unit 2 of Chapter 4.

Description and an emphasis on context

Accounts of qualitative research often include a great deal of detail. Social scenes are described in some depth and people's conversations reported at length. This is because the events described have considerable meaning to the participants in the research. Also, qualitative researchers believe that knowledge of the context in which social life takes place is crucial to a full understanding. For example, people say and do different things in different situations.

Emphasis on process

Quantitative methods such as questionnaires tend to provide a 'snapshot' of social life. They reflect social events and processes at one point in time. However, qualitative researchers are able to achieve a sense of the development of social processes over time. Participant observers may stay 'in the field' for over a year, watching relationships develop and events unfold. Unstructured interviews allow the respondent to reflect freely on their past experiences and feelings.

Flexibility

As outlined above, the aim of qualitative research is to understand the world through the eyes of those being researched. To achieve this, researchers need to let people express themselves in the ways that make sense to them and to focus on the issues that are important to them. This is less likely to be achieved through quantitative methods such as questionnaires because they contain set questions chosen by the researcher and so reflect their priorities. Qualitative approaches in contrast are flexible – interviews are unstructured and resemble 'guided conversations' whilst participant observation requires the sociologist to fit in with the lives of those being studied and to avoid imposing their own concerns.

activity23 *features of qualitative research*

Item A *Through their eyes*

O'Reilly (2000) conducted research on British expatriates living on the Costa del Sol in Spain. She found that the common view that this group are dissatisfied with their lives in the sun and long to return to Britain is not an accurate portrayal of how they see themselves and their situation.

Item B *Flexibility*

In her study of young people with learning difficulties, Davies (1999) reports that she found her interviewees often mentioned food in the course of their conversations. She followed these comments up only in order to develop rapport. However, she gradually came to realise that food was very important to the research. It was a focus for the young people's anxieties about the attempts of people to control them and it also provided opportunities for resistance to that control.

Item C Context

Father and daughter   *Daughter and friend*

Item D Process

McKee and Bell (1985) used unstructured interviews to discover how couples adjusted to long-term male unemployment. They found that couples did not experience immediate changes in their relationship but that adjustments occurred gradually over a long period of time.

Items A, C and D adapted from Bryman, 2004

question

Explain how each of these items illustrates one of the four features of qualitative research.

5.2   Structured observation

Would you always tell an interviewer what you have said and done? Probably not. Asking questions has its limitations. Respondents may not remember their behaviour, miss out important information, say what they think the interviewer wants to hear, or not even be aware of some aspects of their behaviour. Observation offers researchers the opportunity to see social action at first hand.

Observation can be structured, where the researcher counts what they see and hear using a detailed *observation schedule*. This type of observation usually generates quantitative data. Alternatively, the observer can actually join in the activities of a group and observe what they say and do. This type of observation is known as *participant observation* and usually produces qualitative data.

In most cases *structured observation* does not involve the researcher joining in with the group – it is *non-participant*

observation. Because of this, it is often used in social settings where an observer can watch events and complete the observation schedule without attracting too much attention and without affecting behaviour. Examples of these situations include classrooms and sports events.

The researcher designs an observation schedule before the research begins. This identifies the categories of behaviour that are to be observed – see Activity 24.

key terms

Observation schedule A set of categories of behaviour which the observer records when they occur.
Structured observation Non-participant observation using an observation schedule.
Non-participant observation A form of observation in which the researcher does not join those being observed.
Participant observation A form of observation in which the researcher joins in the activities of the group being observed.

activity24 observation schedules

Item A Flanders Interaction Analysis Categories (FIAC)

This observation schedule was developed to observe school classrooms. Every three seconds the observer decides which of the 10 events categorised is occurring - in other words they make 20 categorisations each minute.

Teacher talk in response to pupils
1   Accepts feeling (for example, accepts and clarifies an attitude or the feeling tone of a pupil)
2   Praises or encourages
3   Accepts or uses ideas of pupils

Biology lesson

Teacher talk initiated by teacher

4   Asking questions
5   Lecturing
6   Giving direction
7   Criticising pupils, or justifying authority

Pupil talk

8   Pupil talk – response
9   Pupil talk – initiation

Silence

10 Silence or confusion

Adapted from Flanders, 1970

Item B *Types of job*

Jenkins et al. (1975) used structured observation to compare different kinds of jobs. An observation schedule was devised to assess 20 aspects of a job. Most aspects were covered through more than one indicator, each of which took the form of a question that observers had to answer on a six or seven-point scale. For example, one aspect was 'Worker pace control' and comprised three observational indicators such as: 'How much control does the employee have in setting the pace of his/her work?' Another dimension was 'Autonomy' which was measured by items such as, 'The job allows the individual to make a lot of decisions on his/her own'. Each respondent was observed twice for an hour. The observations were at least two days apart and were made at different times of the day by different observers.

Adapted from Bryman, 2004

questions

1   How might FIAC (Item A) be helpful to those interested in studying teaching?

2   What criticisms can be made of FIAC?

3   How did the researchers in Item B attempt to achieve reliability and validity in their research?

4   Design structured observation schedules for:

a) Customer behaviour in a supermarket.

b) Hostility to the opposition in a football crowd.

5.3   Participant observation

Participant observation involves watching and listening to people whilst at the same time joining in their daily routines and activities. Supporters of this method believe that this is the best way to understand the meanings people give to their own and other's actions – to 'get inside their heads'.

Participant observation is the main method used in *ethnography*. Ethnographic researchers study people and groups in their 'natural' setting, whether this is their own home or simply a place where they spend a lot of time. It is based on the view that research methods need to be *naturalistic* to achieve validity.

Brewer (2000) defines ethnography as: 'the study of people in naturally occurring settings ... by methods of data collection which capture their social meanings and ordinary activities, involving the researcher participating directly in the setting if not also in the activities, in order to collect data in a systematic manner but without meaning being imposed.'

Ethnographic research may involve interviews and the analysis of secondary sources as well as participant observation.

Gaining entry

Participant observation cannot work unless the observer can gain entry to the group and get some degree of acceptance from its members. The process of gaining entry has been examined in Unit 2, pages 151-153. Participant observers face particular problems in becoming accepted when their research focuses on groups who are seen as criminal or deviant by the wider society.

Often the observer will start by building up a relationship with one member of the group who can act as a *gatekeeper*, providing contact with other members and

activity25 ethnographic research

Working as a bank cashier

Over a 16-month period from May 2000 to August 2001, I tried to record every aspect of a cashier's working life, both business and social. I used field diaries, participant observation, oral life histories, individual and group interviews and participation in 'out of work' social activities. In order to be in a position to explain events within the context in which they occurred, I chose to 'go native'. By wearing the uniform and working alongside other cashiers, enduring continuous public rudeness and frequent, unpleasant male sexual advances, I strove to integrate myself as part of the social fabric of the bank. I needed to cement relationships with people in whose natural environment I was researching, and I needed to show trust by using their language, speaking as they speak and doing as they do.

Adapted from Child, S., quoted in David & Sutton, 2004

HSBC Bank, Leadenhall Street, London

question

Explain the ways in which this research can be described as ethnographic.

credibility for the observer, thus allowing them to build up a snowball sample. In many cases, the gatekeeper develops a close relationship with the observer. Members of the group who build up this kind of special relationship with the researcher are known as *key informants*. Key informants can provide valuable information, contacts and introductions to other group members.

Taking a role

Participant observers have to decide early in the research exactly how they will behave in the group and to what extent they will reveal that they are actually researchers. These decisions relate to the *role* they will play in the group.

Should they take an *overt* (open) role by admitting to everyone that they are sociological observers, or should they limit this information to just a small number of key members, or tell nobody at all – a *covert* (hidden) role?

How do participant observers become accepted into a group so that their presence does not affect behaviour? Is it better to join in as many activities as possible or to take a 'fly on the wall' approach? As Lofland and Lofland (1994) put it, in most situations observers need to choose a role somewhere between the 'Martian' (a complete stranger who knows absolutely nothing about the culture) and the 'convert' (a complete believer in everything the group stands for). In practice, the taking of a role is not always a matter of choice. If not fully accepted, the observer may remain on the margins of the group, unable to really enter the world of the members. Alternatively, social pressures

activity26 wheeling and dealing

The following two extracts are from an American study about smuggling and dealing in illegal drugs. Patricia Adler describes how she and her husband gained access to drug smugglers and explains the role of key informants in the research.

Item A Gaining entry

We rented a townhouse near the beach. One of the first friends we made was our closest neighbour, Dave. Dave spent most of his time hanging out or walking on the beach with a variety of friends who visited his house. We started spending much of our free time over at his house, talking, playing board games late into the night and smoking marijuana together. We were glad to find someone from whom we could buy marijuana since we did not know too many people.

One day something happened which forced a breakthrough in the research. Dave had two guys visiting him from out of town and, after snorting quite a bit of cocaine, they turned the conversation to a trip they had just made back from Mexico, where they piloted a load of marijuana back across the border in a small plane. It turned out that Dave was a member of a smuggling crew that was importing a ton of marijuana weekly and 40 kilos of cocaine every few months. We decided to take advantage of the knowledge, access and rapport we had already developed. We therefore discussed the idea of doing a study of the general subculture with Dave and several of his closest friends (now becoming our friends). We assured them of anonymity and confidentiality and they were happy to help.

Item B Key informants

Throughout their relationship with us, several participants became involved with the researcher's perspective. They actively looked for instances of behaviour that filled holes in our concepts and theories. Dave became so intrigued that he conducted a 'natural experiment' entirely on his own, offering an unlimited supply of drugs to a lower-level dealer to see if he could work up to higher levels of dealing.

Our key informants also helped us in widening our circle of contacts. They let us know when someone in whom we might be interested was dropping by, vouching for our trustworthiness and reliability as friends who could be included in business conversations.

Items A and B adapted from Adler, 1993

Smuggled marijuana seized by New York State Police

questions

1 In what ways can Dave be described as a 'gatekeeper'?

2 Explain the ways in which key informants helped Adler's research.

3 What ethical issues are raised in the items? Do you think the researcher's actions are justifiable? Explain your answer.

activity27 overt and covert roles

Item A Advantages and disadvantages

Covert research cannot employ overt research techniques such as interviewing or even certain kinds of observation without arousing suspicion. Fieldnotes, the record of the researcher's observations and conversations, cannot be written up in public. The covert researcher may gain access to people and places impossible to an overt researcher. Those being researched may act more 'normally' in the presence of a covert researcher, thinking the researcher is 'one of them'. However, in most cases being honest and avoiding situations that require deception makes life a lot easier and potentially a lot safer.

Adapted from David & Sutton, 2004

questions

1 Using the items, make a list of the advantages and disadvantages of overt and covert participant observation.

2 How does Adler's research (Item B) show that most participant observation involves both overt and covert roles?

Item B Suspicion and trust

The illegal nature of dealing in illicit drugs and dealers' general level of suspicion made the adoption of an overt research role highly sensitive. In discussing this issue with our key informants, they all agreed that we should be extremely discreet. We carefully approached new individuals before we admitted that we were studying them. With many of these people, we took a covert position in the research setting. However, as non-participants in the business activities, it was difficult to become fully accepted as peers.

After this initial covert phase, we began to feel that some new people trusted us. In some cases, our key informants approached their friends or connections and convinced their associates to talk to us. In other instances, we approached people directly, asking for their help with our project. Sometimes, we had to juggle our overt and covert roles with different people. It was often confusing to separate the people who knew about our study from those who did not, especially in the minds of our key informants who would occasionally make veiled references to the research in front of other people, especially when loosened with intoxicants.

Adapted from Adler, 1993

---

may force them to participate rather more than they would have chosen, causing them to lose focus on the observational aspect of the research.

Gold (1969, originally 1958) identifies four possible roles for a participant observer, based on the extent to which they participate in the group's or organisation's activities.

1 The complete participant The researcher participates fully in everything. This may be possible where the observer is already a member of the group – a teacher researching a school, for example – or where the research is covert and the observer has to join in everything to prevent revealing themselves as a researcher. It may also occur by mistake when an observer 'goes native' and begins to identify too strongly with the group members.

2 The participant as observer Here the observer joins in the routines and activities of the group or organisation but their role is overt – members are aware of the study.

3 The observer as participant In this role the researcher is mainly an observer, interviewer and collector of documents although they do participate in some activities.

4 The complete observer The researcher does not get involved in any way with the group. Members of the group may not be aware of the researcher's presence. In this way the research is *unobtrusive* – not noticeable – and therefore not having any effect on people's behaviour. This role can also occur by mistake if the researcher is not accepted into the group.

In practice, researchers are likely to adopt all of these roles at certain points during their fieldwork.

Recording information

Participant observers cannot remember everything they see and hear. They need to make *fieldnotes* of their observations as soon as possible. This is straightforward in situations where participants may be writing things down anyway, for example an A-level Sociology lesson or a business meeting. However, in less formal situations, especially those involving what society sees as deviant activities, making notes can be a lot more tricky – see Activity 29.

In the early stages of participant observation fieldnotes can be very detailed. This is because the researcher is not sure exactly what they are looking for. Later in the research, theories may be developed (see Unit 1 on grounded theory, pages 148-149). This gives the researcher a clearer focus and they become more aware of which words and actions have the most significance. They are then able to ignore some events.

In fact, the making of fieldnotes can help the researcher develop theories and concepts. This is because the process of writing a record involves reflection on what has been seen and heard, and selection of what exactly to record. This process can provide a focus for future observation.

activity28 taking a role

Item A The Magic Kingdom

In his study of Tokyo Disneyland, Raz (1999) visited the theme park on many occasions, including being part of several official and unofficial tours; interviewed current and former employees; conducted a content analysis of company guidebooks; and organised a focus group with park visitors.

Adapted from Bryman, 2004

Item B The call centre

The journalist Polly Toynbee spent six weeks trying to live on the minimum wage. She lived in a council flat and took a range of jobs including kitchen porter, worker in a cake factory, hospital porter, school dinner assistant and the job she describes here, working in a call centre, 'cold calling' for a London cleaning firm.

I sat in on Melissa's calls for five minutes and then I was on my own. My letter today was G. I had to call all the businesses with central London postcodes starting with the letter G.

'No THANK you!' 'Not today'. 'We are suited thanks.' 'No, you can't talk to anyone.' 'You lot called only a couple of weeks ago. I can't believe you're calling us again after we explained last time that we are very happy with our present cleaning company.' 'Oh God, not another one!' 'Certainly not. How dare you! What a nerve.' 'You should know we fired you a month ago! Your company was a bloody disgrace!' 'Fuck the fuck off, with your fucking phone calls!' It was more surprising that most people were very polite. 'Frightfully sorry, but we've got an awfully good cleaner we're really fond of. But so kind of you to call.'

I have never known the hands of a clock tick by so slowly, slower than double Geography at school, slower than time passed in any other job I did. I ached with boredom as I tapped out number after number, repeating the same phrases over and over again, with ever-sinking spirits. I clocked up 163 calls in my seven working hours that day, and I got just one appointment. It was unbearable, claustrophobic, mind-crushing and soul-wearyingly pointless.

Adapted from Toynbee, 2003

Tokyo Disneyland

Item C Hiding in the Wendy House

In 'The Man in the Wendy House' King explains his research in an infants' school. He used his height to distance himself (literally) from the children and tried to avoid eye contact with them. He also at one stage used the Wendy House as a convenient 'hide'.

Adapted from King, 1984

Item D The skinheads

Most of my fieldwork time was spent with about ten skinheads who made up one group, most of whom lived in the suburbs of Perth, Western Australia. The typical week of fieldwork consisted of outings on Friday and Saturday night, on several weekdays and the occasional Sunday. Typical activities during fieldwork included playing pool and drinking in pubs and nightclubs, walking and sitting in Perth's central pedestrian mall, fighting, standing in groups taking, joking and insulting one another, visiting people, drinking in homes, and eating in late-night fast-food places.

Adapted from Moore, 1994

question

Match each of the items to one of the participant observer roles identified by Gold on page 175. Explain the reasons for your decisions.

activity29 making fieldnotes

Item A Toilet time

Jason Ditton makes the following comments from his participant observation in a bread factory.

I found it impossible to keep everything that I wanted to remember in my head until the end of the working day and so had to take rough notes as I was going along. But I had nowhere to retire to privately to jot things down. Eventually, the wheeze of using innocently provided lavatory cubicles occurred to me. Looking back, all my notes from that third summer were on Bronco toilet paper!

Adapted from Ditton, 1977

Item B Observations of football supporters

My research began without a focus so I decided to record everything. A typical match day Saturday would result in 30 sides of notes handwritten on A4 paper.

Adapted from Armstrong, 1993

Item C Some principles of making fieldnotes

- Write down rough notes as quickly as possible after seeing or hearing something interesting.
- Write up full fieldnotes at the end of the day and include location, who is involved, time of day and so on.
- Notes must be vivid and clear.
- Take a lot of notes - if in doubt, write it down.

Adapted from Bryman, 2004

questions

1 Do you think Ditton (Item A) was an overt or covert observer? Give reasons for your answer.
2 Suggest reasons why Armstrong (Item B) wrote such detailed notes at the beginning of the research.
3 Explain reasons for each of the four principles of making fieldnotes (Item C).

Getting out

When is the right time for participant observation to end? Practical factors can cause the research to end. Funding may run out, or the researcher's personal circumstances change. Adler's research on drug dealing began to wind down when she became pregnant, for example. Sometimes the observer reaches the point where they have found out as much as they can. This situation occurs when new data simply confirms what the researcher already knows. This is known as *theoretical saturation*.

Leaving the field needs to be carefully managed. Relationships with the group need to be respected and members need to be reassured that they will not be misrepresented or harmed by the use of the information they have provided. Contacts may be retained for follow-up research, or because genuine friendships have developed.

Assessing validity

Supporters of participant observation often claim that it is more likely to produce valid data than other research methods. How do they know this? How do they assess the validity of their data? These questions are addressed in Activity 30 and in Section 5.6 at the close of this unit (see pages 183-185).

key terms

Ethnography A study of the 'way of life' of a group, in which people are observed in their 'natural' setting.

Naturalistic observation Observing people in their normal, 'natural' settings.

Gatekeeper Someone who has the power to grant or refuse access to a group by an outsider.

Key informants Members of a group who have a special relationship with the researcher and are an important source of information.

Overt observation The researcher is 'open' and explains what they're doing to the research participants.

Covert observation The researcher hides their true purpose from the research participants.

Fieldnotes The notes taken by observers during their research 'in the field'.

Theoretical saturation This occurs when new data simply confirms what the researcher already knows.

activity30 validity in participant observation

Item A Checking data

The hidden and confidential nature of the drug dealing world made me feel the need for extreme certainty about the validity of my data. I therefore based all my conclusions on independent sources and accounts that we carefully verified. First, we tested information against our own common sense and general knowledge of the scene. We adopted a hard-nosed attitude of suspicion, assuming people were up to more than they would originally admit. Second, we checked our information against a variety of sources. Our own observations of the scene formed a primary source, since we were involved with many of the main participants on a daily basis. Finally, wherever possible, we checked out accounts against hard facts: newspaper and magazine reports; arrest records; material possessions; and visible evidence.

Adapted from Adler, 1993

Item B Assessing validity

Bruyn (1996) lists six criteria to assess the validity of research based on participant observation.

1 **Time** The longer the researcher spends with the group, the greater the validity of the data.

2 **Place** An understanding of physical location enables the researcher to understand the context of actions.

3 **Social circumstances** The more varied the observer's opportunities to interact with the group, the greater will be their understanding.

4 **Language** The more familiar the researcher becomes with the language used by the group, the more accurate their interpretations.

5 **Intimacy** The more the researcher becomes personally involved with the group, the more they are able to understand their meanings and interpretations.

6 **Social consensus** The extent to which the observer is able to indicate how the meanings within the culture are used and shared among people.

Adapted from May, 2001

questions

1 How did Adler (Item A) try to ensure the validity of the information she obtained from drug dealers?

2 Comment on the points made in Item B. Are they likely to lead to greater understanding?

5.4 Qualitative interviews

Sometimes participant observation is not appropriate for qualitative data collection. For example, the research issue may focus on a very specific part of people's lives – food habits for instance. Or it might be concerned with attitudes and past experiences which cannot be observed. In these instances, some form of qualitative interviewing may be used.

Qualitative interviewing is different from the structured interviewing described in Unit 4 in the following ways.

- There is much less structure in the wording and order of questions.
- There is more interest in the respondent's point of view.

- 'Rambling' or going off the point tends to be encouraged as it reveals what is important to the respondent.

- The researcher is looking for 'rich', detailed answers.

- Interviewers are able to be flexible, altering the wording and order of questions and asking new questions in the light of respondents' comments. They are able to *probe* for clarification and more detail.

Qualitative interviews vary in their degree of structure. Unstructured interviews may only have a few broad guidelines for the interviewer, semi-structured interviews are likely to have a list of topics to discuss and some questions may be planned in advance.

activity31 probing

The following extract is taken from an interview with a husband and wife about a visit to Disney World.

Interviewer: OK. What were your views or feelings about the presentation of different cultures, as shown in, for example, Jungle Cruise or It's a Small World at the Magic Kingdom or in World Showcase at Epcot?

Wife: Well I thought the different countries at Epcot were wonderful, but I need to say more than that, don't I?

Husband: They were very good and some were better than others, but that was down to the host countries themselves really, as I suppose each of the countries represented would have been responsible for their own part, so that's nothing to do with Disney, I wouldn't have thought. I mean some of the landmarks were hard to recognise for what they were supposed to be, but some were very well done. China, for example, had an excellent 360 degree film showing parts of China and I found that interesting.

Interviewer: Did you think there was anything lacking about the content?

World Showcase, Epcot Centre, Disney World

Husband: Well I did notice that there weren't many Black people at World Showcase, particularly the American Adventure. Now whether we were there on an unusual day in that respect I don't know ... And there was certainly very little mention of Black history in the American Adventure presentation, so maybe they felt alienated by that, I don't know, but they were noticeable by their absence.

Interviewer: So did you think there were any special emphases?

Husband: Well thinking about it now, because I hadn't really given this any consideration before you started asking about it, but thinking about it now, it was only really representative of the developed world, you know ... and there was nothing of the Third World there. Maybe that's their own fault, maybe they were asked to participate and didn't, but now that I think about it, that does come to me. What do you think, love?

Wife: Well, like you, I hadn't thought of it like that before, but I agree with you.

Adapted from Bryman, 1999

questions

1 How does the interviewer use probing in this extract?
2 How does the probing reveal more about the respondents' views of Disney World?

activity32 types of qualitative interview

Item A Clubbing

Clubbers were usually interviewed twice, with the second interview happening after we had been clubbing together. Both interviews were very much conversational in style and I avoided interview schedules, although all interviews were taped. The first interview was designed to achieve three main goals: to put the clubbers at ease while also explaining fully and clearly in what ways I was hoping for help; to begin to sketch in details of the clubber's clubbing preferences, motivations and histories; and to allow me an opportunity to decide how to approach the night(s) out that I would be spending with the clubber.

Adapted from Malbon, 1999

Newquay, Cornwall

Item B Food

Interviewees were asked to talk about their favourite and most detested foods; whether they thought there was such a thing as 'masculine' or 'feminine' foods or dishes; which types of food they considered 'healthy' or 'good for you' and which not; which types of food they ate to lose weight and which they avoided for the same reason; memories they recalled about food and eating events from childhood and adulthood; whether they liked to try new foods; which foods they had first tasted as an adult; whether there had been any changes in the types of food they had eaten over their lifetime; whether they associated different types of food with particular times, places or people; whether they ever had any arguments about food with others; whether they themselves cooked and if they enjoyed it; whether they ate certain foods when in certain moods and whether they had any rituals about food.

Adapted from Lupton, 1996

question

Identify which of these interviews is semi-structured and which unstructured. Explain the reasons for your answer.

Unstructured interviews

Unstructured interviews tend to be used when the researcher is 'treading new ground' and opening up areas of enquiry. The aim of the unstructured interview 'is to find out what kinds of things are happening rather than to determine the frequency of predetermined kinds of things that the researcher already believes can happen' (Lofland & Lofland, 1994). For this reason unstructured interviews are often used at the start of a study in order to provide direction for later research.

Life history interviews A particular form of unstructured interview is the life history. This is an interview which covers an individual's whole life. Respondents are asked to reflect on their experiences, feelings and relationships. These interviews can last for a very long time. It is estimated that the typical life history interview comprises two or three sessions of between one hour and one and a half hours each (Atkinson, 2004).

Oral history interviews are more specific than life histories. They tend to focus on specific events in the past. As with life history interviews, there is potential for bias here as respondents' may not have accurate recall or they may distort their accounts of events to suit their own purposes. However, oral history interviews have allowed the voices of ordinary people and less powerful groups to be heard.

Semi-structured interviews

This form of questioning involves the use of an *interview guide* – a list of questions or specific topics to cover. In most cases, the questions will be asked using similar wording and in the same order in each interview.

However, the interviewer has the flexibility to move away from the guide to pick up issues raised by the respondent.

Interviewer effect

Interviewers play a different role in quantitative and qualitative interviewing. However, whatever the style of the interview it is possible that the appearance and behaviour

activity33 life history interviews

A sample list of categories for life history interviews
Birth and family of origin
Cultural settings and traditions
Social factors
Education
Love and work
Historical events or periods
Retirement
Inner life and spiritual awareness
Major life themes
Vision of the future
Closure questions

Adapted from Atkinson, 2004

question

Choose four of the categories above. For each write one example of a question suitable for a life history interview.

of the interviewer may have some effect on responses. Answers may be influenced by what the respondent feels the interviewer wants to hear or what they think is socially acceptable. This is known as *interviewer effect* or *interviewer bias*.

One cause of interviewer effect is a sense of social difference between the interviewer and the respondent. Social differences may include differences of ethnicity, age, gender, social class or religion. Another cause is the behaviour of the interviewer. Aggressive styles of interviewing, a willingness to probe for more detail, and previous experience of interviewing, all play a part in influencing the responses of the interviewee (Fielding & Thomas, 2001).

activity34 a semi-structured interview

The following is an extract from an interview guide about training in small businesses.

1 Brief introduction to you and your business
2 Issues of size, number of employees, types of employee (age, qualifications, geographical recruitment and so on).
3 How do you identify the skills that people need to work here?
4 How do you expect/encourage those who work here to gain the skills required?
5 How do you find out about training provision, if at all?
6 How do you gauge the success of your 'on the job' training?
7 What support have you been able to get in promoting staff development?
8 Do you or your company have networked computer facilities? If so, who uses them, how did they get trained, do others working here learn from them, and what are these machines used for?

Adapted from David & Sutton, 2004

questions

1 In what ways is the extract from the interview guide structured?

2 In what ways is it unstructured?

Transcribing interviews

Most interviews are taped and then *transcribed*. This means making an exact written record of the tape. This method of recording interviews has a number of advantages over the traditional method of writing notes.

- It enables the researcher to hear the way respondents answer questions, the pitch and tone of their voice, hesitations and so on.

- It allows the interviewer to concentrate on the respondent's answers rather than note making during the interview.

- It means that the interviewer does not have to select which aspects of answers to note, a process that can reflect the views of the interviewer rather than the respondent.

- Very thorough analysis of what is said can take place.

- The interview data can be examined on several occasions and by different researchers.

- The interview data can be checked.

activity35 interviewer effect

Item A The Ten Commandments of interviewing

1 Never begin cold: always warm up with light, chatty conversation.
2 Remember your purpose.
3 Present a natural front.
4 Demonstrate active listening: be attentive and be seen to be so.
5 Think about appearance.

6 Interview in a comfortable place.
7 Don't be satisfied with monosyllabic answers: use probes and prompts.
8 Be respectful.
9 Practice.
10 Be pleasant and behave appropriately.

Adapted from Berg, 1998

Item B The interview from hell

questions

1 In what way does the interviewer in Item B fail to follow the Ten Commandments of interviewing in Item A?

2 What effect is her approach likely to have on the validity of the data collected?

activity36 transcribing interviews

Everyone we contacted agreed to participate. Interviews took place in participants' offices or in a school lounge and lasted between 45 minutes and three hours. We recorded and transcribed all but two interviews: one participant refused to be taped, and the tape recorder malfunctioned during another interview. For interviews not taped we made detailed notes. We assured all participants that their responses would remain confidential and anonymous and hired someone to transcribe the tapes.

Adapted from Rafaeli et al., 1997

questions

1 What problems of taping interviews are identified in this extract?

2 Suggest ways in which these problems might be overcome.

5.5 Focus groups

A *focus group* is an organised group discussion about an issue chosen by the researcher. Focus groups usually consist of six to ten people and are led by a facilitator who guides the discussion using a topic guide – a list of issues to discuss. Typically focus groups last for one to two hours and are recorded on audio or video tape.

The nature of the research determines the make-up of the focus group. Sometimes they consist of strangers whilst at other times they are made up of existing groups who already know each other. For example, in research about the understanding of AIDS, Kitzinger used existing groups such as members of a retirement club, intravenous drug users and civil engineers to examine how interaction was important in constructing the meaning of AIDS (Kitzinger, 1993).

Bryman (2004) identifies some of the advantages of focus

activity37 focus groups

Item A Boys' talk

'Yeah, I've had loads of girlfriends. Mostly I've dumped them when I've got bored with them or when they started trying to interfere with me going out with my mates.'

'No, I've never had a proper girlfriend. I would really like a girlfriend but I find it hard to talk to girls.'

Item B Talking about shopping

We tried to maintain spontaneity of discussion within the groups and only intervened when it was clear that the conversation was going off track, where there were unproductive silences, or where there was continuous repetition of the same issue. Our interventions were mostly in the form of open questions on themes we had prepared beforehand, but we were careful that these questions should naturally fit in with the general flow of conversation. The themes that we developed for our focus group discussion were as follows.

- Experiences of Wood Green Shopping City and Brent Cross Shopping Centre
- The difference between shopping on high streets and markets and going to a shopping centre
- Gender differences
- Shopping as pleasure, work, or leisure
- Christmas shopping and shopping in sales.

Adapted from Holbrook & Jackson, 1996

questions

1 How does Item A illustrate the problem of gaining valid data from focus groups?

2 What are the advantages and disadvantages of the role adopted by the facilitator of the focus group described in Item B?

3 Draw up a topic guide for a focus group discussion about views of TV soap operas.

groups over one-to-one interviewing.

1 They allow for an understanding of why people feel the way they do. Members of the focus group can examine each other's reasons for holding a particular view and can adjust their views after listening to others.

2 Participants are able to concentrate on the issues they feel are important, as the group itself can control the discussion.

3 Researchers can get a realistic insight into participants' views because members can challenge and argue with each other – this means they have to think quite carefully about the views they express.

4 The researcher can actually see the process of people creating meaning, as in the example of AIDS research above.

Focus groups also have their problems. Members may feel that they have to conform to culturally expected norms. What is more the group context may mean that some individuals may dominate and others withdraw. In this situation a skilful facilitator is vital. There are also practical problems such as difficulties in organising focus groups and in transcribing and analysing the resulting data.

5.6 Evaluating qualitative data collection

Validity

Think of some of the research topics examined in this unit – a study of bank cashiers, smuggling and dealing in illegal drugs, Disney World, working in a call centre, the social world of skinheads, and clubbing. Now imagine designing questionnaires to study these topics. How could you construct meaningful and relevant questions which would give you valid insights into the social world of those concerned? In some cases you might have direct experience of these topics – for example, you may have worked in a call centre or been to Disney World. However, in other cases you may know little or nothing about the social worlds of those you intend to study.

Qualitative research methods such as participant observation and unstructured interviews provide an opportunity of gaining valid insights into social worlds other than your own. They can reveal the concerns of research participants, the meanings which direct their actions and the contexts which influence their behaviour.

Validity is often seen as the main strength of qualitative research. The data results from long periods of time talking to, listening to, observing and interacting with research participants. This gives qualitative data a unique richness and depth.

Assessing validity Claiming that qualitative data is valid is one thing, proving it is another. Researchers use a number of methods to assess validity. Sometimes they use a process known as *respondent validation*. A rough copy of the research findings is given to some or all of the participants and they are asked to comment on its accuracy. This can work as long as the account is easy to understand and the

participants do not feel pressured to agree with the researcher.

An alternative method is the *principle of verifiability*. All social groups have norms – accepted ways of behaving – in terms of which their members are competent. The participant observer should have identified these norms and be able to follow them or provide others with instructions on how to behave 'normally' in particular social settings.

Aaron Cicourel (1976) used this method in his participant observation study of probation officers in California. His aim was to discover the meanings used by probation officers to define particular young people as delinquent. Cicourel claimed that by working as a part-time probation officer, he was able to identify the same young people as delinquents as his full-time colleagues. In other words, he had learned and acted in terms of the norms of those he was researching. This provided support for his interpretation of the meanings they used to define delinquency.

A third method involves researchers comparing their findings with those of others who have conducted similar research using the same or different research methods. This allows them to check their data, especially when it differs from the findings of other researchers. This method was used in Adler's participant observation study of drug dealers and drug smugglers (see Activity 30, Item A, page 178).

Reliability

Research methods and data are reliable when different researchers using the same methods obtain similar results. For example, if the same questionnaire and the same sampling procedure produce similar results when used by different researchers, then the methods and the data are reliable. A reliable method allows studies to be replicated, ie repeated.

Qualitative research is difficult, if not impossible, to replicate. It lacks standardised research tools such as questionnaires which can be used by other researchers. Qualitative methods such as participant observation and unstructured interviews lack standardised procedures. For example, there are no set questions in an unstructured interview. The content and direction of unstructured interviews often vary considerably, even if the same researcher is conducting the interviews. In view of this, it is not possible to replicate unstructured interviews. As such, they lack reliability.

Qualitative research relies heavily on the researcher's judgements, interpretations and social skills. A participant observer often develops close relationships with research participants, relationships which are partly shaped by their personality, gender, class and ethnicity. It is unlikely that researchers who differ in these respects would develop similar relationships and produce the same findings. Again, this makes it difficult to replicate qualitative research. As a result, such research is seen to lack reliability.

wish to interview everybody who gave a particular answer. Or they may simply want to find out who would be willing to be interviewed in more depth. In Annette Lawson's (1990) research on adultery, the use of a postal questionnaire provided her with a large group of respondents willing to participate in qualitative interviews about their experiences of marital unfaithfulness.

6.2 Methodological pluralism

Some researchers combine different research methods and different types of data in order to build up a fuller picture of social life. This approach is known as methodological pluralism.

It recognises that each method and type of data has its particular strengths and weaknesses. Combined they are seen to produce a more comprehensive and rounder picture of social reality. And their combination can also provide new insights and new directions for research.

Some of the strengths of methodological pluralism can be seen from Eileen Barker's (1984) study of the Moonies – the Unification Church. She conducted in-depth interviews, each lasting 6-8 hours, with a number of Moonies. The interviews dealt with their background, why they became a Moonie, their life in the church and the meaning of religion as they saw it. Barker also lived as a participant observer in

several centres with the Moonies at various times during the six years of her research. This enabled her to gain the trust of many members of the church, resulting in information which would not have been given to an outsider. Two years after the start of her research, she constructed a large (41 page) questionnaire based on her findings from interviews and observation. This provided information from a larger sample and was intended to reveal 'social patterns, trends and tendencies and gain a more reliable understanding of regularities between variables – of "what goes with what" '.

Barker claims that combining different methods of investigation gave her a much fuller picture than any one method or data source could have provided.

6.3 Triangulation

Triangulation is a term used to describe various ways of assessing the validity and reliability of research methods and data (Denzin, 1970). It looks at the topic under investigation from different angles and vantage points. Triangulation can take various forms. These include:

1 Investigator triangulation This involves the use of different researchers, eg different observers and interviewers. The aim is to check for observer and interviewer bias by, for example, using interviewers from different social backgrounds.

activity39 methodological pluralism

Our research on victims of crime was based on methodological pluralism. This approach favours neither qualitative or quantitative research methods. It is a position which recognises that different research techniques can uncover different layers of social reality and that the role of the researcher is to look for confirmations and contradictions between those different layers of information.

So, for example, for the first stage of our data-gathering process we walked our two research areas with police officers, we frequented the public houses, and we engaged in in-depth interviews with a variety of people working in the localities.

Then, on the basis of this information, we produced a criminal victimisation survey questionnaire and conducted a survey in each area, and, on the basis of this experience, moved into focus group discussions with survey participants. So, as a research process, we were always moving between quantitative and qualitative data looking for ways of making sense of the different layers of social reality which were being revealed to us.

Adapted from Walklate, 2000

Victims of crime – burgled during their wedding

question

According to this extract, what are the main advantages of methodological pluralism?

2 Data triangulation This involves collecting data at different times from different people in different places. It can also involve combining primary and secondary data. Data triangulation serves as a cross-check for validity. It can also serve as a means of assessing researchers' interpretations and conclusions.

3 Methodological triangulation This takes two forms. 'Within method' triangulation uses a variety of techniques within the same method, for example open and closed questions within a questionnaire. Asking similar questions in a variety of ways can check on the validity of the answers and the reliability of the method. 'Between-method' triangulation refers to the combination of a number of research methods, for example questionnaires, unstructured interviews and participant observation. The data produced by each method can be checked by comparing it with the data produced by the other methods.

The idea of triangulation is illustrated by the following quotation from *Belfast in the 30s: An oral history* (quoted in Macdonald & Tipton, 1993).

'In the first place we carried out ... "investigator triangulation". That is, each transcript was checked by two or three researchers to ensure that it said what people had meant to say. In the second place, we systematically did a cross-method triangulation, in that every piece of oral evidence that could be, was checked against a range of written sources: newspapers, parliamentary reports, documents etc. Finally, there was a considerable amount of data triangulation possible within the oral sources themselves' (Munck & Rolston, 1987).

key terms

Methodological pluralism Combining different research methods and different kinds of data in order to build up a fuller picture of social life.
Triangulation Combining different research methods and different types of data in order to check the validity and reliability of findings.

activity40 triangulation

Carolyn Hoyle's research examined how the police dealt with domestic violence. She used a variety of methods – 'interviews with police officers and victims, observation of officers on duty, and examination of official records were all used to understand the police response to incidents of domestic violence'.

She interviewed victims *after* she had interviewed police officers 'partly to ensure that the police officers had given me an accurate version of the incident and of the wishes of the victims'. She used semi-structured interviews which produced 'quantitative data and qualitative descriptions'.

In discussions with the researcher and talking amongst themselves, police officers sometimes trivialised domestic violence. Dealing with 'domestics' was more trouble than it was worth, it was exasperating because they were 'so griefy'. These comments may reflect the 'canteen culture' of police stations where officers get things off their chests and put on a show of bravado. But, when asked about specific incidents, their replies contradicted these comments. They said they listened carefully to both sides in the dispute and had done their best to deal sympathetically and effectively with the situation. These claims were supported by Carolyn Hoyle's direct observation of officers dealing with domestic violence.

Adapted from Hoyle, 2000

Canteen culture

questions

1   In what ways can Hoyle's research be seen as an example of triangulation?

2   With reference to Hoyle's research, outline the advantages of triangulation.

6.4 Quantitative and qualitative data from the same method

Most methods can produce both quantitative and qualitative data. A questionnaire can include some open questions and participant observation can involve some numerical data – for example, how often a particular type of incident occurred. But perhaps the method most suited to collecting both types of data is the semi-structured interview. James Nazroo's research on marital violence is an excellent example of the collection of both qualitative and quantitative data from semi-structured interviews (see also Activity 38, pages 184-185).

Nazroo's sample consisted of 96 cohabiting couples under retirement age drawn from doctor's patient lists. Open-ended questions were used in order to collect qualitative data about the meaning and context of marital violence. In addition, there were specific questions designed to produce quantitative data about the type and frequency of violent acts. This was linked to a rating scale which operationalised marital violence – for instance, by categorising acts of violence into severe, moderate and mild along with examples of each type. This provided a quantitative measure of marital violence.

activity41 qualitative and quantitative data on marital violence

Item A Quantitative data on marital violence

Acts of violence were measured using a series of categories. All acts of violence were counted including one-off incidents of gentle hitting. In terms of this measure, 38% of men and 55% of women had been violent in their present relationship. However, when these incidents were categorised in terms of dangerous and non-dangerous violence, a very different picture emerges.

'Danger violence' is operationally defined as violence that is undefendable (where victims cannot easily defend themselves) and is either intimidating (used to intimidate or frighten the victim) or injurious (causes physical injury to the victim). In terms of these measures, male violence is far more likely to be dangerous than female violence - 20% of men compared to 6% of women used 'danger violence'. Nazroo uses a further category - 'threatening violence' which he defines as danger violence which is not in self-defence. Again the gender differences are significant - 19% of men compared to 4% of women used threatening violence. In terms of these categories, the quantitative data shows that men's violence in marriage is very different from women's - it is far more likely to be dangerous and threatening.

In terms of the physical consequences of marital violence, only 1% of men compared with 10% of women had been severely injured by their partner. In terms of psychological consequences, women often revealed anxiety symptoms, men did not. Again, this suggests that male violence has a very different meaning than female violence.

Adapted from Nazroo, 1999

Item B Qualitative data on marital violence

This stamp went on sale in the USA in 2003. It sells for 45 cents, 8 cents of which goes to fund programmes to combat domestic violence.

What is immediately apparent when listening to accounts of violence by women, is that the men were easily able to defend themselves from attack. They grab their partners by the arm and hold them off, or pick them up and put them in another room to calm down, or disarm them. They will also not respond at all to their partners' attacks and they will frequently laugh at the audacity of their partners. Some of these men respond in a threatening way, for example one man, describing his response to being slapped, says: 'I shouted and she ran'. None of these men appear to have been intimidated in the least. The ease with which the men appear to be able to defend themselves is undoubtedly partly a result of their greater physical strength. However, it is also partly a result of the nature of the assaults carried out by the women in this group. Unlike the men who used severe violence, the women rarely seem to be seriously intent on harming their partners, never really pushing their attacks home even if they have the advantage of a weapon or surprise.

Adapted from Nazroo, 1999

questions

1 Briefly summarise the data in Items A and B.

2 How does Nazroo's research illustrate the benefits of methodological pluralism?

3 How does Nazroo's research illustrate triangulation?

summary

1. Many researchers use both quantitative and qualitative data, while recognising the strengths and weaknesses of each.
2. Quantitative methods can act as starting points for qualitative research and vice versa.
3. Methodological pluralism combines different research methods and different kinds of data with the aim of producing a more comprehensive picture of social life.

4. Triangulation provides a way of assessing the validity and reliability of research findings. It takes three main forms:
   - Investigator triangulation
   - Data triangulation
   - Methodological triangulation.
5. Methods such as semi-structured interviews provide the opportunity to collect both quantitative and qualitative data.

Unit 7   Secondary sources of data

keyissues

1   What is secondary data?

2   How do sociologists use secondary data?

Secondary data refers to any existing information. Some sources of secondary data – such as official statistics and government reports – are deliberately created to make a public record of the social world. Others are private and personal records, such as diaries and photographs.

Not all secondary data is intended as a record. Songs, novels, buildings, TV programmes and magazines can all tell us something about the society in which they were produced, and the values and motives of the people who produced them.

Secondary data can be used in two ways. First, it can be seen as an accurate record and used to help understand whatever aspect of society it concerns. Second, it can be an object of study in itself – how and why was it created? Whose interests does it serve?

For example, crime statistics can be accepted at face value as an accurate record of the amount of crime. Alternatively, they can be an object of study in themselves by asking questions such as. What factors affect police decisions to stop and search someone? What influences the public's decision whether or not to report a crime?

7.1 Secondary sources as unobtrusive measures

Some sociologists have cast doubt on the validity of all studies based on methods where participants are aware that they are being studied. Webb et al. (1966) argue that these methods are prone to *reactivity*. This means that people's answers in questionnaires and interviews are inevitably distorted by the knowledge that they are being studied. For example, they tend to provide answers that they feel are socially acceptable such as non-sexist and non-racist responses (see Unit 3 on interviewer effect). This point is also relevant for all forms of overt observation. For example, the behaviour of a class of pupils is usually affected by the presence of an observer in the room.

Webb et al. support the use of what they call *unobtrusive measures*. These are sources of data where the researcher can have no effect on the data. Many secondary sources of data can be considered unobtrusive as they are not subject to reactivity. Webb et al. identify two main types of secondary sources as unobtrusive measures.

Physical traces Objects left behind by people in the course of their lives such as rubbish and graffiti (see Activity 44).

Archive material This covers a wide range of secondary data such as official statistics, diaries, novels and newspaper articles.

7.2 Previous research

One source of secondary data which cannot be considered unobtrusive is the data gathered from previous sociological studies. This is because it is derived from methods of primary data collection where reactivity may be a factor – for example, interviews, questionnaires and observation.

Unit 1 covered the use of previous research at the start of a study (see pages 150-151). This section looks at further uses of previous research.

Data-sets These are sets of data collected at regular intervals which provide a bank of information for researchers to draw on. Some of the best known data-sets are the General Household Survey, the British Social Attitudes Survey and the British Household Panel Study. These data-sets are held in the UK Data Archive at the University of Essex. They have two main advantages.

- They use large, nationally representative samples which are beyond the resources of individual researchers.

- They offer opportunities for *longitudinal analysis*. The British Household Panel Study, for example, uses the same 'panel' of respondents over time, so trends and patterns can be identified.

There is also a bank of qualitative data which includes the raw data from some of the most well-known studies of the last 20 years. This is known as Qualidata and is also held at the University of Essex.

Table 1 Data-sets

Title	Data-set details	Topics covered
British Household Panel Survey	A panel study which began in 1991 and is conducted annually by interview and questionnaire with a nationally representative sample of around 10,000 individuals in over 5,000 households. The same individuals are interviewed each year.	Household organisation; labour market behaviour; income and wealth; housing; health and social and economic values.
British Social Attitudes Survey	More or less annual survey since 1983 of a representative sample aged 18 and over by interview and questionnaire. Each survey comprises an hour long interview and a self-completion questionnaire.	Range of social attitudes and behaviour. Some areas are covered annually, some occasionally.
General Household Survey	Annual interviews since 1971 with members over 16 in over 8,000 randomly sampled households.	Tends to cover standard issues such as education and health that are asked each year, plus additional items that vary annually. Large variety of questions relating to social behaviour and attitudes.

Adapted from Bryman, 2004

There are disadvantages associated with the use of data-sets. They are often very complex and it can be difficult to access the information needed. Also, because the data is already collected it may not include exactly what a researcher requires.

Meta-analysis There are a large number of studies on particular social issues but these are often based on limited samples. *Meta-analysis* is an attempt to identify patterns across a number of these studies. It is 'a quantitative method for identifying patterns in findings across multiple studies of the same research question' (Schutt, 1996).

7.3 Official statistics

Official statistics are the quantitative data produced by local and national government. They cover a wide range of

key terms

Reactivity The ways in which the researcher or research tool (eg questionnaire) distort the responses of the research participant.

Unobtrusive measures Data which is not affected by reactivity.

Data-set Sets of data collected at regular time intervals, eg once a year.

Longitudinal analysis An analysis of trends over time.

Meta-analysis An analysis of the findings of a number of studies investigating the same research issue.

behaviour including births, deaths, marriage and divorce, the distribution of income and wealth, crime and sentencing, and work and leisure. Much of the enormous

activity42 a meta-analysis

Item A Broken homes and delinquency

Wells and Rankin (1991) identified 50 studies that tested the hypothesis that young people from broken homes have higher rates of delinquency than those from homes with intact families. Estimates of the increase in delinquency as a result of broken homes ranged from 1 to 50%. In order to explain this variation, Wells and Rankin analysed key characteristics of the studies such as sampling and operationalising of key concepts such as 'delinquency'.

They found that differences in methods accounted for most of the variation in the findings. For example, the effect of broken homes tended to appear greater in studies using official statistics. In general, Wells and Rankin conclude that differences in estimates of the effect of broken homes on delinquency were due primarily to differences in research methods.

Adapted from Schutt, 1996

Item B *What causes what?*

questions

1 What does Item A tell us about the findings of studies concerning the relationship between delinquency and family type?

2 How can the work of Wells and Rankin be described as a meta-analysis?

3 What explanation did they give for the different patterns

they found in the studies?

4 Look at Item B. Despite the apparent relationship between the two, why might the experience of a broken home have little or nothing to do with delinquency? Consider the possibility that both may be caused by a third factor.

---

volume and range of official data can be accessed through the government's website at www.statistics.gov.uk.

Official data can be very helpful to sociologists. These figures 'enable us to understand the dynamics of society – perhaps along race, class, age and gender lines – as well as charting trends within society... This information provides government and social policy formulators with data upon which to base their decisions ... as well as the means to forecast and evaluate the impact of new social policy provisions' (May, 2001).

Critical views During the 1960s and 1970s, a great deal of criticism – often influenced by interpretivist perspectives – was directed at official statistics. They were seen as unreliable and invalid. This criticism was aimed particularly at crime statistics. A detailed discussion of crime statistics can be found on pages 10 17. Criticism became so strong that more attention was paid to how the statistics were constructed than to the levels and trends that the statistics were intended to show.

In defence of official statistics In 1980, Martin Bulmer wrote an article defending the use of official statistics. He argued that much of the criticism of official statistics was based on crime data but the problems these presented were not typical of other official data. In general, the inaccuracies in many official statistics were no worse than those found in sociological studies. In fact, some official

statistics, such as birth and death rates, were probably very accurate.

Today, most sociologists take a balanced view of official statistics. They acknowledge that there are some problems with all official data but accept that this is not a reason to dismiss them out of hand. Each set of official statistics must be judged on its own merits.

7.4 Trace measures

In one story, the famous detective Sherlock Holmes works out that the murderer is tall, left-handed, walks with a limp, wears thick-soled shooting boots and a grey cloak, smokes Indian cigars through a cigar-holder and carries a blunt penknife. He remarks to Watson, 'You know my method. It is founded on the observation of trifles' (quoted in Lee, 2000). *Trace measures* are the 'trifles' that Sherlock Holmes observed so closely.

Every human activity leaves physical traces of its existence. A soccer match leaves litter, lost property such as gloves and scarves, hamburger wrappers or boxes, plastic coffee cups, beer bottles, marks on the pitch and so on. These are all 'traces' which can be analysed. The amount of coffee consumed compared to beer might indicate how cold the day was. The remains of hamburgers and other food consumed might indicate the distance

activity43 crime statistics

Item A Crime statistics

Number of crimes recorded by the police in 2002/03 and 2003/04

Offence group	Number of crimes (thousands)		% change
	2002/03	2003/04	2002/03 to 2003/04
Violence against the person (VAP)	834.9	955.8	14%
More serious VAP	38.3	43.9	15%
Other offences against the person - with injury	349.7	433.4	24%
Other offences against the person - with no injury	447.0	478.5	7%
Sexual offences	48.6	52.1	7%
Robbery	108.0	101.2	-6%
Total violent crime	991.6	1,109.0	12%
Domestic burglary	437.6	402.3	-8%
Other burglary	451.3	416.3	-8%
Thefts of & from vehicles	975.8	889.2	-9%
Other thefts & handling	1,389.4	1,379.0	-1%
Fraud & forgery	330.1	317.9	-4%
Criminal damage	1,109.3	1,205.6	9%
Total property crime	4,693.4	4,610.3	-2%
Drug offences	141.1	141.1	0%
Other offences	72.5	74.2	2%
Total recorded crime	5,898.6	5,934.6	1%

Adapted from Dodd et al., 2004

Item B Two versions of crime statistics

The official version	An alternative version
The law is democratically arrived at and applied equally to all people at all times.	The law changes over time. Further, it is not applied equally to all people at all times.
A criminal act takes place and the law is broken.	A crime is committed but is anyone aware of it – and will they report it?
The crime is known to a member of the public who reports it to the police.	If reported, will the decisions of the police apply in the same way to all similar incidents?
The police treat all situations in a similar way without prejudice.	The crime may be reported but not recorded by the police. Even if recorded, not all offences are included in the statistics.
The offender is detained and charged with the offence.	If recorded, the offender may not be apprehended by the police.
The offender is subject to the decisions of the criminal courts.	If detected, not all people are treated in the same way by officials in the criminal justice system, even when they have committed similar crimes.
The initial act becomes a crime statistic.	Official statistics are compiled which are neither valid nor reliable.

Adapted from May, 2001

Item C Reporting crime

The greatest threat to women comes from those who they come into contact with most, such as family members and friends. Will a woman who is the victim of domestic violence from her partner report it to the police? Studies have shown that women tend to conceal such experiences from the police, as well as from researchers. Therefore, the overall assessment of domestic violence will be affected because the detection of the crime depends upon the victim reporting it without fear of repercussions. In addition, it depends on police practices and their willingness to see the incident as a legitimate part of their normal duties.

Crimes at work are often not reported for fear of losing jobs, or companies not wishing to attract bad publicity, or simply that there is a lack of confidence in the capability of the police to tackle the crime effectively. For these reasons, crime statistics tend to reflect street crimes which are visible, rather than white-collar and domestic crimes which are difficult to detect and take place within private domestic or work environments.

Adapted from May, 2001

questions

1 Summarise the trends and patterns in recorded crime shown in Item A

2 How does the 'alternative' view of criminal statistics in Item B conclude that statistics such as those in Item A are neither reliable nor valid?

3 Apply the descriptions of domestic violence and crimes at work in Item C to the flow chart in Item B. Which view – the 'official' or the 'alternative' – seems more realistic? Explain your answer.

---

supporters travelled to the match – the more food consumed at the ground, the further they may have travelled.

The 1975 film *Jaws* deals with the hunt for a gigantic shark that terrorises a seaside resort. Simon (1981) used trace measures to measure the impact of the film. Counts of the date stamps on books about sharks borrowed from public libraries showed a substantial increase after the film was released. Simon also records that sales of marine novelties such as sharks' teeth, magazine articles about sharks, and visits to museum exhibits dealing with sharks all increased following the film (example provided in Lee, 2000)

But trace measures are rarely adequate in themselves to draw firm conclusions about the social world. You may

activity44 trace measures

Item A Garbology

The Garbage Project is based at the University of Arizona. One piece of research studied the number of condom wrappers found in garbage. After 1984, the researchers found that the numbers increased significantly, a possible indication that public health messages about protection against HIV infection had been successful.

Adapted from Lee, 2000

Item B Graffiti

Klofas and Cutshall (1985) examined graffiti left on the walls of an abandoned borstal for young males. During their stay, boys had been moved to rooms on different corridors. As they moved the conditions in which they lived became progressively less severe. The amount of graffiti per room decreased corridor by corridor and the content of the graffiti changed. In the first corridor, there was a high proportion of 'tags' or personal identifiers. The researchers suggest that this may indicate the boys' attempts to maintain an identity when they first arrived in the institution. Romantic graffiti increased from the earlier to the later corridors, perhaps reflecting one way of coping with being locked away. Political graffiti was most common in the middle corridors. Klofas and Cutshall speculate that it may have been at the middle points in their stay that the boys came into most conflict with the authorities.

Adapted from Lee, 2000

Item C

Gang graffiti after riots in South Central Los Angeles

questions

1 Suggest one other topic of research which could use 'garbology' (Item A). Explain how it could be used.
2 How valid do you consider the interpretation of the graffiti in Item B? Explain your answer.
3 Attempt an analysis of the graffiti in Item C.
4 Suggest trace measures for the following:
   a) The amount of illegal drug taking in a public park
   b) The eating habits of school pupils
   c) The amount of extra reading done by Sociology students at your school or college.

have already noticed that traces can be interpreted in many different ways. For this reason, trace measures need to be combined with other methods to provide a more complete picture.

Trace measures can also be used to check the validity of responses in interviews and questionnaires. For example, trace analysis has revealed that household members are likely to under-report the amount of alcohol they consume. This was discovered by comparing people's answers in surveys with the number of empty bottles in their garbage (Rabow & Neuman, 1984).

7.5 Documents

Documents have been described as the 'sedimentation of social practices' (May, 2001). Sediment is what is deposited and left after something has finished. Documents are all of the written and visual traces left by people in the course of their lives. These include a vast range of items. Following Bryman (2004) we will divide them into the following categories.

- **Personal documents** – such as diaries, letters and photographs.
- **Official documents** – these may be from local or central government or from private businesses and organisations.
- **Mass media output** – TV and radio programmes, newspaper and magazine articles and so on.
- **The Internet** – material such as emails, websites and chat rooms.

John Scott (1990) suggests four criteria for assessing the quality of documents.

- **Authenticity** – is the document genuine or a forgery?
- **Credibility** – is the author of the document 'sincere' or are they deliberately distorting events?
- **Representativeness** – is the document typical?
- **Meaning** – what exactly does the document mean? Can it be understood and what is its significance?

Analysing documents

The point has already been made that secondary data can be an object of analysis as well as a source of information. Sociologists have developed various methods of analysing the content of documents. Ray Pawson (1995) distinguishes three main types of analysis, 1) formal content analysis 2) thematic analysis 3) textual analysis.

Formal content analysis This method attempts to classify and quantify the content of a document in an objective manner. Say you were interested in the portrayal of gender roles in children's fiction published during the last five years. You could take a sample of the books and analyse each in terms of the same pre-set categories. For example, which activities are shared by girls and boys and which are limited to one or the other. The results are then quantified and interpreted. If, for example, preparing food and taking care of younger brothers and sisters is limited to girls, then it could be argued that gender roles remain distinct.

Critics accept that formal analysis can often effectively measure simple straightforward aspects of content. However, they argue that it says little about the meaning of a document, either in terms of its meaning to the audience or the meaning the producer intends to communicate.

Thematic analysis This approach looks for the motives and ideologies which are seen to underlie documents. For example, a news broadcast may reflect the interests of powerful groups in society. The job of the researcher is to uncover this underlying ideology. The Glasgow Media Group combined content and thematic analysis in their analysis of TV news broadcasts in the 1970s and 80s. They made a strong case that there is a pro-management, anti-union bias in the reporting of industrial disputes.

However, there are a number of problems with thematic

analysis. Who is to say that the sociologist's interpretation of the underlying ideology is correct? And if it is correct, does the existence of such ideology matter? Readers of *The Sun*, for instance, may see through or ignore or be unaware of its right-wing views. This may well explain why a significant minority of *Sun* readers regularly vote Labour.

Textual analysis Rather than looking for underlying ideologies, this method involves a close examination of the 'text' of a document to see how it encourages a particular reading and creates a particular impression. Ray Pawson (1995) gives the following example from a newspaper

activity45 *family photographs*

Item A On holiday

Item B Christmas

Item C Photographs of Disneyland

Sutton (1992) argues that photographs distort people's memories of their visits to Disneyland. They take pictures that support their anticipation that Disney theme parks are happy places and ignore the less pleasant aspects of their visit such as queuing. When they return home, they only retain the photographs that remind them of pleasant experiences. In other words, positive feelings are constructed after the visit, partly by the use of photographs. As a result, Sutton argues, the photographs do not provide accurate recollections of a visit, but distorted ones.

Adapted from Bryman, 2004

A happy family - dad's taking the picture

questions

1 Assess the extent to which photographs provide a representative and credible source of secondary data using the examples in Items A and B.

2 How does Item C show that personal documents are often more useful as an object of analysis than a source of accurate information?

Secondary sources do have their disadvantages. Compared to primary sources, they are 'messy'. The researcher has no control over their production. On the other hand, primary data is produced by the researcher using tried and tested methods. The researcher is in control, checking for reliability, validity and representativeness, operationalising and measuring concepts, and creating exactly the kind of data required for a particular piece of research. By comparison, secondary data are just there. As a result, key pieces of information might be unavailable. And available information might not match the specific requirements of the research.

However, these 'disadvantages' of secondary sources can also be seen as advantages. Most secondary sources are unobtrusive, so there is no possibility that reactivity has occurred, that the researcher has influenced or shaped the actual data. A diary, a letter, a TV programme, a newspaper article, a film, a piece of music, a poster, a photograph and a novel are products of the social world. They have not been contaminated by the sociologist. They have not been produced by 'contrived', 'artificial', 'abnormal' or 'unnatural' processes such as questionnaires or interviews. As data, they may be 'messy', but they are actual pieces of social reality as it is lived.

summary

1. Many secondary sources can be seen as unobtrusive measures. As such, they avoid the problem of reactivity.

2. Data-sets provide an important bank of information. They often use large, nationally representative samples.

3. Meta-analyses are useful for identifying patterns across a number of studies on the same topic.

4. Official statistics have often been criticised for lacking reliability and validity. However, some official statistics provide a fairly accurate picture.

5. Trace measures are a valuable source of data, both in themselves and as a means of checking the validity of other forms of data.

6. Documents can be divided into the following categories.
   - Personal documents
   - Official documents
   - Mass media output
   - The Internet.

7. John Scott suggests four criteria for assessing the quality of documents.
   - Authenticity
   - Credibility
   - Representativeness
   - Meaning.

8. There are three main methods of analysing documents.
   - Formal content analysis
   - Thematic analysis
   - Textual analysis.

9. A major advantage of secondary sources is that most are unobtrusive. As a result, they have not been contaminated by the sociologist and not produced by 'artificial' methods such as questionnaires and interviews.

Unit 8 *Interpreting and reporting data*

keyissues

1. How is quantitative data presented and interpreted?
2. How is qualitative data presented and interpreted?
3. How is a typical research report organised and written?
4. What ethical issues are involved in publishing research?

The issues in this unit have already been covered in *Sociology in Focus for OCR AS Level*. However, as they are also part of the A2 specification, they will be repeated here along with some additional material.

8.1 Interpreting quantitative data

Your survey is complete. The questionnaires have been collected and the responses have been coded and quantified. What happens next?

Researchers then:
- describe
- present
- interpret
- analyse and
- evaluate the data.

These steps are interconnected. For example, presenting data in a bar chart involves describing and analysing the data.

Describing and presenting quantitative data

Quantitative data can be described and presented in various ways. The following examples are taken from *Social Trends*.

Tables A table of numbers is a set of numbers arranged and displayed in a logical and systematic way. As the following example shows, a table can pack a large amount of information into a small space.

Table 2 Students in higher education: by type of course and gender

United Kingdom   *Thousands*

	Undergraduate		Postgraduate		All higher education
	Full time	Part time	Full time	Part time	
Males					
1970/71	241	127	33	15	416
1980/81	277	176	41	32	526
1990/91	345	193	50	50	638
2001/02	519	263	94	133	1009
Females					
1970/71	173	19	10	3	205
1980/81	196	71	21	13	301
1990/91	319	148	34	36	537
2001/02	620	412	93	153	1279

Adapted from *Social Trends*, 2004

Table 2 contains the following categories or variables – male, female, full time, part time, undergraduate, postgraduate and year. The data is systematically organised in terms of these categories. The population from which the data is drawn is noted – in this case all students in higher education in the United Kingdom – and the meaning of the numbers is stated – they represent thousands of people.

The table allows certain trends to be identified at a glance – for example, the rapid growth in the numbers of students in higher education, particularly the numbers of female students.

Line graphs These are useful for presenting a visual display of trends over time. The following example clearly illustrates a steady increase in video purchases from 1986 to 2000. The vertical axis (on the left) shows numbers in millions for the UK. The horizontal axis (along the bottom) shows time in years.

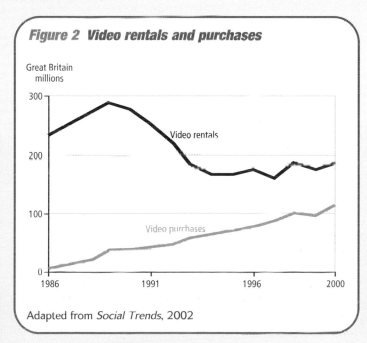

Figure 2 Video rentals and purchases

Great Britain
millions

Adapted from *Social Trends*, 2002

Bar charts These are particularly useful for comparing the behaviour of different groups. In the example below, different age and gender groups are compared in terms of their use of the Internet.

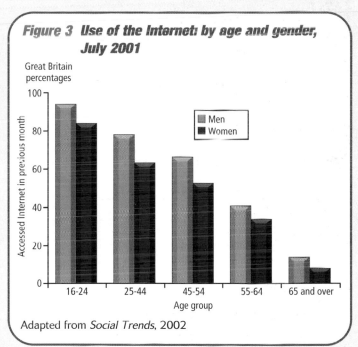

Figure 3 Use of the Internet: by age and gender, July 2001

Great Britain percentages

Adapted from *Social Trends*, 2002

Each bar shows the percentage of men and women for each of the five age groups who had used the Internet at least once during the month before the survey. For example, over 90% of men and over 80% of women in the 16-24 age group had accessed the Internet during the month before the survey. This drops to under 20% of men and 10% of women in the 65 and over age group.

The bar chart clearly shows that age is a major factor affecting Internet use, though gender is also important.

Bar charts are a useful method of organising and presenting data. They provide a simple visual summary of the main points.

Pie charts These are a useful visual aid when illustrating the proportion of each type that makes up the whole category. The pie chart below shows the percentage of each type of household in Britain in 2000. For example, one-person households make up 32% of all households. (Note that the data must be shown as a percentage of 360 in order to work out the angles – eg, the angle for the 32% segment is 32% of 360 which is just over 115°.)

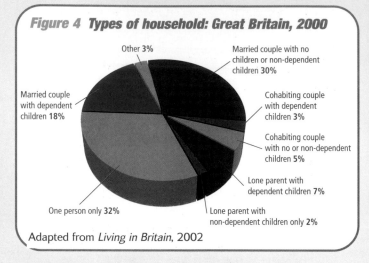

Figure 4 Types of household: Great Britain, 2000

Other 3%

Married couple with no children or non-dependent children 30%

Married couple with dependent children 18%

Cohabiting couple with dependent children 3%

Cohabiting couple with no or non-dependent children 5%

One person only 32%

Lone parent with dependent children 7%

Lone parent with non-dependent children only 2%

Adapted from *Living in Britain*, 2002

Interpreting, analysing and evaluating quantitative data

What does the data mean? What does it indicate? How can it be used? How good is it? These are some of the questions researchers ask when interpreting, analysing and evaluating quantitative data.

Patterns and trends Interpreting and analysing data involves looking for patterns and trends. Often these 'jump out' once the data has been described and presented in tables, graphs and charts.

Look at the table on page 199. It shows a steady increase

activity47 *reading data*

TABLES Look at the table on page 199.
1 How many full-time male undergraduates were there in 2001/02?
2 Compare the growth in the numbers of male and female undergraduates from 1970/71 to 2001/02.

LINE GRAPHS Look at the line graph on page 199.
3 Briefly summarise the rentals and purchases of videos from 1986 to 2000.
4 Suggest possible trends in rentals and purchases.

BAR CHARTS Look at the bar chart on page 199.
5 Both age and gender appear to affect Internet use, with age being the most important factor. How does the bar chart show this?

PIE CHARTS Look at the pie chart above.
6 Work out the angle needed to draw the segment representing married couples with no children or non-dependent children.

in participation in higher education. This increase is particularly marked for females. From 1970/71 to 2001/02, the number of enrolments for men on undergraduate courses more than doubled, for women the increase was over fivefold.

The wider context Interpretation and analysis can go beyond the figures themselves. If patterns and trends have been identified, the next questions are 'What do they show?' 'What do they mean?' Answering such questions involves looking at the data in a wider context and comparing it with additional data.

What does the increased participation of women in higher education indicate? This trend may be interpreted as evidence of greater female participation in mainstream society. This, in turn, may be seen as reflecting a change in women's values – an increasing concern with paid employment outside the home and with career advancement.

Further information can be used to support this interpretation. Official statistics show that employment rates for women have risen from 52% to 70% between 1970 and 2000 (*Social Trends*, 2002). Sociological research indicates that working-class London schoolgirls in the 1970s saw their future mainly in terms of love, marriage and children. By the 1990s, a similar sample attached much more importance than their 1970s counterparts to education, having a job or career, and being able to support themselves (Sharpe, 1976 and 1994).

Interpreting and analysing quantitative data involves:
- looking for patterns and trends in the data
- interpreting these in a wider social context
- bringing in further information to provide a broader picture.

Correlational analysis Quantitative data is data in numbers. As such, it lends itself to correlational analysis. Correlational analysis is a statistical technique which measures the strength of the relationship between two or more variables. A strong correlation does not in itself show a cause and effect relationship. However, it indicates the possibility of a causal relationship. Further analysis may strengthen this possibility, especially if additional data points to a causal relationship.

Validity All the interpretation and analysis in the world is a waste of time if the data is not valid. For example, some researchers have found a high positive correlation between unemployment and crime. But, if the measures of unemployment and crime are not valid, then any correlation is meaningless. Put another way, the analysis is worthless if the data fails to present a true and accurate measurement of unemployment and crime.

The problem of validity is highlighted by a Home Office Research Study entitled *Rape and Sexual Assault of Women: The extent and nature of the problem* (Myhill & Allen, 2002). The study was based on a nationally representative sample of 6,944 women aged 16 to 59. It estimated that nearly one in twenty women in England and Wales have been raped since they were 16 – an appalling 754,000 victims.

activity48 validity

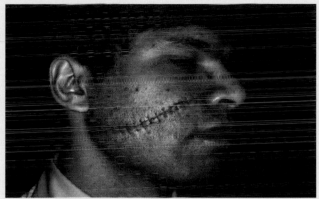

Teacher in Tower Hamlets, London, after being attacked outside an anti-racist concert

Synagogue in Finsbury Park, London, after being vandalised and desecrated

question

With some reference to the pictures, briefly discuss the problems of obtaining valid quantitative data on racial attacks.

The operational definition of rape used in this study is the use of violence, threats or intimidation to force a woman to have sexual intercourse against her will. Is this a valid definition of rape? It seems reasonable. But, only 60% of the women classified as rape victims in terms of this definition were prepared to classify their experience as rape or to see it as a crime. They tended to be women who had been raped by their partner or by a 'date'.

In an article in the *Daily Mail* (July 24, 2002), Melanie Phillips presents a scathing attack on the Home Office research, describing it as 'a load of manipulative, malevolent rubbish'. She claims that the researchers have 'muddied' the concept of rape. A flavour of her argument can be seen from the following quotation.

'Although the study claims the word "forced" implies an assault, it does nothing of the kind. A woman might feel forced to have sex against her will, for example, if her lover tells her that otherwise he will leave her for another woman. Or she might be an unwilling participant because he is

drunk, hasn't had a bath for a week, or she doesn't love him.

The crucial point is that in such circumstances she is participating in sex even though she could choose not to do so. She is therefore not the victim of violence. By any fair-minded or common-sense definition, this is not rape.'

Whether or not the Home Office researchers have produced a valid measure of rape is a matter of judgement. This applies to some extent to every operational definition – from crime to unemployment to marital satisfaction to leisure activity.

8.2 Interpeting qualitative data

Interpreting and evaluating documents

Content analysis Various forms of content analysis were introduced in Unit 7, pages 194-196. This section looks at an example of content analysis in practice. It is based on an analysis of gender roles in six reading schemes, including the *Janet and John* and *Ladybird* series, which were widely used in primary schools during the 1960s and 1970s (Lobban, 1974).

- First, a sample of the materials to be analysed is examined. In terms of the above example, three books from each of the series might be selected.
- Second, categories are created in terms of which the data can be classified and organised. The categories reflect the purpose of the research – in this case an analysis of gender roles. Categories developed from the reading schemes included objects, activities and roles that are linked to girls, those that are linked to boys, and those that are linked to both.
- Third, a larger sample is selected and the researcher classifies data from the books in terms of the various categories. Table 3 presents the results of this analysis for the six reading schemes.

Themes The classification of data into categories is usually only a first step. Once this has been done, further analysis can take place. For example, the researcher might look for themes which are common to many of the categories in Table 3. The following themes might be identified from the way boys and girls are presented in the reading schemes.

- Boys are presented as more adventurous than girls
- As physically stronger
- As having more choices.
- Girls are presented as more caring than boys
- As more interested in domestic matters
- As followers rather than leaders.

The researcher may then widen the focus and, for example, relate these themes to adult roles such as the mother-housewife role and gender divisions in the labour market. For instance, women are concentrated in the caring professions – nursing, social work and primary school teaching. Men outnumber women in leadership roles such as managers. The researcher may then ask how the themes identified in the reading schemes form a part of gender socialisation – the way boys learn to be men and girls learn to be women. For example, how do these themes steer men and women into 'men's jobs' and 'women's jobs'?

Summary This example shows content analysis at work. Data from the reading schemes is coded into various categories such as toys and pets and activities. These categories are then related to gender roles as shown in Table 3. This is a preliminary stage – it is concerned with sifting and sorting the data. Further interpretation and analysis take place when the researcher identifies themes which cut across many of the categories. The researcher may then relate findings from the content analysis to broader issues such as gender roles in adult society.

Illustrations from The Ladybird Key Words Reading Scheme (1972)

Table 3 Gender roles that occurred in three or more of the six schemes

Gender for which role was allocated	Toys and Pets	Activities	Taking the lead in activities that both boys and girls take part in	Learning a new skill	Adult roles presented
Girls only	1 Doll 2 Skipping rope 3 Doll's pram	1 Preparing the tea 2 Playing with dolls 3 Taking care of younger siblings	1 Hopping 2 Shopping with parents 3 Skipping	1 Taking care of younger siblings	1 Mother 2 Aunt 3 Grandmother
Boys only	1 Car 2 Train 3 Aeroplane 4 Boat 5 Football	1 Playing with cars 2 Playing with trains 3 Playing football 4 Lifting or pulling heavy objects 5 Playing cricket 6 Watching adult males in occupational roles 7 Heavy gardening	1 Going exploring alone 2 Climbing trees 3 Building things 4 Taking care of pets 5 Sailing boats 6 Flying kites 7 Washing and polishing Dad's car	1 Taking care of pets 2 Making/building 3 Saving/rescuing people or pets 4 Playing sports	1 Father 2 Uncle 3 Grandfather 4 Postman 5 Farmer 6 Fisherman 7 Business owner 8 Policeman 9 Builder 10 Bus driver 11 Bus conductor 12 Train driver 13 Railway porter
Girls and boys	1 Book 2 Ball 3 Paints 4 Bucket and spade 5 Dog 6 Cat 7 Shop	1 Playing with pets 2 Writing 3 Reading 4 Going to the seaside 5 Going on a family outing			1 Teacher 2 Shop assistant

Adapted from Lobban, 1974

activity49 content analysis

Item A Men looking for women

Professional male 43 articulate, sincere, successful, own business, flat/car, of varied interests seeks intelligent lady companion.

Scotsman, May 1996

Gentleman company director 6ft tall, 54 wishes to meet lady for company and conversation. I am in good health and enjoy life to the full. I smoke and drink in moderation.

Scotsman, May 1996

Analysis About one third of men described themselves in terms of their occupational, educational and economic status. They represented themselves as hard-working, industrious, ambitious, successful achievers, consistent with traditional gender stereotypes of masculinity.

Adapted from Jagger, 2001

Item B Women looking for men

Caring, easy-going, warm, attractive F seeks tall M for walking, talking and cuddles.

Guardian, March 1996

Woman warmth and affection in abundance. Petite, attractive, dark brown hair, eyes that reflect great capacity for kindness, fun, giving and receiving at many levels. Deep understanding of humanity. Act one has ended with lots completed. Act two is to begin. Looking for male companion, 40s plus.

Independent, May 1996

Adapted from Jagger, 2001

Item C Men's magazines

questions

1 Item A presents a textual analysis of dating adverts placed by men. Try to analyse the adverts (placed by women) in Item B in a similar way.

2 Suggest ways of using content analysis to analyse the covers of the men's magazines in Item C. What conclusions might you draw?

Discovering meanings

The analysis of qualitative data often aims to discover the meanings which underlie what people say and do. There is no simple recipe for doing this. It relies heavily on the interpretative skills of the researcher, and is best illustrated by example.

Newspaper headlines Look at the newspaper headlines in Figure 5 on page 204. They refer to men and women infected with AIDS through blood transfusions, and mother to child transmission of AIDS in the womb.

What meanings lie behind these headlines? One interpretation runs as follows. The word 'innocent' crops up again and again. This suggests that the people concerned do not deserve to be infected – it is not their fault. As one headline states, they come from 'ordinary families', and this kind of thing does not, and should not, happen to 'ordinary people'. This implies that unlike 'ordinary people', 'typical' AIDS victims are not so 'innocent' – in some way they deserve their fate, in some way they are guilty for what happens to them.

activity52 talking about families

In the book *Family Understandings* (2001) the researchers used semi-structured interviews to find out what members of families with teenage children thought about family life. One question asked about the importance of family life. The most common themes in the answers were identified and 'representative quotations' used to illustrate each theme. Below are examples of two of the themes or categories identified, followed by representative quotations.

Category	Meaning of category
Positive attributes	• The family as a source of positive ideals, particularly the giving and receiving of care, help and love.
Taken-for-granted	• The family is taken for granted and 'natural'. • Its importance is hard to describe. • However, respondents are able to say that they would be lost without a family.

Happy families

'It just grows with you and grows round you and you are there and you'd hate to be without it.' (Roger Hutchinson, father)

'I wouldn't like not to have the kids and I wouldn't like not to have Stan.' (Linda Barnes, mother)

'Um, you've got people around you who love and care about you.' (Leanne Field, 11)

'It's the caring isn't it, and the love that's there in your family.' (Mandy Lawson, mother)

'I just think it's the right way to be.' (Carol Brook, mother)

'The love that I get from them.' (Kate Baxter, 14)

'I'm not sure really. I don't really know, just – I'm not sure'. (Jayne Towers, mother)

'I wouldn't be the same if I didn't have my family. If I was put up for adoption I would have been an emotional wreck really.' (Andrew Corner, 16)

Adapted from Langford et al., 2001

questions

1 Which quotations illustrate each of the four bullet points in the table?

2 Do you think it would be possible to interpret any of the quotations in a different way? Explain your answer.

3 To what extent do you think the selection of quotations and the analysis of interview data relies on the judgement of the researcher?

Data and methods In this section, the researcher describes the research methods used to collect the data. Table 5 provides an example of points which might be covered. This section should be fairly detailed. It's not enough to say that the study was based on 6 months participant observation or a number of semi-structured interviews. As Table 5 indicates, a lot more information is required.

This section has two main aims.

• First, to present sufficient details about the research methods for another researcher to repeat the study.

• Second, to allow the reader to evaluate the methods and the results. For example, data from a questionnaire given to a sample of five people hardly provides a sound basis for generalisation.

Results This section outlines the main findings of the research. Quantitative data is presented in tables along with statistical analyses. Qualitative data is used for illustration and flavour. For example, typical statements

Table 5 *Data and methods*

Sample size
Sample design
Sampling frame
Date of data collection
How settings selected for observation were chosen
Response rate achieved
Limitations of and possible biases in the data
Sources of secondary data
  (eg, statistics from government surveys)
Basic demographic characteristics of the sample
  (eg, age, gender, ethnicity)
Explanation of any special data analysis techniques used

From Gilbert, 1993

from unstructured interviews are quoted or descriptions from observations provided.

This section assesses the degree to which the results support the hypothesis or meet the aims of the research.

Conclusion This section brings everything together. It relates the results to the questions and issues raised in the introduction. It attempts to explain the results and relates them to various theories. It looks at the implications of the findings for future research. For example, what questions are raised which require further research?

References Throughout the research report, publications have been referred to by author/s and date, eg (Smith, 2003). The references provide full details of the books and articles noted in the text – these include title, author and year of publication. See the references at the back of this book for an illustration.

The following activity gives examples of reporting

research results taken from actual studies. They are based on examples given by Bryman (2001).

Ethical issues

Writing and publishing research reports raises a number of ethical questions. Authors have to ask: Am I protecting the welfare and interests of those who participated in the research? Am I respecting their privacy and maintaining their anonymity? Am I telling the truth? Do I have a duty to publish my results?

Protecting participants When research reports are published anybody can read them, anybody can comment on them – in the press, on radio and on TV. Those who participate in the research may gain or lose as a result of publication. They may be affected as individuals in terms of their job security and promotion prospects – they may lose their jobs, or their career may grind to a halt. They

activity53 reporting results

Item A An introduction

Religion remains a central element of modern life, shaping people's world-views, moral standards, family lives, and in many nations, their politics. But in many Western nations, modernisation and secularisation may be eroding Christian beliefs, with profound consequences that have intrigued sociologists since Durkheim. Yet this much touted secularisation may be overstated – certainly it varies widely among nations and is absent in the United States (Benson, Donahue, and Frickson, 1989; Felling, Peters, and Schreuder, 1991; Firebaugh and Harley, 1991; Stark and Iannaccone, 1994). We explore the degree to which religious beliefs are passed on from generation to generation in different nations.

Kelly & De Graaf, 1997

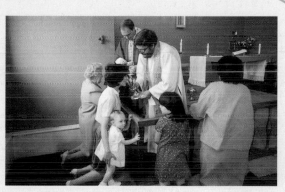

Church of St John the Divine, London

Item B Research methods

The following is a summary of some of the main research methods used in a study of vegetarianism by Beardsworth and Keil (1992).

- Semi-structured interviews and the reasons for using this method
- The number of people interviewed and the context in which the interviews took place
- How the interview data was analysed – this mainly involved identifying themes.

Adapted from Bryman, 2001

Item C Conclusion

The following is an excerpt from the conclusion to the research report on vegetarianism referred to in Item B.

Just as meat tended to imply strongly negative connotations for respondents, concepts like 'fruit' and 'vegetable' tended to elicit positive reactions, although less frequently and in a more muted form than might have been anticipated on the basis of the analysis of the ideological underpinnings of 'wholefoods' consumption put forward by Atkinson (1980, 1983), or on the basis of the analysis of vegetarian food symbolism advanced by Twigg (1983).

Beardsworth & Keil, 1992

questions

1 Look at Item A.
   a) What are the authors trying to do in this introduction?
   b) How well are they doing it?
2 Judging from Item B, does the methods section in this research report do the job?
3 What are the authors doing in Item C?

Promoting vegetarianism at the Earth Summit in Johannesburg, 2002

may also be affected collectively. For example, the organisation they work for may be presented in a good or a bad light. Similarly, groups such as teachers, doctors, police, bakery workers and others may gain or lose in terms of the standing of their professions. For example, the publication of a research report critical of teachers may have a negative effect on the whole profession.

The same applies to various social groups – women, ethnic minorities, older people, gays and so on. A research report may present them in a positive light or, often unwittingly, provide a negative view – for example, by reinforcing stereotypes of older people.

Clearly, researchers must consider these issues carefully before publication. They have responsibilities to those who take part in their research.

Telling the truth There is general agreement that researchers must do their best to tell the truth as they see it. This can produce a conflict of interest – telling the truth may harm research participants. There is no easy way out of this dilemma.

Telling the truth 'as they see it' inevitably involves bias – all researchers are influenced to some extent by their values and beliefs. There is no such thing as a totally objective research report. To guard against extreme bias and to check 'the truth', some researchers argue that research participants should be shown the data and asked to comment on it before publication (Simons, 1984).

Confidentiality and anonymity Codes of conduct for researchers in sociology and other social sciences stress the need for confidentiality and anonymity. Participants are told that anything they say is confidential – that there is no way it can be linked to them when published. One obvious way of doing this is ensuring anonymity – making sure their identities are not disclosed. For example, questionnaire respondents are often identified by number rather than name and sometimes given a false name in the published report. Similarly, places of employment and residence are not mentioned by name or are given invented names.

Researchers are aware of the harm that can be caused by naming names. For example, Holdaway (1982) in his participant observation study of police behaviour disguised people's identities, their place of work, and where events occurred. His reasons? The behaviour he observed could result in disciplinary action, it could ruin careers, or lead to dismissal from the force.

Obligation to publish Some sociologists argue that researchers have a duty to publish for the following reasons.
- To advance knowledge
- To inform government policy
- Because the public has a right to know (Homan, 1991).

Apart from the difficulty of getting a professional journal or book publisher to publish research, there are other barriers to publication. Many organisations who fund

research issue contracts with the right to veto (prevent) publication. This can be used, for example, by governments to prevent publication of views critical of their policy (Willmott, 1980). Similarly, researchers have been prevented from continuing research within organisations because their findings have been critical of the management and/or staff (Platt, 1976).

Conclusion There is growing recognition by researchers that they have duties and obligations to those who participate in their research and to the groups to which the participants belong. The ethical codes which govern sociological research now cover the entire research process – which includes the writing and publication of research.

summary

1. Quantitative data can be described and presented in terms of:
   - Tables
   - Line graphs
   - Bar charts
   - Pie charts.

2. Interpreting and analysing quantitative data involves looking for patterns and trends.

3. Quantitative data lends itself to correlational analysis.

4. Assessing validity is one of the main ways of evaluating quantitative data.

5. Content analysis identifies themes that run through qualitative data.

6. The analysis of qualitative data aims to discover the meanings which underlie what people say and do.

7. Participant observers interpret what they see and hear. They look for patterns of behaviour – aspects of behaviour which fall into a similar pattern.

8. Data from unstructured interviews is analysed in much the same way as other sources of qualitative data. Researchers look for themes and patterns.

9. The analysis of qualitative data relies heavily on the interpretative skills of the researcher. To some extent, this analysis will be influenced by the researcher's values and beliefs.

10. To some extent, all social research is reflexive - it reflects and is shaped by the researcher, by their values and beliefs.

11. When writing a research report, the author's job is to present the evidence and develop an argument based on that evidence.

12. A typical research report contains the following:
   - Title
   - Author
   - Abstract
   - Introduction
   - Theory
   - Data and methods
   - Results
   - Conclusions
   - References.

13. Writing and publishing a research report raises ethical issues. Authors should:
   - Protect participants
   - Tell the truth (as they see it)
   - Maintain confidentiality and make sure participants remain anonymous.

4 *Methodology*

Introduction

The previous chapter took a practical look at the research process. It examined how sociologists actually do research. It looked at the toolkit of research methods at their disposal and the way they apply these methods.

This chapter looks beyond research methods to the theories and assumptions which lie behind the study of human behaviour. This approach is known as methodology. It combines a study of research methods with philosophical questions about the nature of social reality.

What is social reality? How does it differ from the reality of the natural world? To what extent do people direct their own actions? How is it possible to discover the meanings in terms of which human beings see their world? Where do these meanings come from?

There are many answers to these questions. And each answer will affect the way sociologists conduct their research, what they look for and how they interpret their results.

The scientific method - one view of methodology

chaptersummary

▶ **Unit 1** examines positivism and realism.

▶ **Unit 2** looks at interpretivist methodology.

▶ **Unit 3** looks at postmodernist methodology.

▶ **Unit 4** looks at feminist methodology.

▶ **Unit 5** considers the relationship between values and sociological research.

Unit 1 *Positivism and realism*

keyissues

1 Are the methods of the natural sciences appropriate for the study of human behaviour?

2 What are positivist and realist approaches?

Sociology is often referred to as a *social science*. Whether or not it can be seen as a scientific discipline is one of the major debates within the subject. The founding fathers of sociology in the 19th century were, however, in no doubt. By following the rules and logic of the scientific method, sociology could discover the laws underlying the development of human society. And, in this respect, it was a science just like the *natural sciences* of physics and chemistry which seek to discover the laws underlying the behaviour of matter.

1.1 Auguste Comte – positivism

Auguste Comte (1798-1857) is credited with inventing the term sociology. He argued that sociology should be based on the methodology of the natural sciences. This would

result in a 'positive science of society' which would reveal the 'invariable laws' which governed the evolution of human society. Comte's approach is known as *positivism*.

Comte insisted that only directly observable 'facts' were acceptable as evidence in his science of society. Anything that couldn't be directly measured, such as subjective meanings and purposes, was ruled out. The facts of society must be objectively measured and quantified, ie put into a numerical form. It would then be possible to identify cause and effect relationships and discover the laws underlying social evolution.

1.2 Emile Durkheim – the rules of sociological method

Social facts In *The Rules of Sociological Method*, first published in 1895, Durkheim outlined the logic and methods to be followed for sociology to become a science of society. The starting point, 'the first and most fundamental rule is: Consider social facts as things'. Social facts are the institutions, beliefs and values of society. As things, social facts can be treated in the same way as the objects, events and processes of the natural world. They can be objectively measured, quantified and subjected to statistical analysis. Correlations can be drawn between social facts, cause and effect relationships established and theories developed to explain those relationships. In this way 'real laws are discoverable' in the social world as in the natural world.

But how can social facts be treated as things? Aren't beliefs, for example, part of human consciousness? And aren't human beings, because they have consciousness, fundamentally different from the inanimate objects which make up the natural world? In view of this, is natural science methodology appropriate for the study of human behaviour?

External reality Durkheim accepted that social facts form part of our consciousness – they have to for society to exist. Without shared norms and values, for example, society could not operate. But, although they are a part of us, social facts also exist outside of us. In Durkheim's words, 'collective ways of acting and thinking have a reality outside the individuals'. Members of society do not simply act in terms of their particular psychology and personal beliefs. Instead they are directed to act by social facts, by values and beliefs which are over and above the individual and part of the wider society. In this respect social facts 'have a reality outside the individuals' and can therefore be studied 'objectively as external things'.

Thus just as matter is constrained to act by natural forces, so human beings are constrained to act by social forces. Given this, social facts can be studied using the methodology of the natural sciences.

The social facts of suicide Durkheim's *Suicide: A Study in Sociology* was published in 1897. This study exemplified his rules of sociological method. Durkheim argued that the causes of suicide rates (the number of suicides per million of the population) are to be found in society, *not* in the psychology of individuals. Suicide rates are social facts. They are also a product of social facts, of 'real, living, active forces which, because of the way they determine the individual, prove their independence from him'.

Statistical evidence Durkheim examined official statistics on suicide from a number of European countries (see Item A, Activity 1). He found that 1) suicide rates within each country were fairly constant over a number of years and 2) there were significant differences in the rates both between societies and between social groups within the same society.

Correlation and analysis Durkheim found correlations between suicide rates and a wide range of social facts. For example, he found statistical relationships between suicide rates and religion, location, age and family situation. Some of these are illustrated in the following table. In each of the pairs, the group on the left had a higher suicide rate than the group on the right.

Protestants	-	Catholics
City dwellers	-	Rural dwellers
Older adults	-	Younger adults
Unmarried	-	Married
Married without children	-	Married with children

Causation Having established correlations between social facts, Durkheim's next task was to see if he could discover causal connections. He argued that variations in suicide rates were caused by variations in levels of social integration that is the extent to which individuals are part of a wider social group. In the case of the examples given above, the groups on the left have lower levels of social integration, than the groups on the right. For example, older adults are less socially integrated than younger adults because their children have grown up and left home, many of their friends and relatives have died, and if they have retired from work they may well have lost touch with their workmates. Using examples such as this, Durkheim claimed that 'suicide varies inversely with the degree of integration of the social groups of which the individual forms a part' – that is, the higher an individual's social integration the less likely they are to take their own life.

Theory and explanation Durkheim's final task was to explain why suicide rates vary with levels of social integration. Part of his explanation runs as follows. As members of society, people are social beings – they have been socialised to play a part in society. The greater their social isolation the less they can participate in society. Their lives lack meaning and purpose unless they are shared with others. In Durkheim's words, 'The individual alone is not a sufficient end for his activity. He is too little.' In a situation of social isolation, 'the individual yields to the slightest shock of circumstance because the state of society has made him ready prey to suicide'.

Egoistic suicide Durkheim identified various types of suicide. He called the type described above egoistic suicide and argued that it is typical of societies which are making the transition to modernity. In such societies, the individual stands increasingly alone – ego refers to 'I', to the self. These societies have an 'excess of individualism' – people tend to think primarily of themselves, they are less concerned with their duties and obligations to others, and with the opinions of others.

Social currents Durkheim argued that in every society there are underlying *social currents*. These social currents flow through society and shape behaviour. They are the underlying processes and mechanisms that direct human action. However, they cannot be directly observed and measured, they can only be inferred. For example, social currents cannot be observed and quantified in the same way as family size and religious beliefs. But they are just as real and they have the same power over people's behaviour. In this respect, they are social facts.

Egoism is an example of a social current. It is a focus on self, a concern with self, an emphasis on the individual rather than the group. Egoism results in the isolation of the person. For Durkheim, the social current of egoism provides the basic explanation for egoistic suicide.

In Steve Taylor's (1988) words, Durkheim's methodology 'involved searching for the invisible underlying causes of the relationships between things that are observed'. Durkheim believed that his research on suicide proved that scientific methodology was appropriate for the study of society, because it had shown that 'real laws are discoverable'.

1.3 Positivism and realism

Durkheim and positivism

Positivists accept that much of Durkheim's work is scientific. He quantified a number of social facts. His statistical analysis revealed correlations between them and indicated cause and effect relationships. However, they part company with Durkheim on two main counts.

First, Durkheim sometimes failed to provide an operational definition of social facts – that is, a definition which could provide quantifiable data. For example, without an operational definition of social integration, this aspect of Durkheim's theory could not be tested and shown to be true or false (Gibbs & Martin, 1964).

Second, positivists reject Durkheim's view that causes can be found in underlying processes and mechanisms that cannot be directly observed and measured. From a positivist viewpoint, Durkheim's use of unobservable social currents to explain suicide rates is unacceptable and unscientific.

Durkheim and realism

Durkheim's methodology is sometimes described as positivist. As noted earlier, positivists believe that sociology should adopt the methodology of the natural sciences and focus only on directly observable facts. At first sight, this is exactly what Durkheim does. He identifies observable social facts and correlates them with other observable social facts.

However, Durkheim goes further. He looks beyond observable social facts in a search for explanations. He attempts to identify the social currents which ultimately cause the social facts he has observed.

This approach is known as *realism*. Realists argue that the causes of many of the things we observe lie in underlying processes and mechanisms which cannot be directly observed. From a realist viewpoint, both the natural and social sciences operate in much the same way. In this sense, Durkheim's methodology can be seen as scientific.

key terms

Positivism In Comte's view, a method of study based on directly observable facts, objectively measured, from which it is possible to identify cause and effect relationships and discover laws underlying social evolution.
Social facts In Durkheim's view, the institutions, beliefs and values of society, which although they exist within individuals also exist outside of them and direct their behaviour.
Social currents The processes which underlie and ultimately cause observable social facts.
Realism A view of the scientific method which argues that events in both the natural and social world are shaped by underlying processes, mechanisms and structures.

summary

1. Comte believed that sociology should be based on the methodology of the natural sciences. As a positivist, he argued that only directly observable 'facts' were acceptable as evidence.

2. Durkheim argued that social facts have a reality outside individuals. Social facts can therefore be studied as 'things'. This means that the methodology of the natural sciences can be used to study human society.

3. Durkheim argued that his study of suicide supported this view. He claimed to have discovered cause and effect relationships between social facts.

4. Durkheim's approach is known as realism. He argued that there are underlying processes and mechanisms in society which shape behaviour. These are not directly observable.

activity1 a realist approach

Item A Suicide statistics

Rate of suicides per million inhabitants in European countries

	Period			Numerical position in the		
	1866-70	1871-75	1874-78	1st period	2nd period	3rd period
Italy	30	35	38	1	1	1
Belgium	66	69	78	2	3	4
England	67	66	69	3	2	2
Norway	76	73	71	4	4	3
Austria	78	94	130	5	7	7
Sweden	85	81	91	6	5	5
Bavaria	90	91	100	7	6	6
France	135	150	160	8	9	9
Prussia	142	134	152	9	8	8
Denmark	277	258	255	10	10	10
Saxony	293	267	334	11	11	11

Adapted from Durkheim, 1970 (originally published in 1897)

Item B *Alone*

Death from poison – living alone in a one-room attic

questions

1 Durkheim claimed that 'each society is predisposed to contribute a definite quota of voluntary deaths'.

   a) What support for this statement is provided by Item A?

   b) Use Item A to support Durkheim's claim that a science of society is possible.

2 How might Durkheim explain the type of suicide illustrated in Item B?

Unit 2 *Interpretivist methodology*

keyissues

1 How significant are meanings for understanding social action?

2 What are the similarities and differences between the main interpretivist perspectives?

Interpretivist sociology covers a range of theoretical perspectives which see fundamental differences between the natural and social worlds. From an interpretivist perspective, the social world is essentially a world of meaning. Human beings construct their own social reality. Their actions are directed by meanings, their experience is based on meanings. Any understanding of human action must therefore involve an understanding of those meanings. And for many researchers, this means employing methodologies which are very different from those used in the natural sciences.

2.1 Max Weber – social action

Social action Max Weber (1864-1920) defined sociology as 'a science which attempts the interpretive understanding of social action in order thereby to arrive at a causal explanation of its course and effects' (1964). Social action is action which involves other members of society. It is based on meanings in the minds of social actors which direct their actions. Weber was particularly concerned with motives – the intentions and purposes which direct social actors to achieve certain goals.

Verstehen Motives are an important part of any explanation of social action. Weber's method of interpreting motives is known as *verstehen,* which roughly translates as empathetic understanding. Researchers put themselves in the place of social actors and attempt to see the world through their eyes. The problem of course is whether verstehen produces a true picture of the actor's world view. Weber's solution to this problem will be examined shortly.

The Protestant ethic Weber's methodology can be illustrated with his most famous work, *The Protestant Ethic and the Spirit of Capitalism.* Weber was interested in the meanings and motives - the 'spirit of capitalism' – which, he believed, led to the rise of capitalism. On the basis of a wide range of historical documents, he claimed that they developed from early forms of Protestantism which preceded capitalism. Weber identified a Protestant work ethic in terms of which work became a 'calling' which must be pursued with a single mind. Making money is an indication of success in one's calling, it shows that a person has not lost favour in God's sight. Weber argues that the Protestant work ethic is a major cause of the rise of capitalism.

The comparative method How does Weber know that his interpretation of motives – in this case the Protestant work ethic – is correct? His answer is to use the *comparative method* which compares different societies and different groups within the same society. In the absence of a laboratory in which variables can be manipulated and controlled, Weber attempts to find 'natural' laboratories which allow the influence of variables to be measured.

If Weber's interpretation of the Protestant work ethic is correct, then Protestants should have spearheaded the rise of capitalism. He produces evidence which indicates that early capitalism developed within predominantly Protestant rather than Catholic societies, and within those societies the 'business leaders and owners of capital are overwhelmingly Protestant'. From this, Weber claims that his interpretation of the motives of social actors is validated.

2.2 Herbert Blumer – symbolic interactionism

Weber investigated meanings on a wide canvas, often drawing on information from across the world and from different time periods. Symbolic interactionists tend to focus on meanings in the context of small-scale interaction situations. From this point of view, the meanings which direct action are developed and negotiated during the process of social interaction. The job of the sociologist is to discover these meanings.

Discovering meaning Herbert Blumer (1962) has developed a methodology for the study of social interaction. The first step is for researchers to immerse themselves in interaction situations, to observe and interpret the actions of others and attempt to see the world through their eyes. In Blumer's words, this involves 'feeling one's way inside the experience of the actor' in order to 'catch the process of interpretation through which they construct their action'. Blumer is refreshingly honest when discussing how this might be achieved. 'It is a tough job requiring a high order of careful and honest probing, creative yet disciplined imagination, resourcefulness and flexibility in study, pondering over what one is finding, and constant readiness to test and recast one's views and images of the area.'

Structure and meaning Symbolic interactionists accept that to some extent social interaction is structured. Meanings are not constantly reinvented, social interaction is often routine and repetitive rather than creative and spontaneous. But this does not mean that negotiation and interpretation aren't still important aspects of interaction. Nor does it mean that human action is shaped by the structures and mechanisms of the social system, as some sociologists would argue.

Blumer gives the example of family structure and industrialisation to illustrate this point. It has been claimed that industrialisation leads to the replacement of extended families by nuclear families. Blumer objects to this view which tends to see human action as a product of structures and mechanisms. Where in the equation are the meanings people give to family life, where are the interpretations they place on industrialisation? Without these meanings and interpretations sociologists have little chance of grasping social reality.

Blumer argues that the research process must be as systematic, rigorous and objective as possible. Equally important, however, are qualities such as sensitivity and sympathy. Both the tone and substance of Blumer's methodology are a long way from the views outlined in Unit 1.

2.3 Phenomenology

Phenomenological perspectives take the logic of a social reality to its furthest point. They argue that as human beings our only reality consists of meanings. The job of the sociologist is to discover these meanings and nothing more – for the logic of this argument states there is nothing more to discover. The methodology that results from this view will now be examined using the example of suicide.

Discovering suicide In *Discovering Suicide* J. Maxwell Atkinson's basic question is 'How do deaths get categorised as suicide?' When he has answered this question he can go no further because suicide is simply a meaning and has no reality beyond this. Classifications of suicide are not right or wrong, they just are. For example, there is no such thing as a 'real' or objective suicide rate waiting to be discovered. The official statistics are the rate, full stop.

Atkinson's research attempts to discover the meanings used by coroners to classify deaths as suicide. He held discussions with coroners, attended inquests, observed a coroner's officer at work and analysed a coroner's records. He argues that coroners have a 'commonsense theory of suicide' which they use to both classify and explain deaths as suicide. In terms of this theory, the following evidence is seen as relevant for reaching a verdict.

1. Whether suicide threats have been made or suicide notes left.

2. The type of death – hanging, gassing and drug overdose are seen as typical suicide deaths.

3. The location of death – death by gunshot at home is more likely to be seen as suicide than in the countryside where it may well be interpreted as a hunting accident.

4. The biography of the deceased – a recent divorce, the death of a close friend or relative, a history of depression, problems at work, financial difficulties, lack of friends are seen as typical reasons for suicide.

The closer the deceased fits this commonsense theory of suicide, the more likely his or her death will be defined as suicide. In Atkinson's words, coroners 'are engaged in analysing features of the deaths and of the biographies of the deceased according to a variety of taken-for-granted assumptions about what constitutes a "typical suicide", "a typical suicide biography", and so on'.

Having uncovered to his satisfaction the meanings used to classify deaths as suicide, Atkinson's research is finished. There are no more questions to ask.

Causation As outlined in a previous section, Durkheim's research on suicide was concerned with causation, in particular with the causes of variations in suicide rates. Phenomenologists see this as a pointless and misguided

activity2 suicide – a phenomenological view

Item A Contemplating suicide

Item B Homeless, friendless, deserted

The Maniac Father and The Convict Brother Are Gone - The Poor Girl, Homeless, Friendless, Deserted, Destitute and Gin Mad, Commits Self Murder.

Item C Retired coroner

During the War it was something of an understanding that you didn't bring in suicide verdicts unless you really had to. 'Bad for National Morale' – and of course I think most people felt responsible for keeping morale up. I think with suicide at that time we felt it was a kind of 'defeatism', defeatism in the face of the enemy, and that was a cardinal sin, letting the side down, you know. So when there was a verdict of suicide, lots of coroners couldn't resist reading a sermon about moral cowardice. I expect I did.

Quoted in Langley, 1988

questions

1 How does Item A illustrate 'typical suicide deaths'?

2 How does Item B indicate a 'typical suicide biography'?

3 What support does Item C provide for Atkinson's view of suicide?

---

exercise. Suicides are not objective 'social facts' with causes that can be explained, they are meanings. To try and discover the 'causes' of suicide will simply result in uncovering the meanings used to classify a death as suicide. Thus it comes as no surprise that the 'typical suicide biography' – the friendless, divorced loner – is very similar to Durkheim's socially isolated individual. Suicides, like any other aspect of social reality, are simply constructions of meaning.

Conclusion Phenomenology rejects the entire scientific enterprise as it is normally understood. It is a distortion of social reality to treat it as 'social facts', as 'things'. There are no 'structures' or 'mechanisms' operating in human society. There are no objective facts with causes which can be explained. There are only meanings to be uncovered and understood.

2.4 Two sociologies?

It is sometimes argued that there are 'two sociologies' (Halfpenny, 1984). The first is based on 'scientific

methodology', using 'hard' quantitative data and concerned with discovering causal relationships. This approach is sometimes labelled 'positivism'. The second is based on 'interpretivist methodology', using 'soft' qualitative data and concerned with understanding the meanings which make up social reality. This approach is sometimes labelled 'interpretivism', sometimes 'phenomenology'.

Supporting the distinction Some sociologists find this distinction between the two sociologies useful. They claim that there is a tendency for some researchers to adopt a positivist view and see the methods of the natural sciences as the most effective way of acquiring knowledge. And they see a real distinction between this group and those who adopt an interpretivist approach.

Those who support this distinction also claim to detect a tendency for positivists to favour certain research methods, for example survey research based on questionnaires, and certain forms of data, for example quantitative data. On the other hand, those who adopt an interpretivist approach are said to favour methods such as participant observation and unstructured interviews which are seen to produce rich, in-depth qualitative data.

These differences are seen to reflect the aims of the 'two sociologies'. Positivism aims to discover cause and effect relationships. This requires quantitative data so that the strength of relationships between variables can be measured. Interpretivism aims to understand human action. This requires rich, qualitative data in order to discover the meanings which lie behind action.

Opposing the distinction Ray Pawson (1989) rejects this view of the 'two sociologies'. He argues that it gives a false picture of the relationship between theory, research

methods and the actual practice of doing sociology.

Pawson describes the idea of 'two sociologies' as a 'methodological myth'.

In other words, the two sociologies don't exist. Instead, there is a whole range of different views, different assumptions and different methodologies. As previous sections have shown, there are various views of science and its application to the study of human society. And sociologists who are primarily concerned with meanings use a variety of research methods and types of data and often start from different theoretical perspectives. This variety cannot be reduced to 'two sociologies'.

key terms

Interpretivist sociology A range of theoretical perspectives which emphasise the importance of meanings for understanding human action.

Verstehen A term used by Weber for interpreting motives. Roughly translated it means empathetic understanding – ie, attempting to understand motives by putting yourself in the actor's place.

Comparative method Comparing different societies, and different groups within the same society.

Phenomenology A view which states that phenomena – things or events – must be studied in their own right, not as representing something else. Thus, meanings must be studied as meanings – they have no other reality.

summary

1. Interpretivist perspectives emphasise the importance of meanings for understanding social action.

2. However, there are important differences between interpretivist perspectives. Some look for causal explanations of social action, others seek only to discover the meanings used to construct social reality.

3. Some sociologists make a distinction between two sociologies – positivism and interpretivism. They argue that these sociologies differ in terms of theory and methodology.

4. Other sociologists argue that this distinction is false. They see sociology as far more varied in terms of theory and methodology than the idea of two sociologies suggests.

Unit 3 Postmodernist methodology

key issues

1 How does postmodernism challenge sociological research methodology?

2 What alternatives does it offer?

The challenge

Postmodernists directly challenge the entire basis of research methodology in the social sciences. They reject the whole idea of collecting data to support or reject hypotheses or theories. They question the possibility of making any definite statements about social reality. They reject the idea that there is an objective reality 'out there' waiting to be discovered. They argue that the 'facts' and 'knowledge' that fill sociological research reports and textbooks are nothing of the sort. They are simply sociologists' constructions of reality rather than a valid description and analysis of the social world 'out there'.

The following discussion of postmodernist methodology is largely based on Mats Alvesson's excellent book *Postmodernism and Social Research* (2002).

A postmodernist view of reality

From a postmodernist perspective, any description, analysis, view or picture of the social world is simply one view amongst many. And this applies to sociologists as much as anybody else.

Nothing is certain – everything is tentative, doubtful, indeterminate. Take yourself. In one sense you are one person, in another sense you are lots of people. In one sense you have one identity, in another sense you are made up of multiple identities. In various situations you adopt different identities, see things in different ways, operate with different meanings. What you see or say in one situation may contradict what you see or say in another situation.

This applies both to the sociologist and those who participate in his or her research. Nothing is fixed, everything is fluid; nothing is whole, everything is fragmented; there is no single reality, only multiple realities.

Objectivity and research

Sociologists aim to be objective, to present the social world of those they are studying as it really is, to give us the 'facts'. Many sociologists accept that complete objectivity is an ideal that is unattainable. However, they do their best to get there. And they believe their research reports are a lot better than the view of the person in the street.

From a postmodernist view, research reports are not objective. Instead, they are constructions which are designed to persuade, to give the impression of rational, analytic thinking, and to convince the reader that the researcher's view is 'the truth'. And often, the persuasion works. In the words of Mats Alvesson (2002):

'This is made possible through the skilful denial of any relevance of the pre-structured understanding of the researcher, his or her class, gender, nationality, his or her paradigmatic, theoretical and political preferences and biases, the vocabularies employed, the dynamics of the research process, the expectations and more or less politically skilled operations of the informants, the more or less arbitrary decisions about informants, the selective presentation of evidence and rhetorical tricks and conventions of writing.'

Sociologists are a bit like conjurers. They deceive, they play tricks, they create illusions. For example, they skilfully present an illusion of objectivity where none exists.

Sociological categories

Think of the following terms – culture, subculture, norm, value, social class, ethnicity, social structure, social status, social role. These are all categories used by sociologists to order, organise and make sense of the social world. According to postmodernists, the social world is forced into these categories, wedged into these pigeonholes. In this respect, the social world becomes a construction built by sociologists. In this way, researchers impose their own order and framework on the social world.

From a postmodernist viewpoint, the social world is ambiguous rather than clear-cut, fluid rather than fixed, open rather than closed. It cannot be rammed into fixed, predetermined categories.

Is there any alternative to researchers imposing their reality on the social world? Do they have to make sense of human action by using pre-set categories?

Categories as problematic A starting point is to see all categories as problematic, to be aware that they create order where none may exist, that they impose a particular view of reality, that they structure the social world in a particular way.

Defamiliarisation This offers the possibility of getting away from a sociological construction of the social world. *Defamiliarisation* means looking at the familiar in new and novel ways. Instead of assuming human action is natural, rational, patterned, ordered, the observer should try and see it from other viewpoints – as exotic, random, irrational, contradictory, arbitrary, crazy. For example, look back on your schooldays and family life and try and look at them in a fresh and novel way – for example, as an alien from another planet or somebody from the distant past or future.

Multiple interpretations

Postmodernists are particularly scathing and dismissive of

metanarratives – literally 'big stories' such as Marxism and functionalism which offer a single explanation, a single perspective on social reality. Metanarratives have their own set of categories, their own vocabulary (or jargon), they are based on particular values, they define the social world in a particular way, and they wrap it all up in a neat, tidy, rigid framework. A metanarrative is a total package into which all social reality can be accommodated.

But if you buy into one metanarrative, that's all you get. All your research will be coloured by it. What you look for, how you interpret it, will be guided by the big story you believe.

From a postmodernist viewpoint, there are multiple, if not infinite, interpretations of the social world. Who is to say which is 'right' or the 'best'?

Where does this take us? Some would say nowhere – what's the point of doing research if it's no better or worse than any other view – for example, no better or worse than the view of the journalist, novelist, comedian, child, grandparent, Christian, Muslim or Jew?

For some, there is a halfway house. Sociologists should be more humble. They should accept the idea of *multiple interpretations*. They should look at the social world from different vantage points, in terms of different perspectives. And they should allow other voices to be heard in their research publications, particularly the voices of those they are researching.

Evaluation

Much of what postmodernists have to say about sociological methodology is negative. Taken to its extreme, it suggests that sociological research is a waste of time. Worse, it can be seen as an illusion which distorts the social world and deceives the audience.

But have postmodernists got it right? Using their arguments, there's no way of judging whether they're right or wrong. The voice of postmodernism is simply one voice amongst many – neither better nor worse.

Despite this criticism, postmodernism has made sociologists more aware of the problems and pitfalls of research. It has made many researchers more sensitive, more questioning and more humble. Mats Alvesson (2002) presents the following evaluation. Postmodernism 'offers a challenge and an inspiration to revise and make qualitative research more sophisticated and creative. This is not bad, and a strong reason for taking it seriously. But not too seriously.'

key terms

Defamiliarisation Looking at the familiar in new and novel ways.

Metanarratives Big stories or pictures of how the world works. Grand theories produced by the natural and social sciences.

Multiple interpretations Looking at the social world from different vantage points and in terms of different perspectives.

summary

1. From a postmodernist perspective, any description or analysis of the social world is simply one view amongst many.

2. As a result, it is not possible to make any definite statements about social reality. Sociological research is not, and cannot be, objective.

3. Researchers impose their own order and framework on the social world by using pre-set categories.

4. Researchers should regard all categories as problematic. And they should defamiliarise themselves from the social world in order to open their eyes to a variety of interpretations.

5. Postmodernists reject metanarratives, arguing they should be replaced by multiple interpretations of the social world.

6. Using their own arguments, there is no way of judging whether postmodernists are right or wrong.

7. Postmodernism has made sociologists more aware of the problems and pitfalls of research. And it has encouraged them to be more creative and innovative.

activity3 postmodernism and research

Item A The research process – a simple version

1. Collection of data
2. Production of a wealth of information eg, writing up observations and transcribing interviews
3. Structuring the data, reducing mess
4. Analysis and further reduction of material
6. Creating an order and logic to the report
6. Producing a text

Adapted from Alvesson, 2002

Item B The research process – a complex version

2. During the research:
Use of particular research methods
Interaction between researcher & research participants
Presentation of self, impression management
Bias, meanings, interpretations, feelings

3. Broad-brushed selection of research data
Reconstruction & ordering of data

5. Interpretation & analysis of data

1. Researcher brings to research their:
Expectations, understandings, assumptions
Culture, gender, ethnicity, nationality, class, age
Values, attitudes, meanings, political & religious beliefs
Identities, personal experiences
Theoretical background & categories

4. Fine-tuned selection of data
Further reconstruction & ordering

6. Producing a text
Following conventions of a research report
Writing skills
Skills of persuasion

Adapted from Alvesson, 2002

Item C Body ritual among the Nacirema

The Nacirema spend a large part of the day in ritual activity. The focus of this activity is the human body. The basic belief underlying their rituals is that the human body is ugly and has a natural tendency to debility and disease. Every household has a shrine where the body rituals take place.

The focal point of the shrine is a box or chest which contains many charms and magical potions. Beneath the charm-box is a small font where they perform the daily mouth ceremony. The Nacirema have a horror of and fascination with the mouth. Were it not for the rituals of the mouth, they believe that their teeth would fall out, their gums bleed, their friends desert them and their lovers reject them.

Once or twice a year, the Nacirema seek out a holy-mouth man. The ceremony involves almost unbelievable ritual torture. The power of the holy-mouth-man is evident from the fact that his clients return year after year, despite the fact that their teeth continue to decay.

Adapted from Miner, 1965

questions

1 Research is not as simple and straightforward as it seems. Comment on this statement from a postmodernist view with some reference to Items A and B.

2 Item B is an adapted extract from an article by Horace Miner, an American anthropologist. Nacirema is American spelt backwards.

a) How is this description an example of defamiliarisation?

b) Do you find it useful?

c) Write a brief defamiliarised description of an aspect of everyday behaviour.

Unit 4 Feminist methodology

key issues

1 What is feminist methodology?

2 What contribution has it made to sociology?

Over the past 30 years 'women's studies' has become a major growth industry. In university bookshops, shelves are stacked with books about women and their place in history and society. And most of these books are written by women.

What does this mean? Clearly it means that women are seen as more important than before. The growth of women's studies can be seen as a reflection of the rise of feminism and changes in perceptions of women's roles in Western society. There is little doubt that social change and the changes in values which accompany it influence choices about what to study. For many feminists, however, the effects of these changes are a lot more fundamental than simply choice of subject matter.

4.1 Feminism – the weak thesis

Ray Pawson (1992) distinguishes between the 'weak thesis' and the 'strong thesis' of feminist methods. In terms of the 'weak thesis', research methods in sociology are essentially sound. The problem is that in practice they are shot through with sexism. The solution is to purge them of sexism. Eichler's *Non-Sexist Research Methods* (1988) is an example of this approach. She identifies major areas of sexism which infuse the research process. These include:

Androcentricity This means viewing the world from a traditional male perspective, with its assumptions of male dominance and superiority – for example – seeing women as passive objects rather than active subjects. As a result, women are largely 'invisible' – in Sheila Rowbotham's (1973) words, they are 'hidden from history'.

Overgeneralisation Many studies deal only with men but present their findings as though they applied to both men and women. For example, until recently social mobility studies in Britain were based solely on men. Since women's social status was seen to derive from the status of their husbands, there seemed little point in looking at

women in their own right. Their class position could be simply 'read off' from the position of their husband.

Research methods

According to Eichler, the sexist assumptions outlined above are found in all aspects of the research process. This can be seen from her examples of questions taken from questionnaires. The first is an example of a sex specific term when talking about people in general.

- If someone wanted to make a speech in your community claiming that Blacks are inferior, should he be allowed to speak or not?

The next question reflects common assumptions about male dominance.

- Is it acceptable for women to hold important political offices in state and national government? Yes/No.

The solution is to reformulate the questions in a non-sexist way.

Eichler's argument suggests reform rather than radical change. Research methods, in and of themselves, are not sexist. Once researchers learn to use them in a non-sexist way, then the problem will be solved.

4.2 Feminism – the strong thesis

The changes advocated by the strong thesis are more fundamental. Something of their flavour is provided by Ann Oakley's article 'Interviewing Women: A Contradiction in Terms' (1981).

Feminist interviewing

Oakley (1981) argues that the standard approach to interviewing has the following characteristics. '(a) its status as a mechanical instrument of data-collection; (b) its function as a specialised form of conversation in which one person asks the questions and another gives the answers; (c) its characterisation of interviewees as essentially passive individuals and (d) its reduction of interviewers to a question asking and rapport-promoting role'.

Oakley sees this approach as clinical, manipulative, exploitative and hierarchical. The interviewer 'uses' the respondent for 'his' purposes, controlling the content and direction of the interview. The relationship is unequal – the interviewer takes and the respondent gives. A feminist methodology would replace this by a non-hierarchical relationship, with the researcher giving as well as receiving. For example, an interviewer must 'be prepared to invest his or her personal identity in the relationship' which means honesty, sincerity, understanding and compassion between equals. It means that both parties have a say in the content and direction of the interview. Only with this personal involvement will 'people come to know each other and admit others into their lives'.

This example argues for a change in research methods – a new type of interviewing – rather than simply cleansing existing methods of sexism. It argues that research techniques are so imbued with male assumptions and practices that they must be radically changed. These changes are not only morally correct, they will also result in better data.

One reaction to Oakley's views is summed up by Ray Pawson's (1992) query, 'What's new?'. There is a long tradition of interviewing which emphasises sensitivity and non-directive approaches. Whether Oakley's views are significantly different from this is questionable.

Gender politics and methodology

Some feminists argue that the 'women's struggle' and feminist methodology are inseparable. 'Malestream' sociology is so saturated with assumptions of male dominance that a feminist alternative is required. Maria Mies (1993) provides an example of this approach. She argues that a feminist methodology must have the following features.

1 **Conscious partiality** The idea of so-called value free research has to be replaced by conscious partiality, which in practice means that female researchers must positively identify with the women they study.

2 **View from below** This replaces the 'view from above', with its assumptions of male dominance, which supports the existing power structure. Researchers must take the 'view from below' because it is more likely to reflect women's experiences and more likely to empower women in their struggle for liberation.

3 **Action research** Rather than being a detached spectator, a dispassionate observer, the researcher should actively participate in the struggle for women's liberation.

4 **Changing the status quo** From this involvement in their own emancipation, both researchers and the women they study will develop a better understanding of their situation. This is based on the idea, 'If you want to know a thing, you must change it'. Only by challenging and changing patriarchy will its true nature be revealed.

5 **Raising consciousness** Both researchers and the researched must raise their consciousness – become aware of their oppression. In particular, it is the job of the researcher to give women the means to gain insight into and change their situation.

6 **Individual and social history** Part of the process of raising consciousness requires a study of women's individual and social history. This will allow women to reclaim their history from its appropriation by men.

7 **Collectivising experience** Women must collectivise their experience and join together and cooperate in their struggle for liberation. They must overcome the individualism, competitiveness and careerism which characterise the male world.

In terms of these propositions, Maria Mies is claiming that valid knowledge can only emerge from the struggles waged by the oppressed against their oppressors. The journey to truth involves just the opposite of value freedom. In Mies' case it requires a wholehearted commitment to women's liberation.

Mies' views are not new. Marxists have produced similar arguments for the liberation of the working class, as have African Americans for Black liberation in the USA. Whatever the virtues of this point of view, it is unlikely to offer a recipe for sociology as a whole since there is more to human society than oppressors and oppressed.

Standpoint feminism

Mies' views are an example of standpoint feminism. Standpoint theory argues that certain groups, because of their position in society, have a greater chance of gaining valid insights into the social world. For example, some Marxists argue that the position of workers in capitalist society gives them a vantage point from which to reveal the exploitation and oppression of class society. Similarly, Nancy Hartsock (1983) claims that 'women's lives make available a particular and privileged vantage point on male supremacy'. Because of their experience of gender subordination, women are in a better position to uncover the truth about male dominance.

Standpoint feminism argues that women's exclusion from powerful positions in society is actually an advantage when it comes to research. Women's position as 'outsiders' allows them to stand back and take a 'stranger's' view of male-dominated society. Ironically, the marginalisation experienced by female researchers as women provides them with an opportunity to produce unbiased accounts of the social world.

Experience as women, however valuable, is only part of the process of discovering truth. Women's experience can only by fully understood and explained in relation to the wider society. Women 'speaking their truth' do so in the context of power relationships which shape their lives.

This view is reflected in standpoint feminism's approach to research participants. The hierarchy of researcher and researched must be removed. The research process must be democratic and involve the participants as equals. In this way, they are more likely to express their true feelings.

By no means all feminists support the view that it is possible to produce objective, unbiased accounts of the social world. Some critics of standpoint feminism argue that there are many versions of social reality, all of which are equally valid. This position is the starting point for postmodern feminism.

4.3 Postmodern feminism

Women as a category

Feminism is not a single perspective. In its early days, things were fairly simple. Women were the oppressed, men were the oppressors, the target was patriarchy, the aim to liberate women. There was a tendency to see women as a single, undifferentiated category. Groups of women objected to this approach – for example, Black women and lesbian women. OK, they were women, but, they argued, their experiences and social situation distinguished them from women in general. As a result, many of the generalisations about women did not apply, or only partly applied, to them.

Postmodern feminism takes this argument a step further. It rejects the standard feminist metanarrative ('grand story') of women as a homogeneous, undifferentiated category, faced with an oppressive patriarchal system. And it even rejects categories which subdivide the category 'women', such as Black women, lesbian women and working-class women. Instead, postmodern feminists emphasise diversity and variation. They argue that researchers should be open to this diversity rather than approaching it with pre-set, preconceived categories.

Evaluation This approach has been criticised by a number of feminists. Breaking down or rejecting the category 'women' prevents the possibility of making generalisations which apply to most or all women. It also blunts the force of feminist protest and threatens the unity of women as a group. Emphasising variation and uniqueness may lead to 'divide and conquer', so serving male dominance (Alvesson, 2002).

The research process

Research as a construct Postmodern feminists favour interpretivist research methods such as participant observation. They are particularly aware that the results of research are a social construct – they are largely constructed by the researcher from fieldnotes which document their observations. This awareness leads them to revisit, reopen and reinterpret their fieldnotes. As Sara Delamont (2003) states,

> 'fieldnotes are not a closed, completed, final text: rather, they are indeterminate, subject to reading, rereading, coding, recording, interpreting, reinterpreting.'

This is in line with the postmodernist view that there are multiple interpretations of any observation.

Multiple voices As outlined in Unit 3, postmodernists argue that researchers should allow the voices of those they research to be heard. Again, in Sara Delamont's (2003) words, this means 'the text will reproduce the actors' own perspectives and experiences. This may include extended biographical and autobiographical accounts, extended

dialogues between the researcher and informants, and other "documents of life". Typically, there is an emphasis on the kinds of narratives or stories through which social actors construct their own and others' experiences.'

Reflexity The researcher's own voice should be heard loud and clear, expressing her or his thoughts and feelings about the research. This will be a reflexive voice, reflecting on the research process, the author's interpretations, emotions and relationships with the research participants. This reflects the researcher's awareness that they are a part of the social world they are researching, that the results of their research may say as much, if not more, about them as about the research participants they are studying.

Presenting research Postmodernists' focus on multiple identities and multiple interpretations is reflected in their writing styles. Descriptions of social action and social scenes vary from 'cold' to 'hot', from dispassionate to passionate, from clinical to evocative. There is a mix of styles from poetic to descriptive, from the researcher's words to those of the research participants. The intention is to allow the reader to move through a variety of interpretations and observe from a variety of standpoints (Delamont, 2003).

---

key terms

Androcentricity A male-centred view of the world which assumes male superiority and dominance.

Overgeneralisation Generalising further than the evidence allows. For example, generalising from a male sample to both males and females.

Conscious partiality Positively identifying with and favouring a particular group.

Multiple voices Many voices. In this case, it refers to the view that many voices should be heard in the research report.

---

summary

1. There are a number of feminist methodologies.

2. The 'weak thesis' states that androcentricity and overgeneralisation are found in all aspects of the research process.

3. Research methods, in and of themselves, are not sexist. Once researchers learn to use them in a non-sexist way, the problem will be solved.

4. The 'strong thesis' states that feminism requires its own research methods – for example, feminist interviewing.

5. Some feminists see the women's struggle and feminist methodology as inseparable. The feminist researcher should be consciously partial and actively participate in women's liberation.

6. Postmodern feminism rejects pre-set, pre-determined categories. It emphasises diversity and variation.

7. It argues that there are multiple interpretations of any observation and that this should be reflected by multiple voices in research reports.

4.5 Conclusion

Sociology used to be a male subject, run by males and concerned with males. Women were largely absent from sociology departments and in a minority among research participants. When sociologists studied workers, they usually studied male workers. When they studied social mobility, it was men who went up and down the class system – women didn't even make it into the supposedly representative sample. And women's concerns and issues were unlikely to be heard and researched.

Thanks in large part to feminists, women now feature in every area of sociology – as workers, members of ethnic minorities, as voters, as students, as mothers and housewives, as participants in the class system and as members of religious organisations. Women are no longer invisible.

The research process has been largely cleansed of sexism. Researchers are increasingly aware that sexism will produce invalid results.

Feminists have been at the forefront of recent developments in methodology. Many have argued that sociology is not, should not and cannot be value free. They have emphasised the importance of capturing the experience of research participants and of expressing that experience directly. They have argued that emotion has an important part to play in the research process. And they have opened up, questioned, and presented alternatives to established research methodology.

activity4 feminism and methodology

Item A Sexist questionnaires

A study of the lifestyles of adolescent girls and boys included sets of questions about the roles they might identify with (Murdock & Phelps, 1973). Both girls and boys were given a list of roles to choose from, which included 'good pupil', 'rebel', 'good friend' and 'pop fan'. Boys were given a separate list which included 'sports fan' and 'natural leader'. Girls were also given their own list with roles such as 'homemaker' and 'fashion follower'. The girls had no opportunity of choosing from the boys' options and the boys' had no opportunity of choosing from the girls' options.

Adapted from Jones, 1974

Item B Woman-to-woman

Janet Finch describes herself as a feminist sociologist. She conducted two studies based on in-depth interviews in which all the interviewees were women – 1) clergyman's wives and 2) women who used and ran preschool playgroups. She talked to the women in their own homes about marriage, motherhood and childbearing.

She preferred a woman-to-woman discussion in an informal setting 'on both methodological and political grounds'. In her view 1) it works better and 2) it's morally better. Finch found that she gained their trust because she was a woman and because, as a feminist, she treated them as equals. Sharing their gender, both parties shared a subordinate position in society and, as a result, were likely to identify with each other. And, in an equal relationship, the interviewees felt they could talk freely. The women welcomed the interviews and were enthusiastic during the discussions.

As a feminist sociologist, Finch was 'on the side' of the women she studied. In her words, this 'inevitably means an emotional as well as an intellectual commitment to promoting their interests'. Does this bias her research? No more than any other research, since, in her view, 'all social science knowledge is intrinsically political in character'.

Adapted from Finch, 1993

questions

1 a) How can the questions in Item A be seen as sexist?
   b) How might the results of this study simply reproduce traditional gender stereotypes?
2 a) In what ways does Finch's woman-to-woman interviewing style reflect Oakley's 'feminist interviewing'?
   b) What are the advantages of this style of interviewing?

Unit 5 Sociology, methodology and values

keyissues

1 Is an objective, value-free sociology possible?
2 Is it desirable?

What we see, the questions we ask and the way we interpret data are influenced by a range of social and personal factors. They include our class, gender, ethnicity, nationality, culture and our personalities, experiences and life histories. These points will now be developed, focusing on the influence of values on social research.

Values are strongly held beliefs about what is right and wrong, what is good and bad, what is worth fighting for and fighting against, what is worth having and not having, who is worthy of respect and support and who is not.

Can the research process in particular and sociology in general be *value free*? And, going one step further, is a value-free sociology desirable?

The founding fathers of sociology believed that an objective, value-free science of society was both possible and desirable. Despite their many differences, not least in terms of personal values, Comte, Marx and Durkheim each believed his work to be uncontaminated by value judgements. Today's sociologists are a lot less certain. A brief look at the debate about values and the study of deviance illustrates this.

5.1 Values and the study of deviance

In an article entitled 'Whose Side Are We On?' the American sociologist Howard Becker (1970) argues that it is impossible to conduct research 'uncontaminated by personal and political sympathies'. Becker's sympathies lie with the underdog, those who have been labelled deviant. He is critical of the agents of social control who, in his eyes, create deviance by selectively applying labels to the poor and powerless (see page 234). Becker argues that not only the research process but the theories which lie behind it – in his case interactionism – are infused with value judgements. From his standpoint 'interactionist theories look (and are) rather left'.

Like Becker, the American sociologist Alvin Gouldner (1975) believes that a value-free sociology is impossible. However, his values are a lot further to the left than Becker's. From his standpoint, Gouldner accuses the interactionists of adopting a 'bland liberal position' (liberalism advocates reform within the existing structure rather than radical social change). A more radical position would lead to a critical examination of the relationship between deviance and the unequal distribution of power in society.

Gouldner pictures Becker and his interactionist colleagues as White middle-class liberals who 'get their kicks' from a 'titillated attraction to the underdog's exotic difference'. Their sympathies result in no more than mild criticism of the agents of social control. Their bland liberalism prevents a radical critique of the structure of social inequality which creates deviance.

Gouldner argues that values underlie every sociological perspective. And these values influence the way sociologists picture and explain the social world.

Functionalism has often been seen as reflecting a conservative position which advocates the maintenance of the status quo – the way things are. In doing so, it is seen to justify existing social structures. With its view that order, stability and consensus are essential for the smooth running of society and its emphasis on the positive functions of social institutions, it implies that radical change is harmful to society.

Alvin Gouldner (1971) argues that in terms of the logic of functionalism, 'only "evil" – social disorder, tension or conflict – can come from efforts to remove the domination of man by man or make fundamental changes in the character of authority'.

Marxism The values which underlie Marxism are plain for all to see. Marx was committed to socialism. His vision of communism is utopian – a perfect society. He looked forward to an egalitarian society free from the evils of capitalism – free from oppression, exploitation and alienation, with wealth and power shared by all rather than concentrated in the hands of the few. And it is partly in terms of this vision that Marxists see capitalist society. For example, J.C. Kincaid's (1973) solution to poverty states, 'Poverty cannot be abolished in a capitalist society but only in a socialist society under workers' control, in which human needs and not profits determine the allocation of resources'. Marxism replaces the functionalist commitment to the status quo with a commitment to revolutionary change.

5.2 Sociological theory and values

Feminism The previous unit looked at feminist methodology and made the point that most feminist researchers argue that sociology is not, should not, and cannot be value free.

Many feminists wear their hearts and values on their sleeves. They place a high value on gender equality. They regard the present system of patriarchy as unjust and oppressive. They identify with the women they study and seek to empower them in their struggle for liberation. Patriarchy is wrong – the injustices of the system must be spelt out as a first step to overthrowing it.

Feminist research is directed by values which define what is right and wrong and what should be done.

5.3 The question of relativism

If we accept that to some degree value judgements underlie all sociological perspectives, where does this leave the search for 'truth'? Since all perspectives are value based it can be argued that there is no way – apart from our own value judgements – of deciding whether one is superior to another. Some would agree with this argument. They would take a *relativist* position, seeing all knowledge as relative. In terms of this view, there is no such thing as objective knowledge since everything is seen through the lens of our values and culture.

Others argue that just because a perspective is based on values does not necessarily negate its insights and its findings. Taking a relativist view is like dismissing the research findings of Greenpeace and the nuclear industry simply because of the differing values and vested interests of those organisations. And since any view of society can only be partial, differing perspectives in sociology may add breadth to that view. It is this breadth that allows Melvin Tumin (1967) to make the following statement about social stratification. 'The evidence regarding the mixed outcomes of stratification strongly suggests the examination of alternatives. The evidence regarding the possibilities of social growth under conditions of more equal rewarding is such that the exploration of alternatives seems eminently worthwhile.' And here Tumin is referring to evidence produced from a variety of sociological perspectives.

Views of reality

At one extreme, there is the position that objectivity and value freedom are possible. At the other extreme, all knowledge is seen as relative and there is no way of deciding between opposing views of reality. The most radical version of relativism rejects any possibility of objective knowledge, seeing in its place only subjective experience. In this respect, there is no reality outside human perception. What we see is what there is and there is nothing else.

Few, if any, sociologists accept this position – if they did there would be little point in doing sociology. Here is an elegant rejection of relativism by Julia O'Connell Davidson and Derek Layder (1994).

'But the idea that there is no reality separate from the conceptual systems employed by people to grasp it accords quite ludicrous powers to human thought (Trigg, 1989). A tree that falls in a forest falls regardless of whether a person is there to witness and conceptualise the event, children in Somalia die of starvation regardless of whether the governments of the Western world believe that they are providing adequate aid. Many people in Britain and the United States fondly imagine that they live in a meritocratic, post-racist, post-sexist society, but this does not mean that a working-class child or a Black child or a female child is truly blessed with the same chances of obtaining wealth and social power as the middle-class, White, male child. Of course one person's freedom fighter

is another person's terrorist. And of course you can never know with absolute certainty that another person understands what you say in exactly the same way that you understand it. And of course language, concepts and beliefs affect our perception of social reality. But this does not mean that there really is no solid world out there separate from human beings' concepts and beliefs. In practice, as King Canute is purported to have discovered, the object world has a nasty habit of intruding no matter what people may believe about it.'

key terms

Value-free research Research that is free from the values of the researcher. Research that is objective.

Relativism The idea that there can be no objective, value-free knowledge.

summary

1. There is evidence to suggest that values underlie every aspect of the sociological enterprise from the gathering of data to the construction of theories.

2. It can be argued that feminism, functionalism, Marxism and other theories are, at least in part, value based.

3. A relativist position states that an objective, value-free sociology is impossible. Carried to its extreme, this means that there is no way of judging whether research findings are valid or invalid.

4. Many sociologists, while accepting that a value-free sociology is not possible, still retain the ideal of objectivity. This means that research which is rigorous, systematic and reflexive is better than research which is sloppy, unsystematic and uncritical.

activity5 thinking about values

Item A Taking sides

To have values or not to have values: the question is always with us. When sociologists undertake to study problems that have relevance to the world we live in, they find themselves caught in a crossfire. Some urge them not to take sides, to be neutral and do research that is technically correct and value free. Others tell them their work is shallow and useless if it does not express a deep commitment to a value position.

This dilemma, which seems so painful to so many, actually does not exist; for one of its horns is imaginary. For it to exist, one would have to assume, as some apparently do, that it is indeed possible to do research that is uncontaminated by personal and political sympathies. I propose to argue that it is not possible and therefore that the question is not whether we should take sides, since we inevitably will, but rather on whose side we are on.

Adapted from Becker, 1970

Item B Better ways of conducting research

Social researchers draw on their everyday knowledge and on their political and moral values in the process of research; they use them to set the research agenda and to design classification systems; they use their social, as well as professional, skills to obtain information; they employ their knowledge as members of society and their political values to analyse and interpret their findings. But accepting this inevitable and indissoluble link between scientific and everyday thinking and between social theories and moral and political values does not make critical investigation impossible. As Geerz (1973, p30) comments in relation to ethnographic and anthropological work:

'I have never been impressed by the argument that, as complete objectivity is impossible ... one might as well let one's sentiments run loose. As Robert Solow has remarked, that is like saying that as a perfectly aseptic (germ free) environment is impossible, one might as well conduct surgery in a sewer.'

Research that is rigorous and reflexive produces knowledge that is more objective than research which is sloppy and uncritical. Researchers who, as well as being technically competent, consider the impact of their own gender, 'racialised' and class identity upon the research process and who understand that research is itself a form of social interaction will produce a more reliable picture of the social world. In short, there are better and worse ways of conducting research.

From O'Connell Davidson & Layder, 1994

Item C The value of money – a Blackfoot view

One day White men came into our camp to buy our land for dollar bills and put us on reservations with other Indians.

When the White chief had laid all of his money down on the ground and shown how much he would give all of us for signing a treaty with him, our chief took a handful of clay and made a ball of it and put it on the fire and cooked it. And it did not crack. Then he said to the White chief:

'Now, give me some of your money; we will put the money on the fire and the clay alongside of it, and whichever burns the quickest is the cheapest.'

The White chief said:

'My money will burn the quickest, because it is made of paper; so we can't do that.'

Our chief then reached down into his belt pocket and took out a little buckskin bag of sand, and he handed it to the White chief, and said: 'Give me your money. I will count the money, while you count the grains of sand. Whichever can be counted the quickest will be the cheapest.'

The White chief took the sand and poured it out into the palm of his hand, and as he looked at it, he said:

'I would not live long enough to count this, but you can count the money quickly.'

'Then,' our chief said, 'our land is more valuable than your money. It will last forever. It will not even perish by the flames of fire. As long as the sun shines and the waters flow, this land will be here to give life to men and animals. We cannot sell the lives of men and animals; therefore we cannot sell this land. It was put here for us by the Great Spirit, and we cannot sell it because it does not belong to us. You can count your money and burn it within the nod of a buffalo's head, but only the Great Spirit can count the grains of sand and the blades of grass on these plains. As a present to you, we will give you anything we have that you can take with you; but the land, never.'

From Long Lance, 1956

Blackfoot Indians performing a religious ceremony

Item D *King Canute*

King Canute ordering the waves to go back

questions

1 Do you agree with Becker's view in Item A? Give reasons for your answer.
2 'There are better and worse ways of conducting research.' Discuss with reference to Item B.
3 It is useful to look at social life from a variety of standpoints and vantage points. Discuss with some reference to Item C.
4 How does the cartoon in Item D support O'Connell Davidson's and Layder's rejection of relativism? (See page 225.)

5 Social inequality and difference

Introduction

We live on a highly unequal planet. The Human Development Report 2003 records that average life expectancy in Norway is 78.7 years, more than double the figure of 33.1 years for Zimbabwe. In Norway the average annual income is a healthy $30,000, while in Sierra Leone it is a paltry $470. The most glaring inequalities are those between nations. For example, the average North American consumes five times more than a Mexican, ten times more than a Chinese, and thirty times more than an Indian.

Gaps between rich and poor people are also found *within* every country, even an extremely wealthy country like Britain. For example, Hutton (1995) has warned that Britain is dividing into a 40/30/30 society. The top 40% of the working population are *privileged* (in full-time and secure employment), the next 30% are *insecure* or *marginalised* (in part-time or precarious work), and the remaining 30% are *disadvantaged* (unemployed or economically inactive). According to Hutton these divisions within the labour market are creating massive problems, as large numbers have been condemned to conditions of permanent stress and insecurity.

This chapter attempts to make some sense of the social inequalities which exist in Britain. In the following units we shall look at selected dimensions of inequality, chart their patterns and trends, and identify their causes and effects.

Social inequality on a London street

chaptersummary

▶ **Unit 1** looks at two key concepts for the study of social inequality.

▶ **Unit 2** describes the unequal distribution of income and wealth.

▶ **Unit 3** examines workplace changes and their impact on inequalities.

▶ **Unit 4** explains how workplace changes affect class formation and identity.

▶ **Unit 5** describes the main concepts and measures of poverty.

▶ **Unit 6** charts contemporary trends in poverty.

▶ **Unit 7** turns to debates on the 'underclass'.

▶ **Unit 8** evaluates class-based explanations of inequality.

▶ **Unit 9** looks at feminist explanations of gender inequalities.

▶ **Unit 10** considers explanations of ethnic inequalities.

Unit 1 Basic concepts

keyissues

1 What are the basic concepts used to study social inequality?

2 What are the main forms of social inequality?

1.1 Life chances

A useful way of thinking about social inequalities is in terms of *life chances*. Max Weber (1864-1920) used this term to describe people's opportunities for obtaining material goods, services and cultural experiences. In some respects it is just a sociological way of talking about 'living standards'. It covers things like possessions (eg cars, houses), a decent education, access to high quality health care, and even pleasures such as holidays and recreations. But Weber's basic point is that a person's position in society – especially their economic class position – puts limits on their prospects for getting these 'good' things in life. Some social groups are better placed than others to gain access to scarce and valuable resources. In other words, different social groups have different life chances. For example, people born into the middle class have considerable advantages over those born into the working class. They are likely to live longer, gain better educational qualifications and enjoy higher incomes.

Capital Life chances can be linked to a closely related concept, that of *capital*. Capital is an 'asset', and the more capital someone has, the greater their life chances. Social scientists have identified a number of different, but inter-linked, types of capital.

- **Economic capital** This refers to material wealth, money and property. People who possess large amounts of material capital have a much wider range of choice in life, and they can invest to increase their wealth ('money makes money').

- **Cultural capital** Bourdieu (1984) argues that social classes have different sets of tastes, preferences and linguistic competences, and parents pass these down to their children. The cultural 'know-how' of middle-class groups helps to explain their superior performance in education.

- **Human capital** This refers to particular job skills, knowledge and educational qualifications. It can be regarded as a form of investment for future rewards. For example, people study for professional qualifications in anticipation that this will bring them higher income and status in the future.

- **Social capital** Putnam (2000) uses this term to describe the social networks and levels of trust in communities. This, too, can be a valuable asset. For example, the 'old boy network' helps people find jobs and business opportunities (although it excludes those who are not part of the network). More generally, 'There is evidence that communities with a good stock of social capital are more likely to experience lower crime figures, better health, higher educational achievement, and better economic growth' (McDonnell, 2004).

1.2 Stratification

Social inequality seems to be an ever-present feature of societies. Beteille (1977) notes it has existed even among small groups based on hunting and gathering (eg Inuits, Bushmen). But social inequality in these groups was

activity1 two Britains, two life chances

Debbie Brett is a single mother trapped in a fifth-floor flat on a south London council estate, complete with three smashed windows and a broken lavatory. Debbie and her four children have no usable sitting room. They've never had a holiday or been out for a meal as a family. Debbie raises her children on Income Support and she is prey to local loan sharks.

Debbie and her girls look down from their balcony on to the large house and garden of the Confinos. Daniel is an investment banker and his wife Jane is a magistrate. They have a wide circle of friends and are involved in local societies and good causes. Their four children enjoy a range of activities – yoga, dance, art and drama classes. The family has frequent trips to their house in France, weekly outings for meals, visits to the theatre and other treats.

Both families act with great dignity but the contrasts in their lives show that equality of opportunity is a myth in Britain.

Adapted from Graef, 2003

Debbie Brett and her family look down on the prosperous private houses stretching for miles below them.

The Confino family outside their large house with six bedrooms. The scaffolding is a sign of more home improvements.

questions

1 Use the idea of life chances to indicate the prospects of the Bretts and the Confinos.

2 How might the various concepts of capital help to explain their present and future positions?

traditionally a matter of inequalities between individuals or families. These societies were not organised into clearly defined levels or *strata* where whole groups are ranked in a hierarchy of power and privilege. So social inequality is not always expressed in the form of *social stratification*.

Social stratification is the term sociologists use to describe the relatively enduring social divisions of inequality which appear in most societies. The idea of stratification is borrowed from geology where it describes how rocks and minerals are arranged in successive layers (strata) in the earth's crust. Sociologists suggest that this image fits human societies too, since most societies contain a number of social groups organised in some sort of hierarchy, one on top of another. Admittedly, comparisons between the physical world of rocks and the social world of human beings can be misleading. For one thing, human beings have attitudes and feelings – it is difficult to imagine a stone complaining about inequalities and injustices in the rock world! Also, social divisions are not usually as fixed as layers of rock. For one thing, people often move from one level to another – this is called *social mobility*. However, the idea of stratification is a useful image for thinking about the structure of inequalities in society.

Class, gender, ethnicity Social class fits the stratification model rather neatly. In Britain the class structure is often described in terms of an upper class perched above a middle class which rests in turn on the working class, with an underclass occupying the bottom rank or layer. Moreover, social class is about people's positions in the economic marketplace and the division of labour in society, so it has a direct bearing on their life chances.

But class is not the only dimension of stratification in Britain. Cutting across the class hierarchy are two other types: *gender stratification* and *ethnic stratification*. The hierarchy here is not quite as clear-cut or 'vertical' as it is with class. For example, women are found at all class levels, and some members of ethnic minorities are wealthier and more powerful than many members of the White majority. Nevertheless, gender and ethnicity represent major social divisions in society. For example, women and ethnic minorities tend to have lower status,

and less wealth and power than White males. Life chances vary not only with social class, but also along the lines of gender and ethnicity.

In this chapter we shall pay particular attention to class, ethnicity and gender. Often it will be necessary to discuss them one at a time for the sake of simplicity. But it should be remembered that in real life they always interact in complex ways. A person is defined not just by class or gender or ethnicity, but all of these acting together.

key terms

Life chances Opportunities for obtaining material goods and cultural experiences. Prospects for achieving certain living standards.
Capital Assets which enhance life chances. Capital takes different forms: economic, cultural, human and social.
Stratification A system of structured inequality between social groups.
Social class A set of social and material divisions based on people's positions in the economic marketplace.
Gender This refers to male-female differences in behaviour and cultural expectations.
Ethnicity A term used to denote a group distinguished by cultural characteristics, and sometimes by skin colour.

summary

1 A person's life chances are often directly influenced by their class, gender and ethnicity.

2 In general, the greater their economic, cultural, human and social capital, the greater their opportunities and the better their life chances.

3 There are three main forms of social stratification in present-day societies – class, gender and ethnic stratification.

4 Although they can be studied separately, they act together to influence people's lives.

Unit 2 Income and wealth

keyissues

1 What are income and wealth?

2 How are they measured?

3 How are they distributed?

2.1 Income

People's income is usually regarded as the best measure of their economic wellbeing, since it determines how much

they are able to save and spend (*Social Trends*, 2004). Income is the 'flow' of money a person (or family or household) receives within a given time period. A distinction is usually made between *original income* and *disposable income*.

Original income refers to earnings from employment and self-employment, pensions and interest on savings and investments.

Disposable income allows for the effect of flows to and from the state by taking original income and adding any state benefits (eg Income Support) and deducting direct taxes (eg income tax, council tax). The effect of state benefits and direct taxes is to reduce overall income inequalities – richer people pay more tax, poorer people receive more means-tested state benefits.

There are some other things that might be included as income. For example, some economists argue that there are all sorts of state subsidies (eg 'free' NHS treatment, subsidised public transport) which might reasonably be regarded as income, although it is difficult to calculate their cash value. Also, indirect taxes (eg VAT on goods and services) are sometimes taken into account in estimates of income. These indirect taxes hit poorer groups harder by taking a larger share of their disposable income, and this has the effect of increasing overall income inequalities.

Sources of income Income from employment is the most important single component of household income. *Social Trends* (2004) reports that wages and salaries accounted for 50% of all income in the United Kingdom in 2002. Other sources of income, in decreasing order of importance, are 'social benefits' such as pensions and welfare benefits, investment income and self-employment. Of course, the most common sources of income vary according to the particular social group. For example, pensions and investment income are relatively more important for older people, while many lone-parent households rely heavily on Income Support and tax credits. Also, the shares of the various components of household income vary over time. Since 1987, wages and salaries have become slightly less important, and social benefits slightly more important.

Income statistics

Most income statistics are flawed in some way or other.

- Useful information is gathered from surveys such as the *Family Resources Survey* and the *British Household Panel Survey*. But these household surveys do not cover the whole population – for example, they miss people sleeping rough and people living in institutions. Also, people may under-report their income. This might be innocent enough – for example, people tend to underestimate their income from investments and self-employment. Or it might be an attempt to avoid paying tax – for example, people concealing income from 'cash in hand' business deals.

- The *New Earnings Survey* is an annual survey which asks employers to provide information on the earnings of a sample of employees. But employees with earnings below the income tax threshold (mainly women with part-time jobs, and some young people) are less likely to be included in the sample. Also, the survey provides data on the incomes of individual employees but it does not reveal their household income. Clearly, people's living standards are affected not just by their own income but also by the pooled income of all members of their household (although the total sum is not always shared equally or fairly!).

- Average incomes can be misleading. The average figure is boosted by the huge earnings of small but extremely rich groups. So the incomes of as many as two thirds of earners may fall below this so-called 'average'. That is why some researchers prefer to use the median figure. The median is the half-way point in income, with half of all earners falling below this figure, and the other half above it.

- The choice of time period is important. The income of a particular household may change within a relatively short time span (eg moving in or out of employment) as well as over a lifetime (eg the drop in income on retirement). People often smooth out these income fluctuations by saving when their incomes are high, and borrowing or dipping into their savings when times are lean.

Trends Income inequalities showed a slight narrowing from the 1950s to the late 1970s. The richest people lost some of their share of income, although most of the gains were made by those immediately below them in the income league. But then society became much more unequal in the 1980s when there was a reversal of the long-term trend towards income redistribution. This growth in inequality slowed down a little in the early 1990s but then rose once more. As a result, at the beginning of the 21st century income inequality in Britain stood at a record high. It is true that the majority of the population have benefited from a rise in their *real* incomes (allowing for the effect of inflation) and so their *absolute* living standards have improved considerably over the last fifty or so years. But the poorest groups have failed to close the income gap between themselves and the rest of society. If anything, that gap has widened. Between 1979 and 1999, real incomes rose on average by 55%, but those of the bottom tenth of the population rose by only 6%, while those of the top tenth rose by 82% (Aldridge, 2001).

Income and class There is no simple and direct link between income and social class. For example, there is a wide spread of earnings among people doing similar kinds of work. Nevertheless, it is broadly true that income is related to social class (eg for both males and females, nonmanual workers earn more than manual workers). According to *Family Resources Survey* data, the weekly disposable income of households tends to decline as we descend the social class scale.

Executive salaries 'Fat cat' salaries have attracted a great deal of criticism in recent years. Britain increasingly resembles a 'winner takes all' society in which the salaries of top company executives have soared. On top of their basic salaries many of them enjoy generous bonus schemes and share options (the opportunity to purchase company shares at a discount, yielding handsome profits for the lucky few). They also enjoy nice perks such as company cars and free medical insurance. In 2003, the average pay for chief executives of the top 100 companies in Britain was about £1.6m per annum. The most successful ones earn even higher sums. Red Nose Day in 2003 raised £35m for charity but that is less than a quarter of the annual earnings of the tycoon who runs the BHS store chain. Critics have complained that British directors and executives earn inflated sums compared with their counterparts in France and Germany. Moreover, there seems little link between executive pay and company performance. Even unsuccessful executives are often paid off handsomely with 'golden parachute' sums.

Low pay As McKnight (2002) points out, there is no precise definition of low pay. Some researchers apply the term to the lowest 10% or 20% of earners, some use poverty measures (see Unit 5), while others use a fixed wage level such as the National Minimum Wage. One estimate is that there are about 2 million adults on low pay (Palmer et al., 2002). The people most likely to be low paid are women, young people, those with poor qualifications, older male workers, long-term sick and disabled persons, and ethnic minorities. Low pay is concentrated in certain industries (eg agriculture, hotels and catering, and retail) and certain occupations (eg cleaners, catering assistants, security guards). Low paid workers also run a high risk of unemployment and so they are often caught in a pattern where they swing between low pay and no pay.

Table 1 Occupational winners and losers, Great Britain 2002

	Average weekly pay
Top	
Treasurers and financial managers	£1,234
Medical practitioner	£1,159
Solicitor	£899
Police officers (inspectors and above)	£839
Marketing and sales managers	£807
Bottom	
Waiters, waitresses	£211
Petrol pump attendants	£211
Kitchen porters	£209
Launderers and dry cleaners	£207
Retail cash desk and check-out operators	£205

Adapted from *New Earnings Survey*, 2002

Explaining income inequality

There is no single explanation for the widening income inequality in Britain in the 1980s and 1990s. But here are some of the common explanations.

Population changes There was a shift towards 'high risk' groups in society. For example, Britain has an ageing population and this puts increasing numbers of retired people at risk of low incomes (unless they have a good occupational pension and a nest egg of savings). Likewise, the growth in lone-parent households has resulted in increasing numbers dependent on social benefits, if the parent is not in full-time work.

Social benefits These became less generous during the 1980s and 1990s. This was because benefit levels were linked to prices rather than wages, yet wages rose faster than prices. So the living standards of those on benefits fell further behind those of wage-earners.

Tax cuts The government's decision to cut income tax rates during this period was especially beneficial to high earners who previously paid 'super-tax'. These high earners were left with more disposable income as a result of government policy to reduce their 'tax burden'.

The National Minimum Wage It was only in 1999 that this was introduced to create a safety net for the lowest paid workers. Even so, this minimum wage is set rather low, and the *New Earnings Survey* estimated that in 2002 there were some 330,000 people aged 18 or over who were still paid less than the minimum wage rates.

Labour market This is the most important reason for the widening income gap, because the majority of household income is derived from employment. Goodman and Shephard (2002) highlight the following factors.

- Polarisation of 'work rich households' (where both adults work) and 'workless households' (those with no earners, and therefore more dependent on social benefits). Women have joined the workforce in increasing numbers – but most of these women have partners who work and so their households are 'work rich'. On the other hand, the participation rate of men has been declining, and those who drop out of the workforce often have a non-working partner – so these households become 'workless' and their income falls.

- Growth of wage inequality. Technological change (eg computerisation) has created greater demand for skilled and qualified workers. This 'skills premium' boosts the income of skilled workers, while the income of less skilled groups lags behind. Another related factor is that the demand for unskilled labour in Britain has slackened because of competition from cheap labour abroad.

- The membership and power of trade unions were reduced during this period and so they were less able to protect the incomes of low-paid groups. Wage inequality tends to be less marked in industries where there is high union coverage.

activity2 *the distribution of income*

Item A *The pig trough*

At the conference of the Trades Union Congress the president John Edmonds attacked fat cat salaries. 'A company director who takes a pay rise of £50,000 when the rest of the workforce is getting a few hundred is a greedy bastard.' He described executive pay as the 'politics of the pig trough' and called on the government to increase income taxes on the rich. The media described Edmonds as being out of touch with reality. Some pointed out that nobody complained when top footballers or entertainers earned vast sums.

But a survey of the top 100 companies reveals that chief executives have given themselves a rise of 45% in the last year. Their average pay is now over £1 million. But there is a very slim link between pay and company performance or even company size.

The Dutch-born chief executive of drugs giant SmithKline Beecham got £8 million in 1996 and £27 million in 1997. The company does not think he is over-paid – during his leadership, £34 million per day was added to the value of the UK-based company in 1997. SmithKline Beecham maintain that they have to offer top pay in order to recruit top talent so that they can compete internationally.

Adapted from *Sunday Times* 25.10.1998

Item B *Income shares*

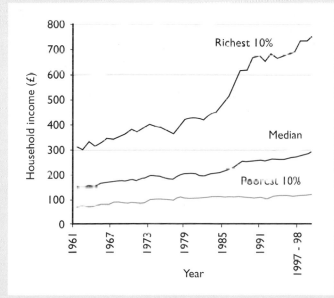

Adapted from Goodman & Shephard, 2002

questions

1 Using Item A, identify the criticisms of and justifications for executive pay.
2 Using Item B, outline the trends in income distribution.
3 Give two reasons why the data in Item B might be inaccurate.
4 Briefly outline and assess the evidence that Britain is becoming a more unequal society.

Figure 1 Breakdown of wealth in Britain

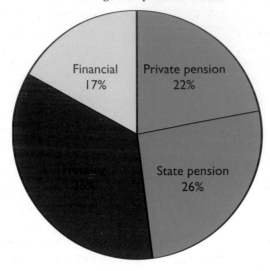

Including state pension wealth

Financial 17%
Private pension 22%
Housing 35%
State pension 26%

Excluding state pension wealth

Private pension 29%
Housing 47%
Financial 24%

Adapted from 1995/96 *Family Resources Survey*

2.2 Wealth

Wealth refers to the total 'stock' of economic resources and possessions at a fixed point in time. It is a measure of the monetary value of assets such as shares, savings, land, buildings and consumer goods. Economists use the term 'marketable wealth' to describe those assets (eg house, car, shares, money) which can be disposed of or sold. Another measure, 'marketable wealth plus pensions', adds on the estimated cash value of pension entitlements. Occupational and state pensions normally cannot be cashed in, but they are genuine assets which boost income after retirement.

In 2002, residential dwellings formed the most important component of personal or household wealth in Britain (*Social Trends*, 2004). Next most important was life assurance and pension funds. Stocks and shares grew between 1987 and 2001 but then fell steeply, as did assurance and pension funds.

Wealth statistics

It is difficult to get accurate figures on the distribution of wealth in Britain. The available sources all have limitations.

- **Surveys** One method is to ask a sample of the population about their wealth. For example, the *Family Resources Survey* provides data on things like people's estimated savings. But people may not feel like revealing their personal details to snooping sociologists and statisticians! Also, surveys rely on people telling the truth, but some individuals (especially rich ones) may wish to conceal their true wealth in order to avoid paying taxes.

- **Rich lists** Another method is to do background research on particular groups. This is the basis of the annual 'rich lists' produced by the *Sunday Times* and the *Mail on Sunday*. The journalists who compile these lists usually trawl through land records, company accounts, shares portfolios and even art collections. This research is time-consuming and complex and it often relies on rough estimates of the value of assets. Researchers are not always able to track down undisclosed wealth (eg assets 'hidden' in offshore accounts). Moreover, the lists refer only to the 'top 500' or so wealthiest individuals in Britain.

- **Inland Revenue** When someone dies, the Inland Revenue calculates the value of their estate in order to assess any inheritance tax that may be due. However, this can result in an under-estimation of the true wealth of the richest people. Many will have taken the precaution earlier in life of spreading their wealth among their children, often in the form of gifts and trust funds. They do this in order to reduce the inheritance tax their children would otherwise have to pay out of the proceeds of the estate. And it is not only the richest groups whose wealth is underestimated. Many people do not leave enough wealth to qualify for inheritance tax, and so they are excluded (as if they had no wealth at all) from the Inland Revenue figures.

Wealth trends

Absolute trends The wealth of Britain's population increased substantially in the second half of the twentieth century. As real incomes rose, many 'ordinary' people were able, for the first time, to buy their homes. Owner occupation increased from 30% of households in 1951 to about 70% by the end of the century. Car ownership spread throughout the population, many people were able to afford foreign holidays, and there was a boom in consumer goods (televisions, washing machines etc). Moreover, the spread of occupational pension schemes made retirement a bit more comfortable for many people.

Also, in the 1980s and 1990s there was a wave of 'popular capitalism' as large numbers of people bought shares in newly privatised public utilities (eg British Gas, British Telecom, British Rail). The demutualisation of high street building societies brought further windfall shares or cash sums for large groups. As a result, the number of adults owning shares increased from 2.5 million in 1980 to 16 million in 1997. So, in absolute terms, the majority of the population saw its wealth grow impressively.

Relative trends Nevertheless, wealth is much more unevenly distributed than income. This is partly because people tend to become wealthier as they grow older and so there is a concentration of wealth among older groups. Also, inheritance tends to reproduce the pattern of inequality – richer groups pass on considerable wealth to their children, while poorer groups have little to inherit from their parents.

It is true that in some respects wealth inequalities narrowed during the twentieth century, at least up until the 1980s. In 1911, the top 1% of the population owned 69% of the country's wealth, but by 2001, this had dropped to 23% (*Social Trends*, 2004). But many of the 'gains' were made by the groups immediately below the top group. The bottom 50% may have enjoyed an increase in absolute wealth but they have not increased their relative share of the nation's wealth.

Furthermore, 'wealth' is sometimes illusory or precarious. In the early years of the 21st century many people carry a huge debt burden (eg large mortgages, high credit card debt, car loans). A spell of unemployment could easily plunge them into a crisis situation. People who are approaching retirement face the prospect of declining state pensions, as many employers have ended their 'final salary' occupational pension schemes. Moreover, the dramatic falls in the stock market in the late 1990s have hit savings and nest eggs. Many of the people who got windfall shares in the 1980s and 1990s have sold them or seen their value drop dramatically. Share ownership is still highly concentrated – most shareholders have a very modest portfolio, and the stock market is dominated by wealthy individuals and investment groups.

Wealth and class Official statistics do not usually list the social class of the wealthiest people. But we can safely assume that wealth and class are linked, since 'wealth is the result of inheritance, saving or accumulation, the legal opportunities for which are clearly related to class' (Reid, 1998). One clue to the class origins of the wealthy comes from the 'rich lists'. The *Mail on Sunday* (2003) notes that 'self-made' men (and a few women) accounted for 60% of the places in the richest 300 people in Britain. But it admits that 11 of the top 20 richest people inherited the bulk of

their fortune. This includes the Duke of Westminster, who owns large tracts of Mayfair in London and is worth a massive £4.3 billion. The *Sunday Times* (2004) describes the background of the top richest 1,000:751 were self-made millionaires, while 249 inherited their wealth. The list included 36 aristocrats: 1 Monarch, 10 Dukes, 5 Marquesses, 14 Earls, 5 Viscounts, 20 Lords, 1 Baroness, 10 Baronets, 61 Knights, 3 Dames and 6 Ladies. It is also worth noting that the *Sunday Times* list contained only 78 women.

Of course, even 'self-made' millionaires may have had a head-start if they were lucky enough to have been born into a comfortable middle-class family. For example, some are able to build a modest family business into a much more lucrative enterprise. But others come from more humble origins. An example of this is David and Victoria Beckham, ranked number 962 in the 2002 *Sunday Times* rich list. On top of his football salary, David has endorsement deals with the likes of Brylcreem, Pepsi and Adidas. Victoria earns substantial sums from her Spice Girls royalties as well as her solo career.

key terms

Income The money a person, family or household receives within a given period of time.
Original income Money received from employment, pensions, savings and investments.
Disposable income Original income minus direct taxes and plus state benefits.
Wealth The economic resources and possessions held by an individual, family or household at a fixed point in time. It is a measure of the value of assets such as shares, savings, land, buildings and consumer goods.

summary

1 Incomes have risen in real terms over the past few decades but the distribution of income has become much more unequal.

2 There is a huge income gap between the low paid and the richest executives.

3 Absolute wealth has increased significantly over the long term and this has resulted in a considerable improvement in people's standards of living. But wealth is much more unevenly distributed than income.

4 Over the past 30 years, there has been a modest redistribution of wealth. However, groups at the bottom have hardly increased their already meagre share.

5 Measurements of income and wealth are often imprecise. It is particularly difficult to estimate people's wealth.

activity3 the distribution of wealth

Item A Polarisation

A survey of 2001 census data by market analysis company CACI reveals that, over the past decade, Britain has experienced a dramatic polarisation. More and more people have climbed the wealth ladder, with the middle classes in particular showing signs of increased affluence. Wealthy achievers have increased from 19% to 25% of the population. In contrast, those of 'moderate means' or 'hard pressed' now comprise 37%, compared with under 33% ten years ago. CACI identifies 5 groups:

Wealthy achievers (25%) Work in managerial or professional occupations. Usually own expensive houses, have more than one car, and enjoy large income and savings.

Urban prosperous (11% of population). Usually younger (25-35 years), university educated, and in well-paid jobs.

Comfortably off (27%) Middle-income owner-occupiers, with children still at home.

Moderate means (15%) Live in traditional terraced houses, work in a shop or factory, and less likely to have savings.

Hard pressed (22%) Live in rented property, travel to work by public transport or on foot. They cope on a tight budget and often need loans to tide them through. Preponderance of single-parent families.

Adapted from Doward et al., 2003

Item B Distribution of wealth, United Kingdom

	1976	1981	1986	1991	1996	2001
% of marketable wealth owned by:						
most wealthy 1%	21	18	18	17	20	23
most wealthy 5%	38	36	36	35	40	43
most wealthy 10%	50	50	50	47	52	56
most wealthy 25%	71	73	73	71	74	75
most wealthy 50%	92	92	90	92	93	95

Adapted from *Social Trends*, 2003, 2004

questions

1 Using Item A, identify two features which demonstrate 'polarisation'.

2 Using Item B, outline two trends in the distribution of wealth.

3 Give two reasons why the data in Item B might be misleading.

Unit 3 Workplace inequalities

keyissues

1 How has the economy changed in recent years?

2 How have these changes affected the labour market?

3 How have changes in the workplace affected class, gender and ethnic inequalities?

The workplace is a highly unequal environment. Some workers enjoy high status, pleasant working conditions and a satisfying degree of autonomy – freedom to organise their own work. Others are less fortunate. Above all, the workplace is the main source of unequal financial rewards. Your position in the labour market has a direct effect on your lifetime earnings, your living standards and your ability to build up a pension, savings and investments. Moreover, this is not just a matter of individual luck. Many of the inequalities run along the lines of class, gender and ethnicity.

But workplace inequalities must first be placed in the context of wider economic changes. Britain's economy has undergone sweeping changes over the past few decades and these have had a major impact on the workplace. As Roberts (2001) points out, economic change alters the kinds of jobs people do, as well as their opportunities to work at all.

3.1 The changing economy

Dramatic economic changes have transformed labour markets almost beyond recognition. These changes include globalisation, sector shifts and the rise of a more flexible 'post-Fordist' labour market.

Globalisation

McGrew (1992) defines globalisation as the process by which decisions and activities in one part of the world come to have significant consequences for people in other parts of the globe. The world becomes more and more 'connected'. Interaction between nations becomes more frequent and intense as goods, capital, people, knowledge, culture, fashions and beliefs flow across territorial boundaries.

Globalisation is not exactly new but the process seems to have speeded up in recent decades. As far as labour markets are concerned, there are a number of reasons for this:

- Multinational firms find it more profitable to use cheap labour in countries like India or China. So they set up their own production centres in those countries, or, more commonly, sub-contract work to firms located in those countries.
- New technologies allow the production process to be broken down into simpler tasks, with components being manufactured in different countries before finally being assembled for the finished product. Cheaper transport costs (eg through containerisation) make this an economic proposition nowadays.
- Information technology has become more sophisticated and it allows the head office of a large company to closely monitor its subsidiary firms or sub-contractors in other countries.
- Trade liberalisation has opened up markets abroad. The World Trade Organisation has tried to get countries to agree to remove trade barriers and so firms find it far easier now to operate in other countries. Multinational companies now span the globe, selling their goods and services wherever they can find a market.

Supporters of the 'free market' welcome the expansion of international production. They say that the removal of trade barriers creates strong international competition and this is good news for producers (who benefit from cheaper labour) and consumers (who benefit from cheaper prices). Competition is supposed to create more jobs and greater prosperity for all. Nevertheless, critics of free markets fear that the 'footloose' nature of capitalist firms threatens wages and jobs. For example, a firm may decide that its British workers are too expensive and so it may scale down its operations in Britain and move production abroad. The fear that a firm may do this creates job insecurity among employees and ensures that they moderate their wage claims.

Sector shifts

The economy consists of three sectors: primary (agriculture, mining), secondary (manufacturing, construction) and tertiary (services). Gallie (2000) describes long-term 'sector shifts' which have transformed the job scene in Britain. First, the primary sector has shrunk. Agriculture already accounted for only a tiny proportion of Britain's workforce as far back as 1900, and mining suffered a sharp decline as the twentieth century proceeded. Second, manufacturing expanded and diversified in the first half of the twentieth century but saw a marked contraction in its workforce during the second half. In 1980, 28% of British jobs were in manufacturing, but by 2000 this had fallen to 16%. But manufacturing output in Britain remains high, even if its workforce has declined. Third, there has been a remarkable and rapid growth in the service sector. By the end of the twentieth century, some 75% of jobs were located in the service sector, largely as a result of the expansion of areas like finance, administration, health and education. Financial and business services now account for about one in five jobs in the UK. But the service sector is actually quite diverse. It also includes workers in 'personal services' (eg hairdressers, shop assistants, cleaners), and even security guards.

Post-Fordism

Some sociologists claim that Britain's labour market has moved from a 'Fordist' to a 'post-Fordist' style of operation. Fordism is the name given to the production pattern developed by Henry Ford in the United States. Ford set up large factories equipped with assembly lines to produce motor cars on a mass scale. The product was uniform and standard (Ford famously said customers could have any colour they wanted, as long as it was black!). The division of labour in the factory was clear and rigid, with each worker performing routine but highly specialised tasks. Many of these workers could expect to have the same job all their working life. The factory was organised along hierarchical lines, with many layers of management between the shop floor and the boardroom. One of the alleged advantages of Fordism was the 'economies of mass production' – if goods are manufactured on a mass scale, the costs of producing them tend to drop. So the Fordist model was quickly adopted by other industries and countries.

However, in the global age there is no longer such a strong demand for standardised goods produced on a mass scale. Rather, consumers have diverse and short-lived tastes. So post-Fordist enterprises aim to cater for the wide range of 'niche' markets across the world. Computerised technology makes it easier for producers to make customised goods in small batches and to respond quickly to changing fashions. Post-Fordism also entails changes in the organisation and skills of the workforce. Management hierarchies have become 'flatter' (that is, fewer layers of managers), and control has become more decentralised. Workers are increasingly expected to be versatile. Instead of a clear division of labour, there is emphasis on 'multi-tasking' and teamwork. Workers may have to re-train and build up a portfolio of multiple skills. Above all, the post-Fordist emphasis is on 'flexibility'.

Table 2 Fordism and post-Fordism

Fordism	Post-Fordism
rigid procedures	flexibility
mass production	small batch production
standardised products	niche products
hierarchical management	flat hierarchies
jobs for life	portfolio careers
clear division of labour	multi-tasking
semi-skilled routine tasks	creativity, versatility
centralised control	decentralised control

A post-Fordist age? The post-Fordist model gives us some insight into the features of the modern economy. Nevertheless, it must be handled with caution.

- Many of the so-called post-Fordist features (eg small batch production) are hardly new – the British labour market has always had flexible features.
- Large factories and mass production continue to operate, even if it is true that they are increasingly located in cheap labour countries.
- It might be a mistake to regard post-Fordism as a powerful, all-embracing trend that sweeps all before it. Post-Fordism is only part of a large and varied economy.

key terms

Globalisation The development of a global society. Events in one part of the world are increasingly likely to affect other parts of the world.
Sectors of the economy The three main sectors of the economy – primary, secondary and tertiary.
Sector shifts Changes in the number of jobs in the three sectors of the economy.
Post-Fordism A change in the organisation of production and labour from the earlier Fordist practices.

activity4 the changing economy

Item A Call Bangalore

Train travellers will be forced to call Bangalore to find out the time of their next connection at Crewe or Clapham Junction, under a plan to shift Britain's national rail enquiries service to India. Train operators intend to educate Indian call centre workers in the details of Britain's railways. Indian staff will need to know about places in Britain as well as the difference between a saver, a supersaver, an off-peak saver and a weekender.

An executive from National Rail Enquiries reports that Indian call centres deliver an excellent service and some operators have 'virtually no Indian accent'. But he has warned that there may well be trade union agitation and a media outcry in Britain, since the move could put 1,700 jobs at risk in the existing call centres in Cardiff, Derby, Newcastle and Plymouth.

The trade union Amicus said it was a myth that jobs could be exported without loss of quality.

Adapted from the *Guardian*, 15.10.2003

Victoria Station, London

Item B Sector shifts

Employee jobs, United Kingdom (percentages)

	Males				Females			
	1971	1983	1993	2003	1971	1983	1993	2003
Distribution, hotels, catering and repairs	13	17	20	22	23	26	26	26
Manufacturing	41	29	24	20	29	16	11	7
Financial and business services	5	12	17	20	7	14	17	19
Transport and communication	10	10	10	8	3	2	2	4
Construction	8	8	7	8	1	2	1	1
Agriculture	2	2	2	1	1	1	1	-
Energy and water supply	5	4	2	1	1	1	1	-
Other services (public administration, education, health and other community, social and personal service activities)	15	17	19	20	35	39	41	42

Adapted from *Social Trends*, 1995, 2004

Item C Fordism

Assembly line at the Ford Motor Company

The picture shows an early version of an assembly line at the Ford Motor Company. The cars were moved from worker to worker – at first by hand and then by machine power when the line became mechanised. Identical cars rolled down the line with each worker carrying out one or more simple tasks, such as fitting windscreens or tightening wheel nuts.

Creating new lace designs

questions

1 How does Item A illustrate globalisation?
2 What evidence of sector shifts does Item B provide?
3 What aspects of Fordism are illustrated in Item C?
4 What aspects of post-Fordism are illustrated in Item D?

Item D Post-Fordism

Mini production

Workers at the BMW factory in Oxford, which produces the Mini, are organised into 'self-steered' teams of between 8 and 15 people. They tackle many production problems themselves, rather than relying on other departments, and rotate tasks between team members. Rather than being management-led, the focus is now on initiative and self-management. The teams aim for continuous improvement and have developed ideas which have saved the company large sums of money.

Adapted from Watkins, 2003

In a factory near Derby, 50 high-tech machines whir 24 hours a day, producing lace that ends up in 3,000 colours, and is incorporated into women's underwear by manufacturers around the world. The factory is owned by Sherwood Group.

Its survival depends on flexibility and creativity. It must be responsive to the lingerie world's thirst for new fashions. And it must specialise in small-batch production to meet the requirements of hundreds of textile companies throughout the world. The factory has a design studio which produces around 200 lace designs each year. And it has equipment which can dye lace in thousands of shades.

Adapted from *Financial Times*, 13.11.2002

3.2 The flexible economy

Post-Fordism refers to how everything has become more flexible – enterprises, labour markets, occupations and workers (Roberts, 2001). In particular, businesses are trying to achieve *functional flexibility* and *numerical flexibility*. Functional flexibility refers to post-Fordist techniques and operating methods. This includes the use of versatile information technology (eg programmable, computerised machines) and a versatile, multi-skilled workforce. Numerical flexibility refers to the various ways in which firms try to match the numbers of workers to the volume of work. Traditionally, firms have sacked workers in times of economic difficulty and hired them when there is an economic upturn. But post-Fordist employers also use the device of *non-standard contracts*.

Numerical flexibility – unemployment

Shedding workers (or 'downsizing') is the most drastic form of numerical flexibility. In the past, redundancy was commonly a result of cyclical downturns in the economy, but increasingly it is a cost-cutting measure even when the business is profitable (Noon & Blyton, 2002). For example, in 2001 Corus (previously British Steel) announced closure of some of its steel-making plants in Britain. About 6,000 jobs were lost, yet the share price of Corus shot up! According to Hutton (2002), shareholders in Britain tend to think of short-term profits rather than the long-term welfare of the company and its workers. So they put pressure on companies to stay 'lean' and sack 'surplus' staff.

Measuring unemployment

The number of people in employment in Britain is measured by means of household surveys and the census. In 2003, it stood at a record high of 28.1 million. However, it is a rather more difficult task to calculate the number of people who are unemployed at any given time. The Office for National Statistics (ONS) publishes two measures – the claimant count and the International Labour Organisation (ILO) measure – but there is a large difference between them and they do not always move in line with one another.

The claimant count This is derived from Job Centre records, and counts only those people who are claiming unemployment-related benefits. Over the years there have been numerous alterations to the benefit rules and this affects the unemployment totals. Some critics accuse governments of 'fiddling' the figures in order to make unemployment seem less of a problem. In the late 1980s, for example, the government effectively removed 16 and 17 year-olds from the unemployment register by declaring that they would no longer qualify for unemployment benefits. Furthermore, the system of benefits regulations is such that women are less likely than men to make unemployment-related claims.

The ILO count This is calculated from the *Labour Force Survey* (LFS), a random survey of people living in private households in the United Kingdom. The ILO count defines the unemployed as those jobless people who want to work, are available for work, and are actively seeking employment. The ILO definition of unemployment is now the official one. Even so, it presents certain problems. For example, a woman may not be regarded as 'available for work' unless she can start a new job almost immediately, yet mothers of young children often need time to make the necessary childcare arrangements. Also, some people may no longer be 'actively seeking work' because they have become dispirited by their fruitless search for a job. Palmer et al. (2002) point out there are about 2.5 million people, many of them sick and disabled, who want paid work but find it extremely difficult to obtain.

In addition, the scale of unemployment is sometimes masked by social trends. For example, in the 1980s and 1990s more young people stayed on in education rather than seeking jobs. There was also an increase in the numbers of people leaving the job market (eg middle-aged people opting for early retirement, and larger numbers of people claiming incapacity benefit). Without these trends, the official unemployment totals would have been much higher.

Unemployment trends

Unemployment soared in Britain in the 1980s and the 1990s, largely as a result of major recessions at the beginning of both of those decades. It reached a peak of just under 3 million in 1993. Since then, unemployment has reduced significantly. In 2003, it stood at about 1.48 million (a rate of about 5.1%) for the ILO measure, and about 926,900 for the claimant count. Britain now has its lowest unemployment rate for 20 years, and one of the highest economic activity rates among the developed nations.

Compared with thirty years ago, the average employee is only slightly more likely to become unemployed. Perhaps only a fifth of the workforce has ever been made redundant. But those who become unemployed are likely to remain so for nearly three times longer than in the past (Gregg & Wadsworth, 1999). Moreover, the threat of unemployment creates a sense of insecurity among the workforce. This insecurity is intensified by the increasing practice of employers offering temporary rather than permanent jobs.

Unemployment figures indicate the 'stock' of unemployed people at a given point in time. But unemployment can also be seen in terms of 'flows' – movement into and out of unemployment. The unemployed population is constantly changing as people lose or find jobs. But the risk of unemployment is different between social groups. Some groups are more likely to enter unemployment and to stay there for a longer time. For most people unemployment is brief, but for a minority it is prolonged. Those most at risk include unskilled and poorly qualified individuals, young people, people with poor health or disabilities, ethnic minorities, and older men (Brown et al., 2002).

key terms

Functional flexibility Post-Fordist techniques and operating methods which aim to make production more flexible and responsive to the market.

Numerical flexibility The ways in which firms try to match the numbers of workers to the volume of work.

The claimant count A count of unemployment based on the number of people claiming unemployment-related benefits.

The ILO count A count of unemployment based on the number of jobless people who want work, are available for work, and are actively seeking employment.

Economically inactive Those people who are neither in employment nor unemployed. This includes full-time students, the voluntarily unemployed (eg looking after a home or an infirm relative) and those unable to work because of chronic illness or disability.

Economically active Those people who are either in employment or, if unemployed, actively looking for work.

In employment This covers employees, self-employed, and those on government training schemes.

activity5 unemployment

Item A Flexibility

The magical, iconic quality in a market economy is flexibility. Flexibility is what makes a market economy work. Financial capital, for example, is mobile and flexible; it has no loyalties, nor does it expect any. Its job is to chase the highest returns.

Over the last thirty years, corporations have increasingly looked for the same quality from their workforces. If a company chooses to run down a branch of production, then it needs the flexibility to extract itself as quickly and cheaply as possible. When it increases output, it needs to do so in such a way that, if market conditions change, it can disinvest quickly. Hiring a worker is not so much a contract with reciprocal obligations as a cash deal – one that employers think they should be able, flexibly, to cancel at will.

Adapted from Hutton, 2002

Item B Unemployment (ILO measure)

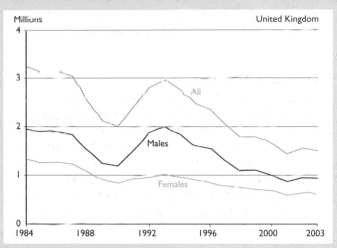

Adapted from *Social Trends*, 2004

questions

1 Using Item A, identify two links between flexibility and unemployment.

2 Briefly summarise the trends in Item B.

3 Give two reasons why the data in Item B might be flawed.

4 Outline the evidence that Britain is becoming more 'flexible'.

Numerical flexibility – non-standard contracts

The 'standard contract' is one where employees work on a full-time and permanent basis. But nowadays, employers seem to be resorting more frequently to 'non-standard contracts' in order to achieve numerical flexibility. They do this by hiring more part-time, temporary and casual staff, and by 'outsourcing' many of their work operations. These non-standard contracts now account for as much as one quarter of the total workforce.

Part-time work This kind of work has become increasingly common. In 2003, there were about 6.3 million part-time workers in the UK out of a total workforce of 28.1 million (*Social Trends*, 2004). Most of these part-timers are women, and part-time work may suit their particular needs, allowing them to combine limited hours of work with their home and childcare commitments. But the arrangement also suits employers who are able to adjust the hours of part-time workers in a flexible manner.

Temporary work Towards the end of the 20th century, the British economy was faced with unpredictable markets, rapidly changing technologies and strong pressures to reduce wage costs. Many employers responded by offering temporary work rather than permanent positions to their employees. Noon and Blyton (2002) estimate there are about 1.7 million workers (7.1% of the total) on temporary contracts. Temporary contracts give employers greater flexibility because they can decide whether or not to renew the contracts at the end of the fixed term.

Casual work Some workers are employed on a 'casual' basis, hired only for limited periods when there is work to

be done (eg seasonal workers in agriculture, or irregular work in the building trade). One version of this is the 'zero hours' contract where shop workers have no guaranteed hours or earnings but are still expected to keep themselves available for employers to call on as and when required.

Outsourcing or subcontracting Employers are increasingly outsourcing – subcontracting much of their work to outside firms or employment agencies. They do this to cut costs (they can switch contracts to the lowest bidder). It also helps them avoid the risks and responsibilities of employing workers directly (eg they can dispense with the services of subcontracted staff without having to give them redundancy pay). The NHS subcontracts a lot of its cleaning and cooking operations to outside firms. Often this means that the NHS is indirectly employing people on low pay and poor terms and conditions it would not dare to offer its own staff (Toynbee, 2003).

Bass the brewers, who own a large chain of pubs, provide an example of outsourcing. They directly employ workers to produce beer – their core business. Everything else is subcontracted – food preparation, cleaning, lighting, music, maintenance, door security. Outsourcing gives the company considerable flexibility. If there is a downturn in business, they can simply reduce the amount of work performed by their subcontractors, so saving the costs of a directly employed workforce (Ward, 2000).

Self-employment This is yet another non-standard form of work. In 2002, about 3 million people were self-employed in Britain, almost double the figure for the 1970s. Self-employment became more widespread in the 1980s and

1990s, partly as a response to the high unemployment at the time. But it was also a response to outsourcing, which created more entrepreneurial opportunities for small businesses.

Myths of flexibility?

Some researchers question whether the economy is quite as flexible as post-Fordists suggest. Indeed, Meadows (1999) exposes certain 'myths' about the so-called 'flexible' job market.

- It is an exaggeration to say that 'jobs for life' have disappeared: many employees still spend a large part of their career with a single employer. Anyway, it is unlikely that 'jobs for life' were ever quite so widespread in the past (eg workers in manufacturing have always been vulnerable to unemployment).

- It is untrue that 'job hopping' is now the norm. The average length of job tenure has fallen only slightly, from 6 years in 1975 to 5.5 years in 1999. Although young people may now have to change jobs more often at the beginning of their working life, most of them eventually land a more settled position.

- Permanent jobs are still much more common than temporary ones. In 1999, about 82% of the workforce were permanent employees. Even if people start on fixed-term contracts, they usually move on to permanent positions.

- The growth of part-time work has been modest, from about 21% of all jobs in 1980 to 26% in 2003. Also, Meadows maintains that most people take part-time jobs because they want to, rather than because they cannot get a full-time job.

3.3 Class and the workplace

As the economic structure of Britain has changed, so have its occupational patterns. 'Since the early 1980s, there has been substantial change in the composition of the workforce: more women, a better qualified workforce, a growing service sector and contracting manufacturing sector, more non-manual jobs and fewer manual jobs, more private sector and less public sector employment, more part-time work' (Bryson & Gomez, 2002).

In this section we explore how these workplace changes have affected class inequalities. The following sections examine the impact of workplace changes on gender and ethnic inequalities.

There is a direct link between social class and the workplace, because class is usually defined by a person's occupation. So it is only to be expected that economic and occupational changes will have a significant impact on class inequalities.

Occupational change Gallie (2000) describes the long-term transformation of the occupational structure in Britain. In the first half of the 20th century there was a growth in clerical work (especially among women) and a significant expansion of professions, but manual work still dominated.

The second half of the century saw a sharp decline in the numbers of manual workers (especially unskilled workers) and a spectacular expansion in professional and managerial groups. So, between 1951 and 1992, manual workers declined from three-quarters to less than 40% of the workforce. By the end of the 20th century, the workforce consisted of a fairly even division between three broad occupational groups: professional/managerial, 'intermediate' (lower ranks of white-collar workers), and manual.

It is not only the size of social classes which has changed. The nature of work, too, has been greatly affected by the move towards a more flexible, post-Fordist economy. For example, manual workers find that the new service sector jobs have a different character: 'The old working class was employed in coal mines, shipyards, steel plants and engineering workshops; the new working class is employed in supermarkets, security firms, contract cleaners, fast food and other catering establishments, and suchlike' (Roberts, 2001).

Class inequalities It is foolish to deny that there is still a hierarchy of occupations and classes in Britain. Class differences in the workplace lead to huge income inequalities (see Unit 2). Roberts (2001) argues that the middle classes still enjoy considerable financial and other advantages, and that is why they are so anxious that their children do not drop down into the working class! Skilled manual workers have suffered from the decline of manufacturing and the move to a flexible economy. Indeed, manual workers in manufacturing have been the main victims of outsourcing abroad over the past twenty or so years. Denny (2003) reports that not all of them have managed to find alternative jobs. In the worst-hit areas, such as the old coal fields, many manual workers took early retirement or went on benefit, with painful consequences for families and communities. Others found jobs that were not as well paid as those they had lost.

In general, then, it is difficult to deny that middle-class workers enjoy marked advantages. For example, semi-skilled and unskilled manual workers are four times more likely than professional and managerial groups to become unemployed (Brown et al., 2002). If working, they are more likely to be on casual, temporary or part-time contracts. And it is extremely unlikely that any executives are asked to live on poverty-level wages.

Middle class deskilling?

The Marxist writer Harry Braverman (1974) argued that many white-collar workers were being *deskilled,* to such an extent that they could be considered working class. Their skills were being eroded by automation, computerisation and the fragmentation of work tasks into simpler routines, and this had implications for their pay, status and power. Moreover, Braverman saw this deskilling as a deliberate management strategy. Under capitalism, employers wish to cut their costs and maximise their profits by replacing workers with machines. Where this is not

activity6 class work

Item A Poverty wages

Barbara Ehrenreich used covert ('hidden') participant observation in order to discover what it was really like to survive in 'dead-end' jobs in the United States. She took on a variety of low paid jobs, including waitress, cleaner, care assistant and supermarket worker. To her surprise, she found that these so called 'unskilled' jobs actually required a wide range of demanding skills. Moreover, the 'working poor' perform valuable services for society – they keep other people's homes spick and span (yet usually live in substandard housing themselves) they look after other people's children (often at the cost of neglecting their own), they provide cheap services for individuals and firms (yet they are treated as insignificant and 'invisible'). Richer people are insulated from poor people and fail to realise the level of hardship they endure.

Ehrenreich struggled to exist on her low wages and she was forced to live in seedy rented accommodation and scrimp on food, clothes and entertainment. She points out that low-paid workers often have to take on more than one job to make ends meet. In spite of working harder than ever before in her life, Ehrenreich found herself sinking deeper into poverty and debt. She describes the energy and dedication of poverty-wage workers and confesses how exhausted she felt at the end of each working day. She deplores the way these workers are robbed of self-respect and dignity by the rest of society. Customers treat them shabbily and employers exploit them and humiliate them daily (eg by insisting on a 'purse search' before the employee leaves work at the end of the day). Ehrenreich concludes that: 'The less people are paid, the more anxious employers are to squeeze every bead of sweat out of their labour, monitoring each second with an indignity that no worker further up the scale would tolerate'.

Adapted from Ehrenreich, 2002

Item B Class and unemployment

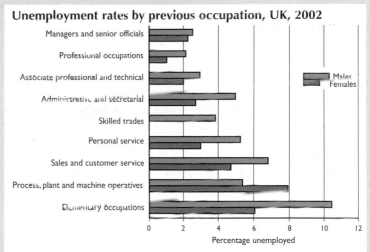

Unemployment rates by previous occupation, UK, 2002

Elementary occupations are those that involve mainly routine tasks and do not require formal qualifications. For skilled trades, the sample size for females was too small for reliable estimates.

Adapted from *Social Trends*, 2003

questions

1   Using Item A, identify two characteristic features of low-paid work.

2   Identify two strengths and two weaknesses of using covert participant observation to study low-paid work.

3   Using Item B, outline the connections between class and unemployment.

---

possible they try to control workers by reducing their autonomy and discretion. One effective way of doing this is by breaking their work down into simple, repetitive tasks.

This is not a totally novel idea. After all, the assembly lines of Henry Ford were organised along similar principles. But Braverman's arguments were controversial because many experts expected the new 'flexible' economy to create a demand for multi-skilled, highly educated and versatile workers, not the 'industrial robots' of the past. Office work has always included some routine and trivial tasks but the introduction of computers was expected to enlarge the range of office skills.

It is not easy to evaluate Braverman's arguments. First of all, he saw deskilling as a broad 'tendency' and accepted that it advanced at an uneven pace in different industries and occupations. So, merely showing there are some exceptions to deskilling does not necessarily disprove his

case. Second, it is not easy to measure skills or to assess whether there has been a net deskilling. Even within any one occupation, some aspects of the job may have been upskilled and others deskilled. Given this complexity, it is not surprising that sociologists have reached different conclusions on the deskilling thesis.

Criticisms of deskilling The following criticisms have been levelled at the deskilling thesis.

• Management strategies are broader and more enlightened than Braverman suggests. For example, managers may feel that 'job enrichment' makes for happier and more productive workers. Investing in 'human capital' (qualifications and skills) can be an effective way of increasing profits.

• Workers are not totally passive. They may organise effectively to resist rigid specialisation and deskilling.

• Deskilling is most common in mass production industries, but only a minority of workers are employed in these industries. Post-Fordists argue that nowadays more people are engaged in 'people work' and in jobs which require flexibility and a widening of skills.

- Braverman neglects the important role of gender. Women's skill levels tend to be under-rated because of the low value attached to 'women's work'.

- Research evidence suggests that deskilling is patchy rather than universal. For example, Gallie et al. (1998) surveyed a large national sample of workers who had been affected by new technologies and managerial strategies. Yet only a small minority reported that their jobs had been deskilled. Almost two thirds felt their jobs had been upskilled (to a modest extent), while a large minority reported no significant change.

McDonaldisation of society There are similarities between Braverman's views and the non-Marxist ideas of George Ritzer (1996). Ritzer argues that the so-called 'rational' principles of the fast-food industry are coming to dominate wider sectors of society (eg health, education, business). These principles are efficiency (speed), calculability (measurable quantities), predictability (sameness) and control (the substitution of humans with technology). Thus, in McDonald's you expect your chips to be served quickly, in standard amounts, and to have the same quality in all branches. Human discretion is minimised as far as possible by the use of technology. Ritzer is broadly critical of the process of deskilling which McDonaldisation introduces into society at large. He says it is inefficient and dehumanising, and it strips people of their creativity and initiative. Moreover, he is not convinced by those who argue that society is actually moving away from McDonaldisation towards post-Fordism or postmodernism. For Ritzer, there is no clean break between Fordism and post-Fordism – they co-exist in contemporary society.

3.4 Gender and the workplace

The gendered workplace The workplace is 'gendered' in the sense that men and women tend to have a different relationship to work. There are broad differences in their employment patterns, industrial locations and earnings (Pilcher, 1999).

Forms of work Men are more likely than women to be self-employed. Of the 3.3 million people who were self-employed in the UK in 2003, over 70% were men. About 16% of male workers were self-employed, compared with about 7% of female workers. Another difference is that women are more likely than men to work part-time. Of the 6.3 million part-time workers in the UK in 2003, 81% were women. About 40% of female employees were part-timers, compared with only about 8% of male employees (*Social Trends*, 2004).

Horizontal segregation Men and women tend to be located in different sorts of industries and occupations. This is called *horizontal segregation* (the barrier between 'male' and 'female' occupations). This segregation is a matter of degree, and it varies between industries. There is some evidence that horizontal segregation has been declining in recent years, and Roberts (2001) suggests that the traffic is mainly in the direction of women moving into men's fields rather than the other way round. Table 3 provides examples of horizontal segregation.

Table 3 Segregation by occupation, Great Britain, 2001

	% women	% men
Taxi drivers, chauffeurs	7	93
Security guards	8	92
Software professionals	16	84
ICT managers	17	83
Police officers up to sergeant	20	80
IT technicians	29	71
Solicitors, lawyers, judges	37	63
Sales representatives	37	63
Medical practitioners	38	62
Chefs and cooks	46	54
Shelf fillers	48	52
Secondary teachers	57	43
Sales assistants	72	28
Waiters and waitresses	77	23
Office assistants and clerks	81	19
Cleaners and domestics	81	19
Primary and nursery teachers	86	14
Hairdressers and barbers	88	12
Nurses	90	10
Care assistants and home carers	90	10
Receptionists	95	5

Adapted from *Labour Force Survey*, 2001

Vertical segregation Within any industry or occupational group, men and women tend to be concentrated at different levels. This is called *vertical segregation*. Again, it is a matter of degree, and both sexes are found at most levels. But women tend to be under-represented at the most senior positions. Middle-class women often proceed so far and then encounter the glass ceiling (they can see where they would like to go next but the ceiling impedes further progress). However, Desai et al. (1999) found that women are starting to break through the glass ceiling, and they predict that the occupational profiles of males and females will converge in future.

Table 4 The glass ceiling

Women are 45% of the workforce in Britain, but they are under-represented at the top. They make up:

- 9% of top company directors
- 13% of council chief executives
- 7% of senior police officers
- 9% of newspaper editors
- 18% of MPs
- 6% of High Court judges
- 29% of secondary school heads

Adapted from EOC, 2004

Career patterns About 25 years ago many women worked full-time before having children, then withdrew from the workforce while the children were young, before eventually returning to work. So their employment pattern had a double hump – a peak of high employment in late teens and early 20s, then a fall for 30 year olds, before rising to another (but lower) peak for those in their late 40s. But Desai et al. (1999) describe significant changes in female employment patterns. By 1998, the double hump pattern had been replaced by a near-flat employment rate of around 70% that only begins to fall after the age of 50. Women are increasingly returning to work after only a brief period of maternity leave, so nowadays they are likely to be more or less continuously involved in paid work.

Earnings There are all sorts of difficulties in making fair comparisons of men's and women's earnings. Obviously, a female doctor will earn far more than a male labourer. But Goodman and Shephard (2002) say it is important to compare male and female wages across similar jobs and to control for other factors such as length of service. Also, women tend not to work as many hours as men, so a distinction has to be made between hourly earnings and weekly earnings. Nevertheless, earnings surveys do show that a 'gender gap' exists – see Activity 7, Item B.

Unemployment It is not easy to decide on 'true' unemployment rates because women are slightly less likely to register as unemployed. Nevertheless, the figures suggest that men are more likely to be unemployed across all age groups. In 2002/03 the unemployment rate (ILO definition) in Britain was 5.1% overall, but 5.6% for men and 4.5% for women.

Female progress

Changes in the economy have transformed the gender composition of the workforce and enabled women to take on a wider range of jobs and careers. 'Economic and occupational trends in the second half of the twentieth century were relatively kind to women' (Roberts, 2001). This progress can be summed up by two major trends – the *feminisation of the workforce*, and a reduction in gender inequalities.

Feminisation of the workforce Throughout the 20th century, there was no time when women comprised less than about 30% of the total labour force. But, from the 1950s onwards, there was a marked trend towards the increasing feminisation of the workforce, and this accelerated during the 1980s and 1990s. Between 1971 and 2003, the numbers of women in employment in Britain increased from 8.8 million to 12.9 million, while the numbers of male workers remained relatively static at around 15.2 million. This trend is largely due to an increase in the numbers of women who are economically active – in work, or unemployed but seeking work. This increase in economic activity even applies to women with pre-school age children. In 1973, only 27% of all women with at least one child under the age of 5 were economically active, but by 2001 this had increased to 53%.

key terms

Horizontal segregation The tendency for men and women to be located in different sorts of industries and occupations.
Vertical segregation The tendency for men and women to be concentrated at different levels – of power, status and pay – within any industry or occupational group.
The glass ceiling The barrier to women's advancement in employment. It is called the glass ceiling because women can see where they would like to go but the ceiling impedes their progress.

activity7 gender and work

Item A Gender and occupation

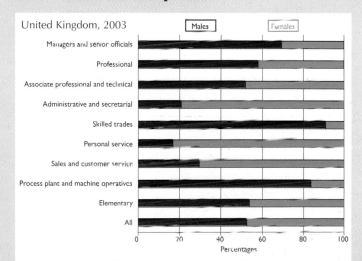

Adapted from *Social Trends*, 2004

Item B Gender and earnings

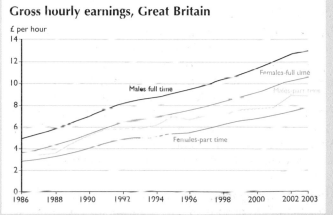

Data are not available for male part-time earnings for 1986 and 1992, nor for female part-time earnings for 1994

Adapted from *Social Trends*, 2004

Item C *The assembly line in the head*

The typical call centre operator is young, female and works in a large, open plan office. Employees are closely monitored and they must conform to acceptable codes of speech. The work is demanding, repetitive and frequently stressful – an 'assembly line in the head'. Promotion prospects and career advancement are limited. Work consists of an uninterrupted and endless sequence of similar conversations with customers she never meets.

The operator has to concentrate hard on what is being said, jump from page to page on a screen, making sure that the details entered are accurate and that she has said the right things in a pleasant manner – 'smile down the phone'. The pressure is intense because she knows her work is being measured, her speech monitored, and it often leaves her mentally, physically and emotionally exhausted.

Call centre for Intelligent Finance – the IF Bank, part of the Halifax

Nevertheless, call centre management need to motivate their staff, maintain quality of service and reduce labour turnover. So they have had to make certain concessions to employees – allowing them to vary the 'script', work part-time, and earn incentive bonuses.

Adapted from Taylor & Bain, 1999

questions

1 Briefly summarise the gender differences shown in Item A.

2 Using Item B, outline two trends in gender-related earnings.

3 Using Item C, identify two characteristic features of call centre work.

4 Using Item A and your wider sociological knowledge, outline the evidence that call centre work is typical of women's work in general.

5 Outline and assess Braverman's and Ritzer's explanations of the 'assembly line in the head'.

Reduction in inequalities Many gender inequalities in the workplace have been reduced, if not removed entirely.

- Horizontal segregation has decreased since the 1970s. Crompton (1997) speculates that, with the decline in manual occupations and traditionally 'male' industries (mining, shipbuilding etc), we might expect to see further decline in gender-typed occupations.

- Vertical segregation is declining. 'As women have increased the level of their labour force participation, so they have also improved the level and extent of their academic and professional qualifications. Over the last ten years, women in all countries have been steadily increasing their representation in professional and managerial occupations' (Crompton, 2000).

- The pay gap has been closing and the figures for 2001 were the narrowest on record. Indeed, Desai et al. (1999) report that 1 in 5 women earn more than their partners, compared with 1 in 14 in the 1970s.

Pilcher (1999) is aware that not all gender inequalities have been swept away. But she claims there have been significant improvements, for the following reasons.

- Economic change. The shift in the economy from heavy industry to services has created more job opportunities for women.

- Political processes. The Equal Pay Act of 1970 and the Sex Discrimination Act of 1975 have outlawed the more blatant forms of sex discrimination in the workplace. Moreover, the government has provided tax credits and benefits to enable lone parents to work.

- Women themselves have changed. Partly as a result of the growing influence of feminism, women are more career-minded nowadays. More effective contraception makes it easier for them to combine work with family responsibilities. Also, the growing instability of family life creates an incentive for them to become financially independent through work.

Redundant men?

At the same time as women have been advancing, some groups of men seem to have been retreating. In fact, the employment rate of men has been declining over the past twenty or thirty years: 'It was mainly men's jobs that were lost as a result of the labour shake-outs from manufacturing and extractive industries' (Roberts, 2001). Beynon (2002) argues that 'de-industrialisation' (the decline of manufacturing) was immensely damaging for many working-class men. 'The old industrial labourers, along with skilled and semi-skilled workers, were rendered obsolete by the technological advances they had helped to implement. Jobs that depended upon physical strength vanished in their millions and in their place came, at best, short-term contracts and part-time work' (Beynon, 2002).

The desperate plight of redundant miners and steelworkers has been highlighted by popular films such as *Brassed Off* and *The Full Monty*. Many of the discarded men appear to be poorly placed to land the new service sector jobs on offer. These men traditionally took pride in their 'masculine' identity, yet many of the new jobs seem to call for more 'feminine' skills (eg the ability to manage people with sensitivity and tact). Moreover, working-class men may lack the educational qualifications which are required for the new jobs.

3.5 Ethnicity and the workplace

Ethnic disadvantage In 2003, the Cabinet Office Strategy Unit published a major review of evidence on ethnic minorities in the labour market. It summarised its findings as follows.

- Ethnic minorities are disadvantaged in many ways – employment and unemployment rates, earnings levels, occupational attainment, and levels of self-employment. The extent of these disadvantages has fluctuated over time but they have not been eliminated.

- The extent and nature of this disadvantage differs significantly by ethnic group. While ethnic minorities in general tend to be disadvantaged, groups such as Indians and Chinese have enjoyed labour market success.

- Within each ethnic group, labour market performance varies considerably according to gender and area of residence. In general, the second generation tend to do better than the first generation.

- The labour market disadvantage of ethnic minorities has many complex causes. The most important are education and skills, limited access to employment opportunities, and discrimination in the workplace.

The ethnic penalty Heath and McMahon (1995) coined the term *ethnic penalty* to refer to all the sources of disadvantage that might lead an ethnic minority group to fare less well than similarly qualified Whites. In other words, when ethnic minority and White groups are matched in terms of class, educational attainment and other relevant factors, an ethnic disadvantage remains. The unexplained sources of this remaining disadvantage form the ethnic penalty.

The firm conclusion of the Cabinet Office report (2003) is that all ethnic minorities suffer an ethnic penalty. Even after like-for-like analysis, there is still an unexplained gap between Whites and minorities in terms of their work situations and job rewards. After taking account of all potentially relevant factors (eg differences in age, qualifications, geographical area), there is still an unexplained gap in their labour market achievements. This gap may be caused by racial discrimination, or possibly it is the result of other, as yet unidentified, factors.

Problems of interpretation Before considering ethnic disadvantage in more detail, it is helpful to bear in mind some of the problems involved in handling ethnic data.

- **Information gap** In many cases there is just not enough detailed information available. Large-scale studies (eg Modood et al., 1997) are very useful but they are few and far between.

- **Limitations of sample size** Ethnic minorities are only 8% of the total population of the United Kingdom and so surveys based on a random sample of the general population will usually contain rather small numbers. A small sample size is a weak basis for making generalisations, so some surveys deliberately over-sample ethnic minorities. Another solution, used by the annual Labour Force Survey, is to group results for a number of years, rather than take results from one year alone.

- **Classifications** How are people assigned to ethnic groups? If researchers use different classification systems, this makes it difficult to compare their findings. The Census and the Labour Force Survey now share the same classification system, asking people to identify their own 'ethnic group' from a list of eleven categories. But this is a large number of categories to handle with ease, and researchers sometimes combine them in different ways.

- **Ethnic diversity** The ethnic minority population of Britain is not only small, it is also extremely diverse. Generalisations which apply to some ethnic groups (eg Indians) may not apply to others (eg Black Caribbeans).

- **Internal diversity** There is diversity within ethnic minority groups as well as between them. There are class divisions within every group, and all groups contain a broad range from the most to the least prosperous.

- **Like-for-like comparisons** Where possible, comparisons should be on a like-for-like basis. Some ethnic groups have a 'younger' age profile than others, and young people tend to earn less than older people. So it is important, when comparing groups, to control for age differences.

Ethnic minority employment

Employment rates Generally speaking, the employment rates for minorities are lower than those for Whites, but it varies between groups. For example, Black women are almost three times more likely than Bangladeshi women to be in employment. Young people from minorities are less likely to be economically active than Whites, but this is partly because they have a larger proportion in full-time education.

Table 5 Employment by ethnic origin, Great Britain, 2001

	In employment (%)
Women	
Black/Black British	58
- Caribbean	63
- African	52
Asian/Asian British	41
- Indian	53
- Pakistani/Bangladeshi	22
Chinese	56
White	68
Men	
Black/Black British	66
- Caribbean	68
- African	65
Asian/Asian British	67
- Indian	73
- Pakistani/Bangladeshi	60
Chinese	63
White	81

Adapted from EOC, 2002

Unemployment The unemployment rate for minorities has consistently run at about twice the level for Whites. However, there are variations between ethnic groups. Unemployment rates partly reflect differences in age profiles, geographical locations and occupational and industrial distribution. But minorities tend to have higher unemployment rates than Whites even when they have similar or even better qualifications, so discrimination cannot be ruled out as a cause.

Industrial sectors Minority men are under-represented in construction and agriculture but they are more likely than White men to work in the service sector. The most striking example of this service sector concentration is found among male Bangladeshi workers, about 52% of whom are in the restaurant industry. The differences between Whites and minorities are less marked among women because women in general tend to be concentrated in the service sector.

Occupations The occupational profile of ethnic minorities differs from that of the White majority and from each other. For example, in 2000 about one in eight male Pakistani workers was a cab driver or chauffeur (compared with the national average of one in a hundred). And six per cent of Indian men were medical practitioners (ten times the national average). The Cabinet Office (2003) reports a slight rise over time in the proportion of all ethnic groups holding professional or managerial jobs. White and Indian men have similar rates of representation in professional and managerial occupations but the remaining ethnic minority groups (with the exception of Chinese) have lower proportions. Similar patterns are found in respect to women, but Indian women have made much more rapid progress than others – in 2000, 16% of working Indian women were in professional or managerial jobs, compared with 15% of White women and 13% of Black Caribbean women.

Self-employment With some exceptions, self-employment is more common among ethnic minority men than among White men. In 2002, one fifth of Pakistani and Bangladeshi men were self-employed, compared with one in ten White people and less than one in ten Black people. Ethnic minority women have much lower levels of self-employment than their male counterparts.

Earnings Just under a half of all ethnic minorities live in the London area where wages are generally higher than in the rest of the country. Nevertheless, the average weekly earnings of most ethnic minority groups are significantly less than those of their White counterparts. In 2000, only Indian men did not earn less than their White equivalents. But Indian and Caribbean women tend to earn more than White women, partly because they are more likely to work full-time.

Ethnic diversity

It would be misleading to regard ethnic minorities as perpetual 'losers' in the job market. Data gathered from the Census and Labour Force Surveys provide clear signs of progress by most ethnic minority groups over the past decade or so. The 4th PSI Survey (Modood et al., 1997) concluded that economic differences *between* minority groups have become more important than the Black-White divide. This has led researchers to reject the 'racial dualism' model which depicted a simple division between all ethnic minorities ('Blacks') on the one hand, and the White majority on the other. As the Cabinet Office report (2003) declares, the old picture of White success and ethnic minority under-performance is now out of date.

Instead of a blanket view of minorities as perpetual victims, there is an increasing recognition of *ethnic diversity* – some minority groups are still struggling in the face of economic adversity and discrimination, but others have moved a considerable distance along the path to economic prosperity. Wadsworth (2001) summarises some of the key research findings on ethnic minority variations:

- Those born in Britain seem to have a better overall labour market performance (in terms of pay and

key terms

Ethnic penalty The unexplained disadvantage suffered by ethnic minorities after most of the relevant factors appear to have been taken into account.
Ethnic diversity The view that there are important differences between ethnic groups – for example, in terms of their position in the labour market.

employment rates) than those born abroad. Nevertheless, they still do relatively worse overall than their White peers.

- There are big differences in the labour market performances of ethnic minority groups. The

Bangladeshi and Pakistani communities do relatively badly, while the Chinese and Indian communities do relatively well. The gains made by the African-Caribbean community seem to have halted among young men but not among young women.

summary

1 The workplace is the main source of unequal financial rewards. Workplace inequalities must be seen in the context of wider economic changes.

2 Economic changes over the past 30 years include:
- Increasing globalisation
- Sector shifts – a decline in jobs in agriculture, mining and manufacturing and an increase in jobs in the service sector
- A move from Fordism to post-Fordism, though this trend may have been exaggerated
- Increasing functional and numerical flexibility.

3 Examples of numerical flexibility include:
- Shedding workers or downsizing
- Part-time work
- Temporary work
- Casual work
- Outsourcing or sub-contracting
- Self-employment.

4 Occupational changes, such as the decline of manual workers and the expansion of professional and managerial groups,

have resulted in changes in the shape of the class structure. However, significant class inequalities remain.

5 It is not clear whether the deskilling of middle-class occupations has moved very far.

6 The workplace is largely gendered in terms of horizontal segregation (men's jobs and women's jobs) and vertical segregation (the under-representation of women at the most senior positions).

7 However, there is evidence that both types of segregation are decreasing, as are other forms of gender workplace inequality – for example, the pay gap is reducing.

8 In general, ethnic minorities are disadvantaged in the workplace – for example, their wages tend to be lower and unemployment rates higher than the White majority.

9 Ethnic minorities still incur the ethnic penalty – this may be due to racial discrimination in the labour market.

10 There is a growing recognition of ethnic diversity – of differences between ethnic groups and their position in the labour market.

activity8 ethnicity and work

Item A *Ethnicity and pay*

Average net weekly pay of men in Britain, 1994 and 2000

Sample size for Black African (1994) too small to be accurate and therefore excluded.

Sample size for Black African (1994), Pakistani (1994) and Chinese (1994), too small to be accurate and therefore excluded. No information available for Bangladeshi women.

Adapted from Cabinet Office, 2003

Average net weekly pay of women in Britain, 1994 and 2000

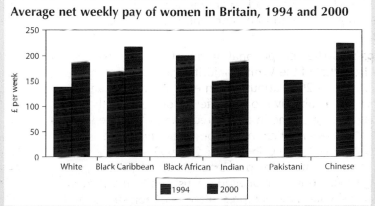

Item B Ethnicity and unemployment

Unemployment rates, UK, 2001/02

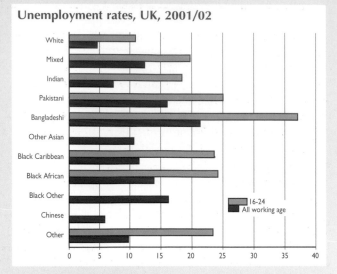

Black Other and Chinese 16-24 year-old samples too small for reliable estimates.

Adapted from *Social Trends*, 2003

Item C Ethnicity and top jobs

Employment in higher managerial and professional jobs, GB, 2001/02

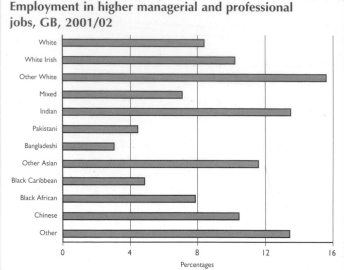

Adapted from *Social Trends*, 2004

Item D Asian shopkeepers

The days of almost every newsagent and corner shop in Britain being Asian-owned are coming to an end. During the past 30 years, Asians came to dominate this sector of the market: they accounted for 65% of Britain's independent retailers by the end of the 1980s. But a PSI report, *Asian Self-employment*, concludes that Asians are not committed to self-employment – for example, many Pakistanis and Bangladeshis only took up self-employment because racial discrimination prevented them from finding employment. Young Asians do not want to work 10 hours a day in the restaurants and grocery stores their parents set up. Besides, the small Asian corner shop faces severe competition from supermarkets, especially after the relaxation of Sunday trading laws. So the next generation of Asians is keen to move into the mainstream labour market.

Adapted from the *Observer*, 24.11.1996

Newsagent and post office

questions

1   In what ways do Items A, B and C indicate:
   a) Ethnic disadvantage
   b) Ethnic diversity?

2   Give two reasons why the type of data in Items A, B and C should be treated with caution.

3 a) Using Item D, identify two reasons for Asians turning away from shopkeeping.
   b) What evidence does Item C contain which suggests that some are doing so?

Unit 4 Class changes

The previous unit described significant changes in the structure of work and occupations in Britain. As Crompton (2002) notes, the occupational structure is not a fixed system of 'slots'. Rather, it is fluid and always in a process of change and development. In this unit we explore the implications of these changes for social classes. They include the following.

- Social class schemes have been revised to reflect the new occupational patterns.

- Social mobility has altered the nature and sizes of social classes. Sociologists call this *class formation* – the processes by which social classes are generated and formed.

- The characteristic values and lifestyles of social classes have changed in some ways, partly as a result of their new composition.

- The old class identities may have been undermined or transformed.

- The impact of class may be stronger in some areas than other.

4.1 Social class schemes

Occupation and class There are a number of reasons why occupation is the most popular way of measuring class. First, information on occupations is easily available and so it is a convenient and simple index to use. Second, it is usually seen as a good predictor of lifestyles and life chances. 'In an industrial society, occupation is an excellent indicator of both levels of material reward and social standing, and over the years such indexes have been found to correlate with a range of factors, such as rates of infant mortality, access to education, voting behaviour, and so on' (Crompton, 1993). And third, people frequently base their class identities on their occupations (eg manual workers may see themselves as 'working class').

At the same time, it has to be recognised that occupation is not a perfect measure of class. For one thing, there is no automatic link between occupation and income – some manual workers earn more than non-manual workers, and even within one occupation there may be a wide range of incomes. Likewise, the link between occupation and power is not always obvious. The 'upper class' may appear on occupational lists as lawyers, managers, etc, but this gives little hint of the substantial economic and political power they possess. Another problem is how to classify people who are 'outside' the occupational system – for example, full-time housewives, people unable to work through chronic disability, and the idle rich. Lastly, postmodern theorists argue that we now have much greater freedom and choice and so there is no longer a close connection between occupation and things like accents, education, cultural attitudes and leisure pursuits. So occupation may have lost some of its predictive power.

Registrar General's Social Class Sociologists and government statisticians still rely on occupational classifications as a means of identifying people's social class. For a long time the most popular classification was the Registrar General's Social Class scheme (see Table 6). This scheme arranged occupations into five social classes, with the split within class 3 representing the division between non-manual ('middle class') and manual ('working class') groups.

However, this scheme faced mounting criticism over the years. It tended to bunch women workers in a few social classes (especially 3NM). Also, it made finer distinctions between men's jobs than women's. For example, different levels of nurse (from untrained auxiliaries to ward sisters) were lumped together in class 2. But the decisive criticism was that the scheme had become outdated and it no longer reflected the emerging occupational structure of Britain.

Table 6 Registrar General's Social Class scheme

Class 1 Professional (eg accountant, doctor, lawyer, surveyor, clergy)

Class 2 Intermediate (eg farmer, MP, schoolteacher, nurse, manager)

Class 3NM Skilled Non-manual (eg secretary, shop assistant, typist, waiter)

Class 3M Skilled Manual (eg plumber, bus driver, butcher, cook, hairdresser)

Class 4 Semi-skilled Manual (eg bar staff, postman/woman, bus conductor/conductress)

Class 5 Unskilled Manual (eg road sweeper, kitchen hand, labourer, cleaner)

ONS Social Class scheme For the 2001 census, the government introduced a revised classification to take account of the changing occupational structure. For example, it recognises the growth of self-employed groups (class 4) as well as the existence of long-term unemployed (class 8).

The ONS (Office of National Statistics) scheme is based mainly on the type of employment contract, and occupations are grouped according to two main criteria:

- Market situation – this refers to employment status (eg employer, employee, manager) and the likely level of material rewards, job security and prospects for promotion associated with the occupation.

- Work situation – this refers to the degree of authority, control and autonomy associated with the occupation.

Unlike the previous scheme it no longer assumes that there is a 'hierarchy' of jobs where some are clearly higher or lower than others (although this is not totally convincing – the top classes do appear to enjoy greater privileges). Also, the manual/non-manual divide is given less emphasis than in the past. While classes 1 and 2 can be regarded as 'middle class', and classes 5, 6 and 7 as 'working class', there are also two 'intermediate' classes (classes 3 and 4). Class 8 may be regarded as an 'underclass'.

Table 7 ONS Social Class scheme

1 Higher managerial and professional occupations (eg company directors, senior managers, police inspectors, doctors, lawyers)

2 Lower managerial and professional occupations (eg junior managers, teachers, journalists, social workers, nurses)

3 Intermediate occupations (eg clerical workers, secretaries, auxiliary nurses, police constables)

4 Small employers and self-employed workers (eg taxi drivers, farmers, shopkeepers, self-employed plumbers, publicans)

5 Supervisory, craft and related occupations (eg construction workers, electricians, train drivers, and supervisors of people in categories 6 and 7)

6 Semi-routine occupations (eg shop assistants, hairdressers, cooks, postal workers, receptionists)

7 Routine occupations (eg porters, waiters, refuse collectors, cleaners, labourers)

8 Never worked/long-term unemployed

4.2 Social mobility

Social mobility occurs whenever people move across social class boundaries or from one occupational level to another. The direction of mobility may be *upwards* or *downwards*. Another distinction is between *intergenerational* mobility (differences between the levels of parents and their children) and *intragenerational mobility* (career shifts within a person's working life, such as promotion from the shop floor to the company boardroom).

Mobility affects the way classes are formed, their size and shape and the firmness of the boundaries between them. Some sociologists argue that if mobility is restricted, then class boundaries become sharper and each of the classes becomes more cohesive. Conversely, if there is a great deal of mobility, then class boundaries become blurred and classes themselves may become more fragmented and diverse.

Mobility studies The basic procedure in mobility studies is to select a sample of people and identify their occupations. These occupations can then be compared with their previous occupations (for intragenerational mobility) or the occupations of their parents (for intergenerational mobility). Some studies are designed especially to investigate mobility but researchers often have to draw relevant data from other surveys such as the General Household Survey or the National Child Development Study.

The measurement of social mobility presents some tricky technical difficulties.

- Occupational classifications have been revised over the years and some occupations have been moved from one class to another. This makes comparisons difficult.
- Assigning people to an occupation is not always straightforward. Parents as well as their adult children may have changed occupations a number of times in the course of their lives. One way round this is to compare their occupations at a certain age (preferably when they have reached 'occupational maturity').
- Certain groups (eg full-time housewives, unemployed people) are awkward to classify. Should they be listed in terms of their previous occupation? Or put in the same occupational group as their partner?

Patterns of social mobility

The Nuffield study One of the landmarks in mobility research was the Nuffield study (Goldthorpe, 1980), based on interviews with over 10,000 men, aged 20 to 64, in England and Wales in 1972. Using his own class scheme (a forerunner of the ONS scheme), Goldthorpe allocated these men to seven social classes. For purposes of simplification they are usually grouped into three clusters: service class, intermediate class, and working class. Goldthorpe regarded the service class and the working class as representing opposite ends of the hierarchy of privilege, and much of his data is based on contrasts between their mobility prospects. The service class includes higher and lower grade professionals, managers and administrators.

Goldthorpe's findings challenged much of the conventional wisdom on mobility. For example, he found that only a minority of the service class had been born into it. There had been such a huge expansion in the service class that it had been forced to recruit heavily from 'below'. Also, long-range mobility (eg from working class to service class) was not uncommon. On the basis of this data, Goldthorpe concluded that *absolute mobility rates* had increased in Britain. Absolute mobility refers to the total mobility which takes place in a society. The Nuffield study and subsequent studies have found surprisingly high rates of absolute mobility and the main reason for this is the transformation of the occupational structure. Technological progress has created a greater demand for non-manual skills and a better educated workforce. Also, there has been a shift from manufacturing industries with their largely manual workforce towards the mainly white-collar service sector. Thus, the number of middle-class occupations has expanded and this has created more 'space' for the working class to move up.

Relative mobility rates, on the other hand, are calculated by comparing the mobility prospects of different social groups at the same point in time. Someone born into the middle class has a good chance of getting a middle class job; someone born into an unskilled manual family has a slimmer chance. So relative mobility rates measure the chances of one group relative to other groups. Now, whereas Goldthorpe argued that absolute mobility prospects had improved, he claimed there had been little change in relative mobility rates. The odds were still weighted in favour of those from the higher classes and so equality of opportunity had not been achieved. Goldthorpe (1980) concluded that: 'No significant reduction in class inequalities has in fact been achieved'.

Class and mobility

The Nuffield study showed that class affects mobility chances. It is not just a matter of individual merit – if someone comes from a socially disadvantaged background, they have a lower chance of landing a service class job. Put another way, class *origins* play a key role in determining people's class *destinations*. This has been contested by Peter Saunders, (1996), who argues that Britain is close to a true *meritocracy* – a society in which people achieve their position on the basis of merit (talent and hard work) (see Unit 8). Nevertheless, there is strong evidence to support the view that the middle classes enjoy considerable advantages in landing the best jobs.

ISER study In a study for the Institute for Social and Economic Research, Ermisch and Francesconi (2002) investigated a sample of around 2,400 men (sons) and 2,300 women (daughters) drawn from the British Household Panel Survey 1991-99. Their findings reveal the importance of class origins. First, people whose parents were in higher-earning occupations are more likely themselves to be in higher-earning occupations. Second, they are also more likely to marry someone whose parents were in higher-earning occupations. This 'assortative mating' (marrying someone from the same educational and occupational level) allows couples to build up valuable cultural and social capital, (knowledge, skills and social networks). People at the top have large amounts of valuable cultural and social capital and well-connected networks and this protects their children from downward mobility, even if they are not very bright. This helps to explain the third finding: downward mobility from the 'top' is less common than upward mobility from the 'bottom'.

Ermisch and Francesconi speculate that today's middle classes (many of whom climbed the social ladder in the 1960s) may even be tightening their grip on high status jobs. The room at the top is no longer growing so fast, and those already in the middle class are making sure their children get middle-class jobs. In effect, they are blocking the ascent of children from lower-class backgrounds.

Gender and mobility

Women have usually been missing from mobility studies.

Goldthorpe and Payne (1986) identify three reasons for this neglect. First, the inclusion of women as well as men requires larger research samples and is time-consuming and expensive. Second, researchers normally prefer all-male samples so that they can make comparisons with previous studies (which share the same bias towards males). And third, women present certain technical difficulties. For example, should the occupation of a woman be compared with that of her father or mother? What is the occupational classification of full-time housewives? How should part-time workers be classified?

Sociologists disagree about the consequences of this neglect of women. Goldthorpe and C. Payne (1986) claim that all-male samples provide a more or less reliable guide to women's mobility patterns. An opposing view is taken by G. Payne and Abbott (1990) who argue that generalisations derived from male samples do not apply to women, because women have a different occupational distribution and different patterns of movement between occupations. Besides, we can make sense of men's and women's mobility patterns only if we see them in relation to one another. For example, if women find it difficult to enter service class occupations, then men have an increased chance of filling these positions. Some surveys (eg Savage & Egerton, 1997) suggest that women are more likely than men to experience downward mobility from privileged social groups (although the daughters of professionals are more successful than the daughters of managers).

A review of research evidence by Aldridge (2001) confirms that women are concentrated in routine white-collar jobs. More room has been found for women in the 'middle' rather than at the 'top'. Nevertheless, over the past few decades, women have enjoyed more favourable social mobility trends than men, and so they are catching up. Aldridge concludes that increased labour force participation by women, along with improved opportunities in the workplace, have had a positive effect on their mobility chances.

Ethnicity and mobility

There have been very few studies of the mobility patterns of ethnic minority groups. Although minorities may be included in larger studies, their sample sizes are often too small to draw confident conclusions. Nevertheless, Aldridge (2001) summarises the scattered findings so far. First, the original migrants to Britain generally suffered downward mobility, compared with their previous occupations or their fathers' occupations. Second, their children in general tend to be *more* socially mobile (upward and downward) than the White population. But third, there are differences between ethnic groups, with Indians and Pakistanis experiencing the most rapid mobility (upward and downward). Fourth, there is evidence that some groups within the ethnic minority population are catching up with the majority White population through rapid upward social mobility, but minority ethnic groups are still relatively disadvantaged in comparison with Whites.

The effect of ethnicity seems to be much smaller than that of social class. Thus, Roberts (2001) suggests that class factors operate in much the same way among minority groups as they do among Whites. Within any ethnic group, the children of middle-class parents have a better chance than those with working-class parents of achieving middle-class jobs.

The significance of social mobility

Do we live in a fair and open society in which everybody has an equal chance of reaching the top? In other words, do we live in an equal opportunity society? Do people reach their position in society on the basis of merit? Do they deserve their position based on their talent and effort? In other words, do we live in a *meritocracy*?

Or, do we live in a relatively closed society in which there are barriers preventing equality of opportunity, a society in which factors other than merit influence our position?

These are important questions – they affect each and everyone of us. Studies of social mobility can help to provide answers.

Absolute mobility There is general agreement that absolute mobility rates for men rose throughout the 20th century. In other words, the total amount of social mobility increased. As noted earlier, this was primarily due to economic changes which led to changes in the occupational structure. As a result, the middle class expanded and the working class contracted – there was more room at the top and less room at the bottom. This led to an increase in upward mobility and a decrease in downward mobility.

But does an increase in absolute mobility rates indicate greater equality of opportunity? Does it move society closer to a meritocracy? Many sociologists argue that absolute mobility rates cannot provide answers to these questions. This is why they turn to relative mobility rates.

Relative mobility As noted earlier, relative mobility rates refer to the relative chances of members of different social classes of moving upwards, downwards, or staying in the same social class – their class of origin. Absolute mobility rates for the 20th century show that men born into the working class have a greater chance of moving into the top classes as the century progressed. *But*, the same applies to members of other social classes. They too have a greater chance of moving up or, if born at the top, a greater chance of remaining there.

Available evidence indicates that relative mobility rates have changed little during the 20th century. The relative chances of members of different social classes of making it to the top have hardly changed at all (Aldridge, 2004).

What does this mean in terms of the questions asked earlier? No change in relative mobility rates suggests that there is no move towards greater equality of opportunity, no trend towards a more meritocratic society. It suggests that, in relative terms, the class people are born into continues to affect their life chances just as it did throughout the 20th century.

key terms

Social mobility The movement from one class to another. Mobility can be upwards (moving from a lower to a higher class), or downwards (moving from a higher to a lower class).
Class of origin The class into which people are born.
Intergenerational mobility Mobility from a person's class of origin. Movement from their parents' class.
Intragenerational mobility Class changes during a person's working life resulting from changes in occupation – for example, from a manual labourer to a teacher.
Absolute mobility rate The total amount of social mobility which takes place in society.
Relative mobility rate The relative chances of members of different social classes of becoming socially mobile.
Meritocracy A society in which people's position is achieved on the basis of merit – for example, on the basis of talent and effort. An open society in which all members have equal opportunities.

4.3 Changing classes – the upper class

The class map of Britain has altered over the years under the impact of deep social and economic changes. There are still some familiar landmarks, such as the huge contrasts between those at the top and those at the bottom. But there have been shifts and movements, too, and so the old maps – upper, middle and working classes – need to be revised in certain ways. This section looks at the upper class.

Towards the end of the 19th century there were three relatively distinct upper classes in Britain – large land-owners, manufacturing capitalists (factory owners and industrialists) and a commercial class of merchants and financiers. But these groups soon merged: 'By the early years of the 20th century it was possible to speak of a unified upper class with its roots in the increasingly intertwined areas of land, commerce and manufacturing' (Scott, 1986). They were drawn together not only by shared economic investments but also by social, cultural and marriage ties and similar lifestyles and values.

But does an upper class still exist in modern Britain? According to some commentators the upper class has more or less disappeared, its exclusiveness eroded by a tide of democracy and its wealth fragmented by inheritance taxes and estate duties. Certainly it is not singled out for special attention in occupational classifications (eg even the richest 'company directors' or 'farmers' are listed as part of the service class). Indeed, Saunders (1990) contends it is really too small – about 1% of the total population – to be regarded as a separate, distinct class.

Nevertheless, sociological evidence supports the idea that there is an upper class in Britain. It may be called by different names (eg the capitalist class, the rich, the Establishment). But whatever it is called, it is distinguished by its massive wealth, its cohesive social networks and its considerable power.

activity9 reaching the top

Item A Humble origins

It is quite common to read newspaper accounts of the careers of very rich people who started with nothing – yet these accounts are often side by side with articles complaining of the rigid class structure in Britain! Joseph Lewis, the richest man in Britain in 1997, was born in an East End pub where his father was the landlord. At least 20 of the top 100 richest people are self-made. They include Jack Walker, the steel magnate; the Barclay twins, who started their professional life as decorators; Ann Gloag, a former nurse who founded the bus company, Stagecoach, with her brother; the musician Paul McCartney; and Bernie Ecclestone (son of a Suffolk trawlerman) who manages Formula One racing. There are six sons of coal miners in the top 500 richest.

Adapted from Bauer, 1997

Bernie Ecclestone (centre)

Ann Gloag

Item B Absolute mobility trends

(based on data from 1964-1997 British Election Surveys)

Men (date of birth)	1900-09	1910-19	1920-29	1930-39	1940-49	1950-59
Percentages						
Stable	39	38	35	34	28	35
Upwardly mobile	29	30	39	38	42	42
Downwardly mobile	21	20	17	18	19	13
Horizontally mobile	11	12	9	10	11	10
(total)	(100)	(100)	(100)	(100)	(100)	(100)

Women (date of birth)	1900-09	1910-19	1920-29	1930-39	1940-49	1950-59
Percentages						
Stable	29	26	28	22	20	17
Upwardly mobile	22	26	23	29	32	36
Downwardly mobile	32	30	28	27	26	27
Horizontally mobile	17	18	21	22	22	20
(total)	(100)	(100)	(100)	(100)	(100)	(100)

Note: horizontally mobile refers to short-range mobility between 'intermediate' classes – eg routine white-collar, skilled manual.

Adapted from Aldridge, 2001

Item C   *Relative mobility*

One aim of the Nuffield mobility study was to discover whether Britain had become a more open society. Have, for example, the chances for a working-class boy to reach the service class improved over the years? The study compared the social mobility rates of men born between 1908-1917 with those born between 1938-1947. Findings on the first group are shown in Box 1 as 'then', those for the second group as 'now'.

The findings of the Nuffield study may be simply expressed as the 1:2:4 Rule of Relative Hope. This rule states that whatever the chance of a working class boy of reaching the service class, a boy from the intermediate class has twice the chance and a boy from the service class four times the chance.

The 1:2:4 rule applies to both groups of men in the survey (ie those born 1908-1917 and those born 1938-1947). Box 1 compares the chances of the two groups of reaching the service class. Although the percentage of working-class boys entering the service class has risen (from 14% to 18%), so has the percentage of those from the intermediate and service classes. The relative chances of children from each social class background have remained unaltered at approximately 1:2:4.

At first glance, this might not make sense. How can considerably more people enter the service class over the years? This is due simply to a change in the occupational structure. During the period covered by the survey, the number of service class occupations had nearly doubled. These changes are shown in Box 2. As a result of changes in the occupational structure, there is far more room at the top of the class system.

Adapted from Kellner & Wilby, 1980

Box 1

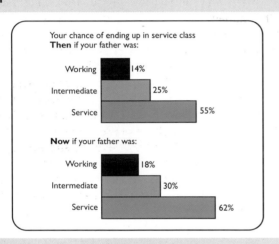

Box 2

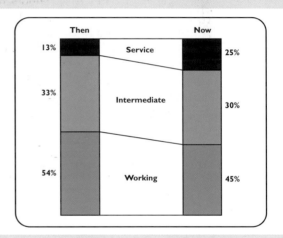

Classes used in the Nuffield study

1   **Service class** People with well-paid jobs with career prospects in the professions, national and local government, senior management and higher technical jobs.

2   **Intermediate class** People with routine non-manual jobs, clerks, sales personnel, self-employed with small businesses, supervisors, low-grade technicians.

3   **Working class** Skilled, semi-skilled and unskilled manual workers, including farm labourers.

questions

1   Using Item A, identify one reason why Britain might be seen as a fairly open society, and one reason why it might be seen as fairly closed.

2   a) Briefly summarise the trends in absolute mobility shown in Item B.

    b) Give two differences in the mobility patterns of men and women.

c) Why might this mobility data be unreliable?

3   With reference to Items B and C, explain how it is possible for absolute mobility rates to rise and relative mobility rates to remain largely unchanged.

4   On the basis of Items B and C, has British society become more meritocratic?

Wealth

At present there are over 57,000 millionaires in Britain. To get in the top 200 requires a fortune of at least £103 million, and £250 million is needed to qualify for the top 100. The richest people are a constant source of

fascination for those who follow their exploits in the gossip columns and glossy magazines. Many of these rich people were born into the upper-class, since Britain's generous inheritance laws allow upper class families to retain much of their wealth. So it is just not true that savage inheritance taxes have destroyed the great landed estates of the aristocracy. Indeed, Robinson (1996) argues that the decline of the aristocracy is entirely imaginary. If anything, they have rallied in the 20th century – some historic estates have increased substantially in size; and members of the aristocracy have not only held on to their great wealth and traditional 'leadership' roles, but also developed new roles in the City and in the arts.

Idle rich? A common image of the rich is that of an idle, feckless group who live a life of unbridled pleasure and self-indulgence. But many of them are actively involved in business enterprise, management and directorships. Even if they were born into great wealth, many members of the upper class follow 'entrepreneurial' lifestyles in spheres such as computer software, the media, the finance sector and service industries (Beresford & Boyd, 1998).

Quite a large proportion of millionaires in Britain are more or less 'self-made'. In 2004, the *Sunday Times* list of the richest 1,000 people in Britain reported that 'old wealth' accounted for only 25%, while the remainder had inherited comparatively little wealth. So, alongside those born into wealth there are people who have moved from rags to riches through a combination of talent, effort and luck. This includes entrepreneurs like Richard Branson. It also includes the 'jet set' or 'pop aristocracy' - people who have earned vast amounts of money in the fields of media, sport or entertainment – for example, Paul McCartney and J. K. Rowling.

Culture

As well as passing on financial wealth to their children the upper class also transmit cultural and social capital. Children born into this class learn its language, customs and values, and they are 'accepted' and sponsored by powerful people who share the same values. According to Scott (1991), the upper class consists of a series of intersecting status circles. What they have in common is a remarkable level of self-confidence and a well-developed sense of their exclusiveness and social superiority. This exclusiveness is reinforced by their close kinship links – not surprisingly, they tend to marry 'people like us' and people with 'money'. They are also connected by a network of prestigious social institutions – the public schools, Oxbridge (the universities of Oxford and Cambridge), gentlemen's clubs, fashionable haunts (night clubs, country house weekends), the social 'season' (Royal Ascot, Henley), favourite pursuits (riding, shooting) and influential magazines (eg *Tatler*). Every so often, newcomers succeed in breaking into upper-class circles, but many of these newcomers are recruited from the public schools and Oxbridge circuits and so they have already been socialised into the appropriate climate of values. Even if the newcomers are vulgar rich (*nouveaux riches*) they usually ensure that their children get an expensive education so that they can move effortlessly in the upper-class world.

Power

One way of assessing the power of the upper class is through the study of elites (people who fill the top positions in the major institutions of society). Most of the sociological debates have centred around economic elites and political elites.

Economic elites One view is that the upper class has gradually lost control of industry and the economy. Many years ago, Burnham (1941) presented the *managerial revolution thesis*, which stated that 'ownership' and 'control' were being separated. The day-to-day running of the economy was passing from wealthy owners to technically qualified experts and managers. This thesis seems to be supported by developments such as the continuing growth of huge corporations and the wider distribution of shareholding. Family firms have given way to large corporations owned by multiple shareholders, including institutional shareholders, such as pension funds, insurance companies and banks.

Scott (1986a) recognises that there has been a fundamental transformation of property ownership towards more impersonal forms of shareholding. But he concludes that the managerial revolution thesis is flawed and he offers an alternative model. He suggests that the control of business enterprises is exercised by a 'constellation of interests' which includes large shareholders (entrepreneurial capitalists) and managers (internal capitalists). It also includes finance capitalists – those who hold top posts in important financial institutions (banks, pension funds etc). All these interests come together in company boards of directors where the strategic decisions are made. Moreover, this control is reinforced by a system of interlocking directorships (directors in one company are often directors in other companies as well) which allows the key participants to exert widespread influence in the economy as a whole. The individuals who form this network (Scott calls them the 'business class') are recruited largely from the upper class, or they soon become members of it.

Political elites The orthodox Marxist position is that the capitalist class is also a *ruling class* – that is, its economic power allows it to control the political state. Capitalists ensure that the state protects their economic interests. They enforce their will on the state either directly (by taking up the top political offices) or indirectly (through manipulation and threats). But Scott (1986) points out that 'not all capitalists are politically active, and not all leading holders of political power are drawn from a business background' (Scott, 1986). He claims it may be more accurate to think in terms of a *power bloc* – an informal coalition of social groups (eg capitalists, government, trade unions) which is based on compromises between the different players. The capitalist business class increasingly finds it can exercise power only by working through these coalitions. Nevertheless, it still manages to retain its dominant position, both economically and politically. In a later work, Scott concludes that 'there is in Britain today a ruling class' (Scott, 1991). He maintains there are two main grounds on which the capitalist class can also be regarded as a ruling class. First, its economic dominance is maintained by the operations of the state (ie the state does little to disturb the economic status quo). Second, its members are still heavily represented among the top political elite (and the power bloc).

The Super Class meritocracy

Adonis and Pollard (1997) detect the emergence of a new group at the 'top' – the Super Class, a professional and managerial elite centred mainly in the City of London. Most of them are lawyers, accountants or executives and they enjoy massive incomes. Adonis and Pollard claim that they constitute a distinct class on the basis of their size, cohesion and uniformity. One of their defining features is that they are largely 'self-made' meritocrats. So they defend their privileges and feel they have earned their luxurious

key terms

Managerial revolution thesis The idea that the day-to-day running of the economy was passing from wealthy owners to technically qualified experts and managers.
Power bloc An informal coalition of powerful groups – eg of capitalists, government departments and trade unions.

lifestyles (servants, opera, exotic foreign holidays). Another feature is their tendency to segregate themselves from the rest of society – they use private schools and private medicine and live in exclusive estates patrolled by private security guards.

activity10 the upper class

Item A The British aristocracy

British aristocracy is a way of life. It is focused around traditional pursuits such as country living, horse racing, field sports, a fruity accent free of regional shadings, house parties, participation in the Season, a code of good manners (however frequently ignored), a horror of state education, respect for the past, indifference to religious enthusiasm and an acceptance of authority. It encompasses a stylish lack of stylishness for men, good grooming for women, a distinct lack of respect for mindless convention and a quiet belief in one's own superiority.

Adapted from Brook, 1997

Henley Regatta

Ladies' Day at Royal Ascot

Item B The Super Class

Clare and Gary moved from central London to the exclusive Wentworth estate in Surrey because they sought privacy and excellent private schools for their three children. The estate has 24-hour security with guards and dog-handlers. Gary works as European manager for a restaurant chain. Claire says, 'Nowadays if you have the money you can buy into this sort of life. Our last home was near Tower Bridge and you could almost watch burglaries and muggings happening from the window'.

Helen and Michael moved to the Wentworth estate after spending six years living in America. Helen runs the house and Michael is a personnel director for a multinational company. They live in a five-bedroom house, have two Mercedes, private health care and will privately educate their two daughters. Helen says, 'It is nice not to live on a main road or with other people breathing down your neck. But, when we first came in and saw all the security systems I felt concerned because nobody wants to live in a prison'. She adds that their status is a result of their earnings and careers: 'We are wealthy and cocooned but we've worked hard to be cocooned'.

Adapted from Rayment & Reeve, 1995

questions

1 With some reference to Item A, suggest how the British aristocracy pass on cultural and social capital to their children.

2 Briefly outline the similarities and differences between the aristocracy and the Super Class.

4.4 Changing classes – the middle classes

Middle class or non-manual groups have grown in spectacular fashion. They accounted for only 30% of the population in 1951 but then doubled to almost 60% by 2001. In the process of expansion, the middle class has also become more diverse. The 'traditional' middle class consisted largely of the established professions (eg law, medicine) and the commercial classes (eg entrepreneurs, traders, shopkeepers). But the second half of the 20th century saw an enormous growth in the new 'salariat' (salaried groups such as office workers, teachers, social workers and civil servants). Of course, this does not mean that the older groups have entirely disappeared. In fact, since the 1970s there has been something of a revival of groups such as small employers and self-employed workers.

The service class

The service class refers to ONS classes 1 and 2. This class has expanded considerably in the post-war period as a result of transformations in the economic and occupational structure. Indeed, in the 1960s and 1970s a number of social scientists (eg Bell, 1976) claimed that a post-industrial society was emerging, based not so much on manufacturing as on the expansion of the service sector (eg financial and banking services, health and education, administration). In a post-industrial society, knowledge and information are the most valuable assets and therefore there is a greater demand for professional, managerial and technical experts.

Assets The service class is a privileged group in terms of income, job security, working conditions and promotion prospects. Savage et al. (1992) describe three main types of assets used by the service class to protect its privileges. *Professionals* rely mainly on cultural assets (eg knowledge, qualifications). They are successful in passing this cultural capital on to their children who usually do well in education and proceed to the better jobs in society. *Managers,* on the other hand, depend on bureaucratic assets (organisational positions) which are more precarious (eg quite often their expertise is based on particular firms and so their asset is not so 'transferable'). The third group, the *petit bourgeoisie* (entrepreneurs, traders) is based on property assets (economic capital) which can be stored and transferred.

In a later work, Savage (2000) concedes that these distinctions have become increasingly blurred (eg the careers of professionals and managers now have a great deal in common). But he argues that the concept of *cultural capital* has become increasingly relevant for understanding all middle-class groups. This concept was popularised by Pierre Bourdieu (1984) who argued that each social class has a characteristic *habitus*, or set of taken-for-granted preferences, which expresses itself in things like their choice of food, music and leisure habits. Moreover, the cultural capital of a class becomes an important 'marker' of its social standing in relation to other groups. Sometimes a social class will deliberately set out to create cultural distinctions between itself and others in order to establish its own cultural superiority. Savage modifies Bourdieu's views in certain ways but he believes cultural capital is becoming ever more important to the middle class. Traditional class markers, such as the divide between manual and non-manual workers, have become weaker, and so the middle classes are developing new forms of cultural capital in order to distinguish themselves from other groups in society.

Individualisation Savage (2000) suggests that middle-class careers have become more individualised. Once, perhaps, middle-class professionals and managers might have anticipated a familiar career path, with promotion following predictably on the basis of seniority and experience. But that is changing. Fewer middle-class people are pursuing conventional careers and increasing numbers are found in 'entrepreneurial' roles (self-employment, consultancy etc). Even those who remain employees find that a career is viewed in a new way. It has become a 'project of the self' and employees are expected to engage in 'self-development' using the resources of the organisation. They are expected to show enterprise and initiative rather than sticking to routine tasks. Annual salary increments are still found in the public sector, but in both private and public sectors there has been a move towards performance-related pay awarded on the basis of the employee's success in meeting targets. Among the effects of these changes is increasing job insecurity and the introduction of a greater element of 'risk-taking' than in the past.

Values Roberts (2001) describes the three main values (or 'preoccupations') of professional and managerial groups. First, they see themselves as having a 'service' relationship with their employers, one that is quite unlike the 'contract' relationship of manual workers. The service class expect to be trusted with autonomy and responsibility, and their salary is seen as a reward for their loyalty and dedication. They are willing to put in extra (unpaid) hours when necessary. Second, they have a strong sense of career and they expect to improve their salary by keeping their qualifications and expertise up to date. Third, they believe in a form of meritocracy where the greatest rewards should go the most highly qualified and energetic individuals. Inequality is not a bad word in their world-view.

Intermediate classes

The new ONS Social Class scheme has relegated semi-routine occupations (eg shop assistants, receptionists, hairdressers) to the working class. Also, it has created two *intermediate classes*, one composed mainly of clerical and secretarial workers, and the other of self-employed and small employers. However, Savage (2000) is sceptical that there is really an intermediate class between the service class and the working class. He says this distinction is difficult to justify in economic terms – there is not much difference, if any, in pay between routine white-collar workers and skilled manual workers. For Savage, the main divide is between the service class and the 'rest'.

Nevertheless, the term intermediate suggests that the groups concerned fall somewhere between the middle ('service') class and the working class. Roberts (2001) shows this in the case of female office workers. Many of these women have modest pay, low job autonomy and poor career prospects, and so they are hardly part of the service class. But they are much better off – in terms of pay, status, job security and pleasant working conditions – than their working-class female counterparts in factories and shops.

Values Roberts (2001) takes the view that the female-dominated ranks of routine office workers have never really developed a distinctive class identity, lifestyle or politics. This is partly because many of them live in 'cross-class' households, where their partner is drawn from another class. However, he describes the male-dominated ranks of the self-employed and small employers as leading markedly work-centred lifestyles. They are the supreme champions of individualism (people should stand on their own feet rather than rely on the state) and hard work and discipline.

Middle-class insecurity

Roberts (2001) describes the growing sense of insecurity and anxiety among the middle classes. Many of them feel their perks and privileges are under threat. Also, they are increasingly desperate to ensure their children do well at school, so they can avoid falling down the social class ladder. Some of these fears may well be exaggerated, but there is little doubt that the middle classes face certain threats.

- Managers are placed at risk by the post-Fordist trend to delayering (cutting out layers of middle management).
- Increased competitive pressures have added to the work burdens of many professionals and managers. Teachers, for example, frequently complain of work stress and burn-out.
- Computerisation and automation pose a threat to the middle classes. This is one of the reasons for the large reductions in the numbers of bank clerks. It is also related to the arguments about deskilling (see pages 242-244).
- Middle-class work (eg call centres, IT processing, insurance work) is at risk of being off-shored. White-collar workers may discover that they are as vulnerable to international competition as steelworkers and shipbuilders a generation ago. Indeed, the trade union Amicus predicts that about 200,000 call centre jobs will be lost by 2010, and a massive 2 million jobs in financial services will be shipped abroad by 2030.

4.5 Changing classes – the working class

The working class is represented by classes 5,6 and 7 in the ONS scheme.

This class has shrunk from 75% of the total population in 1901 to about 43% at the end of the 20th century. But Roberts (2001) points out that its 'decline' should not be exaggerated. It is still the largest single class, larger than either the service class (36%) or the even smaller intermediate class (21%). If we regard the intermediate classes as part of the working class (as the deskilling thesis might suggest), then the middle classes are still in a minority in the population at large. Roberts makes the obvious but important point that not everybody is a stockbroker, accountant or brain surgeon. There is still a high demand for skilled manual workers. Moreover, there is still plenty of 'donkey work' to be performed, and around a quarter of all jobs require no formal qualifications and very little training.

As the working class has become smaller, so too there have been important changes in the lifestyles and values of its members. This is usually described as a move from the 'traditional' working class to the 'new' working class.

The traditional working class

Most sociologists date the traditional working class from around the end of the 19th century until the 1950s or 1960s. Its broad features have been described in a number of classic studies, including those by Hoggart (1957) and Young and Willmott (1957). Hoggart's was largely a 'cultural' reading, while Young and Willmott used a more formal sociological approach based on interviews with a sample of people from Bethnal Green in East London. In spite of their different methods, there is a great similarity in their descriptions.

Work Men usually worked in heavy industries such as mining, steel, shipbuilding and the docks. The physically demanding nature of this work placed a high value on rugged masculinity and male camaraderie. Women were normally expected to become full-time housewives after marriage but financial hardship sometimes forced them into the workforce.

Class consciousness Traditional workers had a strong sense of class solidarity. They adopted 'proletarian' views and gave their loyalties to trade unions and the Labour Party. They distrusted 'them' – bosses, the middle classes, anyone in authority.

Respectability There was an important divide *within* the working class between 'roughs' and 'respectables'. The traditional working class held respectable values (eg honesty, the work ethic) and they tried to maintain decent moral standards.

Community The traditional working class lived in close knit communities ('urban villages'). People had long connections with their locality and they built up large circles of friends and acquaintances. Occasionally there were bitter feuds and conflicts but at least people were not 'anonymous'. 'Bethnal Greeners are not lonely people: whenever they go for a walk in the street, for a drink in the pub, or for a row on the lake in Victoria Park, they know the faces in the crowd' (Young & Willmott, 1957).

Some commentators felt that Hoggart and Young and Willmott were far too nostalgic for the traditional working class and this made them overlook its negative features – for example, recurrent unemployment, financial hardships, and rigid division of roles between men and women. Nevertheless, they succeeded in conveying some of the strengths – the warmth, the sociability, the humour and resilience – of people who lived in difficult material circumstances.

The new working class

In the 1950s and 1960s sociologists sensed that a 'new' working class was emerging, one quite different in character from its predecessor. One of the defining features of this new working class was its greater affluence. The postwar period of full employment was bringing rising incomes and higher living standards – for example, car ownership, and consumer durables such as washing machines and fridges. Indeed, certain sections of the working class seemed to be catching up with and even surpassing some middle-class groups. This was called *embourgeoisement*, the process by which members of the working class seemed to be becoming 'bourgeois' and adopting middle-class lifestyles and living standards.

Embourgeoisement Goldthorpe et al. (1969) tested the embourgeoisement thesis by studying affluent workers in Luton, an economically prosperous area with reasonably high wages based on growth industries. The research sample consisted mainly of male manual workers in the Vauxhall car works. This intensive study used a variety of methods (eg interviewing, observation) to gather data on things like political attitudes, work routines and community lifestyles. The findings were grouped according to the three main 'dimensions' of embourgeoisement.

Economic differences The manual workers in Luton had relatively high earnings compared with the rest of the working class. But they did not earn as much as middle-class groups, who had the added advantage of greater job security and considerable fringe benefits.

Class relationships There was little social mixing between the classes in Luton. They were residentially and socially segregated and they were keenly aware of the status differences between them.

Normative differences This refers to differences in attitudes, values and outlook. The affluent workers were certainly less committed than traditional workers to the trade unions and Labour Party. But they were not totally middle class in outlook either (eg unlike the middle class, they had little sense of a career).

The Luton researchers concluded that the embourgeoisement thesis was deeply flawed, especially as far as economic conditions and class relationships were concerned. Class relationships are not fundamentally changed by a small rise in the pay packet or by the mere purchase of a washing machine. Moreover, Goldthorpe et al. stress that the affluent workers were not modelling themselves on the middle class or actively seeking to become middle class. Rather, there was a process of 'independent convergence' whereby some sections of the working class happened to be moving closer to middle-class lifestyles (eg home-centred rather than community-oriented). At the same time, the middle class was moving closer to certain working-class styles (eg they were becoming more 'collectivist' in the sense of joining middle-class trade unions).

The Luton study discredited the embourgeoisement thesis and many sociologists concluded that the debate was more or less finished. However, more sophisticated versions of the embourgeoisement thesis have surfaced since the original study was conducted. For example, Young and Willmott (1975) introduce the notion of 'embourgeoisement with a time lag' – what the middle class have today, the working class will have tomorrow. And Pahl's (1984) research on the Isle of Sheppey identified the emergence of a 'middle mass' in which the boundaries between lower middle class and the skilled manual class have become increasingly blurred. So perhaps, it would be premature to declare that the embourgeoisement debate has finished.

Working class in the post-Fordist age

Most Marxists agreed that the embourgeoisement thesis was misguided but they took issue with the Luton researchers' view that affluent workers were reasonably contented. According to Goldthorpe et al., the Luton workers found little satisfaction in their jobs but they were willing to trade this in return for a wage packet which gave them a comfortable standard of living outside the job. But Westergaard (1970) insisted that this was exactly what Marx meant by alienation! The only bond the affluent workers had with their work was through the 'cash nexus' – that is, their reward was purely a monetary one and they derived little social or creative pleasure from their work. For Westergaard and other Marxists, the working class faced a bleak future under capitalism. But is this so? Or has post-Fordism rescued the working class from this fate?

A weakened working class? Roberts (2001) accepts that there is an affluent section of the working class. Also, he notes the emergence of a new 'aristocracy of labour' – the technicians and technologists who work in laboratories or in front of computer screens rather than on factory floors. However, he argues that most of these groups are not as affluent as the middle class, and they still tend to identify themselves as working class and support trade unions. So Roberts does not think they signal the decline of the working class. The cohesion of the working class is not being destroyed by affluent groups being lifted 'up' out of its ranks. Rather, Roberts argues that the greatest threat to the working class comes from economic trends such as globalisation and post-Fordism.

These trends have increased the risk of sections of the working class 'dropping down' into unemployment, low-quality jobs and a possible 'underclass'. Overall, the working class has become more fragmented, weakened and disorganised under the impact of post-Fordist economic changes. Since the 1980s, inequalities within the working class have widened, unemployment and job insecurity have increased, and the power of trade unions has been progressively eroded. According to Roberts, these economic changes are bad news for the working class. Increasingly unprotected by trade unions and New Labour, they have lost the capacity to act as a collective force to promote their common interests.

Savage (2000), too, argues that the collective confidence of the working class is being undermined in contemporary society. At one time, they saw themselves collectively as strong and independent, in contrast to the servile, dependent people who worked in the 'office'. But Savage argues that there has been a cultural shift. Nowadays, the working class are no longer in powerful trade unions, and the jobs they have seem somehow less 'heroic' when compared with the collective craft pride of the 'old'

shipbuilders, steelworkers and miners. Manual labour has suffered a loss in status, and it is often regarded as more suitable for young men than for mature adults.

4.6 Class identity

Class identity can be a confusing thing. Mrs Thatcher, a Conservative Prime Minister, once declared that class divisions were meaningless since 'we are all working people now'. Some years later Tony Blair, the Labour Prime Minister, claimed we are all 'middle class'! Clearly they gave different meanings to the terms 'working' and 'middle'. This is a common problem in surveys where people are asked to assign themselves to a social class. We can never be quite sure they are using the terms in the same way. Nevertheless, for a long time sociologists have assumed that most people have a strong sense of their class identity. It is only in recent years that this assumption has been seriously challenged.

Postmodern sociologists claim that class is no longer a major basis for people's identities. The old class identities have crumbled away in the face of postmodern social trends, and nowadays it is lifestyles, individualism and consumption which form the basis of people's identities.

Postmodern lifestyles Pakulski and Waters (1996) argue that postmodern society has 'liberated' people from their class backgrounds. In postmodern societies culture plays a more significant role than class, property and the economic marketplace. What matters most nowadays is 'status', which is based on cultural matters such as gender, ethnicity, values, tastes, opinions, consumption habits and expressive lifestyles. These lifestyles are freely chosen rather than dictated by class positions. Moreover, according to Pakulski and Waters, it is these lifestyles which are the main source of people's identities. Class identities, in comparison, have faded into insignificance.

Individualisation One of the things that helped to make class identities so powerful in the past was their collective nature. People seemed to have a keen sense of loyalty to their class traditions and the working class regularly engaged in joint action (eg industrial strikes) to defend their class interests. However, some sociologists claim that class collectivism has weakened in the age of late modernity. Beck and Beck-Gernsheim (1996) describe the trend

key terms

Post-industrial society A society largely based on the service sector rather than manufacturing.
Embourgeoisement The process by which members of the working class appeared to be becoming middle class.

activity11 the working class

Item A *The traditional working class*

In the 1950s, over 80% of male workers in Bethnal Green in East London were employed in manual occupations. Many worked in the docks as dockers and ship repairers. Others were employed in a multitude of small manufacturers, making everything from furniture, boots and shoes, locks and hinges, to a variety of products for the railway industry.

Trade union membership was high. Class solidarity was strong. Every constituency in East London returned a Labour MP and every council was controlled by the Labour Party. People shared their politics, they spoke the same language with the same accent, they worked with their hands and shared the same kind of life.

Adapted from Young & Willmott, 1957

Item B The new working class

The new working class is employed in shops, or more typically supermarkets and hypermarkets, in restaurants and hotels (the hospitality industries), and other businesses connected with leisure, sport and tourism. There is more work in call centres, in security firms, and with contract cleaners. Some of these jobs look attractive to working-class school-leavers, especially those in hairdressing, fashion and music where work and leisure interests can be fused. Once in these industries, individuals are most likely to find that their work is mundane and low paid, though some young people still enjoy their associations with the industries in question. Many of the new jobs require an emotional input – the work is often demanding, though not skilled in the traditional sense. Employees are required to market themselves – their appearance and demeanour in shops and restaurants are part of the services that the businesses offer. Such work can be stressful and demeaning, it requires personal skills rather than formal qualifications and training. There is still plenty of straight 'donkey work', but many of the new working-class jobs require the occupants to appear human, interested, and committed to the customers' satisfaction.

Adapted from Roberts, 2001

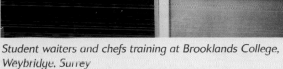

Student waiters and chefs training at Brooklands College, Weybridge, Surrey

Staff training at Tottenham Green Leisure Centre

questions

1 With some reference to Items A and B, outline the differences between the traditional working class and the new working class.

2 How and why might the working class today be 'weaker' than the traditional working class?

---

towards *individualisation* and *detraditionalisation*. Class traditions no longer seem so relevant or appealing in an age when people are increasingly forced to exercise personal choice and take their own individual decisions. Traditional certainties have collapsed and the old 'fixed' categories of class, religion and gender no longer provide detailed guidance on how people should lead their lives. So, according to Beck and Beck-Gernsheim, people must now create their own lives through their own actions (the 'do-it-yourself biography'). People increasingly see themselves as individuals rather than as members of a social class.

Consumption Another threat to class identities comes from the rise of 'consumer culture'. People may once have constructed their identities around work and production but nowadays their identities often seem attached to the worlds of leisure and consumption. Consequently, identities may no longer be based on how people *earn*

their money (a matter of occupation and class) but on how they *spend* it (a matter of consumer lifestyles). These consumer lifestyles do not necessarily run along class lines. At one time, perhaps, consumer lifestyles were more or less a direct expression of class membership. People tended to follow traditional class based leisure pursuits and spending patterns. In contemporary society, however, consumer lifestyles seem to be more diverse and flexible and based on individual tastes and choices. People are usually aware that they are making a cultural 'statement' about themselves through their consumption habits. They signal their personal identities by what they choose to wear, eat, drink, listen to or collect.

The demise of class identity? Is it really true that class identities have declined so dramatically? Marshall (1997) accuses postmodernists of using 'data-free' sociology and wilfully ignoring research evidence which indicates that class identities are still important. Likewise, Crompton

(1998) suggests that the trends to individualisation and detraditionalisation are nothing new (they were previously described by Marx and Weber) and they do not necessarily mean that class analysis is outdated. As for consumption identities, a great deal of consumer behaviour is still a matter of routine shopping for basic needs rather than a form of cultural expression.

Researching class identities

Strong class identities A large-scale survey by Marshall et al. (1988) found that about 60% of the sample thought of themselves as belonging to a particular social class and over 90% could place themselves in a class if prompted. Furthermore, three quarters of the sample agreed that people are born into classes and that it is difficult to move from one class to another. These figures hardly suggest that class awareness has disappeared. On the contrary, Marshall et al. argue that class is still the most common and powerful source of social identity. Other identities may have grown in importance but they have not yet displaced class identities from their central position. However, Marshall's survey has been challenged on methodological grounds for presenting such a large number of 'class' questions to the respondents. This may have loaded the answers by directing the respondents' attention to class issues. If they had been given a free choice they might have rated other identities as having greater significance than class.

Nevertheless, Devine (1997) springs to the defence of Marshall et al. She accepts that people have many different identities but she contends that recent research supports

the view that class identities still exert the strongest influence on things like political attitudes, voting patterns and views on inequality. After reviewing available research findings she concludes that: 'Overall, the evidence suggests that class is the most common and salient social identity in Britain and other social identities such as gender and race have not undermined an affiliation to class' (Devine, 1997).

Weak class identities Savage et al. (2001) studied the class identities of 178 people living in the Manchester area. Few of their sample thought Britain was a classless society, and most of them were well aware of the strong influence of class in the wider society – in the world of politics, the economy and the media. However, many of them hesitated to identify *themselves* as members of any class. Most saw themselves as 'outside' classes, as just 'ordinary' individuals. Savage et al. describe a paradox – class is an important structural force in people's lives, yet class identities are generally weak. Savage (2000) concludes that Britain is not a class-conscious society in the sense that people have well-developed and articulate views about membership of collective class groupings and a clear sense of their place in the class system.

> ## key terms
>
> **Individualisation** The process whereby people see themselves increasingly as individuals rather than as members of social groups.
> **Detraditionalisation** The decline in the influence of tradition on people's views and actions.

activity 12 thinking of class

Item A Respectability

Beverley Skeggs (1997) shows the centrality of class in the lives of 83 working class young women in the North of England. These women were working class in terms of their social background, jobs, housing and income. They had a strong sense that the class system was unjust. They especially resented the way other people pigeon-holed them because of their class. They felt teachers, doctors and employers dismissed them as not worth bothering about. Even assistants in posh department stores seemed to 'look down their noses' at them. The women felt injured and humilated by the way others classified them.

As a result, these women made strenuous efforts to show they were 'respectable'. This bid for respectability took the form of acting middle class. They took particular care in their choice of clothes ('do I look common in this?'), and in their leisure pursuits and home decorations. Skeggs argues they had no real wish to 'become' middle class. Rather, they just did not want to be recognised as working class, because then they would become victims of class prejudices.

Adapted from Skeggs, 1997

Item B Name your class

For many members of the traditional working class, society consisted of 'us and them'. Their class identity was clear – they belonged to 'us', to a working class which was distinct from the rest of society. More recent research on class identity indicates that things are not nearly so clear-cut nowadays.

A sample was asked to identify their social class. Here are some of their answers:
- 'Well, it's not the upper class, I'll tell you that. I, well, I don't know whether you'd put us working class really. I don't think we're middle class but we, I don't know, I don't know where we come in that really.'
- 'I'd just say ordinary.'
- 'I was going to say...I didn't...I wouldn't put myself as...I'm working class...by background and upbringing and I'm still working so in that sense I'm working class. I find it a difficult area to make distinctions in. Again, it's a scale or criteria that I prefer not to use so I don't find it helpful or meaningful.'
- 'I've no experience of the class business, I couldn't comment on it.'

Adapted from Savage, 2000

Item C Postmodern man

1 Using Item A, identify two ways in which class identity was important to the women.
2 What does Item B suggest about the strength of class identity in recent years?
3 Give two reasons why the measurement of class identity is difficult.
4 Using data from this activity, evaluate:
   a) The claim that class identities are weakening
   b) Explanations for this process.
5 How does Item C illustrate postmodernists' view of identity in today's society?

4.7 Life chances – the consequences of class

Postmodern theorists claim not only that class identities are weak but also that class no longer exerts much of an influence on people's lives in general. However, this is contradicted by empirical evidence which suggests a direct link between social class and many aspects of social life. 'The social class into which we are born remains vastly influential in shaping our life course and life chances...' (Breen & Rottman, 1995). Support for this statement can be found in research data which show there are substantial gaps between social classes in terms of social and economic outcomes. Of course, the size of this gap is not the same in every sphere of social life and it also changes over time. For example, Roberts (1997) found that there is certainly less class segregation among youth now than in the past, and they mix more freely in pubs and clubs. But, he adds that class still has a strong influence on the educational and employment fortunes of young people. Middle-class youths continue to enjoy many advantages in life.

The impact of class can be illustrated by looking at empirical evidence in three main areas: economic welfare, personal welfare and life experiences.

Economic welfare

Westergaard (1995) has made a persuasive case that class is mainly about 'who gets what', and he has drawn attention to the way scarce material resources are unequally distributed along class lines.

Income and wealth Class-related inequalities in income and wealth have already been examined in Unit 2. To recap, this showed that most people in Britain have benefited from absolute rises in income and wealth, and to that extent there has been a real and significant improvement in their life chances. At the same time, the distribution of income has become much more unequal, and any redistribution of wealth has occurred only within the top class groups.

Social mobility and jobs Class-related inequalities in economic welfare were also examined in Section 4.2 on social mobility. This section presented evidence that people from the working class have enjoyed a long-term rise in absolute mobility rates but their relative mobility rates still lag behind those of the middle class. This restricts their opportunities to get better jobs and higher incomes.

Home ownership Another example of class inequalities is the pattern of home ownership. In an era of buoyant house prices, a home is an appreciating financial asset and it provides a valuable inheritance for children. Yet middle class people are more likely than the working class to live in owner-occupied property, with all the advantages that brings. In 2000/01, 74% of employers and managers in the UK were buying their home with a mortgage, almost double the proportion for unskilled manual workers.

Personal welfare

Health The middle classes appear to have marked advantages in terms of health. Life expectancy at birth has increased over the past 30 years among all social classes, but greater gains have been made by the middle classes.

Between 1972-76 and 1992-96, the life expectancy gap between professionals and unskilled manual males widened from 5.5 years to 9.5 years, before narrowing again to 7.4 years in 1997-99. There was a similar difference for females (*Social Trends*, 2003). Also, the Acheson Report (1998) found that, among professionals, 17% (men) and 25% (women) reported a long-standing illness. Among unskilled workers, the figures were 48% (men) and 45% (women).

These differences arise partly from the fact that middle-class groups tend to lead healthier lifestyles. For example, in 2000, 39% of men in the unskilled manual group in Great Britain were regular cigarette smokers, compared with only 17% in the professional group. Among women, the proportions were 35% and 14%. But the class differences in health cannot all be attributed to behavioural lifestyles. The Acheson Report concluded that material disadvantage, and especially poverty, is the major factor in explaining the class gap in health. Moreover, the behaviour of social groups is closely linked to their structural situation (eg people are more likely to smoke in situations of stress). Indeed, Wilkinson (1998) argues that societies which are highly unequal and hierarchical have the worst health record and the highest death rates. This is because they increase people's sense of inferiority, shame and incompetence. Wide income inequality leads to low levels of trust and more hostility and violence, lower levels of social support, weaker social networks, and greater domestic conflict. All this takes its toll on health.

Happiness Class also has a bearing on happiness or 'life satisfaction'. Research suggests that the quality of social relationships has a bigger impact than financial income on life satisfaction. But surveys show that, within a country, richer people are happier than those on lower incomes (Donovan & Halpern, 2002). Also, an increase in personal income brings higher levels of satisfaction. However, the overall levels of happiness in Britain have not altered much over the last 30 years, even though the country has become much wealthier. This may be because high levels of inequality are associated with low levels of satisfaction.

Life experiences and opportunities

Poor people often have to endure life's raw experiences. For example, they are more likely to become unemployed. Unemployment rates are about four times higher among unskilled workers than among professional groups. As if to rub salt into the wound, poorer people are also the most likely to become the victims of crime. The Acheson Report notes that, in 1995, 4% of affluent suburban families were burgled, compared with 10% of families living in council and low-income estates. It also notes that, in England and Wales, unskilled workers are four times more likely than professionals to commit suicide.

The middle classes are better positioned to take advantage of opportunities in education. They are more likely to stay on longer in the education system, to perform better in examinations, and to get more advanced qualifications.

summary

1. Social class is usually measured in terms of occupation. In 2001, the government introduced a revised classification – the ONS Social Class scheme – to take account of the changing occupational structure.

2. Absolute social mobility has increased over the past 50 years. This is mainly due to the expansion of service class occupations. However, there has been little change in the rate of relative mobility.

3. This suggests that there is no move towards greater equality of opportunity, no trend towards a meritocratic society.

4. The upper class may be more open now to recruitment from below, but it seems to have retained a great deal of economic and political power, as well as cultural and social capital.

5. The middle class has grown over the past 50 years with changes in the occupational structure. It is a diverse class and certain sections – the intermediate classes – share some of the features of the working class.

6. The manual working class has become smaller over the past 50 years.

7. The traditional working class has been largely replaced by the new working class. However, there is little evidence of embourgeoisement.

8. There is evidence that changes in the economy have weakened working-class solidarity and power.

9. Postmodernists claim that class identity is weak, and that lifestyles, individualism and consumption now form the basis for people's identities. However, some researchers argue that class still exerts an important influence on people's sense of identity.

10. Class still has a significant influence on people's life chances. There is a strong relationship between class and income, wealth, home ownership, educational attainment, health, life expectancy and 'life satisfaction'. Although the 'class gap' changes over time, class inequality remains widespread.

activity13 class matters

Item A Poverty kills

Poverty kills. The effect of poverty on the health of Britain is the same as a plane crashing and killing 115 passengers every day of every year. Poverty kills with subtlety and skill. Poverty will use the damaged emotions of its victims as a deadly weapon, driving them to suicide and to violence against each other. Poverty will inject its victims with stress and anxiety and take away their sleep and watch their hearts slowly succumb to the poison. Poverty will set up accidents – an easy thing to do in homes with no money to pay for fire guards or stair guards or safety rails or window bars, where the parents cannot afford a nanny or an au pair, where the only playground is the street with its company of cars, or where mothers are compelled to light their children's rooms with candles.

Poverty will go straight for the belly of its victims, leaving them with children who are shorter and lighter. Poverty sneaks through the maternity wards. From the poor, it takes 700 babies each year – babies who are stillborn but would have survived if they had had the same chance of life as the babies of more prosperous families. If it misses them in the maternity ward, poverty stalks them in the home, taking 1,500 children during their first year of life – again, children who would have survived if they had had the same life expectancy as those in richer homes. In April 1995, the *British Medical Journal* said that if a chemical plant caused illness on the same scale as poverty in Britain, it would be closed down immediately.

Adapted from Davies, 1997

Item B Life expectancy and class

Life expectancy at birth, England & Wales

Social class	Life expectancy at birth					Years
	1972 -76	*1977 -81*	*1982 -86*	*1987 -91*	*1992 -96*	*1997 -99*
Males						
Professional	72.0	74.7	75.1	76.7	77.7	78.5
Managerial and technical	71.7	72.4	73.8	74.4	75.8	77.5
Skilled non-manual	69.5	70.8	72.2	73.5	75.0	76.2
Skilled manual	69.8	70.0	71.4	72.4	73.5	74.7
Semi-skilled manual	68.4	68.8	70.6	70.4	72.6	72.7
Unskilled manual	66.5	67.0	67.7	67.9	68.2	71.1
All males	69.2	70.0	71.4	72.3	73.9	75.0
Females						
Professional	79.2	79.9	80.4	80.9	83.4	82.8
Managerial and technical	77.0	78.1	78.5	80.0	81.1	81.5
Skilled non-manual	78.0	78.1	78.6	79.4	80.4	81.2
Skilled manual	75.1	76.1	77.1	77.6	78.8	79.2
Semi-skilled manual	75.0	76.1	77.3	77.0	77.7	78.5
Unskilled manual	73.9	74.9	75.3	76.2	77.0	77.1
All females	75.1	76.3	77.1	77.9	79.3	79.7

Note: Life expectancy at birth refers to the number of years a person can expect to live.

Adapted from *Social Trends*, 2003

Item C *Class and educational attainment*

Class and GCSE attainment, 2002

England & Wales					Percentages
	5 or more GCSE Grades A*-C	*1-4 GCSE grades A*-C*	*5 or more GCSE grades D-G*	*1-4 GCSE grades D-G*	*None reported*	*All*
Higher professional	77	13	6	.	3	100
Lower professional	64	21	11	2	2	100
Intermediate	52	25	17	2	4	100
Lower supervisory	35	30	27	4	4	100
Routine	32	32	25	5	6	100

Adapted from *Social Trends*, 2004

questions

1 Give three reasons to justify the claim in Item A that 'poverty kills'.

2 What is the relationship between life expectancy and social class shown in Item B?

3 What is the relationship between educational attainment and social class shown in Item C?

4 What does the evidence in this activity say to those postmodernists who claim that class is no longer a major influence on people's lives?

Unit 5 *Poverty – concepts and measurement*

keyissues

1 What are the main concepts of poverty?

2 How are they measured?

Poverty is at the sharp end of inequality. Even politicians agree that being poor is a terrible thing. It is degrading. It restricts your opportunities and life chances. It is not only bad in itself, it leads to other problems such as crime, poor health and family breakdown. So there is a broad consensus or agreement that there is a condition called 'poverty' and it is something to be avoided.

Beyond that, however, the consensus soon falls apart. Take the key question of whether poverty is a problem in Britain, an enormously wealthy country with one of the strongest economies in the world. In 1996, the Conservative government refused to sign up Britain to a United Nations anti-poverty plan. The government insisted that poverty is found only in Third World countries – some people in Britain might be on 'low incomes' but nobody was actually poor. Yet at the same time as the government took this line, the Child Poverty Action Group claimed that 4.5 million children were living in poverty in Britain!

It seems strange that some people can claim there is zero poverty in Britain while others count the numbers of poor in the millions. But poverty has always been a controversial matter. There are fierce disagreements over its definition, its measurement, its extent and its causes. One of the major lines of division is the basic choice between *absolute* or *relative* concepts of poverty.

5.1 Concepts of poverty

Absolute poverty This can be defined as a level of income which is on or below what is necessary for bare subsistence. It implies the existence of a more or less clear-cut poverty line. Those who fall below the absolute line are poor (living at a minimum standard of existence) while those above it are not poor. The poverty line itself can be determined by identifying the goods and services required for subsistence and then calculating the amount of money required to buy them. This was the basis of the 'basket of goods' approach pioneered by Seebohm Rowntree in the early 20th century. Rowntree estimated the minimum income needed to buy a weekly 'basket of goods' which included only essentials such as food, clothes, fuel and rent.

The absolute concept treats poverty as an *objective*, technical matter. So it requires technical experts to decide on the minimum standards appropriate for different types of people (eg an office worker needs less food than a labourer). Also, it defines poverty mainly in terms of people's *physical* needs and necessities. So it expects people to resist splashing out on 'luxuries' and it assumes they will spend their money wisely (eg buying the most nutritious food at the cheapest prices). Furthermore, the poverty line is set at *subsistence* level, affording only enough for a bare minimum standard of living. So it takes little account of the lifestyles and income enjoyed by those who are not poor. Indeed, absolute means 'without relation to other things'. So absolute poverty is about minimum living standards, not about the general pattern of inequality in society.

The absolute concept has the advantage of presenting a reasonably clear-cut poverty line. Also, it corresponds to what many people think of as poverty. Nevertheless, the calculation of basic needs is still a complex technical task. More importantly, the absolute approach ignores the way people's judgements of basic needs tend to be based on the society's general living standards.

Relative poverty This approach defines poverty in terms of where people stand *relative* to others in the same country. If individuals or families fall well below the average living standards in their society, then they can be regarded as poor. The point is that Britain is an affluent country and so its citizens expect a great deal more from life than merely avoiding starvation. If most people in Britain have cars and colour television, then anyone who cannot afford these things is likely to feel deprived or poor, even though these goods are not absolutely essential.

The relative approach draws attention to *subjective* views and value judgements. These are important because they are the yardstick by which people judge whether they are deprived or not. People will feel poor if their actual living standards fall well below 'reasonable' expectations. These expectations include being able to take part in normal social activities and lifestyles. So the relative concept takes account of *social* tastes and customs (eg magazines, alcohol, sporting activities) even though these are not strictly necessary for survival. Crucially, people's expectations are *relative* – they are formed by making comparisons with their fellow citizens. If their living standards fall way behind those enjoyed by most people, they feel poor.

The relative approach is a more generous measure of poverty, one that allows for some non-essential goods and services. It also has the advantage of recognising that people's needs and expectations tend to rise as a society grows wealthier. But it is criticised for blurring the distinction between 'genuine' poverty (destitution) and inequality. People may feel that poverty is an urgent problem which should be remedied, but they may feel less concerned about the existence of inequality in society. Also, at a practical level, it is unclear where exactly the

relative poverty line should be drawn.

Absolute/relative The distinction between absolute and relative concepts is not hard and fast. It is usually a matter of degree. For example, the absolute approach usually makes some social concessions by allowing certain 'luxuries' and non-essentials (eg newspapers, sweets). It is perhaps best seen as defining poverty in terms of 'minimum' standards and this can sometimes include a narrow selection of 'social' goods and activities. As for the relative approach, it moves in an 'absolute' direction when it attempts to draw an objective poverty line. Without such a line, it would be impossible to count the numbers of poor people. But it usually draws this line somewhere nearer the 'average' than the minimum.

Table 8 *Absolute and relative poverty*

Absolute	Relative
Poverty is a technical, 'scientific' matter. It can be defined *objectively* by experts.	Poverty always involves *subjective* judgements. It is not a purely technical matter, since people's values and politics affect their views on the subject.
Poverty is about *physical* needs. You are poor when you only have enough for physical subsistence.	Poverty involves *social* needs as well as physical needs. You are poor if you cannot afford 'normal' pleasures (TV, going to the pub etc).
Poverty is about *minimum* standards. It is about how close you are to subsistence level.	Poverty is about your relative position – where you stand in relation to others. You are poor if you fall too far below *average* living standards in your society.

5.2 Measuring poverty

How many poor people are there in Britain? The frustrating answer is that estimates range all the way from 'none' to as many as 'a quarter of the population'. Obviously, the answer depends to some extent on the way poverty is defined. An absolute definition will lead towards a low estimate, while a relative definition will arrive at a far higher figure.

As well as deciding on a definition, there are some other issues which researchers need to address:

- Which 'unit of assessment' is appropriate? Researchers can choose to focus on 'individuals', or the 'benefit unit' (eg couple or lone parent with dependent children), or 'households' (ie taking into account the pooled income of all members of the household, including working children).

- The poverty line has to be tailored to fit different circumstances. For instance, a couple with six children will need a higher income than a childless couple. So

activity 14 poverty in mind

Item A The struggling middle classes

Britain is suffering an outbreak of 'luxury fever' – the belief we are poor when we have never had it so good. Despite relatively high incomes, the majority of Britons consider themselves little better off than the struggling poor. In a study by Clive Hamilton, a researcher at Cambridge University, more than 60% of people said they could not afford to buy everything they really need. The middle classes are among the worst affected by this new affliction. Just under half of people who earn more than £35,000 believe they do not have enough money for essentials, whilst 40% of those in the £50,000 plus bracket feel similarly deprived.

The delusion comes despite the fact that Britons today have real incomes nearly three times higher than in 1950. Dr Hamilton believes rising incomes have led many families to aspire to celebrity standards – luxury brands, fancy houses, extravagant lifestyles - making them feel deprived if they have to settle for less. Sunglasses by Gucci and Chanel are bought by people who cannot afford their clothes.

Hamilton contends this emphasis on the tribulations of the middle classes crowds out sympathy for those who are genuinely struggling.

Adapted from Seenan, 2003

'Pity the poor rich, crippled by taxation.' A cartoon from 1947.

Item B Defining poverty

Seebohm Rowntree Primary poverty is where total earnings are insufficient to obtain the minimum necessary for ensuring physical efficiency. Secondary poverty is where total earnings would be sufficient for physical efficiency if people did not spend money on other things.

Joseph and Sumption An absolute standard is defined by reference to the actual needs of the poor and not by reference to the expenditure of those who are not poor. A family is poor if it cannot afford to eat.

Peter Townsend Individuals, families and groups in the population can be said to be in poverty when they lack the resources to obtain the types of diet, participate in the activities and have the living conditions and amenities which are customary, or at least widely encouraged or approved, in the societies to which they belong. Their resources are so seriously below those commanded by the average individual or family that they are, in effect, excluded from ordinary living patterns, customs and activities.

questions

1 Using Item A, identify two reasons why the middle classes are not suffering 'genuine' poverty.

2 Using Item B, identify one absolute and one relative definition of poverty. Give reasons for your choices.

3 Outline and assess the view that poverty is a relative matter.

---

researchers have to work out income equivalents. *Equivalisation* is the process where income levels are adjusted to take account of the size and composition of the household.

• 'Snapshot' surveys tell us who is poor at a given point in time. But it is also important to find out the length of time those people have been in poverty. People may experience short spells of poverty within the course of a year, or they may endure persisting poverty for long periods. These patterns affect our understanding of how poverty impinges on people's lives.

We can now turn to look at the two main sources of poverty figures – official statistics, and special measures developed by social scientists.

Official statistics

Claimant count This measure counts the numbers of

families living on or below benefit levels. The assumption here is that benefits such as Income Support are usually set at a very low level and so people living on or below this level can be considered poor. Indeed, even people living on income between 100% and 140% of benefit levels have been described as living precariously in the 'margins of poverty'.

The government used to publish this claimant count in its Low Income Families statistics but it denied that this was an official measure of poverty. It argued, rather unconvincingly, that claimants are not 'in' poverty, because benefits lift them 'out' of poverty. This is one of the reasons why the Low Income Families series was discontinued in 1985 – although some independent researchers still try to calculate the claimant count.

Households Below Average Income (HBAI) The government now publishes relevant data in the form of HBAI statistics. The HBAI unit of assessment is the household rather than the family or benefit unit. Government statisticians make estimates of household income from sources such as the Family Resources Survey, an annual sample survey of private households in Britain. The British Household Panel Survey is also used for a more 'longitudinal' picture. Households are ranked according to (equivilised) income and then divided into groups of equal size. Groups containing 20% of households are 'quintile groups', and groups containing 10% of households are called 'deciles'.

The statistics are presented in two forms – before housing costs (BHC), and after housing costs (AHC). The AHC measure presents net income after housing costs have been met. It seems fairer to compare AHC household incomes, because housing costs are a fixed commitment which cannot be avoided. Also, housing costs differ greatly between regions (eg mortgage and rent are much higher in South East England).

The HBAI adopts a relative measure of poverty – households are compared with the 'average' and if they fall far below the average household income then they are regarded as poor. Originally the poverty line was 50% of the 'mean' (the figure obtained by adding up all incomes and dividing by the number of households). For example, if the average mean income was £200, then the poverty line would be £100. Averages, of course, can be misleading, since the huge incomes of the richest groups pull up the average. So the government has also adopted a poverty line drawn at 60% of the median – the mid-point of the income distribution, where half the households fall below this figure, and half above.

One advantage of the HBAI is that it adopts a generous relative measure, rather than defining people as poor only if they are leading a very frugal existence. Also, the government produces HBAI figures on a regular basis, so comparisons can be made over time. However, as a poverty line it can lead to rather odd conclusions. Just consider what would happen if there was a sudden economic recession. The average income in society would plunge downwards – and yet the numbers of people in HBAI poverty would be likely to fall, since there would probably be fewer households living on incomes below 50% of this reduced average. So, in absolute terms, more people would be worse off, and yet the poverty figures would appear to have improved!

Social science surveys

Some social scientists have attempted to develop sophisticated measures of poverty, ones which are based on detailed empirical knowledge of how poverty affects people's lives. Examples of this include Townsend's 'deprivation index', Mack and Lansley's 'Breadline Britain' approach, and Bradshaw's 'budget standards'.

Townsend's deprivation index

Peter Townsend is probably the most famous champion of a relative approach to poverty. But he introduces a novel twist by suggesting that the relative poverty line can be measured in a completely objective way. In order to estimate the amount of poverty in Britain, Townsend (1979) conducted a massive survey of 2,000 households which provided him with data on household incomes, resources and lifestyles. From this data he devised a deprivation index (see Table 9), a measure of the extent to which people are able to participate in customary lifestyles and enjoy certain resources that are common in Britain. Townsend then plotted household incomes against deprivation scores. He claims this shows objectively that, as income falls, the deprivation score increases until it reaches a 'deprivation threshold' where there is a 'sudden withdrawal' from the normal activities and customs of the surrounding society. People whose income falls below the threshold are effectively excluded from normal everyday activities. On this basis, Townsend estimated that about 25% of households were in poverty at the time of the survey.

Townsend's approach was highly stimulating but it attracted a number of criticisms.

- Some critics were sceptical that there is an objective point of sudden withdrawal, arguing instead that poverty is a matter of degree. For these critics, values will always intrude into discussions of where the poverty line should be drawn.
- Little explanation is given for Townsend's particular choice of 'indicators'. Why did he select these twelve items?
- There is some confusion over what is 'customary'. On Townsend's own admission, over two thirds of the population go without a cooked breakfast most days of the week!
- Townsend blurs the distinction between choice and constraint. He seems to assume that people have uniform tastes, and if they lack one of his items it is due to financial constraint. But some people may choose not to have a cooked breakfast. Vegetarians choose not to eat meat.

Table 9 Townsend's deprivation index

	% of population going without
Has not had a week's holiday away from home in last year	53%
(adults) Has not had a relative to home for a meal in past month	33%
(adults) Has not been out to relative for meal in past month	45%
(children) Has not had a friend to play or to tea in past month	36%
(children) Did not have a party on last birthday	57%
Has not been out for entertainment in last two weeks	47%
Does not have fresh meat on four days a week	19%
Has gone 1 or 2 days without cooked meal in last fortnight	7%
Has not had a cooked breakfast most days of the week	67%
Household does not have a refrigerator	45%
Household does not usually have Sunday joint	26%
Household does not have sole use of indoor amenities (toilet; sink or washbasin; bath or shower; cooker)	21%

Breadline Britain

Mack and Lansley (1985) conducted research for *Breadline Britain*, a television series on the problem of poverty. They were inspired by Townsend's work, but they felt that his measure was one of inequality rather than poverty. For Mack and Lansley, poverty is not about how close you are to the 'average' but about minimum living standards. It is about lacking the *necessities* of life. But Mack and Lansley do not see this in terms of a bare subsistence minimum. They agree with Townsend that poverty in Britain should be defined in relative terms. So Mack and Lansley resolve this tension between 'minimum' and 'relative' approaches by defining poverty in terms of a *socially acceptable* minimum. It is the minimum level which people consider socially acceptable once the general wealth of the country is taken into account.

In order to find out what is socially acceptable, Mack and Lansley surveyed a sample of just under 1,200 people. Data was gathered on their lifestyles, incomes and possessions. Also, the sample were presented with a list of 35 items and asked whether they considered these as necessary or not. This gives a 'consensus' picture of public opinion. So, if people lack any of the items which are widely considered as necessary, it is likely that this is due to financial constraints rather than 'tastes'. Therefore Mack and Lansley define poverty as 'an enforced lack of socially perceived necessities'. For their final estimates of poverty, Mack and Lansley selected 14 items. If a person lacked 3 or more of these, that was counted as poverty. If people lacked 7 or more they were described as being in intense poverty. Because this measure of poverty is based on what is socially acceptable, we would expect the list of necessary items to expand as society becomes wealthier. Thus, in an update of the Breadline Britain series (Gordon & Pantazis, 1995), some new items were added (eg having children's friends for tea).

The latest in the Breadline Britain series is the Poverty and Social Exclusion survey by Gordon et al. (2000). This brings together data from the General Household Survey 1998-99 and from an ONS survey in 1999. In the Breadline Britain tradition, it defines poverty as a 'lack of items that all adults should be able to afford and which they should not have to do without'. This study not only asked people to identify 'necessary' items and say whether they possessed these items or not. It also asked them if they personally *wanted* the items they lacked. This helped to ensure that their deprivation was based on financial stringency rather than tastes. However, critics pointed out that the public were not asked whether lacking 3 or more items was a good criterion of poverty. This was a definition imposed by Breadline Britain researchers themselves.

Budget standard

Basically this is Rowntree's 'basket of goods' approach, revived and developed by Bradshaw (1993). A budget standard is based on the notion of a basket of goods and services which is required for a family to maintain a certain standard of living. The items covered include food, clothes, housing, heating and transport costs. Experts select the items for the basket and then price it, after making suitable adjustments for household composition and size. Bradshaw has used this idea to produce two budget standards – low-cost and modest-but-adequate.

The low-cost budget buys only the cheapest brands of food, furniture and clothing, only basic haircuts, and no more than two cinema visits a year. It is set slightly above mere subsistence and it permits the purchase of a fridge, washing machine and television. But it is very basic and it does not budget for jewellery, cosmetics, alcohol or smoking. The more generous modest-but-adequate measure allows additional items such as basic cosmetics and jewellery, some alcohol and a one-week annual holiday (the low-cost budget only allowed one day trip to Blackpool!). It makes more allowance for social tastes and lifestyles but it still restricts people to modest lifestyles (eg it does not allow money for smoking or perfume).

The budget standard approach is useful for revealing what people need to live on, whether it is for a low-cost or modest lifestyle. People can be regarded as poor if their actual income falls below that needed to 'buy' the basket of goods. However, Platt (2002) points out that it is a complex process to work out the budget standards, and the measure soon becomes out of date as lifestyles and costs change.

5.3 Social exclusion

At the end of the 20th century, the European Union states moved away from a narrow poverty perspective towards the broader concept of social exclusion. Poverty was increasingly viewed not as a mere lack of income, but rather as a multi-dimensional form of social and economic deprivation. In 1997, the British government set up the Social Exclusion Unit, which defined social exclusion as 'a shorthand label for what can happen when individuals or areas suffer from a combination of linked problems such as unemployment, poor skills, low incomes, poor housing, high crime environments, bad health and family breakdown'.

The social exclusion approach differs from the traditional poverty perspective in the following ways.

- **It is multidimensional** It recognises that poverty or deprivation has many dimensions and takes many different forms. For example, people can be excluded from the labour market (unemployment), from services (poor households may have their gas or electricity disconnected) and from social relations (socialising often requires money).

- **The emphasis is on processes** There is a danger of assuming poverty is a permanent, static condition for the people concerned. The social exclusion approach prefers to look at the dynamic processes involved. For example, there is a high degree of 'churning' – people moving in and out of poverty as their circumstances alter.

activity15 measuring poverty

Item A *Necessary items*

Mack and Lansley (1985)	% of people classifying an item as a necessity
1 Heating to warm living area of the home	97%
2 Indoor toilet (not shared)	96%
3 Damp free home	96%
7 A warm waterproof coat	87%
8 Three meals a day for children	82%
12 Refrigerator	77%
13 Toys for children	71%
28 A telephone	43%
29 An outing for children once a week	40%
34 A car	22%
35 A packet of cigarettes every other day	14%

Item B *Focus groups*

Beresford et al. (1999) used the focus group approach to find out how people judge if someone is in poverty or not. They organised discussion groups of poor people to focus on poverty and share their views. In particular, the group was asked about the criteria they use for deciding if someone is poor. These discussions were taped and analysed. Here is a selection of quotes from the discussion groups.

'I think everybody needs some sort of leisure pursuits and if they've only got enough to pay for what they really need, for basic needs, I would say that was poor.'

'You must go out because if you stay in that causes severe depression – you must go out. And when I say go out, I don't mean socialise, spend so many pounds a night on luxury meals, I simply mean enough money to go out, meet your friends and just get yourself away from those four walls.'

'If you've got enough to put food on the table, that isn't really poor.'

Adapted from Beresford et al., 1999

questions

1 Using Item A, select three items and suggest why they were given this ranking.

2 Using Item B, suggest one advantage and one disadvantage of the focus group approach.

3 Give two reasons why Mack and Lansley rely on 'socially necessary' items.

4 Why does the list of necessary items need to be updated as society grows wealthier?

- **It puts the stress on relationships** rather than treating poverty as something that can be viewed in isolation. It suggests that poverty can be fully understood only by looking at the relationship between the 'victims' and the rest of society.

- **The social exclusion approach does not blame poor people** It sees their plight as a result of the way they are excluded by more powerful groups in society. The responsibility is placed on social institutions to incorporate and include marginalised groups

Measuring social exclusion

In 1999, the Labour government published a White Paper (*Opportunity for All*) where it set out a programme to tackle poverty and social exclusion. Recognising that no single yardstick does justice to the range and depth of deprivation, it identified some 40 poverty and social exclusion measures. These were presented as 'performance indicators' which would be monitored and presented in an annual 'poverty audit'. The government boldly asked to be judged on how far it succeeded in reducing social exclusion. Its targets included the following –

improvements in literacy and numeracy rates; rise in educational qualifications; reduction in truancy and school exclusions; reducing the numbers of people in workless households; reducing the numbers claiming Income Support; increasing healthy life expectancy; reducing smoking and drug misuse; reducing suicide rates; reducing the percentage of households with low incomes; reducing teenage pregnancies; and reducing the numbers of 'rough sleepers'.

These indicators certainly provide a helpful list of some of the pressing problems in society. But critics suggest that the government has stretched the idea of social exclusion so far that it loses any consistent meaning. The long list of diverse indicators even includes obesity! Apart from anything else, this makes the measurement of social exclusion a rather complex and unmanageable affair.

Criticisms

The concept of social exclusion has achieved wide currency in Britain. However, the concept is still a bit fuzzy and unclear, and there are a number of unresolved issues. Here are some of the main criticisms.

- Poverty and social exclusion are sometimes treated as much the same thing. But some social scientists prefer to keep the two terms separate – poverty is about lack of income, while social exclusion is a much broader and more complex matter of social relationships.

- It seems to imply that social exclusion is the main cause of poverty. This may well be the case. For example, racial discrimination may create higher unemployment, and hence poverty, among ethnic minorities. But it is equally possible that poverty leads to social exclusion – for example, poor people are more likely to drop out of school. Probably there is a complex interaction of causal factors which varies from case to case.

- It perhaps exaggerates the extent to which people are really 'excluded' in Britain. Critics maintain that the welfare state more or less ensures that everyone is 'inside' the system. For example, everyone is entitled to free secondary school education and to medical treatment under the NHS. The social exclusion approach places too much stress on rigid boundaries – people are either included or excluded – when in fact it is usually a matter of degree.

- It seems to assume that all exclusion is involuntary. But the rich 'superclass' in Britain is an example of a group which voluntarily withdraws from mainstream state institutions and chooses to use private education, pension schemes and medical treatment. Even when we look at less privileged groups, it is not always clear whether their exclusion is voluntary or involuntary. Have school truants been excluded or have they excluded themselves?

- It seems to suggest that, if exclusion is the problem, then inclusion is the solution. This is not always the case. For example, an unemployed person may eventually find a job, but if that job pays a low wage then the person is not liberated from poverty. Simply including people in the mainstream is not an adequate solution, if that system itself is unjust.

CASE research Hills et al. (2002) report the results of a wide range of research by the Centre for Analysis of Social Exclusion (CASE). The conclusion they reach is that social exclusion is a bit of a myth. Very few people are truly 'excluded' across all the major institutions of society. If social exclusion means that the poor live apart from the rest of society, then that does not tend to happen in Britain. People in low-income households are still able to participate in elections, socialise with friends and families, and take part in community life. Hills et al. admit that the social exclusion strategy may be useful in drawing attention to the wider aspects of deprivation. However,

they suggest that it masks the central problem – lack of money, and a highly unequal distribution of income. Unfortunately, the concept of social exclusion tends to deflect attention from the fact that wages and benefits in Britain are often insufficient to lift people above the poverty line.

key terms

Absolute poverty Living at a bare minimum level of subsistence.
Relative poverty A form of deprivation experienced by those whose income falls below a certain percentage of average income. This means they are unable to participate in the normal activities and lifestyles enjoyed by most people.
Claimant count A measure of poverty based on counting those on or below benefits such as Income Support.
Households Below Average Income (HBAI) A measure of poverty based on a comparison of household incomes.
Deprivation index A measure of the extent to which people are able to participate in lifestyles and enjoy resources which are common in society.
Breadline Britain measure A measure of poverty based on what a representative sample consider to be an acceptable lifestyle and standard of living.
Budget standard A measure of poverty based on the income needed to buy a specified 'basket' of goods and services.
Social exclusion The process by which certain groups are marginalised and disadvantaged by the mainstream institutions of society.

summary

1. Definitions of poverty range from the absolute to the relative.

2. The absolute concept is criticised as being too severe for a wealthy society, but the relative concept is criticised for measuring inequality rather than poverty.

3. Most estimates of poverty rely on the official measure of HBAI.

4. Nevertheless, social scientists have developed their own measures – for example, the Breadline Britain measures and the budget standards.

5. The concept of social exclusion had attracted a great deal of research attention in recent years. The concept is criticised for being ill-defined, including too many things, and for diverting attention from the central problem of poverty – lack of money and a highly unequal distribution of income.

Unit 6 Poverty trends

keyissues

1 What are the trends in poverty?

2 Who are the poor?

3 What is the relationship between poverty and class, gender and ethnicity?

6.1 Poor Britain

The *Poverty and Social Exclusion Survey* (Gordon et al., 2000) delivered a biting criticism of Britain at the end of the 20th century. Its findings, based on the third Breadline Britain study, told a sorry tale.

- 9.5 million people could not afford adequate housing conditions.
- 8 million could not afford two or more essential household goods.
- 7.5 million were too poor to engage in common social activities.
- 10.5 million suffered financial insecurity (eg could not save £10 a month).
- 6.5 million adults went without essential clothing.

- 4 million were not properly fed by today's standards.
- 2 million children lacked at least two basic necessities.

According to these figures, poverty appears to be a significant problem in Britain. Not only that, but there is evidence that it is also a *growing* problem. This rather surprising conclusion is supported by the combined results of the Breadline Britain series of research (see Table 10). This presents a disturbing paradox – Britain has become much wealthier over the past few decades and the majority of people have experienced real rises in their living standards – and yet, in spite of this, poverty seems to have increased rather than diminished.

Table 10 Breadline Britain

% of households in poverty
(lacking 3 or more 'necessary' items)

1983	1990	1999
14%	21%	24%

Some critics refuse to believe that poverty has actually increased at the same time as average living standards have

activity16 poverty today

Item A Life in poverty

Numerous politicians, academics and journalists have declared that there is no such thing as absolute poverty in Britain, that it is a problem of the past. Yet in Hyde Park (Leeds) there are some people who, for at least some of the time, lack at least one of the four essentials of life – food, fuel, shelter and clothing. Yet they are only a minority – they are surrounded by many people in the community who live in real need and who avoid disaster only by exercising rigid self-discipline. They need to measure every penny and plan every action, so that they never give in to temptation by spending the evening in a pub or giving their children new toys or buying new clothes or going out to the cinema. If they control every detail of their lives and strap themselves down within strict limits, then they can cling to the four essentials of life.

But these lives of quiet desperation are always on the edge of disaster. One mistake, one weakness or one extra problem – that is all it takes to plunge them into trouble. An unexpected bill, a crime, a physical sickness, a mental illness, a violent partner, an aggressive neighbour, an accident at home, a bereavement or an addiction. Some stumble over the edge accidentally, like those who make a mistake with their bills, some deliberately jump, like those who blow their entire week's money in one night in the pub, preferring six days of trouble to a lifetime without laughter.

Adapted from Davies, 1997

Homeless and jobless in York

(2000) presents evidence that some women live in poverty even in households with adequate overall incomes. For example, men often have more personal spending money, while women cut back when money is short. Inequalities seem to be greatest where men control the household finances, and least where the partners pool their incomes.

- **Pensions** One of the advantages women enjoy is that they live longer than men. Yet this can increase their risk of poverty in old age, as their dwindling state pensions fail to keep pace with inflation. Women are less likely to have built up occupational pensions, because of their more sporadic career patterns.

key term

Feminisation of poverty thesis The view that more women than men are living in poverty and that the gender gap is increasing.

Ethnicity and poverty

With some notable exceptions (eg Modood et al., 1997; Platt, 2002), there have been very few intensive studies of poverty among Britain's ethnic minorities. Minorities certainly appear in sample surveys (eg the Family Resources Survey) but their numbers are usually too small to allow confident generalisations. Nevertheless, the available evidence does suggest that minorities tend to have higher rates of poverty and disadvantage: 'In comparison to their representation in the population, people from minority ethnic communities are more likely than others to live in deprived areas; be poor; be unemployed, compared with White people with similar qualifications; suffer ill-health and live in overcrowded and unpopular housing' (Social Exclusion Unit, 2000). In many cases the reasons for poverty are the same as those for the White population, although minorities face the added problem of racial discrimination.

A report for the National Children's Bureau (Marsh & Perry, 2003) confirms that all ethnic minority groups have high rates of poverty compared to the general population. Of course, there are more and less successful individuals and families within every group. But ethnic minority children in general are more likely than White children to live in households marked by disadvantage, persistent low income and hardship. However, the report stresses that there are differences between ethnic groups. For example, the poverty of Asians may be intensified by their larger families, while Black Caribbeans may be poor because of their higher incidence of lone-parent households. The report draws on previous research by Modood et al. (1997) and others to sketch the main ethnic differences.

- Indians, on average, are doing almost as well as Whites in terms of employment rates, occupational status and earnings. However, they still contain a substantial

number of people who are on low incomes and vulnerable to unemployment.
- Black Caribbeans have made uneven progress. Black children do have higher rates of poverty, and this is in some part due to living in lone-parent families. However, Black lone parents are more likely than their White counterparts to have paid jobs. Black women in general are more likely to work full-time, and to earn slightly more, than White women.
- The deepest poverty is found among Pakistani and Bangladeshi families. Their plight was documented in the Cantle Report (2001) which followed the outbreak of 'Asian riots' in 2001 in towns in Northern England. The report described the 'parallel lives' of Pakistani and Bangladeshi communities, cut off from the mainstream by a combination of language problems, racial discrimination and persistent poverty.

summary

1 Estimates indicate that poverty in Britain has risen over the past 20 or so years, despite the country growing much wealthier. This is perfectly possible, especially if poverty is defined in relative terms. However, HBAI estimates indicate that poverty has decreased from 2000 onwards.

2 The main groups at risk of poverty in 2002/03 are lone parents and the unemployed.

3 The largest group in poverty in 2002/03 is couples with children.

4 Working-class people run a higher risk of poverty, due to factors such as low wages, recurrent unemployment and ill health.

5 The feminisation of poverty may be real or it may simply be that women's poverty is more visible nowadays. But women are more likely than men to be poor. Female lone parents and older women are especially at risk.

6 Ethnic groups are more likely to suffer poverty, partly as a result of discrimination, partly as a result of class. There are important differences between ethnic groups.

activity17 group poverty

Item A The next meal

The *Guardian* (18.11.97) reported that three men walked into Le Gavroche restaurant to celebrate a business deal. Five hours later their bill for a three-course dinner came to £13,091. Only £216 went on food - cigars and spirits cost £845, and the rest was blown on champagne and fine wine. One wine, costing £4,959, proved 'still a bit young' so they gave it to the staff. Silvano Giraldin, the general manager of the Michelin two-star restaurant in Mayfair, London, said 'I am sure this new record will be broken shortly. There are many more people who can afford it these days. These people, they make fast money, they live in the fast lane.'

Compare this with the diary entry of 'Carol', a poor woman living in Easterhouse, Glasgow: 'Jim and I have been together for six years and always been on Social Security. The last time we went out for a meal together was five years ago on our wedding anniversary. There are things you have to do without. We've never been to the cinema together. I can't go to a hairdresser. You can't take the children out.'

Adapted from Holman, 1998

Item B Poverty and ethnicity

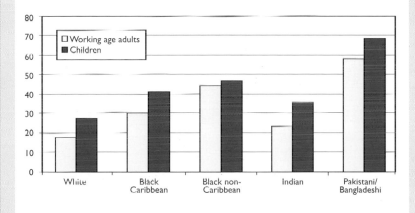

Percentage with household income lower than 60% of the median

Legend: ☐ Working age adults ■ Children

White; Black Caribbean; Black non-Caribbean; Indian; Pakistani/ Bangladeshi

Households Below Average Income, after housing costs.
Adapted from Marsh & Perry, 2003

Le Gavroche Restaurant, Mayfair, London

questions

1 With some reference to Item A, outline the relationship between poverty and class.

2 a) Briefly summarise the ethnic differences shown in Item B.
   b) Give three reasons for these differences.

Unit 7 The underclass

keyissues

1 What are the different views of the underclass?

2 What are their strengths and weaknesses?

The concept of an *underclass*, which first became popular in the 1980s, has been adopted by a wide range of social scientists. They see it as a useful way of describing a group which occupies a low position in the social structure and possibly has different cultural values from the rest of the population. It is normally defined by its economic, social and cultural features.

● The members of an underclass suffer from *economic* disadvantage and material hardship. They are at the very bottom of the class structure – 'under' the working class. As a result, they live in poor housing in deprived areas and they have high rates of poverty and unemployment.

● The *social* features of the underclass are described by

Field (1989) who suggests it recruits from three main groups – the long-term unemployed, lone-parent families and pensioners. Of course, not everybody within these categories belongs to an underclass. A great deal depends on their psychological characteristics and support networks. For example, if poor people get good support from family and community then they are less likely to be trapped in the underclass.

- Sometimes the underclass are described as having a distinctive and rather unattractive set of cultural values – for example, idleness, criminality, lack of ambition. One writer, Charles Murray, even refers to them as the 'new rabble' (see Table 13).

Table 13 Murray's view of the 'new rabble'

- Low-skilled working class, poorly educated
- Lone-parent families are the norm
- Dependent on welfare and 'moonlighting' (informal economy)
- High levels of crime, child abuse and drug abuse
- Great resistance to changing their behaviour
- Exploit welfare benefit system
- Unwilling to get a job
- Children have truancy and discipline problems
- Keen on violent and pornographic films

Adapted from Murray, 1994

7.1 Controversies

Does an underclass exist? The history of the underclass concept is a stormy and troubled one. It seems to have a unique capacity for rousing passions and igniting controversies. There is not even any agreement on whether an underclass actually exists! Some sociologists claim it is a complete myth since there is no empirical evidence for its existence. Some say there are signs that an underclass is slowly emerging although it is not yet clearly visible or fully formed. A minority insist it is already a major problem in Britain.

Blaming the victim Another criticism aimed at the underclass concept is that it revives old and dangerous notions. In the past, the most disadvantaged group in society was described by other labels, many of them moral in tone. For example, Marx referred to the lumpenproletariat (dregs, misfits, vagrants and thieves) and Victorian society expressed its contempt for the 'disreputable poor'. This moral denunciation of poor people was widespread at one time. If people were poor, it was assumed that this was due to their individual failings or vices. Either they were too stupid to get a job, or they were lazy or foolish, idling their lives away and spending the little money they had on drink and gambling. Even today, these attitudes towards the poor are still around, and

Murray's 'rabble' description gives them fresh credibility.

Sociologists call this 'blaming the victim' – putting the blame for poverty on the alleged 'pathological' traits of the poor rather than on structural injustices in society. Many sociologists argue that it is the structure of society which provides the main explanation for why some people and not others are poor. Indeed, some argue that the underclass are no more 'deviant' than any other group, as the following quote shows. 'It is not my wish to glamourise low-income people, to represent them all as good types ranged against the wicked capitalists. Crime, drug abuse, heavy drinking, sexual immorality, neglect of children do occur among the bottom 30% of society. But so they do also amongst the other 70%, including members of that illustrious club, the House of Commons' (Holman, 1997).

So, even if we accept that an underclass exists in Britain, there is a dispute over whether it is basically a 'cultural' or a 'structural' problem. There are major differences between cultural and structural accounts of the underclass.

7.2 The cultural underclass

This version argues that the underclass are poor because they hold certain immoral or inferior values (eg laziness, lack of responsibility) which do not equip them for success in a competitive society. In many ways, this is a revival of the old *culture of poverty* thesis.

Culture of poverty The American anthropologist, Oscar Lewis (1968), popularised the idea that impoverished groups tend to develop their own characteristic culture, one marked by 'deviant' lifestyles such as heavy drinking, drug use, fighting and promiscuous sex, and attitudes such as resignation and fatalism. The culture of poverty thesis was highly controversial and gave rise to endless disputes about whether the main reason for group poverty was cultural (the group's inappropriate values) or situational (lack of structural opportunities) or some combination of the two. Some critics doubted whether the most deprived groups really have a separate culture at all. One interpretation was that poor people actually share mainstream values but have to 'stretch' them a little because of their difficult circumstances. For example, they would like to get married but cannot afford it, so they just set up 'common-law' partnerships.

Charles Murray The American political scientist, Charles Murray (1984, 1994), adopts a largely cultural explanation for the plight of the underclass. For Murray, the underclass represents not so much a degree of poverty but rather a type of poverty. It is a lifestyle rooted in certain undesirable attitudes and deplorable behaviour. This is why critics accuse Murray of 'blaming the victim'. Murray certainly stigmatises the underclass, as we can see from his insensitive use of the term 'rabble'. However, Murray's ideas are rather more complex than that. He concedes that, in some respects, the underclass are behaving perfectly rationally. After all, if the government provides you with generous welfare hand-outs, why be a fool and take a low-paying, boring job? So Murray lays most of the blame on misguided governments which, in his opinion, provide over-generous welfare benefits for the underclass. He maintains that this only encourages dependency and allows the underclass to continue to lead their dissolute lifestyles. Murray advocates right-wing policies of withdrawing or reducing welfare benefits in order to force members of the underclass to take more responsibility for their own lives.

Methodological problems There are several methodological problems in testing whether the underclass have separate cultural values. First, cultures are complex, overlapping affairs and it is extremely difficult to map where one ends and another begins. Second, the selection of samples is a tricky matter. It cannot be assumed that all unemployed people, or all poor people, are members of the underclass. If the criteria used to define an underclass sample are too broad, it is unlikely that significant cultural differences will emerge. Third, how do we measure cultural values? Do we rely on what people *say* (what they tell interviewers) or what they *do* (their actual behaviour)? These kinds of methodological problems help to explain why the research evidence does not always reach firm conclusions.

Evidence against a distinctive culture Does the underclass really have a distinctive set of cultural values? Not according to Dean and Taylor-Gooby (1992), based on their interviews with 85 social security claimants of working age. Although these claimants were dependent on welfare, they were hardly part of a dependency culture. Indeed, they were firm believers in mainstream values and they were keen to participate in the workplace and in family life. They were unemployed through circumstance rather than through choice. In other words, it was their situation rather than their culture which resulted in their unemployment.

Further criticism of the idea of a cultural underclass comes from Westergaard (1996). He contends that there is a large body of research evidence to show that the vast majority of unemployed people want to have paid work but cannot find it. Westergaard also dismisses other alleged cultural features of the underclass. For example, lone-parenthood is spread across society rather than being concentrated among the poorest. As for crime, Westergaard regards it as the *effect* of poverty and structural strain, rather than a cultural value of poor people. According to Westergaard, it is false to allege that there is a single package of cultural features which represents a freely-chosen underclass style of life.

Evidence for a distinctive culture Critics of the cultural underclass sometimes seem to be implying that everyone in society has exactly the same set of values. That would be rather surprising, especially since sociology normally highlights the existence of cultural diversity in society. Indeed, some sociologists argue that it is quite reasonable to expect that the most deprived groups develop distinctive values as they adapt to their particular structural situation. These values may not be the original cause of their

problems but, once they have emerged, they make it harder to break out of the underclass.

Research evidence for underclass values is presented by Buckingham (1999) who analysed the National Child Development Study cohort. This cohort consists of a sample of about seventeen thousand people who were born in 1958 and who have been re-visited at various intervals since. Buckingham looked at the data on the cohort by the time they had reached the age of 33. He argues that within this cohort there is a recognisable group who have the hallmarks of an underclass (eg lack of qualifications, chronic joblessness). They were distinctive in terms of their patterns of family formation (they had higher rates of lone parents and early pregnancies) and work commitment (they were more likely to pack in a job if they didn't like it). Moreover, there was some evidence of intergenerational stability – that is similarities between the sample and their parents. However, Buckingham notes that they were not excluded from participating in society (eg they were just as likely to vote as any other group). Also, his research was unable to confirm whether the distinctive attitudes of the underclass are the cause or the effect of their situation.

A 'tangle of pathologies'

Howard Williamson (1997) studied a sample of what he calls 'Status Zero Youth' (SZY), a group of 16 and 17 year-olds who were not in any form of education, training or formal employment. They survived by 'ducking and diving' and 'making out', by means of a mixture of benefit fraud, stealing, living on hand-outs and finding some casual work in the 'informal' economy. Williamson describes them as caught in a 'tangle of pathologies' – an unhappy childhood, a broken or conflict-ridden home, sexual and physical abuse, sporadic school attendance, drug misuse, temporary homelessness, and brushes with the law. But the exact circumstances varied from individual to individual.

Although SZY might appear a classic example of an underclass, Williamson stresses that they represent only a 'soft' version of it. They were not a fixed group with a solid core and firm group boundaries (there was a great deal of turnover in the membership). Also, they did not display a distinctive set of 'deviant' values and lifestyles. For example, some of them showed a keen entrepreneurial spirit in searching for casual work, and few of them were firmly committed to regular offending. For the most part, their lives were governed by opportunism and short-term goals, but this hardly amounts to an alternative way of life. Most of them still subscribed to dominant mainstream goals – they just didn't know how to get there, or found too many obstacles in their path.

7.3 The structural underclass

Some social scientists reject the underclass concept because it is so closely associated with right-wing views such as those of Murray. Nevertheless, a number of liberal and radical writers do accept that the concept of

activity18 separate culture?

Item A The 'new rabble'

According to Charles Murray, 'When I use the term underclass, I am indeed focusing on a certain type of poor person defined not by his condition, eg long-term unemployed, but by his deplorable behaviour in response to that condition, eg unwilling to take the jobs that are available to him.'

Murray sees births outside marriage 'as the leading indicator of an underclass'. Such births often lead to lone-parent families, the majority of which are headed by women. When lone-parent families become widespread, they form the basis of and the 'breeding ground' for an underclass. And 'proof that an underclass has arrived is that large numbers of young, healthy, low-income males choose not to take jobs'. Many turn to crime (particularly violent street crime) and regular drug abuse. These are further characteristics of an underclass.

Many of these boys have grown up in a family without a father and male wage earner. As a result, they lack the male role models and many of the values of mainstream society. In Murray's words, 'Little boys don't naturally grow up to be responsible fathers and husbands. They don't naturally grow up knowing how to get up every morning at the same time and go to work. They don't naturally grow up thinking that work is not just a way to make money, but a way to hold one's head high in the world.'

Murray believes that the socialisation and role models required to develop these attitudes are often lacking in female-headed, low-income families.

Adapted from Murray, 1984 and 1990

Item B Welfare dependency

THE DRUG   THE PUSHERS   THE ADDICTS

Item C Spiralling crisis

The spiralling crisis in Britain's inner cities has spawned a new underclass. Thousands of people in run-down council estates are condemned to lives of deprivation, drug abuse, violence, educational failure and unemployment. Those growing up on these estates have no belief that their lives could be different from the poverty-stricken, aimless, drug-addled existence of their parents. Shona Trewannie, who works in a community school in Leeds, admits she feels sorry for the generation of young teenagers who make her life hell. 'The kids hitting their teenage years now are third-generation drug addicts, with no experience of parenting. They have never lived in a house where people have gone to work and have no idea of what it means to live without violence and squalor. They're practically wild.'

The problem can be summed up in a single word – poverty. Poverty of income, poverty of opportunity and poverty of expectation.

Adapted from Hill, 2003

questions

1 a) How does Murray define the underclass in Item A?
   b) Why does his argument represent a cultural view of the underclass?

2 How does Item B illustrate Murray's view of the basic cause of underclass behaviour?

3 Using Item C, identify two ways in which the teenagers resemble a cultural underclass.

---

underclass is a valuable tool for exploring issues of social inequality. But they insist that the main reason for the existence of the underclass lies in the structural inequalities of society rather than the cultural values of the poor. In this view, the underclass suffers from an unjust or inefficient social order which fails to ensure a fair distribution of opportunities and resources. For example, Field (1989) argues that the emergence of an underclass in Britain was a direct result of the Thatcherite market policies and economic failures of the 1980s.

Structural break

The idea that there is a *structural break* between the working class and the underclass was developed in detail by Rex and Tomlinson (1979). They argued that the material disadvantage of Britain's ethnic minorities was so severe that they could be regarded as cut off from – and beneath – the White working class. Consigned to the most menial and precarious jobs and victimised by racism, ethnic minorities could be seen as forming a separate underclass at the bottom of society. This idea of a structural break is one of the key assumptions of structural versions of the underclass, whether applied to ethnic minorities or to other groups. It serves to highlight the point that the underclass are the ultimate 'losers' or 'victims' in capitalist society.

Criticisms Is there really a structural break between the underclass and the rest of society? It is one thing to recognise the existence of a disadvantaged group at the bottom of society, but quite another to claim that they constitute a separate class, cut off from the rest of society by a structural break. So the idea of a structural underclass must be treated with caution.

- Westergaard (1996), as we have seen, is critical of the idea of a cultural underclass, but he is equally scathing about the structural version. Westergaard, a Marxist, contends that it is misleading to suggest that there is a sharp split between the underclass and the rest of the working class. The problems of the underclass are simply a slightly harsher version of those faced by the working class as a whole. In a capitalist society, those members of the working class who are in regular work share many common problems with those who are unemployed.

- The idea of a structural break suggests that the members of an underclass are somehow outside or excluded by society. But the British welfare state guarantees certain citizenship rights (eg entitlements to welfare benefits, education, health treatment) to everyone. So poverty or disadvantage is perhaps better understood as a matter of degree, rather than in terms of a dramatic structural break.

7.4 Structure and culture

Combinations of cultural and structural explanations are possible. For example, Dahrendorf (1987) explains the existence of the underclass mainly in terms of structural factors such as large-scale unemployment and economic recession. Nevertheless, he adapts his structural explanation to take account of cultural differences as well. Structural factors explain the emergence of the underclass but after a while this underclass appears to develop its own cultural style. The longer people are part of the underclass, the more likely it is that they will become attached to its cultural values. They become accustomed to dependency and powerlessness and slowly lose the motivation and discipline to improve their living standards.

This interplay of structural and cultural factors can be seen in the following study of 'Southerton'.

Homeless in 'Southerton'

Tom Hall (2003) spent a year on an ethnographic study of youths living in a homelessness hostel or bedsits in 'Southerton' in South East England. By spending a lot of time with these youngsters, he was able to build up a detailed picture of their day-to-day lifestyles and problems. On the surface, these young people closely resembled an underclass. At best, they had brief experience of low-paid and temporary employment, and they were hardly enthusiastic job-seekers. Although many of them relied on the welfare system for support, they were often lazy and deceitful in their dealings with benefit officials. For the most part, they lived a marginalised existence of boredom and frustration, spending hours sitting watching television, hanging out together and doing nothing. Every so often, their routine would be interrupted by waves of enthusiasm (eg over the prospect of a flat) or recurrent crises (eg trouble with the law, broken friendships). But, even then, many of them had an over-riding sense that their days were heading nowhere in particular.

The Southerton youngsters displayed many of the features of an underclass. However, Hall reveals the complexity of their lives. He argues that it is misleading to think that these youngsters have made a simple cultural choice of lifestyle. They also faced formidable structural *constraints* which they were ill equipped to deal with. Many of them came from troubled home backgrounds which had undermined their confidence and motivation. Besides, the local job market offered few opportunities for teenagers with little experience or qualifications. Hall concludes that cause and effect are hopelessly entangled. The constraints lead to the emergence of an underclass way of life. At the same time, the daily choices made by the youngsters make it much harder for them to break out. They are trapped in a mutually reinforcing set of circumstances, a mixture of choice and constraint. So they get by as best they can, bending their behaviour and expectations to fit their difficult circumstances.

7.5 An ethnic underclass?

The idea of an underclass had its origins in studies of African-American ghettos in the United States in the 1960s. These inner-city ghettos harboured some of the most disadvantaged and alienated groups in American society and this lent credibility to the notion of a distinct underclass. As we have already seen, this idea was borrowed by Rex and Tomlinson (1979) and applied to ethnic minorities in Britain. Some ethnic minorities certainly seem to meet many of the criteria for an underclass. They are typically seen as materially disadvantaged and marginalised in terms of the power structure of society. As Pilkington (2003) points out, ethnic minorities face racial discrimination and this makes it more likely that they will experience those forms of disadvantage normally associated with an underclass. Nevertheless, the idea of an ethnic underclass is too sweeping and it fails to take proper account of ethnic diversity.

Ethnic diversity Is there really such a dramatic structural break between ethnic minorities and the rest of society? The 4th PSI Survey (Modood et al., 1997) shows that it is no longer helpful to take a blanket view of minorities as if they were uniformly poor and disadvantaged. Rather, the emphasis now is on ethnic diversity – there are important socio-economic differences between ethnic groups and a wide range of circumstances within each group.

Pilkington (2003) uses the available research evidence to challenge the notion that minorities in general comprise a ethnically defined underclass.

- There is no convincing evidence that minorities have the cultural characteristics of an underclass (eg idleness, or a dependent 'welfare mentality'). Indeed, they possess a great deal of cultural capital and often show great enterprise and initiative.

- The economic position of most minorities has been improving both in absolute terms (eg rising incomes, higher employment rates and better jobs) and in relative terms (ie the gap between Whites and minorities is closing).

- If Britain has an underclass, ethnic minorities form only a small part of it. Pakistanis and, even more so, Bangladeshis are the only groups where the majority of members experience any of the forms of disadvantage thought to be characteristic of an underclass. Even here, however, there is some evidence of relative progress over time.

Pilkington concludes that it makes little sense to regard minorities as a whole as forming an underclass. Admittedly the concept is useful for signalling that *certain* minority groups are trapped in situations where they face higher risks of becoming poor, unqualified or unemployed. But most members of ethnic minorities are not in this position.

7.6 Assessing the underclass concept

The concept of an underclass first emerged from academic research which revealed the existence of a sharply disadvantaged group in society. So it has the merit of highlighting structural inequality in contemporary society. As Saunders (1990) notes, it indicates a group of people who are generally poor, unqualified and irregularly or never employed. Nevertheless, many sociologists have been reluctant to adopt the term, for a number of reasons. For example, the concept lacks clarity and precision. How big is the underclass? Does the underclass consist of a uniform group of people, or is it made up of different social groups with very little else in common? Researchers give no simple or consistent answers to these questions.

Some sociologists reject the term because they feel it is not truly a class. Roberts (2001) is one of those who argue that it does not really pass all the standard class tests. He admits that it qualifies as a class in the sense that people in the underclass have distinctive work situations – mainly unemployment! Also, he accepts that the idea of an underclass does not rely on a complete structural break – there is always a continuum between one class and the next. However, Roberts feels there is not enough evidence that there is a solid underclass core which passes on its lifestyles and life chances to the next generation. There is

quite a bit of mobility in and out of the so-called underclass, so it has not yet developed any class stability. Furthermore, Roberts says the underclass case is totally hopeless when it alleges distinctive cultural characteristics. He maintains that the so-called members of the underclass are just as keen to work as the employed, and there is little evidence that they have a common set of 'deviant' cultural values. Instead of an underclass, Roberts prefers to talk of excluded and disadvantaged groups which have become detached from normal, respectable working-class ways of life. But he allows that an underclass is certainly a 'future possibility'.

key terms

Underclass A disadvantaged group at the bottom of society, below the working class.
Dependency culture A culture based on dependency on state benefits.
Structural break A clear break or division between the underclass and the rest of society.
Cultural underclass An explanation of the underclass which suggests they have separate and inappropriate values, and this is a major cause of their poverty.
Structural underclass An explanation of the underclass which stresses their disadvantaged structural position. It sees a structural break between them and the rest of society, and this restricts their opportunities.

summary

1   The underclass notion draws attention to a severely impoverished and disadvantaged social group. But some social scientists doubt whether this group is distinctive enough to constitute a class.

2   Cultural versions of the underclass (eg Charles Murray) are accused of 'blaming the victim', but some researchers claim there is evidence that the underclass has distinctive values.

3   Structural versions of the underclass are accused of exaggerating the structural break, but again, some researchers insist there is evidence for this.

4   Combinations of structural and cultural explanations are possible. The cultural values of the underclass may not be the original cause of their poverty, but if they live in poverty for long enough, their values may be transformed.

5   Ethnic minorities tend to be disadvantaged, but researchers suggest that it is too sweeping to talk about an 'ethnic underclass'.

activity19 structural constraints

Item A Single mother

Kerry Whyte is a 17 year-old single mother living on benefits in a one-bedroomed council flat. But Kerry does not consider herself a 'social problem'. She is bright, articulate and self-aware and, in her view, a good mother. She has got plans for her future and a much-loved 13-month-old son, Jordan.

She did not get pregnant to jump the council housing queue or because she lacked imagination or to impress her friends. She just made a mistake, but she is facing the consequences and getting on with her life. She is currently studying part-time. Once Jordan is at nursery, she says, she'd like to work in a bank or a building society. What she does not want to do is to manage on £80 a week benefits.

Motherhood has given Kerry a sense of achievement and independence. Sometimes, she admits, she is lonely, and she stays in most nights. But she maintains a good relationship with her boyfriend, who sees his son every week. She hopes one day they will live together as a family, but adds that maybe that sounds like a fairytale.

Adapted from the *Guardian*, 6.3.1997

Item B Erica

A Charles Murray snapshot could portray people like Erica, a low-income, single-parent, as evidence of the underclass, weak characters whose lack of morals and motivation led to her poverty. But seen from the perspective of her life over a long timescale, she comes over as a strong woman who has overcome some enormous setbacks, who cares desperately for her children and who succeeds in bringing them up. People like Erica are not an underclass whose difficulties stem from their wickedness, neglect of children and rejection of work. Rather, they have to be regarded as people born into many disadvantages and whose efforts to survive are handicapped by conditions of deprivation and poverty. Far from creating poverty, they were flung into it. Given the incomes and surroundings of more affluent citizens, they could have avoided much of the distress and want which became the lot of their children.

Adapted from Holman, 1998

Item C

questions

1 Identify two ways in which Item A suggests that the underclass is a structural rather than cultural problem.

2 Using Item B, outline two structural constraints on poor people.

3 Using Items A and B, identify and explain two reasons why it is difficult to separate cultural and structural causes.

4 What view of the underclass – cultural or structural – does Item C support? Explain your answer.

Unit 8 Class explanations

keyissues

1 What are the main explanations for class stratification?

2 What are their strengths and weaknesses?

Sociologists have earned a reputation for being obsessed with social class. The theoretical giants of the discipline, Marx and Weber, showed that the deepest conflicts in society revolve around class issues such as the distribution of income, wealth and power. Clearly, the class structure has changed since Marx and Weber wrote but Savage (2000) identifies reasons why class is still central to explanations of economic inequality. First, he argues that the unequal distribution of wealth in Britain can be explained in terms of the division between a tiny upper class who possess huge amounts of property and a much larger class who rely on income from wages and salary.

Second, the labour market, where classes are formed, remains the main arena for the generation of income. Third, Savage believes that class theory offers the best explanation for economic inequalities, one that is much more convincing than, say, explanations in terms of impersonal market forces.

In this unit we shall examine the relevance of class explanations by looking first at the nature of the stratification system which generates class inequalities. This is followed by an analysis of leading theoretical approaches – Marxism, Weberian theory and functionalism. Finally, the unit ends with a consideration of the 'death of class' thesis which argues that class explanations have lost much of their analytical power.

8.1 Class stratification

Social differences are found in every society. People vary in their personal qualities (eg intelligence, beauty), their social roles (eg occupations) and their general group characteristics (eg gender, age, ethnicity). These differences mean that people have unequal chances of success when they compete for scarce and desirable resources. Some people may have *natural* advantages (eg physical strength) while others may enjoy *social* advantages (eg being born into a rich family). Whatever the reasons, it is clear that societies usually distribute rewards unequally between individuals and groups. These inequalities often take the form of social strata – layers or groups organised in a hierarchy of privilege, where those at the top tend to possess greater wealth, prestige and power.

Stratification takes different forms in different societies and historical periods. The four major systems of stratification are slavery, feudalism, Hindu castes and the social class system of industrialised societies.

Slavery The major division in this system is between free citizens and unfree slaves. Slaves are regarded as the property of their owners and they are deprived of civil, legal and political rights. Slavery was found in ancient Greece and Rome, and in the Americas and West Indies from the 17th century until the abolition of the transatlantic slave trade in the 19th century. It still exists in some modified forms in certain parts of the world today.

Feudalism The feudal system of medieval Europe was organised mainly around the ownership of land. It consisted of three estates – nobles (who were granted large tracts of land by the king), clergy (who earned most of their income from land rent), and 'freemen' (usually in a trade, but they paid a fixed rent to the lord of the manor). Each estate had its own legally defined rights and duties. Serfs, the majority of the population, were not, strictly speaking, an estate. They worked the lord's land and provided him with agricultural produce and military service in return for his protection from rival nobles.

Castes The Hindu caste system in India has four main castes – Brahmins (priests and nobles), Kshatriyas or Rajputs (warriors, landowners), Vaishyas (merchants, farmers) and Shudras (servants, manual workers). These are further broken down into thousands of jatis (subcastes) based on occupations or village or kin groupings. An etiquette system regulates social interaction between these groups and reduces any 'pollution' which would result from close contact with members of a lower caste or from the 'outcasts' or Untouchables.

People cannot move out of their caste of birth, although it is possible for a whole subcaste to improve its relative position in the hierarchy by following a stricter observance of 'pure' practices. The caste system is supported by the religious beliefs and ideas of Hinduism. *Dharma* imposes a duty on Hindus to conduct themselves in a proper, moral manner. *Karma* is the notion that caste membership is a reflection of a person's moral worth – for example, if you behave morally in this life you will be re-born into a higher subcaste in the next round of the reincarnation cycle.

Social class

Social class is the dominant form of stratification in Britain and other modern societies. Class is a matter of economic inequalities and each class consists of people who share similar positions in the economic structure. Every society is a 'class' society to the extent that it contains broad economic divisions. Nevertheless, there are some key differences between the social class system and other stratification systems. In the class system there is generally much greater legal and political freedom – for example, workers have contractual relationships with employers, quite unlike the feudal obligations of serfs or the forced labour of slaves. Second, the class hierarchy does not rely on religious justifications, unlike the caste system, or feudalism's notion of the divine right of kings. Third, there are fewer barriers to social mobility in the class system and so there is greater movement between strata. And lastly, the economic marketplace assumes a much more central and dominant role in class-based societies – it is this that determines social class ranking. This is especially true of capitalist societies.

Class in capitalist society

Capitalism can be defined as 'an economic system in which goods and services are produced for sale, with the intention of making a profit, in a large number of separate firms using privately owned capital goods and wage labour' (Jessop, 1987). Its central mechanism is the market where all the buyers and sellers pursue their own material interests within a competitive framework. The prices of goods and services are fixed according to how much producers are able to charge and what consumers are willing to pay – the laws of supply and demand. The means of production (machinery, factories, capital etc) are mostly privately owned and the owners have a profit motive to raise output. Workers sell their labour to employers in return for a wage and they are contractually free to change employers in the search for higher wages.

Of course, a 'perfect', fully competitive market is rare. For example, capitalists often try to rig the market by setting up monopolies or cartels which allow them to charge higher prices for the goods and services they sell. Because of these 'imperfections', most capitalist societies have imposed legal controls on firms, and established collective bargaining rights for trade unions. Moreover, totally unregulated or 'free' markets run the risk of creating huge social inequalities as well as high rates of unemployment. Therefore social democratic governments have tried to control or regulate the free market in various ways – boosting employment by investing in industry, providing jobs in the public sector, and using the tax and benefit systems to reduce income inequalities.

Structural inequality Inequality is not really surprising or accidental in a capitalist country like Britain. Rather, it is something that is systematically generated by the way society is structured and organised. This works in a number of ways.

- Competitive markets are dominant – people compete with one another for the best jobs, incomes, houses. But some groups have a head start in this competition. For example, middle-class groups have higher economic, social and cultural capital and so they are in a stronger position to grab most of the scarce resources.

- Profit is given higher priority than need. Therefore the system accepts unemployment and low wages, because it is seen as right that employers must protect their profits. The needs of non-workers (those on benefits) are given low priority because they do not create profits for anyone.

- The dominant ideology supports and tolerates inequality. Meritocratic arguments reassure people that the system is fundamentally fair – the successful are seen as deserving their lion's share of rewards, while the less successful are expected to resign themselves to their fate. This ideology masks the unequal opportunities in society – working-class people face greater material and cultural obstacles which hinder their educational and occupational achievements.

- Inequality persists because the present social system serves the interests of the richer and more powerful classes. Once in a position of power, these classes will use this power to protect their privileges. They will adopt *closure strategies*, which make entry from below into their ranks difficult, and resist any major reform to reduce inequality of opportunity or redistribute power or wealth.

Meritocracy Capitalism is not the only type of social structure to generate marked economic inequalities. For example, poverty was just as bad, if not worse, in the old East European communist states. Moreover, perhaps a certain level of inequality is necessary or desirable. Indeed, many people seem to support the idea of a *meritocracy*. A meritocratic system assumes it is the task of social institutions (eg schools, workplace) to set up a 'contest' to identify and select the most talented people. Ideally the contest should be as fair as possible so that everyone can show their true merits. The victors in this contest are then rewarded with the prizes of higher income, status and power.

Unequal but fair?

Saunders (1995, 1996) argues that while Britain is an unequal society it is not necessarily unfair. He blames left-wing sociologists for spreading the SAD thesis – the argument that class-related Social Advantages and Disadvantages, rather than individual merit, are the main factors behind success or failure. According to Saunders, this thesis is false because it rests on the 'myth' of class rigidity. Saunders believes that it is academic ability and personal ambition which shape individual success or failure. If you are bright and willing to work hard you will almost certainly succeed.

In order to test this, Saunders imagines what mobility patterns would look like in a perfect meritocracy, but one where talent tends to be concentrated in higher classes (because brighter people are more successful and have brighter children). He then compares these imaginary patterns with actual mobility patterns in Britain. For this, he draws on research evidence which includes Goldthorpe's work and the National Child Development Study (NCDS). Saunders concludes that there is a remarkably close fit between the two patterns. For example, he claims that the research evidence shows that class origins are only a weak influence on final class destinations. Ability (based on tests at age 11) and motivation (based on tests at age 16) appear to be better predictors of success or failure. However, Saunders admits that the evidence is not fully conclusive – for example, he lacked data on IQ scores and on recruitment into the 'top elite'. He also concedes that social background does play some part. But he still maintains that, in the end, what matters most is not class background but ability and effort. He suggests that the SAD thesis is flawed and that the meritocracy thesis is more plausible. Moreover, Saunders believes most people would agree that a meritocracy is the fairest kind of system.

SAD but true? Marshall and Swift (1996) accuse Saunders of selective reading which ignores a great deal of published evidence that contradicts his arguments. This evidence indicates that class background has a substantial effect on class destinations. It is true that working-class children who are high educational achievers have a good chance of entering service class occupations. But if we take all children with modest educational achievements, then those from working-class backgrounds are less likely than those from a service-class background to land service-class jobs. These differences in relative mobility rates cast strong doubt on the claim that Britain is a meritocracy (see also pages 252-253, 254, 255-256).

Furthermore, Breen & Goldthorpe (1999, 2002) highlight what they regard as 'fatal flaws' in Saunders' arguments. On technical grounds, they criticise him for excluding unemployed people from his analysis, for inadequate measures of social class (ie not using the Goldthorpe class scheme) and for putting too much faith in the NCDS indicators of ability and effort. They also criticise him on conceptual grounds. Breen & Goldthorpe claim that a re-analysis of the NCD data set reveals that, while merit does play a part in determining class destinations, the effect of class origins remains strong. Working-class children need substantially more 'merit' in order to succeed.

Compromise? In reply, Saunders (2002) suggests there is a great deal of common ground between himself and his critics. This leads him to offer some propositions he hopes will win general agreement.

- The amount of movement between classes is not inconsistent with the operation of a system of meritocratic selection.
- The main departure from meritocratic selection is the ability of the middle classes to hold on to their positions and pass them on to their children. This means they are more successful than they 'should' be if a pure meritocracy existed.
- Class origins play only a small role in shaping class destinations in Britain. Individual ability and effort now play a much bigger part.

8.2 Marxist theory

The main theories considered here are Marxism, Weberian theory and functionalism. Some British sociologists describe themselves as Marxists, some work within the Weberian tradition, while others find something of value within every theoretical approach. Sociology is a self-critical discipline and so it is important to identify the limitations of these 'rival' theoretical models. But it is equally important to recognise their respective strengths – every model has something to offer in terms of its particular insights and preoccupations.

Karl Marx (1818-1883) stressed the fundamental importance of economic processes, since every social group must first satisfy its material needs (eg for food, shelter, clothing). So humans are inevitably involved in economic activities such as harnessing natural resources, producing goods, developing new technologies and establishing a division of labour in the workforce. And as people band together to perform these economic tasks, so they enter into social class relationships. According to

*activity*20 *not so SAD*

Item A Differences

It makes some difference whether your father is an unskilled manual worker or a well-paid professional, whether your mother left school early, whether your parents showed an interest in your education, whether your parents left you to find your own way, whether you attended a private school or a state comprehensive, whether you had your own bedroom in which to do your homework. But what matters most is whether you are bright and whether you work hard.

Adapted from Saunders, 1996

Item B The pen of gold

J.K.Rowling is worth about £435 million due to the huge sales of her Harry Potter novels which have sold over 250 million copies worldwide. The associated film rights and merchandising have doubled the fortune she has made from her books. At one time she was a penniless single mother who lived on £70 benefit a week and scribbled her first Harry Potter novel in a café. But her gifted 'pen of gold' has brought her success and fame. Now her family homes include a 6-bedroom Perthshire retreat, a Georgian mansion in Edinburgh and a £4.5 million pad in Kensington, west London. She is the 91st richest person in Britain.

Adapted from *Sunday Times Rich List*, 27.4.2003 and 18.4.2004

J. K. Rowling signing books in Edinburgh

questions

1. Using Item A, identify two examples of class factors which contribute towards success in life.
2. Using Item B, outline two ways in which Rowling provides an example of meritocracy.
3. Give two reasons why it is difficult to measure effort and talent.
4. Outline and assess meritocratic explanations of inequalities.

Marx, the early era of *primitive communism* was reasonably egalitarian because it was based on very simple hunting and gathering techniques. But social classes started to emerge as soon as societies developed a more specialised division of labour and introduced private property. So history can be divided into a number of successive stages (eg ancient slavery, feudalism, capitalism), each stage having a distinctive *mode of production* – the dominant technology of the society and its pattern of class relationships.

Marx was especially interested in capitalist societies with their advanced technology based on steam power, machinery and the factory system. Under capitalism, he argued, there are two major classes – the capitalists (*bourgeoisie*) and the workers (*proletariat*). These classes are defined by their relationship to the *means of production* – productive resources such as land, factories, machinery, raw materials. Capitalists (entrepreneurs, financiers and industrialists) own the means of production and so they are in a highly privileged and powerful economic position. The workers, on the other hand, do not own productive property and so they can survive only by selling their labour power to employers. It is this basic division, between the owners of capital and the workers, which creates major conflicts.

Class conflict

Marx noted the paradox that capitalism has the potential to create wealth for everyone and yet it oppresses and exploits large sections of the population. In Marx's view, it is the workers who create wealth by their sweat and toil but most of the economic rewards are seized by employers and property owners – this is known as the labour theory of value. There is a basic conflict of interests between bosses and workers, since it is in the employer's interests to keep wages low in order to increase profits. This creates all sorts of strains and conflicts within capitalism, and Marx attempted to explore these 'contradictions' in some detail.

- **Polarisation of social classes** Marx expected capitalists to try to maintain their profits by driving down wages or by introducing machinery to replace workers. This would result in sharper contrasts between the living standards of the working class and the capitalist class. Marx's 'immiseration thesis' predicted that the living standards of workers would fall further and further behind those of capitalists. Class divisions would become more polarised as 'intermediate' classes merged with either capitalists or workers. For example, the 'petty bourgeoisie' (eg small shopkeepers) would sink into the working class.

- **Alienation** Capitalism has massive productive power but it fails to make people happy or contented. Instead, it creates *alienation*, an impoverishment of the human spirit. Capitalism is obsessed with the pursuit of profit and so it treats people simply as commodities to be bought and sold. Few people are able to control their

own destinies and few people find any sense of fulfilment in their daily work or their social relationships.

- **Economic crisis** Marx regarded capitalism as an erratic and uncontrollable system which frequently runs into deep economic crisis. Capitalists have no choice but to follow the competitive logic of capitalism but this intense competition simply creates further problems. Marx argued that there was a long-term tendency for profit rates to fall and eventually this would cause the final collapse of the capitalist system.

According to Marx, these contradictions would lead to revolution and the replacement of capitalism with a classless communist society. However, this would happen only if workers first became aware of their 'true' class interests. This is difficult because many workers suffer from *false consciousness* – a flawed view of society and their position within it. They have been fooled into thinking that capitalism is fair and 'natural' and so they are reluctant to challenge it. In a sense they have been brainwashed by the capitalists who have greater control over the 'social superstructure' – the realm of ideas and social consciousness, including religion, law, politics and education.

Criticisms of Marx

It is not always easy to decide what Marx was 'really' arguing, or how he would modify his ideas if he were alive today. But here are some of the common criticisms levelled at his work.

Determinism Marx gave the impression that there were certain scientific 'laws of history'. This implies that the path of history is fairly predictable, with one historical stage leading to the next in some rigid and predetermined fashion. But critics insist that Marx underestimates the freedom of people to alter the course of history. Some neo-Marxists (eg Gramsci) eventually accepted that history involves genuine decisions and choices and the outcome is by no means certain.

Economic determinism Marx attached too much importance to economic factors. He treated the economic 'base' as primary in the sense that it shapes the 'superstructure' of ideas and culture in a society. This implies that the dominant ideas of a society are little more than ideologies which help to maintain the economic position of capitalists. For example, the prevailing religious ideas (eg 'blessed are the poor') reconcile people to the massive inequalities of capitalism. However, critics maintain that culture is not just a direct product of economic forces. Cultural conflicts (eg around gender, nationalism or ethnicity) have their own reality and they cannot always be 'reduced' to economic issues.

Predictions Many of Marx's apparent predictions have not been fulfilled. Instead of deeper poverty and misery, the living standards of workers in capitalist societies have mostly risen. Instead of polarisation, the middle classes have steadily grown. And instead of revolution, workers seem to have reconciled themselves to capitalism. Indeed, the fall of the Berlin Wall in 1989 suggests that it is communism, not capitalism, which has collapsed under its internal contradictions.

Falsely conscious? Perhaps capitalism has survived because, for all its injustices and imperfections, it is still the best available system. It is certainly true that some capitalist societies (eg Nazi Germany) have displayed appalling levels of brutality and cruelty. But Western liberal democracies have a strong track record in terms of material progress, political freedoms and civil liberties. In that case, workers might be perfectly sensible, rather than falsely conscious, in siding with capitalism.

Neo-Marxism

Marx died over a century ago and it is unfair to expect him to have predicted every development since then. Indeed, some Marxists reject the idea that Marxism offers a set of predictions at all. Rather, they see Marxism as a method, one that provides us with a set of relevant concepts and some useful guidelines – for example, if you want to understand a society, start by looking at the economy and class conflict. On the other hand, maybe the method itself is unreliable if it has led to such misleading generalisations. Perhaps Marxism requires substantial revision or modification or at least some updating.

Neo-Marxism is the term used to describe the work of later Marxists who wrestled with the problem of why things did not work out quite as expected – for example, why have workers not overthrown capitalism? Neo-Marxists have taken Marx's ideas in many different directions and there is no single neo-Marxist approach. But most seem to agree that culture deserves far more serious attention than it was given by 'classical' Marxists. Neo-Marxists generally see culture as a force in its own right, one that cannot be treated as a mere reflection of economic forces – although

it is never entirely free of the influence of economic factors.

One example is the French Marxist, Pierre Bourdieu (1984), who describes how cultural tastes play a part in creating boundaries between social classes. Another is the Italian Marxist, Antonio Gramsci (1971) who places as much emphasis on culture and politics as on the economy. Gramsci develops the concept of *hegemony* – dominance by cultural and political means. It refers to the way capitalists use their superior resources (eg control of mass media and education) to win the hearts and minds of workers. They try to convince workers that the capitalist system is legitimate, normal and a matter of common sense. But Gramsci (1971) notes that hegemony is a precarious thing since it is usually contested by rival groups with competing ideologies.

activity21 class conflict

Item A Marx's vision

The ruling class exploits the working class.

The workers' revolution overthrows the ruling class.

Communism replaces capitalism and the state eventually 'withers away'. The result is a classless society.

A successful revolution in one country leads to revolutions in other countries.

Item B *The collapse of communism*

Lenin's statue being dismantled in East Berlin in 1991. Lenin was one of the founders of Soviet communism after the Russian Revolution of 1917.

Opening the Berlin Wall after the collapse of communism in Eastern Europe in 1989. The wall divided communist East Berlin from capitalist West Berlin.

Item C *Union reforms*

Roberts (2001) describes how trade unions and industrial relations in the UK were transformed by sweeping reforms in the 1980s and early 1990s. These reforms included:

- The 'closed shop' (restricted to union members) was banned.
- Ballots were required prior to industrial action.
- Most forms of secondary (sympathetic) industrial action were banned.
- Unions were made responsible for the actions of all their officials, including shop stewards.
- Heavy restrictions were imposed on picketing.
- Union funds were placed at risk in the event of any breaches of these regulations.

Roberts argues that some of these reforms proved to be popular among trade union members. In fact, by the 1990s professionals and managers were more likely than manual workers to be union members. Nevertheless, these reforms have made it harder for workers, as they have weakened organised labour. Employers have found it easier to opt out of national bargaining and to limit workplace negotiations to matters like basic rates of pay and hours of work. Employers now have a much freer hand over working practices, incentive systems and investment decisions.

Adapted from Roberts, 2001

Item D Trade union membership

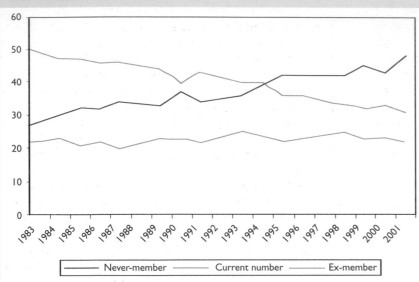

Legend: Never-member —— Current number —— Ex-member

Note: figures on the graph are percentage of employees in the whole economy

Adapted from Bryson & Gomez, 2002

questions

1 Use Items A and B to criticise Marx's vision of the future.

2 Using Item C, identify two examples of class conflict.

3 Using Items C and D, outline two things which seem to fit the Marxist idea of false consciousness.

4 Give two reasons why it is difficult to decide whether workers are falsely conscious or not.

8.3 Weberian theory

Just as there is a Marxist tradition in sociology, so many sociologists work within a Weberian framework. One of the key features of this Weberian tradition is the distinction between *class*, *status* and *party*. Weber treated these as separate (but related) sources of power which have direct effects on people's life chances.

Class Like Marx, Weber (1864-1920) treated social class as basically an economic matter. He agreed that ownership (or non-ownership) of productive property is an important basis for class formation but Weber moved away from Marx's two-class model. Instead, he chose to define class in terms of position in the economic marketplace. The market consists of a great many positions which vary according to the source and amount of income, and differences in occupational skills and educational qualifications. A printer, for example, normally has greater skills and higher income than a labourer and it is oversimplified to describe them both as working class. So Weber's approach allows for a considerable number of finely graded occupational classes, each based on market position. The people within each class share broadly similar life chances.

Status Status refers to the degree of honour or prestige which is attached to social groups in society. Different status groups compete with each other for a greater share of social esteem. Moreover, the members of a status group tend to share common values and lifestyles and form a community. They use *status symbols* to announce their common membership (eg stockbrokers speed around in Porsches, skinheads wear Doc Martens and braces). Status, then, has more to do with social evaluation based on consumption styles (how people spend their money) than with production (how they earn it). So status groups are not quite the same thing as social classes. On the other hand, they are not always sharply separated. For example, the

class position of a group might enhance its social status. Also, each status group adopts strategies to increase its material resources and improve its life chances.

Party When Weber talks about party he is referring to the exercise of power by pressure groups, political parties, trade unions and other organised interest groups. These groups compete for power, which Weber defined as the probability of imposing one's will even against the resistance of others. Parties may form around social classes or status groups, a combination of these, or on some entirely different basis. Parties can use their power to increase their economic wealth but Weber does not accept that economic wealth automatically confers power. For example, a politician or trade union leader might exercise greater power than a rich employer. Indeed, Weber suggested that power in modern society is increasingly concentrated in large bureaucracies rather than in the ownership of the means of production. In a development of Weber's ideas, Scott (1996) suggests that command might be a better term than party. For Scott, class relations are based on material property, status relations on differences in social prestige, and command relationships on different positions in the 'sphere of authority'.

Neo-Weberians

Many British sociologists find the Weberian approach immensely valuable in studying social stratification. One example is John Goldthorpe who has devised classification schemes which are based largely on a Weberian understanding of market positions. Another is John Scott who uses Weberian insights to explore the unequal distribution of income, wealth and property. Neo-Weberian sociologists generally take the view that Marx's two-class model is less useful than Weber's 'market' approach for understanding the complexities of the modern economy and class structure.

Social closure Parkin (1979) regards Weber's concept of *social closure* as especially useful for exploring group conflicts. Social closure refers to strategies for creating and maintaining group privileges. The *exclusion strategy* – placing restrictions in the paths of others – is used by groups anxious to protect their existing privileges. For example, they may insist that new recruits to their ranks possess the right educational credentials or an acceptable culture.

The *usurpation strategy*, on the other hand, is a matter of grabbing some of the privileges enjoyed by others. For example, workers may attempt to improve their position by going on strike for better pay or conditions.

Parkin also applies this closure framework to gender inequalities. Men use exclusion strategies against women – male workers resist female entry into their skilled trades, and employers use 'cultural' arguments ('it's not woman's work'). On the other hand, females have tried to usurp male privileges by mounting campaigns and protests and by pushing for legislative reform – for example, the Sex Discrimination Act and the Equal Pay Act.

Weber vs Marx

Many sociologists find something of value in both the Marxist and the Weberian approaches. Nevertheless, the important debates in stratification often involve clashes between the two perspectives. It is instructive, then, to identify their main differences.

- **Production or market?** Marxists define classes in terms of ownership of the means of production (basically a two-class model), whereas Weberians see classes as positions in the market place (allowing for a wider range of classes). Marxists say Weberians identify too many trivial market-based classes and this merely distracts attention from the basic split between capitalists and workers.

- **View of history** Marx saw history as a long march towards the final goal of a communist society where class antagonisms would no longer exist. But Weber

was sceptical about the possibility of a classless society and he regarded stratification as a more or less permanent source of conflict in every society.

- **Matching dimensions?** Marxists usually portray class, status and power as 'matched' – that is, the capitalist class not only has economic riches but also high status and decisive political power. Weber recognises that these three dimensions frequently overlap but he insists that they are sometimes less closely linked than Marxists suggest. For example, a penniless aristocrat might be high in status but low in class, while a market stallholder might earn good money but still be low in status.

Middle classes Weber's market approach seems better equipped to deal with the existence of middle-class groups. Marxists have great difficulty in fitting middle-class groups into their basic model of capitalists and workers. This is called the 'boundary problem' – where exactly is the boundary line between capitalists and workers? The middle classes are sometimes described as filling 'contradictory class locations' (Wright, 1985).

key terms

Class For Weber, a person's position in the economic marketplace.
Status The degree of honour or prestige attached to social groups.
Power As defined by Weber, the probability of imposing one's will even against the resistance of others.
Status symbols Symbols which represent the status of a particular group in society.
Social closure Strategies for maintaining or creating group privileges.
Exclusion strategy A strategy used by group members to exclude others from their group.
Usurpation strategy A strategy used by a group to obtain some of the privileges held by others.

activity22 status

Item A Gay clubs

In an outbreak of 'heterophobia', bars and clubs in Manchester's thriving Canal Street gay area are turning away the straight and heterosexual people who are attracted to the gay scene in ever larger numbers. Clubs like Poptastic and bars like Manto now employ drag queens and gay doormen to decide whether customers trying to gain entry are really gay. The manager of Poptastic says it is easy to tell who is gay: 'By the way they are dressed, by the way they act, their mannerisms and asking them who they kiss and where they go'.

The clubs see this as essential to the survival of the gay community. The manager of the Paradise Factory says too many straight customers change the atmosphere of the place.

Adapted from the *Independent* 11.10.1997

Gayfest, Canal Street, Manchester

Item B Royal Ascot

Royal Ascot

8.4 Functionalism

Functionalist sociologists often draw a comparison between society and the human body. The body consists of separate but interdependent parts, each part playing a specialised role which contributes to overall physical wellbeing. Likewise, society is depicted as a more or less harmonious and integrated 'whole' with every social institution serving a particular function. The main task of the sociologist, then, is to discover the particular functions performed by each social institution. In the case of stratification, functionalists seek to reveal the contributions it makes to the survival and maintenance of society. This leads them to quite different conclusions from conflict theorists (whether Marxist or Weberian) who regard stratification as a source of conflict and tension. For functionalists, stratification is something which is beneficial and positive.

Davis and Moore

A long running debate on the functions of stratification was opened up by Kingsley Davis and Wilbert E. Moore (1945). They observe that stratification is a permanent and universal feature of human societies and conclude that this is because it is functionally necessary. Stratification is inevitable because every society faces the task of 'placing' people – in particular, ensuring that the most important positions are filled by suitable people. Also, it needs to motivate these people – they must perform their duties in a responsible and conscientious manner. In order to achieve this, societies offer higher rewards (eg income, status) for the most important jobs. Davis and Moore offer certain guidance on how we can identify these jobs. Normally

they are 'unique' (no other occupation can substitute for them). For example, a managing director is more important than a chauffeur because the director could drive the car but the driver probably could not direct a company. Also, the most important jobs tend to have other positions dependent on them – the managing director supervises many people, the chauffeur merely tends to the car.

But functional importance is not the only criterion which decides the distribution of rewards. Davis and Moore add a second criterion, the scarcity of personnel. This refers either to the shortage of people with innate ability (not everyone has the talent to become a brain surgeon) or to the necessity of a long period of job training. In order to tempt capable people to undergo training, society compensates them by guaranteeing financial rewards and high social status at the end of the training period.

Evaluation The functionalist view of stratification has been heavily criticised (but Davis and Moore have replied to many of these criticisms).

- How easy is it to determine the functional importance of a job? Isn't a dustman just as important to our health as a doctor? (Davis and Moore say this criticism overlooks the 'scarcity of personnel' arguments).

- Davis and Moore assume there is a general *consensus* on the pattern of rewards. How, then, do we explain the widespread resentment about the unequal distribution of income and wealth? Inequality is a continuing source of conflict in most modern societies.

- Davis and Moore seem to regard power as a social resource which is distributed throughout society in such a way that it works for the common good. They overlook the way power is used as a *weapon* by some groups to further their own material interests.

- Some of the highest rewards go to wealthy people who do not really perform any 'function' at all but simply live off the interest payments on their wealth. (Davis and Moore accept this criticism).
- Davis and Moore offer a dismal view of human nature which suggests that people will perform tasks only for monetary or status rewards. They overlook other motives such as altruism or sense of service or joy in work. (Davis and Moore reply that, unfortunately, these other motives are usually pretty weak!).
- Davis and Moore neglect the dysfunctions (negative effects) caused by stratification. They assume that stratification is functional for *everyone*. But some people benefit more than others and some suffer greatly from stratification.

After this flood of criticism, many commentators concluded that the functionalist approach had been discredited. However, some writers have returned to the debate. Saunders (1990) maintains that the arguments of Davis and Moore cannot be easily dismissed. Saunders believes they are correct in saying that stratification serves important functions (even if it creates dysfunctions at the same time). Also, even Davis and Moore's critics agree that stratification is more or less universal. The main disagreement arises over the claim that stratification is inevitable in all future societies. Here Saunders sides with the critics in accepting that stratification based on unequal material reward is not inevitable. But Saunders concludes that any alternative would probably require a coercive state willing and able to clamp down on any emerging inequalities: 'capitalist countries often turn out to be more unequal...but socialist countries are always more repressive' (Saunders, 1990). Saunders also suspects that the abolition of unequal rewards would act as a disincentive to entrepreneurship and innovation.

activity23 It's a wonderful world

Item A Success

Capitalism is a successful economic growth machine. It is dynamic, innovative and highly productive, constantly developing new technology.

Capitalism has led to staggering improvements in the living standards of poor and rich alike. It is a myth that it has increased misery for the majority.

Economic growth causes environmental problems (pollution, depletion of natural resources etc) but capitalism also provides the wealth and technology to deal with these problems.

Social systems cannot make people happy but capitalism provides congenial conditions (eg leisure time, freedom from want) in which individuals can pursue happiness.

Adapted from Saunders, 1995

Item C Sir Richard Branson

Sir Richard Branson is the sixth richest person in the UK with an estimated worth of £2,600 million. His Virgin group has airlines, trains, mobile phones and a host of other businesses. He has an estate in Oxfordshire and a private island in the Caribbean.

Adapted from *The Sunday Times Rich List*, 28.04.2004

Sir Richard Branson at the launch of Virgin Wines

Item B Bless the rich

When I arrived in Britain 20 years ago, money was a dirty word. The upper class camouflaged their wealth with their frayed shirt collars, beaten-up Minis and draughty homes. The working class viewed money as the root of all evil, and Marxists portrayed it as the means by which capitalists oppressed the proletariat.

Today, all that is gone. Money is respectable now, and wealth is regarded as a good thing. Even the Left is peeling the stigma from wealth.

On the whole, the rich make our society infinitely better. Those who want to accumulate wealth have to deploy their talents, channel their energies and unfurl their imagination, thereby setting new frontiers in every field. Economic competitiveness has men and women sweating over the design for a more powerful and cheaper car, or the script for a more entertaining television series, and the rest of us benefit.

Rich money may not trickle down to the rest of us, as politicians like to promise, but we can borrow it. Moreover, there are plenty of rich with a social conscience and they give time and money to help those less fortunate. The rich are more generous, more tolerant and more creative. We should cherish them.

Adapted from Odone, 2001

questions

1 Using Item A, identify two 'functions' of capitalism.
2 Using Item B, outline two ways in which inequalities can make things better.
3 Give two reasons why it is difficult to judge whether inequalities are functional or dysfunctional.
4 In terms of Davis and Moore's theory, why should Richard Branson be so well rewarded with wealth and status?

8.5 The death of class?

Heated debates about social class surfaced towards the close of the 20th century when a number of sociologists rejected the assumption that class is still a dominant influence in society. Postmodern theorists, especially, take the view that class is a spent force. In postmodern society, they argue, there is a refreshing degree of diversity, freedom and choice, and this has liberated people from the shackles of class. In view of this, they have pronounced the 'death of class'. Other sociologists, however, reply that the patient is still struggling and kicking, and therefore the obituary notice is more than a tad premature.

Lee and Turner (1996) suggest that the class approach has been challenged in two main ways. One is what they call 'myths of classlessness' and the other is the 'death of class' itself.

Myths of classlessness Every so often some expert alleges that Britain has become a classless society, one where the stamp of class leaves only a faint impression on people's lives. The embourgeoisement thesis was one version of this argument. But that thesis, and others which suggest there has been a 'levelling out' of class differences, have been shown to be greatly exaggerated (see Unit 4). Indeed, Adonis and Pollard (1997) argue that, if class means categorising people by their incomes, well-being and access to power and influence, then Britain is more segregated by class now than at any time since the mid-20th century.

The death of class This argument allows that class inequalities may still exist but it contends that class *analysis* no longer provides convincing explanations of social attitudes and behaviour. It asserts that this type of analysis no longer works as a tool for sociological research since class is no longer a historical force (eg the 'class war' has ended). As one critic says, 'class as a concept is ceasing to do any useful work for sociology' (Pahl, 1989). Although Pahl concedes that capitalism produces class divisions, he nevertheless thinks that class analysis has declined into mere political dogma. Quite simply, it no longer provides valuable sociological insights. It is used mainly as a tool of description rather than as a theoretical explanation.

Goldthorpe and Marshall (1992) have replied to Pahl by putting up a stout defence of class analysis. First, they argue that many criticisms are misplaced. For example, they say it is untrue that class analysis commits sociologists to dogmatic views about the inevitability of class consciousness or class conflict. This is a matter for empirical investigation rather than an eternal truth. Second, they defend the value of research programmes on class, maintaining that this type of research explains a good deal of what happens in society. But they admit that class analysis must remain self-critical. It cannot simply assert that class is an important factor in social life – it must *demonstrate* it.

Class in postmodern society

Many of the criticisms of class analysis come from postmodern sociologists. For example, Pakulski and Waters (1996) argue that class diverts attention away from more important areas such as identity, ethnicity and gender. In their opinion, postmodern societies are no longer class societies, since production and the marketplace are now of minor significance. So class is more or less 'dead'. Inequalities and conflicts still exist but they no longer run along class lines. People are slotted into British society according to their 'status' rather than their class. In a 'status-conventional' society the important things are cultural symbols, consumer lifestyles, value-commitments (eg feminism, environmentalism) and ascribed statuses (eg ethnicity, gender). People's identities are predominantly linked to styles of consumption rather than class and property.

Postmodern theorists are certainly correct in saying that the 'new' divisions in British society – ethnicity, gender, age, lifestyle – deserve the serious attention of sociologists. But as Marshall (1997) points out, only empirical research can determine whether these divisions are more or less important than class differences. Anyway, as Westergaard (1995) observes, these 'new' divisions are always connected to class in some way. For example, many of the disadvantages suffered by women and ethnic minorities are essentially 'class' matters of income, wealth and power.

Marshall (1997) maintains that the pronouncements of postmodern theorists rest on 'data free' sociology. He argues that they tend to proceed by assertion rather than providing firm evidence that class is no longer important. Marshall scornfully notes that their disregard for evidence reduces sociology to the same status as New Age beliefs in reincarnation (ie a matter of subjective faith rather than objective proof). Marshall believes that if they paid more attention to empirical data they would realise that class remains a potent force. For example, Devine (1997) produces strong evidence that social class remains an important influence on people's life chances, collective identities and political actions.

Trains and cars Furlong and Cartmel (1997) accept that contemporary Britain resembles a postmodern society in important respects. Young people are growing up in a world quite different from the one experienced by previous generations. In the past, the metaphor of a railway journey captured the way young people's lives were shaped by social class. Within the school, working-class and middle-class children boarded different trains bound for different destinations. Once on the track, there was little opportunity to switch destinations or to change trains. Nowadays, in contrast, the journey from class origins to class destinations is more likely to be taken by car. In this new postmodern world, young people are constantly faced by choices and they have to make lots of individual decisions: Where shall I head? Which route shall I take? How many stops will I make? Consequently, young people often feel they have some control over their destiny, selecting their routes and steering their car as they choose. Nevertheless, Furlong and Cartmel maintain that class still imposes its influence on their journeys. Some people drive bigger, better and faster cars than others, and some have more petrol money to take them a further distance.

Class and social transformation

Savage (2000) is not convinced by the postmodernist argument that class is now outdated and irrelevant. On the contrary, he thinks class remains massively important. But he is equally unhappy with those who defend 'traditional' class analysis. In Savage's opinion, the theoretical legacy of Marx and Weber is more or less exhausted and it is time to move on. He feels too many class researchers have failed to appreciate the extent to which socio-economic change has transformed and restructured class relations. Indeed, he feels class research is currently facing a crisis – it has become too detached from debates about social inequality, and it has become so 'technical' that it is understood only by dedicated specialists.

So Savage steers a course between those who defend the traditional class approach and those who reject it entirely. His solution is to 'rescue', 'renew' or 'reposition' class analysis in various ways:

- Savage argues that class has been identified too closely with *occupational* groups. This neglects the importance of the *organisations* which employ people. Corporate organisations have undergone huge restructuring over recent decades, and people's fates have hinged on whether or not they occupy 'central' positions within

these organisations. These central positions may be taken up by manual workers as well as professionals and managers.
- He thinks class analysis must incorporate *culture* to a greater extent. Class is always tied up with identities and relationships with others. Savage regards Bourdieu's concept of cultural capital as valuable for exploring the intimate link between culture and class.
- Savage recognises there has been a trend towards 'individualisation' but he does not regard this as signalling the death of class. Rather, he treats individualism as a mode of class identity. What is happening is that, as the nature of their jobs have changed, working-class people have been moving away from the old 'collective' forms towards the more 'individualised' forms typical of the middle class.

For Savage, Britain is not an especially class-conscious society – people do not usually have well-developed views about the class system, and they have no clear sense of their place within it. Nevertheless, the paradox is that, structurally, class is as important as ever, possibly even more important than it was 30 years ago. He claims there is abundant evidence to show that patterns of economic and social inequality are marked in Britain, and that it makes good sense to see them in terms of class. Savage (2000) wishes to reclaim the study of economic inequality as an essential part of class analysis: 'If there is still a role for class analysis it is to continue to emphasise the brute realities of social inequality'.

summary

1. Slavery, feudalism and the caste system are some of the major forms of stratification. Social class is the main form of stratification in capitalist societies.

2. Capitalist societies create structural inequalities between different social classes. As long as these inequalities persist, they prevent equality of opportunity since some classes face greater obstacles than others.

3. Some sociologists (eg Saunders) argue that what matters most in reaching final class destinations is ability and effort rather than class of origin.

4. Others argue that SAD – the social advantages and disadvantages of class – have a major influence on final class destinations.

5. Marxism is a conflict theory. It sees a basic conflict of interest between the two main classes in capitalist society – the (ruling) bourgeoisie and the (subject) proletariat.

6. Marx believed that class polarisation, alienation and economic crises would lead to the downfall of capitalism and result in a classless society – communism.

7. Marx has been criticised for what some see as economic determinism. Neo-Marxists tend to put more emphasis on culture and political power.

8. According to Weber, the stratification system in capitalist

society is made up of three main components – class, status and party. Often, but not always, these overlap. For example, members of the upper class often belong to high status groups.

9. Weber's concept of social closure has proved useful when studying how groups create, maintain and defend their privileges.

10. Davis and Moore argue that stratification is a universal and functionally necessary part of all societies. It ensures the most functionally important positions are filled by the most able candidates.

11. Many postmodernists argue that the growing diversity, freedom and choice in today's society have led to a decline in the significance of class – a decline which may well lead to the death of class. Lifestyles, values, gender and ethnicity are steadily replacing class as a basis for identity.

12. While there may be something to this view, there is considerable evidence to show that class still exerts a major influence on people's life chances and lifestyles.

13. Savage argues that socio-economic change has transformed the class structure. This requires changes in 'traditional' class analysis – for example, more emphasis on cultural capital.

Unit 9 Gender and inequality

keyissues

1. How do the different versions of feminism explain gender inequality?

2 What are their strengths and weaknesses?

It was the emergence of the women's movement in the 1960s and 1970s which fired the imagination of sociologists and inspired them to treat gender as a major dimension of stratification. The women's movement demonstrated the importance of gender divisions in society and it highlighted certain conflicts of interests between men and women. For example, some activists argued that Britain was a *patriarchal society* in which men dominated and exploited women. The women's movement aimed to change the balance of power and secure equal rights and freedoms for women. Their demands included equal pay for equal work, and equal job and educational opportunities.

9.1 Feminism

The movement of the 1960s was powered by women who defined themselves as feminists. There are different versions of feminism but Radcliffe Richards (1982) suggests it is basically a movement for the elimination of gender-based injustices. Most feminists share the assumption that women are disadvantaged in comparison with men. In addition, they normally subscribe to the view that these inequalities are not the direct result of natural differences between men and women. Rather, they are socially constructed. Put another way, sex has to be distinguished from gender.

Sex refers to the biological differences between males and females. Gender, on the other hand, is about cultural differences. Most societies seem to assume that there are basic differences in masculine and feminine temperaments and behaviour, and so they socialise men and women into their respective gender roles. For example, men are more likely to be allocated to breadwinner roles and women to childcare roles. Feminists usually regard these gender differences as socially constructed and socially maintained, and so they say they can be changed. One of the tasks of the women's movement was to challenge all the common gender assumptions and stereotypes, as a necessary first step towards creating a more egalitarian society.

Although feminists agree on many things, there are some sharp divisions between the various 'schools' of feminist thought. Sometimes these schools offer diverging accounts of gender inequalities and propose rather different types of solutions. It is instructive, then, to look at the particular arguments of some major feminist approaches – liberal, socialist and radical.

Liberal feminism

Liberal feminists seek equal rights with men. They argue that people should be treated according to their individual merits (talent, effort etc) rather than on the basis of their sex. Women should be allowed to compete freely with men and they should enjoy the same privileges and opportunities. So liberal feminists campaign for the removal of all those social, economic, political or legal obstacles which deny women the same freedom of choice as men.

Liberal feminism has been highly successful in its campaigns for achieving equality of opportunity between men and women. Legislation has been passed on issues such as equal pay, sexual discrimination and the right to maternity leave. However, liberal feminists argue that gender inequalities still persist. Reasons for this include lingering prejudice (eg cultural stereotypes about the proper roles for males and females) and continuing discrimination in the workplace (eg employers are not always family-friendly: many of them insist on long or unsociable hours at work). Another problem is occupational segregation. Although liberal feminists celebrate the huge strides made by girls in gaining educational qualifications, they complain that all too often this is not followed by the expected occupational success. Too many young women end up in dead-end jobs.

Dual labour market This theory, developed by Barron and Norris (1976), fits in well with liberal feminist explanations of gender inequality. The basic idea is that the labour market can be considered as consisting of two sectors, one much more attractive than the other. Barron and Norris claim that the *primary sector* emerges because employers need to provide superior conditions if they are to attract and retain skilled workers. The theory sees men as concentrated in the primary sector (skilled labour, sound training, high job security, good pay and promotion prospects) while women are mainly confined to the *secondary sector* (with the opposite characteristics).

The dual labour market theory is open to a number of criticisms.

- It is not at all certain that the contemporary labour market can be neatly divided into two clear-cut sectors. In the age of 'flexibility' the labour market has become much more fragmented and complex. Rather than a dual labour market, economists prefer to talk of a 'segmented labour market'.

- It exaggerates the extent to which the two sectors coincide with gender divisions. Women have always been found in both sectors, and their representation in the 'better' jobs has improved over the last few decades.

- It lacks a detailed account of why it is women who come to fill the positions in the secondary sector. Barron and Norris suggested, rather unconvincingly, that it might have something to do with their weak connection with trade unions.

Marxist/socialist feminism

Socialist and Marxist feminists share the view that capitalism is bad for men and women. They see it as an exploitative system which creates huge class inequalities. However, as feminists they recognise that the struggle is not just against capitalism but also against sexism and patriarchy. Although conventional Marxism explains why there is class inequality in capitalist society, it does not go far enough in explaining why sexual discrimination persists. Indeed, some early Marxists thought patriarchy would fade away as capitalism developed. So socialist/ Marxist feminists stress the need to look at gender as well as class factors. They argue that the emergence of capitalism altered the relations between men and women. Capitalism is a competitive system which sets people against each other. Under capitalism, men try to gain control over women in various ways – employers treat women as a *reserve army of labour* to be hired and fired at will; male workers try to exclude females from their trades and crafts; and husbands exploit their wives' unpaid housework.

Class differences One of the strengths of the socialist/Marxist approach is its emphasis upon class divisions. Other feminists often neglect the importance of class. Indeed, Skeggs (1997) accuses many feminists of advancing 'individualist' values and neglecting the constant influence of class in women's lives. There are class differences *between* women and this means they do not all enjoy the same incomes, lifestyles or aspirations. The life chances of the female pharmacist or lawyer are much better than those of the female factory worker or office cleaner. Indeed, in the opinion of one feminist sociologist: 'Women's opportunities have widened, but class differences between women are more powerful than any gender-based similarities' (Delamont, 2001).

Reserve army of labour Marx's theory of the reserve army of labour has been one of the main influences on socialist/Marxist feminists. According to Marx, the reserve army is used by capitalists to suppress workers' demands for higher wages during economic booms when there is a high demand for labour. In that case, capitalists simply recruit extra workers from the reserve army of unemployed people, and this expansion in the labour force helps to keep wages low. When the economy becomes depressed again these extra workers can be sacked and returned to the reserve army in waiting. So the reserve army allows capitalists to protect their profits through boom and bust.

Feminists have taken this theory further by arguing that in the modern world it is mainly women who fill the ranks of the reserve army. Also, socialist/Marxist feminists have moved away from Marx's purely economic explanation by adding some cultural explanations. Married women are often regarded as 'secondary' workers whose main responsibility is to home and children. This 'familist' ideology helps to explain their key role in the reserve army.

As Freedman (2001) notes, married women are 'supposed' to be dependent on their husband's wages and to give priority to their home responsibilities, so this should make them more willing to leave employment if demand drops.

Freedman accepts that the reserve army explanation is 'theoretically appealing' but its crucial failing is that it is not supported by empirical evidence. There is little evidence that women are in fact more likely than men to leave the workforce during economic recession. The ideology of familism is less convincing in an age when many women follow continuous career patterns throughout their working lives.

Radical feminism

Radical feminists believe there is a basic conflict between all men and all women. The main enemy of women is *patriarchy* – 'the combination of social, economic and cultural systems which ensures male supremacy' (Coote & Campbell, 1982). Women could almost be considered a separate class – 'radical feminists argue that women have shared interests because they are all exploited and oppressed by men. Women, then, are said to form a class that is in conflict with another class – men' (Abbott & Wallace, 1990). Men use their collective power to ensure that society is run in their interests. They seize most of the material rewards and social privileges and they inflict physical and sexual violence on women.

Men also exercise control over cultural attitudes and this means they are able to justify their dominance by convincing people that it is natural – it is just 'the way things are'. Many radical feminists agree that there are natural differences between the sexes (ie males and females think, feel and act differently) but they do not accept that male domination is inevitable. Some radical feminists advocate 'separatism' – women can free themselves from patriarchal control by cutting themselves off (sexually and socially) from men.

Patriarchy Some critics are unhappy about the tendency for radical feminists to accept that there are natural differences in temperament and behaviour between men and women. But the main criticism of the radical feminist approach is its reliance on the concept of patriarchy. It is true that many feminists use this term in a loose sense to describe the greater privileges and power of men. But radical feminists tend to adopt a rather rigid and exaggerated view of patriarchy. Rowbotham (1979) has criticised this view on a number of grounds.

- It implies that nothing has really changed over the years (men have always ruled). Yet this overlooks significant historical shifts in male-female relationships. Indeed, Morgan (1996) suggests that the term patriarchy should be replaced by the more flexible concept of sexual stratification.

- It is too one-sided, suggesting that men exercise fixed power over women in all areas of life. This overlooks the possibility of women having greater power or at least equality in some social areas.

- It perpetuates a negative image of men as eternal monsters, bullies, oppressors. This image is unfair and unhelpful.
- It suggests one cause (patriarchy) for women's subordination and a separate cause (capitalism) for men's exploitation. But gender and class cannot be separated so easily.

Dual/triple radical/socialist

These theories were developed by Sylvia Walby (1986, 1990) in an attempt to combine the insights of socialist and radical feminists.

Dual class In her earlier work, Walby (1986) argued that married women occupy a *dual class* position. One class position is formed in the *domestic mode of production*, where husbands and wives constitute separate classes (since husbands exploit the domestic labour of their wives). But women also work in the capitalist mode of production, where class is determined by particular work and employment situations. And whereas 'husbands' and 'wives' form separate classes (in the domestic mode), this is not true of 'men' and 'women' (in the capitalist mode). The capitalist system *divides* women according to their respective social classes. It also *unites* men and women within each class. These two systems – domestic and capitalist – interact in the lives of women.

Triple system In a later work, Walby (1990) identifies three interacting systems – racism, capitalism and patriarchy. But the main difference is that she now places the major emphasis on patriarchy, which she defines as 'a system of social structures and practices in which men dominate, oppress and exploit women' (Walby, 1990). Walby describes patriarchal relations as existing in six interacting 'structures' – domestic life, employment, state policies, male violence against women, sexuality and cultural institutions (eg media, education, religion). Walby dismisses some of the criticisms which have been levelled at the concept of patriarchy. She insists it can take account of class and race variations and she recognises that it changes over time. It has changed in *degree*: improvements in women's educational and employment opportunities have lessened the intensity of patriarchy. It has also changed in *form*: the main site of women's oppression has shifted from the 'private' household to the more 'public' spheres of employment, culture and the state.

According to Freedman (2001), the dual or triple systems approach has the advantage that it does not seek one simple overarching explanation of women's subordination. Rather, it treats capitalism, patriarchy and racism as linked but interacting systems, each making a difference. This recognition of complexity is to be welcomed. Nevertheless, Freedman points out that the dual/triple approach actually widens rather than narrows the search for the basis of women's disadvantage. It raises as many questions as it answers.

activity24 women as a class

Item A New feminism

Girls are doing better than boys at school. More women are in paid work than men. We have seen women become Prime Minister, head of MI5 and Director of Public Prosecutions. We see young female singers talking gleefully about girl power and women taking control of all aspects of their lives – suing employers for discrimination, bringing up children on their own, or deciding not to have children at all.

So is there still a need for a movement for women's rights? I believe the answer is yes. Women are still poorer and less powerful than men. More women than men live on benefits. Women still suffer abuse and violence at the hands of men. Women are still a tiny minority in the British establishment. And women may be working more, but they are still not reaping the rewards: working women are paid less than men.

Adapted from Walter, 1998

Stella Rimington, former head of MI5

Item B Class difference

Class profiles, United Kingdom, 1997-98 (percentages)

	Professional	Managerial technical	Skilled non-manual	Skilled manual	Partly skilled manual	Unskilled manual
Women	2	19	25	6	13	5
Men	7	24	9	25	13	4

Adapted from *Social Focus on Women and Men* EOC/ONS, 1998

questions

1 Using Item A, identify two reasons why there is still a need for a women's movement.

2 Using Item B, outline two differences in the class profiles of men and women.

3 Using Items A and B, give two reasons why it is difficult to decide whether women are disadvantaged compared with men.

4 Assess the view that women should be seen as a class.

9.2 Choice or constraint?

There are many competing explanations of gender inequality but most of them fall into two broad camps – *choice* and *constraint*. Some explanations place much more emphasis on one side than the other, although it is possible to combine them in an overall explanation.

Constraints

This model argues that society imposes unfair constraints on women and this limits their opportunities and life chances. First, men still expect women to shoulder the main burden of childcare and domestic responsibilities, so women may be forced into part-time work in order to juggle home responsibilities with work. Second, women have often been marginalised in the workplace. In the past, men have used their collective power to resist the entry of women into certain crafts (eg printing) or professions (eg medicine). Although legal barriers have now been eliminated, certain workplaces are still unfriendly to women. For example, the 'long hours culture', and the lack of creches, put the mothers of young children at a disadvantage. Third, further pressure is put on women by the prevailing ideology that men are the 'real' breadwinners and women are the 'real' homemakers. Although this ideology is much weaker now than in the past, it still plays a role in shaping women's attitudes, ambitions and behaviour.

The constraint model draws attention to the many obstacles which stand in the way of women achieving full equality and a fair deal in the workplace. One of the most formidable of these obstacles is women's responsibility for housework.

Housework

It seems that increasing numbers of households – especially 'dual career' ones, where both partners work – are paying others to do some of their domestic chores. There is a whole army of domestic helps, au pairs, window cleaners, nannies, even dog-walkers, who rent out their services to tend to other people's children, pets or homes. But most cooking, cleaning, childcare and routine maintenance within households is still performed by the household members themselves. This housework or 'domestic labour' has a number of characteristic features:

- It is not normally regarded as 'real' work since it is unpaid. It is outside the 'formal' economy of wages and taxes.
- It makes a major 'hidden' contribution to the economic welfare of a country. Just imagine what it would cost if a price were placed on all the services given freely in housework.
- It is demanding and time consuming. Convenience foods and labour-saving devices (washing machines, microwaves etc) may have taken some of the drudgery out of housework but it still requires time, energy and patience. Much of it involves routine tasks which have to be repeated again and again.

- There are broad gender differences in housework. For example, housework by men often takes the form of 'helping out' rather than a regular and normal role. Also, men tend to do specialised tasks (household repairs, DIY) and the more pleasant tasks (playing with children rather than changing nappies).

Measuring the housework gap The broad picture of gender inequalities in housework and childcare is pretty clear but there are methodological difficulties in measuring the exact 'gap'. First of all, people may disagree on what constitutes housework. Does it include reading the children a bedtime story, or pottering around in the garden? Leonard (2000) gives one example – women tend to underestimate time spent on child care, while men overestimate it (eg any time spent with children is defined by them as childcare). Also, some studies rely on people's estimates of the time they spend on housework, but their perceptions may not correspond to the reality. Gershuny (1997) notes that different results are obtained if people are asked to keep 'time-use' diaries noting the precise amount of time spent on household chores in a typical week. Even so, recording the time spent on particular tasks is problematic, since people, particularly women, often juggle several tasks at once. Moreover, the diary approach can be criticised for missing out the 'meanings' of tasks (eg the difference between urgent and non-urgent tasks, and between providing help and taking responsibility).

Housework time British Household Panel Survey findings show that men are getting more involved in things like washing up, supermarket shopping and childcare. But household chores are seldom split evenly, although the actual division of labour depends on the particular circumstances of the household. In 2003, BHPS data revealed that, on average, women do about 19 hours of housework a week, compared with 5.5 hours for men. If a woman is part-time and her partner full time, she still spends about 13 hours more than him on housework. But where both partners are in employment they end up working (paid and unpaid) almost the same total amount of time, but with men spending more time in paid work and women in domestic tasks. Indeed, Sullivan (2000) observes

Table 14 *Hours of paid and unpaid work per week (where both husband and wife are employed full-time). Based on diaries kept by couples.*

	1975		1997	
	husband	wife	husband	wife
Paid work	45	36	41	33
Unpaid work	12	25	15	24
All work	57	61	56	57
wife's % of unpaid work	68		62	
wife's % of all work	52		50	

Adapted from Gershuny, 1997

Table 15 Household tasks and gender, Great Britain, 1999

Minutes per person per day	Men	Women
Cooking, washing up	30	74
Cleaning house, tidying	13	58
Gardening, pet care	48	21
Caring for/playing with children	20	45
Maintenance, odd jobs, DIY	26	9
Clothes washing, ironing, sewing	2	25
All	138	232

Adapted from *Social Trends*, 2001

that about one third of full-time employed men actually spend longer overall than their female partner on domestic tasks!

Childcare An EOC report, *Working Fathers* (2003), states that fathers in the United Kingdom carry out about one third of all childcare. The amount of time fathers spend with their children rose from less than 15 minutes on an average weekday in the mid-1970s to 2 hours a day by the late 1990s. At weekends it rises even further to an average of 6 hours each day. Nevertheless, the main burden of childcare tends to fall on women. This unequal division of labour has serious implications for women's work participation, especially when the children are young. For example, the EOC (2002) found that women whose youngest child is aged under 5 have an employment rate of 54%, compared with 70% for women whose youngest child is 5-10 years, and 77% for women whose dependent children are aged 11 or over.

Unequal but fair? Baxter (2000) reports the puzzling findings of a national Australian survey on the division of labour in the home. Although women in the sample did the bulk of the housework, about 59% of these women (and 68% of men) regarded this as 'fair'. Baxter suggests this was because the division of tasks was considered to be more important than the actual time spent on them. Women seemed to be grateful for the 'symbolic value' of men doing some traditionally 'feminine' tasks. Against a background where housework is treated as women's work, any contribution the men made was appreciated, and this took some of the sting out of the unfair allocation of housework time. Another possible interpretation is that loyal women do not like to moan about their partner to some nosy sociologist! Or perhaps those women who resented an unequal division of housework had already left the nest?

Choices

By contrast, the choices model states that women nowadays have genuine freedom to choose their own destinies. Many of the obstacles to women's full participation in work have been removed by legislation,

and by changing social norms and changes in the workplace itself. So women are increasingly able to make a free and 'rational' choice. Yet many of them still decide to give priority to childcare rather than to their careers. Quite simply, there are broad gender differences in orientations towards work. It is these differences in attitudes and aspirations which explain the different occupational profiles of men and women. This *rational choice* or *preferences* model is most famously associated with the work of Catherine Hakim.

The Hakim debate

Feminist sociologists have helped to demolish many of the old myths about women and work. Myths such as 'a woman's place is firmly in the home' or 'women are incapable of doing men's jobs' have slowly toppled one after the other. However, Catherine Hakim (1995) accuses feminists of inventing their own myths about women's work attitudes and behaviour. She claims that empirical research has exposed five 'feminist myths' about women's employment (see Table 16). This has provoked critical replies (eg Ginn et al., 1996) and the controversy shows every sign of continuing far beyond these early exchanges (eg Crompton & Harris, 1998; Hakim, 2000).

Hakim contends that men and women really do have different work orientations – 'all the available research evidence shows that, even by the 1990s, the majority of women in Britain...did not seek continuous lifetime careers but continued to give priority, to varying degrees, to family activities' (Hakim, 1997). Hakim concedes that some women, usually the most highly educated, are strongly committed to full-time work. These women favour 'symmetrical' roles in which responsibilities for home and work are shared equally between men and women. But Hakim maintains that between half and two thirds of adult women still hold 'traditional' views (that is, they accept some sexual division of labour). As a result, their commitment to work is weaker than men's. Some of these women choose to give up work, at least for a period, in order to concentrate on their family responsibilities. Others prefer to take part-time work, a decision which reflects their traditional views – 'The majority of part-timers regard breadwinning as the *primary* (but not exclusive) responsibility of men, and see women as secondary earners whose *primary* (but not exclusive) responsibility is domestic work and homemaking' (Hakim, 1996).

Evaluation Ginn et al. (1996) disagree with Hakim on a number of points. They suggest it is an over-simplification to divide women into two more or less distinct groups with clear-cut values (traditional and symmetrical). There is likely to be considerable overlap between these groups, especially since most women have to juggle with the competing demands of work and family. Also, attitudes towards work fluctuate over time and so the divisions are not fixed. But their main criticism of Hakim is that she offers no convincing explanation of why women are still disadvantaged in employment. They accuse Hakim of treating gender inequalities in pay, working conditions and

activity25 caring

Item A The price of sex

The little baby girl lying in the maternity ward beside the baby boy will pay a heavy price for her sex. Over the course of a lifetime, the cost of being female in Britain is nearly 50% less income than a male. There is no mystery behind the biggest cause of the pay gap. It is women's caring responsibilities that cripple their achievements in the labour market and expose them to the risk of poverty when relationships break down. Women surge ahead in their careers in their 20s but then, after the first child, their working patterns diverge from those of men. They cut back their careers, don't apply for promotions, change their jobs and opt for work they can fit round their children's lives. They take time out of the job market, they lose confidence and skills, and when they go back to work after several years they typically drop three or four skill levels.

In the 1990s, many women have responded by taking part-time work. But this 'mummy track' brings fewer promotion prospects, less interesting work, and a pay gap double that for full-time work.

Adapted from Bunting, 2003

Item B Dividing the work

Minutes per day in cooking and cleaning, Great Britain (based on time-use diary data held by Institute for Social and Economic Research)

	manual/ clerical		professional/ technical	
	1975	1997	1975	1997
Men				
Both full-time	19	29	30	43
Husband full-time and wife part-time	15	28	18	24
Husband full-time and wife not employed	12	18	18	37
Women				
Both full-time	141	93	135	98
Husband full-time and wife part time	208	167	218	146
Husband full-time and wife not employed	256	182	235	162

Adapted from Sullivan, 2000

questions

1 Using Item A, identify two ways in which caring responsibilities interfere with women's careers.
2 Using Item B, outline one example of the difference class makes, and one example of the difference working part time makes.
3 Give two reasons why it is difficult to measure housework time and the allocation of tasks.

career prospects as little more than a reflection of individual attitudes. By placing so much stress on attitudes and orientations, Hakim seems to end up 'blaming the victim'. The implication seems to be that if women are not working, or are trapped in part-time jobs, then it's their own fault – since they are free agents who make their own choices.

Ginn et al. offer an alternative explanation. They argue that women's attitudes to work are largely shaped by the wider social context, a context where male employers discriminate against women, governments provide poor childcare options, and where there are powerful cultural expectations that women will give priority to their families. These pressures place limits on the real choices available to women and force many of them to scale down their work ambitions.

Responding to these criticisms, Hakim has denied that she divides women into two polarised groups. She also allows for an intermediate group ('adaptives' or 'drifters') whose views on work may change as they gain more experience in the workplace. She concedes that women's attitudes are changing but she believes they are doing so much more slowly than feminists imagine. Furthermore,

Hakim denies that non-working or part-time women are always 'victims' – most of them seem reasonably content with the choices they have made. Hakim accuses her feminist critics of arrogance in assuming that they know what is in the best interests of other women.

It is not easy to resolve the Hakim debate. The main difference between Hakim and her critics is their different interpretations of research findings. But the debate raises a number of tricky methodological issues.

- Both sides support their arguments by drawing on a huge body of statistical data and survey findings. But some of the available evidence is contradictory and this leads each side to accuse the other of selecting the most convenient evidence for its case.

- Some of the evidence suffers from technical limitations. For example, 'snapshot' attitude surveys may show that, at a given point of time, older women hold more 'traditional' views than younger women. But only long-term research can show whether this is because of generational effects (younger women have grown up in a more egalitarian age) or life-cycle effects (perhaps women become more conservative as they grow older or have children).

- Delamont (2001) points out that Hakim (like her critics) relies mainly on large-scale survey data. It is not always clear from these studies whether respondents are stating what they think are *ideal* patterns (what ought to be happening) or what actually happens (what they do). People may say one thing and do another, according to the particular circumstances of their lives.

Table 16 The Hakim debate

Myth 1 Women's employment has been rising.

Hakim There has been little or no change in the overall hours worked by women. Although more women have joined the workforce, there has been a shift from full-time to part-time work.

Critics The number of women employed is more significant than the overall 'volume' of hours. When women participate (full-time or part-time) in the workforce, this inevitably has an effect on their attitudes and lives.

Myth 2 Women's work commitment is the same as men's.

Hakim On average, women are still less committed to work than men and this is especially the case for non-working women and part-time working women.

Critics Commitment is not a constant, fixed thing. If women had better employment opportunities and childcare arrangements, then they would be more enthusiastic about full-time work.

Myth 3 Childcare problems are the main barrier to women's employment.

Hakim It all depends on women's priorities. Poor childcare facilities have not prevented large numbers of women from combining full-time work with family responsibilities. But lots of women choose not to work, or to work part-time.

Critics Where women state a preference for non-working or part-time work, this must be seen in the context of family demands on their time and the high cost of childcare arrangements. It is hardly a 'free' choice.

Myth 4 Part-time jobs are low quality.

Hakim It is no longer true that part-time jobs are not 'real' jobs, or that they are exploited and marginalised. Anyway, part-timers often prefer convenience factors over good pay and promotion prospects. Part-time workers have the highest rate of job satisfaction.

Critics The expressed satisfaction of part-timers is likely to reflect their lack of alternatives and their weak bargaining position with employers because of their domestic responsibilities. Part-time work still carries certain marked disadvantages, such as lower pay.

Myth 5 There is no gender difference in labour turnover.

Hakim Women are less stable workers, with higher absenteeism and turnover rates. This is not just a reflection of the types of jobs they do. Women's work orientations are different, and employers have had to provide part-time jobs in order to attract women into the workforce.

Critics Higher turnover and absenteeism rates are not a result of different orientations to work. They may reflect the types of jobs women do. Also, women's continuing childcare responsibilities force them to take time off or stop work.

---

activity26 making choices

Item A Adapting

Charles and James (2003) conducted qualitative interviews with 55 women and 56 men in South Wales. The sample consisted of manual and routine non-manual workers employed in a manufacturing firm, a retail store and a public sector organisation. The findings indicate that orientations to work are highly complex. For example, part-timers (male and female) may be just as committed to work as full-timers. Also, some women who are the main breadwinners in their family may nevertheless subscribe to the ideology of the male breadwinner.

Most of the people in the sample fell into Hakim's 'adaptive' category – their attitudes seemed to shift according to circumstances. These include job insecurity (this can reduce work commitment), changing domestic circumstances (flexibility at work becomes more important when people take on caring responsibilities at home) and stage in the life cycle (eg some older respondents with poor promotion prospects become less work-centred).

Overall, most men and women did not have work as a central life interest. Rather, they were home and family-centred. But men were more likely to express this through taking home a wage (that is the way they 'cared' for their family). Women, on the other hand, were more likely to keep their work identities separate from their home identities.

Adapted from Charles & James, 2003

Item B Changing attitudes

Percentages *disagreeing* with the statement: *A husband's job is to earn the money; a wife's job is to look after the home and the children*

	1984	1989	1991	1994	1998
Men	45	46	42	57	80
Women	41	58	48	61	83
Employed women	59	78	66	77	(no data)

Adapted from various British Social Attitudes surveys

Item C Choice or constraint?

questions

1 Using Item A, identify two factors which affect attitudes to work.

2 Using Item B, outline two trends in attitudes towards gender roles.

3 Using Items A, B and C, give two reasons why it is difficult to measure orientations towards work.

4 Briefly outline and assess choice and constraint explanations for gender differences in work.

9.3 Postfeminist approaches

Gender differences in the workplace were described in Unit 3. It was noted there that many gender inequalities have been reduced and women are now better placed as workers than ever before. Women have already made deep inroads into 'male' areas such as management and the professions, and Roberts (2001) concludes that 'the days of the trail-blazing pioneers are over'. These changes have been accompanied by the rise of *postfeminism* which attempts to make sense of the new gender landscape.

The term postfeminism refers to the new ideas and directions which emerged in the late 1980s and 1990s. For some, it suggests that the women's movement has moved beyond ('post') its original themes and interests to develop new, but still recognisably feminist, ideas. For others, however, postfeminism represents a rejection of all feminist values! So it is a term which can easily lead to confusion since it is used in a number of conflicting ways.

- **The end of feminism** Although many women support the gender reforms of the past few decades, they may feel that equality has at last been achieved. A survey by Sianne and Wilkinson (1995) found that the younger generation of women (aged 18-35) tends to view the gender war as outdated and few of them identify themselves as feminists.

- **A backlash against feminism** Faludi (1992) warns that women's rights are being threatened by a media backlash which spreads scare stories about feminism (eg career women are alleged to miss out on the joys of marriage and motherhood). However, Oakley and Mitchell (1998) question whether there really has been a systematic backlash against women's rights in Britain.

- **Power feminism** This is postfeminist in the sense that, unlike earlier feminism, it no longer treats women as perpetual victims. For example, Wolf (1993) urges women to stop presenting themselves as victims and start celebrating their new found 'girl power'. Equal opportunity has more or less been achieved.

- **Difference feminism** Feminists in the 1960s and 1970s stressed the common 'sisterhood' which unites all women. Postfeminists, by contrast, are much more interested in differences between women. For example, postmodern feminists deny that there is a common

'essence' to women – the individual differences between women are just as striking as the differences between men and women. Postmodernists argue that people have been released from stereotyped gender roles and this gives them greater freedom to choose their own personal lifestyles and identities.

- **New feminism** This term is applied to those feminists (eg Walter, 1998a) who argue that feminism has no right to tell women how to run their private lives. Rather, it confines itself to campaigning on 'public' issues such as material inequalities (eg gender differences in earnings, wealth and career opportunities). Although it accepts that equal rights legislation has been introduced into the workplace, it claims that women still suffer multiple injustices both in the work sphere and in wider public affairs.

The bewildering varieties of postfeminism make it difficult to tie them to a specific explanation. Some postfeminists think gender equality has been won and so there is nothing left to explain! The 'new feminists', by contrast, still draw on many of the explanations already covered in this unit. As for the 'difference feminists', they move away from comparisons between men and women towards a new kind of issue – the differences between women themselves. Indeed, one of the main contributions of postfeminism is its discovery of fresh problems. One of these is the claim that perhaps it is men who are today's 'victims'.

A male crisis?

Some years ago Tolson (1977) identified a *crisis of masculinity* in Britain. He argued that the 'heroic' image of the male breadwinner was less convincing in an age of high male unemployment. Faced with rising challenges to their traditional privileges and responsibilities, many males were confused and unsure of their 'proper' roles and identities. This idea of a male crisis seemed more and more plausible as the 20th century moved on. In the 1990s, many fears were voiced about the growing problem of the 'redundant male'. Young working-class men, it was predicted, would become increasingly marginalised in a feminised world where most jobs no longer required physical strength. Middle-class men, too, looked under some threat, as employers declared that the new service economy needed 'feminine' skills. Women were supposedly more 'people-friendly' and they possessed the sensitive management and communication skills required for the modern world of work. A number of commentators treated these predictions as little more than scare stories, but others thought there were signs of a genuine shift in the balance of gender power.

Sacred cows Ros Coward (1999) attacks the 'sacred cows' of feminism. She believes that feminists are wrong to insist that female oppression is just as bad as it ever was. Coward accepts that there are still specific areas of injustice or unfairness (eg lack of equal pay). But she rejects the idea that there is an over-arching patriarchal system, with men always advantaged and women disadvantaged. There were profound changes in men's lives in the 1990s. They suffered high unemployment, they were further threatened by the steady feminisation of the economy, and girls caught up with then surpassed boys in educational performance. So the idea of a male crisis may well be exaggerated but it cannot be dismissed lightly. Consequently, Coward says it is no longer appropriate to treat women's problems as greater or more pressing than men's. Social changes are creating a new 'gender landscape' and it is one in which men are just as likely as women to emerge as casualties.

key terms

Sex Biological differences between males and females.
Gender Cultural differences between masculine and feminine temperaments, behaviour and attitudes.
Patriarchy Rule by men.
Sexism Treating men and women differently, when gender is not relevant or appropriate.
Feminism A movement for the elimination of gender-based injustices and inequalities.
Dual labour market The idea that there are two labour markets – the primary sector with skilled jobs, high job security, good pay and promotion prospects in which men are concentrated, and the secondary sector with the opposite characteristics in which women are mainly confined.
Reserve army of labour A large number of people outside the main labour market who can be hired when demand for labour is high and fired when demand is low.
Dual class position The idea that women have two class positions, one deriving from their position in the home, the other from their position in the paid labour market.
Crisis of masculinity The idea that many men are facing a crisis in their masculine identity, largely as a result of changes in the labour market.

summary

1. Liberal feminists seek equal rights and opportunities with men. They see a dual labour market with men concentrated in high-skilled jobs with good pay and promotion prospects. Critics argue that the labour market is more complex than this.

2. Socialist and Marxist feminists see capitalism as the major cause of gender inequality. Women are the main occupants of a reserve army of labour which can be drawn on when demand for labour is high and refilled when demand is low. Critics argue that there is little evidence to support this view.

3. Radical feminists argue that there is a basic conflict of interest between men and women, and that women are exploited and oppressed by patriarchy. Critics argue that this view is too sweeping and one-sided, and that it takes little account of social change.

4. Walby argues for a triple systems approach, seeing capitalism, patriarchy and racism each contributing to gender inequality.

5. Explanations of gender inequality tend to fall into two broad categories – constraint and choice.

6. The constraint model argues that society places unjustified constraints on women which limit their opportunities – for example, the demands of housework.

7. The choice model argues that gender differences nowadays are largely a matter of choice. Critics argue that this view ignores the power of cultural expectations which limit women's work ambitions.

8. The term postfeminism has a confusing range of meanings – for example, some postfeminists argue that women have now won equality, others reject the idea that all women should be lumped into a single category since they see important differences between women.

9. Gender inequality is now seen as a problem for many men as well as women.

Unit 10 Ethnicity and inequality

key issues

1 What are the main explanations for ethnic inequality?

2 What are their strengths and weaknesses?

The Parekh Report (2000) urged Britain to officially declare itself a multicultural, multi-ethnic society, as the ethnic composition of the country has been transformed since the 1950s by successive waves of migrants from New Commonwealth countries (eg Jamaica, India, Pakistan). Many of their children and grandchildren, born and raised in Britain, continue the ethnic traditions of their communities. As a result, Britain is not only a 'community of individuals', it is also a 'community of communities'.

The Parekh Report welcomed this cultural diversity and cultural enrichment but it warned that social harmony was threatened by the evil of racism. Members of ethnic minorities too often find themselves the targets of racial discrimination. This is one of the reasons, but not the only one, for the patterns of economic disadvantage among ethnic minorities.

10.1 Terms

There is a great deal of confusion about the best terms for describing and classifying Britain's minority groups. Each term is based on a set of assumptions, some of which are highly suspect. This can be illustrated by looking at the most common terms: races, Black-White groups, ethnic groups, minorities and immigrants.

Table 17 UK population by ethnic group (percentages)

White	92.1
Mixed	1.2
Asian or Asian British	
Indian	1.8
Pakistani	1.3
Bangladeshi	0.5
Other Asian	0.4
Black or Black British	
Black Caribbean	1.0
Black African	0.8
Black other	0.2
Chinese	0.4
Other	0.4
Total minority population	7.9

Adapted from the 2001 census

Races This term classifies humans into separate racial types on the basis of their inherited biological and physical features. At one time, these physical differences were regarded as fixed and so the boundaries between 'pure' races were seen as permanent and rigid. Nowadays, however, the insights of genetics have exposed these fallacies. For instance, it makes little scientific sense to talk about separate races – there is great genetic diversity *within* so-called races and a great deal of overlap and continuity *between* them. Besides, genetic characteristics are constantly altering and mutating. This is not to deny the broad physical differences between human groups. Biological diversity is a reality – but it does not fall neatly into distinct 'races'. The idea of race, then, has little scientific or explanatory value.

Sociologists are interested mainly in the *social* or *folk* meanings of race (Banton, 1979). The physical features of race are not important in themselves – they enter into social life only if people think they are important and act on that belief. Banton uses the term *racialisation* to describe the way people 'frame' the social world in racial terms. People *construct* racial categories which they then impose on their own and other groups. Sometimes they draw the false conclusion that the moral and intellectual achievements of groups are a result of their physical features. These common sense views on race may be unscientific but clearly they have real consequences for the groups concerned.

Sociologists continue to use the term 'race' in its social sense, but usually they are more comfortable using it as an adjective (eg 'racial disadvantage' or 'racial discrimination') rather than a noun.

Black-White This classification, too, is based on a physical feature – skin colour. This is socially significant because people tend to be treated differently according to the colour of their skin. Britain's cultural heritage includes many negative images of Black people and so people with a dark skin are likely to be selected as targets for prejudice and discrimination.

One of the problems with this classification is the uncertainty about which groups are included in the 'Black' category. Does it include Chinese, or 'brown' groups such as South Asians? What about people of 'intermediate' appearance (eg Cypriots, Maltese, Arabs) or people of *mixed* parentage? Sometimes 'Black' refers only to African-Caribbean groups, and at other times it includes other minority groups (many of whom do not identify themselves as Black). In spite of these criticisms, the Black-White distinction is still widely used (eg the census refers to 'Whites' and to a 'Black' category which includes Africans and Caribbeans).

Ethnic groups Ethnic groups are identified according to their distinctive cultural features. The members of an ethnic group usually have a shared sense of history, a common cultural tradition and a collective identity. As the Parekh Report points out, all human beings (including Whites) belong to an ethnic group. In popular usage, however, the term is often reserved only for minorities

Ethnicity is an attractive concept for sociologists because it draws attention to cultural and social features. But it is not easy to allocate people to ethnic groups. Culture is sprawling and untidy and so it is difficult to map the boundaries where one culture ends and another begins. In practice, researchers are faced with a choice of 'marker'. Some choose to classify according to *territory* (eg country of origin) on the assumption that people from the same country will normally share a common culture. But many countries are culturally diverse. People from India, for example, may be Hindus, Sikhs or Muslims. Consequently, some sociologists think it is more sensible to classify according to dominant *culture* or *religion* rather than territory.

Minorities A minority is 'a group of people distinguished by physical or cultural characteristics, subject to different and unequal treatment by the society in which they live and who regard themselves as victims of collective discrimination' (Wirth, 1945). Sometimes minorities are actually a numerical majority, as in the case of the Black population in South Africa under apartheid. So we are dealing with issues of *power* as much as numbers. The idea of a minority implies the existence of a more powerful majority which manages to dominate or marginalise the minority.

In Britain, the term minority is normally used in a loose, imprecise way and it is usually interchangeable with other terms (Black, ethnic etc). A composite term which is becoming more popular is BME (Black and minority ethnic population). But the Parekh Report advises that minority should never be used in the sense of 'less important'.

Immigrants This is a controversial term. Often it is applied only to ethnic minorities, yet most migrants to this country are White and this has been the pattern for a long time. Another problem with the term immigrant is the way it is extended to *all* members of ethnic minorities. This is misleading, since many, and in some cases the majority, were born in this country.

Asylum-seekers are a special case. Unlike 'economic' migrants, they are refugees from persecution in their own countries and they have come to Britain to seek 'asylum' under the terms of the Geneva Convention.

10.2 Explaining racial disadvantage

Disadvantage The picture of ethnic minority disadvantage is fairly clear. Racial and ethnic minorities have higher rates of poverty and unemployment; they are more likely to live in poor quality housing in deprived areas; and they tend overall to have poorer health and educational attainment. Granted, it would be far too sweeping to describe all minorities as an underclass, and there are clear signs of progress in many areas. Also, we must recognise ethnic diversity – there are variations between each group as well as within them.

Multiple factors There are many factors to be taken into account when explaining racial disadvantage. Take, for example, the problem of explaining the higher unemployment rates among minorities. These rates could be a result of racial discrimination (eg employers refusing to recruit people from ethnic minorities). But they could also be a reflection of age differences – ethnic minorities have a younger age profile, and young people run a higher risk of unemployment. Or geography – minorities may be concentrated in those parts of Britain where industries are in decline. Or human capital – perhaps minorities have poorer qualifications and skills. So researchers have to work through the long list of potentially relevant factors in order to assess how much each of them contributes to the final explanation. But this is a difficult task. As Berthoud (2000) notes, all the relevant factors interact, and each factor may have a different outcome depending on the particular group concerned.

Theories Theories of ethnic disadvantage differ according to the factors they select as most important. There are many theories to choose from but the main distinction is between *structural* and *cultural explanations*. Structural approaches usually stress the importance of constraints and factors 'external' to the group concerned. These external factors include racial discrimination, class inequalities and the nature of the labour market. Cultural approaches, on the other hand, give greater attention to the 'internal' features of the group and to the choices they make. Internal features include things like lifestyles, cultural values and family patterns (eg South Asian groups tend to have large families, and African-Caribbean groups have a high rate of single-parent families).

In practice, the distinction between structural constraints and cultural choices can become rather blurred. For example, how do we explain the low economic participation rates of some groups of South Asian women? Is it a matter of choice – have they chosen to devote themselves to their families? Or a matter of constraint – have home responsibilities prevented them from finding suitable employment? In most cases, there is an ongoing interaction between structural and cultural factors, although one side may provide the bulk of the explanation.

In the following sections we consider four broad types of explanation – genetic, cultural, racial discrimination and structural. Some of these are highly controversial, as we shall see!

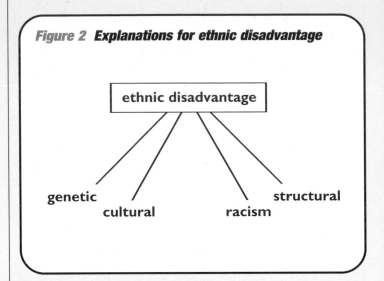

Figure 2 Explanations for ethnic disadvantage

10.3 Genetic explanations

This approach argues that there is a genetic basis for ethnic disadvantage. As such, it seems to mark a return to the old discredited 'race' theories which falsely claimed that the achievements of groups were a direct reflection of their physical and biological characteristics. One example is the work of Herrnstein and Murray (1994) who view 'racial' disadvantage as, at least in part, a reflection of inherited differences in intelligence. Basically, they say that the average IQ scores of Blacks are lower than those of Whites and this explains their relative lack of economic success. Herrnstein and Murray admit there are lots of methodological problems in measuring intelligence. How valid are IQ tests? Are they culturally biased? How can we measure the separate effects of heredity and environment, when in reality they interact? They also accept that there is a wide range of intelligence within every 'racial' group, and great overlap between them. But they nevertheless conclude that Black groups are, on average, less intelligent than Whites (and Asians) and this is why they are less successful.

Evaluation Criticisms of this genetic explanation are summarised by Fraser (1995). Some critics accuse Herrnstein and Murray of dabbling in science fiction rather than science. These critics are not convinced that Herrnstein and Murray are justified in placing such faith in IQ scores, and they remain sceptical that differences in intelligence can be attributed largely to heredity. Intelligence is the product of the *interaction* of heredity and

activity27 multiple factor explanations

Item A *Limitations of data*

Britain's ethnic minority population is extremely diverse, and the trends in education, employment and unemployment, health and housing are shaped not only by ethnicity, but also by gender, and possibly by class. Culture, neighbourhood and peer groups are all likely to have an influence. These factors mean that analytical work in this area is complex. There are also some notable gaps in the information available. There are often limitations in sample size and a lack of socio-economic information to enable thorough investigation of the variations between different ethnic minority groups. Indeed, even within ethnic groups, comparisons on a generational basis are problematised by a lack of data on immigration status, birthplace and length of residence within the UK.

Adapted from Cabinet Office, 2002

questions

1 Using Item A, identify two problems in interpreting ethnic data.
2 a) Summarise the data in Item B.
   b) Why is it important to hold a number of variables (factors) constant?
3 Why do many researchers argue for multiple factor explanations for ethnic disadvantage?

Item B *Male earnings*

The table below shows the weekly earnings of ethnic minority males compared to White males.

- The first line shows actual average earnings.
- The second line shows the gap between White earnings and those of various minority groups.
- The third line shows the gap in earnings when education is held constant – that is, when Whites and ethnic minorities with the same educational qualifications are compared.
- The fourth line shows the gap in earnings when a number of factors are held constant – that is, when Whites and ethnic minorities with the same educational attainment, age, migration status, social class and family structure are compared. This is the closest comparison of like with like.

Weekly male earnings

	White	African Caribbean	African	Indian	Pakistani/ Bangladeshi
Overall	£332	£217	£216	£327	£182
Gap		£115	£116	£5	£150
Gap, controlling for education		£105	£146	£13	£126
Gap, controlling for all variables		£81	£132	£23	£129

Adapted from Berthoud, 2000

environment, and so the nature of the environment has enormous significance for the outcome. Black people have a different (and often difficult) history and they are more likely than Whites to be raised in poor environments. So Herrnstein and Murray are not comparing like-for-like. Any improvement in the social and economic conditions of minority groups would result in a significant boost to their test scores.

Moreover, many critics feel it is mischievous and possibly even racist to suggest that intelligence runs along so-called racial lines. Given the great differences in measured intelligence within groups, and the enormous overlap between them, there is little support among social scientists for the idea that there is a direct link between 'race' and intelligence.

10.4 Cultural explanations

This approach suggests that a great deal of ethnic disadvantage can be explained in terms of the cultural origins and cultural values of ethnic minorities. Culture is seen to be relevant in a number of ways.

- Some ethnic minority groups may have language problems which reduce their chances of finding employment in Britain. Modood et al. (1997) found that three-fifths of Bangladeshi women, half of Pakistani women, and one fifth of Pakistani and Bangladeshi men did not speak English, or only limited English.
- Some patterns of disadvantage may stem from the cultural choices of ethnic groups. For example, Dahya (1974) argued that first-generation Pakistanis deliberately chose to live near each other in the inner city, partly in order to protect and maintain their cultures.
- The cultural traditions of certain ethnic groups may help to account for their economic activity rates. For example, the custom of *purdah* (seclusion of women) is one possible explanation for the low participation rates of South Asian women.
- Research suggests there is ethnic diversity both in education and in the workplace. The different success rates of ethnic groups may be a reflection of their particular cultural assets and traditions. For example, some groups seem to be more entrepreneurial than others.

Entrepreneurship

Members of ethnic minorities may sometimes be forced into setting up their own businesses because racial discrimination limits their opportunities for employment. However, some researchers suggest that certain ethnic groups have a cultural predisposition towards self-employment. For example, East African Sikhs are often described as having a 'spirit of enterprise' and a supportive family network which favours economic success. Asians in Britain have been especially successful in retail and restaurants, and there are growing numbers of wholesalers (mainly in the food sector) and manufacturers (mainly in textiles and clothes manufacturing). African-Caribbeans, on the other hand, have not enjoyed such good fortune, with the major exception of their high levels of success in sport and show business. When they do set up businesses they are more likely to be in services (eg hairdressing, repairs) than in retail. Their entry into the professions and commerce has been rather limited, especially for men.

Roberts (2001) states that cultural explanations of the economic differences between Asians and African-Caribbeans are plausible. Asian immigrants brought strong entrepreneurial traditions with them and these soon found expression in the establishment of ethnic businesses. But the traditional cultures and networks of African-Caribbeans had been weakened by their bitter experience of colonialism and slavery. Indeed, some commentators argue that there is an 'anti-enterprise' attitude among African-Caribbean groups. Cashmore (1991) reports that successful Black entrepreneurs are often treated with suspicion in Britain (eg the Black community may accuse them of 'selling out' or adopting 'White' values). Sewell (1997), a Black educationalist, has attacked the prevailing notion that you can only be an 'authentic' Black person if you are 'street-wise'. This attitude may discourage young Black men (but not so much women) from studying hard and developing careers or businesses.

Ethnic minority women

Mirza (1997) suggests that Black British Feminism has emerged in order to fill in the 'silences' about ethnic minority women who have been largely neglected by mainstream feminism. White feminists have tended to stress the things that unite women ('sisterhood') and so they have given little attention to ethnic differences *between* women. Yet attitudes to things like religion, motherhood, marriage and the sexual division of labour will tend to vary according to the ethnicity of the women concerned. Mirza adds that another task of Black British Feminism is to challenge prevailing stereotypes such as the misleading images of the 'Black superwoman' and the 'submissive Asian woman'.

Black superwoman Reynolds (1997) criticises the widespread myth of the Black superwoman. African-Caribbean women in Britain are generally seen as much more successful than their male counterparts in terms of educational qualifications and occupational achievements.

One reason given for this is that they come from a matrifocal (woman-centred) culture where women have a long tradition of independence from men. So the stereotype depicts Black women as naturally resilient and resourceful 'survivors', and this stands in sharp contrast to the marginalisation and failures of Black men.

Reynolds argues that this stereotype mistakenly treats all Black women as having an inner 'essence' and this overlooks the variations between them. She also challenges many of the misconceptions surrounding Black culture. For example, she criticises the view that the matrifocal family is the ideal norm in African-Caribbean societies. There is certainly a high incidence of lone-parent families among African-Caribbeans in Britain, but the degree of 'male absenteeism' has been greatly exaggerated. Most men have always been heavily involved in family life and have assumed many responsibilities in the home.

Reynolds admits that Black women have high economic participation rates and they do appear to be doing better than men in education and work. But she claims that their success has been exaggerated. In spite of improvements in the numbers gaining good academic and professional qualifications, they are more likely than their White counterparts to be employed in jobs for which they are overqualified. They may have moved away from unskilled and semi-skilled manual labour but many of them are clustered in a narrow range of occupations (eg clerical officers, secretaries) where promotion prospects are slim and earnings modest. Poverty remains a problem for many Black women, and their unemployment rates are not far below those of Black men.

Submissive Asian women South Asian women are frequently portrayed as passive victims who meekly submit to the demands of males in their patriarchal cultures. They tend to have poorer educational qualifications than men in their communities (Modood et al., 1997). Pakistani and Bangladeshi women have especially low economic participation rates, although some of their work may be 'hidden' in the form of homeworking (eg doing piecework at home for an outside contractor). This relative disadvantage of South Asian women is often attributed to their cultural traditions, especially the customs of *purdah* (seclusion of women) and *izzat* (family honour). There may be a cultural reluctance to allow women to mix freely in the world of work, since this exposes them to accusations of disreputable behaviour which would reflect badly on the family honour. Instead, women are expected to give priority to home and family.

But these perceptions may be based on misreadings of the lives of these women. South Asian women are not necessarily as meek as the stereotypes suggest. For example, Charlotte Butler's (1995) study of young Muslim women in the East Midlands revealed 'progressive' attitudes towards work and sexual equality. These young women rejected the idea that women should be confined to the home or discouraged from seeking employment or higher education. Also, the economic activity rate of Muslim females varies according to their socioeconomic skills (the better educated groups from East Africa have higher rates) and the area of settlement in Britain (this affects local employment opportunities). So it is not just culture which shapes their economic participation. For example, the ever-present threat of racism may restrict their job opportunities or even deter them from joining the workforce in the first place.

Pakistani and Bangladeshi women Dale et al. (2002) examined the labour prospects for Pakistani and Bangladeshi women, using data from the 4th PSI survey as well as their own research on 43 ethnic minority women in Oldham. Most of these women subscribed strongly to the centrality of the family and they fully expected to get married and have children. While they enjoyed the freedom that came with a paid job, they accepted they would lose some of their independence when they got married. As one of their respondents said: 'It is the most important thing, family, nothing takes priority over it, people will die for their family here and they will do everything for them…You have to think of them first and then yourself' (Bangladeshi, age 21). Nevertheless, Dale et al. found clear evidence of change across the generations. Younger women were more likely to speak fluent English and more likely to view paid work as a way of establishing their own independence and self-esteem. The Islamic faith, of itself, was not seen as a deterrent to women's economic participation.

*activity*28 *culture*

Item A Chinese

There are about 170,000 Chinese in the UK, most of them from Hong Kong but also from Malaysia, Vietnam and Korea. Twenty years ago they suffered poor health, low wages and bad housing. Now they have the highest level of car ownership, lowest level of unemployment, and they are by far the best educated and highest earning ethnic minority group. The speed with which they achieved this success is remarkable.

There is no single reason for this, but education is a crucial factor. Nancy Park, a Chinese medical student, says: 'We work hard at our study. We know it is the way to get on. Our parents always encourage us to work'. More than a quarter of Chinese in Britain have qualifications beyond A level, twice the figure for the White population.

Gender does not seem to make a difference. In terms of earnings and education, Chinese women are absolutely equal to men. And increasingly they are choosing to have smaller families.

A surprisingly high proportion report that they have no religion. But cultural values are important in their success. Michael Chew, a solicitor, says: 'In part it is Confucianism. We are taught to value the family, to study, to be obedient. We don't just live for today, we have developed a meaning of life.'

Adapted from the *Observer*, 30.3.1997

Chinatown, London

Item B Women's economic activity

Economic activity, employment and ILO unemployment rates of women in Britain, 2000

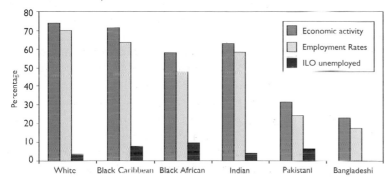

Note: Sample sizes for Bangladeshi unemployment are too small to be included.
Adapted from Cabinet Office, 2003

questions

1 Using Item A, identify two cultural factors which may account for Chinese success.

2 Briefly summarise Item B.

3 Give two reasons why it is difficult to attribute the patterns shown in Item B simply to cultural differences.

4 Outline and assess cultural explanations for ethnic disadvantage.

Evaluating cultural explanations

Few sociologists would deny that culture has some impact on people's ambitions and achievements. But culture is not necessarily the main reason for ethnic disadvantage, even if it cannot be ignored entirely. Moreover, some cultural explanations can be criticised for 'blaming the victim' and for the fallacy of 'ethnic absolutism'.

Blaming the victim One merit of the cultural approach is that it treats ethnic minorities respectfully as active agents who have their own values, priorities and goals. But if taken too far this sort of argument can end up blaming the victim. It can lead to the inflexible attitude that 'they' are totally to blame. If South Asian women in Britain have low economic participation rates, then some people might think 'that's their own fault – it's their culture, keeping women at home'. This effectively removes blame from structural factors such as racism in the workplace, or the lack of suitable employment opportunities in the locality. Likewise, there is a danger of 'pathologising' African-Caribbean cultures, exaggerating their 'weakness' and disorganisation. These cultures may be 'different' rather than 'weak'. So some sense of balance is necessary.

Ethnic absolutism Paul Gilroy (1990) is highly critical of what he calls the *fallacy of ethnic absolutism* – the mistaken assumption that ethnic cultures are somehow 'fixed' and 'final'. This fallacy wrongly assumes that each ethnic culture has a permanent 'essence' which never changes and that every member of the culture is bound forever to it. Against this, Gilroy argues, first, that cultures are dynamic rather than static – they are always evolving. Second, they are not mutually exclusive – they frequently borrow from one another, and there is great overlap. Third, no culture is uniform and homogeneous – it always contains internal diversity and individual differences in lifestyles and values. And fourth, Gilroy argues that cultures are formed, maintained and changed within particular social contexts – so the culture of a group can never satisfactorily be understood in isolation from its position in the social structure.

Clearly, Gilroy is recommending an understanding of culture which is radically different from crude cultural approaches which end up blaming the victim.

10.5 Racism

This explanation argues that the economic disadvantages suffered by ethnic minorities are largely or partly the result of racism. Even in contemporary Britain, where anti-discrimination legislation has been passed, members of ethnic minorities may find themselves the victims of racial prejudice and racial discrimination. For example, some researchers argue that teachers often have low expectations of Black pupils and this undermines the pupils' confidence and motivation to achieve good academic qualifications. Also, there is evidence that ethnic minorities are unfairly treated by employers who refuse to recruit or promote them according to their merits. So it can be an uphill struggle for ethnic minorities to establish themselves in an environment which stereotypes or marginalises them.

Defining racism

As Miles (1989) observes, *racism* is a contested concept, with fierce disagreements over its definition and its extent. He also criticises the way the term has been progressively broadened to cover more and more things. For Miles, this has resulted in the term losing much of its precision and meaning. Nevertheless, most sociologists agree that racism involves attitudes and behaviour. So we can distinguish at least two types of racism – *cultural racism* and *racial discrimination*.

Cultural racism This refers to negative stereotypes and hostile or derogatory attitudes towards ethnic minorities. These attitudes are 'out there' in the wider culture of the society. Not everyone subscribes to these racist attitudes but they are still aware of them, they see them circulated by the mass media, and they hear them passed on as common sense by other people. Some of these attitudes take the form of organised belief systems. One example of this is the doctrine of 'biological racism' which has been handed down from colonial times.

Biological racism depicts racial minorities as culturally inferior, uncivilised or backward on account of their allegedly less advanced position in the scale of biological evolution. This 'old' form of racism has been scientifically discredited – there is no direct link between the biology of a group and its social and cultural achievements. However, Barker (1982) maintains that a more sophisticated form of racism – *new racism* – has emerged to take its place. New racism does not describe racial minorities as inferior. Rather, it objects to minorities on the grounds that they are *culturally different*, and it alleges that their cultures are incompatible with 'traditional' or 'White' British culture. The mere presence of ethnic minorities in Britain is treated as a threat to the 'British way of life'.

Some writers doubt whether new racism really represents a distinct break from older versions of racism. Mason (1992) suggests that new racism is hardly new (it is one of the oldest forms of racism) and hardly non-biological (it draws on sociobiology to support its dubious claim that it is 'natural' to maintain culturally exclusive barriers).

Table 18 Self-reported racial prejudice, British Social Attitudes Surveys

% of people saying they are:

	1985	1987	1989	1991	1994	1998	2001
Very prejudiced	5	5	4	2	2	2	2
A little prejudiced	29	34	32	29	34	24	23
Not at all prejudiced	65	64	63	68	64	74	75

Adapted from Evans, 2002

Racial discrimination This is a matter of behaviour rather than attitudes – although racist attitudes and racist behaviour tend to reinforce one another. Racial discrimination occurs when a socially-defined 'racial' group is treated differently or unequally, and where this treatment is unfair and against the wishes of those who are disadvantaged by it. Thus, if an employer refuses to give a job to a suitably qualified Black person simply because of that person's skin colour, then that is an example of direct racial discrimination. The 1976 Race Relations Act bans not only *direct discrimination* but also *indirect discrimination* – treatment which is 'equal' in a formal sense but which unfairly puts certain groups at a disadvantage. For example, imposing a difficult language test on applicants for a labouring job is unnecessary, and it may handicap those whose first language is not English.

Measuring racial discrimination

Measuring racial discrimination is no easy task. Racism is no longer respectable or even legal in Britain and so people may try to conceal their racist views and actions. Sometimes researchers have to resort to undercover experiments such as sending actors from different ethnic groups after the same jobs. Since these actors are usually matched in every other respect (age, qualifications etc), any differences in their success rates might be seen as indicating racial discrimination by the employer.

PEP/PSI surveys Valuable information on racial discrimination is provided by the large-scale surveys conducted by PEP/PSI. In the first of these surveys, Daniel (1968) used 'situation tests' in which matched African-Caribbean, Asian and White actors applied for jobs. Daniel's conclusion was that discrimination in employment ranged from the substantial to the massive. In the second survey, also using situation tests, Smith (1977) concluded that discrimination had lessened a little but it still occurred. For example, Black workers encountered discrimination when applying for non-manual jobs and unskilled manual jobs and this could not be explained away simply by lack of qualifications. The third PSI survey (Brown, 1984) did not measure discrimination directly through situation tests but relied on the weaker evidence provided by what people told the interviewers. But it concluded that 'racialism and direct racial discrimination continue to have a powerful effect on the lives of Black people' (Brown, 1984). As for the fourth survey (Modood et al., 1997), this, too, relied on people's opinions and perceptions. African Caribbeans (95%) were more likely than Whites (90%) and Bangladeshis (51%) to say they thought at least some employers refuse jobs for racial or religious reasons. About a fifth of economically active members of ethnic minorities felt this had happened to them personally.

Recruitment practices A study by Jenkins (1986) sheds light on the way racist attitudes enter into recruitment decisions. Jenkins interviewed a sample of managers and personnel officers to find out how they assessed job applicants. The two main criteria they used were 'suitability' (eg relevant skills and qualifications, ability to

do the job) and 'acceptability' (eg 'manner', 'appearance' and 'attitude'). Even if minority candidates passed the suitability hurdle, they were likely to be disqualified on the grounds of acceptability. This seemed to be largely based on the managers' gut feelings and racial stereotypes (eg 'Asians are clannish', 'West Indians have a chip on their shoulder'). Also, minorities were placed at a disadvantage because these organisations often hired staff by means of internal recruitment and 'word of mouth' recommendations. If these workforces were already predominantly White, this meant Blacks were unlikely to hear of job opportunities. The Cabinet Office (2003) describes this in terms of social capital – ethnic minorities may lack the 'bridging' social capital (social connections and networks) to get jobs with White employers.

The ethnic penalty Berthoud (2000) studied Labour Force Survey data on 8,590 young minority men. His analysis showed that some minority groups suffer an *ethnic penalty* in employment, even after taking account of relevant factors such as differences in education and skills, or variations in local employment opportunities. For example, Whites tend to fare better in the labour market than minorities with the same or even better educational qualifications. The ethnic penalty refers to the disadvantage which is left over after taking the most obvious and straightforward factors into account. The strong suspicion exists that this is the result of racial discrimination, although Berthoud states that discrimination is not the only possible explanation for the observed ethnic penalty. There may be other, as yet unidentified, factors at play. He also points out that the ethnic penalty is larger for some groups than others (eg Indians and Chinese have higher earnings and employment rates than Africans and Pakistanis). Possibly this is because some groups encounter higher levels of racial discrimination than others. Or it may arise because some groups are more successful in dealing with it.

The decline of racial discrimination?

After reviewing the available evidence, the Cabinet Office Strategy Unit (2003) concluded that racial discrimination was an important factor in explaining racial disadvantage in the labour market. However, there is a danger of over-stretching this kind of explanation. First, as Berthoud (2000) notes, we cannot just assume that the ethnic penalty is totally explained by racial discrimination. It is very difficult to disentangle all the interacting factors which lead to ethnic disadvantage, and it is perfectly possible that other sorts of explanations are more appropriate. Second, there is some reason to believe that racial discrimination is weaker now than in the past. For example, Evans (2002) reports that successive British Social Attitudes surveys reveal a growth in tolerance towards racial minorities, especially but not exclusively among young people. Also, anti-discrimination legislation is much tighter now. Indeed, firms now have to prove that they are taking steps to ensure a fair representation of ethnic minorities in the workplace.

activity29 discriminating

Item A Perceptions

A Mori Poll survey included the following responses.

'They place a lot of emphasis on socialising and because I don't go out drinking of a Friday night with them, they think I am a bit strange and that I have nothing in common with them.' (Pakistani female, Manchester)

'Say if an Asian girl went for a job and a White girl. They might think, oh well, you know, just assume that the Asian girl, she's going to get to a certain age, she'll get married, you know, so we won't have her, she won't be here long.' (Asian female, Watford)

'I was turned down and there was no reason for it as I had the qualifications, I had the necessary experience. I had a friend, a White guy who worked in that company and he told me that they employed someone White who had less qualifications than me.' (Pakistani male, Manchester)

'These big companies are all White organisations, and they're obviously going to go for people that they can relate more to. You will have all the ideas and you might have all the experience and so forth, but you find you've been interviewed by a White person who can't really relate to you or understand where you're coming from.' (Black male, Watford)

Cited in Cabinet Office, 2002

Item B Situation tests

Brown and Gay (1985) used the 'situation test' approach by sending off letter and telephone applications for non-manual and skilled manual jobs. The matched applicants were White, African Caribbean and Asian, and their different ethnic groups were indicated by their name or early biography (in the letters) or a slight accent (by telephone). The researchers varied the order in which applications were made, and they rotated the format of the letters, in order to randomise any bias. The table below lists the interview offers for these three groups:

	White	Asian	African Caribbean
All job types			
Offer of interview	90%	63%	63%
Total applications	335	335	335

Adapted from Brown & Gay, 1985

questions

1 Using Item A, identify two ways in which firms discriminate against ethnic minorities.

2 Using Item B, give two examples of discrimination.

3 Suggest one advantage and one disadvantage of 'perceptions' (Item A) and 'situation tests' (Item B) as measures of discrimination.

10.6 Structural explanations

Structural approaches argue that ethnic disadvantage is the outcome of the way society is organised. Capitalist society is based on market principles, the profit motive and competition, and this kind of structure automatically generates inequalities between groups. Racial minorities tend to be less powerful and so they lose out in the harsh struggle for money, jobs and power.

Structural theorists normally make the following kinds of links between social structure and ethnic disadvantage.

- In the 1950s and 1960s, Britain faced a labour shortage which was eased by the recruitment of workers from the New Commonwealth. Although these workers made a valuable contribution to the British economy, the jobs they filled were often low-skilled and low-paid. Once trapped near the bottom of the class structure, the unequal opportunity structures of capitalism made it difficult for them to improve their situation, and so their disadvantage was handed down to their children.

- Britain is a society which has deep structural strains and conflicts, and this kind of situation breeds racism. White people may feel they are in direct competition with ethnic minorities and so they may try to gain an 'edge' by supporting racial discrimination. Capitalists and employers also have a vested interest in racism: if ethnic minority workers are seen as 'inferior', this makes it easier to exploit them as a source of cheap labour. Also, employers might hope to use ethnic minorities as a 'reserve army' to prevent White workers from pressing for higher wages.

Ethnicity and class

Structural approaches suggest it makes little sense to study ethnicity in isolation from class factors. Table 19 gives an example of the importance of class for explaining the low educational attainment of certain ethnic minority groups.

Both Marxist and Weberian sociologists have attempted to describe the nature of this relationship between ethnicity and class.

Marxist model Marxist analyses of ethnic stratification are based on a distinctive view of capitalism and the class system. In this view, capitalism creates a deep rift between the privileged ruling class and the oppressed working class. Most ethnic minorities are members of the exploited working class and it is this, rather than their ethnic features, which largely dictates their economic fate. In other words, conflicts and inequalities cannot be taken at face value as

Table 19 Social class factors affecting the educational attainment of certain ethnic minority groups

- Poverty and/or low occupational status and low education of parents
- Low expectations and aspirations of parents, teachers or the pupils themselves
- Lack of parental engagement in their children's education, either due to lack of time, cultural barriers, or lack of ability to do so
- Anti-academic culture and peer pressure
- Residence in deprived areas where schools tend to have poor outcomes
- Disproportionate likelihood of parental or pupil illness
- Pressure on children to enter employment as soon as possible to supplement family income

Adapted from Cabinet Office, 2003

if they were important in themselves. Rather, they are usually the symptoms of some deeper, underlying problem – the class struggle. So economic or class conflicts are primary, and the ethnic problems which they create are merely secondary. It is capitalism which assigns ethnic minorities to the ranks of the working class and it is capitalism which 'racialises' their situation by encouraging 'racial' divisions and 'racial' hostility.

A number of criticisms have been levelled at Marxist explanations.

- Marxists claim that racism is much more intensive under capitalism or even that it is found *only* in capitalist societies. But critics of this view say that it is true only because Marxists have defined 'racism' and 'capitalism' in very selective ways in order to make it so. Racist beliefs and doctrines probably predated capitalism and they also exist in present day non-capitalist societies.
- Some Marxists (eg Sivanandan, 1982) seem to offer a crude 'economic reductionist' argument which explains everything in terms of economic and class factors. But others argue that race relations have 'relative autonomy' – racial conflicts are certainly connected to class struggles but they also need to be treated as important in their own right.
- It is not at all clear that there is a single 'logic of capitalism' which makes racism necessary and inevitable. It is quite possible to imagine capitalism working without any racism at all. Indeed, ethnic conflict may undermine social harmony and to that extent it is a threat to the capitalist order.

Weberian model Weberian sociologists define classes in terms of economic market positions. Although members of ethnic minorities are distributed across all social classes, they are likely to be concentrated in certain locations including underclass positions. Sometimes Weberians also

treat an ethnic minority as a status group – a community who share a similar degree of prestige or respect. Minority groups in Britain may have lower status than Whites, due to the influence of racist ideologies. Nevertheless, Weber's notion of social closure can be used to show how ethnic groups engage in a constant struggle for power, status, income and wealth. They mobilise themselves to protect their existing privileges by excluding other groups and they also try to usurp the privileges of groups who are better off.

The Weberian view of an ethnic underclass has already been criticised in an earlier unit. But the Weberian approach is generally more flexible than the Marxist model. It seems better able to deal with the scattered class positions and economic progress of some ethnic minorities – for example it is not true that all minorities are economically disadvantaged. Marxists would probably accuse Weberians of taking too descriptive an approach and for failing to recognise the basic problem – the exploitative nature of capitalism.

Institutional racism

Institutional racism is currently the most influential version of the structural approach. The term suggests that racism is a basic feature of Britain's social institutions (eg government, schools, employment and housing markets). According to this view, racist assumptions are built in to the rules and routines of these institutions. Consequently, they neglect the needs of their ethnic minority clients, or even discriminate against them. As employing agencies, they fail to recruit minorities in sufficient numbers, and minorities are under-represented at their higher levels.

Now, this does not necessarily mean that every individual working within these institutions supports racist attitudes and behaviour. But regardless of their personal views on racism, they tend to reinforce it just by going about their normal business. Racism is taken for granted and habitual – it has become so institutionalised that it is not even recognised as racism. Yet it has serious consequences for ethnic minorities as it reinforces their socio-economic disadvantage. Indeed, institutional racism can be defined as 'any situation in which groups, socially defined as races, are systematically disadvantaged in respect of social rewards, capacities or opportunities' (Mason, 1982).

Evaluation Institutional racism is a highly controversial concept. It is a prime example of *conceptual inflation* where the meaning of racism has been stretched beyond attitudes and behaviour to include socio-economic disadvantage as well. Some sociologists feel it is little more than a political slogan which has limited analytical usefulness. Here are some of the main criticisms levelled at it.

- The term implies that all racial disadvantage is the result of racism. But there may be other causes, such as cultural or class factors. So perhaps it is better to use the term ethnic or 'racial' disadvantage and keep an open mind on possible causes.

activity30 ethnicity and class

Item A Super rich

Tony Blair attended a gathering of Britain's 200 wealthiest Asians in central London last night. He described them as a credit to the country as a whole. Between them, they are worth £7.5 billion, own a number of household brands and employ 300,000 people around the world. Leading the way are the Mittal brothers, who own a multinational steel company worth £2 billion, followed by the Hinduja family, worth £1.2 billion, with extensive interests in industry and oil. Others include Shami Ahmed, owner of the Joe Bloggs fashion label, valued at £60 million.

But some observers say the publication of the list of 'super-rich' Asians paints a misleading picture. Few in the top 10 made their money in Britain, and many on the list come from wealthy families.

Reuben Singh (right) winner of the Asian Business entrepreneur of the year, 2002

Suresh Grover, of the Southall Monitoring Group, said: 'While there is no doubt that there are some success stories, we also have to ask the question, at what price? Many Asian workers are poorly paid and work in terrible conditions, often in companies owned by other Asians. At the end of the day, a businessman is a businessman and it doesn't matter what the race is.'

Kamaljeet Jandu, at the Trades Union Congress, said: 'This list does not give a complete picture and there is a danger of replacing old stereotypes with new ones. Not all Asians are wealthy and many have limited opportunities.'

Adapted from the *Guardian*, 26.3.1998

Item B Class distribution

Male occupations (percentages)

	White	Caribbean	Indian	African Asian	Pakistani	Bangladeshi	Chinese
Professional/ managerial	30	11	19	26	14	7	41
Intermediate/ junior	21	20	28	31	18	22	26
Total non-manual	51	31	47	57	32	29	67
Skilled manual	31	37	23	22	36	2	5
Semi-skilled	14	26	22	17	28	65	20
Unskilled	4	6	7	3	4	4	8
Total manual	49	69	52	42	68	71	33

Adapted from Modood et al., 1997

questions

1 Using Item A, identify two ways in which Asian 'success stories' might be misleading. Refer to Item B in your answer.

2 Using Item B, select two groups and describe their class patterns.

3 Provide a structural explanation for the class patterns shown in Item B.

- It includes situations where there is no conscious intention to discriminate. Some sociologists think this is unfair and bizarre. For example, it implies there is no difference between apartheid-era South Africa (where racial discrimination was intentional and legal) and contemporary Britain (where racial discimination is illegal). Both cases are presented as examples of institutional racism.

- It presents a rather simplistic view of stratification in which Whites are always the winners and ethnic minorities the losers. As Pilkington (2001) points out, this takes insufficient account of ethnic diversity.

Pilkington (2003) concludes that the concept of institutional racism is too loose and ill-defined. It causes confusion by packing together too many things – beliefs within the institution which legitimise racial inequality ('occupational culture'), racially discriminatory practices ('indirect discrimination'), and patterns of racial disadvantage (the staffing structure of the institution).

The Lawrence Report

For a long time there was great resistance to accepting the idea that institutional racism was a problem in Britain. However, there was a major shift in attitudes after the publication of the Macpherson Inquiry (1999) into the brutal murder of a Black youth, Stephen Lawrence, in 1993. Macpherson described the murder as an unprovoked racist attack by White youths, but he also concluded that the failure to bring Stephen's killers to justice was the result not just of police incompetence but also of institutionalised racism within the police force. Macpherson provided a detailed definition of this concept (see Table 20).

The Report recommended a number of measures to stamp out institutional racism both within the criminal justice system and in the wider society. One almost immediate result of the Report was the admission by many police forces and other bodies (eg hospitals, the armed services, education) that institutional racism was a problem within their organisations. Moreover, it led to legislation in 2001, when the Race Relations Acts were extended to cover public bodies such as police. This legislation imposed a statutory duty on public bodies to take active measures to establish racial justice and ensure equal opportunities.

However, some critics (eg Green, 2000; Dennis et al., 2000) remain unconvinced that Macpherson has really proved the existence of institutional racism. These critics have great sympathy for the suffering of the Lawrence family but they say this should not blind us to the shortcomings of Macpherson's arguments.

- Macpherson produced no substantial evidence that the police officers involved in the Lawrence investigation had acted in a racist manner. Yet his concept of institutional failure seems to brand all officers as racist (even although Macpherson says this is not his intention).

- It is undoubtedly the case that some police officers hold racist attitudes and act in a racist manner. But that does not mean the institution approves or tolerates their racism. Indeed, Macpherson recognised that the policies of the Metropolitan Police were anti-racist. So it may be unfair to brand the institution as racist.

- Incompetence is not the same thing as racism. Macpherson collapses these two things together in an unhelpful way. It is not certain that the 'collective failure' of the investigation would have been any different if it was a White youth who had been murdered.

- Macpherson casts his net so wide that it inevitably brands everyone as racist. Is there anyone, White or ethnic minority, who is entirely free of 'unwitting ignorance' or 'stereotypes'? His definition is so wide it becomes meaningless and useless – no organisation could ever really 'prove' it was not racist in his terms.

In spite of these possible flaws in Macpherson's approach, many observers welcome the impact of his report. It has spurred organisations to examine their own ethnic composition and to review their practices and procedures with a view to eradicating racism.

Table 20 *Institutional racism*

- Institutional racism consists of the collective failure of an organisation to provide an appropriate and professional service to people because of their colour, culture or ethnic origin. It can be seen or detected in processes, attitudes and behaviour which amount to discrimination through unwitting prejudice, ignorance, thoughtlessness and racist stereotyping which disadvantage minority ethnic people.

- Unwitting racism can arise from lack of understanding, ignorance or mistaken beliefs. It can arise from well-intentioned but patronising words or action. It can arise from unfamiliarity with the behaviour or cultural traditions of people or families from minority ethnic communities. It can arise from racist stereotyping of Black people as potential criminals or troublemakers.

Macpherson Report (The Stephen Lawrence Inquiry), 1999

key terms

Races Classifications of peoples on the basis of their broad physical and biological characteristics. Now generally regarded as unscientific.

Racialisation The way people construct 'racial' categories. The social construction of 'racial' groups.

Ethnic penalty The portion of ethnic disadvantage which cannot be accounted for by more obvious quantifiable factors such as class and educational attainment, and may be due in part to racial discrimination.

Ethnic absolutism The fallacy that ethnic cultures are fixed, internally homogeneous and mutually exclusive. The mistaken view that ethnic cultures are unchangeable, the same for every member of the ethnic group and exclusive to each particular group.

Cultural racism Negative stereotypes of and hostile attitudes towards ethnic minorities, which form part of the mainstream culture.

New racism An objection to ethnic minorities based on the view that their cultures are different and don't fit with mainstream culture.

Racial discrimination Negative treatment of members of a socially defined 'racial' group, simply because they are seen to belong to that group.

Institutional racism A set of routine practices within institutions which results in marked patterns of disadvantage among certain ethnic groups.

summary

1. A variety of terms have been used to describe and classify ethnic groups. Sometimes they are used interchangeably. However, to some extent, each term is based on different assumptions.

2. In general, ethnic minorities are disadvantaged compared to the White majority. However, there is considerable ethnic diversity, both within and between ethnic groups.

3. Multiple factor explanations are often used to explain ethnic disadvantage – that is, a range of factors such as class, educational attainment, ethnic cultures and discrimination combine to cause disadvantage.

4. Genetic explanations claim that ethnic disadvantage is partly a reflection of inherited differences in intelligence. This view is largely discredited today – there is little reason to suppose that intelligence runs along ethnic lines.

5. Cultural explanations see both ethnic disadvantage and advantage in terms of ethnic cultures. However, the use of cultural explanations can lead to 'blaming the victim' and to the creation of stereotypes such as the 'Black superwoman' and the 'submissive Asian woman'.

6. Explanations based on racism argue that ethnic disadvantage is, at least in part, due to racial discrimination. Although discrimination is difficult to prove, there is evidence to support this view.

7. Structural explanations argue that ethnic disadvantage is due to the way society is structured and organised. For example, the unequal opportunity structures of capitalist society make it difficult for at least some ethnic minorities to improve their position.

8. Some researchers argue that racism is embedded in the organisation and routine practices of institutions such as the criminal justice system. Critics argue that this view of institutional racism is ill-defined, vague and unproven.

References

Abbott, P. & Wallace, C. (1990). *Introduction to sociology*. London: Routledge.

Abraham, J. (1994). Bias in science and medical knowledge: The Opren controversy. *Sociology, 28,* 717-736.

Abraham, J. (1995). *Divide and school: Gender and class dynamics in comprehensive education*. London: Falmer.

Acheson, Sir D. (1998). *Inequalities in health report*. London: Stationery Office.

ACPO (Association of Chief Police Officers) (2000). *A guide to identifying and combating hate crime*. London: ACPO.

Adams, C. (2000). Suspect data: Arresting research. In R.D. King & E. Wincup (Eds.), *Doing research on crime and justice*. Oxford: Oxford University Press.

Adler, P.A. (1993). *Wheeling and dealing: Ethnography of an upper level drug dealing and smuggling community*. New York: Columbia University Press.

Adonis, A. & Pollard, A. (1997). *A class act*. London: Hamish Hamilton.

Aldridge, S. (2001). *Social mobility*. London: Performance & Innovation Unit, Cabinet Office.

Aldridge, S. (2004). *Life chances and social mobility: An overview of the evidence*. London: Prime Minister's Strategy Unit, Cabinet Office.

Allan, J., Livingstone, S. & Reiner, R. (1997). The changing generic location of crime in film. *Journal of Communication, 47,* 4, 1-13.

Althusser, L. (1972). Ideology and ideological state apparatuses: Notes towards an investigation. In B.R. Cosin (Ed.), *Education, structure and society*. Harmondsworth: Penguin.

Alvesson, M. (2002). *Postmodernism and social research*. Buckingham: Open University Press.

Annual abstract of statistics (2004). London: TSO.

Arber, S. (2001). Designing samples. In N. Gilbert (Ed.), *Researching social life* (2nd ed.). London: Sage.

Armstrong, G. (1993). Like that Desmond Morris? In D. Hobbs & T. May (Eds.), *Interpreting the field: Accounts of ethnography*. Oxford: Clarendon Press.

Atkinson, J.M. (1978). *Discovering suicide*. London: Macmillan.

Atkinson, P. (2004). Life story interview. In M.S. Lewis-Beck, A. Bryman & T.F. Liao (Eds.), *The Sage encyclopaedia of social science research methods* (vols 1-3). Thousand Oaks, CA: Sage.

Ball, S.J. (2003). *Class strategies and the education market: The middle classes and social advantage*. London: RoutledgeFalmer.

Ballantine, J. & Spade, J. (2001). *Schools and society*. Belmont: Wadsworth.

Banton, M. (1979). Analytical and folk concepts of ethnicity, *Ethnic and Racial Studies, 2,* 2.

Barclay, G. & Tavares, C. (1999). *Digest 4: Information on the criminal justice system in England and Wales*. London: HMSO.

Barker, E. (1984). *The making of a Moonie*. Oxford: Blackwell.

Barker, M. (1982). *The new racism*. London: Junction Books.

Barron, R. & Norris, G. (1976). Sexual divisions and the dual labour market. In D. Barker & S. Allen (Eds.), *Dependence and exploitation in work and marriage*. London: Longman.

Bauer, P. (1997). *Class on the brain*. London: Centre for Policy Studies.

Baxter, J. (2000). The joys and justice of housework, *Sociology, 34,* 4.

Baym, N.K. (1995). From practice to culture on Usenet. In S.L. Star (Ed.), *The cultures of computing*. Oxford: Blackwell.

Beardsworth, A. & Keil, T. (1992). The vegetarian option: Varieties, conversions, motives and careers, *Sociological Review, 40,* 253-293.

Beck, U. & Beck-Gernsheim, E. (1996). Individualization and precarious freedoms. In P. Heelas et al. (Eds.), *Detraditionalization*. Oxford: Blackwell.

Becker, H.S. (1963). *Outsiders: Studies in the sociology of deviance*. London: Macmillan.

Becker, H.S. (1970). Whose side are we on? In H.S. Becker, *Sociological work*. New Brunswick: Transaction Books.

Becker, H.S. (1971). Social-class variations in teacher-pupil relationship. In B.R. Cosin, I.R. Dale, G.M. Esland & D.F. Swift (Eds.), *School and society*. London: Routledge.

Bell, D. (1976). *The coming of post-industrial society*. London: Penguin, Harmondsworth.

Beresford, P. & Boyd, S. (1998). Britain's richest 1,000. *Sunday Times*, 19th April.

Beresford, P. & Boyd, S. (2004). The Sunday Times rich list 2004. *Sunday Times*, 18th April.

Beresford, P., Green, D., Lister, R. & Woodward, K. (1999). *Poverty first hand*. London: CPAG.

Berg, B.L. (1990). *Qualitative research methods for the social sciences*. Needham Heights, MA: Allyn & Bacon.

Bernstein, B. (1971). Education cannot compensate for society. In B.R. Cosin et al. (Eds.), *School and society*. London: Routledge & Kegan Paul.

Bernstein, B. (1973). *Class, codes and control*. London: Paladin.

Berthoud, R. (2000). Ethnic employment penalties in Britain, *Journal of Ethnic and Migration Studies, 26,* 3.

Beteille, A. (1977). *Inequality among men*. Oxford: Basil Blackwell.

Beynon, J. (1985). *Initial encounters in a comprehensive school*. London: Falmer.

Beynon, J. (2002). *Masculinities and culture*. Buckingham: Open University Press.

Bird, C. (1980). Deviant labelling in school: The pupils' perspective. In P. Woods (Ed.), *Pupil strategies*. London: Croom Helm.

Blumer, H. (1962). Society as symbolic interaction. In A.M. Rose (Ed.), *Human behaviour and social processes*. London: Routledge.

Blumer, H. (1969). *Symbolic interactionism: Perspective on method*. Englewood Cliffs: Prentice Hall.

Bordua, D. (1962). A critique of sociological interpretations of gang delinquency. In M.E. Wolfgang, L. Savitz & N. Johnston (Eds.), *The sociology of crime and delinquency*. New York: John Wiley & Sons.

Bottomley, A. & Coleman, C. (1981). *Understanding crime rates*. Farnborough: Saxon House.

Bottoms, A.E. & Wiles, P. (2002). Environmental criminology. In M. Maguire, R. Morgan and R. Reiner (Eds.), *The Oxford handbook of criminology* (3rd ed.). Oxford: Oxford University Press.

Bottoms, A.E., Mawby, R. L. & Xanthos, P. (1989). A tale of two cities. In D. Downes (Ed.), *Crime and the city*. London: Macmillan.

Bourdieu, P. (1984). *Distinction: A social critique of the judgement of taste*. London: Routledge.

Bourdieu, P. (1990). *The logic of practice*. Cambridge: Polity Press.

Bourdieu, P. & Passeron, J. (1977). *Reproduction in education, society and culture*. London: Sage.

Bourgois, P. (1995). *In search of respect*. Cambridge: Cambridge University Press.

Bourne, J., Bridges, L. & Searle, C. (1994). *Outcast England: How schools exclude Black children*. London: Institute of Race Relations.

Bowles, S. & Gintis, H. (1976). *Schooling in capitalist America*. London: Routledge & Kegan Paul.

Bowling, B. & Phillips, C. (2002). *Racism, crime and justice*. London: Longman.

Box, S. (1983). *Power, crime and mystification*. London: Tavistock.

Bradshaw, J. (Ed.), (1993). *Budget standards for the United Kingdom*. Aldershot: Avebury.

Brantingham, P.J. & Brantingham, P.L. (1984). *Patterns of crime*. New York: Macmillan.

Braverman, H. (1974). *Labour and monopoly capitalism*. New York: Monthly Review Press.

Breen, R. & Goldthorpe, J. (1999). Class inequality and meritocracy. *British Journal of Sociology, 50,* 1.

Breen, R. & Goldthorpe, J. (2002). Merit, mobility and method. *British Journal of Sociology, 53,* 4.

Breen, R. & Rottman, D. (1995). *Class stratification*. London: Harvester Wheatsheaf.

Brewer, J. (2000). *Ethnography*. Buckingham: Open University Press.

British Crime Survey (BCS) see Simmons & Dodd (2003).

British Sociological Association website www.bsa.org.uk

Brook, S. (1997). *Class: Knowing your place in modern Britain*. London: Victor Gollancz.

Brown, C. (1984). *Black and White Britain*. London: Heinemann.

Brown, C. & Gay, P. (1985). *Racial discrimination*. London: Policy Studies Institute.

Brown, P., Halsey, A.H., Lauder, H. & Wells, A. (1997). The transformation of education and society: An introduction. In A.H. Halsey et al. (Eds.), *Education: Culture, economy, society*. Oxford: Oxford University Press.

Brown, U. Scott, G., Money, G. & Duncan, B. (2002). *Poverty in Scotland 2002*. London: CPAG.

Brownlee, I. (1998). *Community punishment: A critical introduction*. Harlow: Longman.

Brunsdon, C., Johnson, C., Moseley, R. & Wheatley, H. (2001). Factual entertainment on British television. *European Journal of Cultural Studies, 4*.

Bryman, A. (1999). Global Disney. In P. Taylor & D. Slater (Eds.), *The American century*. Oxford: Blackwell.

Bryman, A. (2001). *Social research methods*. Oxford: Oxford University Press.

Bryman, A. (2004). *Social research methods* (2nd ed.). Oxford: Oxford University Press.

Bryson, A. & Gomez, R. (2002). Marching on together? In A. Park, J. Curtice, K. Thomson, L. Jarvis & C. Bromley, *British social attitudes 19th report*. London: Sage.

Buchanan. A. (2001). Fathers involvement and outcomes in adolescence and adulthood. ESRC. (can be accessed on www.literacytrust.org.uk)

Buckingham, A. (1999). Is there an underclass in Britain? *British Journal of Sociology, 50*, 1.

Bulmer, M. (1980). Why don't sociologists make more use of official statistics? *Sociology, 14*, 505-523.

Bulmer, M. (2001). The ethics of social research. In N. Gilbert (Ed.), *Researching social life* (2nd ed.). London: Sage Publications.

Bunting, M. (2003). Why can women still expect to earn only half as much as men? *The Guardian*, 10th October.

Burgess, R.G. (1983). *Experiencing comprehensive education*. London: Methuen.

Burgess, R.G. (1989). Grey areas: Ethical dilemmas in educational ethnography. In R.G. Burgess (Ed.), *The ethics of educational research*. Brighton: Falmer Press.

Burnham, J. (1941). *The managerial revolution*. New York: John Day.

Bush, T., Coleman, M. & Glover, D. (1993). *Managing autonomous schools: The grant-maintained experience*. London: Paul Chapman.

Butcher, B. & Dodd, P. (1983). The Electoral Register – Two surveys. *Population Trends, 31*, 15-19.

Butler, C. (1995). Religion and gender, *Sociology Review, 4*, 3.

Bynner, J., Ferri, E. & Wadsworth, M. (2003). *Changing Britain, changing lives*. London: Institute of Education.

Cabinet Office Strategy Unit (2002). *Ethnic minorities and the labour market interim report*. Cabinet Office.

Cabinet Office Strategy Unit (2003). *Ethnic minorities and the labour market final report*. Cabinet Office.

Campbell, B. (1993). *Goliath: Britain's dangerous places*. London: Macmillan.

Cantle, T. (2001). *Community cohesion*. Home Office.

Carlen, P. (1983). *Women's imprisonment*. London: Routledge.

Carlen, P. (1988). *Women, crime and poverty*. Buckingham: Open University Press.

Carlen, P. (1990). *Alternatives to women's imprisonment*. Buckingham: Open University Press.

Carrabine, E., Cox, P., Lee, M. & South, N. (2002). *Crime in modern Britain*. Oxford: Oxford University Press.

Carter, R.L. & Hill, K.Q. (1979). *The criminal's image of the city*. New York: Pergamon Press.

Cashmore, E. (1987). *The logic of racism*. London: Allen & Unwin.

Cashmore, E. (1991). Flying business class. *New Community, 17*, 3.

Caspi, A. & Moffit, T. (1995). The continuity of maladaptive behaviour: From description to understanding in the study of anti-social behaviour. In D. Cicchetti & D. Cohen (Eds.), *Developmental psychology*. New York: Wiley.

Cavadino, M. & Dignan, J. (2002). *The penal system* (3rd ed.). London: Sage.

Chahal, K. & Julienne, L. (1999). *We can't all be White: Racist victimisation in the UK*. York: Joseph Rowntree Foundation.

Chambliss, W. (1969). *Crime and the legal process*. New York: McGraw-Hill.

Charles, N. & James, E. (2003). Gender and work orientations in conditions of job insecurity, *British Journal of Sociology, 54*, 2.

Chaudhary, V. & Walker, M. (1996). The petty crime war. *The Guardian*, 21 November.

Chibnall, S. (1977). *Law and order news*. London: Tavistock.

Chitty, C. (1997). Choose...education? *Sociology Review*, April.

Chitty, C. (2002). *Understanding schools and schooling*. London: RoutledgeFalmer.

Chubb, J. & Moe, T. (1997). Politics, markets and the organisation of schools. In A.H. Halsey et al. (Eds.), *Education: Culture, economy, society*. Oxford: Oxford University Press.

Cicourel, A.V. (1976). *The social organisation of juvenile justice*. London: Heinemann.

Clancy, A., Hough, M., Aust, R. & Kershaw, C. (2001). *Crime, policing and justice: The experience of ethnic minorities: Findings from the 2000 British Crime Survey, Home Office Research Study 223*. London: Home Office.

Clarke, R.V.G (2003). 'Situational' crime prevention: Theory and practice. In E. McLaughlin, J. Muncie & G. Hughes (Eds.), *Criminological perspectives: Essential readings* (2nd ed.). London: Sage.

Clarke, R.V.G. (1995). Situational crime prevention. In M. Tonry & D. Farrington (Eds.), *Building a safer society*. Chicago: University of Chicago Press.

Clinard, M. (1974). *Sociology and deviant behaviour* (4th ed.). New York: Holt, Rinehart and Winston.

Cloward, R. & Ohlin, L. (1961). *Delinquency and opportunity*. Glencoe: The Free Press.

Coffey, A. (2001). *Education and social change*. Buckingham: Open University Press.

Cohen, A. (1955). *Delinquent boys*. Glencoe: The Free Press.

Cohen, L.E. & Felson, M. (1979). Social change and crime rates: A routine activities approach. *American Sociological Review, 44*, 588-608

Cohen, P. (1984). Against the new vocationalism. In I. Bates et al. (Eds.), *Schooling for the dole?* London: Macmillan.

Cohen, S. (1987). *Folk devils and moral panics* (2nd ed.). Oxford: Blackwell.

Cohen, S. (2003). Human rights and crimes of the state: The culture of denial. In E. McLaughlin, J. Muncie & G. Hughes (Eds.), *Criminological perspectives: Essential readings* (2nd ed.). London: Sage.

Coleman, C. & Moynihan, J. (1996). *Understanding crime data*. Buckingham: Open University Press.

Collier, R. (1998). *Masculinities, crime and criminology*. London: Sage.

Collins, R. (1972). Functional and conflict theories of educational stratification. In B.R. Cosin (Ed.), *Education: Structure and society*. Harmondsworth: Penguin.

Commission for Racial Equality (1992). *Set to fail? Setting and banding in secondary schools*. London: Commission for Racial Equality.

Connolly, P. (1998). *Racism, gender identities and young children*. London: Routledge.

Connor, H. & Dewson, S. (2001). Social class and higher education: Issues affecting decisions on participation by lower social class groups. *DfEE Report 267*. London: DfEE.

Cook, D. (2001). Safe and sound? Crime, disorder and community safety policies. In M. May, R. Page & E. Brunsdon (Eds.), *Understanding social problems: Issues in social policy*. Oxford: Blackwell.

Coote, A. & Campbell, B. (1982). *Sweet freedom*. London: Pan.

Couper, M.P. (2000). Web surveys: A review of issues and approaches. *Public Opinion Quarterly, 64*, 464-494.

Cowan, R. (2004). Police failing to tackle domestic abuse. *Guardian*, 19 February.

Coward, R. (1999). *Sacred cows*. London: Harper Collins.

CPAG (2004). *Poverty: the facts* (5th ed.). London: CPAG.

Crawford, A., Jones, T., Woodhouse, T. & Young, J. (1990). *Second Islington Crime Survey*. London: Middlesex Polytechnic.

Critcher, C. (2003). *Moral panics and the media*. Buckingham: Open University Press.

Croall, H. (2001). *Understanding white collar crime*. Buckingham: Open University Press.

Crompton, R. (1993). *Class and stratification*. Cambridge: Polity Press.

Crompton, R. (1997). *Women and work in modern Britain*. Oxford: Oxford University Press.

Crompton, R. (1998). *Class and stratification* (2nd ed.). Cambridge: Polity Press.

Crompton, R. (2000). The gendered restructuring of the middle class. In R. Crompton et al. (Eds.), *Renewing Class Analysis*. Oxford: Basil Blackwell.

Crompton, R. & Harris, F. (1998). Explaining women's employment patterns. *British Journal of Sociology, 4*, 1.

Cronin, A. (2001). Focus groups. In N. Gilbert (Ed.), *Researching social life* (2nd ed.). London: Sage.

Cumberbatch, G., Woods, S. & Maguire, A. (1995). *Crime in the news*. Birmingham: Aston University.

Dahrendorf, R. (1987). The erosion of citizenship. *New Statesman*, 12th June.

Dahya, B. (1974). The nature of Pakistani ethnicity. In A. Cohen (Ed.), *Urban ethnicity*. London: Tavistock.

Dale, A., Fieldhouse, E., Shaheen, N. & Kalra, V. (2002). The labour market prospects for Pakistani and Bangladeshi women, *Work, Employment and Society, 16*, 1.

Daniel, W.W. (1968). *Racial discrimination in England*. Harmondsworth: Penguin.

David, M. & Sutton, C. (2004). *Social research: The basics*. London: Sage Publications.

Davies, N. (1994). Dirty business: Red light for Blue Squad. *The Guardian*, 29 November.

Davis, K. (1961). Prostitution. In R. Merton & R. Nisbet (Eds.), *Contemporary social problems*. New York: The Free Press.

Davis, K. & Moore, W.H. (1945). Some principles of stratification, *American Sociological Review, 10*.

Davis, N. (1997). *Dark heart*. London: Chatto & Windus.

De Vaus, D. (2001). *Research design in social research*. London: Sage.

Dean, H. & Taylor-Gooby, P. (1992). *Dependency culture*. Hemel Hempstead: Harvester Wheatsheaf.

Delamont, S. (2001). *Changing women, unchanged men?* Buckingham: Open University Press

Delamont, S. (2003). *Feminist sociology*. London: Sage.

Demack, S., Drew, D. & Grimsley, M. (2000). Minding the gap: Ethnic, gender and social class differences in attainment at 16, 1988-95. *Race, Ethnicity and Education, 3*, 117-143.

Dench, G. (1997). *Rewriting the sexual contract*. London: Institute of Community Studies.

Denman, S. (2001). *The Denman report – Race discrimination in the Crown Prosecution Service*, London: Crown Prosecution Service.

Dennis, N., Erdos, G. & Al-Shahi, A. (2000). *Racist murder and pressure group politics*. London: Institute for Study of Civil Society.

Denny, C. (2003). Profits of loss. *Guardian*, 25th November.

Denzin, N.K. (1970). *The research act in sociology*. London: Butterworths.

Desai, T., Gregg, P., Steer, J. & Wadsworth, J. (1999). Gender and the labour market. In P. Gregg & J. Wadsworth (Eds.), *The state of working Britain*. Manchester: Manchester University Press.

Devine, F. (1997). *Social class in America and Britain*. Edinburgh University Press.

Devine, F. & Heath, S. (1999). *Sociological research methods in context*. Basingstoke: Macmillan.

DfEE (1997). *Excellence in schools*. (Cmnd 3861). London: HMSO.

DfES (2003). *Widening participation in higher education*. London: DfES.

DfID (Department for International Development) (2000). *Viewing the world: A study of British television coverage of developing countries*. DfID.

Ditton, J. (1977). *Part-time crime: An ethnography of fiddling and pilferage*. Basingstoke: Macmillan.

Dobash, R., Schlesinger, P., Dobash, R. & Weaver, C. (1998). Crimewatch UK. In M. Fishman & G. Cavender (Eds.), *Entertaining crime*. New York: Aldine De Gruyter.

Dodd, T., Nicholas, S., Povey, D. & Walker, A. (2004). *Crime in England and Wales 2003/2004*. London: Home Office.

Donnison, D. (2001). The changing face of poverty. In M. May, R. Page & E. Brunsdon (Eds.), *Understanding social problems: Issues in social policy*. Oxford: Blackwell.

Donovan, N. & Halpern, D. (2002). *Life satisfaction*. Cabinet Office Strategy Unit.

Douglas, J.W.B. (1964). *The home and the school*. London: MacGibbon & Kee.

Doward, J., Reilly, T. & Graham, F. (2003). *Census exposes unequal Britain. Observer*, 23rd November.

Downes, D. & Morgan, M. (2002). The skeletons in the cupboard: The politics of law and order at the turn of the millennium. In M. Maguire, R. Morgan & R. Reiner (Eds.), *The Oxford handbook of criminology* (3rd ed.). Oxford: Oxford University Press.

Downes, D. & Rock, P. (2003). *Understanding deviance* (4th ed.) Oxford: Clarendon Press.

Durkheim, E. (1961). *Moral education*. Glencoe: The Free Press.

Durkheim, E. (1964). *The rules of sociological method*. New York: The Free Press.

Durkheim, E. (1970). *Suicide: A study in sociology*. London: Routledge & Kegan Paul.

Ehrenreich, B. (2002). *Nickel and dimed*. London: Granta.

Eichler, M. et al., (1988). *Non-sexist research methods*. London: Allen & Unwin.

EOC (2002). *Facts about women and men in Great Britain 2002*. EOC.

EOC (2003). *Working fathers*. EOC.

EOC (2004). *Sex and power. Who runs Britain?* EOC

Epstein, D., Elwood, J., Hey, V. & Maw, J. (Eds.) (1998). *Failing boys? Issues in gender and achievement*. Buckingham: Open University Press.

Ermisch, J. & Francesconi, M. (2002). *Intergenerational social mobility and assortative mating in Britain*. University of Essex: Working Papers of the Institute for Social and Economic Research.

Evans, G. (2002). In search of tolerance. In A. Park, J. Curtice, K. Thomson, L. Jarvis & C. Bromley (Eds.), *British social attitudes 19th report*. London: Sage.

Eysenck, H.J. (1971). *Race, intelligence and education*. London: Temple Smith.

Eysenck, H.J. (1987). Personality theory and the problem of criminology. In B. McGurk, D. Thornton & M. Williams (Eds.), *Applying psychology to imprisonment*. London: HMSO.

Faludi, S. (1992). *Backlash*. London: Chatto & Windus.

Farnworth, M., Thornberry, T., Krohn, M. & Lizotte, A. (1994). Measurement in the study of class and delinquency. *Journal of Research in Crime and Delinquency, 31*, 32-61.

Farrington, D. & Morris, A. (1983). Sex, sentencing and reconviction. *British Journal of Criminology, 23*.

Feinstein, L. (2003). Inequality in the early cognitive developments of British children in the 1970 cohort. *Economica, 70*, 277.

Ferri, E., Bynner, J. & Wadsworth, W. (2003). *Changing Britain, changing lives*. London: Institute of Education.

Field, F. (1989). *Losing out.* Oxford: Basil Blackwell.

Fielding, N. & Thomas, H. (2001). Qualitative interviewing. In N. Gilbert (Ed.), *Researching social life* (2nd ed.). London: Sage.

Finch, J. (1993). 'It's great to have someone to talk to': Ethics and politics of interviewing women. In M. Hammersley (Ed.), *Social research: Philosophy, politics and practice.* London: Sage.

Finn, D. (1987). *Training without jobs.* London: Macmillan.

Flaherty, J., Veit-Wilson, J. & Dornan, P. (2004). *Poverty: The facts.* (5th ed.). London: CPAG.

Flanders, N. (1970). *Analysing teacher behaviour.* Reading, MA: Addison Wesley.

Flick, U. (1998). *An introduction to qualitative research.* London: Sage.

Foster, P. (1990). *Policy and practice in multicultural and antiracist education.* London: Routledge.

Fowler, F. (1988). *Survey research methods.* London: Sage.

Francis, P. (2000). Getting criminological research started. In V. Jupp, P. Davies and P. Francis (Eds.), *Doing criminological research.* London: Sage.

Fraser. S. (Ed.), (1995). *The bell curve wars.* New York: Basic Books.

Freedman, J. (2001). *Feminism.* Buckingham: Open University Press.

Frosh, S., Phoenix, A. & Pattman, R. (2002). *Young masculinities.* London: Palgrave.

Furlong, A. & Cartmel, F. (1997). *Young people and social change.* Philadelphia: Open University Press.

Gabor, T. (1994). *Everybody does it.* Toronto: University of Toronto Press.

Gaine, C. & George, R. (1999). *Gender, 'race' and class in schooling: A new introduction.* London: Falmer.

Galindo-Rueda, F., Marcenaro-Gutierrez, O. & Vignoles, A. (2004). *The widening socio-economic gap in UK higher education.* Centre for the Economics of Education Discussion Paper. London: London School of Economics and Political Science.

Gallie, D. (2000). The labour force. In A.H. Halsey (Ed.), *Twentieth century British social trends.* Basingstoke: MacMillan.

Gallie, D., White, M., Cheng, Y. & Tomlinson, M. (1998). *Restructuring the employment relationship.* Oxford: Clarendon Press.

Garner, R. (2004). Education audit: Secondary schools. *The Independent,* 5 January.

Gershuny, J. (1997). Distribution of work in the household. In G. Dench (Ed.), *Rewriting the sexual contract.* London: Institute of Community Studies.

Gewirtz, S., Ball, S.J. & Bowe, R. (1995). *Markets, choice and equity in education.* Milton Keynes: Open University Press.

Gibbs, J. & Martin, W. (1964). *Status integration and suicide.* Oregon: University of Oregon Press.

Giddens, A. (1998). *The Third Way: The renewal of social democracy.* Cambridge: Polity Press.

Gilbert, N. (1993). Writing about social research. In N. Gilbert (Ed.), *Researching social life.* London: Sage.

Gilbert, N. (Ed.) (2001). *Researching social life* (2nd ed.). London: Sage Publications.

Gillborn, D. (1990). *'Race', ethnicity and education: Teaching and learning in multi-ethnic schools.* London: Unwin Hyman.

Gillborn, D. & Drew, D. (1992). 'Race', class and school effects. *New Community, 18,* 4.

Gillborn, D. & Mirza, H.S. (2000). *Educational inequality: Mapping race, class and gender.* London: OFSTED.

Gillborn, D. & Youdell, D. (2001). The new IQism: Intelligence, 'ability' and the rationing of education. In J. Demaine (Ed.), *Sociology of education today.* Basingstoke: Palgrave.

Gilroy, P. (1983). Police and thieves. In Centre for Contemporary Cultural Studies *The empire strikes back.* London: Hutchinson.

Gilroy, P. (1990). The end of anti-racism, *New Community, 17.*

Ginn, J., Arber, S., Brannen, J., Dale, A., Dex, S., Elias, P., Moss, P., Pahl, J., Roberts, C. & Rubery, J. (1996). Feminist fallacies, *British Journal of Sociology, 47,* 1.

Giordano, P.C. (1995). The wider circle of friends in adolescence. *American Journal of Sociology, 101,* 661-697.

Glaser, B.G. & Strauss A.L. (1967). *The discovery of grounded theory: Strategies for qualitative research.* Chicago: Aldine.

Glasgow Media Group (1976). *Bad news.* London: Routledge & Kegan Paul.

Goffman, E. (1968). *Asylums.* Harmondsworth: Penguin.

Gold, R. (1969). Roles in sociological field observation. In G. McCall & J. Simmons (Eds.), *Issues in participant observation: A text and reader.* London: Addison Wesley.

Goldthorpe, J.H. (1980). *Social mobility and class structure in modern Britain.* Oxford: Oxford University Press.

Goldthorpe, J.H., Lockwood, D., Bechofer, F. & Platt, J. (1969). *The affluent worker in the class structure.* Cambridge: Cambridge University Press.

Goldthorpe, J.H. & Marshall, G. (1992). *The promising future of class analysis, Sociology, 26,* 3.

Goldthorpe, J.H. & Payne, C. (1986). On the class mobility of women, *Sociology, 20,* 4.

Goodman, A. & Shephard, A. (2002). *Inequality and living standards in Britain.* Institute for Fiscal Studies Briefing Note, 19.

Gordon, D. & Pantazis, C. (1995). *Breadline Britain in the 1990s.* Bristol University Press.

Gordon, D. et al. (2000). *Poverty and social exclusion in Britain.* York: Joseph Rowntree Foundation.

Gottfredson, M. & Hirschi, T. (1990). *General theory of crime.* Stanford: Stanford University Press.

Gouldner, A.W. (1971). *The coming crisis of Western sociology.* London: Heinemann.

Gouldner, A.W. (1975). *For sociology.* Harmondsworth: Penguin.

Graef, R. (1990). *Talking blues.* London: Fontana.

Graef, R. (2003). A tale of two Britains. *Observer,* 20th July.

Graham, J. & Bowling, B. (1995). *Young people and crime, Home Office Research Study,145.* London: Home Office.

Gramsci, A. (1971). *Selections from the prison notebooks.* London: Lawrence & Wishart.

Green, D. (Ed.), (2000). *Institutional racism and the police.* London: Institute for the Study of Civil Society.

Gregg, P. & Wadsworth, J. (Eds.), (1999). *The state of working Britain.* Manchester: Manchester University Press.

Hakim, C. (1995). 5 feminist myths about women's employment, *British Journal of Sociology, 46,* 1.

Hakim, C. (1996). The sexual division of labour and women's heterogeneity, *British Journal of Sociology, 47,* 1.

Hakim, C. (1997). Diversity and choice. In G. Dench (Ed.), *Rewriting the sexual contract.* London: Institute of Community Studies.

Hakim, C. (2000). *Work-lifestyle choices in the 21st century.* Oxford: Oxford University Press.

Halfpenny, P. (1984). *Principles of method.* York: Longman.

Hall, S., Critcher, C., Jefferson, T., Clarke, J. & Roberts, B. (1978). *Policing the crisis.* London: Macmillan.

Hall, T. (2003). *Better times than this.* London: Pluto Press.

Halsey, A.H., Floud, J. & Anderson, C.A. (1961). *Education, economy and society.* New York: Free Press.

Halsey, A.H., Heath, A. & Ridge, J.M. (1980). *Origins and destinations: Family, class and education in modern Britain.* Oxford: Clarendon.

Halsey, A.H., Lauder, H., Brown, P. & Wells, A. (1997). *Education: Culture, economy, society.* Oxford: Oxford University Press.

Hargreaves, D.H. (1967). *Social relations in a secondary school.* London: Routledge & Kegan Paul.

Hargreaves, D.H. (1975). *Interpersonal relations and education.* London: Routledge & Kegan Paul.

Hargreaves, D.H. (1982). *The challenge for the comprehensive school.* London: Routledge & Kegan Paul.

Harris, S. (2004). Wipe out middle-class advantage. *Daily Mail*, 12 November.

Hartsock, N. (1983). The feminist standpoint: Developing the ground for a specifically feminist historical materialism. In S. Harding & M. Hintikka (Eds.), *Discovering reality in feminist perspectives on epistemology, metaphysics, methodology and philosophy of science*. Dordrecht: D.D. Reidel, 1983.

Heath, A. & McMahon, D. (1995). *Education and occupational attainments*. London: Centre for Research into Elections and Social Trends.

Heath, A. & Payne, C. (2000). Social mobility. In A. Halsey (Ed.), *Twentieth Century British Social Trends*. Basingstoke: Macmillan.

Heidensohn, F. (1996). *Women and crime* (2nd ed.). London: Macmillan.

Heidensohn, F. (2002). Gender and crime. In M. Maguire et al. (Eds.), *The Oxford handbook of criminology* (3rd ed.). Oxford: Clarendon Press.

Herrnstein, R. & Murray, C. (1994). *The bell curve*. New York: Free Press.

Hey, V. (1997). *The company she keeps*. Milton Keynes: Open University Press.

Hill, A. (2003). Council estate decline spawns new underclass, *Observer*, 30th November.

Hills, J., Le Grand, J. & Piachaud, D. (2002). *Understanding social exclusion*. Oxford: Oxford University Press.

Hirschi, T. (1969). *Causes of delinquency*. Berkeley CA: University of California Press.

HMIC (Her Majesty's Inspectorate of Constabulary) (2001). *Winning the race: Embracing diversity*. London: Home Office.

Hobbs, D. (1988). *Doing the business*. Oxford: Oxford University Press.

Hobbs, D., Hadfield, P., Lister, S. & Winlow, S. (2003). *Bouncers*. Oxford: Oxford University Press.

Hoggart, R. (1957). *The uses of literacy*. London: Chatto & Windus.

Holbrook, B. & Jackson, B. (1996). Shopping around: Focus group research in North London, *Area, 28*, 136-142.

Holdaway, S. (1982). An inside job: A case study of covert research on the police. In M. Bulmer (Ed.), *Social research ethics*. London: Macmillan.

Holdaway, S. (1988). *Crime and deviance*. London: Macmillan.

Holdaway, S. (1996). *The racialisation of British policing*. London: Macmillan.

Holman, B. (1997). *Towards equality*. London: SPCK.

Holman, B. (1998). *Faith in the poor*. Oxford: Lion.

Homan, R. (1991). *The ethics of social research*. Harlow: Longman.

Home Office (2000). *Code of practice on reporting and recording racist incidents*. London: Home Office.

Home Office (2002). *Statistics on race and the criminal justice system*. London: Home Office.

Home Office (2003). *Statistics on women and the criminal justice system*. London: Home Office.

Hood, R. (1992). *Race and sentencing*. Oxford: Clarendon Press.

Hood, R. & Sparks, R. (1970). *Key issues in criminology*. London: Weidenfeld & Nicholson.

Howard, M., Garnham, A., Finister, G. & Veit-Wilson, J. (2001). *Poverty: the facts*. London: CPAG.

Hoyle, C. (2000). Being 'a nosy bloody cow': Ethical and methodological issues in researching domestic violence. In R.D. King & E. Wincup (Eds.), *Doing research on crime and justice*. Oxford: Oxford University Press.

Hudson, B. (1993). Racism and criminology: Concepts and controversies. In D. Cook & B. Hudson (Eds.), *Racism and criminology*. London: Sage.

Hughes, G. (2000). Understanding the politics of criminological research. In V. Jupp, P. Davies & P. Francis (Eds.), *Doing criminological research*. London.

Hughes, G. (2000). What are the futures of crime control? *Sociology Review, 9*.

Hughes, G. (2001). The competing logics of community sanctions: Welfare, rehabilitation and restorative justice. In McLaughlin, E. & Muncie, J. (Eds.), *Controlling crime* (2nd ed.). London: Sage.

Hughes, G. & Langan, M. (2001). Good or bad business?: Exploring corporate and organised crime. In J. Muncie & E. McLaughlin (Eds.), *The problem of crime* (2nd ed.). London: Sage.

Hughes, G., Leisted R. & Pilkington, A. (1996). *An independent evaluation of the Northamptonshire Diversion Unit*. Northampton: Nene Centre for Research.

Human Development Report (2003). Oxford University Press: UN Development Report.

Hutton, W. (1995). *The state we're in*. London: Jonathan Cape.

Hutton, W. (2002). *The world we're in*. London: Abacus.

Ireson, J. & Hallam, S. (2001), *Ability grouping in education*. London: Sage.

Jackson, D. (1998). Breaking out of the binary trap: Boys' underachievement, schooling and gender relations. In D. Epstein et al. (Eds.), *Failing boys? Issues in gender and achievement*. Buckingham: Open University Press.

Jacobson, J. (1998). *Islam in transition: Religion and identity among British Pakistani youth*. London: Routledge.

Jagger, E. (2001). *Marketing Molly and Melville*. Sociology, 35, 639-659.

Jefferis, B.J., Power, C. & Hertzman, C. (2002). Birth weight, childhood socioeconomic environment and cognitive development in the 1958 British birth cohort study. *British Medical Journal, 325*, No. 7359.

Jenkins, R. (1986). *Racism and recruitment*. Cambridge: Cambridge University Press.

Jensen, A.R. (1973). *Educational differences*. London: Methuen.

Jessop, B. (1987). The future of capitalism. In R.J. Anderson et al. (Eds.) *Classic disputes in sociology*. London: Allen Unwin.

Jones, I. (1974). A critique of Murdock and Phelps' 'Mass media and the secondary school'. Unpublished dissertation, School of Education, University of Leicester.

Jones, K. (1998). Death of a Princess. *Sociology Review*, September.

Jones, S (1998). *Criminology*. London: Butterworth.

Jones, T., McLean, B. & Young, J. (1986). *The Islington Crime Survey*. Aldershot: Gower.

Jupp, V., Davies, P. & Francis, P. (Eds.) (2000). *Doing criminological research*. London: Sage Publications.

Kalra,V. (2003). Police lore and community disorder: Diversity in the criminal justice system. In D. Mason (Ed.), *Explaining ethnic differences*. Bristol: The Policy Press.

Kaluzynska, E. (1980). Wiping the floor with theory. *Feminist Review, 7*.

Keddie, N. (1973). Classroom knowledge. In N. Keddie (Ed.), *Tinker, tailor ... the myth of cultural deprivation*. Harmondsworth: Penguin.

Kellner, P. & Wilby, P. (1980). The 1:2:4 rule of class in Britain. *Sunday Times*, 13th January.

Kelly, J. & De Graaf, N.D. (1997). National context, parental socialisation and religious belief: Results from 15 nations. *American Sociological Review, 62*, 639-659.

Kerr, J. (1994). *Understanding football hooliganism*. Buckingham: Open University Press.

Kincaid, J.C. (1973). *Poverty and equality in Britain*. Harmondsworth: Penguin.

King, R. (1984). The man in the Wendy House: Researching infant schools. In R.G. Burgess (Ed.), *The research process in educational settings: Ten case studies*. Lewes: Falmer.

Kirton, A. (1998). Labour and education: The story so far. *S magazine*, September.

Kitzinger, J (1993). Understanding AIDS. In J. Eldridge (Ed.), *Getting the message: News, truth and power*. London: Routledge.

Labov, W. (1973). The logic of nonstandard English. In N. Keddie (Ed.), *Tinker, tailor ... the myth of cultural deprivation*. Harmondsworth: Penguin.

Lacey, C. (1970). *Hightown Grammar*. Manchester: Manchester University Press.

Lander, B. (1962). An ecological analysis of Baltimore. In M.E. Wolfgang, L. Savitz & N. Johnston (Eds.), *The sociology of crime and delinquency*. New York: John Wiley & Sons.

Langford, W., Lewis, C., Soloman, Y. & Warin, J. (2001). *Family understandings*. London: Joseph Rowntree Foundation.

Langham, S. (2002). Feminism and the classroom. *Sociology Review*, November.

Langley, P. (Ed.) (1988). *Discovering sociology*. Ormskirk: Causeway Press.

Lawson, A. (1989). *Adultery: An analysis of love and betrayal*. Oxford: Oxford University Press.

Layton-Henry, Z. (1992). *The politics of immigration*. Oxford: Blackwell.

Lea, J. & Young, J. (1982). The riots in Britain: Urban violence and political marginalisation. In D. Cowell, T. Jones & J. Young (Eds.), *Policing the riots*. London: Junction Books.

Lea, J. & Young, J. (1993). *What is to be done about law and order?* (2nd ed.). London: Pluto Press.

Lee, D., Marsden, D., Rickman, P. & Dunscombe, J. (1990). *Scheming for youth: A study of YTS in the enterprise culture*. Milton Keynes: Open University Press.

Lee, D. & Turner, B. (1996). *Conflicts about class*. London: Longman.

Lee, R. (2000). *Unobtrusive measures in social research*. Buckingham: Open University Press.

Lemert, E.M. (1972). *Human deviance, social problems and social control* (2nd ed.). Englewood Cliffs NJ: Prentice Hall.

Leonard, M. (2000). Back to the future?, *Sociology Review, 10*, 2.

Levi, M. (1993). *The investigation, prosecution and trial of serious fraud, Research Study, 14*. London: Royal Commission on Criminal Justice.

Lewis, O. (1968). *La Vida*. London: Panther Books.

Light, A. (Ed.) (1998). *Tupac Ama Ru Shakur, 1971-1996*. London: Plexus.

Lobban, G. (1974). Data report on British reading schemes. *Times Educational Supplement*, March 1.

Lofland, J. & Lofland, L. (1994). *Analysing social settings*. Belmont, CA: Wordsworth.

Lombroso, C. (1876). *L'uomo delinquente*. Milan: Hoepli.

Long Lance, Chief Buffalo Child. (1956). *Long Lance*. London: Corgi.

Lupton, D. (1996). *Food, the body and the self*. London: Sage.

Mac an Ghaill, M. (1988). *Young, gifted and Black: Student-teacher relations in the schooling of Black youth*. Milton Keynes: Open University Press.

Mac an Ghaill, M. (1992). Coming of age in 1980s England: Reconceptualising black students' schooling experience. In D. Gill, B. Mayor & M. Blair (Eds.). *Racism and education: Structures and strategies*. London: Sage.

Mac an Ghaill, M. (1994). *The making of men: Masculinities, sexualities and schooling*. Buckingham: Open University Press.

Macdonald, K. & Tipton, D. (1993). Using documents. In N. Gilbert (Ed.), *Researching social life*. London: Sage.

MacGregor, S. (2001). The problematic community. In M. May, R. Page & E. Brunsdon (Eds.), *Understanding social problems: Issues in social policy*. Oxford: Blackwell.

Machin, S. (2003). Unto them that hath … *Centrepiece, 8*, 4-9.

Mack, J. & Lansley, S. (1985). *Poor Britain*. London: Allen & Unwin.

Macpherson, W. (1999). *The Stephen Lawrence Inquiry*. London: HMSO.

Maguire, M. (2002). Crime statistics. In M.Maguire et al. (Eds.), *The Oxford handbook of criminology* (3rd ed.). Oxford: Clarendon Press.

Mahony, P. (1998). Girls will be girls and boys will be first. In D. Epstein et al. (Eds.), *Failing boys? Issues in gender and achievement*. Buckingham: Open University Press.

Malbon, B. (1999). *Clubbing: Dancing, ecstasy and vitality*. London: Routledge.

Malcom X (1966). *The autobiography of Malcolm X*. New York: Grove Press.

Mandel, E. (1984). *Delightful murder: A social history of the crime story*. London: Pluto.

Marks, G. & Houston, D. (2002). Attitudes towards work and motherhood held by working and non-working mothers. *Work, Employment and Society, 16*, 2.

Marquand, D. (1998). *The unprincipled society: New demands and old politics*. London: Fontana.

Marsh, A. & Perry, J. (2003). Ethnic minority families – poverty and disadvantage. In C. Kober (Ed.), *Black and ethnic minority children and poverty*. London: National Children's Bureau.

Marshall, G. (1997). *Repositioning class*. London: Sage.

Marshall, G. & Rose, D. (1989). Reply to Saunders. *Network: Newsletter of the British Sociological Association, 44*, 4-5.

Marshall, G. & Swift, A. (1996). Merit and mobility, *Sociology, 30*, 2.

Marshall, G., Rose, D., Newby, H. & Vogler, C. (1988). *Social class in modern Britain*. London: Unwin Hyman.

Martin, C. (2000). Doing research in a prison setting. In V. Jupp, P. Davies & P. Francis (Eds.), *Doing criminological research*. London: Sage.

Mason, D. (1982). Some problems with the concepts of race and racism. University of Leicester Discussion Papers in Sociology S92/5.

Matza, D. (1964). *Delinquency and drift*. London: Wiley.

Matza, D. & Sykes, G.M. (1961). Juvenile delinquency and subterranean values. *American Sociological Review, 26*, 5.

Mauer, M. (1997). *Intended and unintended consequences: State racial disparities in imprisonment*. Washington DC: The Sentencing Project.

May, T. (2001). *Social research: Issues, methods and process*. Buckingham: Open University Press.

Mayhew, P. (2000). Researching the state of crime: Local, national and international victim surveys. In R.D. King & E. Wincup (Eds.), *Doing research on crime and justice*. Oxford: Oxford University Press.

Mayhew, P., Aye Maung, N. & Mirrlees-Black, C. (1993). *The 1992 British Crime Survey, Home Office Research Study, 132*. London: HMSO.

Mayhew, P., Mirrlees-Black, C. & Aye Maung, N. (1994). *Trends in crime : Findings from the 1994 British Crime Survey, Home Office Research and Statistics Department Research Findings, 18*. London: HMSO.

McDonnell, B. (2004). What is social capital?, *Sociology Review, 13*, 3.

McGrew, A. (1992). A global society. In S. Hall et al. (Eds.). *Modernity and its futures*. Cambridge: Polity Press.

McKenzie, J. (2001). Changing education: *A sociology of education since 1944*. Harlow: Pearson Education.

McKnight, A. (2002). Low-paid work. In J. Hills et al. (Eds.). *Understanding social exclusion*. Oxford: Oxford University Press.

McKnight, A. (2005). Employment: Tackling poverty through 'work for those who can'. In J. Hills & K. Stewart (Eds.), *A more equal society? New Labour, poverty, inequality and exclusion*. Bristol: The Policy Press.

McKnight, A., Glennerster, H. & Lupton, R. (2005). Education, education, education …: An assessment of Labour's success in tackling education inequalities. In J. Hills & K. Stewart (Eds.), *A more equal society? New Labour, poverty, inequality and exclusion*. Bristol: The Policy Press.

McLaughlin, E. & Muncie, J. (2001). Introduction. In McLaughlin, E. & Muncie, J. (Eds.), *Controlling crime* (2nd ed.). London: Sage.

Meadows, P. (1999). *The flexible labour market*. London: National Association of Pension Funds.

Merton, R.K. (1968). Social structure and anomie. In R.K. Merton *Social theory and social structure*. New York: The Free Press.

Messerschmidt, J. (1993). *Masculinities and crime*. Lanham: Rowman & Littlefield.

Meyenn, R.J. (1980). School girls' peer groups. In P. Woods (Ed.), *Pupil strategies*. London: Croom Helm.

Midwinter, E. (1975). The community school. In J. Rushton & J.D. Turner (Eds.), *Education and deprivation*. Manchester: Manchester University Press.

Mies, M. (1993). Towards a methodology for feminist research. In M. Hammersley (Ed.), *Social research: Philosophy, politics and practice*. London: Sage.

Miles, M.B. & Huberman, A.M. (1994). *Qualitative data analysis*. Thousand Oaks, CA: Sage.

Miles, R. (1989). *Racism*. London: Routledge.

Miller, D. et al. (1998). *Shopping, place and identity*. London: Routledge.

Miller, W.B. (1958) Lower class culture as a generating milieu of gang delinquency, *Journal of Social Issues, 14*.

Miner, M. (1965). Body ritual among the Nacirema. In W.A. Lessa & E.Z Vogt (Eds.), *Reader in comparative religion: An anthropological approach* (2nd ed.). New York: Harper & Row.

Mirrlees-Black, C. & Byron, C. (2000). *Domestic violence: Findings from the BCS self-completion questionnaire. Research Findings no. 86*. Home Office Research, Development and Statistics Directorate.

Mirza, H. (1992). *Young, female and Black*. London: Routledge.

Mirza, H. (Ed.) (1997). *Black British feminism*. London: Routledge.

Modood, T., Berthoud, R., Lakey, J., Nazroo, P., et al. (Eds.) (1997). *Ethnic minorities in Britain: Diversity and disadvantage*. London: Policy Studies Institute.

Mollard, C. (2001). *Asylum: The truth behind the headlines*. Oxfam.

Moore, D. (1994). *The lads in action: Social process in an urban youth subculture*. Aldershot: Ashgate.

Morgan, D. (1996). *Family connections*. Cambridge: Polity.

Morris, T.P. (1957). *The criminal area: A study in social ecology*. London: Routledge & Kegan Paul.

Morton, D.C. & Watson, D.R. (1973). Compensatory education and contemporary liberalism in the US: A sociological view. In J. Raynor & J. Harden (Eds.), *Equality and city schools, Volume 2*. London: Routledge & Kegan Paul.

Muggleton, D. (2000). *Inside subculture: The postmodern meaning of style*. London: Berg.

Muncie, J. (1987) Much ado about nothing? The sociology of moral panics, *Social Studies Review, 3*.

Muncie, J. (2001). The construction and deconstruction of crime. In J. Muncie & E. McLaughlin (Eds.), *The problem of crime*. London: Sage.

Munck, R. & Rolston, W. (1987). *Belfast in the 30s: An oral history*. Belfast: Blackstaff Press.

Murray, C. (1984). *Losing ground*. New York: Basic Books.

Murray, C. (1990). *The emerging British underclass*. London: Institute of Economic Affairs.

Murray, C. (1994). The new Victorians and the new rabble. *Sunday Times*, 29th May.

Murray, C. (1996). *Charles Murray and the underclass: The developing debate*. London: Institute of Economic Affairs.

Myhill, A. & Allen, J. (2002). *Rape and sexual assault of women: The extent and nature of the problem*. London: Home Office Research, Development and Statistics Directorate.

Naffine, N. (1987). *Female crime*. Sydney: Allen & Unwin.

National Children's Bureau www.ncb.org.uk

National Prisons Survey see Walmsley et al. (1992).

Nazroo, J. (1999). Uncovering gender differences in the use of marital violence: The effect of methodology. In G. Allan (Ed.), *The sociology of the family: A Reader*. Oxford: Blackwell.

Newark, P. (1980). *The illustrated encyclopedia of the old West*. London: André Deutsch.

Nightingale, C. (1993). *On the edge*. New York: Basic Books.

Noon, M. & Blyton, P. (2002). *The realities of work*. Basingstoke: Palgrave.

O'Connell Davidson, J. & Layder, D. (1994). *Methods, sex and madness*. London: Routledge.

Oakley, A. (1981). Interviewing women: A contradiction in terms. In H. Roberts (Ed.), *Doing feminist research*. London: Routledge & Kegan Paul.

Oakley, A. & Mitchell, J. (1998). *Who's afraid of feminism?* London: Penguin.

Odone, C. (2001). It's good to be rich, *The Observer*, 25th March.

Olds, D.L. et al. (1997). Long-term effects of home visitation on material life course and child abuse and neglect: Fifteen year follow-up of a randomised trial. *Journal of the American Medical Association, 278*, 637-643.

Page, R.M. (2002). New Labour and the welfare state. In M. Holborn (Ed.), *Developments in Sociology, Volume 18*. Ormskirk: Causeway Press.

Pahl, J. (2000). Social polarisation in the electronic economy. In R. Crompton et al. (Eds.), *Renewing class analysis*. Oxford: Blackwell.

Pahl, R.E. (1984). *Divisions of labour*. Oxford: Basil Blackwell.

Pahl, R.E. (1989) Is the emperor naked?, *International Journal of Urban and Regional Research, 13*.

Painter, K. & Farrington, D. (1999). Street lighting and crime: Diffusion of benefits in the Stoke-on-Trent Project. In K. Painter & D. Farrington (Eds.), *Surveillance of public space: CCTV, street lighting and crime prevention*. Monsey, NY: Criminal Justice Press.

Pakulski, J. & Waters, M. (1996). *The death of class*. London: Sage.

Palmer, G., Rahman, M. & Kenway, P. (2002). *Monitoring poverty and social exclusion 2002*. York: JRF.

Parekh, B. (2000). *The future of multi-ethnic Britain*. London: Profile Books.

Parkin, F. (1979). *Marxism and class theory*. London: Tavistock.

Parsons, T. (1951). *The social system*. New York: The Free Press.

Parsons, T. (1955). The American family: Its relations to personality and social structure. In T. Parsons & R. Bales (Eds.), *Family, socialisation and interaction process*. New York: The Free Press.

Parsons, T. (1961). The school class as a social system. In A. H. Halsey et al. (Eds.), *Education, economy and society*. New York: Free Press.

Pawson, R. (1989). Methodology. In M. Haralambos (Ed.), *Developments in sociology, Volume 5*. Ormskirk: Causeway Press.

Pawson, R. (1992). Feminist methodology. In M. Haralambos (Ed.), *Developments in sociology, Volume 8*. Ormskirk: Causeway Press.

Pawson, R. (1995). Methods of content/document/media analysis. In M. Haralambos (Ed.), *Developments in sociology, volume 11*. Ormskirk: Causeway Press.

Paxton, W. & Dixon, M. (2004). *The state of the nation: An audit of injustice in the UK*. London: Institute for Public Policy Research.

Payne, G. & Abbott, P. (1990). *The social mobility of women*. London: Falmer Press.

Payne, J. (2001). *Patterns of participation in full-time education after 16: An analysis of the England and Wales Youth Cohort Study*. London: DfEE.

Pearson, G. (1983). *Hooligan: A history of respectable fears*. London: Macmillan.

Pease, K. (2002). Crime reduction. In M. Maguire, R. Morgan & R. Reiner (Eds.), *The Oxford handbook of criminology* (3rd ed.). Oxford: Oxford University Press.

Phillips, C. & Bowling, B. (2002). Racism, ethnicity and criminal justice. In M. Maguire et al. (Eds.), *The Oxford handbook of criminology* (3rd ed.) Oxford: Clarendon Press.

Philo, G. (1993). Getting the message: Audience research in the Glasgow University Media Group. In J. Eldridge (Ed.), *Getting the message: News, truth and power*. London: Routledge.

Philo, G. & Miller, D. (2002). Circuits of communication and power: Recent developments in media sociology. In M. Holborn (Ed.), *Developments in Sociology, Volume 18*. Ormskirk: Causeway Press.

Pilcher, J. (1999). *Women in contemporary Britain*. London: Routledge.

Pilkington, A. (2001). Institutional racism and social exclusion: The experience of minority ethnic groups in the labour market. In M. Haralambos (Ed.), *Developments in Sociology, Volume 17*. Ormskirk: Causeway Press.

Pilkington, A. (2003). *Racial disadvantage and ethnic diversity in Britain*. Basingstoke: Palgrave.

Platt, J. (1976). *Realities of social research: An empirical study of British sociologists*. London: Chatto and Windus.

Platt, L. (2002). Parallel lives? London: CPAG

Plummer, G. (2000). *Failing working-class girls*. Stoke on Trent: Trentham Books.

Plummer, K. (1979). Misunderstanding labelling perspectives. In D. Downes & P. Rock (Eds.), *Deviant interpretations*. Oxford: M. Robertson.

Pryce, K. (1979). *Endless pressure*. Harmondsworth: Penguin.

Pullinger, J. & Summerfield, C. (1998). *Social focus on women and men*. London: EOC/ONS.

Punch, K. (1998). *Introduction to social research*. London: Sage.

Putnam, R. (2000). *Bowling alone*. New York: Simon & Schuster.

Quinton, D., Pickles, A., Maughan, B. & Rutter, M. (1993). Partners, peers and pathways: Assortative pairing and continuities in conduct disorder. *Development and psychopathology, 5*, 763-783.

Rabow, J. & Neuman, C.E. (1984). Garbaeology as method for cross-validating interviews data on sensitive topics. *Sociology and Social Research, 68*, 480-497.

Radcliffe Richards, J. (1982). *The sceptical feminist*. Harmondsworth: Penguin.

Rafaeli, A., Dutton, J., Harquail, C.V. & Mackie-Lewis, S. (1997). Navigating by attire: The use of dress by female administrative employees. *Academy of Management Journal, 40*, 9-45.

Rayment, T. & Reeve, S. (1995). The overclass. *Sunday Times*, 27th August.

Raynor, P. (2002). Community penalties: Probation, punishment and 'what works'. In M. Maguire, R. Morgan & R. Reiner (Eds.), *The Oxford handbook of criminology* (3rd ed.). Oxford: Oxford University Press.

Reay, D. (1998). *Class work: Mothers' involvement in their children's primary schooling*. London: UCL Press.

Reid, I. (1998). *Class in Britain*. Cambridge: Polity Press.

Reiner, R. (1993). Race, crime and justice: Models of interpretation. In L. Gelsthorpe (Ed.), *Minority ethnic groups in the criminal justice system*. Cambridge: Institute of Criminology.

Reiner, R. (1994). Policing and the police. In M. Maguire et al. (Eds.), *The Oxford handbook of criminology* (1st ed.). Oxford: Clarendon Press.

Reiner, R. (2000). Police Research. In R.D. King & E. Wincup (Eds.), *Doing research on crime and justice*. Oxford: Oxford University Press.

Reiner, R. (2002). Media made criminality. In M. Maguire et al. (Eds.), *The Oxford handbook of criminology* (3rd ed.). Oxford: Clarendon Press.

Reiner, R., Livingstone, S. & Allen, J. (2000). No more happy endings? The media and popular concern about crime since the Second World War. In T. Hope & R. Sparks (Eds.), *Crime, risk and insecurity*. London: Routledge.

Rengert, G. & Wasilchick, J. (2000). *Suburban burglary: A tale of two suburbs* (2nd ed.), Springfield, Ill: Charles C. Thomas.

Rex, J. & Tomlinson, S. (1979). *Colonial immigrants in a British city*. London: Routledge Kegan Paul.

Reynolds, T. (1997). Misrepresenting the Black woman. In H. Mirza (Ed.), *Black British feminism*. London: Routledge.

Rist, R. (1970). Student social class and teacher expectations: The self-fulfilling prophecy in ghetto education. *Harvard Educational Review, 40*.

Ritzer, G. (1996). *The McDonaldization of society*. London: Pine Forge Press.

Roberts, K. (1997). Same activities, different meanings. *Leisure Studies, 16*.

Roberts, K. (2001). *Class in modern Britain*. Basingstoke: Palgrave.

Robinson, J. (1996). Still the top class, *Spectator*, 16th November.

Rock, P. (1979). Sociology of crime. In D. Downes & P. Rock (Eds.), *Deviant interpretations*. Oxford: M. Robertson.

Rosenberg, M. (1979). *Conceiving the self*. New York: Basic Books.

Rosenthal, R. & Jacobson, L. (1968). *Pygmalion in the classroom*. New York: Holt, Rinehart & Winston.

Rowbotham, S. (1973). *Woman's consciousness: Man's world*. Harmondsworth: Penguin.

Rowbotham, S. (1979). The trouble with patriarchy, *New Stateman*, 21st December.

Royle, E. (1997). *Modern Britain: A social history 1750-1997*. London: Hodder Headline.

Rutter, M. & Smith, D.J. (Eds.) (1995). *Psychosocial disorders in young people: Time trends and their causes*. Chichester: Wiley.

Sacks, J. (2003). *The dignity of difference*. London: Continuum.

Sainsbury, R., Ditch, J. & Hutton, S. (1993). Computer assisted personal interviewing. *Social Research Update, Issue 3*. Department of Sociology, University of Surrey.

Sallybanks, J. (2000). Assessing the police use of decoy vehicles. *Police Research Series, 137*. London: Home Office.

Sampson, R.J. & Laub, J.H. (1990). Crime and deviance over the life course: The salience of adult social bonds. *American Sociological Review, 55*, 609-627.

Sampson, R.J. & Raudenbush, S. (1999). Systematic social observation of public spaces: A new look at disorder in urban neighbourhoods. *American Journal of Sociology*.

Saunders, P. (1989). Left write in Sociology. *Network: Newsletter of the British Sociological Association, 44*, 3-4.

Saunders, P. (1990). *Social class and stratification*. London: Routledge.

Saunders, P. (1995). *Capitalism: A social audit*. Buckingham: Open University Press.

Saunders, P. (1995). Might Britain be a meritocracy?, *Sociology, 29*, 1.

Saunders, P. (1996). *Unequal but fair? A study of class barriers in Britain*. London: IEA.

Saunders, P. (2002). Reflections on the meritocracy debate in Britain, *British Journal of Sociology, 53*, 4.

Savage, M. (2000). *Class analysis and social transformation*. Buckingham: Open University Press.

Savage, M., Bagnall, G. & Longhurst, B. (2001). Ordinary, ambivalent and defensive, *Sociology, 35*, 1.

Savage, M., Barlow, J., Dickens, P. & Fielding, T. (1992). *Property, bureaucracy and culture*. London: Routledge.

Savage, M. & Egerton, M. (1997). Social mobility, individual ability and the inheritance of class inequality, *Sociology, 31*, 4.

Scarman, L. (1981). *The Scarman Report: The Brixton disorders*. London: HMSO.

Schuerman, L. & Kobrin, S. (1986). Community careers in crime. In A.J. Reiss & M. Tonry (Eds.), *Communities and crime*. Chicago: University of Chicago Press.

Schuman, H. & Presser, S. (1981). *Questions and answers in attitude surveys: Experiments in question form, wording and context*. San Diego: Academic Press.

Schutt, R. (1996). *Investigating the social world*. London: Sage.

Schweinhart, L.J., Barnes, H.V. & Weikart, D.P. (1993). *Significant benefits: The High Scope Perry preschool study through age 27*. Ypsilanti, Michigan: High Scope Press.

Scott, J. (1986). Does Britain still have a ruling class?, *Social Studies Review, 2*, 1.

Scott, J. (1986a). The debate on ownership and control, *Social Studies Review, 1*, 3.

Scott, J. (1990). *A matter of record*. Cambridge: Polity Press.

Scott, J. (1991). *Who rules Britain?* Cambridge: Polity Press.

Scott, J. (1996). *Stratification and power*. Cambridge: Polity Press.

Seenan, G. (2003). Pity the poor struggling middle classes, *The Guardian*, 5th September.

Seitz, V. (1990). Intervention programmes for impoverished children: A comparison of educational and family support models. *Annals of Child Development, 7*, 73-103.

Sewell, T. (1997). *Black masculinities and schooling.* Stoke on Trent: Trentham Books.

Sharpe, K. (2000). Street corner research with prostitutes. In R.D. King & E. Wincup (Eds.), *Doing research on crime and justice.* Oxford: Oxford University Press.

Sharpe, S. (1976). *Just like a girl: How girls learn to be women.* Harmondsworth: Penguin.

Sharpe, S. (1994). *Just like a girl: How girls learn to be women: The 70s to the 90s.* Harmondsworth: Penguin.

Shaw, C.R. & McKay, H.D. (1942). *Juvenile delinquency and urban areas.* Chicago: University of Chicago Press.

Sianne, G. & Wilkinson, H. (1995). *Gender, feminism and the future.* London: Demos.

Simmons, J. & Dodd, T. (2003). *Crime in England and Wales 2002/2003.* London: ONS.

Simmons, R. (2001). Questionnaires. In N. Gilbert (Ed.), *Researching social life* (2nd ed.). London: Sage.

Simón, A. (1981). A quantitative, non-reactive study of mass behaviour with emphasis on the cinema as behavioural catalyst. *Psychological Reports,* 475-485.

Simons, H. (1984). Guidelines for the conduct of an independent evaluation. In C. Adelman (Ed.), *The politics and ethics of evaluation.* London: Croom Helm.

Sinclair, S. (2003). Poverty and social exlcusion. In M. Holborn (Ed.), *Developments in Sociology, Volume 19.* Ormskirk: Causeway Press

Sivanandan, A. (1982). *A different hunger.* London: Pluto Press.

Skeggs, B. (1997). *Formations of class and gender.* London: Sage.

Skogan, W.G. (1990). *Disorder and decline: Crime and the spiral of decay in American neighbourhoods.* New York: The Free Press.

Smart, C. (1977). *Women, crime and criminology.* London: Routledge.

Smart, C. & Neale, B. (1999). *Family fragments.* Cambridge: Polity.

Smith, D.J. (1977). *Racial disadvantage in Britain.* Harmondsworth: Penguin.

Smith, D.J. (1997). Ethnic origins, crime and criminal justice. In M. Maguire, R. Morgan & R. Reiner (Eds.), *The Oxford handbook of criminology* (2nd ed.). Oxford: Oxford University Press.

Smith, D.J. (2002). Crime and the life course. In M. Maguire, R. Morgan & R. Reiner (Eds.), *The Oxford handbook of criminology* (3rd ed.). Oxford: Oxford University Press.

Smith, D.J. & Gray, J. (1995). *Police and people in London.* Aldershot: Gower.

Smith, D.J. & McVie, S. (2003). Theory and method in the Edinburgh study of youth transitions and crime. *British Journal of Criminology, 43,* 169-195.

Smith, D.J. & Tomlinson, S. (1989). *The school effect: A study of multi-racial comprehensives.* London: Policy Studies Institute.

Smith, T. & Noble, M. (1995). *Poverty and schooling in the 1990s.* London: CPAG.

Social Exclusion Unit (2000). *Minority ethnic issues in social exclusion and neighbourhood renewal.* London: SEU.

Soothill, K., Francis, B. & Fligelstone, R. (2002). Patterns of offending behaviour: A New Approach. *Home Office Research Findings, 171.* London: Home Office.

Stanko, E. (1994) Challenging the problem of men's individual violence. In T. Newburn & E. Stanko (Eds.), *Just boys doing business?* London: Routledge.

Stets, J.E. & Straus, M.A. (1990). Gender differences in reporting marital violence and its medical and psychological consequences. In M.A. Straus & R.J. Gelles (Eds.), *Physical violence in American families.* London: Transaction.

Strathdee, R. (2003). Labour market change, vocational education and training, and social class. In M. Holborn (Ed.), *Developments in Sociology, Volume 19.* Ormskirk: Causeway Press.

Straus, M.A., Gelles, R.J. & Steinmetz, S. (1980). *Behind closed doors: Violence in the American family.* New York: Anchor.

Sugarman, B. (1970). Social class, values and behaviour in schools. In M. Craft (Ed.), *Family, class and education.* London: Longman.

Sukhnandan, L. & Lee, B. (1998). *Streaming, setting and grouping by ability.* Slough: NFER.

Sullivan, A. (2001). Cultural capital and educational attainment. *Sociology, 35,* 4.

Sullivan, O. (2000). The division of domestic labour, *Sociology, 34,* 3.

Sutherland, E. (1949). *White collar crime.* New York: Holt, Rinehart & Winston.

Sutherland, H., Sefton, T. & Piachaud, D. (2003). *Poverty in Britain.* York: Joseph Rowntree Foundation.

Sykes, G.M. & Matza, D. (1962). Techniques of neutralisation: A theory of delinquency. In M.E. Wolfgang, E. Savitz & N. Johnston (Eds.), *The sociology of crime and delinquency.* New York: John Wiley & Sons.

Taraborrelli, P. (1993). Becoming a carer. In N. Gilbert (Ed.), *Researching social life.* London: Sage.

Taylor, I., Walton, P. & Young, J. (1973). *The new criminology.* London: Routledge.

Taylor, M. (2005). School league tables. *The Guardian,* 13 January.

Taylor, P. & Bain, P. (1999). An assembly line in the head, *Industrial Relations Journal, 30,* 2.

Taylor, S. (1988). *Suicide.* London: Longman.

Tolson, A. (1977). *The limits of masculinity.* London: Tavistock.

Townsend, P. (1979). *Poverty in the United Kingdom.* Harmondsworth: Penguin.

Toynbee, P. (2003). *Hard work: Life in low pay Britain.* London: Bloomsbury.

Tumin, M. (1967). *Social stratification: The forms and functions of social inequality.* Englewood Cliffs: Prentice-Hall.

von Hirsch, A. (1976). Giving criminals their just deserts. *Civil Liberties Review, 3,* 23-35.

Wadsworth, J. (2001). The labour market performance of ethnic minorities in Britain. In R. Dickens, J. Wadsworth & P. Gregg (Eds.), *The state of working Britain update 2001.* LSE: Centre for Economic Performance.

Walby, S. (1986). Gender politics and social theory, *Sociology, 22.*

Walby, S. (1990). *Theorising patriarchy.* Oxford: Blackwell.

Walklate, S. (2000). Researching victims. In R.D. King & E. Wincup (Eds.), *Doing research on crime and justice.* Oxford: Oxford University Press.

Walklate, S. (2003). *Understanding criminology: Current theoretical debates* (2nd ed.). Buckingham: Open University Press.

Walmsley, R., Howard, L. & White, S. (1992). *The National Prison Survey 1991: Main Findings.* Home Office Research Study, 128. London: HMSO.

Walter, N. (1998). Girls! New feminism needs you! *New Statesman,* 16th January.

Walter, N. (1998a). *The new feminism.* London: Little, Brown & Co.

Ward, T. (2000). The new reserve army of domestic labour, *Sociology Review, 10,* 1.

Watkins, J. (2003). A Mini adventure. *People Management,* 6th November.

Webb, E.J., Campbell, D.T., Schwartz, R.D. & Sechrest, L. (1966). *Unobtrusive measures: Nonreactive measures in the social sciences.* Chicago: Rand McNally.

Weber, M. (1948). Class, status, party. In H. Gerth & C.W.Mills (Eds.), *From Max Weber.* London: Routledge.

Weber, M. (1958). *The Protestant ethic and the spirit of capitalism.* New York: Charles Scribner's Sons.

Weber, M. (1964). *The theory of social and economic organisations.* New York: The Free Press.

Wellings, K., Field, J., Johnson, A. & Wadsworth, J. (1994). *Sexual behaviour in Britain: The national survey of sexual attitudes and lifestyles.* Harmondsworth: Penguin.

Westergaard, J. (1970). The rediscovery of the cash nexus. In R. Miliband & J. Saville (Eds.), *The Socialist Register.* London: Merlin Press.

Westergaard, J. (1995). *Who gets what?* Cambridge: Polity Press.

Westergaard, J. (1996). Class in Britain since 1979. In D. Lee & B. Turner (Eds.), *Conflict about class.* London: Longman.

White, L. (1998). Boys will be boys – and failures. *The Sunday Times*, 11 January.

Wiles, P. & Costello, A. (2000). The 'road to nowhere': The evidence for travelling criminals. *Home Office Research Study, 207*. London: Home Office.

Wilkinson, R. (1998). Why inequality is bad for you. *Marxism Today*, November.

Williams, P. and Dickinson, J. (1993). Fear of crime: Read all about it? *British Journal of Criminology, 33*.

Williamson, H. (1997). Status zero: Youth and the underclass. In R. MacDonald (Ed.), *Youth, the underclass and social exclusion*. London: Routledge.

Willis, P. (1977). *Learning to labour: How working-class kids get working-class jobs*. Farnborough: Saxon House.

Willmott, P. (1980). A view from an independent research institute. In M. Cross (Ed.), *Social research and public policy: Three perspectives*. Social Research Association.

Wilson, J.Q. (1975). *Thinking about crime*. New York: Basic Books.

Wilson, J.Q. (1983). *Thinking about crime* (2nd ed.). New York: Basic Books.

Wilson, J.Q. & Hernstein, R. (1985). *Crime and human nature*. New York: Simon & Schuster.

Wilson, J.Q. & Kelling, G. (2003). Broken windows: The police and neighbourhood safety. In E. McLaughlin et al. (Eds.), *Criminological perspectives* (2nd ed.). London: Sage.

Winant, H. (1994). Racial formation and identity. In A. Rattansi & S. Westwood (Eds.), *Racism, modernity and identity*. Cambridge: Polity Press.

Winlow,S. (2001). *Badfellas*. Oxford: Berg.

Wirth, L. (1945). The problem of minority groups. In R. Linton (Ed.), *The science of man in the world crisis*. New York: Columbia University Press.

Wolf, N. (1993). *Fire with fire*. London: Chatto & Windus.

Woolf, A. (2002). *Does education matter: Myths about education and economic growth*. Harmondsworth: Penguin.

Wright, C. (1986). School processes – An ethnographic study. In S.J. Eggleston, D. Dunn & M. Angali (Eds.), *Education for some*. Stoke on Trent: Trentham Books.

Wright, C. (1992). Early education: Multiracial primary school classrooms. In D. Gill, B. Mayor & M. Blair (Eds.), *Racism and education*. London: Sage.

Wright, E.O. (1985). *Classes*. London: Verso

Wright, R.T. & Decker, S.H. (1994). *Burglars on the job: Street life and residential break-ins*. Boston, MA: Northeastern University Press.

Young, J. (1971). *The drugtakers*. London: Paladin.

Young, J. (1986). The failure of criminology: The need for a radical realism. In R. Matthews & J. Young (Eds.), *Confronting crime*. London: Sage.

Young, J. (1992). Ten points of realism. In J. Young & R. Matthews (Eds.), *Rethinking criminology: The realist debate*. London: Sage.

Young, J. (1997). Left realist criminology. In M. Maguire et al. (Eds.), *The Oxford handbook of criminology* (2nd ed.). Oxford: Clarendon Press.

Young, J. (1999). *The exclusive society: Social exclusion, crime and difference in late modernity*. London: Sage.

Young, J. (2002). Crime and social exclusion. In M. Maguire, R. Morgan & R. Reiner (Eds.), *The Oxford handbook of criminology* (3rd ed.). Oxford: Oxford University Press.

Young, M. & Willmott, P. (1957). *Family and kinship in East London*. Harmondsworth: Penguin.

Young, M. & Willmott, P. (1975). *The symmetrical family*. Harmondsworth: Penguin.

Zeller, R.A. (1997). In J.P. Keeves (Ed.). *Educational research methodology and measurement: An international handbook* (2nd ed.). Oxford: Elsevier.

Zigler, E. & Styfco, S.J. (1993). Using research and theory to justify and inform Head Start expansion. *Social Policy Report, Society for Research in Child Development, 7*, 1-21.

Author index

Subject index